AA Pet Friendly

Places to Stay 2008

Reprinted 2008
This 7th edition published 2007 © Automobile Association Developments Limited 2007. Automobile Association Developments Limited retains the copyright in the current edition © 2007 and in all subsequent editions, reprints and amendments to editions. The information contained in this directory is sourced entirely from the AA's establishment database, Information Research, AA Hotel Services. The contents of this publication are believed correct at the time of printing. Nevertheless, the publishers cannot be held responsible for any errors or omission or for changes in the details given in this guide or for the consequences of any reliance on the information provided by the same. This does not affect your statutory rights. Assessments of AA inspected establishments and campsites are based on the experience of the Hotel and Restaurant Inspectors and Campsite Inspectors on the occasion(s) of their visit(s) and therefore descriptions given in this guide necessarily contain an element of subjective opinion which may not reflect or dictate a reader's own opinion on another occasion.

The AA strives to ensure accuracy in this guide at the time of printing. Due to the constantly evolving nature of the subject matter the information is subject to change. The AA will gratefully receive any advice from our readers of any necessary updated information.

Please contact Advertisement Sales: advertisingsales@theaa.com
Editorial Department: lifestyleguides@theaa.com
AA Hotel & Guest Accommodation enquiries: 01256 844455
AA Campsite enquiries: 01256 491577

Main cover photograph courtesy of Chris Rose/Alamy

Typeset/Repro by Servis, Manchester
Printed in Italy by Printer Trento SRL, Trento.

Directory compiled by the AA Hotel Services Department and generated from the AA establishment database.
www.theAA.com

Published by AA Publishing, a trading name of Automobile Association Developments Limited, whose registered office is Fanum House, Basing View, Basingstoke, Hampshire RG21 4EA.
Registered number 1878835

A CIP catalogue record for this book is available from the British Library

ISBN 10: 0 7495 5426 6
ISBN 13: 978 0 7495 5426 2
A03716

Maps prepared by the Mapping Services Department of The Automobile Association. Maps © Automobile Association Developments Limited 2007.

647.9441
2008

Contents

There are tough new rules for keeping a pet. You know, giving them food, water, that sort of thing.

Common sense surely? Apparently not. The vast majority of cases we deal with aren't down to a lack of love. They're down to a lack of understanding.

Now, more than ever, it's important that you learn about your pet. The new Animal Welfare Act will mean that your pet's needs are protected by law. And it'll mean that pet owners are responsible for knowing what those needs are. Don't worry, it's not rocket science. As well as a proper diet, you'll need to make sure your pet has enough room to move around in,

shelter and access to veterinary care. Oh, and because some animals need company for their well-being, you'll need to know whether your pet should live with or apart from other animals.

You see, we believe that all pets deserve a good life. But in order to achieve that all pet owners must have a good understanding of their needs.

As always, the RSPCA is here to help with guidance and support. So, if you have any questions about how to look after your pet, or the changes in the law, please give us a call on 0870 333 5999 or pay us a visit at rspca.org.uk/petcare

RSPCA

The aims of the RSPCA are to prevent cruelty and promote kindness to animals. Reg. charity no 219099. BT provided calls: max. 8p/min. 3p set-up fee from residential lines. Mobile and other provider may vary.

Welcome to the Guide

This guide is perfect for pet owners who are reluctant to put their animals into kennels or catteries while they go on holiday. In these pages you can find not only places where dogs and cats are welcome, but also where horses can be stabled on site or very close by.

Hints on booking your stay

As this guide shows, there are a great many hotels, bed and breakfasts and campsites that offer a warm welcome and an extensive range of facilities to both pet lovers and their animal companions. Though all the establishments listed have told us they are happy to admit animals, some go out of their way to make you and your pet feel at home, offering animal welcome packs, comfortable dog baskets, water bowls, special blankets, home-made treats and comprehensive information on local country walks.

Do remember though, that even the pet-friendliest of proprietors appreciate advance warning if you intend to bring your animal with you. See pages 12-17 for helpful hints and tips on planning your trip. While summer is an obvious time to book a holiday, you might like to consider taking an off-peak break when animals – dogs in particular – are more likely to enjoy cooler temperatures and crowd-free destinations.

And just a friendly word of warning. On sending us information for this guide many establishments stated that they very much welcome pets but they must be accompanied by well behaved owners!

How to Use the Guide

1 Locations The guide is divided into countries. Each country is listed in county order and then alphabetically in town/village order within a county.

2 Map reference Each town/village is given a map reference for the atlas section at the back of the guide. For example:

MAP 05 TG20

05 refers to the page number of the atlas section at the back of the guide

TG is the National Grid lettered square (represents 100,000sq metres) in which the location will be found

2 is the figure reading across the top or bottom of the map page

0 is the figure reading down each side of the map page.

Campsites (and some B&Bs) include a 6-figure National Grid reference as many are located in remote areas.

A county map appears before the atlas section at the back of the guide.

3 Which pets are accepted Five symbols show at a glance what type of animal is welcome – dogs, cats, small caged animals, caged birds and horses. (⌂) indicates places that provide kennels.

4 Establishment rating & name For further information on AA ratings and awards see page 10. If the name of the establishment appears in italic type this indicates that not all the information has been confirmed for 2008.

Within each location hotels are listed first, in descending order of stars and % score, followed by B&Bs in descending orders of stars, then campsites in order of their pennant rating (see page 10).

5 Contact details

6 Directions Short details of how to find the establishment or campsite.

---

1 NORWICH   MAP 05 TG20 **2**

3 (symbols)

4 ★★ 85% HOTEL

Stower Grange

School Rd, Drayton NR8 6EF

☎ 01603 860210 📠 01603 860464

5 e-mail: enquiries@stowergrange.co.uk
web: www.stowergrange.co.uk

6 Dir: *Norwich ring road N to Asda supermarket. Take A1067 Fakenham Rd at Drayton, right at traffic lights*

7 PETS: **Bedrooms** unattended **Public areas** except restaurant **Grounds:** accessible disp bin **Facilities:** food (pre-bookable) pet sitting dog walking washing fac cage storage walks info vet info **On request:** torch towels

8 Resident Pets: Saffy (Staffordshire Bull Terrier)

15

14

13

Expect a warm welcome at this 17th-century, ivy-clad property situated in a peaceful residential area close to the city centre and airport. The individually decorated bedrooms are generally quite spacious; each one is tastefully furnished and equipped with many thoughtful touches. Public rooms include a smart open-plan lounge bar and an elegant restaurant.

9 **Rooms** 11 en suite (1 fmly) ⊘ in all bedrooms S £75; D £95-£150 (incl. bkfst) ✳ **Facilities** 🛶 Wi-fi available New Year **Parking** 40 **Notes** LB

10   **11**   **12**

7 Pet facilities (PETS:)

Bedrooms GF Ground floor bedrooms; **unattended** indicates that the establishment allows a pet to be left unattended in the bedroom; **sign** indicates that a sign is provided to hang on the door stating an animal is in the room.

Sep accomm (separate accommodation) some places have kennels or outbuildings available. Do ask for more information when you book to check that this is suitable for your pet.

Charges £ (€ Republic of Ireland) Some establishments charge a fee for accommodating a pet: the price shown is the charge per animal per night and/or per animal per week (unless otherwise stated).

Grounds Establishments may allow pets access to their gardens or grounds, or in the case of campsites there may be specified areas for exercise.

Exercise area The type of area available (ie fields, beach, coastal path etc) and the distance from the establishment (ie 100yds).

Facilities Information and specific facilties that guests who are staying with their pets might find useful. Campsites may sell certain pet related items in their on-site shop.

Other Additional information supplied by the establishment.

Restrictions Certain establishments have rules on the number of pets, or the size or the breed of dog allowed.* We strongly advise readers to check with the hotel, B&B or campsite at the time of booking that their pet will be permitted to accompany them during their stay.

*Some establishments have stated that they do not accept 'dangerous dogs'. The following breeds are covered under the Dangerous Dogs Act 1991 – Pit Bull Terrier, Japanese Tosa, Dogo Argentino and Fila Brazilierio.

⑧ Resident Pets Lists the names and breeds of the proprietors' own pets.

⑨ Rooms The number of bedrooms, and whether they are en suite, family or ground floor rooms. **Prices** These are per room per night. These are given by the proprietors in good faith, and are indications only, not firm quotations. (✳ indicates 2007 prices). At the time of going to press up-to-date prices for campsites were not available. Please check the AA website **www.theAA.com** for current information. (**Hotels only** – colour TV is provided in all bedrooms unless otherwise indicated).

⑩ Facilities **Leisure facilities** are as stated in the entries. **Child Facilities** (Ch fac), these vary from

place to place so please check at the time of booking that the establishment can meet your requirements.

⑪ Parking Shows the numbers of spaces available for the use of guests'. This may include covered, charged spaces.

⑫ Notes This section can include the following:
No Children followed by an age indicates that a minimum age is required (ie No children 4yrs)
RS (Restricted Service) Some establishments have a restricted service during quieter months and some of the listed facilities may not be available.
LB Some establishments offer leisure breaks.
Dinner (B&Bs only) indicates that an evening meal is available, although prior notice may be needed. **Licensed** (B&Bs only) indicates that the establishment is licensed to serve alcohol.
Payment 🕾 The majority of establishments in this guide accept credit and debit cards. We have shown only those that don't.

⑬ Decription This is written by the AA Inspector at the time of their visit.

⑭ Photograph Establishments may choose to include a photograph in their entry.

⑮ Hotel logo If a symbol appears in the entry it indicates that the hotel belongs to a group or consortium (see page 18).

Symbols and Abbreviations

Key to symbols

⊕	Dogs	⊘	No smoking
🐱	Cats	⊘	No credit cards
🐰	Small caged animals e.g, rabbits, hamsters	✳	2007 prices
🐦	Caged birds	🏊	Indoor swimming pool
🐕	Kennels available	🏊	Heated indoor swimming pool
🐴	Stabling available	🏊	Outdoor swimming pool
★	The best hotels (see page 10)	🏊	Heated outdoor swimming pool
☆	The best B&Bs (see page 10)	🎾	Tennis court/s
★	Hotel and B&B rating (see page 10)	🏏	Croquet lawn
%	Merit score (see page 10)	⛳	Golf course
U	AA Rating not confirmed (see page 11)	🎵	Entertainment
◎	AA Rosette Award for quality of food		

Bed & Breakfast only

►	Campsite rating (see page 11)
⌂	Holiday Centre (see page 11)

⟐   A very special breakfast, with an emphasis on freshly prepared local ingredients

⟐   A very special dinner, with an emphasis on freshly prepared local ingredients

Key to abbreviations

Air con	Air conditioning		RS/rs	Restricted services
BH/bank hols	Bank Holidays		S	Single room
Ch fac	Special facilities for children		STV	Satellite television in bedrooms
D	Double bedroom		Spa	Establishment has own spa facilities
Etr	Easter		Whit	Whitsun Bank Holiday
Fmly	Family bedroom		Wi-fi	Wireless network access
Fr	From		wk	Week
FTV	Freeview television in bedrooms		wkend	Weekend
GF	Ground floor bedroom		Xmas	Special Christmas programme
hrs	Hours			
incl. bkfst	Including breakfast		**Bed & Breakfast only**	
LB	Special leisure breaks		Cen ht	Full central heating
m	Miles		Last d	Last time dinner can be ordered
mtrs	Metres		pri facs	Bedroom with separate, private facilities
mdnt	Midnight		rms	Bedrooms in main building
New Year	Special New Year programme		Tea/coffee	Tea & coffee making facilities
No Children	No children can be accommodated		TVB	Televisions in bedrooms
rdbt	Roundabout		TVL	Television lounge

AA Classifications & Awards

Hotel & Guest Accommodation Ratings

In 2006 the AA, in association with the National Tourist Boards, introduced new common standards for rating accommodation. All Hotels and B&Bs in this guide will have received an inspection under these standards.

AA Hotel Ratings

If you stay in a **one-star** hotel you should expect a relatively informal yet competent style of service and an adequate range of facilities. The majority of the bedrooms are en suite, with a bath or shower room always available. A **two-star** hotel is run by smartly and professionally presented management and offers at least one restaurant or dining room for breakfast and dinner, while a **three-star** hotel includes direct-dial telephones, a wide selection of drinks in the bar and last orders for dinner no later than 8pm. A **four-star** hotel is characterised by uniformed, well-trained staff, with additional services, a night porter and a serious approach to cuisine. A **five-star** hotel, offers many extra facilities, attentive staff, top quality rooms and a full concierge service.

The Merit Score (%) AA inspectors supplement their reports with an additional quality assessment of everything the hotel offers, including hospitality, based on their findings as a 'mystery guest'. This results in a overall Merit Score. Shown as a pecentage score beside the hotel name, you can see at a glance that a hotel with a percentage score of 69% offers a higher standard than one in the same star classification but with a percentage score of 59%. To gain AA recognition initially, a hotel must achieve a minimum quality score of 50%.

Red stars The very best hotels within each star category are indicated by red stars.

There are six descriptive designators for establishments in the Hotel Recognition scheme:

HOTEL Formal accommodatiom with full service. Minimum of six guest bedrooms but more likely to be in excess of 20.

TOWN HOUSE HOTEL A small, individual city or town centre property, which provides a high degree or personal service and privacy.

COUNTRY HOUSE HOTEL A rurally and quietly located establishment with ample grounds.

SMALL HOTEL Has less than 20 bedrooms and is personally run by the proprietor.

METRO HOTEL A hotel in an urban location that does not offer dinner.

BUDGET HOTEL Group lodge accommodation, usually purpose built units by main roads and motorways and in town or city centres.

AA Guest Accommodation Ratings

Stars in the AA Guest Accommodation scheme reflect five levels of quality, from one at the simplest level to five offering the highest quality. The criteria for eligibility is guest care plus the quality of the accommodation rather than the choice of extra facilities. Guests should receive a prompt, professional check in and check out, comfortable accommodation equipped to modern standards, regularly changed bedding and towels, a sufficient hot water supply at all times, well-prepared meals and a full continental breakfast.

Yellow stars The top 10% of three, four and five star establishments are indicated by yellow stars.

There are six descriptive designators for establishments in this scheme:

B&B A private house run by the owner with accommodation for no more than six paying guests.

GUEST HOUSE Run on a more commercial basis than a B&B, the accommodadtion provides for more than six paying guests and there are more services.

FARMHOUSE The B&B or guest house accommodation is part of a working farm or smallholding.

INN The accommodation is provided in a fully licensed establishment. The bar will be open to non-residents and provide food in the evenings.

RESTAURANT WITH ROOMS This is a destination restaurant offering overnight accommodation, with dining being the main business, and open to non-residents. The restaurant should offer a high

standard of food, and restaurant service at least five nights a week. A liquor licence and maximum of 12 bedrooms.

GUEST ACCOMMODATION Any establishment that meets the minimum entry requirements is eligible for this general category.

◉ AA Rosettes

The AA awards Rosettes for the quality of food. These range from one Rosette for food prepared with care, understanding and skill, up to five Rosettes for the very finest cooking that stands comparison with the best cuisine in the world.

AA Campsite Ratings

AA sites are classified from one to five pennants according to their style and the range of facilities they offer. 1 pennant – these parks offer a fairly simple standard of facilities. 2 pennants – offer an increased level of facilities, services, customer care, security and ground maintenance. 3 pennants – have a wide range of facilities and are of a very good standard. 4 pennants – these parks achieve an excellent standard throughout that will include landscaped grounds, natural screening and immaculately maintained toilets. 5 pennant Premier Parks – the very best parks with superb mature landscaping and all facilities, customer care and security will be of exceptional quality.

Campsites have shortened entries in this guide. For more detailed information visit our website www.theAA.com and follow the 'Places to Stay' link.

Holiday Centres

This category indicates parks which cater for all holiday needs including cooked meals and entertainment.

[U] A small number of establishments in the guide have this symbol because their star or pennant rating was not confirmed at the time of going to press. This may be because there has been a change of ownership, or because the establishment has only recently joined one of the AA rating schemes.

To find out more about AA ratings and awards please visit our website www.theAA.com

Useful Information

Britain

Fire Regulations

The Fire Precautions Act does not apply to the Channel Islands, Republic of Ireland, or the Isle of Man, which have their own rules. As far as we are aware, all establishments listed in Great Britain have applied for and not been refused a fire certificate.

Licensing laws

These laws differ in England, Wales, Scotland, Northern Ireland, the Republic of Ireland, the Isle of Man, the Isles of Scilly and the Channel Islands.

Public houses are generally open from mid morning to early afternoon, and from about 6 or 7pm until 11pm, although closing times may be earlier or later and some pubs are open all afternoon. Unless otherwise stated, hotels listed in this guide are licensed. (For guest accommodation, please refer to the individual gazetteer entry. Note that licensed premises are not obliged to remain open throughout the permitted hours.) Hotel residents can obtain alcoholic drinks at all times, if the licensee is prepared to serve them. Non-residents eating at the hotel restaurant can have drinks with meals. Children under 14 (or 18 in Scotland) may be excluded from bars where no food is served. Those under 18 may not purchase or consume alcoholic drinks. A club licence means that drinks are served to club members only. 48 hours must elapse between joining and ordering.

Prices

The AA encourages the use of the Hotel Industry Voluntary Code of Booking Practice, which aims to ensure that guests know how much they will have to pay and what services and facilities that includes, before entering a financially binding agreement. If the price has not previously been confirmed in writing, guests should be given a card stipulating the total obligatory charge when they register at reception.

The Tourism (Sleeping Accommodation Price Display) Order of 1977 compels hotels, travel accommodation, guest houses, farmhouses, inns and self-catering accommodation with four or more letting bedrooms, to display in entrance halls the minimum and

maximum prices charged for each category of room. Tariffs shown are the minimum and maximum for one or two persons but they may vary without warning.

Facilities for disabled guests

The final stage (Part III) of the Disability Discrimination Act (access to Goods and Services) came into force in October 2004. This means that service providers may have to consider making permanent physical adjustments to their premises.

For further information, see the government website **www.disability.gov.uk/dda**. We indicate in entries if an establishment has ground floor rooms, and if a hotel tells us that they have disabled facilities this is included in the description. The establishments in this guide should all be aware of their responsibilities under the Act. We recommend that you telephone in advance to ensure that the establishment you have chosen has appropriate facilities.

Useful websites:

www.disability.gov.uk/disabledpeople/fs/en
www.holidaycare.org.uk
www.dptac.gov.uk/door-to-door

Smoking regulations

We have tried to obtain accurate information on smoking restrictions within establishments, but the situation may change during the currency of this guide. If the freedom to smoke or to be in a non-smoking atmosphere is important to you, check the rules when you book. If bedroom has been allocated for smokers the establishment is obliged to clearly indicate that this is the case.

Useful websites for pet owners:

www.the-kennel-club.org.uk The Kennel Club provides lots of information on microchipping and runs a pet reunification scheme.
www.missingpetsbureau.com A national missing pets register.
www.europetnet.com For lost micro-chipped pets: The European Pet Network has access to several animal databases from various European countries. If a lost micro-chipped and registered pet is found, the EPN aims to find the owner.
www.defra.gov.uk/animalh/quarantine/index.htm for details of the Pet Travel Scheme and for comprehensive information and advise on travelling with your pet.
www.rcvs.org.uk website of the Royal College of Veterinary Surgeons that will help you find a vet near your holiday destination.

Northern Ireland & Republic of Ireland
Licensing Regulations
Northern Ireland:

Public houses open Mon-Sat 11.30-23.00. Sun 12.30-22.00. Hotels can serve residents without restriction. Non-residents can be served 12.30-22.00 on Christmas Day. Children under 18 are not allowed in the bar area and may neither buy nor consume liquor in hotels.

Republic of Ireland:

General licensing hours are Mon-Thu 10.30-23.30, Fri & Sat 10.30-00.30. Sun 12.30-23.00 (or 00.30 if the following day is a Bank Holiday). There is no licensed service (except for hotel residents) on Christmas Day or Good Friday.

Fire Regulations

The Fire Services (NI) Order 1984. This covers establishments accommodating more than six people, which must have a certificate from the Northern Ireland Fire Authority. Places accommodating fewer than six people need adequate exits. AA inspectors check emergency notices, fire fighting equipment and fire exits here.

The Republic of Ireland safety regulations are a matter for local authority regulations. For your own and others' safety, read the emergency notices and be sure you understand them.

Telephone numbers

Area codes for numbers in the Republic of Ireland apply only within the Republic. If dialling from outside check the telephone directory (from the UK the international dialling code is 00 353). Area codes for numbers in Britain and Northern Ireland cannot be used directly from the Republic.

For the latest information on the Republic of Ireland visit the AA Ireland's website: **www.AAireland.ie**

Bank and Public Holidays 2008

1st January	New Year's Day
2nd January (Scotland)	New Year's Holiday
21st March	Good Friday
24th March	Easter Monday
5th May	May Day Bank Holiday
6th May	Spring Bank Holiday
4th August (Scotland)	August Holiday
25th August	Late Summer Holiday
25th December	Christmas Day
26th December	Boxing Day

Pet Patrol

At first, the prospect of taking your pet away with you may seem a little daunting. There is their welfare to think of and the responsibility of trying to ensure they fit comfortably into their new surroundings. Many proprietors have cats and dogs of their own and will quickly build up a good rapport with your pet. This can play a vital role in the success of your holiday, and if all goes well, owners who are genuine animal lovers will be welcoming you back year after year. On the whole, proprietors report favourably on their pet guests, often commenting that their behaviour is at least as good as their owners!

We all love our pets and want to give them the care they deserve, but holidays can mean a certain amount of stress for us and also for our pets. Changes in routine can upset an animal as much as its owner. This is why we ask our pet owners to take special care of their animals when staying away. Keep them to their regular mealtimes if possible, take plenty of water for them on your journey, especially in hot weather.

Planning ahead

Always remember to advise the proprietor when booking that you intend bringing your pet with you. This gives you both the opportunity to establish whether the accommodation really is suitable for your pet's needs. Some establishments impose restrictions on the type, size or number of animals permitted; for example, those that accept dogs may not accommodate the larger breeds. Many estabishments can provide foods but is it advisable to take the food your pet is familiar with.

Not all rooms will necessarily be available to guests with animals and some rooms may be set aside for people with allergies.

When booking, you should also check the establishment's supervision policy. Some may require your pet to be caged when unattended, or may ask you not to leave your pet alone at all.

The gazetteer entry in this guide indicates whether you should expect to pay an additional charge or deposit for your pet, but we recommend that you confirm the amount when booking.

The countryside

For your family holiday to be a complete success, you'll need to do a little research and planning. As well as finding somewhere suitable to stay, you might like to contact the tourist board for leaflets and brochures on pet-friendly places of interest, or you might find the ideal place listed in the AA Days Out guide. Remember to 'Mind that Pet!' and keep your dog under tight control when visiting local attractions.

Time to adjust

Remember that an animal shut in a strange hotel room for long periods may become distressed. We have stories from our hotels and B&Bs of dogs chewing up furniture or howling mournfully while their owners are out and these are symptoms of boredom and separation anxiety, particularly if your pet is a rescue animal.

On arrival, give your pet time to adjust to the new surroundings and if you think he will be upset and bark or howl, don't leave him alone in your room.

Watching our pets let off steam in a different environment is one of the pleasures of a good holiday, but although they are cherished members of the family who provide many hours of fun and enjoyment, owners have a duty to ensure that their pet is kept under proper control at all times.

In the case of dogs, allowing them to socialise with people and other animals from an early age means that, under your supervision, they will be at ease with other residents and their pets during your stay. It's not uncommon to end up swapping dog stories with guests or even members of staff. Lasting friendships are sometimes formed this way!

House rules

Unless otherwise indicated by the management, please don't allow your pet on the furniture, or in the bed. If he or she likes to sleep on the bed, remember to take a sheet, a blanket or a bedspread of your own, unless the proprietor provides one. Remember also to take an old towel to dry your pet after a walk in the rain and don't use the bath or shower for washing your animal.

Clean up after your pet immediately – inside the room and out – and leave no trace of them on departure. Take a supply of supermarket carrier bags with you and poop scoop anywhere in the hotel or grounds. Management will advise on disposal of the bags – some hotels/B&Bs have an animal toilet area and provide bags. If something has been damaged by your pet, notify the management immediately. It's really a case of simple common sense.

If the hotel/B&B allows you to take animals into public areas, be sure that you keep your pet under control at all times. Keep dogs on leads, especially when around small children. Your dog may be easily distracted by the sights and smells of unfamiliar surroundings, and may not respond to your commands as well as at home.

Bear in mind that dogs need to be exercised regularly – even on holiday – and time should be set aside for this as often as possible, especially if they have been travelling with you in the car for most of the day. Most country hotels and B&Bs will have plenty of good walks on the doorstep, which makes the chore of exercising your dog that much more enjoyable.

A lot of the establishments listed in this guide are surrounded by farmland so please remember to keep your dog under strict control near livestock – even letting your dog walk in the same field as farm animals may be considered as "worrying". (Remember a farmer is entitled to kill your dog if it is worrying livestock).

Just in case

One final tip is to check your insurance for the level of cover it offers before taking your pet away. Pet insurance may not cover personal liability but your house insurance might. Should your pet chew the furniture or take a nip at a passing ankle, you would be well advised to have covered this eventuality by having the appropriate, up-to-date insurance policy.

The AA offers Pet Insurance.
Please visit **www.theAA.com** or call **0870 242 0219** for further information.

The Pet Travel Scheme (PETS)

Pets are on the move. They now travel more often with their owners in the United Kingdom and, because of changes in quarantine regulations, pets can now be taken abroad and then return to the UK, subject to certain conditions. This guide includes over 1,400 pet-friendly hotels, guest houses and campsites throughout the UK, solving the problem of what to do with your pet when you want to go on holiday. But what happens if you plan to go further afield – abroad perhaps? What are the regulations?

The Pets Travel Scheme gives information about the countries involved in the scheme; regulations; documentation required; microchip ID tags; help finding a vet; guidance on looking after pets during transportation; bringing your pet from a long-haul country; authorised routes; approved transport companies; charges; a latest news section and lots more besides.

Pets that are resident anywhere in the UK can travel unrestricted within Britain, and are not subject to quarantine regulations or to the PETS rules unless they are entering this country from overseas. There are no requirements for pets travelling directly between the UK and the Republic of Ireland.

The PETS scheme, which only applies to dogs (including assistance dogs), cats, ferrets, and certain other pets, enables pets resident in the UK to enter, without quarantine restrictions, certain (listed) countries throughout the world and then return to Britain. Thanks to the relaxation of quarantine controls in this country, they can go straight home on arrival. In order to bring your pet into, or back into, the UK from one of the listed countries the scheme requires

that your pet must be fitted with a microchip, be vaccinated against rabies, pass a blood test and be issued with a pet passport (or hold a valid pet certificate dated before 1/10/2004). Before entering the UK, your animal will also need to receive both tapeworm and tick treatments. Naturally, careful thought should be given to the welfare of your pet and whether a holiday abroad is appropriate, but if you decide to go ahead, remember it is necessary for your pet to have passed a satisfactory blood test at least 6 calendar months before travel commences. Your pet cannot travel under this scheme unless this time has elapsed.

For detailed information about the PETS scheme contact:
PETS Helpline: 0870 241 1710
(8.30-17.00 Monday to Friday)
E-mail: pets.helpline@dfra.gsi.gov.uk
Website: www.defra.gov.uk/animalh/quarantine/pets/

Remember, whether in the UK or abroad animals can die if left in a vehicle in direct sunlight or high temperatures.

Hotel Groups

Bespoke
0870 890 3740
www.bespokehotels.com

Best Western
08457 737 373
www.bestwestern.co.uk

Crerar Hotels
08700 554 433
www.crerarhotels.com

Campanile
020 8326 1500
www.envergure.fr

Choice
0800 44 44 44
www.choicehotelseurope.com

Classic British
0845 070 7090
www.classicbritishhotels.com

Copthorne
0800 41 47 41
www.millenniumhotels.com

Corus
0845 602 6787
www.corushotels.com

Days Inn
0800 028 0400
www.daysinn.com

Exclusive
01276 471 774
www.exclusivehotels.co.uk

Folio Hotels
0870 903 0007
www.foliohotels.co.uk

Forestdale Hotels
0808 144 9494
www.forestdale.com

Ibis
0870 609 0963
www.ibishotel.com

Independents
0800 885 544
www.theindependents.co.uk

Irish Country Hotels
00 353 1 295 8900
www.irishcountryhotels.com

Manor House
00 353 1 295 8900
www.manorhousehotels.com

Marriott
00800 1927 1927
www.marriott.co.uk

Mercure
0870 609 0965
www.mecure.com

Novotel
0870 609 0962
www.novotel.com

Old English Inns
0800 917 3085
www.oldenglishinns.co.uk

Oxford Hotels & Inns
0871 376 9900
www.oxfordhotelsandinns.com

Paramount
0870 168 8833
www.paramount-hotels.co.uk

Peel Hotels
0845 601 7335
www.peelhotels.co.uk

Pride of Britain
0800 089 3929
www.prideofbritainhotels.com

 Principal
0870 242 7474
www.principal-hotels.com

 Scotland's Hotels of Distinction
01333 360 888
www.hotels-of-distinction.com

 QHotels
0845 074 0060
www.qhotels.co.uk

 Small Luxury Hotels of the World
00800 5254 8000
www.slh.com

 Ramada
0845 2070 100
www.ramadajarvis.co.uk

 The Circle
0845 345 1965
www.circle-hotels.co.uk

 Red Carnation
0845 634 2665
www.redcarnationhotels.com

 Venture Hotels
www.venturehotels.co.uk

 Relais et Chateaux
00800 2000 0002
www.relaischateaux.com

 Von Essen
01761 240 121
www.vonessenhotels.co.uk

 Richardson Hotels
www.richardsonhotels.co.uk

 Welcome Break
01908 299 705
www.welcomebreak.co.uk

England

ENGLAND

BEDFORDSHIRE

ASPLEY GUISE
MAP 04 SP93

★★★ 71% HOTEL

Best Western Moore Place
The Square MK17 8DW
☎ 01908 282000 📠 01908 281888
e-mail: manager@mooreplace.com
Dir: *M1 junct 13, take A507 signed Aspley Guise & Woburn Sands. Hotel on left in village square*

PETS: Bedrooms (GF) **Stables** nearby **Charges** charge for damage **Public areas** lounge only on leads **Grounds** accessible on leads disp bin **Facilities** cage storage walks info vet info **On Request** fridge access torch

This impressive Georgian house, set in delightful gardens in the village centre, is very conveniently located for the M1. Bedrooms do vary in size, but consideration has been given to guest comfort, with many thoughtful extras provided. There is a wide range of meeting rooms and private dining options.

Rooms 35 en suite 27 annexe en suite (16 GF) ⊗ in 43 bedrooms **Facilities** FTV Wi-fi in bedrooms **Parking** 70 **Notes** RS 27-31 Dec

---

BEDFORD
MAP 04 TL04

★★★★ ⊛ 🍽 INN

Knife & Cleaver
The Grove, Houghton Conquest MK45 3LA
☎ 01234 740387 📠 01234 740900
e-mail: info@knifeandcleaver.com
web: www.knifeandcleaver.com
Dir: *5m S of Bedford. Off A6, opp Houghton Conquest church*

PETS: Bedrooms (GF) unattended **Charges** £6 per night, charge for damage **Grounds** accessible on leads **Facilities** food (pre-bookable) food bowl water bowl cage storage walks info vet info **On Request** fridge access towels **Resident Pets:** McCoy (Wheaten Terrier)

In a pleasant village setting, this relaxing inn has a cosy bar and an elegant conservatory-restaurant. Interesting dishes are complemented by a good wine list. Bedrooms, located in a garden annexe, come in a variety of styles, all comfortably appointed and well equipped; the de luxe rooms are particularly good.

Rooms 9 annexe en suite (1 fmly) (9 GF) ⊗ in 2 bedrooms S £59-£69; D £69-£84✶ **Facilities** STV TVB tea/coffee Direct dial from bedrooms Cen ht Dinner Last d 9.30pm Wi-fi available **Parking** 35 **Notes** No coaches Closed 27-30 Dec

---

BERKSHIRE

CHIEVELEY
MAP 04 SU47

★★★★ ⊛⊛ RESTAURANT WITH ROOMS

The Crab at Chieveley
Wantage Rd RG20 8UE
☎ 01635 247550 📠 01635 247440
e-mail: info@crabatchieveley.com
Dir: *1.5m W of Chieveley on B4494*
PETS: Please telephone for details

The individually themed bedrooms at this former pub have been appointed to a very high standard and include a full range of modern amenities. Ground-floor rooms have a small private patio area complete with a hot tub. The restaurant is divided into a modern Fishbar brasserie area and a more formal dining area. Both offer an extensive and award-winning range of fish and seafood dishes.

Rooms 15 en suite 7 annexe en suite (17 GF) ⊗ S £80-£140; D £90-£210✶ **Facilities** STV FTV TVB tea/coffee Direct dial from bedrooms Cen ht Dinner Last d 10pm Wi-fi available Sauna Gymnasium **Parking** 80 **Notes** LB

FINCHAMPSTEAD   MAP 04 SU76

►►► California Chalet & Touring Park

(SU788651)

Nine Mile Ride RG40 4HU

☎ 0118 973 3928 🗎 0118 932 8720

e-mail: enquiries@californiapark.co.uk

web: www.californiapark.co.uk

Dir: *From A321 (S of Wokingham), right onto B3016 to Finchampstead. Follow Country Park signs on Nine Mile Ride to site*

PETS: Charges £1 charge for 2+ dogs per night
Exercise area adjacent woods **Facilities** walks info vet info
Other prior notice required

Open all year Booking advisable Jul & Aug Last arrival 20.00hrs Last departure noon

A peaceful woodland site with secluded pitches among the trees, adjacent to the country park. Several pitches have a prime position beside the lake with their own fishing area. A 5.5-acre site with 30 touring pitches, 30 hardstandings.

HUNGERFORD   MAP 04 SU36

★★★ BED & BREAKFAST
Beacon House

Bell Ln, Upper Green, Inkpen RG17 9QJ

☎ 01488 668640 🗎 01488 668640

e-mail: l.g.cave@classicfm.net

web: www.beaconhouseinkpen.com

Dir: *4m SE of Hungerford. Off A4 S into Kintbury, left onto Inkpen Rd, 1m over x-rds, right to common, 3rd left after Crown & Garter pub*

PETS: Bedrooms unattended **Charges** charge for damage
Grounds accessible on leads disp bin **Exercise area** 100yds
Facilities food (pre-bookable) food bowl water bowl bedding
feeding mat leads washing facs cage storage walks info
On Request fridge access torch towels **Resident Pets:** Bilbo & Sevie (Cocker Spaniels), Jennie & Clare (donkeys)

This large house is set in peaceful countryside. Dinner is available in the winter months. Bedrooms are comfortably furnished and overlook fields. As well as the lounge, there is usually an art exhibition and sale

featuring watercolours, textiles, printmaking and pottery in the adjoining Gallery. Guests are always invited to view.

Rooms 3 rms ⊘ S £32; D £64 **Facilities** TVB Cen ht TVL Dinner Last d 4pm **Parking** 6 **Notes LB** ⊛

MAIDENHEAD   MAP 04 SU88

★★ 72% HOTEL
Elva Lodge

Castle Hill SL6 4AD

☎ 01628 622948 🗎 01628 778954

e-mail: reservations@elvalodgehotel.co.uk

web: www.elvalodgehotel.co.uk

Dir: *A4 from Maidenhead towards Reading. Hotel at top of hill on left*

PETS: Bedrooms (GF) **Charges** £5 per night **Public areas** except restaurant on leads **Grounds** accessible on leads disp bin
Facilities bedding walks info vet info **On Request** fridge access
towels **Resident Pets:** Buster (Terrier)

Within easy reach of the town centre, this family-run hotel offers a warm welcome and friendly service. Bedrooms are pleasantly decorated, continually maintained, and equipped with thoughtful extras. Spacious public areas include a smart, stylish lounge, a bar, and the Lion's Brassiere, which offers a wide range of popular dishes.

Rooms 26 rms (23 en suite) (1 fmly) (5 GF) ⊘ in all bedrooms
S £55-£95; D £70-£108 (incl. bkfst)✻ **Facilities** FTV Wi-fi in bedrooms
Reduced rates at local Leisure Centre **Parking** 32 **Notes LB** Closed
24-30 Dec

MEMBURY MOTORWAY   MAP 04 SU37
SERVICE AREA (M4)

BUDGET HOTEL
Days Inn Membury

Membury Service Area RG17 7TZ

☎ 01488 72336 🗎 01488 72336

e-mail: membury.hotel@welcomebreak.co.uk

web: www.daysinn.com

Dir: *M4 between junct 14 & 15*

PETS: Bedrooms Public areas only access for bedrooms
Grounds accessible

This modern building offers accommodation in smart, spacious and well-equipped bedrooms, suitable for families and business travellers, and all with en suite bathrooms. Continental breakfast is available and other refreshments may be taken at the nearby family restaurant. For further details see the Hotel Groups page.

Rooms 38 en suite

ENGLAND

RISELEY   MAP 04 SU76

►►► **Wellington Country Park** *(SU728628)*
RG7 1SP
☎ 0118 932 6444 📠 0118 932 6445
e-mail: info@wellington-country-park.co.uk
web: www.wellington-country-park.co.uk
Dir: *Signed off A33 between Reading and Basingstoke, 4m S of M4 junct 11*
PETS: Stables nearby (1m) **Charges** £1 per night **Public areas Exercise area** on site adjacent car park **Facilities** on site shop vet info
Open Mar-Nov Booking advisable peak periods Last arrival 17.30hrs Last departure 13.00hrs
A peaceful woodland site set within an extensive country park, which comes complete with lakes, nature trails, deer farm and boating. Ideal for M4 travellers. An 80-acre site with 72 touring pitches, 10 hardstandings.
Notes No open fires

WINDSOR   MAP 04 SU97

★★★★ 71% HOTEL
Royal Adelaide
46 Kings Rd SL4 2AG
☎ 01753 863916 📠 01753 830682
e-mail: royaladelaide@meridianleisure.com
web: www.meridianleisure.com
Dir: *M4 junct 6, A322 to Windsor. 1st left off rdbt into Clarence Rd. At 4th lights right into Sheet St and into Kings Rd. Hotel on right*
PETS: Bedrooms (GF) sign **Stables** nearby **Charges** £10 per night, charge for damage **Facilities** leads pet sitting dog walking walks info vet info **On Request** torch towels **Restrictions** small dogs only **Resident Pets:** Zahra (Toy Poodle)
This attractive Georgian-style hotel enjoys a quiet location yet is only a short walk from the town centre; and has some off-road parking. Bedrooms vary in size but have all been refurbished. Public areas are tastefully appointed and include a range of meeting rooms, a bar and an elegant restaurant.
Rooms 38 en suite 4 annexe en suite (5 fmly) (8 GF) ⊗ in 30 bedrooms S £69-£109; D £79-£139 (incl. bkfst) **Facilities** STV Wi-fi in bedrooms 25% discount for residents at Windsor leisure centre Xmas **Services** air con **Parking** 22 **Notes** LB

★★★ GUEST HOUSE
Clarence Guest House
9 Clarence Rd SL4 5AE
☎ 01753 864436 📠 01753 857060
e-mail: clarence.hotel@btconnect.com
web: www.clarence-hotel.co.uk
Dir: *M4 junct 6, dual-carriageway to Windsor, left at 1st rdbt onto Clarence Rd*
PETS: Bedrooms Facilities walks info vet info
On Request towels
This Grade II listed Victorian house is in the heart of Windsor. Space in some rooms is limited, but all are well maintained and offer excellent value for money. Facilities include a lounge with a well-stocked bar, and a steam room. Breakfast is served in the dining room overlooking attractive gardens.
Rooms 20 en suite (6 fmly) (2 GF) S £40-£68; D £45-£79✱
Facilities FTV TVB tea/coffee Licensed Cen ht TVL Wi-fi available Sauna Steam room **Parking** 4

BRISTOL

BRISTOL   MAP 03 ST57

★★★★ 70% HOTEL
Novotel Bristol Centre
Victoria St BS1 6HY
☎ 0117 976 9988 📠 0117 925 5040
e-mail: H5622@accor.com
web: www.novotel.com
Dir: *at end of M32 follow signs for Temple Meads station to rdbt. Final exit, hotel immediately on right*
PETS: Bedrooms unattended **Charges** £8 per night
Public areas not in food areas except assist dogs, muzzled and on leads **Exercise area** 5 mins walk **Facilities** walks info vet info
On Request towels
This city centre hotel has been refurbished and transformed to provide smart, contemporary style accommodation. Most of the bedrooms demonstrate the latest Novotel 'Novation' style with unique swivel desk, internet access, air-conditioning and a host of extras. The hotel is convenient for the mainline railway station and also has its own car park.
Rooms 131 en suite (20 fmly) ⊗ in 119 bedrooms S £139; D £139✱
Facilities STV Gym Wi-fi available **Services** Lift **Parking** 120 (charged)
Notes LB

★★★ 77% HOTEL
Berkeley Square

CLASSIC
BRITISH HOTELS

15 Berkeley Square, Clifton BS8 1HB
☎ 0117 925 4000 📠 0117 925 2970
e-mail: berkeley@cliftonhotels.com
web: www.cliftonhotels.com/chg.html

Dir: *M32 follow Clifton signs. 1st left at traffic lights by Nills Memorial Tower (University) into Berkeley Sq*

PETS: Bedrooms unattended **Charges** charge for damage **Grounds** accessible on leads **Exercise area** adjacent

Set in a pleasant square close to the university, art gallery and Clifton Village, this smart, elegant Georgian hotel has modern, stylishly decorated bedrooms that feature many welcome extras. There is a cosy lounge and stylish restaurant on the ground floor and a smart, contemporary bar in the basement. A small garden is also available at the rear of the hotel.

Rooms 43 en suite (4 GF) ⊗ in 30 bedrooms **Facilities** STV use of local gym and swimming pool £5 day pass **Services** Lift **Parking** 20 **Notes** LB

★★★ 75% ● HOTEL
Arno's Manor

470 Bath Rd, Arno's Vale BS4 3HQ
☎ 0117 971 1461 📠 0117 971 5507
e-mail: arnos.manor@forestdale.com
web: www.forestdale.com

Dir: *From end of M32 follow signs for Bath, hotel on right side of A4 after 2m. Next to ITV West television studio*

PETS: Bedrooms unattended **Charges** £7.50 per night **Public areas** except restaurant & bar

Once the home of a wealthy merchant, this historic 18th-century building is now a comfortable hotel that offers spacious, well-appointed bedrooms with plenty of workspace. The lounge was once the chapel and has many original features, while meals are taken in the atmospheric, conservatory-style restaurant.

Rooms 73 en suite (5 fmly) (7 GF) ⊗ in 50 bedrooms **Facilities** STV Wi-fi in bedrooms Xmas New Year **Services** Lift **Parking** 200 **Notes**

★★★ 66% HOTEL
Henbury Lodge

Station Rd, Henbury BS10 7QQ
☎ 0117 950 2615 📠 0117 950 9532
e-mail: contactus@henburylodgehotel.com
web: www.henburylodgehotel.com

Dir: *M5 junct 17/A4018 towards city centre, 3rd rdbt right into Crow Ln. At end turn right & hotel 200mtrs on right*

PETS: Bedrooms unattended **Charges** £5 per night **Grounds** accessible

This comfortable 18th-century country house has a delightful home-from-home atmosphere and is conveniently situated with easy access to the M5 and the city centre. Bedrooms are available both within the main house and in the adjacent converted stables; all are attractively decorated and well equipped. The pleasant dining room offers a selection of carefully prepared dishes using fresh ingredients.

Rooms 12 en suite 9 annexe en suite (4 fmly) (6 GF) ⊗ in all bedrooms **Facilities** STV **Parking** 24 **Notes** LB

★★★ GUEST HOUSE
Washington

11-15 St Pauls Rd, Clifton BS8 1LX
☎ 0117 973 3980 📠 0117 973 4740
e-mail: washington@cliftonhotels.com

Dir: *A4018 into city, right at lights opp BBC, house 200yds on left*

PETS: Bedrooms unattended **Charges** charge for damage **Exercise area** park 0.5m

This large terrace house is within walking distance of the city centre and Clifton village. The bedrooms, many refurbished, are well equipped for business guests. Public areas include a modern reception lounge and a bright basement breakfast room. The property has secure parking and a rear patio garden.

Rooms 46 rms (40 en suite) (4 fmly) (10 GF) ⊗ in 13 bedrooms **Facilities** STV TVB tea/coffee Direct dial from bedrooms Licensed Cen ht Reduced rate pass for local health club **Parking** 20 **Notes** Closed 23 Dec-3 Jan

BUCKINGHAMSHIRE

BUCKINGHAM — MAP 04 SP63

★★★ 66% HOTEL
Best Western Buckingham Hotel

Best Western

Buckingham Ring Rd MK18 1RY
☎ 01280 822622 📠 01280 823074

Dir: *Follow A421 for Buckingham, take ring road S towards Brackley & Bicester. Hotel on left*

PETS: Bedrooms unattended **Charges** £10 per night

A purpose-built hotel, which offers comfortable and spacious rooms with well designed working spaces for business travellers. There are also extensive conference facilities. The open-plan restaurant and bar offer a good range of dishes, and the well-equipped leisure suite is popular with guests.

Rooms 70 en suite (6 fmly) (31 GF) ⊗ in 64 bedrooms S £65-£99; D £118✱ **Facilities** STV ⊙ supervised Gym Wi-fi in bedrooms Xmas New Year **Parking** 200 **Notes** LB

GAYHURST MAP 04 SP84

★★★ FARM HOUSE
Mill Farm *(SP852454)*
MK16 8LT

☎ 01908 611489 & 07714 719640 📠 01908 611489

Mrs K Adams

e-mail: adamsmillfarm@aol.com

web: www.millfarmgayhurst.co.uk

Dir: *B526 from Newport Pagnell, 2.5m left onto Haversham Rd, Mill Farm 1st on left*

PETS: Bedrooms Sep Accom pen, kennel **Stables** on site **Grounds** accessible **Resident Pets:** Peter (Terrier), Hector (Dachshund), Alfie (Labrador)

Within easy reach of Newport Pagnell and the M1, this historic farmhouse has a peaceful setting with wonderful views over farmland. Bedrooms are decorated in a homely style and have a host of thoughtful extras. The sumptuous lounge-dining room is enhanced with fine antiques, and the extensive grounds include a tennis court.

Rooms 3 rms (2 en suite) 1 annexe en suite (1 fmly) (1 GF) ⊗ in 1 bedroom S £25-£30; D £50-£60 **Facilities** TVB tea/coffee Cen ht TVL ⚲ Fishing ⚑ **Parking** 13 **Notes** 550 acres mixed ⊗

MILTON KEYNES MAP 04 SP83

★★★ 73% HOTEL
Novotel Milton Keynes
Saxon St, Layburn Court, Heelands MK13 7RA

☎ 01908 322212 📠 01908 322235

e-mail: H3272@accor-hotels.com

web: www.novotel.com

Dir: *M1 junct 14, follow Childsway signs towards city centre. Right into Saxon Way, straight across all rdbts, hotel on left*

PETS: Bedrooms Charges £10 per night **Grounds** accessible **Exercise area** 50mtrs **Facilities** water bowl

Contemporary in style, this purpose-built hotel is situated on the outskirts of the town, just a few minutes' drive from the centre and mainline railway station. Bedrooms provide ample workspace and a good range of facilities for the modern traveller, and public rooms include a children's play area and indoor leisure centre.

Rooms 124 en suite (40 fmly) (40 GF) ⊗ in 105 bedrooms **Facilities** STV ⊛ Gym Steam bath **Services** Lift **Parking** 130 **Notes** LB

★★★ 67% TOWN HOUSE HOTEL
Swan Revived THE INDEPENDENTS
High St, Newport Pagnell MK16 8AR

☎ 01908 610565 📠 01908 210995

e-mail: info@swanrevived.co.uk

web: www.swanrevived.co.uk

Dir: *M1 junct 14 onto A509 then B526 into Newport Pagnell for 2m. Hotel on High St*

PETS: Bedrooms (GF) unattended **Public areas** except restaurant **Exercise area Facilities** water bowl walks info vet info **On Request** fridge access

Once a coaching inn and dating from the 17th century, this hotel occupies a prime location in the centre of town. Well-appointed bedrooms are mostly spacious, individually styled and have good levels of comfort. Public areas include a popular bar and a restaurant offering a variety of freshly prepared dishes.

Rooms 42 en suite (2 fmly) **Facilities** STV **Services** Lift **Parking** 51 **Notes** RS 25 Dec-1 Jan

---

BUDGET HOTEL
Campanile
40 Penn Rd, Fenny Stratford, Bletchley MK2 2AU **Campanile**

☎ 01908 649819 📠 01908 649818

e-mail: mk@campanile-hotels.com

web: www.envergure.fr

Dir: *M1 junct 14, follow A4146 to A5. Southbound on A5. 4th exit at 1st rdbt to Fenny Stratford. Hotel 500yds on left*

PETS: Please telephone for details

This modern building offers accommodation in smart, well-equipped bedrooms, all with en suite bathrooms. Refreshments may be taken at the informal Bistro. For further details consult the Hotel Groups page.

Rooms 80 en suite

NEWPORT PAGNELL MAP 04 SP84
MOTORWAY SERVICE AREA (M1)

BUDGET HOTEL
Welcome Lodge Newport Pagnell
Newport Pagnell MK16 8DS **Welcome Break**

☎ 01908 610878 📠 01908 216539

e-mail: newport.hotel@welcomebreak.co.uk

web: www.welcomebreak.co.uk

Dir: *M1 junct 14-15. In service area - follow signs to Barrier Lodge*

PETS: Bedrooms (GF) unattended **Grounds** accessible **Facilities** walks info vet info

This modern building offers accommodation in smart, spacious and well-equipped bedrooms, suitable for families and business travellers, and all with en suite bathrooms. Refreshments may be taken at the nearby family restaurant. For further details consult the Hotel Groups page.

Rooms 90 en suite

TAPLOW   MAP 04 SU98

★★★★★ ◉◉◉ COUNTRY HOUSE HOTEL

Cliveden

SL6 0JF

von Essen hotels
A PRIVATE COLLECTION
www.vonessenhotels.com

☎ 01628 668561 🖷 01628 661837

e-mail: reservations@clivedenhouse.co.uk

web: www.vonessenhotels.co.uk

Dir: *M4 junct 7, follow A4 towards Maidenhead for 1.5m, turn onto B476 towards Taplow, 2.5m, hotel on left*

PETS: Bedrooms (GF) unattended **Charges** charge for damage **Public areas** except restaurant on leads **Grounds** accessible on leads disp bin **Facilities** food (pre-bookable) food bowl water bowl bedding pet sitting dog walking washing facs cage storage walks info vet info **On Request** fridge access torch towels

This wonderful stately home stands at the top of a gravelled boulevard. Visitors are treated as house-guests and staff recapture the tradition of fine hospitality. Bedrooms have individual quality and style, and reception rooms retain a timeless elegance. Both restaurants here are awarded AA rosettes - The Terrace with its delightful views has two rosettes, and Waldo's, offering innovative menus in discreet, luxurious surroundings, has three. Exceptional leisure facilities include cruises along Cliveden Reach and massages in the Pavilion.

Rooms 39 en suite (8 GF) ⊘ in 12 bedrooms D £423-£1169 (incl. bkfst) ✻ **Facilities Spa** STV ⊗ ↘ ⏛ Squash Gym 🏊 Wi-fi available Full range of beauty treatments, 3 vintage launches ♫ Xmas **Services** Lift **Parking** 60 **Notes** LB

CAMBRIDGESHIRE

BURWELL   MAP 05 TL56

▶▶▶ **Stanford Park** *(TL578675)*

Weirs Drove CB25 0BP

☎ 01638 741547 & 07802 439997

e-mail: enquiries@stanfordcaravanpark.co.uk

web: www.stanfordcaravanpark.co.uk

Dir: *Signed from B1102*

PETS: Public areas Exercise area on site & adjacent to site

Open all year Booking advisable BH Last arrival 20.00hrs Last departure 11.00hrs

A secluded site on the outskirts of Burwell set in four large fields with several attractive trees. The amenities are modern and well kept, and there are eight new hardstandings hedged with privet. A 20-acre site with 100 touring pitches, 20 hardstandings.

Notes ✇ Adults only, no group bookings

CAMBRIDGE   MAP 05 TL45

★★★★ 81% ◉◉ HOTEL

Hotel Felix

Whitehouse Ln CB3 0LX

☎ 01223 277977 🖷 01223 277973

e-mail: help@hotelfelix.co.uk

web: www.hotelfelix.co.uk

Dir: *N on A1307, right at The Travellers Rest*

PETS: Bedrooms (GF) unattended **Charges** charge for damage **Grounds** accessible on leads **Exercise area** nearby

A beautiful Victorian mansion set amidst three acres of landscaped gardens, this property was originally built in 1852 for a surgeon from the famous Addenbrookes Hospital. The contemporary-style bedrooms have carefully chosen furniture and many thoughtful touches, whilst public rooms feature an open-plan bar, the adjacent Graffiti restaurant and a small quiet lounge.

Rooms 52 en suite (5 fmly) (26 GF) ⊘ in all bedrooms S £140-£195; D £175-£285 (incl. bkfst)✻ **Facilities** STV Wi-fi in bedrooms Xmas New Year **Services** Lift **Parking** 90 **Notes** LB

CAMBRIDGE CONTINUED

★★★ 78% HOTEL
Best Western Gonville Hotel

Gonville Place CB1 1LY
☎ 01223 366611 & 221111 📠 01223 315470
e-mail: all@gonvillehotel.co.uk
web: www.bw-gonvillehotel.co.uk
Dir: *M11 junct 11, on A1309 follow city centre signs. At 2nd mini rdbt right into Lensfield Rd, over junct with lights. Hotel 25yds on right*
PETS: Bedrooms (GF) Charges charge for damage
Grounds accessible on leads Facilities vet info
This hotel is situated on the inner ring road, a short walk across the green from the city centre. Well-established, with regular guests and very experienced staff, the Gonville is popular for its relaxing, informal atmosphere. The air-conditioned public areas are cheerfully furnished, and include a lounge bar and brasserie; bedrooms are well appointed and appealing, offering a good range of facilities for both corporate and leisure guests.
Rooms 73 en suite (1 fmly) (5 GF) ⊘ in 38 bedrooms S £89-£140; D £99-£160✶ Facilities FTV Wi-fi available New Year Services Lift Parking 80 Notes LB RS 24-29 Dec

★★★ 77% HOTEL
Royal Cambridge

Trumpington St CB2 1PY
☎ 01223 351631 📠 01223 352972
e-mail: royal.cambridge@forestdale.com
web: www.forestdale.com
Dir: *M11 junct 11, signed city centre. 1st mini rdbt left into Fen Causeway. Hotel 1st right*
PETS: Bedrooms sign Charges £7.50 per night Public areas except restaurant on leads Facilities food food bowl cage storage water bowl walks info vet info
This impressive Georgian hotel enjoys a central location. Bedrooms are well equipped and comfortable, and include superior bedrooms/apartments. Public areas are traditionally decorated to a good standard; the elegant restaurant is a popular choice and the lounge/bar serves evening snacks. Parking and conferencing are added benefits.
Rooms 57 en suite (9 fmly) ⊘ in 28 bedrooms Facilities STV Wi-fi available Xmas New Year Services Lift Parking 80

▶▶▶ Cambridge Camping & Caravanning
Club Site *(TL455539)*

19 Cabbage Moor, Great Shelford CB2 5NB
☎ 01223 841185
web: www.campingandcaravanningclub.co.uk/cambridge
Dir: *M11 junct 11 onto A1309 signed Cambridge. At 1st lights turn right. After 0.5m follow site sign on left*
PETS: Exercise area on site Facilities disp bin walks info vet info
Other prior notice required
Open 13 Mar-3 Nov Booking advisable BH & peak periods Last arrival 21.00hrs Last departure noon
A popular, open site close to Cambridge and the M11, surrounded by high hedging and trees, with well-maintained toilet facilities. The large rally field is well used. An 11-acre site with 120 touring pitches.
Notes site gates closed 23.00-07.00hrs

ELY   MAP 05 TL58

★★★ 72% HOTEL
Lamb

2 Lynn Rd CB7 4EJ
☎ 01353 663574 📠 01353 662023
e-mail: lamb.ely@oldenglishinns.co.uk
web: www.oldenglish.co.uk
Dir: *from A10 into Ely, hotel in town centre*
PETS: Bedrooms Charges charge for damage
Public areas except restaurant on leads Exercise area 5 mins walk Facilities walks info vet info On Request towels
This 15th-century former coaching inn is situated in the heart of this popular market town. The hotel offers a combination of light, modern and traditional public rooms, whilst the bedrooms provide contemporary standards of accommodation. Food is available throughout the hotel - the same menu provided in the bar and restaurant areas.
Rooms 31 en suite (6 fmly) ⊘ in 24 bedrooms Facilities STV Parking 20 Notes LB

★★★ GUEST HOUSE
Castle Lodge

50 New Barns Rd CB7 4PW
☎ 01353 662276 📠 01353 666606
e-mail: castlelodgehotel@supanet.com
Dir: *Off B1382 (Prickwillow Rd) NE from town centre*
PETS: Bedrooms unattended Charges £5 per stay per night
Public areas except restaurant Exercise area field nearby
Facilities food
Located within easy walking distance of the cathedral, this extended Victorian house offers well-equipped bedrooms in a variety of sizes.

Public areas include a traditionally furnished dining room and a comfortable air-conditioned bar lounge. Service is friendly and helpful.

Rooms 11 rms (6 en suite) (3 fmly) S £32.50-£55; D fr £75✳
Facilities TVB tea/coffee Direct dial from bedrooms Licensed Cen ht TVL Dinner Last d 9pm **Parking** 6 **Notes** ⊛ No coaches

HUNTINGDON   MAP 04 TL27

★★★★ 75% HOTEL
Huntingdon Marriott Hotel   **Marriott**
                                              HOTELS & RESORTS
Kingfisher Way, Hinchingbrooke Business Park PE29 6FL

☎ 01480 446000 📄 01480 451111

e-mail: mhrs.cbghd.front.office@marriotthotels.com

web: www.marriott.co.uk

Dir: *on A14, 1m from Huntington centre close to Brampton racecourse*

PETS: Bedrooms unattended **Public areas Grounds** accessible **Exercise area** park nearby

With its excellent road links, this modern, purpose-built hotel is a popular venue for conferences and business meetings, and is convenient for Huntingdon, Cambridge and racing at Newmarket. Bedrooms are spacious and offer every modern comfort, including air conditioning. Leisure facilities are also impressive.

Rooms 150 en suite (45 GF) ⊗ in 60 bedrooms S £67-£170; D £94-£180 (incl. bkfst)✳ **Facilities** STV ⓢ supervised Gym Wi-fi available ♫ Xmas New Year **Services** Lift air con **Parking** 200 **Notes** LB

[U]
George
                                              (logo)
George St PE29 3AB   OLD ENGLISH INNS
                                              GREENE KING
☎ 01480 432444 📄 01480 453130

e-mail: george.huntingdon@oldenglishinns.co.uk

web: www.oldenglish.co.uk

Dir: *Leave A14 at Huntingdon racecourse exit. Then 3m to junct with ring road. Hotel opposite*

PETS: Bedrooms unattended **Charges** £5 per night **Public areas** except not at food service **Exercise area**

At the time of going to press, the star classification for this hotel was not confirmed. Please refer to the AA internet site www.theAA.com for current information.

Rooms 24 en suite (3 fmly) ⊗ in all bedrooms **Facilities** ♫ **Parking** 55 **Notes** LB

►►► **Huntingdon Boathaven & Caravan Park** *(TL249706)*

The Avenue, Godmanchester PE29 2AF

☎ 01480 411977 📄 01480 411977

e-mail: boathaven.hunts@virgin.net

web: www.huntingdonboathaven.co.uk

Dir: *S of town. Exit A14 at Godmanchester junct, through Godmanchester on B1043 to site (on left by River Ouse)*

PETS: Public areas except shower block **Exercise area** on site & field adjacent 500yds **Facilities** vet info **Other** prior notice required

Open all year open in winter only when weather permits Booking advisable Last arrival 21.00hrs

Small, well laid out site overlooking a boat marina and the River Ouse, set close to the A14 and within walking distance of Huntingdon town centre. Clean, well kept toilets. A pretty area has been created for tents beside the marina, with wide views across the Ouse Valley. Weekend family activities organized throughout the season. A 2-acre site with 24 touring pitches, 18 hardstandings.

Notes ⊛ no cars by tents

►►► **The Willows Caravan Park** *(TL224708)*

Bromholme Ln, Brampton PE28 4NE

☎ 01480 437566

e-mail: willows@willows33.freeserve.co.uk

web: www.willowscaravanpark.com

Dir: *Exit A14/A1 signed Brampton, follow Huntingdon signs. Site on right close to Brampton Mill pub*

PETS: Charges 1st dog free, 50p per extra dog per night (£3 per extra dog per week) **Public areas** on leads, except playground & amenities block **Exercise area** adjacent **Facilities** washing facs walks info vet info **Other** prior notice required rabbits also accepted **Restrictions** no Rottweillers, Pit Bulls/Staffordshire Terriers, German Shepherds, Dobermans **Resident Pets:** Cat

Open all year (rs Nov-Feb 10 pitches only plus 6 storage spaces) Booking advisable BH & school hols Last arrival 22.00hrs Last departure noon

A small, friendly site in a pleasant setting beside the River Ouse, on the Ouse Valley Walk. Bay areas have been provided for caravans and motorhomes, and planting for screening is gradually maturing. There are launching facilities and free river fishing. A 4-acre site with 50 touring pitches.

Notes ⊛ no cars by tents, ball games on field provided, no generators, one-way system 5mph, no groundsheets

KIRTLING
MAP 05 TL65

★★★ BED & BREAKFAST
Hill Farm Guest House
CB8 9HQ
☎ 01638 730253 📠 01638 731957

Dir: *0.5m NW of Kirtling*

PETS: Bedrooms sign **Charges** £3 per night, charge for damage **Public areas** on leads **Grounds** accessible on leads disp bin **Exercise area** on site **Facilities** feeding mat walks info vet info **On Request** torch **Resident Pets:** Ben (Terrier), 6 retired racehorses

Located on arable land south of Newmarket, in the heart of horse-breeding country, this 400-year-old property retains many original features. Public areas are furnished in keeping with the building's character, and hearty breakfasts are served at a family table in the elegant dining room.

Rooms 3 rms (2 en suite) ⊘ S £32; D £60✳ **Facilities** TVB tea/coffee Direct dial from bedrooms Cen ht TVL Wi-fi available ⅃ **Parking** 15 **Notes** LB ⊕

PETERBOROUGH
MAP 04 TL19

★★★ 78% ⊛ HOTEL
Best Western Orton Hall
Orton Longueville PE2 7DN
☎ 01733 391111 📠 01733 231912
e-mail: reception@ortonhall.co.uk

Dir: *off A605 E opposite Orton Mere*

PETS: Bedrooms unattended **Charges** £5 per night **Public areas** except restaurants **Grounds** accessible **Exercise area** on site

Impressive country house hotel set amidst 20 acres of woodland on the outskirts of town. The building work is due for completion in November 2007 and will include 12 further bedrooms, a purpose-built function space for up to 150 delegates, and a swimming pool with steam and sauna rooms. The spacious and relaxing public areas have many original features that include The Great Room and 17th-century oak panelling in the Huntly Restaurant. The Ramblewood Inn offers an alternative informal dining and bar option.

Rooms 65 en suite (2 fmly) (15 GF) ⊘ in 42 bedrooms S £70-£140; D £85-£170✳ **Facilities** STV Wi-fi available Three quarter size snooker table Xmas New Year **Parking** 200 **Notes** LB

ST NEOTS
MAP 04 TL16

►►► St Neots Camping & Caravanning Club Site *(TL182598)*
Hardwick Rd, Eynesbury PE19 2PR
☎ 01480 474404

web: www.campingandcaravanningclub.co.uk/stneots

Dir: *From A1 take A428 to Cambridge, 2nd rdbt left to Tesco's, past Sports Centre. Follow International Camping signs to site*

PETS: Public areas except buildings **Exercise area** adjacent disp bin **Facilities** walks info vet info **Other** prior notice required

Open 13 Mar-3 Mar Booking advisable BH & peak periods Last arrival 21.00hrs Last departure noon

A level meadowland site adjacent to the River Ouse on the outskirts of St Neots, with well maintained and modern facilities, and helpful, attentive staff. An 11-acre site with 180 touring pitches, 33 hardstandings.

Notes Gates closed 23.00-07.00hrs

SIX MILE BOTTOM
MAP 05 TL55

★★★ 82% ⊛ HOTEL
Swynford Paddocks
CB8 0UE
☎ 01638 570234 📠 01638 570283
e-mail: info@swynfordpaddocks.com
web: www.swynfordpaddocks.com

Dir: *M11 junct 9, take A11 towards Newmarket, then onto A1304 to Newmarket, hotel 0.75m on left*

PETS: Bedrooms Charges please call for details **Exercise area** on site 2 acres of garden **Facilities** water bowl

This smart country house is set in attractive grounds, within easy reach of Newmarket. Bedrooms are comfortably appointed, thoughtfully equipped and include some delightful four-poster rooms. Imaginative, carefully prepared food is served in the elegant restaurant; service is friendly and attentive. Meeting and conference facilities are available.

Rooms 15 en suite (1 fmly) D £135-£195 (incl. bkfst)✳ **Facilities** STV ⅃ Wi-fi in bedrooms **Parking** 100 **Notes** LB

WISBECH
MAP 05 TF40

★★★ 73% HOTEL
Elme Hall
Elm High Rd PE14 0DQ
☎ 01945 475566 📄 01945 475666
e-mail: elmehallhotel@btconnect.com
web: www.elmehall.co.uk
Dir: *off A47 onto A1101 towards Wisbech. Hotel on right*
PETS: Bedrooms Stables nearby (5m) **Charges** charge for damage **Grounds** accessible on leads **Facilities** vet info **On Request** fridge access **Restrictions** no large dogs

An imposing, Georgian-style property conveniently situated on the outskirts of the town centre just off the A47. Individually decorated bedrooms are tastefully furnished with quality reproduction pieces and equipped to a high standard. Public rooms include a choice of attractive lounges, as well as two bars, meeting rooms and a banqueting suite.

Rooms 8 en suite (3 fmly) ⊘ in all bedrooms S £48-£52; D £68-£245 (incl. bkfst)✳ **Facilities** FTV Wi-fi available ♫ **Parking** 200 **Notes**

►►► Little Ranch Leisure *(TF456062)*
Begdale, Elm PE14 0AZ
☎ 01945 860066 📄 01945 860114
web: www.littleranchleisure.co.uk
Dir: *From rdbt on A47 (SW of Wisbech) take Redmoor Lane to Begdale*
PETS: Charges £1 per night **Public areas Exercise area** on site 10 acre orchard disp bin **Facilities** washing facs vet info

Open all year Booking advisable BH

A friendly family site set in an apple orchard, with 25 fully-serviced pitches and a beautifully designed, spacious toilet block. The site overlooks a large fishing lake, and the famous horticultural auctions at Wisbech are nearby. A 10-acre site with 25 touring pitches, 25 hardstandings.

Notes 🐾

AUDLEM
MAP 07 SJ64

★★★★ FARM HOUSE
Little Heath Farm *(SJ663455)*
CW3 0HE
☎ 01270 811324 Mrs H M Bennion
e-mail: hilaryandbob@ukonline.co.uk
Dir: *Off A525 in village onto A529 for 0.3m. Farm opposite village green*
PETS: Bedrooms Charges £5 per night **Grounds** accessible **Exercise area** on site

The 200-year-old brick farmhouse retains much original character, including low beamed ceilings. The traditionally furnished public areas include a cosy sitting room and a dining room where you dine family style. The refurbished bedrooms are stylish, and the friendly proprietors create a relaxing atmosphere.

Rooms 3 en suite (1 fmly) ⊘ S £30-£35; D £50-£60✳ **Facilities** TVB tea/coffee Cen ht TVL Dinner Last d 10am **Parking** 6 **Notes** LB 50 acres beef dairy mixed Closed Xmas & New Year 🐾

BURWARDSLEY
MAP 07 SJ55

★★ 81% HOTEL
Pheasant Inn
Higher Burwardsley CH3 9PF
☎ 01829 770434 📄 01829 771097
e-mail: info@thepheasantinn.co.uk
web: www.thepheasantinn.co.uk
Dir: *from A41, left to Tattenhall, right at 1st junct and left at 2nd to Higher Burwardsley. At post office left, hotel signed*
PETS: Bedrooms unattended **Public areas** at manager's discretion **Grounds** accessible **Exercise area** surrounding countryside

This delightful 300-year-old inn sits high on the Peckforton Hills and enjoys spectacular views over the Cheshire Plain. Well-equipped, comfortable bedrooms are housed in an adjacent converted barn. Creative dishes are served either in the stylish restaurant or in the traditional, beamed bar. Real fires are lit in the winter months.

Rooms 2 en suite 10 annexe en suite (2 fmly) (5 GF) ⊘ in all bedrooms S £65-£90; D £85-£130 (incl. bkfst)✳ **Facilities** Fishing Wi-fi in bedrooms **Parking** 80

FRODSHAM

MAP 07 SJ57

★★★ 77% HOTEL

Forest Hill Hotel & Leisure Complex

THE INDEPENDENTS
HOTEL ASSOCIATION

Overton Hill WA6 6HH

☎ 01928 735255 🖹 01928 735517

e-mail: info@foresthillshotel.com

web: www.foresthillshotel.com

Dir: *at Frodsham turn onto B5151. After 1m right into Manley Rd, right into Simons Ln after 0.5m. Hotel 0.5m past Frodsham golf course*

PETS: Bedrooms unattended sign Stables nearby (0.25m) Charges £5 per night, charge for damage Grounds accessible on leads disp bin Exercise area 40mtrs Facilities cage storage walks info vet info On Request fridge access

This modern, purpose-built hotel is set high up on Overton Hill, so offering panoramic views. There is a range of spacious, well-equipped bedrooms, including executive rooms. Guests have a choice of bars and there is a tasteful split-level restaurant, as well as conference facilities and a very well equipped leisure suite and gym.

Rooms 58 en suite (4 fmly) ⊘ in all bedrooms S £55-£90; D £70-£130 Facilities STV ③ Gym Wi-fi in bedrooms Nightclub, Dance studio, Aerobics/pilates Xmas New Year Parking 350 Notes LB

GLAZEBROOK

MAP 07 SJ69

★★★ 75% HOTEL

Rhinewood Country House

Glazebrook Ln, Glazebrook WA3 5BB

☎ 0161 775 5555 🖹 0161 775 7965

e-mail: info@therhinewoodhotel.co.uk

web: www.therhinewoodhotel.co.uk

Dir: *M6 junct 21, A57 towards Irlam. Left at Glazebrook sign, hotel 0.25m on left*

PETS: Bedrooms Grounds accessible Exercise area 5 min walk

A warm welcome and attentive service are assured at this privately owned and personally run hotel. It stands in spacious grounds and gardens and is located between Warrington and Manchester. Facilities here include conference and function rooms and the hotel is also licensed for civil wedding ceremonies.

Rooms 32 en suite (4 fmly) (16 GF) ⊘ in 16 bedrooms Facilities STV Wi-fi in bedrooms Complimentary membership to nearby health spa Parking 120

KNUTSFORD

MAP 07 SJ77

★★ 80% HOTEL

The Longview Hotel & Restaurant

55 Manchester Rd WA16 0LX

☎ 01565 632119 🖹 01565 652402

e-mail: enquiries@longviewhotel.com

web: www.longviewhotel.com

Dir: *M6 junct 19 take A556 W towards Chester. Left at lights onto A5033, 1.5m to rdbt then left. Hotel 200yds on right*

PETS: Bedrooms (GF) unattended Charges £10 per night, charge for damage Exercise area 20mtrs Facilities vet info On Request fridge access torch towels

This friendly Victorian hotel offers high standards of hospitality and service. Attractive public areas include a cellar bar and foyer lounge area. The restaurant has a traditional feel and offers an imaginative selection of dishes. Bedrooms, some located in a superb renovation of nearby houses, are individually styled and offer a great range of thoughtful amenities, including broadband internet access.

Rooms 13 en suite 19 annexe en suite (1 fmly) (5 GF) S £60-£129; D £82-£149 (incl. bkfst)✷ Facilities Wi-fi in bedrooms Parking 20

MACCLESFIELD

MAP 07 SJ97

★★★★ 74% HOTEL

Paramount Shrigley Hall

🇯🇵 PARAMOUNT
GROUP OF HOTELS

Shrigley Park, Pott Shrigley SK10 5SB

☎ 01625 575757 🖹 01625 573323

e-mail: shrigleyhall@paramount-hotels.co.uk

web: www.paramount-hotels.co.uk

Dir: *off A523 at Legh Arms towards Pott Shrigley. Hotel 2m on left before village*

PETS: Bedrooms unattended Charges Public areas except dining room Grounds accessible Exercise area on site Resident Pets: Barney (cat)

Originally built in 1825, Shrigley Hall is an impressive hotel set in 262 acres of mature parkland and commands stunning views of the countryside. Features include a championship golf course. There is a wide choice of bedroom size and style. The public areas are spacious, combining traditional and contemporary decor, and include a well-equipped gym.

Rooms 150 en suite (8 fmly) ⊘ in 28 bedrooms S £74-£179✷ Facilities STV ③ supervised ♨ 18 ♨ Fishing Gym Putt green Wi-fi available Beauty salon Hydro centre ♫ Xmas New Year Services Lift Parking 300

►►► Capesthorne Hall *(SJ840727)*

Siddington SK11 9JY

☎ 01625 861221 📠 01625 861619

e-mail: info@capesthorne.com

web: www.capesthorne.com

Dir: *On A34, 1m S of A537*

PETS: Public areas except Hall & Gardens **Exercise area** on site
park land **Facilities** vet info **Other** prior notice required
Restrictions no dangerous dog breeds (see page 7)

Open Mar-Oct Booking advisable BH Last arrival 16.30hrs Last
departure noon

Set in the magnificent grounds of the historic Capesthorpe Hall, with
access to the lakes, gardens and woodland walks free to site users.
Pitches in the open parkland are spacious and can take the larger
motorhomes, and the clean toilet facilities are housed in the old stable
block. The beautiful Cheshire countryside is easily explored. No tents
or trailer tents. A 5.5-acre site with 30 touring pitches, 5 hardstandings.

Notes 🐾 No tents

NANTWICH   MAP 07 SJ65

★★ 71% HOTEL

Best Western Crown Hotel & Restaurant

High St CW5 5AS

☎ 01270 625283 📠 01270 628047

e-mail: info@crownhotelnantwich.com

web: www.crownhotelnantwich.com

Dir: *A52 to Nantwich, hotel in centre of town*

PETS: Bedrooms Public areas on leads **Facilities** cage storage
walks info vet info **On Request** fridge access towels
Resident Pets: Bertie (dog)

Ideally set in the heart of this historic and delightful market town, The
Crown has been offering hospitality for centuries. It has an abundance
of original features and the well-equipped bedrooms retain an old
world charm. There is also a bar with live entertainment throughout
the week and diners can enjoy Italian food in the atmospheric
brasserie.

Rooms 18 en suite (2 fmly) ⊘ in 2 bedrooms S fr £76; D fr £86✳
Facilities FTV Putt green Wi-fi in bedrooms ♫ **Parking** 18 **Notes** LB

RUNCORN   MAP 07 SJ58

BUDGET HOTEL
Campanile

Lowlands Rd WA7 5TP

Campanile

☎ 01928 581771 📠 01928 581730

e-mail: runcorn@envergure.co.uk

web: www.envergure.fr

Dir: *M56 junct 12, take A557, then follow signs for Runcorn rail
station/Runcorn College*

PETS: Please telephone for details

This modern building offers accommodation in smart, well-equipped
bedrooms, all with en suite bathrooms. Refreshments may be taken at
the informal Bistro. For further details consult the Hotel Groups page.

Rooms 53 en suite

TARPORLEY   MAP 07 SJ56

★★★★ FARM HOUSE
Hill House Farm *(SJ583626)*

Rushton CW6 9AU

☎ 01829 732238 📠 01829 733929 Mrs C Rayner

e-mail: aa@hillhousefarm-cheshire.co.uk

web: www.hillhousefarm-cheshire.co.uk

Dir: *1.5m E of Tarporley. Off A51/A49 to Eaton, take Lower Ln,
continue E for Rushton, right onto The Hall Ln, farm 0.5m*

PETS: Bedrooms Sep Accom kennels **Stables** on site
Charges please call for details **Public areas Grounds** accessible
Exercise area on site **Resident Pets:** 2 Springer Spaniels, 2
Labradors, Patterdale Terrier, Wallace & Grommit (cats), horses

This impressive brick farmhouse stands in very attractive gardens
within 14 acres of rolling pastureland. The stylish bedrooms have
en suite facilities, and there is a spacious lounge and a traditionally
furnished breakfast room. The proprietors are especially friendly.

Rooms 3 en suite 1 annexe en suite (1 fmly) ⊘ S £40-£50; D £70-£95✳
Facilities TVB tea/coffee Cen ht TVL **Parking** 6 **Notes** LB 14 acres
non-working Closed Xmas & New Year

WARRINGTON
MAP 07 SJ68

★★ 74% HOTEL
Paddington House

VENTURE HOTELS

514 Old Manchester Rd WA1 3TZ

☎ 01925 816767 📠 01925 816651

e-mail: hotel@paddingtonhouse.co.uk

web: www.paddingtonhouse.co.uk

Dir: *1m from M6 junct 21, off A57, 2m from town centre*

PETS: Bedrooms (GF) unattended **Charges** £5 per night, charge for damage **Grounds** accessible on leads disp bin **Facilities** water bowl vet info **On Request** fridge access towels **Restrictions** no large dogs

This busy, friendly hotel is conveniently situated just over a mile from the M6. Bedrooms are attractively furnished, and include four-poster and ground-floor rooms. Guests can dine in the wood-panelled Padgate restaurant or in the cosy bar. Conference and function facilities are available.

Rooms 37 en suite (9 fmly) (6 GF) ⊗ in 17 bedrooms S £50-£80; D £60-£90 (incl. bkfst) **Facilities** STV Wi-fi in bedrooms **Services** Lift **Parking** 50 **Notes** LB

WYBUNBURY
MAP 07 SJ64

★★★ FARM HOUSE
Lea Farm *(SJ717489)*

Wrinehill Rd CW5 7NS

☎ 01270 841429 Mrs J E Callwood

e-mail: leafarm@hotmail.co.uk

Dir: *1m E of Wybunbury village church on unclassified road*

PETS: Bedrooms Sep Accom outdoor kennel, barns **Stables** on site **Charges** £2 per night, charge for damage **Grounds** accessible on leads disp bin **Exercise area** adjacent **Facilities** food bowl water bowl bedding washing facs cage storage walks info vet info **On Request** fridge access torch towels **Resident Pets:** Lucy (Collie)

The working dairy farm is surrounded by delightful gardens and beautiful Cheshire countryside. The spacious bedrooms have modern facilities and there is a cosy lounge. Hearty breakfasts are served in the attractive dining room, which looks out over the garden, with its resident peacocks.

Rooms 3 rms (2 en suite) (1 fmly) ⊗ S £28-£35; D £48-£54✳ **Facilities** TVB tea/coffee Cen ht TVL Fishing Pool Table **Parking** 24 **Notes** 150 acres Dairy & beef ⊜

CORNWALL &
ISLES OF SCILLY

ASHTON
MAP 02 SW62

►►► **Boscrege Caravan & Camping Park**

(SW595305)

TR13 9TG

☎ 01736 762231

e-mail: enquiries@caravanparkcornwall.com

web: www.caravanparkcornwall.com

Dir: *From Helston on A394 turn right at Ashton next to Post Office. 1.5m along lane signed Boscreage.*

PETS: Exercise area on site 6 acre meadow Dogs on leads disp bin **Facilities** washing facs walks info vet info **Other** prior notice required

Open Mar-Nov Booking advisable Jul-Aug Last arrival 22.00hrs Last departure 11.00hrs

A quiet and bright little touring park divided into small paddocks with hedges, and offering plenty of open spaces for children to play in. The family-owned park offers clean, well-painted toilets facilities and neatly trimmed grass. In an Area of Outstanding Natural Beauty at the foot of Tregonning Hill. A 12-acre site with 50 touring pitches and 26 statics.

BLACKWATER
MAP 02 SW74

►►► Chiverton Park (SW743468)
East Hill TR4 8HS

☎ 01872 560667 📠 01872 560667

e-mail: chivertonpark@btopenworld.com

web: www.chivertonpark.co.uk

Dir: *Exit A30 at Chiverton rdbt (Little Chef) onto unclass road signed Blackwater (3rd exit). 1st right & park 300mtrs on right*

PETS: Charges £2 per night Public areas Facilities disp bin walks info vet info

Open 3 Mar-3 Nov (rs Mar-May & mid Sep-Nov limited stock kept in shop) Booking advisable mid Jul-Aug Last arrival 21.00hrs Last departure noon

A small, well-maintained site with some mature hedges dividing pitches, sited midway between Truro and St Agnes. Facilities include a good toilet block and a steam room, sauna and gym. A new games room with pool table, and children's outside play equipment should prove popular with families. A 4-acre site with 12 touring pitches, 10 hardstandings and 50 statics.

Notes No ball games

BODMIN
MAP 02 SX06

►►► Bodmin Camping & Caravanning Club Site (SX081676)
Old Callywith Rd PL31 2DZ

☎ 01208 73834

web: www.campingandcaravanningclub.co.uk/bodmin

Dir: *A30 from N, at sign for Bodmin turn right crossing dual carriageway in front of industrial estate, turn left at international sign, site left*

PETS: Public areas except buildings disp bin Exercise area on site Facilities walks info vet info Other prior notice required

Open 13 Mar-3 Nov Booking advisable BH & peak periods Last arrival 21.00hrs Last departure noon

Undulating grassy site with trees and bushes set in meadowland close to the town of Bodmin with all its attractions. The site is close to the A30 and makes a very good touring base. An 11-acre site with 130 touring pitches, 12 hardstandings.

Notes Gates closed 23.00-07.00

BOSCASTLE
MAP 02 SX09

★★★★ GUEST ACCOMMODATION
Old Coach House
Tintagel Rd PL35 0AS

☎ 01840 250398 📠 01840 250346

e-mail: jackiefarm@btinternet.com

web: www.old-coach.co.uk

Dir: *In village at junct B3266 & B3263*

PETS: Bedrooms (GF) Charges £5 per stay charge for damage Grounds accessible disp bin Exercise area 250mtrs Facilities walks info vet info

Over 300 years old, the Old Coach House has lovely views over the village and the rolling countryside. The comfortable bedrooms are well equipped and include two rooms on the ground floor. A hearty breakfast is served in the conservatory, which overlooks the well-kept garden.

Rooms 8 en suite (3 fmly) (2 GF) ⊗ S £30-£42; D £48-£60✳
Facilities TVB tea/coffee Cen ht TVL Parking 9 Notes LB Closed Xmas

BUDE
MAP 02 SS20

★★ 74% SMALL HOTEL
Penarvor
Crooklets Beach EX23 8NE

☎ 01288 352036 📠 01288 355027

e-mail: hotel.penarvor@boltblue.com

Dir: *From A39 towards Bude for 1.5m. At 2nd rdbt right, pass shops. Top of hill, left signed Crooklets Beach*

PETS: Bedrooms Charges £2 per night, charge for damage Public areas except restaurant on leads Grounds accessible on leads disp bin Facilities vet info On Request fridge access Resident Pets: Bonnie (Old English/Border Collie cross), Charlie (Cocker Spaniel)

Adjacent to the golf course and overlooking Crooklets Beach, this family owned hotel has a relaxed and friendly atmosphere. Bedrooms vary in size but are all equipped to a similar standard. An interesting selection of dishes, using fresh local produce, is available in the restaurant; bar meals are also provided.

Rooms 16 en suite (6 fmly) ⊗ in all bedrooms S £34-£40; D £68-£80 (incl. bkfst)✳ Parking 20 Notes LB

BUDE CONTINUED

★★★★ GUEST HOUSE
Cliff

Maer Down, Crooklets Beach EX23 8NG

☎ 01288 353110 & 356833 ▤ 01288 353110

web: www.cliffhotel.co.uk

Dir: *A39 through Bude, left at top of High St, pass Somerfields, 1st right between golf course, over x-rds, premises at end*

PETS: Bedrooms (GF) unattended **Stables** nearby **Charges** £2.50 per night **Grounds** accessible **Facilities** cage storage walks info vet info **On Request** fridge access torch towels **Resident Pets:** Janus & Crystal (Boxers), 13 rabbits

Overlooking the sea from a clifftop location, this friendly and efficient establishment provides spacious, well-equipped bedrooms. The various public areas include a bar and lounge and an impressive range of leisure facilities. Delicious dinners and tasty breakfasts are available in the attractive dining room.

Rooms 15 en suite (15 fmly) (8 GF) ✆ S £57.30-£63.30; D £95.50-£105.50✳ **Facilities** TVB tea/coffee Direct dial from bedrooms Licensed Cen ht TVL Dinner Last d 6pm ✆ ☕ Gymnasium Pool Table ♿ **Parking** 18 **Notes** LB No coaches Closed Nov-Mar

►►► Willow Valley Holiday Park (SS236078)

Bush EX23 9LB

☎ 01288 353104

e-mail: willowvalley@talk21.com

web: www.willowvalley.co.uk

Dir: *On A39, 0.5m N of junct with A3072 at Stratton*

PETS: Charges £1 per night **Public areas Exercise area** on site field available disp bin **Facilities** on site shop food vet info **Other** prior notice required

Open Mar-Dec Booking advisable Jul & Aug Last arrival 21.00hrs Last departure noon

A small sheltered park in Strat Valley with a stream running through and level grassy pitches. The friendly family owners have improved all areas of this attractive park, which has direct access off the A39, and only 2 miles from the sandy beaches at Bude. A 4-acre site with 41 touring pitches and 4 statics.

Notes ✆

CAMELFORD   MAP 02 SX18

►►► Lakefield Caravan Park (SX095853)

Lower Pendavey Farm PL32 9TX

☎ 01840 213279

e-mail: lakefield@pendavey.fsnet.co.uk

web: www.lakefieldcaravanpark.co.uk

Dir: *From A39 in Camelford turn right onto B3266, then right at T-junct, site 1.5m on left*

PETS: Stables on site (loose box) **Charges** horses £25 (stables), £5 (grass) per night **Public areas Exercise area** on site disp bin **Facilities** on site shop horse feed and bedding wash facs vet info **Other** drive with caution on site - many resident animals, prior notice required **Resident Pets:** Mo & Bill (Border Terriers), Spock (Papillon), Meg (Jack Russell), Puss-Puss (cat), 40 horses

Open Etr or Apr-Oct Booking advisable Jul-Aug Last arrival 22.00hrs Last departure noon

Set in a rural location, this friendly park is part of a specialist equestrian centre, and offers good quality services. Riding lessons and hacks always available, with BHS qualified instructor. A 5-acre site with 40 touring pitches.

CARLYON BAY   MAP 02 SX05

►►► East Crinnis Camping & Caravan Park (SX062528)

Lantyan, East Crinnis PL24 2SQ

☎ 01726 813023 ▤ 01726 813023

e-mail: eastcrinnis@btconnect.com

web: www.crinniscamping.co.uk

Dir: *From A390 (Lostwithiel to St Austell) take A3082 signed Fowey at rdbt by Britannia Inn, site on left*

PETS: Charges 1 pet free, 2 or more pets £1 **Public areas** except children's area & shower block **Exercise area** on site walks around park **Facilities** walks info vet info **Other** prior notice required

Open Etr-Oct Booking advisable Jul & Aug Last arrival 21.00hrs Last departure 11.00hrs

A small rural park with spacious pitches set in individual bays about one mile from the beaches at Carlyon Bay. The friendly owners keep the site very clean, and the Eden Project is just 2m away. A 2-acre site with 25 touring pitches, 6 hardstandings.

ENGLAND

CAWSAND   MAP 02 SX45

★★★ GUEST ACCOMMODATION
Wringford Down
Hat Ln PL10 1LE
☎ 01752 822287
e-mail: a.molloy@virgin.net
web: www.cornwallholidays.co.uk
Dir: *A374 onto B3247, pass Millbrook, right towards Cawsand & sharp right, 0.5m on right*
PETS: Bedrooms (GF) sign **Sep Accom** kennel **Stables** nearby (0.5m) **Charges** £4 per night £25 per week charge for damage **Grounds** accessible on leads disp bin **Exercise area** on site 100mtrs **Facilities** washing facs cage storage walks info vet info **On Request** fridge access torch towels **Resident Pets:** Danny & Daisy (Golden Retrievers), Sylvester, Truffle, Toffee (ponies), Billy & Baby (cats)
This family-run establishment has a peaceful location near Rame Head and the South West Coast Path, and is particularly welcoming to families. There is a nursery, swimming pool, games room, and gardens with play areas. A range of rooms, and some suites and self-catering units are available. Breakfast and dinner are served in the dining room.
Rooms 7 en suite 5 annexe en suite (9 fmly) (4 GF) ⊘ S £42.50-£50; D £65-£90✹ **Facilities** TVB tea/coffee Cen ht TVL Dinner Last d 8pm ⊗ ☒ Pool Table **Parking** 20 **Notes** LB ⊗ ch fac

COVERACK   MAP 02 SW71

►►► Little Trevothan Caravan & Camping Park *(SW772179)*
Trevothan TR12 6SD
☎ 01326 280260
e-mail: sales@littletrevothan.co.uk
web: www.littletrevothan.co.uk
Dir: *From A3083 onto B3293 signed Coverack, approx 2m after Goonhilly ESS, right at Zoar Garage on unclass road. Across Downs approx 1m then take 3rd left. Site 0.5m on left*
PETS: Charges £1.50 per night **Public areas** on leads & waste must be removed except children's play areas **Exercise area** on site fenced off area coastal walks disp bin **Facilities** on site shop washing facs walks info vet info **Other** prior notice required **Restrictions** No Pitt Bulls or Rottweilers
Resident Pets: 2 Weimaraners, 2 cats & 2 rabbits
Open Mar-Oct Booking advisable Aug Last arrival 21.00hrs Last departure noon
A secluded site near the unspoilt fishing village of Coverack, with a large recreation area. The nearby sandy beach has lots of rock pools for children to play in, and the many walks both from the park and the village offer stunning scenery. A 10.5-acre site with 70 touring pitches and 40 statics.

CRANTOCK   MAP 02 SW76

★★★ 75% HOTEL
Crantock Bay
West Pentire TR8 5SE
☎ 01637 830229 🖷 01637 831111
e-mail: stay@crantockbayhotel.co.uk
web: www.crantockbayhotel.co.uk
Dir: *at Newquay A3075 to Redruth. After 500yds right towards Crantock, follow signs to West Pentire*
PETS: Please telephone for further details
This family-run hotel has spectacular sea views and a tradition of friendly and attentive service. With direct access to the beach from its four acres of grounds, and its extensive leisure facilities, the hotel is a great place for families. There are separate lounges, a spacious bar and enjoyable cuisine is served in the dining room.
Rooms 31 en suite (3 fmly) (9 GF) S £59-£105; D £118-£210 (incl. bkfst & dinner)✹ **Facilities** ⊗ ☒ Gym ⏌ Putt green Wi-fi available Children's games room Xmas New Year **Parking** 40 **Notes** LB Closed 2 wks Nov & Jan RS Dec & Feb

★★ 75% SMALL HOTEL
Fairbank
West Pentire Rd TR8 5SA
☎ 01637 830424 🖷 01637 830424
e-mail: enquiries@fairbankhotel.co.uk
web: www.fairbankhotel.co.uk
Dir: *A3075 1st exit towards Redruth turn right after 500mtrs signed Crantock. Follow signs for West Pentire, hotel on right leaving Crantock village.*
PETS: Bedrooms 2 bedrooms only **Grounds** accessible **Exercise area** 5 min walk to dog friendly beach
Most of the Fairbank Hotel bedrooms have spectacular views over Crantock Bay. Honest home cooking is served in the dining room, which with the bar and conservatory also benefit from the stunning views. Guests receive and warm welcome from the resident owners who create a relaxed and friendly atmosphere.
Rooms 14 en suite (3 fmly) ⊘ in all bedrooms S £37.50-£42.50; D £75-£95 (incl. bkfst) **Facilities** FTV Wi-fi in bedrooms **Parking** 16 **Notes** LB Closed Xmas & 3-31 Jan RS end Feb/early Mar

CRANTOCK CONTINUED

►►► Crantock Plains Touring Park

(SW805589)

TR8 5PH

☎ 01637 830955 & 831273

web: www.crantock-plains.co.uk

Dir: *Leave Newquay on A3075, take 3rd right signed to park & Crantock. Park on left in 0.75m on narrow road*

PETS: Public areas Exercise area on site disp bin **Facilities** on site shop disp bags

Open Etr-Oct Booking advisable Jul-Aug Last arrival 22.00hrs Last departure noon

A small rural park with pitches on either side of a narrow lane, surrounded by mature trees for shelter. The family-run park has modern toilet facilities appointed to a good standard. A 6-acre site with 60 touring pitches.

Notes ⊗ No skateboards

FALMOUTH

MAP 02 SW83

★★★ 78% HOTEL
Best Western Falmouth Beach Resort Hotel

Gyllyngvase Beach, Seafront TR11 4NA

☎ 01326 310500 📠 01326 319147

e-mail: info@falmouthbeachhotel.co.uk

web: www.bw-falmouthbeachhotel.co.uk

Dir: *A39 to Falmouth, follow seafront signs.*

PETS: Bedrooms unattended **Charges** £10 per night **Grounds** accessible **Exercise area** coast paths; beach in winter only

Enjoying wonderful views, this popular hotel is situated opposite the beach and within easy walking distance of Falmouth's attractions and port. A friendly atmosphere is maintained and guests have a good choice of leisure and fitness, entertainment and dining options. Bedrooms, many with balconies and sea views, are well equipped and comfortable.

Rooms 120 en suite (20 fmly) (4 GF) ⊘ in all bedrooms S £62-£72; D £124-£144 (incl. bkfst)✳ **Facilities** Spa FTV ③ supervised ♨ Gym Wi-fi available Steam room, Hair & beauty salon ♫ Xmas New Year **Services** Lift **Parking** 88 **Notes** LB

★★★ 77% HOTEL
Green Lawns

THE INDEPENDENTS

Western Ter TR11 4QJ

☎ 01326 312734 📠 01326 211427

e-mail: info@greenlawnshotel.com

web: www.greenlawnshotel.com

Dir: *on A39*

PETS: Bedrooms (GF) unattended **Charges** £12.50 per night **Exercise area** 0.25m **Facilities** food food bowl water bowl cage storage walks info vet info **On Request** fridge access torch towels

This attractive property enjoys a convenient location close to the town centre and within easy reach of the sea. Spacious public areas include inviting lounges, an elegant restaurant, conference and meeting facilities and a leisure centre. Bedrooms vary in size and style but all are well equipped and comfortable. The friendly service is particularly noteworthy.

Rooms 39 en suite (8 fmly) (11 GF) ⊘ in 24 bedrooms S £60-£105; D £90-£180 (incl. bkfst)✳ **Facilities** ③ ♨ Squash Gym Wi-fi in bedrooms Sauna Solarium Jacuzzi Spa bath New Year **Parking** 69 **Notes** LB Closed 24-30 Dec

---

★★★ 75% ⊛ HOTEL
Falmouth

RICHARDSON

Castle Beach TR11 4NZ

☎ 01326 312671 & 0800 019 3121 📠 01326 319533

e-mail: reservations@falmouthhotel.com

web: www.falmouthhotel.com

Dir: *take A30 to Truro then A390 to Falmouth. Follow signs for beaches, hotel on seafront near Pendennis Castle*

PETS: Bedrooms unattended **Charges Public areas Grounds** accessible **Exercise area** countryside; beach in winter

This spectacular beach front Victorian property affords wonderful sea views from many of its comfortable bedrooms, some of which have their own balconies. Spacious public areas include a number of inviting lounges, beautiful leafy grounds, a choice of dining options and an impressive range of leisure facilities.

Rooms 69 en suite (13 fmly) ⊘ in 50 bedrooms S £65-£75; D £98-£210 (incl. bkfst)✳ **Facilities** STV FTV ③ Gym Putt green Wi-fi available Beauty salon & Therapeutic rooms Xmas New Year **Services** Lift **Parking** 120 **Notes** LB

★★★ 71% HOTEL
Penmorvah Manor
Budock Water TR11 5ED
☎ 01326 250277 📠 01326 250509
e-mail: reception@penmorvah.co.uk
web: www.penmorvah.co.uk
Dir: *A39 to Hillhead rdbt, take 2nd exit. Right at Falmouth Football Club, through Budock and hotel opposite Penjerrick Gardens*

PETS: Bedrooms (GF) **Charges** £7.50 per night
Public areas except restaurants on leads **Grounds** accessible disp bin **Facilities** water bowl cage storage vet info
On Request torch towels **Resident Pets:** Millie (Cocker Spaniel), Toffee & Minky (cats)

Situated within two miles of central Falmouth, this extended Victorian manor house is a peaceful hideaway, set in six acres of private woodland and gardens. Penmorvah is well positioned for visiting the local gardens, and offers many garden-tour breaks. Dinner features locally sourced, quality ingredients such as Cornish cheeses, meat, fish and game.

Rooms 27 en suite (1 fmly) (10 GF) ⊘ in all bedrooms S fr £65;
D £100-£150 (incl. bkfst)✳ **Facilities** Xmas **Parking** 100 **Notes** LB Closed 31 Dec-31 Jan

★★★★ 🔔 GUEST ACCOMMODATION
Prospect House
1 Church Rd, Penryn TR10 8DA
☎ 01326 373198 📠 01326 373198
e-mail: stay@prospecthouse.co.uk
web: www.prospecthouse.co.uk
Dir: *Off A39 at Treluswell rdbt onto B3292, past Crosskeys pub & over lights, after 50yds right through white gates next to phone box*

PETS: Bedrooms Charges £5 per night **Grounds** accessible
Exercise area 150mtrs **Facilities** food **Other** Small friendly dogs only **Resident Pets:** Jerry (cat)

Situated close to the waterside, Prospect House is an attractive building, which was built for a ship's captain around 1820. The original charm of the house has been carefully maintained. The attractive bedrooms are well equipped. A comfortable lounge is available, and freshly cooked breakfasts are served in the elegant dining room.

Rooms 3 en suite ⊘ S £37.50; D £65✳ **Facilities** TVB tea/coffee Cen ht TVL Dinner Last d 9.30pm **Parking** 4 **Notes** LB

★★★★ GUEST ACCOMMODATION
The Rosemary
22 Gyllyngvase Ter TR11 4DL
☎ 01326 314669
e-mail: therosemary@tiscali.co.uk
web: www.therosemary.co.uk
Dir: *A39 Melvill Rd signed to beaches & seafront, right onto Gyllyngvase Rd, 1st left*

PETS: Bedrooms Public areas except restaurant on leads
Grounds accessible **Exercise area** 400mtrs **Facilities** walks info vet info **On Request** fridge access **Resident Pets:** Rifca (Black Labrador)

Centrally located with splendid views over Falmouth Bay, this friendly establishment provides comfortable accommodation. The attractive bedrooms are thoughtfully equipped; some with the benefit of the views. Guests can relax in the lounge with a drink from the well stocked bar. Also available is a sunny decking area at the rear in the pretty garden, facing the sea.

Rooms 10 en suite (4 fmly) ⊘ S £36-£41; D £62-£72✳ **Facilities** TVB tea/coffee Cen ht TVL Wi-fi available **Parking** 3 **Notes** Closed Nov-Jan

►►► Pennance Mill Farm Touring Park
(SW792307)
Maenporth TR11 5HJ
☎ 01326 317431 📠 01326 317431
web: www.pennancemill.co.uk
Dir: *(From A39 (Truro-Falmouth) follow brown camping signs towards Maenporth Beach. At Hill Head rdbt take 2nd exit for Maenporth Beach)*

PETS: Charges £1.50 to £2 per night **Public areas**
Exercise area on site & 100mtrs **Facilities** on site shop walks info vet info **Other** prior notice required

Open Etr-Xmas Booking advisable Last arrival 22.00hrs Last departure 10.00hrs

Set approximately half a mile from the safe, sandy Bay of Maenporth this is a mainly level, grassy park in a rural location sheltered by mature trees and shrubs and divided into three meadows. It has a modern toilet block. A 6-acre site with 75 touring pitches, 8 hardstandings and 4 statics.

Notes ⊛

ENGLAND

FOWEY MAP 02 SX15

★★★ 83% ●● HOTEL

Fowey Hall

Hanson Dr PL23 1ET

von Essen hotels
A PRIVATE COLLECTION
www.vonessenhotels.com

☎ 01726 833866 📠 01726 834100

e-mail: info@foweyhallhotel.co.uk

web: www.vonessenhotels.co.uk

Dir: *In Fowey, over mini rdbt into town centre. Pass school on right, 400mtrs right into Hanson Drive*

PETS: **Bedrooms Charges** £7 per night **Public areas** on leads **Grounds** accessible **Exercise area** beach **Facilities** food bowl bedding **Restrictions** only 2 dogs in hotel at any one time **Resident Pets:** Millie (Collie/Spaniel cross)

Built in 1899, this listed mansion looks out on to the English Channel. The imaginatively designed bedrooms offer charm, individuality and sumptuous comfort; the Garden Wing rooms adding a further dimension to staying here. The beautifully appointed public rooms include the wood-panelled dining room where accomplished cuisine is served. Enjoying glorious views, the well-kept grounds have a covered pool and sunbathing area.

Rooms 28 en suite 8 annexe en suite (30 fmly) (8 GF) D £175-£550 (incl. bkfst & dinner)✷ **Facilities** STV ⊙ ⌖ Wi-fi available Table tennis Basketball Trampoline ch fac Xmas New Year **Parking** 40 **Notes** LB

★★★★ GUEST ACCOMMODATION

Trevanion

70 Lostwithiel St PL23 1BQ

☎ 01726 832602

e-mail: alisteve@trevanionguesthouse.co.uk

web: www.trevanionguesthouse.co.uk

Dir: *A3082 into Fowey, down hill, left onto Lostwithiel St, Trevanion on left*

PETS: Please telephone for details

This 16th-century merchant's house provides friendly, comfortable accommodation within easy walking distance of the historic town of Fowey and is convenient for visiting the Eden Project. A hearty farmhouse-style cooked breakfast, using local produce, is served in the attractive dining room and other menu options are available.

Rooms 5 rms (4 en suite) (1 pri facs) (2 fmly) (1 GF) ✷ S £35; D £50-£65✷ **Facilities** TVB tea/coffee Cen ht **Parking** 5 **Notes** LB ✐

▶▶▶ **Penmarlam Caravan & Camping Park**

(SX134526)

Bodinnick PL23 1LZ

☎ 01726 870088 📠 01726 870082

e-mail: info@penmarlampark.co.uk

web: www.penmarlampark.co.uk

Dir: *From A390 at East Taphouse take B3359 signed Looe & Polperro. Follow signs for Bodinnick & Fowey, via ferry. Site on right at entrance to Bodinnick*

PETS: **Stables** nearby (4m) **Public areas** assist dogs only in shower/toilet block **Exercise area** on site several walks adjacent disp bin **Facilities** on site shop food dog chews cat treats disp bags washing facs walks info vet info **Resident Pets:** Rusty (Border Terrier), Pippa (Collie cross)

Open Apr-Oct (& Easter 2008) Booking advisable BH, Jul-Aug Last departure Noon

A tranquil park set above the Fowey Estuary in an Area of Outstanding Natural Beauty, with access to the water. Pitches are level, and sheltered by trees and bushes in two paddocks, while the toilets are well maintained. A 4-acre site with 65 touring pitches and 1 static.

GOONHAVERN MAP 02 SW75

▶▶▶▶ **Penrose Farm Touring Park**

(SW795534)

TR4 9QF

☎ 01872 573185 📠 01872 573185

web: www.penrosefarm.co.uk

Dir: *From Exeter take A30, past Bodmin and Indian Queens. Just after Wind Farm take B3285 towards Perranporth, site on left on entering Goonhavern*

PETS: **Charges** free except 21 Jul-31 Aug £2 per night **Public areas Exercise area** on site field available local countryside & beach disp bin **Facilities** on site shop food food bowl water bowl dog chews walks info vet info **Other** prior notice required

Open Apr-Oct Booking advisable Jul & Aug Last arrival 21.30hrs

A quiet sheltered park set in five paddocks divided by hedges and shrubs, only a short walk from the village. Lovely floral displays enhance the park's appearance, and the grass and hedges are neatly trimmed. Four cubicled family rooms are very popular, and there is a good laundry. A 9-acre site with 100 touring pitches, 8 hardstandings and 8 statics.

Notes No skateboards/rollerskates. Families & couples only

►►► Roseville Holiday Park *(SW787540)*

TR4 9LA

☎ 01872 572448 🖹 01872 572448

web: www.rosevilleholidaypark.co.uk

Dir: *From mini-rdbt in Goonhavern follow B3285 towards Perranporth, site 0.5m on right*

PETS: Stables nearby (1m) **Charges** £1-£2 per night in high season **Public areas Exercise area** on site field available disp bin **Facilities** vet info **Restrictions** No Rottweilers, Pitt Bulls or Staffordshire Bull Terriers

Open Whit-Oct (rs Apr-Jul, Sep-Oct shop closed) Booking advisable Jul-Aug Last arrival 21.30hrs Last departure 11.00hrs

A family park set in a rural location with sheltered grassy pitches, some gently sloping. The toilet facilities are modern, and there is an attractive outdoor swimming pool complex. Approximately 2 miles from the long sandy beach at Perranporth. An 8-acre site with 95 touring pitches and 5 statics.

Notes 🐾 Families only site

GORRAN   MAP 02 SW94

►►► Treveague Farm Caravan & Camping Site *(SX002410)*

PL26 6NY

☎ 01726 842295 🖹 01726 842295

e-mail: treveague@btconnect.com

web: www.infotreveaguefarm.co.uk

Dir: *From St Austell take B3273 towards Mevagissey, past Pentewan at top of hill, turn right signed Gorran. Past Heligan Gardens towards Gorran Churchtown. Follow brown tourist signs from fork in road*

PETS: Public areas on leads **Exercise area** on site field available adjacent farm disp bin **Facilities** on site shop vet info

Open Apr-Oct Booking advisable at all times Last arrival 21.00hrs Last departure noon

Spectacular panoramic coastal views are a fine feature of this rural park, which is well equipped with modern facilities. A stone-faced toilet block with a Cornish slate roof is an attractive and welcome feature of the park. A footpath leads to the fishing village of Gorran Haven in one direction, and the secluded sandy Vault Beach in the other. A 4-acre site with 40 touring pitches.

Notes 🐾

GORRAN HAVEN   MAP 02 SX04

►► Trelispen Caravan & Camping Park
(SX008421)

PL26 6NT

☎ 01726 843501 🖹 01726 843501

e-mail: trelispen@care4free.net

web: www.trelispen.co.uk

Dir: *B3273 from St Austell towards Mevagissey, on hilltop at x-roads before descent into Mevagissey turn right on unclass road to Gorran. Through village, 2nd right towards Gorran Haven, site signed on left in 250mtrs*

PETS: Public areas Exercise area nearby lane **Facilities** vet info

Open Etr & Apr-Oct Booking advisable Last arrival 22.00hrs Last departure noon

A sheltered campsite in a beautiful, quiet location within easy reach of the beaches. The dated toilets have plenty of hot water, and there is a small laundry. Pubs and shops are nearby. A 2-acre site with 40 touring pitches.

Notes 🐾

GWITHIAN   MAP 02 SW54

►►► Gwithian Farm Campsite *(SW586412)*

Gwithian Farm TR27 5BX

☎ 01736 753127

e-mail: camping@gwithianfarm.co.uk

web: www.gwithianfarm.co.uk

Dir: *Exit A30 at Hayle rdbt, take 4th exit signed Hayle, 100mtrs. At 1st mini-rdbt turn right onto B3301 signed Portreath. Site 2m on left on entering village*

PETS: Stables nearby (0.5m) **Charges** £1 per night £7 per week **Public areas** on leads **Exercise area** 100mtrs disp bin **Facilities** on site shop walks info vet info **Resident Pets:** Spud (Dog)

Open 31 Mar-1 Oct Booking advisable Jul-Aug Last arrival 22.00hrs Last departure 17.00hrs

An unspoilt site located behind the sand dunes of Gwithian's golden beach, which can be reached directly by footpath from the site. The site boasts a superb toilet block with excellent facilities including a bathroom and baby-changing unit. There is a good pub opposite. A 7.5-acre site with 87 touring pitches, 4 hardstandings.

HAYLE

MAP 02 SW53

►►► Treglisson Camping & Caravan Park

(SW581367)

Wheal Alfred Rd TR27 5JT

☎ 01736 753141

e-mail: enquiries@treglisson.co.uk

web: www.treglisson.co.uk

Dir: *4th exit off rdbt on A30 at Hayle. 100mtrs, turn left at 1st mini-rdbt. 1.5km past golf course, site sign on left*

PETS: Public areas on leads **Exercise area** 100mtrs to beach disp bin **Facilities** washing facs walks info vet info **Other** prior notice required **Resident Pets:** Poppy (Border Collie), Tabby, Rosie & Jim (cats)

Open Etr-Oct Booking advisable Jul-Aug Last arrival 20.00hrs Last departure 11.00hrs

A small secluded site in a peaceful wooded meadow, a former apple and pear orchard. This quiet rural site has a well-planned modern toilet block and level grass pitches, and is just 2 miles from the glorious beach at Hayle with its vast stretch of golden sand. A 3-acre site with 30 touring pitches.

Notes Max 6 people to a pitch

HELSTON

MAP 02 SW62

►►► Poldown Caravan Park *(SW629298)*

Poldown, Carleen TR13 9NN

☎ 01326 574560

e-mail: stay@poldown.co.uk

web: www.poldown.co.uk

Dir: *From Helston follow Penzance signs for 1m then right onto B3302 to Hayle, 2nd left to Carleen, 0.5m to site*

PETS: Charges £1 per night **Public areas Exercise area** adjacent dog friendly beaches nearby **Facilities** washing facs walks info vet info **Other** prior notice required **Resident Pets:** 1 dog (Retriever)

Open Apr-Sep Booking advisable Jul-Aug Last arrival 22.00hrs Last departure noon

A small, quiet site set in attractive countryside with bright toilet facilities. All of the level grass pitches have electricity, and the sunny park is sheltered by mature trees and shrubs. A 2-acre site with 13 touring pitches and 7 statics.

Notes ☺

► Skyburriowe Farm *(SW698227)*

Garras TR12 6LR

☎ 01326 221646

e-mail: bkbenney@hotmail.co.uk

web: www.skyburriowefarm.co.uk

Dir: *From Helston take A3083 to The Lizard. After Culdrose naval airbase continue straight at rdbt, after 1m left at Skyburriowe Lane sign. In 0.5m right at sign Skyburriowe B&B/Campsite sign. Continue past bungalow to farmhouse. Site on left.*

PETS: Stables nearby (4m) (loose box) **Public areas** on leads **Exercise area** adjacent **Facilities** walks info vet info **Other** prior notice required **Resident Pets:** Finlee & Candy (Golden Retrievers)

Open Apr-Oct Booking advisable Last arrival 22.00hrs Last departure 11.00hrs

A leafy no-through road leads to this picturesque farm park in a rural location on the Lizard Peninsula. The facilities are fairly basic, but most pitches have electricity. There are some beautiful coves and beaches nearby. A 4-acre site with 30 touring pitches.

Notes ☺ quiet after 23.00hrs

HOLYWELL BAY

MAP 02 SW75

Trevornick Holiday Park

(SW776586)

TR8 5PW

☎ 01637 830531 ▤ 01637 831000

e-mail: info@trevornick.co.uk

web: www.trevornick.co.uk

Dir: *3m from Newquay off A3075 towards Redruth. Follow Cubert & Holywell Bay signs*

PETS: Charges £3.45 - £3.75 per night £24.15 - £26.25 per week **Public areas** on leads **Exercise area** on site fields available & in 0.25m **Facilities** on site shop food food bowl water bowl dog chews cat treats dog scoop/disp bags walks info vet info **Other** prior notice required

Open Etr & mid May-mid Sep Booking advisable Jul-Aug Last arrival 21.00hrs Last departure 10.00hrs

A large seaside holiday complex with excellent facilities and amenities. There is plenty of entertainment including a children's club and an evening cabaret, adding up to a full holiday experience for all the family. A sandy beach is a 15-minute footpath walk away. The park has 68 ready-erected tents for hire. A 20-acre site with 593 touring pitches, 6 hardstandings.

Notes Families and couples only

KENNACK SANDS   MAP 02 SW71

▶▶▶ **Chy-Carne Holiday Park** *(SW725164)*

Kuggar, Ruan Minor TR12 7LX

☎ 01326 290200 & 291161

e-mail: enquiries@chy-carne.co.uk

web: www.chy-carne.co.uk

Dir: *From A3083 turn left on B3293 after Culdrose Naval Air Station. At Goonhilly ESS right onto unclass road signed Kennack Sands. Left in 3m at junct*

PETS: Charges 50p-75p per night **Public areas Exercise area** on site 2.5 acre field **Facilities** on site shop food food bowl water bowl washing facs dog grooming off site walks info vet info **Resident Pets:** Armstrong (Labrador), Amy (Pitbull) Polly and Candy (cats)

Open Etr-Oct Booking advisable Aug Last arrival dusk

Small but spacious park in quiet, sheltered spot, with extensive sea and coastal views from the grassy touring area. A village pub with restaurant is a short walk by footpath from the touring area, and a sandy beach is less than 0.5 miles away. A 6-acre site with 14 touring pitches and 18 statics.

▶▶▶ **Silver Sands Holiday Park** *(SW727166)*

Gwendreath TR12 7LZ

☎ 01326 290631 📠 01326 290631

e-mail: enquiries@silversandsholidaypark.co.uk

web: www.silversandsholidaypark.co.uk

Dir: *From Helston follow signs to Goonhilly. 300yds after Goonhilly Earth Station turn right at x-roads signed Kennack Sands, 1.5m, left at Gwendreath sign, park 1m*

PETS: Charges £1.10 - £1.80 per night **Public areas** except toilet block & reception **Exercise area** on site field available 20yds disp bin **Facilities** washing facs walks info vet info **Other** prior notice required loose box **Resident Pets:** Larch & Willow (Border Terriers), Chrissie & Puff Fluff (cats)

Open Etr-Sep Booking advisable Jul-Aug Last arrival 20.00hrs Last departure 11.00hrs

A small park in a remote location, with individually screened pitches providing sheltered suntraps. A footpath through the woods from the family-owned park leads to the beach and the local pub. A 9-acre site with 34 touring pitches and 16 statics.

Notes No groups

LAND'S END   MAP 02 SW32

★★★ 64% HOTEL

The Land's End Hotel

TR19 7AA

☎ 01736 871844 📠 01736 871599

e-mail: reservations@landsendhotel.wanadoo.co.uk

web: www.landsendhotel.co.uk

Dir: *from Penzance take A30 and follow Land's End signs. After Sennen 1m to Land's End*

PETS: Bedrooms unattended for short periods only **Charges** £20 per night **Public areas** except food areas and bar **Grounds** accessible **Exercise area** many coastal walks

This famous location provides a very impressive setting for this well-established hotel. Bedrooms, many with stunning views of the Atlantic, are pleasantly decorated and comfortable. A relaxing lounge and attractive bar are provided. The Longships restaurant with far reaching sea views offers fresh local produce, and fish dishes are a speciality.

Rooms 33 en suite (2 fmly) S £50-£92; D £100-£184 (incl. bkfst & dinner) ✳ **Facilities** STV Free entry Land's End Visitor Centre Xmas New Year **Parking** 1000 **Notes** LB

LANIVET   MAP 02 SX06

▶▶▶ **Mena Caravan & Camping Site**

(SW041626)

Mena Farm PL30 5HW

☎ 01208 831845

e-mail: mena@campsitesincornwall.co.uk

web: www.campsitesincornwall.co.uk

Dir: *Exit A30 at Innes Downs rdbt onto A391 signed St Austell. 0.5m 1st left, then 0.75m turn right (before bridge) signed Fowey/Lanhydrock. 0.5m to staggered junct & monument stone, sharp right, 0.5m down hill, right into site*

PETS: Charges £1 - £2 per night £7 - £14 per week **Public areas Exercise area** on site adjacent fields and woods disp bin **Facilities** washing facs walks info vet info

Open Etr-Sep Booking advisable Jul-Aug Last arrival 22.00hrs Last departure noon

Set in a secluded, elevated location with high hedges for shelter, and plenty of peace. This grassy site is about 4 miles from the Eden Project, and midway between N and S coasts. On site is a small coarse fishing lake. A 4-acre site with 25 touring pitches and 2 statics.

Notes 🐕

ENGLAND

LAUNCESTON
MAP 03 SX38

★★ 69% SMALL HOTEL
Eagle House
Castle St PL15 8BA
☎ 01566 772036 & 774488 ▤ 01566 772036
e-mail: eaglehousehotel@aol.com
Dir: *from Launceston on Holsworthy Rd follow brown hotel signs*
PETS: Bedrooms Grounds accessible **Exercise area** on site
Next to the castle, this elegant Georgian house dates back to 1767 and is within walking distance of all the local amienties. Many of the bedrooms have wonderful views over the Cornish countryside. A short carte is served each evening in the restaurant.

Rooms 14 en suite (1 fmly) S fr £37; D fr £64 (incl. bkfst)✳
Facilities STV **Parking** 100 **Notes** ⊗

LISKEARD
MAP 02 SX26

★★★★ BED & BREAKFAST
Redgate Smithy
Redgate, St Cleer PL14 6RU
☎ 01579 321578
e-mail: enquiries@redgatesmithy.co.uk
web: www.redgatesmithy.co.uk
Dir: *3m NW of Liskeard. Off A30 at Bolventor/Jamaica Inn onto St Cleer Rd for 7m, B&B just past x-rds*
PETS: Bedrooms unattended **Public areas** except at breakfast
Exercise area adjacent **Facilities** food bowl bedding dog chews dog scoop/disp bags washing facs walks info vet info
On Request towels **Restrictions** no Rottweilers, Rhodesian Ridgebacks or German Shepherds **Resident Pets:** Sinbad (Cocker Spaniel)
This 200-year-old converted smithy is on the southern fringe of Bodmin Moor near Golitha Falls. The friendly accommodation offers smartly furnished, cottage style bedrooms with many extra facilities. There are several dining options nearby, and a wide chice of freshly cooked breakfasts are served in the conservatory.

Rooms 3 rms (2 en suite) (1 pri facs) ⊗ S fr £40; D fr £60
Facilities TVB tea/coffee Cen ht **Parking** 3 **Notes** LB No children 12yrs Closed Xmas & New Year 🕾

LOOE
MAP 02 SX25

★★★ 64% HOTEL
Hannafore Point
THE INDEPENDENTS
Marine Dr, West Looe PL13 2DG
☎ 01503 263273 ▤ 01503 263272
e-mail: stay@hannaforepointhotel.com
Dir: *A38, left onto A385 to Looe. Over bridge turn left. Hotel 0.5m on left*
PETS: Bedrooms Charges £8 per night **Public areas** except food service areas **Exercise area** beach and coastal walks
Facilities food
With panoramic coastal views of St George's Island around to Rame Head, this popular hotel provides a warm welcome. The wonderful view is certainly a feature of the spacious restaurant and bar, providing a scenic backdrop for both dinners and breakfasts. Additional facilities include a heated indoor pool, squash court and gym.

Rooms 37 en suite (5 fmly) S £50-£70; D £100-£140 (incl. bkfst)✳
Facilities ⊙ Gym ♫ Xmas New Year **Services** Lift **Parking** 32
Notes LB

★★ 76% HOTEL
Fieldhead
THE INDEPENDENTS
Portuan Rd, Hannafore PL13 2DR
☎ 01503 262689 ▤ 01503 264114
e-mail: enquiries@fieldheadhotel.co.uk
web: www.fieldheadhotel.co.uk
Dir: *In Looe pass Texaco garage, cross bridge, left to Hannafore. At Tom Sawyer turn right & right again into Portuan Rd. Hotel on left*
PETS: Bedrooms (GF) unattended sign **Charges** £5 per night charge for damage **Grounds** accessible on leads **Facilities** walks info vet info **Restrictions** small dogs preferred
Resident Pets: Trudy (King Charles Spaniel), Baby (Cockatoo), Charlie (Cockatiel), Albi (Budgie), Connie & Pippa (Guinea Pigs)
Overlooking the bay, this engaging hotel has a relaxing atmosphere. Bedrooms are furnished with care and many have sea views. Smartly presented public areas include a convivial bar and restaurant, and outside there is a palm-filled garden with a secluded patio and swimming pool. The fixed-price menu changes daily and features quality local produce.

Rooms 16 en suite (2 fmly) (2 GF) S £36-£60; D £73-£125 (incl. bkfst)✳
Facilities ⊀ Wi-fi in bedrooms New Year **Parking** 15 **Notes** LB Closed Xmas

★★★★ ➾ GUEST HOUSE

South Trelowia Barns

Widegates PL13 1QL

☎ 01503 240709

e-mail: madley.cornwall@virgin.net

Dir: *A387 W from Hessenford, 1m left signed Trelowia, 0.75m down lane on right*

PETS: Bedrooms (GF) **Charges** £2 (Etr-Oct) per night **Public areas Grounds** accessible disp bin **Facilities** food bowl water bowl bedding dog scoop/disp bags washing facs cage storage walks info vet info **On Request** fridge access torch towels **Resident Pets:** Daisy (Terrier cross), Henry & Victor (cats)

Set in a very peaceful rural location, this home offers a relaxing environment and is full of character. The proprietors provide a warm welcome and guests are made to feel at home. The comfortable bedrooms have lots of extra facilities. Cooking is accomplished and features home-grown and local produce.

Rooms 1 en suite 1 annexe en suite (2 fmly) ⊗ S £27-£44; D £50-£54 **Facilities** TV1B tea/coffee Cen ht TVL Dinner Last d 10.30am **Parking** 6 **Notes** LB No coaches ⊛

►►► Camping Caradon Touring Park

(SX218539)

Trelawne PL13 2NA

☎ 01503 272388 🖃 01503 272858

e-mail: enquiries@campingcaradon.co.uk

web: www.campingcaradon.co.uk

Dir: *Site signed from B3359 near junct with A387, between Looe and Polperro*

PETS: Charges £1 - £2 per night **Public areas** except shop, bar & club room **Exercise area** 0.25m disp bin **Facilities** on site shop food food bowl water bowl disp bags leads walks info vet info

Open all year (rs Oct-Etr by booking only) Booking advisable Jul-Aug Last arrival 22.00hrs Last departure noon

Set in a quiet rural location between the popular coastal resorts of Looe and Polperro, this family-run park is just 1.5m from the beach at Talland Bay. The owners have upgraded the bar and restaurant, and are continuing to improve the park. A 3.5-acre site with 85 touring pitches, 23 hardstandings.

►►► Polborder House Caravan & Camping Park *(SX283557)*

Bucklawren Rd, St Martin PL13 1NZ

☎ 01503 240265

e-mail: reception@peaceful-polborder.co.uk

web: www.peaceful-polborder.co.uk

Dir: *Approach Looe from E on A387, follow B3253 for 1m, left at Polborder & Monkey Sanctuary sign. Site 0.5m on right*

PETS: Stables nearby (2m) (loose box) **Public areas Exercise area** 10yds disp bin **Facilities** on site shop food dog scoop/disp bags leads washing facs walks info vet info **Other** prior notice required

Open all year Booking advisable Jul-Aug Last arrival 22.00hrs Last departure 11.00hrs

A very neat and well-kept small grassy site on high ground above Looe in a peaceful rural setting. Friendly and enthusiastic owners. A 3.5-acre site with 31 touring pitches, 15 hardstandings and 5 statics.

►►► Tregoad Park *(SX272560)*

St Martin PL13 1PB

☎ 01503 262718 🖃 01503 264777

e-mail: info@tregoadpark.co.uk

web: www.cornwall-online.co.uk/tregoad

Dir: *Signed with direct access from B3253, or from E on A387 follow B3253 for 1.75m towards Looe. Site on left*

PETS: Stables nearby **Exercise area** on site dog walk in 2m disp bin **Facilities** on site shop food water bowl dog chews dog scoop/disp bags washing facs walks info vet info **Other** prior notice required **Resident Pets:** Jack & Frodo (Border Collies), Sprite (cat)

Open Etr-Jan Bistro open in high and mid season Booking advisable Jul & Aug Last arrival 20.00hrs Last departure 11.00hrs

A smartly upgraded, terraced park with extensive sea and rural views, about 1.5m from Looe. All pitches are level, and the facilities are well maintained. There is a licensed bar with bar meals served in the conservatory. A 55-acre site with 200 touring pitches, 60 hardstandings and 3 statics.

ENGLAND

LOSTWITHIEL

MAP 02 SX15

►►► Powderham Castle Holiday Park

(SX083593)

PL30 5BU

☎ 01208 872277

e-mail: info@powderhamcastletouristpark.co.uk

web: www.powderhamcastletouristpark.co.uk

Dir: *1.5m SW of Lostwithiel on A390 turn right at brown/white sign in 400mtrs*

PETS: **Charges** £1 - £2 per night **Public areas** **Exercise area** on site field set aside disp bin **Facilities** walks info vet info **Other** prior notice required **Restrictions** no Dobermans, Rottweilers, German Shepherds or Staffordshire Bull Terriers **Resident Pets:** Pippin (Cairn Terrier)

Open Etr or Apr-Oct Booking advisable Jul-Aug Last arrival 22.00hrs Last departure 11.30hrs

A grassy park set in attractive paddocks with mature trees. A gradual upgrading of facilities is well under way, and both buildings and grounds are carefully maintained. This park is ideally located for visiting the Eden Project, the nearby golden beaches and sailing at Fowey. A 12-acre site with 72 touring pitches, 12 hardstandings and 38 statics.

Notes 🐾

MARAZION

MAP 02 SW53

★★ 72% SMALL HOTEL
Godolphin Arms

TR17 0EN

☎ 01736 710202 📠 01736 710171

e-mail: enquiries@godolphinarms.co.uk

web: www.godolphinarms.co.uk

Dir: *from A30 follow Marazion signs for 1m to hotel. At end of causeway to St Michael's Mount*

PETS: **Bedrooms** unattended **Public areas** except restaurant **Grounds** accessible **Exercise area** 100yds **Facilities** food bowl **On Request** towels

This 170-year-old waterside hotel is in a prime location where the stunning views of St Michael's Mount provide a backdrop for the restaurant and lounge bar. Bedrooms are colourful, comfortable and spacious. A choice of menu is offered in the main restaurant and the Gig Bar, all with an emphasis on local seafood.

Rooms 10 en suite (2 fmly) (2 GF) ⊘ in all bedrooms S £65-£110; D £85-£145 (incl. bkfst) **Facilities** STV Wi-fi available Direct access to large beach New Year **Parking** 48 **Notes** LB Closed 23-27 Dec

►►► Wheal Rodney Holiday Park *(SW525315)*

Gwallon Ln TR17 0HL

☎ 01736 710605

e-mail: reception@whealrodney.co.uk

web: www.whealrodney.co.uk

Dir: *Turn off A30 at Crowlas, signed Rospeath. Site 1.5m on right. From Marazion centre turn opposite Fire Engine Inn, site 500mtrs on left.*

PETS: **Charges** £1.50 per night **Public areas** except buildings **Exercise area** 200yds disp bin **Facilities** on site shop food food bowl water bowl washing facs walks info vet info **Other** prior notice required **Resident Pets:** Citroen, Harry, Badger (Sheep dogs), Naughty Ralph (cat), chickens

Open Etr-Oct Booking advisable Last arrival 20.00hrs Last departure 11.00hrs

Set in a quiet rural location surrounded by farmland, with level grass pitches and well-kept facilities. Just half a mile away are the beach at Marazion and the causeway or ferry to St Michael's Mount. A cycle route is just 400yds away. A 2.5-acre site with 30 touring pitches.

Notes Quiet after 10pm.

MAWNAN SMITH

MAP 02 SW72

★★★ 85% ⊛ COUNTRY HOUSE HOTEL
Meudon

TR11 5HT

☎ 01326 250541 📠 01326 250543

e-mail: wecare@meudon.co.uk

web: www.meudon.co.uk

Dir: *from Truro A39 towards Falmouth at Hillhead (anchor & cannons) rdbt, follow signs to Maenporth Beach. Hotel on left 1m after beach*

PETS: **Bedrooms** unattended **Charges** £7.50 per night **Grounds** accessible 9-acres **Exercise area** private beach **Resident Pets:** Felix (cat)

This charming late Victorian mansion is a relaxing place to stay, with its friendly hospitality and attentive service. It sits in impressive nine-acre gardens that lead down to a private beach. The spacious and comfortable bedrooms are situated in a more modern building than the main house. The cuisine features the best of local Cornish produce and is served in the conservatory restaurant.

ENGLAND

Rooms 29 en suite (2 fmly) (15 GF) ⊘ in all bedrooms S £70-£120; D £140-£240 (incl. bkfst & dinner)✳ **Facilities** FTV Fishing Riding Wi-fi available Private beach Hair salon Yacht for skippered charter Sub-tropical gardens Xmas **Services** Lift **Parking** 52 **Notes** LB Closed Jan

See advert on this page

MEVAGISSEY   MAP 02 SX04

►►►►► Seaview International Holiday Park *(SW990412)*

Boswinger PL26 6LL

☎ 01726 843425 🖻 01726 843358

e-mail: holidays@seaviewinternational.com

web: www.seaviewinternational.com

Dir: *From St Austell take B3273 signed Mevagissey. Turn right before entering village. Follow brown tourist signs to site*

PETS: Charges £3 per dog per night **Public areas** except pool area **Exercise area** on site disp bin **Facilities** on site shop food dog chews cat treats disp bags walks info vet info **Restrictions** No dangerous dogs (see page 7)

Open Mar-Oct Booking advisable Jul-Sep Last arrival 21.00hrs Last departure 10.00hrs

AA Campsite of the Year for England and overall winner of the AA Best Campsite of the Year 2007. An attractive holiday park set in a beautiful environment overlooking Veryan Bay, with colourful landscaping including attractive flowers and shrubs. It continues to offer an outstanding holiday experience, with its luxury family pitches, super toilet facilities, new takeaway, and refurbished shop. The beach and sea are just half a mile away. A 28-acre site with 189 touring pitches, 13 hardstandings and 38 statics.

MULLION

★★★ 77% HOTEL
Polurrian

TR12 7EN

☎ 01326 240421 🖻 01326 240083

e-mail: relax@polurrianhotel.com

web: www.polurrianhotel.com

PETS: Bedrooms (GF) unattended sign **Stables** nearby (2m) **Charges** £8 per night, charge for damage **Grounds** accessible on leads disp bin **Exercise area** adjacent **Facilities** dog scoop/disp bags walks info vet info **On Request** fridge access

With spectacular views across St Mount's Bay, this well managed hotel has undergone extensive upgrading. Guests are assured of a warm welcome and a relaxed atmosphere from the friendly team of staff. In addition to the formal eating option, the High Point restaurant offers a more casual approach, open all day and into the evening. The popular leisure club has a good range of equipment. Bedrooms vary in size, and sea view rooms always being in demand.

Rooms 39 en suite (4 fmly) (8 GF) ⊘ in all bedrooms S £53-£123; D £106-£184 (incl. bkfst & dinner)✳ **Facilities** ⊗ ⊼ ⦿ Squash Gym Wi-fi available Children's games room ch fac Xmas New Year **Parking** 100

Mullion Holiday Park *(SW699182)*
Ruan Minor TR12 7LJ

☎ 01326 240428 & 0870 444 5344 🖻 01326 241141

e-mail: bookings@weststarholidays.co.uk

web: www.weststartouring.co.uk/aa

Dir: *A30 onto A39 through Truro towards Falmouth. A394 to Helston, A3083 for The Lizard. Park 7m on left*

PETS: Charges £5 per night **Public areas** except buildings, on leads **Exercise area** on site adjacent walks disp bin **Facilities** on site shop food food bowls disp bags leads walks info vet info **Other** prior notice required **Restrictions** No dangerous dogs (see page 7)

Open 5 Apr-28 Oct Booking advisable Jul-Aug & bank holidays Last arrival 22.00hrs Last departure 10.00hrs

A comprehensively-equipped leisure park geared mainly for self-catering holidays, and set close to the sandy beaches, coves and fishing villages on the Lizard Peninsula. There is plenty of on-site entertainment for all ages, with indoor and outdoor swimming pools. A 49-acre site with 150 touring pitches, 8 hardstandings and 327 statics.

ENGLAND

NEWQUAY MAP 02 SW86

★★★★ 77% 🏵 HOTEL
Headland
Fistral Beach TR7 1EW
☎ 01637 872211 🖨 01637 872212
e-mail: office@headlandhotel.co.uk
web: www.headlandhotel.co.uk
Dir: *off A30 onto A392 at Indian Queens, approaching Newquay follow signs for Fistral Beach, hotel adjacent*
PETS: Bedrooms unattended **Charges** dogs £9-11 per night
Public areas on leads except restaurant **Grounds** accessible on leads disp bin **Exercise area** beach 50yds **Facilities** water bowl bedding dog chews feeding mat dog scoop/disp bags tinned & dried food for dogs staying in hotel walks info vet info
Resident Pets: Milly & Twiglet (Airedale Terriers)

This Victorian hotel enjoys a stunning location overlooking the sea on three sides - views can be enjoyed from most of the windows. Bedrooms are comfortable and spacious. Grand public areas, with impressive floral displays, include various lounges and in addition to the formal dining room, Sands Brasserie offers a relaxed alternative. A unique collection of self-catering cottages is available, using hotel facilities, including bars and eating options.

Rooms 104 en suite (40 fmly) S £81-£148; D £83-£326 (incl. bkfst)✶ **Facilities** STV ⓢ ⌖ ♨9 ♨ ✦ Wi-fi in bedrooms Children's outdoor play area, Harry Potter playroom, Surf school ♫ ch fac New Year **Services** Lift **Parking** 400 **Notes** LB Closed 24-27 Dec

★★★ 78% HOTEL
Best Western Hotel Bristol
Narrowcliff TR7 2PQ
☎ 01637 875181 🖨 01637 879347
e-mail: info@hotelbristol.co.uk
web: www.hotelbristol.co.uk
Dir: *off A30 onto A392, then onto A3058. Hotel 2.5m on left*
PETS: Please telephone for details

This hotel is conveniently situated and many of the bedrooms enjoy fine sea views. Staff are friendly and provide a professional and attentive service. There is a range of comfortable lounges, ideal for relaxing prior to eating in the elegant dining room. There are also leisure and conference facilities.

Rooms 74 en suite (23 fmly) ⊗ in 41 bedrooms **Facilities** STV ⓢ Table tennis ch fac **Services** Lift **Parking** 105 **Notes** LB

★★★ 68% HOTEL
Hotel California
Pentire Crescent TR7 1PU
☎ 01637 879292 & 872798 🖨 01637 875611
e-mail: info@hotel-california.co.uk
web: www.hotel-california.co.uk
Dir: *A392 to Newquay, follow signs for Pentire Hotels & Guest Houses*
PETS: Bedrooms (GF) unattended **Stables** nearby (1m)
Charges £8 per night **Grounds** accessible disp bin **Facilities** food (pre-bookable) walks info vet info **On Request** fridge access torch

This hotel is tucked away in a delightful location, close to Fistral Beach and adjacent to the River Gannel. Many rooms have views across the river towards the sea, and some have balconies. There is an impressive range of leisure facilities, including indoor and outdoor pools, and ten-pin bowling. Cuisine is enjoyable and menus offer a range of interesting dishes.

Rooms 70 en suite (27 fmly) (13 GF) S £32.50-£54.50; D £65-£109 (incl. bkfst)✶ **Facilities** ⓢ ⌖ Squash 10 pin bowling alley ♫ Xmas New Year **Services** Lift **Parking** 66 **Notes** LB Closed 3 wks Jan

★★ 76% HOTEL
Whipsiderry

Trevelgue Rd, Porth TR7 3LY

☎ 01637 874777 & 876066 📠 01637 874777

e-mail: info@whipsiderry.co.uk

Dir: *right onto Padstow road (B3276) out of Newquay, in 0.5m right at Trevelgue Rd*

PETS: Bedrooms unattended **Public areas** except restaurant **Grounds** accessible **Exercise area** 100mtrs **Other** reptiles accepted

Quietly located, overlooking Porth Beach, this friendly hotel offers bedrooms in a variety of sizes and styles, many with superb views. A daily-changing menu offers interesting and well-cooked dishes with the emphasis on fresh, local produce. An outdoor pool is available, and at dusk guests may be lucky enough to watch badgers in the attractive grounds.

Rooms 20 rms (19 en suite) (5 fmly) (3 GF) ⊘ in all bedrooms S £55-£67; D £110-£134 (incl. bkfst & dinner)✳ **Facilities** ⤥ American Pool room Xmas **Parking** 30 **Notes LB** Closed Nov-Etr (ex Xmas)

★★★★ GUEST HOUSE
Dewolf Guest House

100 Henver Rd TR7 3BL

☎ 01637 874746

e-mail: holidays@dewolfguesthouse.com

Dir: *A392 onto A3058 at Quiatrell Downs Rdbt, Guesthouse on left just past mini rdbts*

PETS: Bedrooms (GF) certain rooms only **Charges** charge for damage **Grounds** accessible disp bin **Exercise area** beach, walks less than 5 mins **Facilities** walks info vet info **On Request** towels **Other** one bedroom with private enclosed area Prior notice required **Restrictions** no very large dogs

Making you feel welcome and at home is the priority here. The bedrooms in the main house are bright and well equipped, and there are two more in a separate single storey building at the rear. The cosy lounge has pictures and items that reflect the host's interest in wildlife. The guest house is just a short walk from Porth Beach.

Rooms 4 en suite 2 annexe en suite (2 fmly) (3 GF) ⊘ S £22-£44; D £44-£90✳ **Facilities** TVB tea/coffee Licensed Cen ht TVL **Parking** 6 **Notes LB** No coaches

★★★ GUEST ACCOMMODATION
The Three Tees

21 Carminow Way TR7 3AY

☎ 01637 872055 📠 01637 872055

e-mail: greg@3tees.co.uk

web: www.3tees.co.uk

Dir: *A30 onto A392 Newquay. Right at Quintrell Downs rdbt signed Porth, over double mini rdbt & 3rd right*

PETS: Bedrooms (GF) **Charges** £1 per night **Public areas** except dining room **Grounds** accessible disp bin **Exercise area** 2 mins walk **Facilities** water bowl dog chews cage storage walks info vet info **Restrictions** no very large dogs **Resident Pets:** Poppy (Border Collie), Parker (cat)

Located in a quiet residential area just a short walk from the town and beach, this friendly family-run accommodation is comfortable and well equipped. There is a lounge, bar and a sun lounge for the use of guests. Breakfast is served in the dining room, where snacks are available throughout the day. Light snacks are available in the bar during the evenings.

Rooms 8 rms (7 en suite) (1 pri facs) 1 annexe en suite (4 fmly) (2 GF) ⊘ D £60-£70✳ **Facilities** TVB tea/coffee Cen ht TVL Wi-fi available **Parking** 11 **Notes LB** Closed Nov-Feb

►►► **Trebellan Park** *(SW790571)*

Cubert TR8 5PY

☎ 01637 830522 📠 01637 830277

e-mail: treagofarm@aol.com

web: www.treagofarm.co.uk

Dir: *4m S of Newquay, turn W off A3075 at Cubert sign. Left in 0.75m onto unclass road*

PETS: Stables nearby (5m) **Charges** £1 per night **Public areas** on leads **Exercise area** adjacent disp bins **Facilities** shops 0.5m washing facs walks info vet info **Other** max 2 large dogs per pitch **Resident Pets:** Little Ginge, Missus, B.C & Bob (cats), peacocks, aviary birds

Open May-Oct Booking advisable Jul-Aug Last arrival 21.00hrs Last departure 10.00hrs

A terraced grassy rural park within a picturesque valley with views of Cubert Common, and adjacent to the Smuggler's Den, a 16th-century thatched inn. This park has excellent coarse fishing on site. An 8-acre site with 150 touring pitches and 7 statics.

Notes Families and couples only

►►► Treloy Touring Park (SW858625)

TR8 4JN

☎ 01637 872063 & 876279 🖹 01637 872063

e-mail: treloy.tp@btconnect.com

web: www.treloy.co.uk

Dir: *Off A3059 (St Columb Major-Newquay road)*

PETS: Charges £1 - £2 per night Exercise area on site dog walk area disp bin Facilities on site shop food vet info Other prior notice required Restrictions no Pitt Bull Terriers or similar breeds

Open 25 May-15 Sep (rs Sep pool, takeaway, shop & bar) Booking advisable Jul-Aug Last arrival 21.00hrs Last departure 10.00hrs

Attractive site with fine countryside views, within easy reach of resorts and beaches. The pitches are set in four paddocks with mainly level but some slightly sloping grassy areas. Maintenance and cleanliness are very high. A 12-acre site with 195 touring pitches, 24 hardstandings.

►►► Trethiggey Touring Park (SW846596)

Quintrell Downs TR8 4QR

☎ 01637 877672 🖹 01637 879706

e-mail: enquiries@trethiggey.co.uk

web: www.trethiggey.co.uk

Dir: *From A30 take A392 signed Newquay at Quintrell Downs rdbt, turn left onto A3058 past pearl centre to site 0.5m on left*

PETS: Charges telephone for details Public areas except playground Exercise area on site disp bin Facilities on site shop food food bowl water bowl dog chews cat treats dog scoop/disp bags vet info Other prior notice required

Open Mar-Dec Booking advisable Jul-Aug Last arrival 22.00hrs Last departure 10.30hrs

A family-owned park in a rural setting that is ideal for touring this part of Cornwall. Pleasantly divided into paddocks with maturing trees and shrubs, and offering coarse fishing and tackle hire. A 15-acre site with 145 touring pitches, 35 hardstandings and 12 statics.

PADSTOW

MAP 02 SW97

★★★★ 71% ❀ HOTEL

The Metropole

RICHARDSON

Station Rd PL28 8DB

☎ 01841 532486 🖹 01841 532867

e-mail: info@the-metropole.co.uk

web: www.the-metropole.co.uk

Dir: *M5/A30 pass Launceston, turn off & follow signs for Wadebridge & N Cornwall. Take A39 & follow signs for Padstow*

PETS: Bedrooms (GF) unattended sign Charges £7 per night Public areas on leads except restaurant Grounds accessible Facilities walks info vet info On Request torch

This long-established hotel first opened its doors to guests back in 1904 and there is still an air of the sophistication and elegance of a bygone age. Bedrooms are soundly appointed and well equipped; dining options include the informal Met Café Bar and the main restaurant, with its enjoyable cuisine and wonderful views over the Camel estuary.

Rooms 58 en suite (3 fmly) (2 GF) ✪ in 10 bedrooms S £68-£84; D £136-£168 (incl. bkfst)✱ Facilities ↘ Wi-fi available Swimming pool open Jul & Aug only Xmas New Year Services Lift Parking 36 Notes LB

★★ 72% HOTEL

The Old Ship Hotel

Mill Square PL28 8AE

☎ 01841 532357 🖹 01841 533211

e-mail: stay@oldshiphotel-padstow.co.uk

web: www.oldshiphotel-padstow.co.uk

Dir: *from M5 take A30 to Bodmin then A389 to Padstow, follow brown tourist signs to car park*

PETS: Bedrooms Charges £5 per night Public areas on leads Grounds accessible on leads disp bin Facilities water bowl dog chews washing facs walks info vet info On Request fridge access torch towels Resident Pets: Stella & Harley (Boxers), Sox (cat)

This attractive inn is situated in the heart of the old town's quaint and winding streets, just a short walk from the harbour. A warm welcome is assured, accommodation is pleasant and comfortable, and public areas offer plenty of character. Freshly caught fish features on both the bar and restaurant menus. On site parking is a bonus.

Rooms 14 en suite (4 fmly) ⊘ in all bedrooms S £35-£50; D £70-£100 (incl. bkfst) **Facilities** STV Wi-fi in bedrooms ♫ Xmas New Year **Parking** 20

▶▶▶ Dennis Cove Camping (SW919743)

Dennis Ln PL28 8DR

☎ 01841 532349

e-mail: denniscove@freeuk.com

web: www.denniscove.co.uk

Dir: Approach Padstow on A389, turn right at Tesco into Sarah's Lane, 2nd right to Dennis Lane, follow lane to site at end

PETS: Charges £1.30 - £2 per night **Public areas** on leads **Exercise area** adjacent disp bin **Facilities** walks info vet info **Other** prior notice required **Resident Pets:** Milly (Border Collie), Fanny (Schnauzer)

Open Apr-Sep Booking advisable throughout season Last arrival 21.00hrs Last departure 11.00hrs

Set in meadowland with mature trees, this site overlooks Padstow Bay, with access to the Camel Estuary and the nearby beach. The centre of town is just a 10 minute walk away, and bike hire is available on site, with the famous Camel Trail beginning right outside. A 3-acre site with 42 touring pitches.

Notes ⊛ Arrivals from 2pm

▶▶▶ Padstow Touring Park (SW913738)

PL28 8LE

☎ 01841 532061

e-mail: mail@padstowtouringpark.co.uk

web: www.padstowtouringpark.co.uk

Dir: 1m S of Padstow, on E side of A389 (Padstow to Wadebridge road)

PETS: Charges £1.50 per night £10.50 per week **Public areas** **Exercise area** on site dog walking area adjacent public footpaths disp bin **Facilities** on site shop food food bowl water bowl dog chews cat treats dog scoop/disp bags walks info vet info **Other** prior notice required **Resident Pets:** Lottie (Border Terrier), Tinkie & Poppy (Yorkshire Terriers)

Open all year Booking advisable Jul-Aug Last arrival 21.30hrs Last departure 11.00hrs

Set in open countryside above the quaint fishing town of Padstow which can be approached by footpath directly from the park. This level grassy site is divided into paddocks by maturing bushes and hedges to create a peaceful and relaxing holiday atmosphere. A 13.5-acre site with 180 touring pitches, 14 hardstandings.

Notes No groups.

PENTEWAN   MAP 02 SX04

▶▶▶▶▶ Sun Valley Holiday Park (SX005486)

Pentewan Rd PL26 6DJ

☎ 01726 843266 & 844393 🖹 01726 843266

e-mail: reception@sunvalley-holidays.co.uk

web: www.sunvalleyholidays.co.uk

Dir: From St Austell take B3273 towards Mevagissey. Park is 2m on right

PETS: Public areas Exercise area on site disp bin **Facilities** on site shop food food bowl water bowl bedding dog chews dog scoop/disp bags washing facs walks info vet info **Other** prior notice required **Resident Pets:** Jenny & Joe (donkeys), rabbits

Open all year Booking advisable May-Sep Last arrival 22.00hrs Last departure noon

In a picturesque valley amongst woodland, this neat park is kept to an exceptionally high standard. The extensive amenities include tennis courts, indoor swimming pool, licensed clubhouse and restaurant. The sea is 1m away, and can be accessed via a footpath and cycle path along the river bank. A 20-acre site with 29 touring pitches, 4 hardstandings and 75 statics.

Notes No motorised scooters/ skateboards

PENZANCE   MAP 02 SW43

★★★ 83% ⊛⊛ HOTEL

Hotel Penzance

Britons Hill TR18 3AE

☎ 01736 363117 🖹 01736 350970

e-mail: enquiries@hotelpenzance.com

web: www.hotelpenzance.com

Dir: from A30 pass heliport on right, left at next rdbt for town centre. 3rd right onto Britons Hill and hotel on right

PETS: Bedrooms Charges £5 per night **Public areas** except restaurant **Grounds** accessible **Exercise area** 300mtrs **Resident Pets:** Thomas & Jerry (Birman cats)

This Edwardian house has been tastefully redesigned, particularly in the contemporary Bay Restaurant. The focus on style is not only limited to the decor, but is also apparent in the award-winning cuisine that is based upon fresh Cornish produce. Bedrooms have been appointed to modern standards and are particularly well equipped; many have views across Mounts Bay.

Rooms 24 en suite (2 GF) ⊘ in all bedrooms S £60-£75; D £110-£160 (incl. bkfst)✴ **Facilities** STV FTV ↘ Wi-fi in bedrooms Xmas New Year **Parking** 14 **Notes** LB

ENGLAND

★★★ 71% HOTEL
Queen's
The Promenade TR18 4HG
☎ 01736 362371 📠 01736 350033
e-mail: enquiries@queens-hotel.com
web: www.queens-hotel.com
Dir: *A30 to Penzance, follow signs for seafront pass harbour and into promenade, hotel 0.5m on right*
PETS: Charges £10 per night **Exercise area** near promenade

With views across Mounts Bay towards Newlyn, this impressive Victorian hotel has a long and distinguished history. Comfortable public areas are filled with interesting pictures and artefacts, and in the dining room guests can choose from the daily-changing menu. Bedrooms, many with sea views, are of varying style and size.

Rooms 70 en suite (10 fmly) **Facilities** STV Yoga weekends **Services** Lift **Parking** 50 **Notes** LB

★★★ INN
Mount View
Longrock TR20 8JJ
☎ 01736 710416 📠 01736 710416
Dir: *Off A30 at Marazion/Penzance rdbt, 3rd exit signed Longrock. On right after pelican crossing*
PETS: Bedrooms unattended **Public areas** bar only
Exercise area 50yds field & beach **Facilities** walks info vet info
Resident Pets: Muppet (Beagle)

The Victorian inn, just a short walk from the beach and 0.5m from the Isles of Scilly heliport, is a good base for exploring West Cornwall. Bedrooms are well equipped, including a hospitality tray, and the bar is a popular with locals. Breakfast is served in the dining room and a dinner menu is available.

Rooms 5 rms (3 en suite) (2 fmly) S £20-£27.50; D £40-£55✻
Facilities TVB tea/coffee Dinner Last d 8.30pm Pool Table **Parking** 8
Notes RS Sun

★★★ GUEST ACCOMMODATION
Penmorvah
61 Alexandra Rd TR18 4LZ
☎ 01736 363711 & 07875 675940
Dir: *A30 to Penzance, at railway station follow road along harbour front onto Promenade Rd. Right onto Alexandra Rd, Penmorvah on right*
PETS: Bedrooms (GF) **Charges** charge for damage
Public areas except dining room on leads **Grounds** accessible
Exercise area 400yds **Facilities** dog chews walks info vet info
On Request fridge access torch **Resident Pets:** Sooty, Smokey & Minky (rabbits)

Situated in a quiet, tree-lined road just a short walk from the seafront and town centre, and convenient for the ferry port, the Penmorvah has a friendly and relaxing atmosphere. Bedrooms are well appointed and equipped with many thoughtful extras. Well-cooked breakfasts are served in the attractive dining room.

Rooms 8 en suite (2 fmly) (1 GF) ⊘ S £22-£27; D £44-£54
Facilities FTV TVB tea/coffee Cen ht TVL

►►► Bone Valley Caravan & Camping Park
(SW472316)
Heamoor TR20 8UJ
☎ 01736 360313 📠 01736 360313
e-mail: enquiries@bonevalleycandcpark.co.uk
Dir: *A30 to Penzance, then towards Land's End, at 2nd rdbt right into Heamoor, 300yds right into Josephs Lane, 1st left, site 500yds on left*
PETS: Public areas on leads **Exercise area** field 100yds
Facilities on site shop walks info vet info **Other** prior notice required **Resident Pets:** Toby (Lakeland Terrier/Border cross)

Open all year Booking advisable Jul-Aug Last arrival 22.00hrs Last departure 11.00hrs

A compact grassy park on the outskirts of Penzance, with well maintained facilities. It is divided into paddocks by mature hedges, and a small stream runs alongside. A 1-acre site with 17 touring pitches, 2 hardstandings and 5 statics.

►►► Higher Chellew Holiday Park
(SW496353)

Higher Trenowin, Nancledra TR20 8BD

☎ 01736 364532 📠 01736 332380

e-mail: higherchellew@btinternet.com

web: www.higherchellewcamping.co.uk

Dir: *From A30 turn towards St Ives, left at mini-rdbt towards Nancledra. Left at B3311 junct, through Nancledra. Site 0.5m on left*

PETS: **Charges** £2 per night **Public areas** on leads **Exercise area** adjacent field **Facilities** vet info **Other** prior notice required

Open 21 Mar-Oct Booking advisable mid Jul-Aug Last arrival Noon Last departure 10.30hrs

A small rural park quietly located just four miles from the golden beaches at St Ives, and a similar distance from Penzance. This well sheltered park occupies an elevated location, and all pitches are level. A 1.25-acre site with 30 touring pitches.

Notes

PERRANPORTH   MAP 02 SW75

►►► Perranporth Camping & Touring Park
(SW768542)

Budnick Rd TR6 0DB

☎ 01872 572174 📠 01872 572174

Dir: *0.5m E off B3285*

PETS: **Charges** 50p per night **Public areas** **Exercise area** adjacent **Facilities** on site shop food walks info vet info

Open Whit-Sep (rs Whit & mid-end Sep shop & club facilities closed) Booking advisable Jul-Aug Last arrival 23.00hrs Last departure noon

A mainly tenting site with few level pitches, located high above a fine sandy beach which is much-frequented by surfers. The park is attractive to young people, and is set in a lively town on a spectacular part of the coast. A 6-acre site with 120 touring pitches, 4 hardstandings and 9 statics.

►►► Tollgate Farm Caravan & Camping Park *(SW768547)*

Budnick Hill TR6 0AD

☎ 01872 572130 & 0845 166 2126

e-mail: enquiries@tollgatefarm.co.uk

web: www.tollgatefarm.co.uk

Dir: *Off A30 onto B3285 to Perranporth. Site on right 1.5m after Goonhavern*

PETS: **Stables** nearby (loose box) **Public areas** **Exercise area** on site large heath adjacent beach 100yds disp bin **Facilities** on site shop food washing facs walks info vet info **Resident Pets:** 4 dogs, 3 goats, 2 pigs, rabbits, guinea pigs, chickens

Open Etr-Sept Booking advisable Whit, Jul-Aug Last arrival 21.00hrs Last departure 11.00hrs

A quiet site in a rural location with spectacular coastal views. Pitches are divided into four paddocks sheltered and screened by mature hedges. Children will enjoy the play equipment and pets' corner. The three miles of sand at Perran Bay are just a walk away through the sand dunes, or a 0.75m drive. A 10-acre site with 102 touring pitches, 10 hardstandings.

Notes No large groups

POLPERRO   MAP 02 SX25

★★★ 🛏 GUEST ACCOMMODATION
Penryn House

The Coombes PL13 2RQ

☎ 01503 272157 📠 01503 273055

e-mail: chrispidcock@aol.com

web: www.penrynhouse.co.uk

Dir: *A387 to Polperro, at minirdbt left down hill into village (ignore restricted access). Hotel 200yds on left*

PETS: **Bedrooms** unattended **Stables** nearby (5m) **Public areas** except restaurant **Grounds** accessible on leads disp bin **Exercise area** 200yds **Facilities** food bowl water bowl leads pet sitting washing facs cage storage walks info vet info **On Request** fridge access torch towels **Resident Pets:** Ella (Great Dane)

Penryn House has a relaxed atmosphere and offers a warm welcome. Every effort is made to ensure a memorable stay. Bedrooms are neatly presented and reflect the character of the building. After a day exploring, enjoy a drink at the bar and relax in the comfortable lounge.

Rooms 12 rms (11 en suite) (1 pri facs) (3 fmly) ⊘ S £35-£40; D £70-£90 **Facilities** TVB tea/coffee **Parking** 13 **Notes** LB

POLZEATH   MAP 02 SW97

►►► Tristram Caravan & Camping Park

(SW936790)

PL27 6TP

☎ 01208 862215 ▤ 01208 862080

e-mail: info@tristramcampsite.co.uk

web: www.polzeathcamping.co.uk

Dir: *From B3314 take unclass road signed Polzeath. Through village, up hill, site 2nd turn on right*

PETS: Charges £2 per night **Public areas** on leads
Exercise area 100yds **Facilities** vet info **Other** prior notice required

Open Mar-Nov Booking advisable Jul, Aug & school hols Last arrival 21.00hrs Last departure 10.00hrs

An ideal family site, positioned on a gently sloping cliff with grassy pitches and glorious sea views. There is direct, gated access to the beach, where surfing is very popular. The local amenities of the village are only a few hundred yards away. A 10-acre site with 100 touring pitches.

Notes No ball games, no disposable BBQs, no noise between 23.00hrs-07.00hrs

---

PORTHTOWAN   MAP 02 SW64

►►►► Porthtowan Tourist Park *(SW693473)*

Mile Hill TR4 8TY

☎ 01209 890256

e-mail: admin@porthtowantouristpark.co.uk

web: www.porthtowantouristpark.co.uk

Dir: *Exit A30 at junct signed Redruth/Porthtowan. Take 3rd exit from rdbt. 2m & right at T-junct. Park on left at top of hill*

PETS: Charges free (peak season: £1 per night)
Public areas except amenities block & play area **Exercise area** on site short walks and fenced area disp bin **Facilities** on site shop disp bags walks info vet info **Other** prior notice required

Open Etr-Sep Booking advisable Jul-Aug Last arrival 21.30hrs Last departure 11.00hrs

A neat, level grassy site on high ground above Porthtowan, with plenty of shelter from mature trees and shrubs. The superb toilet facilities considerably enhance the appeal of this peaceful rural park, which is almost midway between the small seaside resorts of Portreath and Porthtowan, with their beaches and surfing. A 5-acre site with 80 touring pitches, 4 hardstandings.

Notes ⊛ No bikes/skateboards during Jul-Aug

►►► Wheal Rose Caravan & Camping Park

(SW717449)

Wheal Rose TR16 5DD

☎ 01209 891496

e-mail: les@whealrosecaravanpark.co.uk

web: www.whealrosecaravanpark.co.uk

Dir: *Exit A30 at Scorrier sign, follow signs to Wheal Rose. Park 0.5m on left, Wheal Rose to Porthtowan road*

PETS: Public areas except play area on leads
Exercise area adjacent disp bin **Facilities** on site shop food food bowl water bowl dog chews cat treats disp bags washing facs walks info vet info

Open Mar-Dec Booking advisable Aug Last arrival 21.00hrs Last departure 11.00hrs

A quiet, peaceful park in a secluded valley setting, central for beaches and countryside, and 2m from the surfing beaches of Porthtowan. The friendly owners work hard to keep this park immaculate, with a bright toilet block and well-trimmed pitches. A 6-acre site with 50 touring pitches, 6 hardstandings and 3 statics.

Notes ⊛ 5mph speed limit, minimum noise after 23.00hrs, gates locked 23.00hrs

---

PORT ISAAC   MAP 02 SW98

★★★★ BED & BREAKFAST
The Corn Mill

Port Isaac Rd, Trelill PL30 3HZ

☎ 01208 851079

Dir: *Off B3314, between Pendoggett and Trelill*

PETS: Bedrooms Charges £2 per night **Grounds** accessible on leads **Resident Pets:** Digger (Jack Russell), Mugsy & Millie (cats), Rosie (Retreiver), geese & ducks

Dating from the 18th century, this mill has been lovingly restored to provide a home packed full of character. The bedrooms are individually styled and personal touches create a wonderfully relaxed and homely atmosphere. The farmhouse kitchen is the venue for a delicious breakfast.

Rooms 3 rms (2 en suite) (1 fmly) ⊗ D £70-£75✴ **Facilities** TV1B tea/coffee Cen ht **Parking** 3 **Notes** Closed 24 Dec-5 Jan ⊛

PORTSCATHO   MAP 02 SW83

Rosevine

TR2 5EW

☎ 01872 580206 🖹 01872 580230

e-mail: info@rosevine.co.uk

Dir: *from St Austell take A390 for Truro. Left onto B3287 to Tregony. Then A3078 through Ruan High Lanes. Hotel 3rd left*

PETS: Bedrooms Public areas assist dogs only
Grounds accessible **Exercise area** beach

At the time of going to press, the star classification for this hotel was not confirmed. Please refer to the AA internet site www.theAA.com for current information.

Rooms 11 en suite 6 annexe en suite (7 fmly) (3 GF) S £80-£180; D £160-£262 (incl. bkfst)✶ **Facilities** ⓢ Wi-fi available Outdoor table tennis & play area ♪ Xmas **Parking** 20 **Notes** LB Closed 28 Dec-4 Feb

REDRUTH   MAP 02 SW64

★★ 67% HOTEL

Crossroads Lodge

THE INDEPENDENTS
HOTEL ASSOCIATION

Scorrier TR16 5BP

☎ 01209 820551 🖹 01209 820392

e-mail: crossroads@hotelstruro.com

web: www.hotelstruro.com/crossroads

Dir: *turn off A30 onto A3047 towards Scorrier*

PETS: Bedrooms unattended **Charges** £4.50 per night
Public areas except restaurant **Grounds** accessible
Exercise area surrounding area

Situated on an historic stanary site and conveniently located just off the A30, Crossroads Lodge has a smart appearance. Bedrooms are soundly furnished and include executive and family rooms. Public areas include an attractive dining room, a quiet lounge and a lively bar. Conference, banqueting and business facilities are also available.

Rooms 36 en suite (2 fmly) (8 GF) ⊘ in 8 bedrooms **Facilities** STV **Services** Lift **Parking** 140 **Notes** LB

►►► Lanyon Holiday Park *(SW684387)*

Loscombe Ln, Four Lanes TR16 6LP

☎ 01209 313474

e-mail: jamierielly@btconnect.com

web: www.lanyonholidaypark.co.uk

Dir: *Signed 0.5m off B2397 on Helston side of Four Lanes village*

PETS: Charges £2 per night **Public areas Exercise area** on site 1 acre area & in 200mtrs disp bin **Facilities** on site shop food dog chews cat treats disp bags washing facs walks info vet info **Other** prior notice required **Resident Pets:** Coco, Smudge & Sandy (Cocker Spaniels)

Open Mar-Oct Booking advisable Jul & Aug Last arrival 21.00hrs Last departure noon

---

Small, friendly rural park in an elevated position with fine views to distant St Ives Bay. This family owned and run park is being upgraded in all areas, and is close to a cycling trail. Stithian's Reservoir for fishing, sailing and windsurfing is two miles away. A 14-acre site with 25 touring pitches and 49 statics.

REJERRAH   MAP 02 SW75

 ### Monkey Tree Holiday Park *(SW803545)*

Scotland Rd TR8 5QR

☎ 01872 572032 🖹 01872 573577

e-mail: enquiries@monkeytreeholidaypark.co.uk

web: www.monkeytreeholidaypark.co.uk

Dir: *Exit A30 onto B3285 to Perranporth, 0.25m right into Scotland Rd, site on left in 1.5m*

PETS: Stables nearby (3m) (loose box) **Charges** £20 per week **Public areas** except play area & restaurant **Exercise area** on site disp bin **Facilities** on site shop food food bowl water bowl dog scoop/disp bags leads walks info vet info **Other** prior notice required

Open all year Booking advisable Jul & Aug Last arrival 22.00hrs Last departure 10.00hrs

A busy holiday park with plenty of activities and a jolly holiday atmosphere. Set close to lovely beaches between Newquay and Perranporth, it offers an outdoor swimming pool, children's playground, two bars with entertainment, and a good choice of eating outlets including a restaurant and a takeaway. A 56-acre site with 505 touring pitches.

Notes Family park

►►►► Newperran Holiday Park *(SW801555)*

TR8 5QJ

☎ 01872 572407 🖹 01872 571254

e-mail: holidays@newperran.co.uk

web: www.newperran.co.uk

Dir: *4m SE of Newquay & 1m S of Rejerrah on A3075. Or A30 Redruth, turn off B3275 Perranporth, at 1st T-junct turn right onto A3075 towards Newquay, site 300mtrs on left*

PETS: Stables nearby (2m) (loose box) **Charges** £2.50 per night **Public areas** except play areas **Exercise area** on site dog walks & field 2.5m disp bin **Facilities** on site shop food food bowl water bowl dog chews cat treats litter tray & dog scoop/disp bags washing facs walks info vet info **Other** prior notice required **Resident Pets:** Hamish (West Highland Terrier)

Open Etr-Oct Booking advisable Jul-Aug Last arrival mdnt Last departure 10.00hrs

A family site in a lovely rural position near several beaches and bays. This airy park offers screening to some pitches, which are set in paddocks on level ground. High season entertainment is available in the park's country inn, and the café has an extensive menu. A 25-acre site with 371 touring pitches, 14 hardstandings and 5 statics.

ROSUDGEON MAP 02 SW52

▶▶▶ **Kenneggy Cove Holiday Park**

(SW562287)

Higher Kenneggy TR20 9AU

☎ 01736 763453

e-mail: enquiries@kenneggycove.co.uk

web: www.kenneggycove.co.uk

Dir: *On A394 between Penzance & Helston, turn S into signed lane to site & Higher Kenneggy*

PETS: Charges dogs £2 per night **Public areas** except shop, laundry, toilets & play area **Exercise area** adjacent & beach disp bin **Facilities** on site shop food food bowl water bowl disp bags washing facs walks info vet info **Restrictions** no dangerous breeds (see page 7) **Resident Pets:** Hugo & Tickle (Wire Haired Dachshunds), Ginger & Mollie (cats), Rosie (rabbit)

Open May-Oct Booking advisable Jul-Aug Last arrival 21.00hrs Last departure 11.00hrs

Set in an Area of Outstanding Natural Beauty with spectacular sea views, this family-owned park is quiet and well kept. A short walk along a country footpath leads to the Cornish Coastal Path, and on to the golden sandy beach at Kenneggy Cove. A 4-acre site with 50 touring pitches and 9 statics.

Notes No large groups

ST AGNES MAP 02 SW75

★★★ 77% COUNTRY HOUSE HOTEL

Rose in Vale Country House

Mithian TR5 0QD

☎ 01872 552202 📄 01872 552700

e-mail: office@rose-in-vale-hotel.co.uk

web: www.rose-in-vale-hotel.co.uk

PETS: Bedrooms (GF) **Stables** nearby (3m) **Charges** £4.95 per night, charge for damage **Public areas** on leads **Grounds** accessible on leads disp bin **Facilities** walks info vet info **Resident Pets:** Hetty (Black Labrador)

Peacefully located in a wooded valley this Georgian manor house has a wonderfully relaxed atmosphere and abundant charm. Guests are

assured of a warm welcome. Accommodation varies in size and style; several rooms are situated on the ground floor. An imaginative fixed-price menu featuring local produce is served in the spacious restaurant.

Rooms 18 en suite (10 fmly) (3 GF) in all bedrooms S £75-£125; D £130-£300 (incl. bkfst) **Facilities** Wi-fi available Xmas **Parking** 52 **Notes** LB

★★★★ GUEST ACCOMMODATION

Driftwood Spars

Trevaunance Cove TR5 0RT

☎ 01872 552428 📄 01872 553701

e-mail: driftwoodspars@hotmail.com

Dir: *A30 to Chiverton rdbt, right onto B3277 and follow road through village. Located 200yds before beach*

PETS: Bedrooms (GF) unattended **Stables** nearby (3m) **Charges** £3 per night £21 per week charge for damage **Public areas** except restaurant on leads **Grounds** accessible **Exercise area** 500yds beach **Facilities** vet info **On Request** fridge access **Resident Pets:** Purdy (cat)

Partly built from ship wrecked timbers, this 18th century inn attracts locals and visitors alike. The attractive bedrooms, some in an annexe, are decorated in bright, sea side style and have many interesting features. Local produce served in the informal pub dining room or in the restaurant ranges from hand pulled beers to delicious, locally landed seafood.

Rooms 9 en suite 6 annexe en suite (4 fmly) (5 GF) S £43-£60; D £86-£98 **Facilities** TVB tea/coffee Direct dial from bedrooms Cen ht TVL Dinner Last d 9.30pm Wi-fi available **Parking** 41 **Notes** RS Xmas

▶▶▶ **Beacon Cottage Farm Touring Park**

(SW705502)

Beacon Dr TR5 0NU

☎ 01872 552347 & 553381

e-mail: beaconcottagefarm@lineone.net

web: www.beaconcottagefarmholidays.co.uk

Dir: *From A30 at Threeburrows rdbt, take B3277 to St Agnes, left into Goonvrea Road & right into Beacon Drive, follow brown sign to park*

PETS: Charges £2 per night **Public areas Exercise area** on site field available disp bin **Facilities** washing facs walks info vet info **Resident Pets:** Rusty (cat), Folly (horse)

Open Apr-Oct (rs Etr-Whit shop closed) Booking advisable Jul-Aug Last arrival 20.00hrs Last departure noon

A neat and compact site on a working farm, utilizing a cottage and outhouses, an old orchard and adjoining walled paddock. The unique location on a headland looking NE along the coast comes with stunning views towards St Ives, and the keen friendly family owners keep all areas very well maintained. A 5-acre site with 70 touring pitches.

Notes No large groups

ENGLAND

▶▶▶ Presingoll Farm Caravan & Camping Park *(SW721494)*

TR5 0PB

☎ 01872 552333 📄 01872 552333

e-mail: pam@presingollfarm.fsbusiness.co.uk

web: www.presingollfarm.fsbusiness.co.uk

Dir: *From A30 Chiverton rdbt (Little Chef) take B3277 towards St Agnes. Park 3m on right*

PETS: Stables nearby (1m) **Exercise area** on site adjacent meadow **Facilities** walks info vet info **Resident Pets:** various farm animals

Open Etr/Apr-Oct Booking advisable Jul & Aug Last departure 10.00hrs

An attractive rural park adjoining farmland, with extensive views of the coast beyond. Family owned and run, with level grass pitches, and modernised toilet block in smart converted farm buildings. There is also a campers' room with microwave and free coffee and tea. A 5-acre site with 90 touring pitches.

Notes 😊 No large groups

ST AUSTELL   MAP 02 SX05

▶▶▶▶ River Valley Holiday Park *(SX010503)*

London Apprentice PL26 7AP

☎ 01726 73533 📄 01726 73533

e-mail: river.valley@tesco.net

web: www.cornwall-holidays.co.uk

Dir: *Direct access to park signed on B3273 from St Austell at London Apprentice*

PETS: Charges £25 per week **Public areas** pool area **Exercise area** 100yds disp bin **Facilities** on site shop food food bowl water bowl washing facs walks info vet info **Other** prior notice required

Open end Mar-Sep Booking advisable Jul-Aug Last arrival 22.00hrs Last departure 11.00hrs

A neat, well-maintained family-run park set in a pleasant river valley. The quality toilet block and attractively landscaped grounds make this a delightful base for a holiday. A 2-acre site with 45 touring pitches and 40 statics.

▶▶▶ Old Kerrow Farm Holiday Park *(SX020573)*

Stenalees PL26 8GD

☎ 01726 851651 📄 01726 852826

e-mail: oldkerrowfarmholidaypark@hotmail.com

web: www.oldkerrowfarmholidaypark.co.uk

Dir: *Exit A30 at Innis Downs rdbt onto A391 to Bugle. Left at lights onto unclassified road. Site on right approx 1m just after sign for Kerrow Moor*

PETS: Stables nearby (6m) (loose box) **Charges** £1 for 2nd dog per night **Exercise area** on site adjacent walks and woodland disp bin **Facilities** on site shop food bowl water bowl dog chews cat treats washing facs walks info vet info **Other** prior notice required separate area of site for pet owners

Open all year Booking advisable Last arrival 20.00hrs Last departure noon

A rapidly improving park set on a former working farm, with good toilet facilities. The touring area is divided into two paddocks - one especially for dog owners with an extensive dog walk. Cycle hire can be arranged, and there is a cycle track to the Eden Project four miles away. Future plans include a swimming pool. A 20-acre site with 50 touring pitches, 11 hardstandings.

Notes No noise as quiet, peaceful location

▶▶ Court Farm Holidays *(SW953524)*

St Stephen PL26 7LE

☎ 01726 823684 📄 01726 823684

e-mail: truscott@ctfarm.freeserve.co.uk

web: www.courtfarmcornwall.co.uk

Dir: *From St Austell take A3058 towards Newquay. Through St Stephen (pass Peugeot garage). Right at 'St Stephen/Coombe Hay/Langreth/Industrial site' sign. 400yds, site on right*

PETS: Public areas on leads (site on sheep farm) **Exercise area** on site adjacent fields **Facilities** vet info **Other** prior notice required **Resident Pets:** Bess (Sheep dog), Boots (cat)

Open Apr-Sep Booking advisable Jul-mid Sep Last arrival by dark Last departure 11.00hrs

Set in a peaceful rural location, this large camping field offers plenty of space, and is handy for the Eden Project and the Lost Gardens of Heligan. Coarse fishing and use of a large telescope are among the attractions. A 4-acre site with 20 touring pitches, 5 hardstandings.

Notes No noisy behaviour after dark

ST BLAZEY GATE · MAP 02 SX05

►►► Doubletrees Farm (SX060540)

Luxulyan Rd PL24 2EH

☎ 01726 812266

e-mail: doubletrees@eids.co.uk

web: www.eids.co.uk/doubletrees

Dir: *On A390 at Blazey Gate. Turn by Leek Seed Chapel, almost opposite BP filling station. After approx 300yds turn R by public bench into site.*

PETS: Public areas Exercise area on site disp bin **Resident Pets:** Pansy (cat), chickens

Open all year Booking advisable Last arrival 22.30hrs Last departure 11.30hrs

A popular park with terraced pitches offering superb sea and coastal views. Close to beaches, and the nearest park to the Eden Project, it is very well maintained by friendly owners. A 1.75-acre site with 32 touring pitches, 6 hardstandings.

Notes ☺

ST COLUMB MAJOR · MAP 02 SW96

►►► Southleigh Manor Naturist Park

(SW918623)

TR9 6HY

☎ 01637 880938 📄 01637 881108

e-mail: enquiries@southleigh-manor.com

Dir: *Leave A30 at jctn with A39 signed Wadebridge. At Highgate Hill rdbt take A39. At Halloon rdbt take A39. At Trekenning rdbt take 4th exit 500 mtrs along on right*

PETS: Charges £1.50 per night **Public areas** on leads **Facilities** walks info vet info

Open Etr-Oct Shop open peak times only Booking advisable Jun-Aug Last arrival 20.00hrs Last departure 10.30hrs

A very well maintained naturist park in the heart of the Cornish countryside, catering for families and couples only. Seclusion and security are very well planned, and the lovely gardens provide a calm setting. A 4-acre site with 50 touring pitches.

Notes ☺ Naturist site

ST GENNYS · MAP 02 SX19

►►► Bude Camping & Caravanning Club Site (SX176943)

Gillards Moor EX23 0BG

☎ 01840 230650

web: www.campingandcaravanningclub.co.uk/bude

Dir: *From N on A39 site on right in lay-by, 9m from Bude. From S on A39 site on left in lay-by 9m from Camelford. Approx 3m from B3262 junct*

PETS: Public areas except buildings **Exercise area** on site disp bin **Facilities** walks info vet info **Other** prior notice required

Open 28 Apr-29 Sep Booking advisable BH & peak periods Last arrival 21.00hrs Last departure noon

A well-kept, level grass site with good quality facilities. Located midway between Bude and Camelford in an area full of sandy coves and beaches with good surfing. A 6-acre site with 100 touring pitches, 9 hardstandings.

Notes Site gates closed 23.00-07.00

ST HILARY · MAP 02 SW53

►►► Trevair Touring Park (SW548326)

South Treveneague TR20 9BY

☎ 01736 740647

e-mail: info@trevairtouringpark.co.uk

web: www.trevairtouringpark.co.uk

Dir: *A30 onto A394 signed Helston. 2m to rdbt, left onto B3280. Through Goldsithney. Left at brown site sign. Through 20mph zone to site, 1m on right*

PETS: Public areas except toilet block & house **Exercise area** nearby disp bin **Other** prior notice required

Open Etr-Nov Booking advisable Jul-Aug Last arrival 22.00hrs Last departure 11.00hrs

Set in a rural location adjacent to woodland, this park is level and secluded, with grassy pitches. Marazion's beaches and the famous St Michael's Mount are just three miles away. The friendly owners live at the farmhouse on the park. A 3.5-acre site with 40 touring pitches and 2 statics.

Notes ☺

ST IVES   MAP 02 SW54

★★★★ GUEST HOUSE
Old Vicarage

Parc-an-Creet TR26 2ES

☎ 01736 796124

e-mail: stay@oldvicarage.com

web: www.oldvicarage.com

Dir: *Off A3074 in town centre onto B3306, 0.5m right into Parc-an-Creet*

PETS: Bedrooms Public areas Grounds accessible **Exercise area** on site **Other** pets must be well behaved

This former Victorian rectory stands in secluded gardens in a quiet part of St Ives and is convenient for the seaside, town and the Tate. The bedrooms are enhanced by modern facilities. A good choice of local produce is offered at breakfast, plus home-made yoghurt and preserves.

Rooms 5 en suite (4 fmly) ⊗ S £55-£57; D £76-£80 **Facilities** TVB tea/coffee Licensed Cen ht TVL ⚓ **Parking** 12 **Notes** No coaches Closed Oct-Etr

►►► Penderleath Caravan & Camping Park

(SW496375)

Towednack TR26 3AF

☎ 01736 798403

e-mail: holidays@penderleath.co.uk

web: www.penderleath.co.uk

Dir: *From A30 take A3074 towards St Ives. Left at 2nd mini-rdbt, approx 3m to T-junct. Left then immediately right. Left at next fork*

PETS: Charges £1 - £2 per night **Public areas** except toilets, bar & shop **Exercise area** on site (not available in Aug) nearby beach **Facilities** on site shop food food bowl water bowl dog scoop/disp bags walks info vet info **Other** prior notice required, dogs must be well behaved and on leads at all times

Resident Pets: Buster (Jack Russell)

Open Etr-Oct Booking advisable Jul-Aug Last arrival 21.30hrs Last departure 10.30hrs

Set in a rugged rural location, this tranquil park has extensive views towards St Ives Bay and the north coast. Facilities are all housed in modernised granite barns, and include a quiet licensed bar with beer garden, breakfast room and bar meals. The owners are welcoming and helpful. A 10-acre site with 75 touring pitches.

►►► Trevalgan Touring Park *(SW490402)*

Trevalgan TR26 3BJ

☎ 01736 792048 📠 01736 798797

e-mail: recept@trevalgantouringpark.co.uk

web: www.trevalgantouringpark.co.uk

Dir: *From A30 follow holiday route to St Ives. B3311 through Halsetown to B3306. Left towards Land's End. Site signed 0.5m on right*

PETS: Charges £1.75 per night **Public areas** except playground **Exercise area** 100mtrs disp bin **Facilities** on site shop food food bowl water bowl dog scoop/disp bags washing facs walks info vet info space for loose box

Open Apr-Sep (rs Apr-May & Sep shop & takeaway closed) Booking advisable mid Jul-Aug Last arrival 22.00hrs Last departure 10.00hrs

An open park next to a working farm in a rural area on the coastal road from St Ives to Zennor. The park is surrounded by mature hedges, but there are extensive views out over the sea. There are very good toilet facilities including family rooms, and a large TV lounge and recreation room with drinks machine. A 4.75-acre site with 120 touring pitches.

►► Balnoon Camping Site *(SW509382)*

Halsetown TR26 3JA

☎ 01736 795431

e-mail: nat@balnoon.fsnet.co.uk

Dir: *From A30 take A3074, at 2nd mini-rdbt take 1st left signed Tate St Ives. After 3m turn right after Balnoon Inn*

PETS: Public areas Facilities on site shop walks info vet info **Other** prior notice required **Restrictions** no Staffordshire Bull Terriers or similar breeds

Open Etr-Oct Booking advisable Jul-Aug Last arrival 20.00hrs Last departure 11.00hrs

Small, quiet and friendly, this sheltered site offers superb views of the adjacent rolling hills. The two paddocks are surrounded by mature hedges, and the toilet facilities are kept spotlessly clean. The beaches of Carbis Bay and St Ives are about 2 miles away. A 1-acre site with 23 touring pitches.

Notes ⊛

ENGLAND

ST JUST (NEAR LAND'S END) MAP 02 SW33

►►► Kelynack Caravan & Camping Park

(SW374301)

Kelynack TR19 7RE

☎ 01736 787633 🗎 01736 787633

e-mail: kelynackholidays@tiscali.co.uk

Dir: *1m S of St Just, 5m N of Land's End on B3306*

PETS: Charges £1 per night **Public areas** except play area **Exercise area** adjacent disp bin **Facilities** on site shop food food bowl water bowl disp bags washing facs walks info vet info **Other** prior notice required **Resident Pets:** Jack (Border Collie), Max (King Charles Cavalier Spaniel), Titch (Yorkshire Terrier), Bracken, Carmen, Ned & Scrumpy Jack (donkeys), Pedro (Shetland Pony)

Open Apr-Oct Booking advisable Jul-Aug Last arrival 22.00hrs Last departure 10.00hrs

A small secluded park nestling alongside a stream in an unspoilt rural location. The level grass pitches are in two areas, and the park is close to many coves, beaches, and ancient villages. A 3-acre site with 20 touring pitches, 4 hardstandings and 13 statics.

Notes 🐾

►►► Trevaylor Caravan & Camping Park

(SW368222)

Botallack TR19 7PU

☎ 01736 787016

e-mail: bookings@trevaylor.com

web: www.trevaylor.com

Dir: *On B3306 (St Just -St Ives road), site on right 0.75m from St Just*

PETS: Stables nearby (200mtrs) (loose box) **Exercise area** 50mtrs **Facilities** on site shop food dog chews cat treats disp bags leads washing facs walks info vet info **Other** prior notice required

Open 21 Mar-Oct Booking advisable Jul & Aug Last departure noon

A sheltered grassy site located off the beaten track in a peaceful location at the western tip of Cornwall. The dramatic coastline and the pretty villages nearby are truly unspoilt. Clean, well-maintained facilities and a good shop are offered along with a bar serving bar meals. A 6-acre site with 50 touring pitches.

ST JUST-IN-ROSELAND MAP 02 SW83

►►► Trethem Mill Touring Park *(SW860365)*

TR2 5JF

☎ 01872 580504 🗎 01872 580968

e-mail: reception@trethem.com

web: www.trethem.com

Dir: *From Tregony on A3078 to St Mawes. 2m after Trewithian, follow signs to park*

PETS: Charges £1 per night **Public areas** except buildings **Exercise area** on site 5 acre dog walk disp bin **Facilities** on site shop food walks info vet info

Open Apr-Oct Booking advisable Jul-Aug Last arrival 20.00hrs Last departure 11.00hrs

A quality park in all areas, with upgraded amenities including a reception, shop, laundry, and disabled/family room. This carefully-tended and sheltered park is in a lovely rural setting, with spacious pitches separated by young trees and shrubs. The very keen family who own it are continually looking for ways to enhance its facilities. An 11-acre site with 84 touring pitches, 45 hardstandings.

ST KEVERNE MAP 02 SW72

★★★ GUEST HOUSE

Gallen-Treath Guest House

Porthallow TR12 6PL

☎ 01326 280400 🗎 01326 280400

e-mail: gallentreath@btclick.com

Dir: *1.5m S of St Keverne in Porthallow*

PETS: Bedrooms (GF) unattended **Charges** £2 per pet per night £14 per week charge for damage **Public areas** on leads **Grounds** accessible disp bin **Exercise area** 2 mins walk beach **Facilities** food (pre-bookable) food bowl water bowl bedding dog chews cat treats disp bags washing facs walks info vet info **On Request** fridge access torch towels **Resident Pets:** J.D. (Bearded Collie/Lurcher cross)

Gallen-Treath has super views over the countryside and sea from its elevated position above Porthallow. Bedrooms are individually decorated and feature many personal touches. Guests can relax in the large, comfortable lounge complete with balcony. Hearty breakfasts and dinners (by arrangement) are served in the bright dining room.

ENGLAND

Rooms 5 rms (4 en suite) (1 pri facs) (1 fmly) (1 GF) S £23-£28; D £46-£56✱ **Facilities** TVB tea/coffee Licensed Cen ht TVL Dinner Last d at breakfast **Parking** 6

ST MABYN
MAP 02 SX07

▶▶▶ 79% **Glenmorris Park** *(SX055733)*

Longstone Rd PL30 3BY

☎ 01208 841677 🖹 01208 841514

e-mail: info@glenmorris.co.uk

web: www.glenmorris.co.uk

Dir: *S of Camelford on A39, left after BP garage onto B3266 to Bodmin, 6m to Longstone, right at x-rds to St Mabyn, site approx 400mtrs on right*

PETS: Charges Exercise area nearby disp bin **Facilities** on site shop food disp bags leads walks info vet info

Open Etr-Oct (rs Etr-mid May & mid Sep-Oct swimming pool closed) Booking advisable Jul-Aug (all year for statics) Last arrival 23.30hrs Last departure 10.30hrs

A very good, mainly level park in a peaceful rural location offering clean and well-maintained facilities - a small games room, heated outdoor swimming pool and sunbathing area, and shop. An ideal location for visiting this unspoilt area. An 11-acre site with 80 touring pitches and 11 statics.

Notes Quiet after 22.00hrs

ST MAWES
MAP 02 SW83

★★★ 86% 🏵🏵 HOTEL

Idle Rocks

Harbour Side TR2 5AN

☎ 01326 270771 🖹 01326 270062

e-mail: reception@idlerocks.co.uk

web: www.idlerocks.co.uk

Dir: *off A390 onto A3078, 14m to St Mawes. Hotel on left*

PETS: Bedrooms unattended **Charges** £7 per night **Public areas**

This hotel has splendid sea views overlooking the attractive fishing port. The lounge and bar also benefit from the views and in warmer months service is available on the terrace. Bedrooms are individually styled and tastefully furnished to a high standard. The daily-changing menu served in the restaurant features fresh, local produce in imaginative cuisine.

Rooms 23 en suite 4 annexe en suite (6 fmly) (2 GF) S £78-£118; D £156-£346 (incl. bkfst & dinner)✱ **Facilities** Wi-fi available Xmas New Year **Parking** 4(charged)

SALTASH
MAP 02 SX45

★★★ INN

Crooked Inn

Stoketon Cross, Trematon PL12 4RZ

☎ 01752 848177 🖹 01752 843203

e-mail: info@crooked-inn.co.uk

Dir: *1.5m NW of Saltash. A38 W from Saltash, 2nd left to Trematon, sharp right*

PETS: Please telephone for details

The friendly animals that freely roam the courtyard add to the relaxed country style of this delightful inn. The spacious bedrooms are well

CONTINUED

SALTASH CONTINUED

equipped, and freshly cooked dinners are available in the bar and conservatory. Breakfast is served in the cottage-style dining room.

Rooms 18 annexe rms (15 en suite) (5 fmly) (7 GF) ⊗ in 7 bedrooms S £45; D £70✳ **Facilities** TVB tea/coffee Cen ht Dinner ➘ **Parking** 45 **Notes** Closed 25 Dec

See advert on page 61

SENNEN　　　　　　　　　　MAP 02 SW32

►►► Sennen Cove Camping & Caravanning Club Site *(SW378276)*

Higher Tregiffian Farm TR19 6JB

☎ 01736 871588

web: www.campingandcaravanningclub.co.uk/sennencove

Dir: *A30 towards Land's End. Right onto A3306 St Just/Pendeen Rd. Site 200yds on left*

PETS: Public areas except buildings **Exercise area** on site **Facilities** walks info vet info **Other** prior notice required

Open 28 Mar-29 Sep Booking advisable BH & peak periods Last arrival 21.00hrs Last departure noon

Set in a rural area with distant views of Carn Brae and the coast just 2 miles from Land's End, this very good club site is well run with modern, clean facilities. It offers a children's playfield, late arrivals area and a dog-exercising paddock. A 4-acre site with 75 touring pitches, 6 hardstandings.

Notes Gates closed 23.00-07.00

SUMMERCOURT　　　　　　　MAP 02 SW85

► Carvynick Country Club

TR8 5AF

☎ 01872 510716 ▤ 01872 510172

e-mail: info@carvynick.co.uk

web: www.carvynick.co.uk

Dir: *Off B3058*

PETS: Public areas on leads **Exercise area** adjacent lane **Facilities** walks info vet info dogs must be exercised off site

Open all year (rs Jan/Feb Restricted leisure facilities) Booking advisable

Set within the gardens of an attractive country estate this spacious dedicated American RV Park (also home to the 'Itchy Feet' retail company) provides all full facility pitches on hard standings. The extensive on site amenities, shared by the high quality time share village, include an excellent restaurant with lounge bar, indoor leisure area with swimming pool, fitness suite and badminton court. 32 touring pitches.

TINTAGEL　　　　　　　　　MAP 02 SX08

★★★ INN

Port William Inn

Trebarwith Strand PL34 0HB

☎ 01840 770230 ▤ 01840 770936

PETS: Bedrooms Charges £5 per night **Public areas Exercise area** coastal path

The Port William has a superb location, perched on the cliff-side just south of Tintagel. The smartly appointed bedrooms all have wonderful sea views with the sound of the waves below ensuring a restful sleep. The spacious bar-restaurant has a conservatory and outside area, where the extensive menu can be enjoyed along with the spectacular scenery.

Rooms 8 en suite (1 fmly) ⊗ D £89-£105 **Facilities** TVB tea/coffee Cen ht Dinner Last d 8.45pm Pool Table **Parking** 45 **Notes** LB

TREGURRIAN　　　　　　　　MAP 02 SW86

►►► Tregurrian Camping & Caravanning Club Site *(SW847654)*

TR8 4AE

☎ 01637 860448

web: www.campingandcaravanningclub.co.uk/tregurrian

Dir: *A30 onto A3059, 1.5m turn right signed Newquay Airport. Left at junct after airport, then right at grass triangle, follow signs to Watergate Bay*

PETS: Public areas except buildings **Facilities** disp bin walks info vet info **Other** prior notice required

Open 28 Apr-29 Sep Booking advisable BH & peak periods Last arrival 21.00hrs Last departure noon

A level grassy site close to the famous beaches of Watergate Bay, with a modern amenity block. This upgraded club site is an excellent touring centre for the Padstow-Newquay coast. A 4.25-acre site with 90 touring pitches, 8 hardstandings.

Notes Site gates closed 23.00-07.00.

TRURO — MAP 02 SW84

★★★ 81% ◉◉ HOTEL

Alverton Manor

Tregolls Rd TR1 1ZQ

☎ 01872 276633 📄 01872 222989

e-mail: reception@alvertonmanor.co.uk

web: www.connexions.co.uk/alvertonmanor/index.htm

Dir: *from at Carland Cross take A39 to Truro*

PETS: Bedrooms (GF) **Charges** £3 per night **Public areas** except restaurant on leads **Grounds** accessible on leads **Exercise area** Malpas Park 1m **Facilities** washing facs cage storage walks info vet info **On Request** fridge access torch towels **Resident Pets:** chickens, beehive

Formerly a convent, this impressive sandstone property stands in six acres of grounds, within walking distance of the city centre. It has a wide range of smart bedrooms, combining comfort with character. Stylish public areas include the library and the former chapel, now a striking function room. An interesting range of dishes, using the very best of local produce (organic whenever possible) is offered in the elegant restaurant.

Rooms 32 en suite (3 GF) ⊘ in 10 bedrooms **Facilities** STV ♫ 18 Xmas **Services** Lift **Parking** 120 **Notes** Closed 28 Dec RS 4 Jan

★★★ FARM HOUSE

Polsue Manor Farm *(SW858462)*

Tresillian TR2 4BP

☎ 01872 520234 📄 01872 520616 Mrs G Holliday

e-mail: geraldineholliday@hotmail.com

Dir: *2m NE of Truro. Farm entrance on A390 at S end of Tresillian*

PETS: Bedrooms Grounds accessible **Exercise area** on site **Other** dogs in non en suite bedrooms only **Resident Pets:** Polly & Penny (Yellow Labradors)

The 190-acre sheep farm is in peaceful countryside a short drive from Truro. The farmhouse provides a relaxing break from the city, with hearty breakfasts and warm hospitality. The spacious dining room has pleasant views and three large communal tables. Bedrooms do not offer televisions but there is a homely lounge equipped with a television and video recorder with a selection of videos for viewing.

Rooms 5 rms (2 en suite) (3 fmly) (1 GF) ⊘ S £27-£35; D £50-£56 **Facilities** tea/coffee TVL **Parking** 5 **Notes** LB 190 acres mixed, sheep, horses, working Closed 21 Dec-2 Jan

VERYAN — MAP 02 SW93

►►► **Veryan Camping & Caravanning Club Site** *(SW934414)*

Tretheake Manor TR2 5PP

☎ 01872 501658

web: www.campingandcaravanningclub.co.uk/veryan

Dir: *Left off A3078 at filling station signed Veryan/Portloe on unclass road. Site signed on left*

PETS: Public areas except buildings **Exercise area** on site disp bin **Facilities** walks info vet info **Other** prior notice required

Open 13 Mar-3 Nov Booking advisable BHs & peak periods Last arrival 21.00hrs Last departure noon

A quiet park on slightly undulating land with pleasant views of the surrounding countryside. A tranquil fishing lake holds appeal for anglers, and the site is just 2.5 miles from one of Cornwall's finest sandy beaches. A 9-acre site with 150 touring pitches, 24 hardstandings.

Notes Site gates will be closed from 23.00-07.00.

WADEBRIDGE — MAP 02 SW97

►►► **The Laurels Holiday Park** *(SW957715)*

Padstow Rd, Whitecross PL27 7JQ

☎ 01209 313474

e-mail: jamierielly@btconnect.com

web: www.thelaurelsholidaypark.co.uk

Dir: *Off A389 (Padstow road) near junct with A39, W of Wadebridge*

PETS: Charges £2 per night £14 per week **Public areas** except toilets & laundry on leads **Exercise area** on site fenced area & in 1m disp bin **Facilities** walks info vet info **Other** prior notice required

Open Apr/Etr-Oct Booking advisable Jun-Sep Last arrival 20.00hrs Last departure 10.00hrs

A very smart and well-equipped park with individual pitches screened by hedges and young shrubs. The dog walk is of great benefit to pet owners, and the Camel cycle trail and Padstow are not far away. A 2.25-acre site with 30 touring pitches.

Notes 🐾

ENGLAND

WATERGATE BAY   MAP 02 SW86

★★★ 73% HOTEL
The Hotel and Extreme Academy Watergate Bay

TR8 4AA

☎ 01637 860543 ▤ 01637 860333

e-mail: hotel@watergatebay.co.uk

web: www.watergatebay.co.uk

Dir: *A30 onto A3059. Follow airport/Watergate Bay signs*

PETS: Bedrooms unattended **Charges** £10 per night **Public areas** except food area & playground **Exercise area** 2m of sandy beach **Facilities** vet info

With its own private beach, which is home to the 'Extreme Academy' of beach and watersports activities, this hotel boasts a truly a spectacular location. The style here is relaxed with a genuine welcome for all the family. Public areas are stylish and contemporary. Many bedrooms share the breathtaking outlook and a number have balconies. Several dining options are on offer, including the Beach Hut, Brasserie and Jamie Oliver's restaurant, Fifteen Cornwall.

Rooms 50 en suite 17 annexe en suite (36 fmly) **Facilities** STV ⊗ ⤣ ⤦ Wi-fi available Surfing Badminton Table tennis Billiards Mountain boarding Wave ski-ing ch fac **Services** Lift **Parking** 72

▶▶▶▶ **Watergate Bay Tourist Park**

(SW850653)

Watergate Bay TR8 4AD

☎ 01637 860387 ▤ 01637 860387

e-mail: email@watergatebaytouringpark.co.uk

web: www.watergatebaytouringpark.co.uk

Dir: *4m N of Newquay on B3276 (coast road)*

PETS: Charges free (Jul-Aug £2 per night) **Public areas** except pool area, club room, café & recreation area **Exercise area** on site 2 acre exercise field disp bin **Facilities** on site shop food walks info vet info **Other** prior notice required

Open Mar-Oct (rs Mar-22 May & 13 Sep-Nov restricted bar,cafe,shop & swimming pool) Booking advisable Jul-Aug Last arrival 22.00hrs Last departure noon

A well-established park above Watergate Bay, where acres of golden sand, rock pools and surf are seen as a holidaymaker's paradise. Toilet facilities are to a high standard, and there is a wide range of activities including a regular entertainment programme in the clubhouse. A 30-acre site with 171 touring pitches, 14 hardstandings.

WIDEMOUTH BAY   MAP 02 SS20

 Widemouth Bay Caravan Park *(SS199008)*

EX23 0DF

☎ 01271 866766 ▤ 01271 866791

e-mail: bookings@jfhols.co.uk

web: www.johnfowlerholidays.com

Dir: *Take Widemouth Bay coastal road off A39, turn left. Park on left*

PETS: Charges £3 per night £20 per week **Public areas** except buildings **Exercise area** on site acres of open grassland disp bin **Facilities** on site shop food food bowl water bowl dog chews cat treats walks info vet info **Other** prior notice required

Open Etr-Oct Booking advisable All dates Last arrival Dusk Last departure 10.00hrs

A partly sloping rural site set in countryside overlooking the sea and one of Cornwall's finest beaches. Nightly entertainment in high season with emphasis on children's and family club programmes. This park is located less than half a mile from the sandy beaches of Widemouth Bay. A 58-acre site with 220 touring pitches, 90 hardstandings and 200 statics.

ZENNOR   MAP 02 SW43

★★★ ⊖ INN
The Gurnard's Head

Treen TR26 3DE

☎ 01736 796928

e-mail: enquiries@gurnardshead.co.uk

Dir: *5m from St Ives on B3306*

PETS: Bedrooms unattended **Public areas** except restaurant **Grounds** accessible **Exercise area** adjacent **Facilities** food bowl dog toys

Ideally located for enjoying the beautiful coastline, this inn offers atmospheric public areas. The style is relaxed and very popular with walkers, keen to rest their weary legs. A log fire in the bar provides a warm welcome on colder days and on warmer days, outside seating is available. Lunch and dinner, featuring local home cooked food, is available either in the bar or the adjoining restaurant area. The dinner menu is not extensive but there are interesting choices and everything is home made, even the bread. Breakfast is served around a grand farm-house table.

Rooms 7 en suite ⊘ S £55-£67.50; D £82.50✳ **Facilities** Dinner Last d 9.30pm **Parking** 40 **Notes** No coaches

CUMBRIA

ALSTON   MAP 12 NY74

★★ 76% HOTEL
Nent Hall Country House Hotel
CA9 3LQ
☎ 01434 381584 📠 01434 382668
web: www.nenthall.com
Dir: *from main cobbled street turn left at top onto A689. Hotel 2m on right*
PETS: Bedrooms Charges £10 per night **Grounds** accessible
This delightful old house stands in well-kept gardens. Warm and friendly hospitality is provided, with well-appointed and comfortable accommodation, some rooms being on the ground floor and others being suitable for families. There are two comfortable lounges and a pleasant bar serving bar meals and light snacks as well as a more formal dining room.
Rooms 18 en suite (2 fmly) (9 GF) ⊘ in all bedrooms **Parking** 100 **Notes** ⊗

AMBLESIDE   MAP 07 NY30

★★★★ 75% TOWN HOUSE HOTEL
Waterhead
Lake Rd LA22 0ER
☎ 015394 32566 📠 015394 31255
e-mail: waterhead@elhmail.co.uk
web: www.elh.co.uk/hotels/waterhead.htm
Dir: *A591 into Ambleside, hotel opposite Waterhead Pier*
PETS: Bedrooms (GF) **Charges** £15 per night **Public areas** bar only on leads **Grounds** accessible on leads **Exercise area** 50yds **Facilities** food bowl water bowl walks info vet info **On Request** fridge access torch towels **Restrictions** no dangerous dogs (see page 7) & no Rottweilers
With an enviable location opposite the bay, this well-established hotel offers contemporary and comfortable accommodation with CD/DVD players, plasma screens and internet access. There is a bar with a garden terrace overlooking the lake and a stylish restaurant serving classical cuisine with a modern twist. Staff are very attentive and friendly. Guests can enjoy full use of the Low Wood Hotel leisure facilities nearby.
Rooms 41 en suite (3 fmly) (7 GF) ⊘ in 35 bedrooms S £49-£98; D £98-£236 (incl. bkfst)✳ **Facilities** STV Wi-fi available Complimentary use of leisure club at the Lowwood Xmas New Year **Parking** 43 **Notes** LB

★★★ 80% ⊛ HOTEL
Regent
Waterhead Bay LA22 0ES
☎ 015394 32254 📠 015394 31474
e-mail: info@regentlakes.co.uk
Dir: *1m S on A591*
PETS: Bedrooms unattended **Charges** £6 per night **Public areas** except restaurant, bar & lounges **Exercise area** nearby
This attractive holiday hotel, situated close to Waterhead Bay, offers a warm welcome. Bedrooms come in a variety of styles, including three suites and five bedrooms in the garden wing. There is a modern swimming pool and the restaurant offers a fine dining experience in a tasteful contemporary setting.
Rooms 30 en suite (7 fmly) ⊘ in all bedrooms S £75-£95; D £100-£140 (incl. bkfst) **Facilities** ⊗ Wi-fi available Xmas **Parking** 39 **Notes** LB Closed 19-27 Dec

★★★ 75% HOTEL
Skelwith Bridge
Skelwith Bridge LA22 9NJ
☎ 015394 32115 📠 015394 34254
e-mail: info@skelwithbridgehotel.co.uk
web: www.skelwithbridgehotel.co.uk
Dir: *2.5m W on A593 at junct with B5343 to Langdale*
PETS: Bedrooms Charges £5 per night **Public areas** except restaurant **Grounds** accessible **Exercise area** 100mtrs **Resident Pets:** Purdey (Black Labrador)
This 17th-century inn is now a well-appointed tourist hotel located at the heart of the Lake District National Park and renowned for its friendly and attentive service. Bedrooms include two rooms with four-poster beds. Spacious public areas include a choice of lounges and bars and an attractive restaurant overlooking the gardens to the bridge from which the hotel takes its name.
Rooms 22 en suite 6 annexe en suite (2 fmly) (1 GF) ⊘ in all bedrooms S £43-£63; D £38-£58 (incl. bkfst)✳ **Facilities** Xmas New Year **Parking** 60

AMBLESIDE CONTINUED

★★★★ GUEST ACCOMMODATION
Brathay Lodge
Rothay Rd LA22 0EE
☎ 015394 32000
e-mail: brathay@globalnet.co.uk
web: www.brathay-lodge.com
Dir: *One-way system in town centre, Lodge on right opp church*
PETS: Bedrooms (GF) Stables nearby (2m) Charges £5 per night
£10 per week charge for damage Exercise area 100 metres
Facilities water bowl washing facs cage storage vet info
On Request fridge access torch towels

Brathay Lodge is a high-amenity, limited-service operation. The
traditional property has been refurbished in a bright contemporary
style offering smart pine furnished bedrooms. Some share a
communal balcony and some ground-floor rooms have their own
entrance. All have spa baths. The self-service canteen-style continental
breakfast can be taken informally in the lounge/breakfast room or in
your bedroom.
Rooms 17 en suite 4 annexe en suite (3 fmly) (6 GF) ⊘ Facilities TVB
tea/coffee Cen ht TVL use of Langdale Country Club Parking 23

APPLEBY-IN-WESTMORLAND MAP 12 NY62

►►►►► **Wild Rose Park** *(NY698165)*
Ormside CA16 6EJ
☎ 017683 51077 📠 017683 52551
e-mail: reception@wildrose.co.uk
web: www.wildrose.co.uk
Dir: *Signed on unclass road to Great Ormside, off B6260*
PETS: Charges Public areas except shop Exercise area on site
fenced exercise area adjacent Facilities on site shop food food
bowl water bowl bedding dog chews cat treats dog scoop/disp
bags leads free disposal bags washing facs walks info vet info
Other prior notice required Restrictions No dangerous dogs (see
page 7) & no Rottweilers, Pitt Bull Terriers or Dobenmans
Open all year (rs Nov-Mar shop & swimming pool closed)
Booking advisable bank & school hols Last arrival 22.00hrs
Last departure noon
Situated in the Eden Valley, this large family-run park has been carefully
landscaped and offers superb facilities maintained to an extremely high

standard. There are several individual pitches, and extensive views
from most areas of the park. Traditional stone walls and the planting of
lots of indigenous trees help it to blend into the environment, and
wildlife is actively encouraged. An 85-acre site with 240 touring pitches,
140 hardstandings and 273 statics.
Notes No unaccompanied teenagers, no group bookings

ARMATHWAITE MAP 12 NY54

★★★ INN
The Dukes Head Inn
Front St CA4 9PB
☎ 016974 72226
e-mail: info@dukeshead-hotel.co.uk
web: www.dukeshead-hotel.co.uk
Dir: *In village centre opp Post Office*
PETS: Bedrooms unattended Stables nearby (1m) Charges £5
per stay charge for damage Public areas except for lounge bar &
restaurant Grounds accessible disp bin Facilities day kennels
nearby walks info vet info Restrictions dogs not to be fed in
bedrooms
Located in the peaceful village of Armathwaite close to the River Eden,
the Dukes Head offers comfortable accommodation in a warm friendly
atmosphere. There is a relaxing lounge bar with open fires and a wide
choice of meals are available either here or in the restaurant.
Rooms 5 rms (3 en suite) (2 pri facs) ⊘ S fr £38.50; D fr £58.50✱
Facilities TV4B tea/coffee Cen ht Dinner Last d 9pm Parking 20
Notes LB Closed 25 Dec

AYSIDE MAP 07 SD38

►►► **Oak Head Caravan Park** *(SD389839)*
LA11 6JA
☎ 015395 31475
web: www.oakheadcaravanpark.co.uk
Dir: *M6 junct 36, A590 towards Newby Bridge, 14m. Park sign on
left, 1.25m past High Newton*
PETS: Exercise area nearby disp bin Facilities vet info
Restrictions no Rottweilers
Open Mar-Oct Booking advisable BH Last arrival 22.00hrs Last
departure noon
A pleasant terraced site with two separate areas - grass for tents and all
gravel pitches for caravans and motorhomes. The site is enclosed
within mature woodland and surrounded by hills. A 3-acre site with 60
touring pitches, 30 hardstandings and 71 statics.
Notes ⊛ No open fires

BARROW-IN-FURNESS   MAP 07 SD26

★★★ 77% ◉ HOTEL
Clarence House Country Hotel & Restaurant
Skelgate LA15 8BQ

☎ 01229 462508 📄 01229 467177

e-mail: clarencehsehotel@aol.com

web: www.clarencehouse-hotel.co.uk

Dir: *A590 through Ulverston & Lindal, 2nd exit at rdbt & 1st exit at next. Follow signs to Dalton, hotel at top of hill on right*

PETS: Bedrooms Charges £10 per night **Grounds** accessible **Exercise area** on site **Other** well behaved dogs in cottage rooms only

This hotel is peacefully located in its own ornamental grounds with unrestricted countryside views. Bedrooms are individually themed with those in the main hotel being particularly stylish and comfortable. The public rooms are spacious and also furnished to a high standard. The popular conservatory restaurant offers well-prepared dishes from extensive menus. There is a delightful barn conversion that is ideal for weddings.

Rooms 7 en suite 12 annexe en suite (1 fmly) (5 GF) ⊘ in 11 bedrooms
S £82-£85; D £110-£115 (incl. bkfst) **Facilities** STV 🎵 New Year
Parking 40 **Notes LB** Closed 25-26 Dec

★★ 64% HOTEL
Lisdoonie
307/309 Abbey Rd LA14 5LF

☎ 01229 827312 📄 01229 820944

e-mail: lisdoonie@aol.com

Dir: *on A590, at 1st set of lights in town (Strawberry pub on left) continue for 100yds, hotel on right*

PETS: Bedrooms Exercise area 10 min walk
Resident Pets: Peggy (German Wirehaired Pointer)

This friendly hotel is conveniently located for access to the centre of the town and is popular with commercial visitors. The comfortable bedrooms are well equipped, and vary in size and style. There are two comfortable lounges, one with a bar and restaurant adjacent. There is also a large function suite.

Rooms 12 en suite (2 fmly) **Parking** 30 **Notes** Closed Xmas & New Year

BASSENTHWAITE   MAP 11 NY23

★★★★ 80% ◉ COUNTRY HOUSE HOTEL
Armathwaite Hall
CA12 4RE

☎ 017687 76551 📄 017687 76220

e-mail: reservations@armathwaite-hall.com

web: www.armathwaite-hall.com

Dir: *M6 junct 40/A66 to Keswick rdbt then A591 signed Carlisle. 8m to Castle Inn junct, turn left. Hotel 300yds*

PETS: Bedrooms (GF) unattended sign **Stables** on site
Charges £15 per night charge for damage **Grounds** accessible on leads disp bin **Facilities** food (pre-bookable) bedding dog chews cat treats dog scoop/disp bags pet sitting dog walking washing facs cage storage walks info vet info **On Request** torch
Resident Pets: Ben & Millie (Belgium Shepherds), Chrissy (Labrador)

Enjoying fine views over Bassenthwaite Lake, this impressive mansion, dating from the 17th century, is peacefully situated amid 400 acres of deer park. Comfortably furnished bedrooms are complemented by a choice of public rooms featuring splendid wood panelling and roaring log fires in the cooler months.

Rooms 42 en suite (4 fmly) (8 GF) S £130-£160; D £210-£350 (incl. bkfst)
☀ **Facilities** Spa STV 🏹 supervised ♨ Fishing Gym ⛳ Putt green
Wi-fi available Archery, Beauty salon, Clay shooting, Quad bikes, Falconry, Mountain Bikes Xmas New Year **Services** Lift **Parking** 100 **Notes LB**

BASSENTHWAITE *CONTINUED*

★★★ 81% ❀ HOTEL

The Pheasant

CA13 9YE

☎ 017687 76234 📄 017687 76002

e-mail: info@the-pheasant.co.uk

web: www.the-pheasant.co.uk

Dir: *Midway between Keswick & Cockermouth, signed from A66*

PETS: Please telephone for details

Enjoying a rural setting, within well-tended gardens, on the western side of Bassenthwaite Lake, this friendly 500-year-old inn is steeped in tradition. The attractive oak-panelled bar has seen few changes over the years and features log fires and a great selection of malt whiskies. The individually decorated bedrooms are stylish and thoughtfully equipped.

Rooms 13 en suite 2 annexe en suite (2 GF) ⊘ in all bedrooms S £75-£90; D £150-£186 (incl. bkfst)✷ Facilities New Year Parking 40 Notes LB No children 12yrs Closed 25 Dec

★★★ 77% HOTEL

Best Western Castle Inn

CA12 4RG

☎ 017687 76401 📄 017687 76604

e-mail: gm@castleinncumbria.co.uk

web: www.castleinncumbria.co.uk

Dir: *A591 to Carlisle, pass Bassenthwaite village on right & hotel is on left side of T-junct.*

PETS: Bedrooms (GF) unattended Charges £5 per night charge for damage Grounds accessible on leads disp bin Facilities dog chews dog scoop/disp bags walks info On Request towels

Conveniently located for Bassenthwaite, Keswick and the Lake District, guests are offered beautiful views, friendly service, comfortable bedrooms and a wide choice of both indoor and outdoor leisure facilities. Hearty meals are served in Ritsons Restaurant or the newly refurbished Lakers Bar.

Rooms 48 en suite (8 fmly) (4 GF) ⊘ in all bedrooms S £99-£110; D £105-£125 (incl. bkfst)✷ Facilities Spa FTV ⚂ supervised ⛳ Gym Putt green Wi-fi in bedrooms Table tennis Pool table Xmas New Year Parking 80 Notes LB

BORROWDALE

MAP 11 NY21

★★★ 73% HOTEL

Borrowdale

CA12 5UY

☎ 017687 77224 📄 017687 77338

e-mail: theborrowdalehotel@yahoo.com

Dir: *3m from Keswick, on B5289 at S end of Lake Derwentwater*

PETS: Bedrooms unattended Sep Accom kennels Public areas except restaurant, & bar at lunchtime Grounds accessible Exercise area 50mtrs Facilities food

Situated in the beautiful Borrowdale Valley overlooking Derwentwater, this traditionally styled hotel has been family-run for over 30 years. Extensive public areas include a choice of lounges, a stylish dining room, and a lounge bar, plus a popular conservatory. There is a wide variety of bedroom sizes and styles; some rooms are rather spacious, including two that are particularly suitable for less able guests.

Rooms 34 en suite 2 annexe en suite (9 fmly) (2 GF) Facilities Xmas New Year Parking 100

BRAMPTON

MAP 12 NY56

★★★ ❀❀ HOTEL

Farlam Hall

CA8 2NG

☎ 016977 46234 📄 016977 46683

e-mail: farlam@relaischateaux.com

web: www.farlamhall.co.uk

RELAIS & CHATEAUX

Dir: *On A689 (Brampton to Alston). Hotel 2m on left, (not in Farlam village*

PETS: Bedrooms (GF) Charges charge for damage Public areas except restaurant Grounds accessible disp bin Facilities food bowl water bowl fresh food by request cage storage walks info vet info On Request torch towels Resident Pets: 4 llamas, 4 rare breed sheep

This delightful family-run country house dates back to 1428. Steeped in history, the hotel is set in beautifully landscaped Victorian gardens complete with an ornamental lake and stream. Lovingly restored over many years, it now provides the highest standards of comfort and hospitality. Gracious public rooms invite relaxation, whilst every thought has gone into the beautiful bedrooms, many of which are simply stunning.

Farlam Hall

Rooms 11 en suite 1 annexe en suite (2 GF) ⊘ in all bedrooms
S £150-£175; D £280-£330 (incl. bkfst & dinner)✶ **Facilities** 🐾 Wi-fi
available New Year **Parking** 35 **Notes** LB No children 5yrs Closed
24-30 Dec

CARLISLE MAP 11 NY45

★★★ 70% HOTEL
Lakes Court
Court Square CA1 1QY
☎ 01228 531951 📠 01228 547799
e-mail: reservations@lakescourthotel.co.uk
web: www.lakescourthotel.co.uk
Dir: *M6 junct 43, to city centre, then follow road to left & railway
station*

PETS: Bedrooms (GF) **Charges** £10-£20 per night
Public areas except dining room on leads **Facilities** walks info
vet info

This Victorian building is located in the heart of the city centre, adjacent
to the railway station. The bedrooms, including a four-poster room, are
modern in style and mostly spacious. There are extensive conference
facilities and a secure car park. A comfortable bar serves light meals
and a wide range of drinks.

Rooms 70 en suite (3 fmly) ⊘ in 19 bedrooms S £60-£75; D £80-£100
(incl. bkfst)✶ **Facilities** STV Wi-fi available Xmas New Year **Services** Lift
Parking 20 **Notes** LB

★★★ 67% HOTEL
The Crown & Mitre
4 English St CA3 8HZ   **PEEL HOTELS**
☎ 01228 525491 📠 01228 514553
e-mail: info@crownandmitre-hotel-carlisle.com
web: www.peelhotel.com
Dir: *A6 to city centre, pass station & Woolworths on left. Right into
Blackfriars St. Rear entrance at end*

PETS: Bedrooms Public areas except restaurant
Exercise area 5 min walk **On Request** towels

Located in the heart of the city, this Edwardian hotel is close to the
cathedral and a few minutes' walk from the castle. Bedrooms vary in
size and style, from smart executive rooms to more functional standard

---

rooms. Public rooms include a comfortable lounge area and the lovely
bar with its feature stained-glass windows.

Rooms 75 en suite 20 annexe en suite (4 fmly) ⊘ in 55 bedrooms
S £69-£92; D £90-£108 (incl. bkfst)✶ **Facilities** STV 🛝 supervised Wi-fi
available Xmas New Year **Services** Lift **Parking** 42

★★★ 🛏 GUEST ACCOMMODATION
Angus House & Almonds Restaurant
14-16 Scotland Rd CA3 9DG
☎ 01228 523546 📠 01228 531895
e-mail: hotel@angus-hotel.co.uk
web: www.angus-hotel.co.uk
Dir: *0.5m N of city centre on A7*

PETS: Bedrooms unattended **Charges** £5 per night
Public areas except restaurant **Exercise area** nearby
Facilities walks info vet info **On Request** fridge access

Situated just north of the city, this family-run establishment is ideal for
business and leisure. A warm welcome is assured and the
accommodation is well equipped. Almonds Restaurant provides
enjoyable food and home baking, and there is also a lounge and a
large meeting room.

Rooms 11 en suite (2 fmly) ⊘ S £40-£52; D £60-£70 **Facilities** TVB
tea/coffee Direct dial from bedrooms Cen ht Dinner Last d 8.45pm Wi-fi
available **Notes** LB

►►► Green Acres Caravan Park *(NY416614)*
High Knells, Houghton CA6 4JW
☎ 01228 675418
web: www.caravanpark-cumbria.com
Dir: *Leave M6/A74(M) at junct 44, take A689 towards Brampton
for 1m. Left at Scaleby sign and site 1m on left*

PETS: Public areas Exercise area on site walks & wooded area
disp bin **Facilities** vet info **Resident Pets:** Kim (mongrel)

Open Etr-Oct Booking advisable BH Last arrival 21.00hrs Last
departure Noon

A small family touring park in rural surroundings with distant views of
the fells. This pretty park is run by keen, friendly owners who maintain
high standards throughout. A 3-acre site with 30 touring pitches, 25
hardstandings.

Notes ⊗

CLEATOR

MAP 11 NY01

★★★ 75% HOTEL

Ennerdale Country House

CA23 3DT

☎ 01946 813907 📄 01946 815260

e-mail: reservations.ennerdale@ohiml.com

web: www.oxfordhotelsandinns.com

Dir: *M6 junct 40 to A66, join A5086 for 12m, hotel on left in Cleator*

PETS: Bedrooms unattended **Facilities** food

This fine Grade II listed building lies on the edge of the village and has landscaped gardens. Impressive bedrooms, including split-level suites and four-poster rooms, are richly furnished, smartly decorated and offer an amazing array of facilities. Attractive public areas include an elegant restaurant, an inviting lounge and an American themed bar, which offers a good range of bar meals.

Rooms 30 en suite (2 fmly) (10 GF) ⊘ in 23 bedrooms S £60-£99; D £70-£139 (incl. bkfst) **Facilities** STV Xmas New Year **Parking** 40 **Notes** LB

COCKERMOUTH

MAP 11 NY13

★★★ 81% ⊛ HOTEL

The Trout

Crown St CA13 0EJ

☎ 01900 823591 📄 01900 827514

e-mail: enquiries@trouthotel.co.uk

web: www.trouthotel.co.uk

Dir: *next to Wordsworth House*

PETS: Bedrooms (GF) unattended **Charges** £10 per night **Grounds** accessible disp bin **Exercise area** parks nearby **Facilities** food vet info

Dating back to 1670, this privately owned hotel has an enviable setting on the banks of the River Derwent. The well-equipped bedrooms, some contained in a wing overlooking the river, are mostly spacious and comfortable. The Terrace Bar and Bistro, serving food all day, has a sheltered patio area. There is also a cosy bar, a choice of lounge areas and an attractive, traditional-style dining room that offers a good choice of set-price dishes.

Rooms 47 en suite (4 fmly) (15 GF) ⊘ in 12 bedrooms S fr £59.95; D £109-£159 (incl. bkfst)✳ **Facilities** STV Fishing Wi-fi in bedrooms Xmas New Year **Parking** 40 **Notes** LB

★★★ 70% HOTEL

Shepherds Hotel

Lakeland Sheep & Wool Centre, Egremont Rd CA13 0QX

☎ 01900 822673 📄 01900 820129

e-mail: reception@shepherdshotel.co.uk

web: www.shepherdshotel.co.uk

Dir: *at junct of A66 & A5086 S of Cockermouth, entrance off A5086, 200mtrs off rdbt*

PETS: Bedrooms (GF) unattended **Grounds** accessible disp bin **Exercise area** on site **Facilities** cage storage walks info vet info **Resident Pets:** dogs, sheep, geese, Jersey cow

This hotel is modern in style and offers thoughtfully equipped accommodation. The property also houses the Lakeland Sheep and Wool Centre, with live sheep shows from Easter to mid November. A restaurant serving a wide variety of meals and snacks is open all day.

Rooms 26 en suite (4 fmly) (13 GF) ⊘ in all bedrooms S £54-£65; D £54-£70 (incl. bkfst)✳ **Facilities** FTV Wi-fi in bedrooms Pool table, Small childs play area **Services** Lift **Parking** 100 **Notes** Closed 25 Dec, 4-14 Jan

---

★★★★ 🏚 GUEST HOUSE

Croft Guest House

6-8 Challoner St CA13 9QS

☎ 01900 827533

e-mail: info@croft-guesthouse.com

Dir: *In town centre off Main St*

PETS: Bedrooms Charges £2.50 per night **Grounds** accessible **Exercise area** 200mtrs to park **Other** dogs in certain rooms only

Croft Guest House, one of the town's oldest buildings, lies in the heart of Cockermouth. It has been carefully upgraded to offer generally spacious, stylish accommodation. Bedrooms are comfortable, well equipped and retain some original features. There is a cosy ground-floor lounge next to the spacious dining room, where delicious breakfasts from the extensive blackboard menu are served at individual tables.

Rooms 6 en suite (1 fmly) ⊘ S £38; D £60✳ **Facilities** TVB tea/coffee Cen ht **Parking** 5 **Notes** LB No coaches

★ ★ ★ ★ 🏠 BED & BREAKFAST

Highside Farmhouse

Embleton CA13 9TN

☎ 01768 776893 🖨 01768 776893

e-mail: enquiries@highsidefarmhouse.co.uk

web: www.highsidefarmhouse.co.uk

Dir: *A66 Keswick to Cockermouth, left at sign Lorton/Buttermere, left at T-junct. 300yds turn right opp church, farm at top of hill*

PETS: Bedrooms Charges £2 per night **Public areas** on leads **Grounds** accessible on leads disp bin **Exercise area** 20mtrs **Facilities** cage storage walks info vet info **On Request** fridge access torch towels **Resident Pets:** Jaz (Border Collie), 2 cats

True to its name, this 17th-century farmhouse stands over 600 feet up Ling Fell with breathtaking views across to the Solway Firth and Scotland. Add warm hospitality, great breakfasts, an inviting lounge-dining room with open fire in winter, and pine-furnished bedrooms, and the trip up the narrow winding road is well worth it.

Rooms 2 en suite ⊘ S £38-£40; D £56-£60⋇ **Facilities** TVB tea/coffee Cen ht **Parking** 2 **Notes** No children 10yrs ⊛

★ ★ ★ ★ GUEST HOUSE

Rose Cottage

Lorton Rd CA13 9DX

☎ 01900 822189 🖨 01900 822189

e-mail: bookings@rosecottageguest.co.uk

Dir: *A5292 from Cockermouth to Lorton/Buttermere, Rose Cottage on right*

PETS: Bedrooms (GF) **Public areas** except for dining room on leads **Exercise area** 200mtrs **Facilities** food (pre-bookable) food bowl water bowl bedding dog chews feeding mat leads cage storage walks info vet info **On Request** fridge access torch towels **Resident Pets:** Fergus (Irish Wolfhound)

This former inn is on the edge of town and has been refurbished to provide attractive, modern accommodation. The smart, well-equipped en suite bedrooms include a self-contained studio room with external access. There is a cosy lounge, and a smart dining room where delicious home-cooked dinners are a highlight.

Rooms 6 en suite 1 annexe en suite (2 fmly) (3 GF) ⊘ **Facilities** TVB tea/coffee Licensed Cen ht Dinner Last d 5pm **Parking** 12 **Notes** Closed 7-29 Feb RS 24-27 Dec

CROOKLANDS

MAP 07 SD58

►►► Waters Edge Caravan Park *(SD533838)*

LA7 7NN

☎ 015395 67708

e-mail: dennis@watersedgecaravanpark.co.uk

web: www.watersedgecaravanpark.co.uk

Dir: *From M6 follow signs for Kirkby Lonsdale A65, at 2nd rdbt follow signs for Crooklands/Endmoor. Site 1m on right at Crooklands garage, just beyond 40mph limit*

PETS: Public areas except bar area & reception **Exercise area** walks and canal banks 300yds **Facilities** on site shop food water bowl disp bags vet info **Restrictions** dogs must be kept on leads at all times

Open Mar-14 Nov (rs Low Season Bar not open on weekdays) Booking advisable BH Last arrival 22.00hrs Last departure noon

A peaceful, well-run park close to the M6, pleasantly bordered by streams and woodland. A Lakeland-style building houses a shop and bar, and the attractive toilet block is clean and modern. Ideal either as a stopover or for longer stays. A 3-acre site with 26 touring pitches and 20 statics.

CROSTHWAITE

MAP 07 SD49

★ ★ ★ 68% HOTEL

Damson Dene

LA8 8JE

☎ 015395 68676 🖨 015395 68227

e-mail: info@damsondene.co.uk

web: www.bestlakesbreaks.co.uk

Dir: *M6 junct 36, A590 signed Barrow-in-Furness, 5m right onto A5074. Hotel on right in 5m*

PETS: Bedrooms (GF) unattended **Public areas** except restaurant/leisure club on leads **Grounds** accessible on leads disp bin **Facilities** walks info vet info **On Request** fridge access torch

A short drive from Lake Windermere, this hotel enjoys a tranquil and scenic setting. Bedrooms include a number with four-poster beds and jacuzzi baths. The spacious restaurant serves a daily-changing menu, with some of the produce coming from the hotel's own kitchen garden. Real fires warm the lounge in the cooler months and leisure facilities are available.

Rooms 37 en suite (4 fmly) (9 GF) ⊘ in 29 bedrooms S £69-£89; D £98-£138 (incl. bkfst)⋇ **Facilities** Spa ⓢ Squash Gym Beauty salon Xmas New Year **Parking** 45 **Notes** LB

ENGLAND

ENGLAND

CROSTHWAITE *CONTINUED*

★★★★ GUEST HOUSE
Crosthwaite House
LA8 8BP

☎ 015395 68264 📄 015395 68264

e-mail: bookings@crosthwaitehouse.co.uk
web: www.crosthwaitehouse.co.uk

Dir: *A590 onto A5074, 4m right to Crosthwaite, 0.5m turn left*

PETS: Bedrooms unattended **Grounds** accessible
Exercise area 100mtrs **Resident Pets:** Pepper (Labrador), Fidge
(Labrador/Collie cross), Bertie (cat)

Having stunning views across the Lyth Valley, this friendly Georgian house is a haven of tranquillity. Bedrooms are spacious and offer a host of thoughtful extras. The reception rooms include a comfortable lounge and a pleasant dining room with polished floorboards and individual tables.

Rooms 6 en suite ⊘ S £27.50-£29.50; D £55-£59✳ **Facilities** FTV TVB tea/coffee Licensed Cen ht TVL Dinner Last d 5pm **Parking** 10 **Notes** No coaches Closed mid Nov-Dec RS early Nov & Feb-Mar

DALSTON   MAP 11 NY35

►►► Dalston Hall Holiday Park *(NY378519)*
Dalston Hall CA5 7JX

☎ 01228 710165

web: www.dalstonhall.co.uk

Dir: *2.5m SW of Carlisle, just off B5299 & signed*

PETS: Charges £1 per night **Exercise area** on site fenced area disp bin **Facilities** on site shop food food bowl water bowl walks info vet info

Open Mar-Oct Booking advisable BH, Jul-Aug Last arrival 22.00hrs Last departure Noon

A neat, well-maintained site on level grass in the grounds of an estate located between Carlisle and Dalston. All facilities are to a very high standard, and amenities include a 9-hole golf course, a bar and clubhouse serving breakfast and bar meals, and salmon and trout fly fishing. A 5-acre site with 60 touring pitches, 26 hardstandings and 17 statics.

Notes No commercial vans. Gates closed 22.00-07.00.

ESKDALE GREEN   MAP 06 NY10

►►► Fisherground Farm Campsite *(NY152002)*
CA19 1TF

☎ 01946 723349 📄 01946 723349

e-mail: camping@fishergroundcampsite.co.uk
web: www.fishergroundcampsite.co.uk

Dir: *Leave A595 at Gosforth or Holmrook, follow signs on unclass road to Eskdale Green then Boot. Site signed on left*

PETS: Public areas on leads **Facilities** disp bin walks info vet info

Open Mar-Oct Last arrival 21.30hrs Last departure 11.00hrs

A mainly level grassy site on farmland amidst beautiful scenery, in Eskdale Valley below Hardknott Pass, between Eskdale and Boot. It has its own railway halt on the Eskdale-Ravenglass railway, 'The Ratty'. A large heated boot drying locker offered free in the laundry is an obvious bonus for walkers and climbers. A 9-acre site with 215 touring pitches.

Notes 🚭 No caravans, no noise after 22.30hrs

GLENRIDDING   MAP 11 NY31

★★★ 77% ⊛ HOTEL
The Inn on the Lake
Lake Ullswater, Glenridding CA11 0PE

☎ 017684 82444 📄 017684 82303

e-mail: info@innonthelakeullswater.co.uk
web: www.innonthelakeullswater.com

Dir: *M6 junct 40, then A66 to Keswick. At rdbt take A592 to Ullswater Lake. Along lake to Glenridding. Hotel on left on entering village*

PETS: Bedrooms unattended **Charges** £7.50 per night
Public areas only in bar **Grounds** accessible
Exercise area countryside **Other** pets in certain rooms only
Resident Pets: Chrissy (Black Labrador)

In a picturesque lakeside setting, this restored Victorian hotel is a popular leisure destination as well as catering for weddings and conferences. Superb views may be enjoyed from the bedrooms and from the garden terrace where afternoon teas are served during warmer months. There is a popular pub in the grounds and moorings for yachts are available to guests. Sailing tuition can be arranged.

Rooms 46 en suite (6 fmly) (1 GF) ⊘ in all bedrooms S £79; D £69-£108 (incl. bkfst) **Facilities** STV ♨9 ☺ Fishing Gym ♩ Putt green Wi-fi available Sailing, 9 hole pitch and putt, Bowls, Lake Bathing ch fac Xmas New Year **Services** Lift **Parking** 200 **Notes** LB

★★★ 73% HOTEL

Best Western Glenridding Hotel

CA11 0PB

☎ 01768 482228 🖨 01768 482555

e-mail: glenridding@bestwestern.co.uk

Dir: *Northbound M6 exit 36, A591 Windermere then A592 for 14m. Southbound M6 exit 40, A592 for 13m*

PETS: Bedrooms unattended **Charges** £5 per night
Public areas except dining areas **Exercise area** nearby
Facilities food bedding dog treats & a friendly welcome!

This friendly hotel benefits from a picturesque location in the village centre, and many of the bedrooms have fine views of the lake and fells. Public areas are extensive and include a choice of restaurants and bars, a coffee shop including a cyber café, and smart leisure facilities. The Garden Room is an ideal venue for weddings and functions.

Rooms 36 en suite (9 fmly) ⊘ in all bedrooms S £65-£90; D £130-£155 (incl. bkfst)✳ **Facilities** STV 🅣 ♨ Wi-fi in bedrooms Billiards 3/4 Snooker table Table tennis Xmas New Year **Services** Lift **Parking** 38 **Notes**

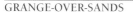

GRANGE-OVER-SANDS   MAP 07 SD47

★★★ 80% HOTEL

Netherwood

Lindale Rd LA11 6ET

☎ 015395 32552 🖨 015395 34121

e-mail: enquiries@netherwood-hotel.co.uk

web: www.netherwood-hotel.co.uk

Dir: *on B5277 before station*

PETS: Bedrooms Charges £3.75 per night **Public areas**
Grounds accessible **Exercise area** 200mtrs

This imposing hotel stands in terraced grounds and enjoys fine views of Morecambe Bay. Though a popular conference and wedding venue, good levels of hospitality and service ensure all guests are well looked after. Bedrooms vary in size but all are well furnished and have smart modern bathrooms. Magnificent woodwork is a feature of the public areas.

Rooms 32 en suite (5 fmly) ⊘ in all bedrooms S £95-£115; D £100-£200 (incl. bkfst)✳ **Facilities** 🅣 supervised Gym ♨ Beauty salon Steam room Spa bath Sunbed New Year **Services** Lift **Parking** 100

GRASMERE   MAP 11 NY30

★★ 76% ⚘ HOTEL

Grasmere

Broadgate LA22 9TA

☎ 015394 35277 🖨 015394 35277

e-mail: enquiries@grasmerehotel.co.uk

web: www.grasmerehotel.co.uk

Dir: *A591 north from Ambleside, 2nd left into Grasmere town centre. Follow road over humpback bridge, past playing field. Hotel on left*

PETS: Bedrooms (GF) unattended **Charges** £5 per stay charge for damage **Grounds** accessible on leads **Exercise area** park adjacent **Facilities** washing facs cage storage walks info vet info **On Request** fridge access torch towels **Other** some bedrooms not suitable for large dogs **Restrictions** no dangerous dogs - see page 7

Attentive and hospitable service contribute to the atmosphere at this family-run hotel, set in secluded gardens by the River Rothay. There are two inviting lounges (one with residents' bar) and an attractive dining room looking onto the garden. The thoughtfully prepared dinner menu makes good use of fresh ingredients. Pine furniture is featured in most bedrooms, along with welcome personal touches.

Rooms 13 en suite 1 annexe en suite (2 GF) ⊘ in all bedrooms S £50-£60; D £100-£190 (incl. bkfst)✳ **Facilities** Wi-fi available Free fishing permit available Xmas New Year **Parking** 14 **Notes** No children 10yrs Closed 3 Jan-early Feb

Ⓤ

Oak Bank

Broadgate LA22 9TA

☎ 015394 35217 🖨 015394 35685

e-mail: info@lakedistricthotel.co.uk

web: www.lakedistricthotel.co.uk

Dir: *N'bound: M6 junct 36 onto A591 to Windermere, Ambleside, then Grasmere. S'bound: M6 junct 40 onto A66 to Keswick, A591 to Grasmere*

PETS: Bedrooms Charges £10 per night **Public areas** only in front lounge **Grounds** accessible **Exercise area** across road

At the time of going to press, the star classification for this hotel was not confirmed. Please refer to the AA internet site www.theAA.com for current information.

Rooms 15 en suite (2 fmly) (1 GF) ⊘ in all bedrooms S £65-£95; D £90-£150 (incl. bkfst)✳ **Facilities** Wi-fi in bedrooms Xmas New Year **Parking** 15 **Notes** LB Closed 2-22 Jan

GRIZEDALE — MAP 07 SD39

★★★★ GUEST ACCOMMODATION
Grizedale Lodge

LA22 0QL
☎ 015394 36532 ▤ 015394 36572
e-mail: enquiries@grizedale-lodge.com
web: www.grizedale-lodge.com
Dir: *From Hawkshead signs S to Grizedale, Lodge 2m on right*

PETS: Bedrooms unattended **Public areas** except dining room
Grounds accessible **Exercise area** 250yds **Other** Breakfast doggie
bag

Set in the heart of the tranquil Grizedale Forest Park, this charming
establishment provides particularly comfortable bedrooms, some with
four-poster beds and splendid views. Hearty breakfasts are served in
the attractive dining room, which leads to a balcony for relaxing on in
summer.

Rooms 8 en suite (1 fmly) (2 GF) ❷ **Facilities** TVB tea/coffee Cen ht
Dinner Last d 8.30pm **Parking** 20

HAWKSHEAD — MAP 07 SD39

★★★ INN
Kings Arms Hotel

LA22 0NZ
☎ 015394 36372 ▤ 015394 36006
e-mail: info@kingsarmshawkshead.co.uk
web: www.kingsarmshawkshead.co.uk
Dir: *In main square*

PETS: Bedrooms (GF) **Stables** nearby **Public areas** except dining
room **Grounds** accessible disp bin **Facilities** food bowl water
bowl washing facs walks info vet info **On Request** fridge access
torch towels

A traditional Lakeland inn in the heart of a conservation area. The cosy,
thoughtfully equipped bedrooms retain much character and are
traditionally furnished. A good choice of freshly prepared food is
available in the lounge bar and the neatly presented dining room.

Rooms 9 rms (8 en suite) (3 fmly) **Facilities** TVB tea/coffee Direct dial
from bedrooms Cen ht Dinner Last d 9.30pm Fishing **Parking** available
Notes Closed 25 Dec

HELTON — MAP 12 NY52

★★★★ GUEST ACCOMMODATION
Beckfoot Country House

CA10 2QB
☎ 01931 713241 ▤ 01931 713391
e-mail: info@beckfoot.co.uk
Dir: *M6 junct 39, A6 through Shap & left to Bampton. Through
Bampton Grange and Bampton, house 2m on left*

PETS: Bedrooms Charges £1.50 per night **Grounds** accessible
on leads disp bin **Facilities** food bowl water bowl bedding dog
chews **Resident Pets:** Turbo & Tweaky (cats), Storm & Fleur
(Shetland ponies)

This delightful Victorian country house stands in well-tended gardens
surrounded by beautiful open countryside, yet is only a short drive
from Penrith. Bedrooms are spacious and particularly well equipped.
The four-poster room is particularly impressive. Public areas include an
elegant drawing room, where guitar workshops are occasionally held,
an oak-panelled dining room and a television lounge.

Rooms 7 en suite (1 fmly) S £35-£45; D £74-£100✻ **Facilities** STV TVB
tea/coffee Cen ht TVL Play area for children. **Parking** 12 **Notes LB**
Closed Dec-Feb

KENDAL — MAP 07 SD59

★★★ 70% HOTEL
Riverside Hotel Kendal

Beezon Rd, Stramongate Bridge LA9 6EL
☎ 01539 734861 ▤ 01539 734863
e-mail: info@riversidekendal.co.uk
web: www.bestlakesbreaks.co.uk
Dir: *M6 junct 36 Sedburgh, Kendal 7m, left at end of Ann St, 1st
right onto Beezon Rd, hotel on left*

PETS: Bedrooms (GF) unattended **Public areas** except restaurant
& leisure areas on leads **Exercise area** 100yds **Facilities** walks
info vet info **On Request** fridge access torch

Centrally located in this market town, and enjoying a peaceful riverside
location, this 17th-century former tannery provides a suitable base for
both business travellers and tourists. The comfortable bedrooms are
well equipped, and open-plan day rooms include the attractive
restaurant and bar. Conference facilities are available, and the
state-of-the-art leisure club has a heated pool, sauna, steam room,
solarium and gym.

Rooms 47 en suite (18 fmly) (10 GF) ❷ in 20 bedrooms S £69-£89;
D £108-£148 (incl. bkfst)✻ **Facilities** STV ⓣ supervised Gym Xmas
New Year **Services** Lift **Parking** 60 **Notes LB**

►►► Kendal Camping & Caravanning Club Site *(SD526948)*

Millcrest, Shap Rd LA9 6NY

☎ 01539 741363

web: www.campingandcaravanningclub.co.uk/kendal

Dir: *On A6, 1.5m N of Kendal. Site 100yds N of Skelsmergh sign*

PETS: Public areas except buildings **Exercise area** on site
disp bin **Facilities** walks info vet info **Other** prior notice required

Open 13 Mar-3 Nov Booking advisable BH & peak periods
Last arrival 21.00hrs Last departure noon

A sloping grass site, set in hilly wood and meadowland, with some level all-weather pitches. Very clean, well kept facilities and attractive flower beds and tubs make a positive impression. The park is handy for nearby Kendal, with its shops and laundry (there is no laundry on site). A 3.5-acre site with 50 touring pitches, 6 hardstandings.

Notes Site gates closed 23.00-07.00

KESWICK   **MAP 11 NY22**

★★★★ GUEST HOUSE
Cragside

39 Blencathra St CA12 4HX

☎ 017687 73344   017687 73344

e-mail: wayne-alison@cragside39blencathra.fsnet.co.uk

Dir: *A591 Penrith Rd into Keswick, under railway bridge, 2nd left*

PETS: Bedrooms Charges charge for damage
Public areas except dining room on leads **Exercise area** 200mtrs
Facilities walks info vet info

Expect warm hospitality at this guest house, located within easy walking distance of the town centre. The attractive bedrooms are well equipped, and many have fine views of the fells. Hearty Cumbrian breakfasts are served in the breakfast room, which overlooks the small front garden. Visually or hearing impaired guests are catered for, with Braille information, televisions with teletext, and a loop system installed in the dining room.

Rooms 4 en suite (2 fmly) ⊗ S £30-£35; D £45-£50 **Facilities** TVB tea/coffee Cen ht **Notes** No coaches

---

★★★★ GUEST ACCOMMODATION
Hazelmere

Crosthwaite Rd CA12 5PG

☎ 017687 72445   017687 74075

e-mail: info@hazelmerekeswick.co.uk

web: www.hazelmerekeswick.co.uk

Dir: *Off A66 at Crosthwaite rdbt (A591 junct) for Keswick, Hazelmere 400yds on right*

PETS: Bedrooms Facilities cage storage walks info vet info

This large Victorian house is only a short walk from Market Square and within walking distance of Derwentwater and the local fells. The attractive bedrooms are comfortably furnished and well equipped. Hearty Cumbrian breakfasts are served at individual tables in the ground-floor dining room, which has delightful views.

Rooms 6 en suite (1 fmly) ⊗ S £30-£35; D £56-£70✳ **Facilities** TVB tea/coffee Cen ht Wi-fi available **Parking** 7 **Notes LB** No children 8yrs

---

★★★ BED & BREAKFAST
Low Nest Farm B&B

Castlerigg CA12 4TF

☎ 017687 72378

e-mail: info@lownestfarm.co.uk

Dir: *2m S of Keswick, off A591 Windermere Rd*

PETS: Bedrooms (GF) **Sep Accom** dedicated kennel per bedroom stables **Charges** £5 per stay **Public areas** except dining room **Grounds** disp bin **Exercise area** 5-acre field adjacent **Facilities** water bowl food bowl bedding dog chews pet sitting dog walking heated dog bath dog grooming cage storage walks info vet info **On request** torch towels
Resident Pets: Sophie, Dillie, Erik & Max (Weimaraners), Pepsi (Poodle)

Low Nest Farm is a small, family-run farm set in some typically breathtaking Cumbrian scenery. Bedrooms are comfortable, en suite and benefit from views of the aforementioned landscape. There are of course, any number of walks available in the area, and Keswick is just two miles away.

Rooms 3 en suite (3GF) ⊗ **Facilities** tea/coffee Cen ht TVL Wi-fi available **Parking** 10 **Notes** No children 16yrs RS Nov-Mar ☜

ENGLAND

KESWICK CONTINUED

►►►► Castlerigg Hall Caravan & Camping Park *(NY282227)*

Castlerigg Hall CA12 4TE

☎ 017687 74499 📄 017687 74499

e-mail: info@castlerigg.co.uk

web: www.castlerigg.co.uk

Dir: *1.5m SE of Keswick on A591, turn right at sign. Site 200mtrs on right past Heights Hotel*

PETS: **Public areas** except recreation field on leads
Exercise area on site disp bin **Facilities** on site shop food food bowl water bowl dog chews cat treats disp bags leads walks info vet info **Restrictions** dogs must not be left unattended
Resident Pets: Jack, Holly, Bells (dogs), Walter & Toby (cats), Amy (Shetland Pony), goats, pot belly pigs, ducks

Open mid Mar-7 Nov Booking advisable touring caravans only Last arrival 21.00hrs Last departure 11.30hrs

Spectacular views over Derwentwater to the mountains beyond are among the many attractions at this lovely Lakeland park. Old farm buildings have been tastefully converted into excellent toilets with private washing and family bathroom, reception and a well-equipped shop, and there is a kitchen/dining area for campers with a courtyard tearoom which also serves breakfast. An 8-acre site with 48 touring pitches, 48 hardstandings.

►►►► Gill Head Farm Caravan & Camping Park *(NY380269)*

Troutbeck CA11 0ST

☎ 017687 79652 📄 017687 79130

e-mail: enquiries@gillheadfarm.co.uk

web: www.gillheadfarm.co.uk

Dir: *From M6 junct 40 take A66, then A5091 towards Troutbeck. Turn right after 100yds, then right again*

PETS: **Public areas** **Exercise area** on site riverside field
Facilities on site shop washing facs walks info vet info

Open Apr-Oct Booking advisable BH Last arrival 22.30hrs Last departure noon

A family-run park on a working hill farm with lovely fell views. It has level touring pitches, and a new log cabin dining room that is popular with families. Tent pitches are gently sloping in a separate field. A 5.5-acre site with 42 touring pitches and 17 statics.

Notes 🐾 No fires

►►► Burns Farm Caravan Park *(NY307244)*

St Johns in the Vale CA12 4RR

☎ 017687 79225 & 79112

e-mail: linda@burns-farm.co.uk

web: www.burns-farm.co.uk

Dir: *Exit A66 signed Castlerigg Stone Circle/Youth Centre/Burns Farm. Site on right in 0.5m*

PETS: **Public areas** on leads **Exercise area** adjacent **Facilities** vet info **Other** prior notice required

Open Mar-4 Nov Booking advisable school hols, Jul/Aug Last departure noon

Lovely views of Blencathra and Skiddaw can be enjoyed from this secluded park, set on a working farm which extends a warm welcome to families. This is a good choice for exploring the beautiful and interesting countryside. Food can be found in the pub at Threlkeld. A 2.5-acre site with 32 touring pitches.

Notes 🐾

►►► Derwentwater Camping & Caravanning Club Site *(NY262232)*

Crow Park Rd CA12 5EN

☎ 01768 772579

web: www.campingandcaravanningclub.co.uk/derwentwater

Dir: *Signed off B5289 in town centre*

PETS: **Public areas** except buildings **Facilities** walks info vet info **Other** prior notice required

Open Mar-14 Nov Booking advisable BH & peak period Last arrival 21.00hrs Last departure noon

A peaceful location close to Derwentwater for this well-managed and popular park which is divided into two areas for tourers. Keswick, with its shops and pubs, is just a 5 minute walk away. A 16-acre site with 44 touring pitches, 17 hardstandings and 160 statics.

Notes Site gates closed 23.00-07.00

►►► Keswick Camping & Caravanning Club Site (NY258234)

Crow Park Rd CA12 5EP

☎ 01768 772392

web: www.campingandcaravanningclub.co.uk/keswick

Dir: *From Penrith on A66 into Main Street (Keswick), right to pass 'Lakes' bus station, past rugby club, turn right, site on right*

PETS: Exercise area on site dog walks disp bin **Facilities** on site shop walks info vet info **Other** prior notice required

Open Feb-Nov Booking advisable BH & peak period Last arrival 21.00hrs Last departure noon

A well situated lakeside site within walking distance of the town centre. Boat launching is available from the site onto Derwentwater, and this level grassy park also offers a number of all-weather pitches. A 14-acre site with 250 touring pitches, 95 hardstandings.

Notes Site gates closed 23.00-07.00

KIRKBY STEPHEN MAP 12 NY70

★★★★ GUEST HOUSE

Brownber Hall Country House

Newbiggin-on-Lune CA17 4NX

☎ 01539 623208

e-mail: enquiries@brownberhall.co.uk

web: www.brownberhall.co.uk

Dir: *6m SW of Kirkby Stephen. Off A685 signed Great Asby, 60yds right through gatehouse, 0.25m sharp left onto driveway*

PETS: Bedrooms Public areas under supervision **Grounds** accessible **Exercise area** on site **Resident Pets:** Sooty & Polar Bear (cats)

Having an elevated position with superb views of the surrounding countryside, Brownber Hall, built in 1860, has been restored to its original glory. The en suite bedrooms are comfortably proportioned, attractively decorated and well equipped. The ground floor has two lovely reception rooms, which retain many original features, and a charming dining room where traditional breakfasts, and by arrangement delicious dinners, are served. There is also a lift.

Rooms 6 en suite (1 GF) ⊘ **Facilities** TVB tea/coffee Lift Cen ht Dinner Last d 24hrs in advance **Parking** 12

★★★ FARM HOUSE

Southview Farm (NY785105)

Winton CA17 4HS

☎ 01768 371120 & 07801 432184 Mrs J Marston

e-mail: southviewwinton@hotmail.com

Dir: *1.5m N of Kirkby Stephen. Off A685 signed Winton*

PETS: Bedrooms unattended **Stables** on site **Public areas** except dining room **Grounds** accessible disp bin **Exercise area** 200 yds **Facilities** feeding mat dog scoop/disp bags washing facs cage storage walks info vet info **On Request** fridge access torch towels **Restrictions** no Dobermans

A friendly family home, Southview lies in the centre of Winton village, part of a terrace with the working farm to the rear. Two well-proportioned bedrooms are available, and there is a cosy lounge-dining room where traditional breakfasts are served around one table.

Rooms 2 rms (2 fmly) ⊘ S £25; D £42✳ **Facilities** TV1B tea/coffee TVL Dinner Last d 8am **Parking** 2 **Notes** 280 acres beef, dairy ⊚

LAMPLUGH MAP 11 NY02

►►► Inglenook Caravan Park (NY084206)

Fitz Bridge CA14 4SH

☎ 01946 861240 📠 01946 861240

e-mail: enquiry@inglenookcaravanpark.co.uk

web: www.inglenookcaravanpark.co.uk

Dir: *On left of A5086 towards Egremont*

PETS: Stables nearby (0.5m) **Public areas** except shop & shower block **Exercise area** fields adjacent **Facilities** on site shop food vet info

Open all year (rs Oct-Etr) Booking advisable at all times Last arrival 20.00hrs Last departure noon

An ideal touring site, well-maintained and situated in beautiful surroundings. The picturesque village of Lamplugh is close to the western lakes of Ennerdale, Buttermere and Loweswater, and a short drive from sandy beaches. A 3.5-acre site with 12 touring pitches, 12 hardstandings and 40 statics.

LONGTOWN MAP 11 NY36

►► Camelot Caravan Park (NY391666)

CA6 5SZ

☎ 01228 791248 📠 01228 791248

Dir: *Leave M6 junct 44. Site 5m N on A7, 1m S of Longtown*

PETS: Public areas on leads **Exercise area** on site **Facilities** washing facs walks info vet info

Open Mar-Oct Booking advisable Jul-Aug Last arrival 22.00hrs Last departure noon

Very pleasant level grassy site in a wooded setting near the M6, with direct access from the A7. This park is an ideal stopover site. A 1.5-acre site with 20 touring pitches and 2 statics.

Notes ⊚

ENGLAND

LOWESWATER — MAP 11 NY12

★★ 69% SMALL HOTEL

Grange Country House

CA13 0SU

☎ 01946 861211 & 861570

e-mail: info@thegrange-loweswater.co.uk

Dir: *left off A5086 for Mockerkin, through village. After 2m left for Loweswater Lake. Hotel at bottom of hill on left*

PETS: Bedrooms (GF) unattended **Charges** £3 - £5 per night **Public areas** except dining room **Facilities** water bowl leads washing facs cage storage walks info vet info food disp bin **On Request** fridge access **Resident Pets:** Toby (Labrador/Collie cross)

This delightful country hotel is set in a quiet valley at the north-western end of Loweswater and continues to prove popular with guests seeking peace and quiet. It has a friendly and relaxed atmosphere, and the cosy public areas include a small bar, a residents' lounge and an attractive dining room. The bedrooms are well equipped and comfortable.

Rooms 8 en suite (2 fmly) (1 GF) ⊗ in 4 bedrooms **Facilities** National Trust boats & fishing Xmas **Parking** 22 **Notes** RS Jan-Feb ⊛

MEALSGATE — MAP 11 NY24

►►►► **Larches Caravan Park** *(NY205415)*

CA7 1LQ

☎ 016973 71379 & 71803 📠 016973 71782

Dir: *On A595, Carlisle to Cockermouth road*

PETS: Stables nearby (6m) (loose box) **Public areas** except toilets & shop **Exercise area** on site fenced disp bin walks nearby **Facilities** on site shop food food bowl water bowl litter dog scoop/disp bags washing facs dog grooming nearby walks info vet info **Resident Pets:** Holly (German Shepherd/ Labrador cross), Trudy (White Belgian Shepherd), Tiger-Lil, Tibby, Blackie (cats)

Open Mar-Oct (rs early & late season) Booking advisable Etr, Spring bank hol & Jul-Aug Last arrival 21.30hrs Last departure noon

This over 18s-only park is set in wooded rural surroundings on the fringe of the Lake District National Park. Touring units are spread out over two sections. The friendly family-run park offers well cared for facilities, and a small indoor swimming pool. A 20-acre site with 73 touring pitches, 30 hardstandings and 100 statics.

Notes ⊛ Adults only

NEAR SAWREY — MAP 07 SD39

★★★★★ ⊛ ≘ ⊜ GUEST HOUSE

Ees Wyke Country House

LA22 0JZ

☎ 015394 36393

e-mail: mail@eeswyke.co.uk

web: www.eeswyke.co.uk

Dir: *On B5285 on W side of village*

PETS: Bedrooms Grounds accessible **Exercise area** adjacent **Facilities** food (charge) **Resident Pets:** Teddy & Harry (Old English Sheepdogs)

A warm welcome awaits you at this elegant Georgian country house with views over Esthwaite Water and the surrounding countryside. The thoughtfully equipped bedrooms have been decorated and furnished with care. There is a charming lounge with an open fire, and a splendid dining room where a carefully prepared five-course dinner is served. Breakfasts have a fine reputation due to the skilful use of local produce.

Rooms 8 en suite (1 GF) ⊗ **Facilities** TVB tea/coffee Licensed Cen ht Dinner Last d noon **Parking** 12 **Notes** No children 12yrs No coaches

PATTERDALE — MAP 11 NY31

►►► **Sykeside Camping Park** *(NY403119)*

Brotherswater CA11 0NZ

☎ 017684 82239 📠 017684 82239

e-mail: info@sykeside.co.uk

web: www.sykeside.co.uk

Dir: *Direct access off A592 (Windermere to Ullswater road) at foot of Kirkstone Pass*

PETS: Stables nearby (loose box) **Charges** £1.50 per night **Public areas Exercise area** on site fenced disp bin **Facilities** on site shop food food bowl water bowl washing facs walks info vet info **Other** prior notice required

Open all year Booking advisable BH & Jul-Aug Last arrival 22.30hrs Last departure 14.00hrs

A camper's delight, this family-run park is sited at the foot of Kirkstone Pass, under the 2000ft Hartsop Dodd in a spectacular area with breathtaking views. The park has mainly grass pitches with a few hardstandings, and for those campers without a tent there is bunkhouse accommodation. A small camper's kitchen and bar serves breakfast and bar meals. There is abundant wildlife. A 5-acre site with 86 touring pitches, 5 hardstandings.

PENRITH — MAP 12 NY53

★★★★ GUEST HOUSE
Glendale

4 Portland Place CA11 7QN

☎ 01768 210061

e-mail: glendaleguesthouse@yahoo.co.uk

web: www.glendaleguesthouse.com

Dir: *M6 junct 40, town centre signs. Pass castle, turn left before town hall*

PETS: Bedrooms Charges £5 per night **Public areas** except dining room **Exercise area** across road **Facilities** food throws **Resident Pets:** Rip (Collie cross), Kia (Border Terrier)

This friendly family-run guest house is part of a Victorian terrace only a stroll from the town centre and convenient for the lakes and Eden Valley. Drying facilities are available. Bedrooms vary in size, but all are attractive, and well equipped and presented. Hearty breakfasts are served at individual tables in the charming ground-floor dining room.

Rooms 7 rms (6 en suite) (1 pri facs) (4 fmly) ⊛ S £35; D £60✳
Facilities TVB tea/coffee Cen ht Wi-fi available

RAVENGLASS — MAP 06 SD09

►►► Ravenglass Camping & Caravanning Club Site *(SD087964)*

CA18 1SR

☎ 01229 717250

web: www.campingandcaravanningclub.co.uk/ravenglass

Dir: *From A595 turn W for Ravenglass. Before village turn left into site*

PETS: Public areas except buildings **Exercise area** adjacent footpaths disp bin **Facilities** on site shop walks info vet info **Other** prior notice require

Open 12 Jan-Nov Booking advisable BH Last arrival 21.00hrs Last departure noon

A pleasant wooded park peacefully located in open countryside, a short stroll from the charming old fishing village of Ravenglass. The Club have improved the park to a high standard with new level gravel pitches, upgraded toilet block and new reception. Muncaster Castle & gardens, the Eskdale/Ravenglass Steam Railway and the coast are all within easy reach. A 5-acre site with 66 touring pitches, 56 hardstandings.

Notes Site gates closed 23.00-07.00

RAVENSTONEDALE — MAP 07 SD09

★★ 68% HOTEL
The Fat Lamb

Crossbank CA17 4LL

☎ 015396 23242 🖷 015396 23285

e-mail: fatlamb@cumbria.com

web: www.fatlamb.co.uk

Dir: *on A683, between Kirkby Stephen and Sedbergh*

PETS: Bedrooms (GF) **Public areas** except restaurant **Grounds** accessible **Facilities** leads cage storage vet info **On Request** fridge access

Open fires and solid stone walls are a feature of this 17th-century inn, set on its own nature reserve. There is a choice of dining options with an extensive menu available in the traditional bar or a more formal dining experience in the restaurant. Bedrooms are bright and cheerful and include family rooms and easily accessible rooms for guests with limited mobility.

Rooms 12 en suite (4 fmly) (5 GF) ⊛ in all bedrooms S £46-£52; D £76-£84 (incl. bkfst)✳ **Facilities** Wi-fi available Private 5-acre nature reserve Xmas **Parking** 60

ROSTHWAITE — MAP 11 NY21

★ 72% HOTEL
Royal Oak

CA12 5XB

☎ 017687 77214 🖷 017687 77214

e-mail: info@royaloakhotel.co.uk

web: www.royaloakhotel.co.uk

Dir: *6m S of Keswick on B5289 in centre of Rosthwaite*

PETS: Bedrooms (GF) **Public areas** except dining room **Grounds** accessible **Facilities** food bowl water bowl leads cage storage walks info vet info **On Request** fridge access torch towels

Set in a village in one of Lakeland's most picturesque valleys, this family-run hotel offers friendly and obliging service. There is a variety of accommodation styles, with particularly impressive rooms being located in a converted barn across the courtyard and backed by a stream. Family rooms are available. The cosy bar is for residents and diners only. A set home-cooked dinner is served at 7pm.

Rooms 8 en suite 4 annexe en suite (5 fmly) (4 GF) ⊛ in all bedrooms D £41-£56 (incl. dinner)✳ **Facilities** no TV in bdrms **Parking** 15
Notes LB Closed 6-24 Jan & 7-27 Dec

ST BEES   MAP 11 NX91

►►►► Seacote Park *(NX962117)*

The Beach CA27 0ET

☎ 01946 822777 📄 01946 824442

e-mail: reception@seacote.com

web: www.seacote.com

Dir: *From St Bees main street follow signs to beach. Take road past Seacote Hotel, through public car park to site*

PETS: Stables nearby (loose box) **Charges** £3 per night £20 per week **Exercise area** on site dog walks leading to beach adjacent to park **Facilities** on site shop disp bags walks info vet info **Other** prior notice required

Open Mar-14 Nov Booking advisable Last arrival 18.00hrs Last departure 11.00hrs

An ideal family holiday park with sweeping sea views, beach access and cliff walks, set in the charming village of St Bees. A smart toilet block with private cubicles is an obvious asset. The facilities of an adjacent hotel are open to park visitors, and include restaurant and bar meals, games room and live entertainment. A 20-acre site with 40 touring pitches, 40 hardstandings and 200 statics.

SILLOTH   MAP 11 NY15

Stanwix Park Holiday Centre

(NY108527)

Greenrow CA7 4HH

☎ 016973 32666 📄 016973 32555

e-mail: enquiries@stanwix.com

web: www.stanwix.com

Dir: *1m SW on B5300. From A596 (Wigton bypass), follow signs to Silloth on B5302. In Silloth follow signs to site, approx 1m on B5300*

PETS: Charges £3 per night £21 per week **Public areas** on leads except leisure areas **Exercise area** 15 min walk to beach **Facilities** on site shop food food bowl water bowl bedding dog chews cat treats dog scoop/disp bags leads walks info vet info pet toys **Other** prior notice required **Restrictions** max 2 dogs per pitch

Open all year (rs Nov-Feb (ex New Year) no entertainment/ shop closed) Booking advisable Etr, Spring bank hol, Jul-Aug & New Year Last arrival 22.00hrs Last departure 11.00hrs

A large well-run family park within easy reach of the Lake District. Attractively laid out, with lots of amenities to ensure a lively holiday, including a 4-lane automatic 10-pin bowling alley. A 4-acre site with 121 touring pitches, 100 hardstandings and 212 statics.

►►►► Hylton Caravan Park *(NY113533)*

Eden St CA7 4AY

☎ 016973 31707 📄 016973 32555

e-mail: enquiries@stanwix.com

web: www.stanwix.com

Dir: *On entering Silloth on B5302 follow signs Hylton Caravan Park, approx 0.5m on left, (end of Eden St)*

PETS: Charges £3 per night £21 per week **Public areas** on leads except leisure areas **Exercise area** 15min walk to beach **Facilities** walks info vet info **Other** prior notice required **Restrictions** max 2 dogs per pitch

Open Mar-15 Nov Booking advisable school hols Last arrival 21.00hrs Last departure 11.00hrs

A smart, modern touring park with excellent toilet facilities including several bathrooms. This high quality park is a sister site to Stanwix Park, which is just a mile away and offers all the amenities of a holiday centre. An 18-acre site with 90 touring pitches and 213 statics.

Notes Families only

TEBAY   MAP 07 NY60

★★★ INN

Cross Keys

CA10 3UY

☎ 01539 624240 📄 01539 629922

e-mail: stay@crosskeys-tebay.co.uk

web: www.crosskeys-tebay.co.uk

Dir: *M6 junct 38, A685 into village*

PETS: Bedrooms Public areas except at meal times **Grounds** accessible **Exercise area** on site **Facilities** food

Situated in the centre of the village, only a short drive from the motorway, this one-time coaching inn has original low-beamed ceilings and open fires. A wide selection of popular dishes is available in the bar and the smart dining room. The bedrooms are comfortably proportioned and traditionally furnished, with three attractive bedrooms in a converted barn at the rear.

Rooms 9 rms (3 en suite) (1 fmly) (6 GF) ⊘ in 3 bedrooms **Facilities** TVB tea/coffee Cen ht TVL Dinner Last d 9pm Pool Table **Parking** 30 **Notes** RS out of season

▶▶▶ **Westmorland Caravan Park** *(NY609060)*

Orton CA10 3SB

☎ 01539 711322 📠 015396 24944

e-mail: caravans@westmorland.com

web: www.westmorland.com

Dir: *Exit M6 at Westmorland Services, 1m from junct 38. Site accessed through service area from either N'bound or S'bound carriageways. Follow park signs*

PETS: Stables nearby (3m) **Public areas Exercise area** on site walks around woods & grass land surrounding countryside disp bin **Facilities** washing facs walks info vet info

Open Mar-Oct Booking advisable Jul-Aug & wknds Last arrival anytime Last departure noon

An ideal stopover site adjacent to the Tebay service station on the M6, and handy for touring the Lake District. The park is screened by high grass banks, bushes and trees, and is within walking distance of a shop and restaurant. A 4-acre site with 70 touring pitches, 70 hardstandings and 7 statics.

Notes no cars by tents

TROUTBECK MAP 11 NY32
(NEAR KESWICK)

▶▶▶▶ **Troutbeck Camping and Caravanning Club Site** *(NY364270)*

Hutton Moor End CA11 0SX

☎ 01768 779615

web: www.campingandcaravanningclub.co.uk/troutbeck

Dir: *On A66 (Penrith to Keswick) turn left at Wallthwaite sign*

PETS: Public areas except buildings **Exercise area** on site **Facilities** walks info vet info disp bin **Other** prior notice required

Open Mar-15 Nov Booking advisable BH Last arrival 21.00hrs Last departure noon

Beautifully situated between Penrith and Keswick, this quiet, pleasant Lakeland park offers a sheltered touring field with serviced pitches enjoying extensive views of the surrounding fells. The toilet block has been upgraded to a very high standard including two family cubicles, and the new log cabin stocks local and organic produce. A 4.5-acre site with 54 touring pitches, 24 hardstandings and 20 statics.

Notes Site gates closed 23.00-07.00

ULVERSTON MAP 07 SD27

★★★★ BED & BREAKFAST

Church Walk House

Church Walk LA12 7EW

☎ 01229 582211

e-mail: martinchadd@btinternet.com

Dir: *In town centre opp Stables furniture shop*

PETS: Bedrooms Public areas Grounds accessible disp bin **Facilities** dog scoop/disp bags owners must bring bowls/bedding cage storage walks info vet info **On Request** fridge access **Restrictions** St Bernard breed is max size permitted, pets must not use furniture, including beds

This Grade II listed 18th-century residence stands in the heart of the historic market town. Stylishly decorated, the accommodation includes attractive bedrooms with a mix of antiques and contemporary pieces. A peaceful atmosphere prevails with attentive service, and there is a small herbal garden and patio.

Rooms 3 rms (2 en suite) ⊘ S £25-£40; D £55-£65 **Facilities** tea/coffee Cen ht TVL **Notes** LB ⊛

WATERMILLOCK MAP 12 NY42

★★★★ ⇔ INN

Brackenrigg

CA11 0LP

☎ 017684 86206 📠 017684 86945

e-mail: enquiries@brackenrigginn.co.uk

web: www.brackenrigginn.co.uk

Dir: *6m from M6 onto A66 towards Keswick & A592 to Ullswater, right at lake & continue 2m*

PETS: Bedrooms Charges £10 per stay **Public areas** bar only **Grounds** accessible **Exercise area** surrounding area

An 18th-century coaching inn with superb views of Ullswater and the surrounding countryside. Freshly prepared dishes and daily specials are served by friendly staff in the traditional bar and restaurant. The bedrooms include six attractive rooms in the stable cottages.

Rooms 11 en suite 6 annexe en suite (8 fmly) (3 GF) S £38-£48; D £69-£80❈ **Facilities** TVB tea/coffee Cen ht Dinner Last d 9pm **Parking** 40 **Notes** LB

ENGLAND

WATERMILLOCK CONTINUED

►►► Cove Caravan & Camping Park

(NY431236)

Ullswater CA11 0LS

☎ 017684 86549 📄 017684 86549

e-mail: info@cove-park.co.uk

web: www.cove-park.co.uk

Dir: *M6 junct 40 take A592 for Ullswater. Right at lake junct, then right at Brackenrigg Hotel. Site 1.5m on left*

PETS: Charges £1 per dog per night **Public areas** on leads **Exercise area** on site 2 dog walks **Facilities** washing facs walks info vet info **Resident Pets:** Daisy (Cocker Spaniel)

Open Mar-Oct Booking advisable bank & school hols Last arrival 21.00hrs Last departure noon

A peaceful family site in an attractive and elevated position with extensive fell views and glimpses of Ullswater Lake. The ground is gently sloping grass, but there are also hardstandings for motorhomes and caravans. A 3-acre site with 50 touring pitches, 17 hardstandings and 39 statics.

Notes ⊖ No open fires

WINDERMERE MAP 07 SD49

★★★★ ®®® COUNTRY HOUSE HOTEL

Holbeck Ghyll Country House

Holbeck Ln LA23 1LU

☎ 015394 32375 📄 015394 34743

e-mail: stay@holbeckghyll.com

Dir: *3m N of Windermere on A591, right into Holbeck Lane (signed Troutbeck), hotel 0.5m on left*

PETS: Bedrooms (GF) unattended **Stables** nearby (1.5m) **Charges** £8 per night, charge for damage **Public areas** front hall only **Grounds** accessible disp bin **Facilities** food (pre-bookable) food bowl water bowl bedding dog chews feeding mat dog scoop/disp bags leads dog walking washing facs cage storage walks info vet info **On Request** fridge access torch towels **Resident Pets:** Solie & Brook (Black Labradors)

With a peaceful setting in extensive grounds, this beautifully maintained hotel enjoys breathtaking views over Lake Windermere and the Langdale Fells. Public rooms include luxurious, comfortable lounges and two elegant dining rooms, where memorable meals are served. Bedrooms are individually styled, beautifully furnished and many have balconies or patios. Some in an adjacent, more private lodge are less traditional in design and have superb views. The professionalism and attentiveness of the staff is exemplary.

Rooms 23 en suite (3 fmly) (3 GF) ⊘ in all bedrooms S £145-£325; D £250-£550 (incl. bkfst & dinner)✳ **Facilities** Spa STV ⌕ Gym ⌣ Putt green Wi-fi available Steam room Treatment rooms Beauty Massage Xmas New Year **Parking** 28 **Notes** LB

★★★★ 75% ®® HOTEL

Storrs Hall

Storrs Park LA23 3LG

☎ 015394 47111 📄 015394 47555

e-mail: storrshall@elhmail.co.uk

web: www.elh.co.uk/hotels/storrshall

Dir: *on A592 2m S of Bowness, on Newby Bridge road*

PETS: Bedrooms Charges £15 per night charge for damage **Grounds** accessible on leads disp bin **Facilities** water bowl cage storage walks info vet info **On Request** torch

Set in 17 acres of landscaped grounds by the lakeside, this imposing Georgian mansion is delightful. There are numerous lounges to relax in, furnished with fine art and antiques. Individually styled bedrooms are generally spacious and boast impressive bathrooms. Imaginative cuisine is served in the elegant restaurant, which offers fine views across the lawn to the lake and fells beyond.

Rooms 30 en suite ⊘ in all bedrooms S £113-£177; D £176-£304 (incl. bkfst) **Facilities** Fishing ⌣ Wi-fi in bedrooms Use of nearby sports/ beauty facilities. Xmas New Year **Parking** 50 **Notes** LB No children 12yrs

---

★★★ ®®® COUNTRY HOUSE HOTEL

Linthwaite House Hotel

Crook Rd LA23 3JA

☎ 015394 88600 📄 015394 88601

e-mail: stay@linthwaite.com

web: www.linthwaite.com

Dir: *A591 towards The Lakes for 8m to large rdbt, take 1st exit (B5284), 6m, hotel on left. 1m past Windermere golf club*

PETS: Sep Accom outdoor kennel & caged run **Grounds** accessible disp bin **Exercise area** on site **Facilities** water bowl food on request cage storage walks info vet info **On Request** fridge access torch towels

Linthwaite House is set in 14 acres of hilltop grounds and enjoys stunning views over Lake Windermere. Inviting public rooms include an attractive conservatory and adjoining lounge, a smokers' bar and an elegant restaurant. Bedrooms, which are individually decorated, combine contemporary furnishings with classical styles. All are thoughtfully equipped and include CD players. Service and hospitality are attentive and friendly.

Rooms 27 en suite (1 fmly) (7 GF) ⊘ in all bedrooms S £120-£170; D £170-£320 (incl. bkfst & dinner)✳ **Facilities** STV Fishing ⌣ Putt green Wi-fi in bedrooms Beauty treatments Xmas New Year **Parking** 40 **Notes** LB ⊗

★★★ 81% HOTEL

Langdale Chase

Langdale Chase LA23 1LW

☎ 015394 32201 🖹 015394 32604

e-mail: sales@langdalechase.co.uk

web: www.langdalechase.co.uk

Dir: *2m S of Ambleside and 3m N of Windermere, on A591*

PETS: Bedrooms (GF) unattended **Public areas** except restaurant & bar on leads **Grounds** accessible on leads disp bin **Facilities** food (pre-bookable) food bowl water bowl pet sitting dog walking washing facs cage storage walks info vet info **On Request** fridge access torch towels **Resident Pets:** Nobby (Boxer)

Enjoying unrivalled views of Lake Windermere, this imposing country manor has been trading as a hotel for over 70 years. Public areas feature beautifully carved fireplaces, oak panelling and an imposing galleried staircase. Bedrooms have stylish, spacious bathrooms and outstanding views.

Rooms 20 en suite 7 annexe en suite (2 fmly) (1 GF) ⊗ in all bedrooms S £80-£140; D £90-£210 (incl. bkfst)✳ **Facilities** Fishing ⮑ Putt green Mini golf Xmas New Year **Parking** 50 **Notes** LB

★★★★ 🛏 GUEST HOUSE

The Coppice

Brook Rd LA23 2ED

☎ 015394 88501 🖹 015394 42148

e-mail: chris@thecoppice.co.uk

web: www.thecoppice.co.uk

Dir: *0.25m S of village centre on A5074*

PETS: Bedrooms Charges £5 per night **Grounds** accessible **Exercise area** 50yds

This attractive detached house lies between Windermere and Bowness. There are colourful public rooms and bedrooms, and a restaurant serving freshly prepared local produce. The bedrooms vary in size and style and have good facilities.

Rooms 9 en suite (2 fmly) (1 GF) ⊗ **Facilities** TVB tea/coffee Licensed Cen ht Dinner Last d 10am Wi-fi available Private leisure club membership **Parking** 10 **Notes** No coaches

►►►► **Windermere Camping & Caravanning Club Site** *(SD479964)*

Ashes Ln LA8 9JS

☎ 01539 821119

web: www.campingandcaravanningclub.co.uk/windermere

Dir: *Signed off A591, 0.75m from rdbt with B5284 towards Windermere*

PETS: Public areas except buildings **Exercise area** on site disp bin **Facilities** walks info vet info **Other** prior notice required

Open 13 Mar-3 Nov Booking advisable BH & peak periods Last arrival 21.00hrs Last departure noon

A top Club site in a beautifully landscaped setting bordered by bluebell woods. Many mature trees and shrubs add to the natural beauty, and there are rocky outcrops and lovely views to be enjoyed. First class toilet facilities, good security, a large adventure playground, and a bar (The Whistling Pig) serving breakfasts, snacks and hot meals all add to the popularity of this very well-redeveloped site. A 24-acre site with 250 touring pitches, 88 hardstandings and 75 statics.

Notes Site gates closed 23.00-07.00

WORKINGTON　　　　　　　　　MAP 11 NY02

★★★ 75% HOTEL

Hunday Manor Country House

Hunday, Winscales CA14 4JF

☎ 01900 61798 🖹 01900 601202

e-mail: info@hunday-manor-hotel.co.uk

Dir: *A66 onto A595 towards Whitehaven, hotel 3m on right, signed*

PETS: Bedrooms unattended **Grounds** accessible **Exercise area** nearby fields

Delightfully situated and enjoying distant views of the Solway Firth, this charming hotel has well-furnished rooms with lots of extras. The open-plan bar and foyer lounge boast welcoming open fires, and the attractive restaurant overlooks the woodland gardens. The provision of a function suite makes the hotel an excellent wedding venue.

Rooms 24 en suite (1 fmly) ⊗ in all bedrooms S £58-£85; D £99-£125 (incl. bkfst)✳ **Facilities** Wi-fi in bedrooms **Parking** 50

DERBYSHIRE

ASHBOURNE   MAP 07 SK14

★★★★ FARM HOUSE
Mercaston Hall *(SK279419)*
Mercaston DE6 3BL
☎ 01335 360263 Mr & Mrs A Haddon
e-mail: mercastonhall@btinternet.com
Dir: *Off A52 in Brailsford onto Luke Ln, 1m turn right at 1st x-rds, house 1m on right*
PETS: Bedrooms Sep Accom barn **Stables** on site **Charges** £2 per night charge for damage **Public areas** except dining room **Grounds** accessible disp bin **Exercise area** adjacent fields **Facilities** food bowl water bowl leads washing facs cage storage walks info vet info **On Request** fridge access torch towels
Located in a pretty hamlet, this medieval building retains many original features. Bedrooms are homely, and additional facilities include an all-weather tennis court and a livery service. This is a good base for visiting local stately homes, the Derwent Valley mills and Dovedale.
Rooms 3 en suite ⊘ S £45; D £66✱ **Facilities** TVB tea/coffee Cen ht ⏣ **Parking** 3 **Notes** No children 12yrs 60 acres mixed Closed Xmas ⊜

▶ Carsington Fields Caravan Park *(SK251493)*
Millfields Ln, Near Carsington Water DE6 3JS
☎ 01335 372872
web: www.carsingtoncaravaning.co.uk
Dir: *From Belper towards Ashbourne on A517 turn right approx 0.25m past Hulland Ward into Dog Lane. 0.75m right at x-roads signed Carsington. Site on right after approx 0.75m*
PETS: Public areas except toilet areas **Exercise area** on site grass dog run **Facilities** vet info **Other** prior notice required
Open end Mar-mid Oct Booking advisable Last arrival 21.00hrs Last departure 18.00hrs
A very well presented and spacious park with a good toilet block, open views and a large fenced pond that attracts plenty of wildlife. The popular tourist attraction of Carsington Water is a short stroll away, with its variety of leisure facilities including fishing, sailing, windsurfing and children's play area. The park is also a good base for walkers. A 6-acre site with 10 touring pitches, 10 hardstandings.
Notes ⊜ No large groups

BAKEWELL   MAP 08 SK26

★★★ 70% ◉ HOTEL
Rutland Arms
The Square DE45 1BT
☎ 01629 812812 🖹 01629 812309
e-mail: rutland@bakewell.demon.co.uk
Dir: *M1 junct 28 to Matlock, A6 to Bakewell. Hotel in town centre*
PETS: Bedrooms (GF) unattended **Exercise area** 5 mins **Facilities** vet info

This 19th-century hotel lies at the very centre of Bakewell and offers a wide range of quality accommodation. The friendly staff are attentive and welcoming, and The Four Seasons candlelit restaurant serves interesting fine dining in elegant surroundings.
Rooms 18 en suite 17 annexe en suite (2 fmly) ⊘ in 12 bedrooms S £44-£65; D £76-£115 (incl. bkfst) **Facilities** Wi-fi in bedrooms Xmas New Year **Parking** 25 **Notes** LB

★★ 75% HOTEL
Monsal Head Hotel
Monsal Head DE45 1NL
☎ 01629 640250 🖹 01629 640815
e-mail: enquiries@monsalhead.com
web: www.monsalhead.com
Dir: *A6 from Bakewell to Buxton. After 2m turn into Ashford in the Water, take B6465 for 1m*
PETS: Bedrooms unattended **Charges** £5 per night **Public areas** lounge & bar only **Grounds** accessible on leads **Exercise area** country walks & paths
Popular with walkers, this friendly hotel commands one of the most splendid views in the Peak Park, overlooking Monsal Dale and the walking path along the disused railway line. Bedrooms are well equipped, and four have superb views down the valley. Imaginative food is served in either an attractive modern restaurant or separate original pub, which also offers a range of fine wines and real ales.
Rooms 7 en suite (1 fmly) ⊘ in all bedrooms S £45-£55; D £50-£70 (incl. bkfst)✱ **Facilities** Xmas New Year **Parking** 20 **Notes** LB

★★★★ GUEST HOUSE
Croft Cottages
Coombs Rd DE45 1AQ
☎ 01629 814101
e-mail: croftco@btopenworld.com

Dir: *A619 E from town centre over bridge, right onto Station Rd & Coombs Rd*

PETS: Bedrooms unattended Grounds accessible on leads
Facilities walks info vet info On Request towels
Resident Pets: Steffi (Belgian Shepherd)

A warm welcome is assured at this Grade II listed stone building close to the River Wye and town centre. Thoughtfully equipped bedrooms are available in the main house or in an adjoining converted barn suite. Breakfast is served in a spacious lounge dining room.

Rooms 3 rms (2 en suite) (1 pri facs) 1 annexe en suite (1 fmly) ⊘
D £56-£75 Facilities TVB tea/coffee Cen ht Parking 2 Notes LB
No coaches ⊛

BELPER   MAP 08 SK34

★★★★ 71% HOTEL
Makeney Hall Hotel
Makeney, Milford DE56 0RS
folio Hotels
☎ 01332 842999 🖨 01332 842777
e-mail: makeneyhall@foliohotels.com
web: www.foliohotels.com/makeneyhall

Dir: *off A6 at Milford, signed Makeney. Hotel 0.25m on left*

PETS: Bedrooms Charges £5 per night Grounds accessible
Exercise area fields Other dogs in courtyard rooms only

This restored Victorian mansion stands in six acres of landscaped gardens and grounds above the River Derwent. Bedrooms vary in style and are generally very spacious. They are divided between the main house and the ground floor courtyard. Comfortable public rooms include a lounge, bar and spacious restaurant with views of the gardens.

Rooms 28 en suite 18 annexe en suite (3 fmly) ⊘ in 14 bedrooms
Facilities STV Wi-fi available Services Lift Parking 150 Notes

---

BUXTON   MAP 07 SK07

★★★ 78% ⊛ HOTEL
Best Western Lee Wood
The Park SK17 6TQ
☎ 01298 23002 🖨 01298 23228
e-mail: leewoodhotel@btconnect.com
web: www.leewoodhotel.co.uk

Dir: *NE on A5004, 300mtrs beyond Devonshire Royal Hospital*

PETS: Bedrooms unattended Charges £8 per night
Grounds accessible Exercise area local walks

This elegant Georgian hotel offers high standards of comfort and hospitality. Individually furnished bedrooms are generally spacious, with all of the expected modern conveniences. There is a choice of two comfortable lounges and a conservatory restaurant. Quality cooking, good service and fine hospitality are noteworthy.

Rooms 35 en suite 5 annexe en suite (4 fmly) ⊘ in 25 bedrooms
Facilities STV FTV Wi-fi in bedrooms Services Lift Parking 50

★★★ BED & BREAKFAST
Wellhead Farm
Wormhill SK17 8SL
☎ 01298 871023 🖨 0871 236 0267
e-mail: wellhead4bunkntrough@cbits.net

Dir: *Between Bakewell and Buxton. Off A6 onto B6049 signed Millers Dale/Tideswell & left to Wormhill*

PETS: Bedrooms Public areas except dining room
Grounds accessible disp bin Exercise area adjacent
Facilities feeding mat litter tray etc leads pet sitting washing facs cage storage walks info vet info On Request fridge access torch towels Resident Pets: Zack (Retriever), Murphy (Border Terrier), Zoro & Billy (cats)

This 16th-century farmhouse is in a peaceful location, and has low beams and two comfortable lounges. The bedrooms, some with four poster beds, come with radios, beverage trays and many thoughtful extras. The proprietors provide friendly and attentive hospitality in their delightful home.

Rooms 4 en suite (1 fmly) S £40-£46; D £58-£68✳ Facilities tea/coffee
Cen ht TVL Dinner Last d 9am Parking 4 Notes LB ⊛

ENGLAND

▶▶▶▶ Lime Tree Park (SK070725)

Dukes Dr SK17 9RP

☎ 01298 22988 📠 01298 22988

e-mail: info@limetreeparkbuxton.co.uk

web: www.limetreeparkbuxton.co.uk

Dir: *1m S of Buxton, between A515 & A6*

PETS: Charges £2 per night Public areas on leads
Exercise area on site field available Facilities on site shop food
Other prior notice required

Open Mar-Oct Booking advisable BH, Jul-Aug Last arrival
21.00hrs Last departure noon

A most attractive and well-designed site, set on the side of a narrow
valley in an elevated location. Its backdrop of magnificent old railway
viaduct and views over Buxton and the surrounding hills make this a
sought-after destination. A 10.5-acre site with 99 touring pitches, 8
hardstandings and 43 statics.

▶▶ Cottage Farm Caravan Park (SK122720)

Beech Croft, Blackwell in the Peak SK17 9TQ

☎ 01298 85330

e-mail: mail@cottagefarmsite.co.uk

web: www.cottagefarmsite.co.uk

Dir: *Off A6 midway between Buxton and Bakewell. Site signed*

PETS: Public areas except toilets Exercise area bridlepath 100yds
Facilities on site shop food food bowl water bowl walks info vet
info

Open mid Mar-Oct (rs Nov-Mar hook up & water tap only)
Booking advisable BH, school hols Last arrival 21.30hrs

A small terraced site in an attractive farm setting with lovely views.
Hardstandings are provided for caravans, and there is a separate field
for tents. An ideal site for those touring or walking in the Peak District.
A 3-acre site with 30 touring pitches, 25 hardstandings.

Notes 🐾

▶▶ Thornheyes Farm Campsite (SK084761)

Thornheyes Farm, Longridge Ln, Peak Dale SK17 8AD

☎ 01298 26421

Dir: *1.5m from Buxton on A6 turn E for Peak Dale. After 0.5m S at
x-rds to site on right*

PETS: Public areas on leads at all times Exercise area adjacent
Facilities vet info Other prior notice required Resident Pets: Bart
(Alsation), 4 cats

Open Etr-Oct Booking advisable BH, high season Last arrival
21.30hrs Last departure evenings

A pleasant mainly-sloping farm site run by a friendly family team in the
central Peak District. Toilet and other facilities are very simple but
extremely clean. A 2-acre site with 10 touring pitches.

Notes 🐾 Adults only (site not suitable for children), no ball games, no
bicycles, unisex showers

CALVER   MAP 08 SK27

★★★★ GUEST ACCOMMODATION
Valley View

Smithy Knoll Rd S32 3XW

☎ 01433 631407

e-mail: sue@a-place-2-stay.co.uk

web: www.a-place-2-stay.co.uk

Dir: *A623 from Baslow into Calver, 3rd left onto Donkey Ln*

PETS: Bedrooms Exercise area adjacent open fields where dogs
can run off lead Other tortoises accepted

This detached stone house is in the heart of the village. It is very
well-furnished throughout and delightfully friendly service is provided.
A hearty breakfast is served in the cosy dining room, which is
well-stocked with local guide books.

Rooms 3 en suite (1 fmly) ⊗ D £50-£70 Facilities TVB tea/coffee
Cen ht Wi-fi available Parking 6 Notes LB No children 5yrs

CASTLETON   MAP 07 SK18

★★★★ GUEST ACCOMMODATION
The Rising Sun Hotel

Thornhill Moor, Bamford S33 0AL

☎ 01433 651323 📠 01433 651601

e-mail: info@the-rising-sun.org

Dir: *On A625 from Sheffield to Castleton*

PETS: Please telephone for details

Located at Thornhill Moor within the Hope Valley, this 18th-century inn
has been renovated to provide high standards of comfort and facilities.
Spacious luxury bedrooms offer quality furnishings and efficient
modern bathrooms, and some have stunning views of the surrounding
countryside. The staff are friendly and capable, and imaginative food is
offered in the comfortable public areas.

Rooms 12 en suite (2 fmly) Facilities TVB tea/coffee Cen ht Dinner
Last d 10pm Parking 120

See advert on opposite page

The Rising Sun

THIS IS NOT JUST ANOTHER HOTEL. THIS IS AN EXPERIENCE!

The Rising Sun, an 18th Century Inn situated in the heart of the Peak District National Park, is privately owned and family run. The hotel has been sympathetically restored with 12 individually designed de luxe bedrooms yet maintains its authentic country inn atmosphere. Fresh flowers in abundance and antiques together with friendly and efficient staff make this the place to stay. Quality fresh food, real ales and fine wines served daily in a relaxed and comfortable bar. Civil ceremonies & wedding receptions a speciality.

The Rising Sun, Thornhill Moor, Hope Road, Nr. Bamford, Hope Valley, Derbyshire S33 0AL
Telephone: 01433 651323 • Fax: 01433 651601
E-Mail: info@the-rising-sun.org • www.the-rising-sun.org

"The Inn of the Peaks"

*Weddings are our speciality.
Hold your Civil Ceremony
in our Oak Panelled
Chatsworth Suite.*

CROWDEN
MAP 07 SK09

►► Crowden Camping & Caravanning Club Site (SK072992)
Woodhead Rd SK13 1HZ
☎ 01457 866057
web: www.campingandcaravanningclub.co.uk/crowden
Dir: *A628 (Manchester to Barnsley road). At Crowden follow sign for car park/youth hostel & camp site. Site approx 300yds from main road*
PETS: **Public areas** except buildings **Exercise area** adjacent to site disp bin **Facilities** walks info vet info **Other** prior notice required
Open 13 Mar-29 Sep Booking advisable BH & peak periods Last arrival 21.00hrs Last departure noon
A beautifully located moorland site, overlooking the reservoirs and surrounded by hills. Tents only, with backpackers' drying room. A 2.5-acre site with 45 touring pitches.
Notes Site gates closed 23.00-07.00

DERBY SERVICE AREA (A50)
MAP 08 SK42

BUDGET HOTEL
Days Inn Donnington
DAYS INN
Welcome Break Services, A50 Westbound DE72 2WA
☎ 01332 799666 📠 01332 794166
e-mail: derby.hotel@welcomebreak.co.uk
web: www.daysinn.com
Dir: *M1junct 24/24a, onto A50 towards Stoke/Derby. Hotel between juncts 1 & 2*
PETS: **Bedrooms** (GF) **Public areas** on leads **Grounds** accessible on leads
This modern building offers accommodation in smart, spacious and well-equipped bedrooms, suitable for families and business travellers, and all with en suite bathrooms. Continental breakfast is available and other refreshments may be taken at the nearby family restaurant. For further details see the Hotel Groups page.
Rooms 47 en suite

GLOSSOP
MAP 07 SK09

★★★ FARM HOUSE
Kings Clough Head Farm (SK018899)
Back Rowarth SK13 6ED
☎ 01457 862668 Mrs S Keegan
e-mail: kingscloughheadfarm@hotmail.com
Dir: *Monks Rd off A624 near Grouse Inn*
PETS: **Bedrooms Facilities** bedding
Situated in the hills with stunning country views, this 18th-century stone house provides thoughtfully furnished bedrooms and a modern efficient bathroom. Breakfast is served at one table in an antique-furnished dining room and a warm welcome is assured.
Rooms 3 rms (1 pri facs) ⊗ S £25-£28; D £46-£54✱ **Facilities** TVB tea/coffee Cen ht TVL **Parking** 4 **Notes** 26 acres cattle geese Closed Xmas ◉

★★★ BED & BREAKFAST
The Old House
Woodhead Rd, Torside SK13 1HU
☎ 01457 857527
e-mail: oldhouse@torside.co.uk
Dir: *2m N of Glossop. On B6105 between sailing club & hairpin bend*
PETS: **Bedrooms Stables** on site **Charges** no charge for dogs, £5 for horses per night **Public areas Grounds** accessible **Exercise area** 25yds **Facilities** food bowl **Resident Pets:** 12 dogs, horses & chickens
Nestling on the northwest-facing slopes above a reservoir, this smallholding commands superb views and offers all mod cons, including a drying room for people who are walking the nearby Pennine Way. Oak beams and rough plastered walls date from the 17th century, and hospitality is warm.
Rooms 3 en suite (1 fmly) (1 GF) **Facilities** tea/coffee Cen ht TVL **Parking** 5 **Notes** ◉

HAYFIELD
MAP 07 SK08

►► Hayfield Camping & Caravanning Club Site (SK048868)
Kinder Rd SK22 2LE
☎ 01663 745394
web: www.campingandcaravanningclub.co.uk/hayfield
Dir: *Off A624, Glossop to Chapel-en-le-Frith (Hayfield by-pass). Well signed into village, follow wood-carved signs to site*
PETS: **Public areas** except buildings **Facilities** walks info vet info disp bin **Other** prior notice required
Open 13 Mar-3 Nov Booking advisable BH & peak periods Last arrival 21.00hrs Last departure noon

On level ground along the River Sett valley, a peaceful location overlooked on three sides by mature woodland, with the hills of the North Derbyshire moors on the fourth side. The camping area is in two fields with central amenities. A 6-acre site with 90 touring pitches.

Notes Site gates closed 23.00-07.00

HOPE MAP 07 SK18

★★★ GUEST HOUSE

Round Meadow Barn

Parsons Ln S33 6RB

☎ 01433 621347 & 07836 689422 📄 01433 621347

e-mail: rmbarn@bigfoot.com

Dir: *Off A625 Hope Rd N onto Parsons Ln, over railway bridge, 200yds right into Hay barnyard, through gates, across 3 fields, house on left*

PETS: Bedrooms Stables on site **Charges** dogs £2.50, horses £7 per night **Grounds** accessible **Exercise area** on site **Resident Pets:** Puzzle (Jack Russell), Cayli, Sparky, Joe & Rocket (Welsh ponies)

This converted barn, with original stone walls and exposed timbers, stands in open fields in the picturesque Hope Valley. The bedrooms are large enough for families and there are two modern bathrooms. Breakfast is served at one large table adjoining the family kitchen.

Rooms 4 rms (1 en suite) (1 fmly) ⊘ S £30-£35; D £50-£60 **Facilities** TVB tea/coffee Cen ht Golf 18 Riding **Parking** 8 **Notes LB** No coaches ✉

►► **Pindale Farm Outdoor Centre** *(SK163825)*

Pindale Rd S33 6RN

☎ 01433 620111 📄 01433 620729

e-mail: bookings@pindale.fsbusiness.co.uk

web: www.pindale.fsbusiness.co.uk

Dir: *From A625 in Hope turn into Pindale Lane between church & Woodroffe Arms. Pass cement works, over bridge, site in 400yds, well signed*

PETS: Stables nearby (5m) **Public areas** on leads **Exercise area** 5 min walk **Facilities** washing facs walks info vet info **Other** prior notice required

Open Mar-Oct Booking advisable Last departure 11.00hrs

An ideal base for walking, climbing and various outdoor pursuits, offering excellent facilities for campers and with a self-contained bunkhouse for up to 60 people. The heated toilet facilities are very good on this well-run campsite. A 1-acre site with 10 touring pitches.

Notes ✉

LONGFORD MAP 07 SK23

★★★★ BED & BREAKFAST

Russets

Off Main St DE6 3DR

☎ 01335 330874 📄 01335 330874

e-mail: geoffreynolan@btinternet.com

web: www.russets.com

Dir: *A516 in Hatton onto Sutton Ln, at T-junct right onto Long Ln, next right into Longford & right before phone box on Main St*

PETS: Bedrooms unattended **Public areas Grounds** accessible **Exercise area** 200yds **Facilities** food **Resident Pets:** Honey (Bearded Collie), Lottie (Miniature Dachshund), Ollie (Blue Persian cat)

An indoor swimming pool is available at this beautifully maintained bungalow, which is in a peaceful location near Alton Towers. Bedrooms are well-equipped and have smart modern bathrooms. Comprehensive breakfasts are served at a family table in a homely dining room, and a comfortable lounge is available.

Rooms 2 en suite (1 fmly) (2 GF) ⊘ S £30-£50; D £50 **Facilities** STV TVB tea/coffee Cen ht TVL ☒ Gymnasium **Parking** 4 **Notes** Closed 3rd wk Dec-1st wk Jan ✉

MATLOCK MAP 08 SK36

★★★ FARM HOUSE

Farley *(SK294622)*

Farley DE4 5LR

☎ 01629 582533 & 07801 756409 📄 01629 584856 Mrs Brailsford

e-mail: eric.brailsford@btconnect.com

Dir: *1m N of Matlock. From A6 rdbt towards Bakewell, 1st right, right at top of hill, left up Farley Hill, 2nd farm on left*

PETS: Bedrooms Stables on site **Charges** pony £15, horse £20 per night inc feed/bedding **Public areas** except dining room **Grounds** accessible **Facilities** food (pre-bookable) food bowl water bowl bedding leads pet sitting dog walking washing facs dog grooming cage storage vet info **On Request** fridge access torch towels **Restrictions** Telephone for details **Resident Pets:** 5 Border Terriers, 1 Labrador, 4 horses, 10 cats (ferrel)

You can expect a warm welcome at this traditional stone farmhouse. In addition to farming, the proprietors also breed dogs and horses. The bedrooms are pleasantly decorated and equipped with many useful extras. Breakfast is served round one large table (dinner is available by arrangement).

Rooms 2 en suite (2 fmly) S £25-£35; D £50-£55✱ **Facilities** TVB tea/coffee Cen ht TVL Dinner Last d 5pm Riding **Parking** 8 **Notes LB** 165 acres arable beef dairy ✉

MATLOCK CONTINUED

▶▶▶▶ Lickpenny Caravan Site *(SK339597)*

Lickpenny Ln, Tansley DE4 5GF

☎ 01629 583040 📄 01629 583040

e-mail: lickpenny@btinternet.com

web: www.lickpennycaravanpark.co.uk

Dir: *From A615 between Alfreton & Matlock, approx 1m N of Tansley. Turn into Lickpenny Lane at x-rds*

PETS: Public areas Exercise area on site disp bin **Facilities** on site shop food bowl water bowl disp bags walks info vet info

Open all year Booking advisable Last arrival 20.00hrs Last departure noon

A picturesque site in the grounds of an old plant nursery with areas broken up and screened by a variety of shrubs, and spectacular views. Pitches, several fully serviced, are spacious and well marked, and facilities are to a very good standard. A bistro/coffee shop is popular with visitors. A 16-acre site with 80 touring pitches, 80 hardstandings.

NEWHAVEN   MAP 07 SK16

▶▶▶ Newhaven Holiday Camping & Caravan Park *(SK167602)*

SK17 0DT

☎ 01298 84300 📄 01332 726027

web: www.newhavencaravanpark.co.uk

Dir: *Between Ashbourne & Buxton at A515 & A5012 junct*

PETS: Public areas except shop **Exercise area** on site woodland walks adjacent **Facilities** on site shop food food bowl water bowl dog chews cat treats dog scoop/disp bags walks info **Resident Pets:** Basil & Harvey (Border Collies)

Open Mar-Oct Booking advisable public hols & wknds Last arrival 23.00hrs Last departure anytime

Pleasantly situated within the Peak District National Park, with mature trees screening the three touring areas. Very good toilet facilities cater for touring vans and a large tent field, and there's a restaurant adjacent to the site. A 30-acre site with 125 touring pitches, 18 hardstandings and 73 statics.

ROSLISTON   MAP 08 SK21

▶▶ Beehive Woodland Lakes *(SK249161)*

DE12 8HZ

☎ 01283 763981 📄 01283 763981

e-mail: info@beehivefarm-woodlandlakes.co.uk

web: www.beehivefarm-woodlandlakes.co.uk

Dir: *Turn S off A444 at Castle Gresley onto Mount Pleasant Road, follow Roliston signs. Park on left at T-junct at end of Linton road*

PETS: Charges £1 per night **Public areas** except around lakes **Exercise area** 800yds disp bin **Facilities** on site shop food bowl water bowl dog chews cat treats litter leads washing facs dog grooming by appointment walks info vet info **Other** prior notice required

Open Mar-Nov Booking advisable Last arrival 20.00hrs Last departure 10.30hrs

A small, informal caravan area secluded from an extensive woodland park in the heart of The National Forest. There is a newly constructed amenity block of good quality. Young children will enjoy the on-site animal farm and playground, whilst anglers will appreciate fishing the three lakes within the park. The Honey Pot tearoom provides snacks and is open most days. A 2.5-acre site with 25 touring pitches, 3 hardstandings.

ROWSLEY   MAP 08 SK26

★★★ 88% ⊛⊛ HOTEL

The Peacock at Rowsley

Bakewell Rd DE4 2EB

☎ 01629 733518 📄 01629 732671

e-mail: reception@thepeacockatrowsley.com

web: www.thepeacockatrowsley.com

Dir: *A6, 3m before Bakewell, 6m from Matlock towards Bakewell*

PETS: Bedrooms unattended **Charges** £10 per dog per night charge for damage **Grounds** accessible **Exercise area** 0.25m **Facilities** food (pre-bookable) water bowl walks info vet info **On Request** torch towels

Owned by Haddon Hall this hotel is a smart contemporary destination, but still retains many original historic features. The menus are well balanced and use local produce. Dry fly fishing is a great attraction here as the hotel owns fishing rights in the area. Staff are delightful and deliver high standards of service.

Rooms 16 en suite (5 fmly) ⊘ in all bedrooms S £75-£100; D £145-£210 (incl. bkfst)✳ **Facilities** STV Fishing 🦮 Wi-fi in bedrooms Free use of Woodlands Fitness Centre 🎵 New Year **Parking** 25

SWADLINCOTE MAP 08 SK21

★★★ BED & BREAKFAST
Overseale House

Acresford Rd, Overseal DE12 6HX

☎ 01283 763741 🖹 01283 760015

e-mail: oversealehouse@hotmail.com

web: www.overseale.co.uk

Dir: *On A444 between Burton upon Trent & M42 junct 11*

PETS: Bedrooms (GF) **Stables** nearby (arrangements can be made) **Grounds** accessible **Facilities** walks info vet info **On Request** fridge access torch towels

Located in the village, this well-proportioned Georgian mansion, built for a renowned industrialist, retains many original features including a magnificent dining room decorated with ornate mouldings. The period-furnished ground-floor areas include a cosy sitting room, and bedrooms contain many thoughtful extras.

Rooms 4 en suite 1 annexe rms (3 fmly) (2 GF) ⊗ S £20-£30; D £50-£60✳ **Facilities** TVB tea/coffee Cen ht **Parking** 6 **Notes** ⊛

THORPE (DOVEDALE) MAP 07 SK15

★★★ 79% ⊛ HOTEL
Izaak Walton

Dovedale DE6 2AY

☎ 01335 350555 🖹 01335 350539

e-mail: reception@izaakwaltonhotel.com

web: www.izaakwaltonhotel.com

Dir: *A515 onto B5054, to Thorpe village, continue straight over cattle grid & 2 small bridges, 1st right & sharp left*

PETS: Bedrooms unattended **Charges** £15 per stay **Public areas**

This hotel is peacefully situated, with magnificent views over the valley of Dovedale to Thorpe Cloud. Many of the bedrooms have lovely views, and the executive rooms are particularly spacious. Meals are served in the bar area, with more formal dining in the Haddon Restaurant. Staff are friendly and efficient. Fishing on the River Dove can be arranged.

Rooms 35 en suite (6 fmly) (8 GF) ⊗ in 33 bedrooms S £110-£138; D £130-£210 (incl. bkfst & dinner) **Facilities** STV Fishing ⌣ Wi-fi in bedrooms ch fac Xmas New Year **Parking** 80 **Notes** LB

TIDESWELL MAP 07 SK17

★★★ GUEST ACCOMMODATION
Poppies

Bank Square SK17 8LA

☎ 01298 871083

e-mail: poptidza@dialstart.net

Dir: *On B6049 in village centre opp NatWest bank*

PETS: Bedrooms Public areas Exercise area 200yds

A friendly welcome is assured at this non-smoking house, located in the heart of a former lead-mining and textile community, a short walk from the 14th-century parish church. Bedrooms are homely and the excellent breakfast features good vegetarian options.

Rooms 3 rms (1 en suite) (1 fmly) ⊗ D £42-£51✳ **Facilities** TVB tea/coffee Cen ht Dinner Last d previous day **Notes** ⊛

YOULGREAVE MAP 08 SK26

► Bakewell Camping & Caravanning Club Site *(SK206632)*

c/o Hopping Farm DE45 1NA

☎ 01629 636555

web: www.campingandcaravanningclub.co.uk/bakewell

Dir: *A6/B5056, after 0.5m turn right to Youlgreave. Turn sharp left after church down Bradford Lane, opposite George Hotel. 0.5m to sign turn right*

PETS: Public areas except buildings **Exercise area** on site **Facilities** walks info vet info **Other** prior notice required

Open 13 Mar-3 Nov Booking advisable BH & peak periods Last arrival 21.00hrs Last departure noon

Ideal for touring and walking in the Peak District National Park, this gently sloping grass site is accessed through narrow streets and along unadopted hardcore. Own sanitary facilities essential. A 14-acre site with 100 touring pitches, 6 hardstandings.

Notes Site gates closed 23.00-07.00.

ENGLAND

DEVON

ASHBURTON
MAP 03 SX77

★★★ 79% ◉◉ COUNTRY HOUSE HOTEL

Holne Chase
Two Bridges Rd TQ13 7NS
☎ 01364 631471 📄 01364 631453
e-mail: info@holne-chase.co.uk
web: www.holne-chase.co.uk
Dir: *3m N on unclass Two Bridges/Tavistock road*

PETS: Bedrooms (GF) unattended sign **Stables** on site
Charges £7.50 per night £52.50 per week charge for damage
Public areas except restaurant **Grounds** accessible disp bin
Facilities food (pre-bookable) food bowl water bowl bedding
dog chews cat treats feeding mat litter tray dog scoop/disp bags
leads pet sitting dog walking washing facs dog grooming cage
storage walks info vet info **On Request** fridge access torch
towels **Resident Pets:** Batty II (Beagle)

This former hunting lodge is peacefully situated in a secluded position, with sweeping lawns leading to the river and panoramic views of the moor. Bedrooms are attractively and individually furnished, and there are a number of split-level suites available. Enjoyable meals using local ingredients, some produced on the owners' farm, feature on the daily-changing menu.

Rooms 10 en suite 7 annexe en suite (9 fmly) (1 GF) ⊘ in all bedrooms
Facilities STV Fishing Riding ⛳ Putt green Fly fishing Riding Beauty
treatments Xmas New Year **Parking** 40

★★ 63% HOTEL

Dartmoor Lodge
Peartree Cross TQ13 7JW
☎ 01364 652232 📄 01364 653990
e-mail: dartmoor.ashburton@newbridgeinns.co.uk
web: www.oldenglish.co.uk
Dir: *Exit A38 at 2nd exit for Ashburton, turn right across bridge, turn left at garage, hotel on right.*

PETS: Bedrooms (GF) unattended **Charges** £10 (dependent on length of stay) **Grounds** accessible **Exercise area** on site
Other ground floor bedrooms only

Situated midway between Plymouth and Exeter, this popular hotel is close to the bustling town of Ashburton and ideally placed for exploring Dartmoor and the South Devon coast. Bedrooms, including two with four-poster beds, are well equipped, whilst public areas include the popular bar and smart restaurant where a range of dishes can be enjoyed.

Rooms 29 en suite (7 fmly) (9 GF) ⊘ in 11 bedrooms **Facilities** STV
Services Lift **Parking** 100 **Notes** LB

★★★★ 🛏 INN

The Rising Sun
Woodland TQ13 7JT
☎ 01364 652544 📄 01364 654202
e-mail: risingsun.hazel@btconnect.com
Dir: *2m E of Ashburton. Off A38 signed Woodland & Denbury, Rising Sun 1.5m on left*

PETS: Bedrooms unattended **Public areas** **Grounds** accessible
Exercise area 50yds **Resident Pets:** peacocks

Peacefully situated in scenic south Devon countryside, this inn is just a short drive from the A38. A friendly welcome is extended to all guests, business, leisure and families alike. Bedrooms are comfortable and well equipped. Dinner and breakfast feature much local and organic produce. A good selection of home-made puddings, West Country cheeses, local wines and quality real ales are available.

Rooms 4 en suite (1 fmly) (2 GF) **Facilities** TVB tea/coffee Cen ht
Dinner Last d 9.15pm **Parking** 40

►►►► Parkers Farm Holidays *(SX779713)*

Higher Mead Farm TQ13 7LJ

☎ 01364 654869 📄 01364 654004

e-mail: parkersfarm@btconnect.com

web: www.parkersfarm.co.uk

Dir: *From Exeter on A38, take 2nd left after Plymouth 26m sign, at Alston, signed Woodland-Denbury. From Plymouth on A38 take A383 Newton Abbot exit, turn right across bridge and rejoin A38, then as above.*

PETS: Stables nearby (0.5m) **Charges** £2 per night **Public areas** except play area & main bar **Exercise area** on site large exercise fields **Facilities** on site shop food food bowl water bowl dog chews cat treats disp bags leads washing facs walks info vet info **Other** prior notice required **Resident Pets:** dogs, horses, sheep, goats, pigs, rabbits, chickens, ducks, guinea pigs

Open Etr-end Oct Booking advisable Etr, Whitsun & school hols Last arrival 22.00hrs Last departure 10.00hrs

A well-developed site terraced into rising ground. Part of a working farm, this park offers beautifully maintained, quality facilities. Large family rooms with two shower cubicles, a large sink and a toilet are especially appreciated by families with small children. There are regular farm walks when all the family can meet and feed the various animals. An 8-acre site with 100 touring pitches, 5 hardstandings and 16 statics.

►►►► River Dart Country Park *(SX734700)*

Holne Park TQ13 7NP

☎ 01364 652511 📄 01364 652020

e-mail: info@riverdart.co.uk

web: www.riverdart.co.uk

Dir: *From M5 take A38 towards Plymouth, turn off at second junct Ashburton following brown signs to River Dart Country Park. Site 1m on left*

PETS: Charges £2.50 per night **Public areas** except amenity block, shop & café **Exercise area** on site disp bin **Facilities** on site shop food food bowl dog scoop/disp bags washing facs walks info vet info **Other** prior notice required **Resident Pets:** Harry (Jack Russell)

Open Apr-Sep (rs Etr & Sep café bar restricted opening hours) Booking advisable Spring bank hol & Jul-Aug Last arrival 21.00hrs Last departure 11.00hrs

Set in 90 acres of magnificent parkland that was once part of a Victorian estate, with many specimen and exotic trees, and in spring a blaze of colour from the many azaleas and rhododendrons. There are numerous outdoor activities for all ages including abseiling, caving and canoeing, plus high quality, well-maintained facilities. The open moorland of Dartmoor is only a few minutes away. A 90-acre site with 170 touring pitches, 12 hardstandings.

★★★ ◉◉ HOTEL

Blagdon Manor Hotel & Restaurant

EX21 5DF

☎ 01409 211224 📄 01409 211634

e-mail: stay@blagdon.com

web: www.blagdon.com

Dir: *Take A388 N of Launceston towards Holsworthy. Approx 2m N of Chapman's Well take 2nd right for Ashwater. Next right beside Blagdon Lodge, hotel 0.25m*

PETS: Bedrooms Charges £5 per night **Public areas** except restaurant **Grounds** accessible disp bin **Facilities** food bowl water bowl bedding dog chews feeding mat dog scoop/disp bags washing facs cage storage walks info vet info **On Request** fridge access torch towels **Resident Pets:** Nutmeg & Cassia (Chocolate Labradors)

Located on the borders of Devon and Cornwall within easy reach of the coast and in its own beautifully kept yet natural gardens, this small and friendly hotel offers a charming home-from-home atmosphere. The tranquillity of the secluded setting, the character and charm of the house and its unhurried pace ensures calm and relaxation. High levels of service, personal touches and thoughtful extras are all part of a stay here. Steve Morey cooks with passion and his commitment on using only the finest local ingredients speaks volumes.

Rooms 7 en suite ⊘ in all bedrooms S £85; D £125 (incl. bkfst)✳
Facilities ⅃ Boules, giant chess/draughts **Parking** 11 **Notes** No children 12yrs Closed 2wks Jan/Feb & 2wks Oct/Nov

AXMINSTER MAP 03 SY29

★★★ 74% ◎◎ HOTEL
Fairwater Head Country House Hotel
Hawkchurch EX13 5TX

☎ 01297 678349 📠 01297 678459

e-mail: info@fairwaterheadhotel.co.uk

web: www.fairwaterheadhotel.co.uk

Dir: off B3165, Crewkerne to Lyme Regis road. Hotel signed to Hawkchurch

PETS: Bedrooms (GF) unattended **Charges** £5 per night charge for damage **Public areas** except dining room on leads **Grounds** accessible on leads **On Request** towels **Resident Pets:** Hector (Boxer)

Peacefully located in the countryside this charming hotel provides attractive gardens and stunning views. The proprietors and staff provide friendly and attentive service in a relaxing environment. Bedrooms are individually decorated, spacious and comfortable, and guests can enjoy best quality local ingredients cooked with great care.

Rooms 10 en suite 6 annexe en suite (8 GF) ⊘ in all bedrooms S £50-£100; D £100-£200 (incl. bkfst & dinner)✳ **Facilities** ♨ Wi-fi available ♫ Xmas **Parking** 25 **Notes** LB Closed 27 Dec-11 Feb

★★★ FARM HOUSE
Apple Tree B&B at Sellers Wood Farmhouse
(SY274941)

Combpyne Rd, Musbury EX13 8SR

☎ 01297 552944 Mr & Mrs Pemberton

e-mail: sellerswood@hotmail.com

web: www.sellerswood.co.uk

Dir: 3m SW of Axminster. Off A358 into Musbury village centre, onto Combpyne Rd, 0.75m left onto driveway

PETS: Bedrooms Stables nearby **Charges** £5 per night **Public areas** except dining room **Grounds** accessible **Exercise area** 100yds **Other** Small dogs only **Resident Pets:** Laird (Black Labrador), Scruffy (Jack Russell), 2 sheep, chickens

Situated on the edge of Musbury with sweeping views over the Axe valley to the cliffs of Beer, this delightful 16th-century farmhouse has a wealth of beams and flagstone floors. Tasty farmhouse dinners using home-grown vegetables are available by arrangement.

Rooms 4 rms (1 en suite) (1 pri facs) (2 fmly) ⊘ **Facilities** tea/coffee Cen ht TVL Dinner Last d before 9am ⬆ **Parking** 6 **Notes** 3 acres (small holding) ⊘

▶▶▶▶ **Andrewshayes Caravan Park**
(ST248088)

Dalwood EX13 7DY

☎ 01404 831225 📠 01404 831893

e-mail: info@andrewshayes.co.uk

web: www.andrewshayes.co.uk

Dir: On A35, 3m from Axminster. Turn N at Taunton Cross signed Stockland/Dalwood. Site 150mtrs on right

PETS: Charges £1.50 - £2 per night **Public areas** except bar on leads **Exercise area** on site 2 adjacent fields in 300mtrs disp bin **Facilities** on site shop disp bags walks info vet info **Other** prior notice required

Open Mar-Nov (rs Sep-Nov shop hrs limited,pool closed Sep-mid May) Booking advisable Spring bank hol & Jul-Aug Last arrival 22.00hrs Last departure noon

A lively park within easy reach of Lyme Regis, Seaton, Branscombe and Sidmouth in an ideal touring location. This popular park boasts an attractive bistro beside the swimming pool, a bar, laundry and shop. A 12-acre site with 150 touring pitches, 105 hardstandings and 80 statics.

BARNSTAPLE MAP 02 SS53

★★★★★ 🏠 🍴 GUEST ACCOMMODATION
Halmpstone Manor
Bishop's Tawton EX32 0EA

☎ 01271 830321 & 831003 📠 01271 830826

e-mail: jane@halmpstonemanor.co.uk

web: www.halmpstonemanor.co.uk

Dir: 3m SE of Barnstaple. Off A377 E of river & rail bridges

PETS: Bedrooms unattended **Stables** nearby **Public areas** except restaurant **Grounds** accessible disp bin **Facilities** washing facs cage storage walks info vet info **On Request** fridge access torch towels **Resident Pets:** Barley (Cocker Spaniel)

The manor was mentioned in the Domesday Book and parts of the later medieval manor house survive. Halmpstone Manor now provides quality accommodation, personal service and fine cuisine. Delightful day rooms include a spacious lounge complete with deep sofas and a roaring fire, and a creative, daily changing menu is offered in the elegant restaurant. Superb hospitality and excellent value make this a great choice for a restful break.

Rooms 4 en suite ⊘ S £70; D £100-£140✳ **Facilities** TVB tea/coffee Dinner Last d 7.30pm **Parking** 12 **Notes** Closed Xmas & New Year

★★★ GUEST HOUSE
Cresta Guest House
26 Sticklepath Hill EX31 2BU
☎ 01271 374022 📠 01271 374022
e-mail: Pdavis.cresta@hotmail.co.uk

Dir: *On A3215 0.6m W of town centre, top of hill on right*
PETS: Bedrooms (GF) **Charges** £10 per stay **Grounds** accessible on leads disp bin **Facilities** vet info **Restrictions** no large dogs

A warm welcome is assured at this family-run establishment, situated on the western outskirts of Barnstaple. The well-equipped bedrooms are comfortably appointed and include ground floor rooms. A hearty breakfast is served in the dining room.

Rooms 8 rms (6 en suite) (2 fmly) (2 GF) ⊘ S £25-£30; D £50-£60✳
Facilities TVB tea/coffee Cen ht **Parking** 6 **Notes** No coaches Closed 2 wks Xmas

►►► **Tarka Holiday Park** *(SS533346)*
Braunton Rd, Ashford EX31 4AU
☎ 01271 343691 📠 01271 326355
e-mail: info@tarkaholidaypark.co.uk
web: www.tarkaholidaypark.co.uk

Dir: *2m from Barnstaple on A361 towards Chivenor. (NB This is a fast dual-carriageway & care should be taken)*
PETS: Charges £15 per night £40 per week **Public areas**
Exercise area on site disp bin **Facilities** on site shop washing facs walks info vet info space for loose box **Other** prior notice required

Open 22 Jan-1 Jan Booking advisable all year Last arrival 22.00hrs Last departure noon

A gently-sloping grass park near the banks of the River Taw, and close to the Tarka cycle trail. It offers a licensed bar for food and drink with occasional entertainment, a putting green, a bouncy castle and children's playground. The site is about 5m from sandy beaches. A 10-acre site with 35 touring pitches, 16 hardstandings and 82 statics.

BICKINGTON
(NEAR ASHBURTON)
MAP 03 SX87

►►►► **Lemonford Caravan Park** *(SX793723)*
TQ12 6JR
☎ 01626 821242 & 821263 📠 01626 821263
e-mail: mark@lemonford.co.uk
web: www.lemonford.co.uk

Dir: *From Exeter A38 take A382, then 3rd exit on rdbt , follow Bickington signs*
PETS: Charges £1.20 per dog per night **Public areas** on leads
Exercise area 10yds **Facilities** on site shop food food bowl water bowl walks info vet info **Other** prior notice required
Restrictions some breeds not accepted

Open Mar-Oct Booking advisable school hols Last arrival 22.00hrs Last departure 11.00hrs

Small, secluded and well-maintained park with a good mixture of attractively laid out pitches. The friendly owners pay a great deal of attention to detail, and the toilets in particular are kept spotlessly clean. This good touring base is only 1m from Dartmoor and 10m from the seaside at Torbay. A 7-acre site with 85 touring pitches, 55 hardstandings and 28 statics.

Notes ☺

BIDEFORD
MAP 02 SS42

★★ 79% ⊛ HOTEL
Yeoldon Country House
Durrant Ln, Northam EX39 2RL
☎ 01237 474400 📠 01237 476618
e-mail: yeoldonhouse@aol.com
web: www.yeoldonhousehotel.co.uk

Dir: *A39 from Barnstaple over River Torridge Bridge. At rdbt right onto A386 towards Northam, then 3rd right into Durrant Lane*
PETS: Bedrooms Charges £5 (1 night), £3 per night for longer stay, charge for damage **Public areas** lounge only & on lead **Grounds** accessible disp bin **Exercise area** N Devon coastal path nearby **Facilities** dog food available (beef & gravy occasionally) washing facs cage storage walks info vet info **On Request** fridge access torch towels **Resident Pets:** Muttley & Shaz (Collie cross)

In a tranquil location with superb views over the River Torridge and attractive grounds, this is a charming Victorian house. The well-equipped bedrooms are individually decorated and some have balconies with breathtaking views. The public rooms are full of character with many interesting features and artefacts. The daily-changing dinner menu offers imaginative dishes.

Rooms 10 en suite ⊘ in all bedrooms S £72.50-£75; D £110-£125 (incl. bkfst) **Parking** 20 **Notes** LB Closed 24-27 Dec

BIDEFORD CONTINUED

★★★★ GUEST ACCOMMODATION
Pines at Eastleigh
The Pines, Eastleigh EX39 4PA
☎ 01271 860561 ▤ 01271 861689
e-mail: pirrie@thepinesateastleigh.co.uk
Dir: A39 onto A386 signed East-The-Water. 1st left signed Eastleigh, 500yds next left, 1.5m to village, house on right
PETS: Bedrooms (GF) **Stables** nearby **Charges** charge for damage **Grounds** accessible on leads disp bin
Exercise area adjacent **Facilities** bowls, dog & cat food on request pet sitting dog walking washing facs cage storage walks info vet info **On Request** torch towels **Other** dogs can be off lead if no sheep in paddock
Friendly hospitality is assured at this Georgian farmhouse, set in 7 acres of gardens. Two of the comfortable bedrooms are located in the main house, the remainder in converted barns around a charming courtyard, with a pretty pond and well. A delicious breakfast featuring local and home-made produce is served in the dining room and a lounge and honesty bar are also available.
Rooms 6 en suite (3 fmly) (4 GF) ⊘ S £40-£45; D £75-£95✱
Facilities TVB tea/coffee Direct dial from bedrooms Cen ht Wi-fi available 🎱 Table Tennis, Archery, Table Football **Parking** 20 **Notes** LB No children 9yrs

BISHOPSTEIGNTON   MAP 03 SX97

★★ 68% HOTEL
Cockhaven Manor Hotel
THE INDEPENDENTS
HOTEL ASSOCIATION

Cockhaven Rd TQ14 9RF
☎ 01626 775252 ▤ 01626 775572
e-mail: cockhaven@btconnect.com
web: www.cockhavenmanor.com
Dir: M5/A380 towards Torquay, then A381 towards Teignmouth. Left at Metro Motors. Hotel 500yds on left
PETS: Bedrooms unattended **Public areas** except restaurant on leads **Grounds** accessible disp bin **Facilities** walks info vet info **On Request** fridge access torch towels other pet facilities available on request **Resident Pets:** Bitsy (dog)
A friendly, family-run inn that dates back to the 16th century. Bedrooms are well equipped and many enjoy views across the beautiful Teign estuary. A choice of dining options is offered, and traditional and interesting dishes along with locally caught fish are popular.
Rooms 12 en suite (2 fmly) ⊘ in 10 bedrooms S £42-£56; D £60-£72 (incl. bkfst)✱ **Facilities** Wi-fi available Petanque **Parking** 50 **Notes** LB RS 25-26 Dec

BRANSCOMBE   MAP 03 SY18

★★ 79% ❀ HOTEL
The Masons Arms
EX12 3DJ
☎ 01297 680300 ▤ 01297 680500
e-mail: reception@masonsarms.co.uk
Dir: off A3052 towards Branscombe, hotel in valley at hill bottom
PETS: Bedrooms Charges £5 per night charge for damage **Public areas** except restaurants on leads **Grounds** accessible on leads disp bin **Exercise area** 300yds **Facilities** water bowl washing facs walks info vet info **On Request** fridge access towels **Resident Pets:** Maisy (Parson Russell Terrier)
This delightful 14th-century village inn is just half a mile from the sea. The bedrooms in the thatched annexed cottages tend to be more spacious and have patios with seating; those in the inn reflect much period charm. In the bar, an extensive selection of dishes, which includes many local specialities is available, and the restaurant offers an imaginative range of dishes.
Rooms 8 en suite 14 annexe en suite (1 fmly) ⊘ in all bedrooms S £80-£160; D £80-£160 (incl. bkfst)✱ **Facilities** Xmas New Year **Parking** 43 **Notes** LB

BRAUNTON   MAP 02 SS43

►►►► **Hidden Valley Park** (SS499408)
EX34 8NU
☎ 01271 813837 ▤ 01271 814041
e-mail: relax@hiddenvalleypark.com
web: www.hiddenvalleypark.com
Dir: Direct access off A361, 8m from Barnstaple & 2m from Mullacott Cross
PETS: Charges max £2 per night **Public areas** except shop & coffee shop **Exercise area** on site exercise field and woods dunes 5m disp bins **Facilities** food food bowl water bowl disp bags washing facs walks info vet info dogs toys
Open all year (rs 15 Nov-15 Mar all weather pitches only) Booking advisable peak season Last arrival 21.30hrs Last departure 10.00hrs
A delightful, well-appointed family site set in a wooded valley, with superb facilities and a cafe. The park is set in a very rural, natural position not far from the beautiful coastline around Ilfracombe. A 25-acre site with 135 touring pitches, 74 hardstandings.

▶▶▶ Lobb Fields Caravan & Camping Park

(SS475378)

Saunton Rd EX33 1EB

☎ 01271 812090 📠 01271 812090

e-mail: info@lobbfields.com

web: www.lobbfields.com

Dir: *At x-rds in Braunton take B3231 to Croyde. Site signed on right leaving Braunton*

PETS: Public areas Exercise area on site disp bin **Facilities** vet info

Open 15 Mar-26 Oct Booking advisable Jul-Aug, Spring BH Last arrival 21.00hrs Last departure 10.30hrs

A bright, tree-lined park with the gently-sloping grass pitches divided into two open areas. Braunton is an easy walk away, and the golden beaches of Saunton Sands and Croyde are within easy reach. A 14-acre site with 180 touring pitches, 7 hardstandings.

Notes No under 18s unless accompanied by an adult

BRENDON
MAP 03 SS74

★★★★ GUEST ACCOMMODATION

Leeford Cottage

EX35 6PS

☎ 01598 741279 📠 01598 741392

e-mail: g.linley@virgin.net

web: www.leefordcottage.com

Dir: *4.5m E of Lynton. Off A39 at Brendon sign, cross packhorse bridges and village green, over x-rds, Leeford Cottage on left*

PETS: Bedrooms Sep Accom small stable & paddock for horses **Charges** charge for damage **Public areas** except dining room **Grounds** accessible disp bin **Exercise area** adjacent **Facilities** food food bowl water bowl bedding dog scoop/disp bags leads washing facs cage storage walks info vet info **On Request** fridge access torch towels **Resident Pets:** Meg (Labrador), Benny, Milly & Molly (goats), Smudge (cat), Marcus (cockerel), ducks, chickens

Situated in the quiet hamlet of Brendon, this 400-year-old cottage has great character. The welcoming proprietors grow their own vegetables and rear hens, which provide the breakfast eggs. Bedrooms are cosy, there's a beamed lounge; no wonder guests return regularly.

Rooms 3 rms (1 en suite) (2 pri facs) ⊗ D £51-£53☀ **Facilities** tea/coffee Cen ht TVL **Parking** 10 **Notes** LB Closed 3-31 Jan 🐾

BRIDGERULE
MAP 02 SS20

▶▶ Highfield House Camping & Caravanning *(SS279035)*

Holsworthy EX22 7EE

☎ 01288 381480

e-mail: nikki@highfieldholidays.freeserve.co.uk

Dir: *Exit A3072 at Red Post x-rds onto B3254 towards Launceston. Direct access just over Devon border on right*

PETS: Public areas Exercise area on site disp bin **Facilities** on site shop washing facs walks info vet info **Restrictions** no Staffordshire Bull Terriers **Resident Pets:** Tilly (West Highland White Terrier), Duke (German Shepherd), goats, pigs

Open all year Booking advisable

Set in a quiet and peaceful rural location, this park has extensive views over the valley to the sea at Bude, five miles away. The friendly young owners, with small children of their own, offer a relaxing holiday for families, with the simple facilities carefully looked after. A 4-acre site with 20 touring pitches and 3 statics.

Notes 🐾

BRIXHAM
MAP 03 SX95

★★★ 70% HOTEL

Berry Head

THE INDEPENDENTS
HOTEL ASSOCIATION

Berry Head Rd TQ5 9AJ

☎ 01803 853225 📠 01803 882084

e-mail: stay@berryheadhotel.com

Dir: *From marina, 1m, hotel on left*

PETS: Bedrooms Charges £8 per night **Public areas** lounge only at certain times **Grounds** accessible **Exercise area** 20yds

From its stunning cliff-top location, this imposing property that dates back to 1809, has spectacular views across Torbay. Public areas include two comfortable lounges, an outdoor terrace, a swimming pool, together with a bar serving a range of popular dishes. Many of the bedrooms have the benefit of the splendid sea views.

Rooms 32 en suite (7 fmly) S £62-£78; D £124-£156 (incl. bkfst) **Facilities** ⓢ ⌇ Petanque sailing Deep sea fishing ♫ Xmas New Year **Parking** 200 **Notes** LB

ENGLAND

BUCKFASTLEIGH　　MAP 03 SX76

★★★ INN
Dartbridge Inn
Totnes Rd TQ11 0JR
☎ 01364 642214 ▤ 01364 643839
e-mail: dartbridgeinn@oldenglishinns.co.uk
Dir: *0.5m NE of town centre. A38 onto A384, 250yds on left*
PETS: Bedrooms　Charges £10 per night　**Grounds** accessible
on leads　**Exercise area** river & woods nearby
Situated close to the beautiful river Dart, this popular inn is ideally
placed for exploring Dartmoor and South Devon. The atmosphere is
friendly and relaxed with open fires and oak beams adding to the
charm. Bedrooms are soundly appointed and an extensive menu is
offered along with daily specials.
Rooms 10 en suite (1 fmly)　**Facilities** TV available tea/coffee Direct dial
from bedrooms Last d 9.30pm　**Parking** 100

★★★ INN
Kings Arms
15 Fore St TQ11 0BT
☎ 01364 642341
Dir: *In town centre opp tourist office & The Valiant Soldier*
PETS: Bedrooms　Public areas except restaurant
Grounds accessible on leads　**Exercise area** 200yds
This long-established, friendly and popular inn has been refurbished
and now provides a well-appointed base from which to explore this
picturesque area. Bedrooms are comfortably furnished, while public
areas include a choice of bars, dining area and an attractive patio and
garden.
Rooms 4 rms (1 en suite) S £35-£45; D £50-£75✶　**Facilities** TVB tea/
coffee Dinner Last d 8.30pm　**Parking** 1　**Notes** No coaches

BUDLEIGH SALTERTON　　MAP 03 SY08

★★★★★ ⌂ GUEST ACCOMMODATION
Downderry House
10 Exmouth Rd EX9 6AQ
☎ 01395 442663 ▤ 01395 442663
e-mail: info@downderryhouse.co.uk
web: www.downderryhouse.co.uk
Dir: *From M5 signed for Budleigh Salterton. From A303 exit at
Daisy Mount and follow B3180*
PETS: Bedrooms 1 ground room only　**Charges** £5 per night
Grounds accessible on leads disp bin　**Exercise area** adjacent
Facilities cage storage walks info vet info　**On Request** torch
towels　**Resident Pets:** Bertie (Beagle)
Just a short stroll from the town and seafront, this lovely house stands
in an acre of gardens with views across meadows. Quality is the
hallmark here with spacious and stylish bedrooms offering impressive
levels of comfort. In addition, the luxurious bathrooms come complete
with robes and fluffy towels. Breakfast provides a wonderful taste of
the local area, served in the attractive dining room overlooking the
gardens. An elegant guest lounge is also available, complete with
honesty bar.
Rooms 5 en suite (1 GF) ⊘ S £65-£75; D £75-£95✶　**Facilities** FTV TVB
tea/coffee Cen ht Wi-fi available ⬇ **Parking** 9　**Notes** LB No children
10yrs

CHAGFORD　　MAP 03 SX78

★★★★ ◉◉◉◉ COUNTRY HOUSE HOTEL
Gidleigh Park
TQ13 8HH
☎ 01647 432367 ▤ 01647 432574
e-mail: gidleighpark@gidleigh.co.uk
web: www.gidleigh.com
Dir: *from Chagford, right at Lloyds Bank into Mill St. After 150yds
fork right, follow lane 2m to end*
PETS: Bedrooms (GF) unattended　**Charges** charge for damage
Grounds accessible disp bin　**Facilities** food bowl water bowl
bedding feeding mat dog scoop/disp bags leads washing facs
cage storage walks info vet info　**On Request** torch towels
Other certain bedrooms only available 75yds from main house &
one cottage

Set in 45 acres of lovingly tended grounds this world-renowned hotel
has been rejuvenated following a multi-million pound refurbishment.
None of the timeless charm and many revered features of the house

have been lost and it retains a very endearing, homely atmosphere. Individually styled bedrooms are sumptuously furnished; some with separate seating areas, some with balconies and many enjoying panoramic views. Public areas are spacious featuring antique furniture, beautiful flower arrangements and magnificent artwork. The outstanding cuisine created by Michael Caines, together with the top quality wine list, will make a stay here a truly memorable experience. Michael Caines has been awarded the AA Chefs' Chef of the Year for 2008.

Rooms 21 en suite 3 annexe en suite (4 fmly) (4 GF) ⊘ in all bedrooms S £340-£480; D £440-£1200 (incl. bkfst & dinner)✳ **Facilities** STV FTV ⌁ Fishing ⌁ Putt green Wi-fi in bedrooms Bowls Xmas New Year **Parking** 25

★★ ◉◉ HOTEL
Mill End
Dartmoor National Park TQ13 8JN
☎ 01647 432282 🖹 01647 433106
e-mail: info@millendhotel.com
web: www.millendhotel.com

Dir: *from A30 at Whiddon Down follow A382 to Moretonhampstead. After 3.5m hump back bridge at Sandy Park, hotel on right by river*

PETS: Bedrooms Charges £10 per night **Grounds** accessible **Exercise area** on site 2-3 acre dog paddock **Facilities** leads dog room **On Request** towels **Resident Pets:** Harry & Orvis (Labradors), Devon & Poppy (cats)

In an attractive location, Mill End, an 18th-century working water mill sits by the River Teign that offers six miles of angling. The atmosphere is akin to a family home where guests are encouraged to relax and enjoy the peace and informality. Bedrooms are available in a range of sizes and all are stylishly decorated and thoughtfully equipped. Dining is certainly a highlight of a stay here; the menus offer exciting dishes featuring local produce.

Rooms 14 en suite (3 GF) ⊘ in all bedrooms S £95; D £95-£155 (incl. bkfst) **Facilities** FTV Fishing ⌁ Wi-fi available Xmas New Year **Parking** 25 **Notes** LB

★★ 69% HOTEL
Three Crowns Hotel
High St TQ13 8AJ
☎ 01647 433444 🖹 01647 433117
e-mail: threecrowns@msn.com
web: www.chagford-accom.co.uk

Dir: *exit A30 at Whiddon Down. Hotel in town centre opposite church*

PETS: Bedrooms unattended **Charges** £2.50 per night **Public areas** except restaurant **Exercise area** 200mtrs to common

This 13th-century inn is located in the heart of the village. Exposed beams, mullioned windows and open fires are all part of the charm which is evident throughout. There is a range of bedrooms; all are comfortable and several have four-poster beds. A choice of bars is available along with a pleasant lounge and separate dining room.

Rooms 17 en suite (1 fmly) ⊘ in 8 bedrooms S £55-£85; D £110-£170 (incl. bkfst)✳ **Facilities** STV Pool table in bar Xmas New Year **Parking** 20 **Notes** LB

★★★ INN
The Sandy Park Inn
TQ13 8JW
☎ 01647 433267
e-mail: sandyparkinn@aol.com
Dir: *1m NE of Chagford off A382*

PETS: Bedrooms unattended **Charges** £5 per night **Grounds** accessible **Exercise area** 20yds

This popular, thatched country inn is conveniently located a short drive from the A30. The busy bar is full of character and is well stocked. There is a separate restaurant and smaller cosy rooms. Bedrooms are contemporary in style and well appointed with comfortable furnishings. A good choice of hearty dishes is also available.

Rooms 5 rms (2 en suite) (3 pri facs) S fr £60; D fr £98✳ **Facilities** TVB tea/coffee Cen ht Dinner Last d 9pm Wi-fi available Fishing **Parking** 4 **Notes** No coaches

---

CHAPMANS WELL
MAP 02 SX39

▶▶▶ **Chapmanswell Caravan Park** *(SX354931)*
PL15 9SG
☎ 01409 211382 🖹 01409 211154
e-mail: george@chapmanswellcaravanpark.co.uk
web: www.chapmanswellcaravanpark.co.uk
Dir: *Off A388, midway between Launceston & Holsworthy*

PETS: Public areas Exercise area 50yds disp bin **Facilities** on site shop food washing facs walks info vet info

Open all year Booking advisable Jul - Aug

Set on the borders of Devon and Cornwall in peaceful countryside, this park is just waiting to be discovered. It enjoys extensive views towards Dartmoor from level pitches, and is within easy driving distance of Launceston (7m) and the golden beaches at Bude (14m). A 10-acre site with 50 touring pitches, 35 hardstandings and 50 statics.

CHAWLEIGH
MAP 03 SS71

★★★ 🏠 BED & BREAKFAST
The Barn-Rodgemonts
Rodgemonts EX18 7ET
☎ 01769 580200
e-mail: pyerodgemonts@talktalk.net
web: www.devon-barn-accommodation.co.uk
Dir: *1m NW of Chawleigh. Off A377 onto B3042 to Chawleigh, 1.5m left onto B3096 for Chulmleigh, 0.5m signed Chawleigh Week, fork left 250yds, Rodgemonts on right*
PETS: Bedrooms Public areas except main house
Grounds accessible **Exercise area** front garden, woods & surrounding area **Resident Pets:** Leo (German Shepherd cross)

Set in peaceful countryside, surrounded by the sights and sounds of nature, this attractive house offers friendly hospitality. Bedrooms are located in the thatched, converted hay barn, each with views of the orchard from which the proprietors produce their own apple juice which serves as part of the delightful breakfasts.

Rooms 2 en suite (1 fmly) ⊗ S £28-£33; D £46-£56 **Facilities** TVB tea/coffee Cen ht TVL **Parking** 3 **Notes LB** 🐾

CHIVENOR
MAP 02 SS53

►►► **Chivenor Caravan Park** *(SS501351)*
EX31 4BN
☎ 01271 812217 📄 01271 812644
e-mail: chivenorcp@lineone.net
web: www.chivenorcaravanpark.co.uk
Dir: *On rdbt at Chivenor Cross, take right exit to caravan park.*
PETS: Charges £1 per night £5 per week **Public areas** except shop & shower block **Exercise area** 100mtrs **Facilities** on site shop disp bags walks info vet info **Other** prior notice required dog crèche nearby **Resident Pets:** 2 dogs, 2 gerbils, 1 tortoise

Open mid Mar-mid Jan Booking advisable Jun-Aug Last arrival 21.00hrs Last departure noon

A nicely maintained grassy park with some hard pitches, set in a good location for touring North Devon, and handy for the bus stop into Barnstaple. The site is about 5 miles from sandy beaches. A 3.5-acre site with 30 touring pitches, 5 hardstandings and 10 statics.

COLYFORD
MAP 03 SY29

★★★★ BED & BREAKFAST
Lower Orchard
Swan Hill Rd EX24 6QQ
☎ 01297 553615
e-mail: robin@barnardl.demon.co.uk
Dir: *On A3052 in Colyford, between Lyme Regis & Sidmouth*
PETS: Bedrooms unattended **Charges** charge for damage
Public areas on leads **Grounds** accessible on leads disp bin
Exercise area 200mtrs **Facilities** cage storage walks info vet info
On Request fridge access **Resident Pets:** Biene & Sasha (Tibetan Terriers)

This modern ranch-style family home looks over the Axe valley. The spacious ground-floor bedrooms are very well equipped. Breakfast is served in the lounge-dining room with patio doors leading to a private sun terrace, well-tended gardens and splash pool. The owners have also created a motoring memories museum and a classic car showroom nearby.

Rooms 2 rms (1 en suite) (1 pri facs) (2 GF) ⊗ S £40-£50; D £50-£60 **Facilities** TVB tea/coffee Cen ht TVL ⤴ **Parking** 3 **Notes** No children 🐾

COMBE MARTIN
MAP 02 SS54

►►► **Newberry Valley Park** *(SS576473)*
Woodlands EX34 0AT
☎ 01271 882334
e-mail: relax@newberryvalleypark.co.uk
web: www.newberryvalleypark.co.uk
Dir: *From M5 junct 27, take A361 to North Aller rdbt. Right onto A399, through Combe Martin to sea. Left into site*
PETS: Public areas Exercise area on site exercise field beach 300yds disp bin **Facilities** on site shop food bowl water bowl disp bags walks info vet info **Other** prior notice required
Resident Pets: Taz (Labrador/Shepherd cross), Amber (German Shepherd), Teyha (Utonagan/Wolf Dog cross)

Open Mar-Sep Booking advisable Peak season & BHols Last arrival 20.45hrs Last departure 10.00hrs

A family owned and run touring park on the edge of Combe Martin, with all its amenities just five minutes walk away. The park is set in a wooded valley with its own coarse fishing lake. The safe beaches of Newberry and Combe Martin are reached by a short footpath opposite the park entrance, where the South West coast path is located. A 20-acre site with 125 touring pitches.

Notes No camp fires

DARTMEET

MAP 03 SX67

★★★ GUEST ACCOMMODATION

Brimpts Farm

PL20 6SG

☎ 01364 631450 📄 01364 631179

e-mail: info@brimptsfarm.co.uk

web: www.brimptsfarm.co.uk

Dir: *Dartmeet at E end of B3357, establishment signed on right at top of hill*

PETS: Bedrooms (GF) **Stables** on site **Public areas Grounds** accessible **Exercise area** adjacent **Facilities** water bowl washing facs walks info vet info **On Request** fridge access torch towels **Resident Pets:** Billy (Border Collie), Kipper (Jack Russell)

A popular venue for walkers and lovers of the great outdoors, Brimpts is peacefully situated in the heart of Dartmoor and has been a Duchy of Cornwall farm since 1307. Bedrooms are simply furnished and many have wonderful views across Dartmoor. Dinner is served by arrangement. Additional facilities include a children's play area and sauna and spa. Brimpts is also home to the Dartmoor Pony Heritage Trust.

Rooms 10 en suite (2 fmly) (7 GF) S £30; D £50-£60✷ **Facilities** TV1B tea/coffee Cen ht TVL Dinner Last d 24hrs notice Wi-fi available Sauna Pool Table Farm walks & trails **Parking** 50 **Notes** LB

DAWLISH

MAP 03 SX97

★★★ 77% HOTEL

Langstone Cliff

THE INDEPENDENTS
HOTEL ASSOCIATION

Dawlish Warren EX7 0NA

☎ 01626 868000 📄 01626 868006

e-mail: reception@langstone-hotel.co.uk

web: www.langstone-hotel.co.uk

Dir: *1.5m NE off A379 Exeter road to Dawlish Warren*

PETS: Bedrooms unattended **Public areas** except pool area & restaurant **Grounds** accessible on leads **Exercise area** country walks & seafront

A family owned and run hotel, the Langstone Cliff offers a range of leisure, conference and function facilities. Bedrooms, many with sea views and balconies, are spacious, comfortable and well equipped. There are a number of attractive lounges and a well stocked bar. Dinner is served, often carvery style, in the restaurant.

Rooms 62 en suite 4 annexe en suite (52 fmly) (10 GF) ⌀ in all bedrooms S £71-£88; D £112-£136 (incl. bkfst) **Facilities** STV ❄ ⤷ 🏊 Gym Wi-fi in bedrooms Table tennis, Golf practice area, Hair and beauty salon 🎵 ch fac Xmas **Services** Lift **Parking** 200 **Notes** LB

Lady's Mile Holiday Park *(SX968784)*

EX7 0LX

☎ 01626 863411 📄 01626 888689

e-mail: info@ladysmile.co.uk

web: www.ladysmile.co.uk

Dir: *1m N of Dawlish on A379*

PETS: Charges £1.50 - £3.25 per night **Public areas** except bar & shop **Exercise area** on site fenced area disp bin **Facilities** on site shop food vet info

Open 17 Mar-27 Oct Booking advisable BH & Jul-Aug Last arrival 20.00hrs Last departure 11.00hrs

A holiday site with all grass touring pitches, and plenty of activities for everyone. Two swimming pools with waterslides, a large adventure playground, 9-hole golf course, and a bar with entertainment in high season all add to the enjoyment of a stay here. Facilities are kept clean, and the surrounding beaches are easily accessed. A 16-acre site with 243 touring pitches and 43 statics.

Peppermint Park *(SX978788)*

Warren Rd EX7 0PQ

☎ 01626 863436 📄 01626 866482

e-mail: info@peppermintpark.co.uk

web: www.peppermintpark.co.uk

Dir: *From A379 at Dawlish follow signs for Dawlish Warren. Site 1m on left at bottom of hill*

PETS: Stables nearby (2m) (loose box) **Charges** £2 - £6 per night **Public areas** except play area, swimming pool & club house **Exercise area** 750yds disp bin **Facilities** on site shop food water bowls food bowls disp bags walks info vet info

Open Etr-Oct (rs early/late season shop, pool, club closed) Booking advisable Spring bank hol & Jul-Aug Last arrival 18.00hrs Last departure 11.00hrs

Well managed, attractive park close to the coast, with excellent facilities including club and bar which are well away from pitches. Nestling close to sandy beaches, the park offers individually marked pitches on level terraces in pleasant, sheltered grassland. The many amenities include a heated swimming pool and water chute, coarse fishing and launderette. A 26-acre site with 250 touring pitches, 24 hardstandings and 75 statics.

ENGLAND

DREWSTEIGNTON · MAP 03 SX79

►► Woodland Springs Adult Touring Park

(SX695912)

Venton EX6 6PG

☎ 01647 231695

e-mail: enquiries@woodlandsprings.co.uk
web: www.woodlandsprings.co.uk

Dir: *Exit A30 at Whiddon Down Junction, left onto A382 towards Moretonhampstead. Site 1.5m on left*

PETS: Public areas except toilet block & shop
Exercise area on site 1 acre open area adjacent disp bin
Facilities on site shop walks info vet info

Open all year Booking advisable Jul-Aug, Xmas Last arrival 22.00hrs Last departure 11.00hrs

An attractive park in a rural area within Dartmoor National Park. This site is surrounded by woodland and neighbouring farmland, and is very peaceful. Children are not admitted. A 4-acre site with 85 touring pitches, 34 hardstandings.

Notes @ Adults only, no fires, no noise 23.00hrs-08.00hrs

EAST ALLINGTON · MAP 03 SX74

►►► Mounts Farm Touring Park *(SX757488)*

The Mounts TQ9 7QJ

☎ 01548 521591

e-mail: mounts.farm@lineone.net
web: www.mountsfarm.co.uk

Dir: *A381 from Totnes towards Kingsbridge. (ignore signs for East Allington). At 'Mounts' site is 0.5m on left*

PETS: Public areas except play area **Exercise area** public footpaths adjacent **Facilities** on site shop food bowl water bowl dog chews cat treats disp bags washing facs walks info vet info **Resident Pets:** 3 cats

Open 15 Mar-Oct Booking advisable BH & peak hol season Last arrival anytime Last departure flexible

A neat grassy park divided into four paddocks by mature natural hedges. Three of the paddocks house the tourers and campers, and the fourth is the children's play area. The toilet facilities have been refurbished, and the laundry and well-stocked little shop are in converted farm buildings. A 7-acre site with 50 touring pitches.

EAST ANSTEY · MAP 03 SS82

►►►► Zeacombe House Caravan Park

(SS860240)

Blackerton Cross EX16 9JU

☎ 01398 341279

e-mail: enquiries@zeacombeadultretreat.co.uk
web: www.zeacombeadultretreat.co.uk

Dir: *M5 junct 27 onto A361 signed Barnstaple, turn right at next rdbt onto A396 signed Dulverton/Minehead. In 5m at Exeter Inn turn left onto B3227 towards South Molton, site in 7m on left*

PETS: Public areas except toilet block & shop **Exercise area** on site fenced disp bin **Facilities** on site shop washing facs walks info vet info **Other** prior notice required **Restrictions** No American Pit Bulls

Open 7 Mar-Oct Booking advisable BH's & Jul-Aug Last arrival 21.00hrs Last departure noon

Set on the southern fringes of Exmoor National Park, this 'garden' park is nicely landscaped in a tranquil location, and enjoys panoramic views towards Exmoor. This adult-only park offers a choice of grass or hardstanding pitches, and a unique restaurant-style delivery service allows you to eat an evening meal in the comfort of your own unit. A 5-acre site with 50 touring pitches, 12 hardstandings.

Notes Adults only

EXETER · MAP 03 SX99

★★★★ 72% ⊛ TOWN HOUSE HOTEL

Alias Hotel Barcelona

Magdalen St EX2 4HY

☎ 01392 281000 🖹 01392 281001

e-mail: barcelona@aliashotels.com
web: www.aliasbarcelona.com

Dir: *from A30 Okehampton follow city centre signs. At Exe Bridges rdbt right for city centre, up hill, on at lights. Hotel on right*

PETS: Bedrooms (GF) **Charges** £15 per stay, charge for damage **Grounds** accessible on leads **Exercise area** 25yds **Facilities** walks info vet info

Situated within walking distance of the city centre, this hotel was once an eye hospital before its total transformation into stylish accommodation in a glamorous setting. Public areas include Café Paradiso, an informal eatery with a varied menu, a night club, a range of meeting rooms and a delightful garden terrace ideal for alfresco dining.

Rooms 46 en suite (2 GF) ⊛ in all bedrooms S fr £95; D fr £135 **Facilities** STV Xmas **Services** Lift **Parking** 35 **Notes** LB

★★★ 75% ☺☺ HOTEL

Best Western Lord Haldon Country House

Dunchideock EX6 7YF

☎ 01392 832483 📄 01392 833765

e-mail: enquiries@lordhaldonhotel.co.uk

web: www.lordhaldonhotel.co.uk

Dir: *M5 junct 31, 1st exit off A30 and follow signs through Ide to Dunchideock.*

PETS: Bedrooms Charges £5 per night Public areas except restaurant & lounge Grounds accessible Facilities walks info vet info On Request fridge access Resident Pets: Jake (cat)

Set amidst rural tranquillity, this attractive country house goes from strength to strength. Guests are assured of a warm welcome from the professional team of staff and the well-equipped bedrooms are comfortable, many with stunning views. The daily-changing menu features skilfully cooked dishes with most of the produce sourced locally.

Rooms 23 en suite (3 fmly) ⊘ in all bedrooms S £70-£80; D £95-£115 (incl. bkfst)✳ Facilities Wi-fi in bedrooms Xmas New Year Parking 120 Notes LB

★★★★ GUEST HOUSE

The Edwardian

30-32 Heavitree Rd EX1 2LQ

☎ 01392 276102

e-mail: michael@edwardianexeter.co.uk

web: www.edwardianexeter.co.uk

Dir: *M5 junct 29, right at lights signed city centre, on left after Exeter University School of Education*

PETS: Bedrooms Charges £10 per pet per night Public areas except dining room Exercise area 200yds Resident Pets: Tara (dog)

The friendly proprietors offer a warm welcome to their guests at this attractive Edwardian terrace property, which is situated within easy walking distance of the city centre. The 13 bedrooms vary in size, are well presented and comfortable, and offer a range of extra accessories. Breakfast is served in the spacious dining room, while the separate inviting lounge offers comfort and relaxation.

Rooms 13 en suite (3 fmly) (14 GF) ⊘ S fr £55; D fr £70✳ Facilities FTV TVB tea/coffee Direct dial from bedrooms Cen ht Wi-fi available Parking 5 Notes No coaches

★★★★ FARM HOUSE

Rydon *(SX999871)*

Woodbury EX5 1LB

☎ 01395 232341 📄 01395 232341 Mrs S Glanvill

e-mail: sallyglanvill@aol.com

web: www.rydonfarmwoodbury.co.uk

Dir: *A376 & B3179 from Exeter into Woodbury, right before 30mph sign*

PETS: Bedrooms Grounds accessible disp bin Exercise area 20mtrs Facilities cage storage walks info vet info On Request fridge access torch towels

Dating from the 16th century, this Devon longhouse has been run by the same family for eight generations. The farmhouse provides spacious bedrooms, which are equipped with many useful extra facilities and one has a four-poster bed. There is a television lounge and a delightful garden in which to relax. Breakfast is served in front of an inglenook fireplace.

Rooms 3 rms (2 en suite) (1 pri facs) (1 fmly) ⊘ S £40-£50; D £60-£70 Facilities FTV TVB tea/coffee Cen ht TVL Parking 3 Notes LB 450 acres dairy

EXMOUTH   MAP 03 SY08

►►►► Webbers Farm Caravan & Camping Park *(SY018874)*

Castle Ln, Woodbury EX5 1EA

☎ 01395 232276 📄 01395 233389

e-mail: reception@webberspark.co.uk

web: www.webberspark.co.uk

Dir: *From M5 junct 30 take A376, then B3179 to Woodbury. Site 500yds E of village*

PETS: Public areas except shop Exercise area on site disp bin Facilities on site shop food dog scoop/disp bags walks info vet info Other prior notice required

Open mid Mar-Oct Booking advisable peak season & BHs Last arrival 20.00hrs Last departure 11.00hrs

An unspoilt family park set in three areas, offering a quiet and relaxing touring location. A high quality toilet block provides en suite family rooms and plenty of smart private facilities. The park has good views towards the Haldon Hills, and plenty to explore including 3,000 acres of Woodbury Common and nearby beaches. An 8-acre site with 115 touring pitches and 4 statics.

EXMOUTH CONTINUED

►► St Johns Caravan & Camping Park

(SY027834)

St Johns Rd EX8 5EG

☎ 01395 263170 📄 01395 273004

e-mail: stjohns.farm@virgin.net

Dir: M5 junct 30 follow A376/Exmouth signs. Left through Woodbury towards Budleigh Salterton on B3179 & B3180. Turn right 1m after Exmouth exit

PETS: Public areas Exercise area on site disp bin Facilities on site shop disp bags walks info vet info Other prior notice required Resident Pets: 4 dogs, 2 cats

Open mid Feb-Dec Booking advisable school summer hols Last arrival 22.00hrs Last departure noon

A quiet rural site with attractive country views, only 2 miles from Exmouth's sandy beaches, and half a mile from Woodbury Common. The owners offer a warm welcome to visitors. A 6-acre site with 45 touring pitches, 8 hardstandings.

GULWORTHY
MAP 02 SX47

★★★ 85% ⊛⊛⊛ HOTEL

Horn of Plenty

PL19 8JD

☎ 01822 832528 📄 01822 834390

e-mail: enquiries@thehornofplenty.co.uk

web: www.thehornofplenty.co.uk

Dir: from Tavistock take A390 W for 3m. Right at Gulworthy Cross. After 400yds turn left and after 400yds hotel on right

PETS: Bedrooms unattended Charges £10 per night Exercise area nearby

With stunning views over the Tamar Valley, The Horn of Plenty maintains its reputation as one of Britain's best country-house hotels. The bedrooms are well equipped and have many thoughtful extras with the garden rooms offering impressive levels of comfort and quality. Cuisine here is also impressive and local produce provides interesting and memorable dining.

Rooms 4 en suite 6 annexe en suite (3 fmly) (4 GF) ⊛ in all bedrooms S £150-£240; D £160-£250 (incl. bkfst) Facilities FTV New Year Parking 25 Notes Closed 24-26 Dec

HAYTOR VALE
MAP 03 SX77

★★ 76% ⊛ HOTEL

Rock Inn

TQ13 9XP

☎ 01364 661305 & 661465 📄 01364 661242

e-mail: inn@rock-inn.co.uk

web: www.rock-inn.co.uk

Dir: off A38 onto A382 to Bovey Tracey, after 0.5m turn left onto B3387 to Haytor

PETS: Bedrooms unattended Charges £5.50 per night Exercise area woods adjacent Other dogs in 3 rooms only, not allowed in public rooms

Dating back to the 1750s, this former coaching inn is in a pretty hamlet on the edge of Dartmoor. Each named after a Grand National winner, the individually decorated bedrooms have some nice extra touches. Bars are full of character, with flagstone floors and old beams and offer a wide range of dishes, cooked with imagination and flair.

Rooms 9 en suite (2 fmly) ⊛ in 2 bedrooms S £66.95; D £76.95-£116.95 (incl. bkfst) Facilities STV New Year Parking 20 Notes LB Closed 25-26 Dec

HOLSWORTHY
MAP 02 SS30

► Noteworthy Caravan and Campsite

(SS303052)

Noteworthy, Bude Rd EX22 7JB

☎ 01409 253731

e-mail: enquiries@noteworthy-devon.co.uk

web: www.noteworthy-devon.co.uk

Dir: On A3072 between Holsworthy & Bude. 3m from Holsworthy on right

PETS: Stables (loose box) Charges £2 per week Public areas except play area Exercise area on site dog walks disp bin space for loose box Facilities washing facs dog grooming walks info vet info Resident Pets: 4 British miniature horses

Open all year Booking advisable Aug

A newly established campsite owned by a friendly young couple with their own small children. There are good views from the quiet rural location, and simple toilet facilities. A 5-acre site with 5 touring pitches and 1 static.

Notes ⊛ No open fires

HONITON

MAP 03 ST10

★★★ ◉◉ HOTEL

Combe House Hotel & Restaurant

Gittisham EX14 3AD

☎ 01404 540400 📠 01404 46004

e-mail: stay@thishotel.com

web: www.thishotel.com

Dir: *off A30 1m S of Honiton, follow Gittisham Heathpark signs*

PETS: Bedrooms unattended **Stables** on site (but may depend on local availability) **Charges** £7 per night charge for damage **Public areas** except restaurant **Grounds** accessible on leads **Exercise area** on site **Facilities** food bowl water bowl dog walking washing facs cage storage walks info vet info **On Request** fridge access torch towels **Resident Pets:** Maverick (cat), Arabian horses in park

Standing proudly in an elevated position, this Elizabethan mansion enjoys uninterrupted views over acres of its own woodland, meadow and pasture. Bedrooms are a blend of comfort and quality with relaxation being the ultimate objective; the Linen Room suite combines many original features with contemporary style. A range of atmospheric public rooms retain all the charm and history of the old house. Dining is equally impressive - a skilled kitchen brigade maximises the best of local and home-grown produce, augmented by excellent wines.

Rooms 15 en suite 1 annexe en suite (1 fmly) S £139-£340; D £168-£450 (incl. bkfst)✳ **Facilities** FTV Wi-fi available Xmas New Year **Parking** 39 **Notes** LB Closed 14-27 Jan

★★★★ GUEST ACCOMMODATION

Ridgeway Farm

Awliscombe EX14 3PY

☎ 01404 841331 📠 01404 841119

e-mail: jessica@ridgewayfarm.co.uk

Dir: *3m NW of Honiton. A30 onto A373, through Awliscombe to end of 40mph area, right opp Godford Farm, farm 0.25m up narrow lane*

PETS: Bedrooms Stables on site **Public areas Grounds** accessible **Exercise area** surrounding farmland **Other** pets not allowed on beds **Resident Pets:** Puzzle (Border Terrier), Teazle (Lurcher), Chaos (Labrador) & 3 horses

This 18th-century farmhouse has a peaceful location on the slopes of Hembury Hill, and is a good base for exploring nearby Honiton and the east Devon coast. Renovations have brought the cosy accommodation to a high standard and the atmosphere is relaxed and homely. The proprietors and their family pets assure a warm welcome.

Rooms 2 en suite S £30-£34; D £52-£58 **Facilities** TVB tea/coffee Cen ht TVL Dinner Last d morning **Parking** 4 **Notes** LB

ILFRACOMBE

MAP 02 SS54

★★ 69% SMALL HOTEL

Darnley

3 Belmont Rd EX34 8DR

☎ 01271 863955 📠 01271 864076

e-mail: darnleyhotel@yahoo.co.uk

web: www.darnleyhotel.co.uk

Dir: *M5 junct 27 then A361 to Barnstaple/Ilfracombe. Left at Church Hill then first left into Belmont Rd.*

PETS: Bedrooms (GF) unattended **Public areas** except restaurant on leads **Grounds** accessible on leads disp bin **Exercise area** 400yds **Facilities** water bowl feeding mat cage storage walks info vet info **On Request** fridge access torch towels **Resident Pets:** Pepsi (cat)

Standing within award winning, mature gardens, with a wooded path to the High Street and the beach (about a five minute stroll away), this former Victorian gentleman's residence offers friendly, informal service. The individually furnished and decorated bedrooms vary in size. Dinners feature honest home cooking, with 'old fashioned puddings' always proving popular.

Rooms 10 rms (7 en suite) (2 fmly) (2 GF) ⊘ in all bedrooms S £36-£38; D £56-£86 (incl. bkfst)✳ **Facilities** Xmas New Year **Parking** 10

ILFRACOMBE CONTINUED

★★★★ GUEST ACCOMMODATION

Strathmore

57 St Brannock's Rd EX34 8EQ

☎ 01271 862248 📄 01271 862248

e-mail: peter@small6374.fsnet.co.uk

web: www.the-strathmore.co.uk

Dir: *A361 from Barnstaple to Ilfracombe, Strathmore 1.5m from Mullacot Cross entering Ilfracombe*

PETS: Bedrooms Charges £5 per night (breakfast included) **Public areas** bar & lounge only **Grounds** accessible **Exercise area** 0.25m **Facilities** water bowl water & biscuits provided, welcome letter for dogs **Resident Pets:** Holly (Sheltie)

Situated within walking distance of the town centre and beach, this charming Victorian property offers a very warm welcome. The attractive bedrooms are comfortably furnished, while public areas include a well-stocked bar, an attractive terraced garden, and an elegant breakfast room.

Rooms 8 en suite (3 fmly) ⊛ S £30-£35; D £56-£76 **Facilities** TVB tea/coffee Cen ht **Parking** 7 **Notes** LB

▶▶▶▶ Hele Valley Holiday Park *(SS533472)*

Hele Bay EX34 9RD

☎ 01271 862460 📄 01271 867926

e-mail: holidays@helevalley.co.uk

web: www.helevalley.co.uk

Dir: *M5 junct 27 onto A361. Through Barnstaple & Braunton to Ilfracombe. Then A399 towards Combe Martin. Follow brown Hele Valley signs. 400mtrs sharp right, then to T-junct. Reception on left.*

PETS: Charges £2.85 - £4 per night £20 - £28 per week **Public areas Exercise area** on site dog walk provided many walks adjacent **Facilities** on site shop food food bowl water bowl dog chews dog scoop/disp bags walks info vet info **Other** prior notice required **Resident Pets:** Anna (Rottweiler)

Open May-Sep Booking advisable at all times Last arrival 18.00hrs Last departure 11.00hrs

A deceptively spacious park set in a picturesque valley with glorious tree-lined hilly views from most pitches. High quality new toilet facilities are provided, and the park is close to a lovely beach, with the harbour and other attractions of Ilfracombe just a mile away. A 17-acre site with 58 touring pitches, 8 hardstandings and 80 statics.

Notes No groups

ILSINGTON

MAP 03 SX77

★★★ 85% ◉◉ HOTEL

Best Western Ilsington Country House

Ilsington Village TQ13 9RR

☎ 01364 661452 📄 01364 661307

e-mail: hotel@ilsington.co.uk

web: www.ilsington.co.uk

Dir: *M5 onto A38 to Plymouth. Exit at Bovey Tracey. 3rd exit from rdbt to 'Ilsington', then 1st right. Hotel in 5m by Post Office*

PETS: Bedrooms unattended **Stables** on site **Charges** £8 per night **Grounds** accessible **Exercise area** 5 min walk

This friendly, family owned hotel, offers tranquillity and far-reaching views from its elevated position on the southern slopes of Dartmoor. The stylish suites and bedrooms, some on the ground floor, are individually furnished. The restaurant provides a stunning backdrop for the innovative, daily changing menus which feature local fish, meat and game.

Rooms 25 en suite (4 fmly) (8 GF) ⊛ in all bedrooms S £92-£98; D £136-£144 (incl. bkfst)✱ **Facilities** ➲ supervised Gym Wi-fi in bedrooms Steam room Xmas New Year **Services** Lift **Parking** 100 **Notes** LB

KENNFORD

MAP 03 SX98

▶▶▶▶ Kennford International Caravan Park *(SX912857)*

EX6 7YN

☎ 01392 833046 📄 01392 833046

e-mail: ian@kennfordint.fsbusiness.co.uk

web: www.kennfordint.co.uk

Dir: *At end of M5, take A38, site signed at Kennford slip road*

PETS: Charges £1 per dog per night **Public areas** on leads **Exercise area** on site small field provided disp bin **Facilities** walks info vet info **Resident Pets:** Jade (Rottweiler), Tigger (cat), Ollie (parrot), guinea pigs

Open all year Booking advisable Last arrival 21.00hrs Last departure 11.00hrs

Screened by trees and shrubs from the A38, this park offers many pitches divided by hedging for privacy. A high quality toilet block complements the park's facilities. A good, centrally-located base for touring the coast and countryside of Devon, and Exeter is easily accessible via a nearby bus stop. A 15-acre site with 127 touring pitches and 15 statics.

KENTISBEARE MAP 03 ST00

►►►► Forest Glade Holiday Park *(ST100075)*

Cullompton EX15 2DT

☎ 01404 841381 📠 01404 841593

e-mail: enquiries@forest-glade.co.uk

web: www.forest-glade.co.uk

Dir: *Tent traffic from A373, signed at Keepers Cottage Inn, 2.5m E of M5 junct 28. Touring caravans via Honiton/Dunkeswell road: phone for access details*

PETS: Charges £1.50 per night **Public areas** except pool, shop & toilets **Exercise area** on site surrounding woodland adjacent disp bin **Facilities** on site shop food food bowl water bowl dog chews washing facs walks info vet info **Other** prior notice required

Open 2 wks before Etr-end Oct (rs low season limited shop hours) Booking advisable school hols Last arrival 21.00hrs

A quiet, attractive park in a forest clearing with well-kept gardens and beech hedge screening. One of the main attractions is the immediate proximity of the forest, which offers magnificent hillside walks with surprising views over the valleys. Please telephone for route details. A 15-acre site with 80 touring pitches, 40 hardstandings and 57 statics.

Notes Families and couples only

LEWDOWN MAP 02 SX48

★★★ ◉◉◉ HOTEL
Lewtrenchard Manor

EX20 4PN

von Essen hotels

☎ 01566 783256 & 783222 📠 01566 783332

e-mail: info@lewtrenchard.co.uk

web: www.vonessenhotels.co.uk

Dir: *A30 from Exeter to Plymouth/Tavistock road. At T-junct turn right, then left onto old A30 Lewdown road. After 6m left signed Lewtrenchard*

PETS: Bedrooms Charges £10 per night **Exercise area** nearby

This Jacobean mansion was built in the 1600s, with many interesting architectural features, and is surrounded by its own idyllic grounds in a quiet valley close to the northern edge of Dartmoor. Public rooms include a fine gallery, as well as magnificent carvings and oak panelling. Meals can be taken in the dining room where imaginative and carefully prepared dishes are served using the best of Devon produce. Bedrooms are comfortably furnished and spacious.

Rooms 14 en suite (2 fmly) (3 GF) ⊗ in all bedrooms S £125-£240; D £150-£270 (incl. bkfst)✳ **Facilities** Fishing 🏌 Clay pigeon shooting Falconry Beauty therapies Xmas New Year **Parking** 50 **Notes** LB

LIFTON MAP 03 SX38

★★★ 81% ◉◉ HOTEL
Arundell Arms

PL16 0AA

☎ 01566 784666 📠 01566 784494

e-mail: reservations@arundellarms.com

Dir: *1m off A30, 3m E of Launceston*

PETS: Bedrooms unattended **Charges** £5 per night plus food **Public areas** except restaurant **Grounds** accessible **Exercise area** 0.5m **Facilities** food **Restrictions** dogs not allowed on riverbank

This former coaching inn, boasting a long history, sits in the heart of a quiet Devon village. It is internationally famous for its country pursuits such as winter shooting and angling. The bedrooms offer individual style and comfort. Public areas are full of character and present a relaxed atmosphere, particularly around the open log fire during colder evenings. Award-winning cuisine is a celebration of local produce.

Rooms 21 en suite (4 GF) ⊗ in all bedrooms S £99-£114; D £160-£190 (incl. bkfst)✳ **Facilities** STV Fishing Wi-fi in bedrooms Skittle alley Shooting (in winter) Fly fishing school New Year **Parking** 70 **Notes** LB Closed 3 days Xmas

LYDFORD MAP 02 SX58

►►► Lydford Camping & Caravanning Club Site *(SX512853)*

EX20 4BE

☎ 01822 820275

web: www.campingandcaravanningclub.co.uk/lydford

Dir: *From A30 take A386 signed to Tavistock & Lydford. Past Fox & Hounds on left, right at Lydford sign. Right at war memorial, keep right to site in 200yds*

PETS: Public areas except buildings **Exercise area** on site disp bin **Facilities** walks info vet info **Other** prior notice required

Open 13 Mar-3 Nov Booking advisable BH & peak periods Last arrival 21.00hrs Last departure noon

Site on mainly level ground looking towards the western slopes of Dartmoor at the edge of the village, near the spectacular gorge. This popular park is close to the Devon coast to coast cycle route, between Tavistock and Okehampton. A 7.75-acre site with 90 touring pitches, 27 hardstandings.

Notes Site gates closed 23.00-07.00

LYNMOUTH MAP 03 SS74

★★★ 73% ⊕ HOTEL

Tors

EX35 6NA

☎ 01598 753236 📠 01598 752544

e-mail: torshotel@torslynmouth.co.uk

web: www.torslynmouth.co.uk

Dir: *adjacent to A39 on Countisbury Hill just before entering Lynmouth from Minehead*

PETS: Bedrooms unattended Charges £5 per night
Public areas except restaurant, pool area & luxury suite
Exercise area surrounding woodland

In an elevated position overlooking Lynmouth Bay, this friendly hotel is set in five acres of woodland. The majority of the bedrooms benefit from the superb views, as do the public areas; which are generous and well presented. Both fixed-price and short carte menus are offered in the restaurant.

Rooms 31 en suite (6 fmly) ⊘ in 1 bedroom S £76-£195; D £112-£250 (incl. bkfst)✳ Facilities ⚘ Table tennis, Pool table Xmas New Year Services Lift Parking 40 Notes Closed 4-31 Jan

★★ 69% HOTEL

Bath

Sea Front EX35 6EL

☎ 01598 752238 📠 01598 753894

e-mail: bathhotel@torslynmouth.co.uk

Dir: *M5 junct 25, follow A39 to Lynmouth*

PETS: Bedrooms unattended Public areas except restaurant
Exercise area 200yds Resident Pets: Boadecia & Polyanna (Persian cats)

This well-established, friendly hotel is situated near the harbour and offers lovely views from the attractive, sea-facing bedrooms and an excellent starting point for scenic walks. There are two lounges and a sun lounge. The restaurant menu is extensive and features daily changing specials, making good use of fresh produce and local fish.

Rooms 22 en suite (9 fmly) ⊘ in 1 bedroom S £37-£59; D £74-£134 (incl. bkfst)✳ Facilities ch fac Parking 12 Notes LB Closed Jan & Dec RS Feb-Mar and Nov

★★★ GUEST ACCOMMODATION

Countisbury Lodge

6 Tors Park, Countisbury Hill EX35 6NB

☎ 01598 752388

e-mail: paulpat@countisburylodge.co.uk

Dir: *Off A39 Countisbury Hill just before Lynmouth centre, signed Countisbury Lodge*

PETS: Bedrooms Exercise area country walks Facilities vet info
Resident Pets: Jessica & Magic (Golden Retrievers), Eric (cat)

From its peaceful elevated position high above the town, this former Victorian vicarage has spectacular views of the harbour and countryside. The atmosphere is friendly and informal but with attentive service. The comfortable bedrooms are attractively decorated, and breakfast is served in the pleasant dining room.

Countisbury Lodge

Rooms 4 en suite (1 fmly) ⊘ S £32; D £56-£60 Facilities FTV TVB tea/coffee Cen ht TVL Dinner Last d breakfast Parking 6

LYNTON MAP 03 SS74

★★★ 69% ⊕⊕ HOTEL

Lynton Cottage

Northwalk EX35 6ED

☎ 01598 752342 📠 01598 754016

e-mail: mail@lyntoncottage.co.uk

Dir: *M5 junct 23 to Bridgewater, then A39 to Minehead & follow signs to Lynton. 1st right after church and right again.*

PETS: Bedrooms (GF) Public areas except restaurant on leads
Grounds accessible on leads disp bin Facilities walks info vet info Restrictions no breeds larger than a retriever
Resident Pets: Mango (Retriever), Chloe & Charlie (cats)

Boasting simply breathtaking views, this wonderfully relaxing and friendly hotel stands some 500 feet above the sea and provides a peaceful hideaway. Bedrooms are individual in style and size, with the added bonus of scenic views, whilst public areas have charm and character in equal measure. Accomplished cuisine is also on offer with taste-laden dishes constructed with care and considerable skill.

Rooms 16 en suite (1 fmly) (1 GF) ⊘ in all bedrooms S fr £58.80; D £84-£156 (incl. bkfst)✳ Parking 20 Notes Closed 2 Dec-12 Jan

★★ 78% SMALL HOTEL
Seawood

North Walk EX35 6HJ

☎ 01598 752272

e-mail: seawoodhotel@aol.com

web: www.seawoodhotel.co.uk

Dir: *turn right at St. Mary's Church in Lynton High St for hotel, 2nd on left*

PETS: Bedrooms Stables nearby (1m) **Charges** £3 per night charge for damage **Grounds** accessible on leads disp bin **Exercise area** 20yds **Facilities** dog chews feeding mat washing facs walks info vet info **On Request** torch towels
Resident Pets: Libby & Millie (Cocker Spaniels)

Tucked away in a quiet area and spectacularly situated 400 feet above the seashore, the Seawood enjoys magnificent views, and is set in delightful grounds. Bedrooms, many with sea views and some with four-poster beds, are comfortable and well equipped. At dinner, the daily-changing menu provides freshly prepared and appetising dishes.

Rooms 12 en suite ⊘ in all bedrooms **Facilities** Xmas **Parking** 12
Notes No children 10yrs Closed Dec-Feb

►►►► Channel View Caravan and Camping Park *(SS724482)*

Manor Farm EX35 6LD

☎ 01598 753349 🖷 01598 752777

e-mail: relax@channel-view.co.uk

web: www.channel-view.co.uk

Dir: *A39 E for 0.5m on left past Barbrook*

PETS: Public areas Exercise area on site exercise field provided **Facilities** on site shop food washing facs walks info vet info **Other** prior notice required

Open 15 Mar-15 Nov Booking advisable Jul-Aug Last arrival 22.00hrs Last departure noon

On the top of the cliffs overlooking the Bristol Channel, a well-maintained park on the edge of Exmoor, and close to both Lynton and Lynmouth. Pitches can be selected from a hidden hedged area, or with panoramic views over the coast. A 6-acre site with 76 touring pitches, 15 hardstandings and 31 statics.

Notes Groups by prior arrangement only

►►► Lynton Camping & Caravanning Club Site *(SS703481)*

Caffyns Cross EX35 6JS

☎ 01598 752379

web: www.campingandcaravanningclub.co.uk/lynton

Dir: *M5 junct 27 onto A361 to Barnstable. Turn right to Blackmoor Gate signed Lynmouth & Lynton. Approx 5m to Caffyns Cross, immediately right to site in 1m*

PETS: Public areas except buildings **Exercise area** adjacent walks disp bin **Facilities** walks info vet info **Other** prior notice required

Open 13 Mar-29 Sep Booking advisable BH & peak periods Last arrival 21.00hrs Last departure noon

Set on high ground with excellent views over the Bristol Channel, and close to the twin resorts of Lynton & Lynmouth. This area is known as Little Switzerland because of its wooded hills, and the park is ideal for walking, and cycling on the nearby National Cycle Network. A 5.5-acre site with 105 touring pitches, 10 hardstandings.

Notes Site gates closed 23.00-07.00

MODBURY   MAP 03 SX65

►►► California Cross C&C Club Site

(SX705530)

PL21 0SG

☎ 01548 821297

web: www.campingandcaravanningclub.co.uk/californiacross

Dir: *Leave A38 at Wrangton Cross onto A3121, continue to x-rds. Cross over onto B3196, left after California Cross sign before petrol station, site on right*

PETS: Public areas except buildings **Facilities** walks info vet info disp bin **Other** prior notice required

Open 13 Mar-3 Nov Booking advisable BH & peak periods Last arrival 21.00hrs Last departure noon

A gently sloping site with some terracing, set in a rural location midway between Ivybridge and Kingsbridge. This well ordered site is protected by high hedging, and is an ideal base for exploring the lovely South Devon countryside. A 3.75-acre site with 80 touring pitches, 7 hardstandings.

Notes Site gates closed 23.00-07.00

MOLLAND · MAP 03 SS82

►►► Yeo Valley Holiday Park (SS788265)

EX36 3NW

☎ 01769 550297 📄 01769 550101

e-mail: info@yeovalleyholidays.com

web: www.yeovalleyholidays.com

Dir: *From A361 onto B3227 towards Bampton. Follow brown signs for Blackcock Inn. Site opposite*

PETS: Stables nearby (4m) (loose box) **Charges** £1 per night £7 per week **Public areas Exercise area** on site disp bin **Facilities** on site shop disp bags walks info vet info **Other** prior notice required

(rs Sep-Mar swimming pool closed) Booking advisable Jul-Aug Last arrival 22.30hrs Last departure 10.00hrs

Set in a beautiful secluded valley on the edge of Exmoor National Park, this family-run park has easy access to both the moors and the north Devon coastline. The park is adjacent to the Blackcock Inn (under the same ownership), and has a very good heated indoor pool. A 7-acre site with 65 touring pitches, 16 hardstandings and 5 statics.

MORETONHAMPSTEAD · MAP 03 SX78

★★★★ BED & BREAKFAST

Hazlecott Bed & Breakfast

Manaton TQ13 9UY

☎ 01647 221521 & 07800 994928 📄 01647 221405

e-mail: hazelcott@dartmoordays.com

web: www.dartmoordays.com

Dir: *A38 onto A382 through Bovey Tracey to Manaton. Pass Kestor Inn, right at x-rds, 0.5m past church*

PETS: Bedrooms Charges £5 per night **Grounds** accessible **Exercise area** 15yds **Resident Pets:** Misty & Muffin (cats)

A home from home is provided at this delightful house secluded on the edge of Dartmoor. Rooms vary in size but all have superb views of the locality. Breakfasts are a feature, when local produce is used confidently. This is an ideal venue for ramblers. Wi-fi connection is also now available here.

Rooms 3 en suite (1 fmly) (1 GF) ⊘ S fr £40; D £60-£80 **Facilities** TVB tea/coffee Cen ht TVL Dinner Last d previous day Wi-fi available **Parking** 6 **Notes** LB

MORTEHOE · MAP 02 SS44

►►► Easewell Farm Holiday Parc & Golf Club (SS465455)

EX34 7EH

☎ 01271 870343 📄 01271 870089

e-mail: goodtimes@woolacombe.com

web: www.woolacombe.com

Dir: *Take B3343 to Mortehoe. Turn right at fork, site 2m on right*

PETS: Stables nearby (1.5m) **Charges** £1.50 per night £10 per week **Public areas Exercise area** on site dog run provided countryside & beach adjacent **Facilities** on site shop food walks info vet info

Open Etr-Oct (rs Etr) Booking advisable Jul-Aug, Etr, Whitsun Last arrival 22.00hrs Last departure 10.00hrs

A peaceful clifftop park with full facility pitches for caravans and motorhomes, and superb views. The park offers a range of activities including indoor bowling and a golf course, and all the facilities of the three other nearby holiday centres within this group are open to everyone. A 17-acre site with 302 touring pitches, 50 hardstandings and 1 static.

►►► North Morte Farm Caravan & Camping Park (SS462455)

North Morte Rd EX34 7EG

☎ 01271 870381 📄 01271 870115

e-mail: info@northmortefarm.co.uk

web: www.northmortefarm.co.uk

Dir: *From B3343 into Mortehoe, right at post office. Park 500yds on left*

PETS: Charges £1.50 per night **Public areas** on leads at all times **Exercise area** on site areas provided coastal path & beach **Facilities** on site shop vet info

Open Apr-Sep (rs Oct caravan owners only) Last arrival 22.30hrs Last departure noon

Set in spectacular coastal countryside close to National Trust land and 500yds from Rockham Beach. This attractive park is very well run and maintained by friendly family owners, and the quaint village of Mortehoe with its cafés, shops and pubs, is just a 5 minute walk away. A 22-acre site with 180 touring pitches, 18 hardstandings and 73 statics.

Notes No large groups

►►► Warcombe Farm Caravan & Camping Park (SS478445)

Station Rd EX34 7EJ

☎ 01271 870690 & 07774 428770 📄 01271 871070

e-mail: info@warcombefarm.co.uk

web: www.warcombefarm.co.uk

Dir: *N towards Mortehoe from Mullacot Cross rdbt at A361 junct with B3343. Site 2m on right*

PETS: Charges £1.50 per night **Public areas** except play area & toilet block **Exercise area** on site 14 acre field provided disp bin **Facilities** on site shop food food bowl water bowl dog chews cat treats dog scoop/disp bags leads walks info vet info **Other** prior notice required

Open 15 Mar-Oct Booking advisable Jul-Aug Last arrival 22.00hrs Last departure noon

Extensive views over the Bristol Channel can be enjoyed from the open areas of this attractive park, while other pitches are sheltered in paddocks with maturing trees. The superb sandy beach with Blue Flag award at Woolacombe Bay is only 1.5m away, and there is a fishing lake with access from some pitches. A 19-acre site with 250 touring pitches, 10 hardstandings.

Notes No groups unless booked in advance

NEWTON ABBOT   MAP 03 SX87

★★★★ FARM HOUSE
Bulleigh Park (SX860660)

Ipplepen TQ12 5UA

☎ 01803 872254 📄 01803 872254 Mrs A Dallyn

e-mail: bulleigh@lineone.net

web: www.southdevonaccommodation.co.uk

Dir: *3.5m S of Newton Abbot. Off A381 at Parkhill Cross by Power station for Compton, continue 1m, signed*

PETS: Stables on site **Charges** dog £5 & horse £5 per night £30 per week charge for damage **Public areas** restaurant & lounge **Grounds** accessible disp bin **Facilities** food (pre-bookable) food bowl water bowl dog chews dog scoop/disp bags leads hay & straw for horses washing facs cage storage walks info vet info **On Request** fridge access torch towels **Resident Pets:** Nippy (Jack Russell cross)

Bulleigh Park is a working farm producing award-winning Aberdeen Angus beef. The owners have also won an award for green tourism by reducing the impact of the business on the environment. Expect a friendly welcome at this family home set in glorious countryside, where breakfasts are notable for the wealth of fresh, local and home-made produce, and the porridge is cooked to a secret recipe.

Rooms 2 en suite 1 annexe en suite S £38-£40; D fr £66 **Facilities** FTV TVB tea/coffee Cen ht TVL **Parking** 6 **Notes** LB ⊗ 60 acres beef, sheep RS Dec-Jan

►►►►► Dornafield (SX838683)

Dornafield Farm, Two Mile Oak TQ12 6DD

☎ 01803 812732 📄 01803 812032

e-mail: enquiries@dornafield.com

web: www.dornafield.com

Dir: *Take A381 (Newton Abbot-Totnes) for 2m. At Two Mile Oak Inn turn right, then left at x-roads in 0.5m to site on right*

PETS: Charges £1-£1.80 per night **Public areas Exercise area** on site 2 exercise areas provided disp bin **Facilities** on site shop food food bowl water bowl dog chews cat treats dog scoop/disp bags walks info vet info **Other** prior notice required **Resident Pets:** cat

Open 15 Mar-4 Jan Booking advisable BH & Jul-Aug Last arrival 22.00hrs Last departure 11.00hrs

An immaculately kept park in a tranquil wooded valley between Dartmoor and Torbay, offering either de-luxe or fully-serviced pitches. A lovely 15th-century farmhouse sits at the entrance, and the park is divided into three separate areas, served by two superb, ultra-modern toilet blocks. The friendly family owners are always available. A 30-acre site with 135 touring pitches, 97 hardstandings.

►►►►► Ross Park (SX845671)

Park Hill Farm, Ipplepen TQ12 5TT

☎ 01803 812983 📄 01803 812983

e-mail: enquiries@rossparkcaravanpark.co.uk

web: www.rossparkcaravanpark.co.uk

Dir: *Off A381, 3m from Newton Abbot towards Totnes, signed opposite 'Power' garage towards 'Woodland'*

PETS: Public areas except main restaurant (except assist dogs) **Exercise area** on site various areas provided disp bin **Facilities** on site shop food free disposal bags walks info vet info **Other** dog shower room **Restrictions** certain breeds not accepted **Resident Pets:** Baloo & Monty (Labradors)

Open Mar-2 Jan (rs Nov-Feb & 1st 3wks of Mar restaurant/bar closed (ex Xmas/New Year)) Booking advisable Jul, Aug & BHs Last arrival 21.00hrs Last departure 10.00hrs

A top-class park in every way, with large secluded pitches, high quality toilet facilities and lovely floral displays throughout the 26 acres. The beautiful tropical conservatory also offers a breathtaking show of colour. This very rural park enjoys superb views of Dartmoor, and good quality meals to suit all tastes and pockets are served in the restaurant. A 26-acre site with 110 touring pitches, 82 hardstandings.

Notes ⊗ Bikes, Skateboards/scooters only allowed on leisure field

NEWTON ABBOT CONTINUED

▶▶▶ Twelve Oaks Farm Caravan Park

(SX852737)

Teigngrace TQ12 6QT

☎ 01626 352769 📠 01626 352769

e-mail: info@twelveoaksfarm.co.uk

web: www.twelveoaksfarm.co.uk

Dir: *A38 from Exeter left signed Teigngrace (only), 0.25m before Drumbridges rdbt. 1.5m, through village, site on left. From Plymouth pass Drumbridges rdbt, take slip road for Chudleigh Knighton. Right over bridge, rejoin A38 towards Plymouth. Left for Teigngrace (only), then as above*

PETS: Public areas Exercise area on site disp bin Facilities on site shop walks info vet info

Open all year Booking advisable Last arrival 21.00hrs Last departure 11.00hrs

An attractive small park on a working farm close to Dartmoor National Park, and bordered by the River Teign. The tidy pitches are located amongst trees and shrubs, and the modern facilities are very well maintained. Children will enjoy all the farm animals, and nearby is the Templar Way walking route. A 2-acre site with 35 touring pitches, 17 hardstandings.

OKEHAMPTON   MAP 02 SX59

★★★★ 🍽 GUEST HOUSE

Higher Cadham

Jacobstowe EX20 3RB

☎ 01837 851647 📠 01837 851410

e-mail: info@highercadham.co.uk

web: www.highercadham.co.uk

Dir: *1m N of Jacobstowe. A3072 onto B3216, sharp right after church & continue 0.5m*

PETS: Bedrooms Charges £2 per night Public areas on leads Grounds accessible

Guests return for the excellent hospitality and enjoyable food, and the location is great for cycling or walking breaks. Children will enjoy the animals and the large play area. Ground-floor bedrooms are available, two with easier access, and there is a comfortable bar.

Rooms 9 en suite (4 fmly) (4 GF) ⊘ Facilities TVB tea/coffee Licensed Cen ht TVL Dinner Last d 5pm Parking 30 Notes Closed 21 Dec-10 Jan RS Sun

OTTERY ST MARY   MAP 03 SY19

★★ BED & BREAKFAST

Fluxton Farm

Fluxton EX11 1RJ

☎ 01404 812818 📠 01404 814843

web: www.fluxtonfarm.co.uk

Dir: *2m SW of Ottery St Mary. B3174 W from Ottery over river, left, next left to Fluxton*

PETS: Bedrooms Sep Accom pens for cats only

Grounds accessible on leads Exercise area opposite

Facilities washing facs walks info vet info On Request fridge access Resident Pets: The farm is a cat rescue sanctuary. 18 cats, geese, chickens

A haven for cat lovers, Fluxton Farm offers comfortable accommodation with a choice of lounges and a large garden, complete with pond and ducks. Set in peaceful farmland four miles from the coast, this 16th-century longhouse has a wealth of beams and open fireplaces.

Rooms 7 rms (6 en suite) (1 pri facs) (1 fmly) ⊘ S £25-£27.50; D £50-£55✳ Facilities TVB tea/coffee Cen ht TVL Parking 15 Notes LB No children 8yrs RS Nov-Apr ⊠

PAIGNTON   MAP 03 SX86

★★★ GUEST ACCOMMODATION

Bay Cottage

4 Beach Rd TQ4 6AY

☎ 01803 525729

e-mail: info@baycottagehotel.co.uk

Dir: *Along B3201 Esplanade Rd past Paignton Pier, Beach Rd 2nd right*

PETS: Bedrooms unattended Charges £10 per week

Public areas except dining room Exercise area 100yds

With easy level access to the beach, theatre and the shops, Bay Cottage offers friendly accommodation. In the bedrooms, the best possible use has been made of available space. Home-cooked dinners, by arrangement, are served in the pleasant pine-furnished dining room, and there is also a comfortable lounge.

Rooms 8 en suite (3 fmly) ⊘ S £20-£25; D £40-£50✳ Facilities TVB tea/coffee Cen ht TVL Dinner Last d 9.30am Notes LB Closed 20 Dec-3 Jan ⊠

★★★ GUEST ACCOMMODATION

Park Hotel

Esplanade Rd TQ4 6BQ

☎ 01803 557856 📄 01803 555626

e-mail: stay@parkhotel.me.uk

Dir: *On Paignton seafront, nearly opp pier*

PETS: Bedrooms (GF) **Charges** charge for damage
Public areas except restaurant on leads **Grounds** accessible on
leads **Facilities** cage storage walks info vet info
On Request fridge access torch towels

This large establishment has a prominent position on the seafront with
excellent views of Torbay. The pleasant bedrooms are all spacious and
available in a number of options, and several have sea views.
Entertainment is provided on some evenings in the lounge. Dinner and
breakfast are served in the spacious dining room, which overlooks the
attractive front garden.

Rooms 47 rms (33 en suite) (5 fmly) (3 GF) **Facilities** TVB tea/coffee
Lift Cen ht Dinner Last d 6pm games room with 3/4 snooker table & table
tennis **Parking** 35

PLYMOUTH   MAP 02 SX45

★★★ 71% HOTEL

Novotel Plymouth

Marsh Mills PL6 8NH

☎ 01752 221422 📄 01752 223922

e-mail: h0508@accor.com

web: www.novotel.com

Dir: *Exit A38 at Marsh Mills, follow Plympton signs, hotel on left*

PETS: Bedrooms (GF) unattended **Charges** £6 per night
Public areas except restaurant on leads **Grounds** accessible on
leads **Facilities** vet info

Conveniently located on the outskirts of the city, close to Marsh Mills
roundabout, this modern hotel offers good value accommodation. All
rooms are spacious and designed with flexibility for family use. Public
areas are open-plan with meals available throughout the day in either
the Garden Brasserie, the bar, or from room service.

Rooms 100 en suite (17 fmly) (18 GF) ⊘ in 80 bedrooms **Facilities** STV
ᴿ Xmas New Year **Services** Lift **Parking** 140

★★★ GUEST ACCOMMODATION

The Cranbourne

278-282 Citadel Rd, The Hoe PL1 2PZ

☎ 01752 263858 & 224646 📄 01752 263858

e-mail: cran.hotel@virgin.net

web: www.cranbournehotel.co.uk

PETS: Bedrooms Public areas except dining room on leads
Exercise area 60yds **Resident Pets:** Harry (Golden Retriever)

This attractive Georgian terrace house has been extensively renovated,
and is located just a short walk from The Hoe, The Barbican and the
city centre. Bedrooms are practically furnished and well equipped.
Hearty breakfasts are served in the elegant dining room and there is
also a cosy bar.

Rooms 40 rms (28 en suite) (5 fmly) (1 GF) ⊘ S £25-£45; D £45-£60✱
Facilities TVB tea/coffee Cen ht TVL **Parking** 14

★★★ GUEST ACCOMMODATION

The Lamplighter

103 Citadel Rd, The Hoe PL1 2RN

☎ 01752 663855 & 07793 360815 📄 01752 228139

e-mail: stay@lamplighterplymouth.co.uk

web: www.lamplighterplymouth.co.uk

Dir: *Near war memorial*

PETS: Bedrooms Charges £5 minimum per night
Public areas except dining room on leads **Exercise area** 50mtrs
Facilities cage storage walks info vet info

With easy access to The Hoe, The Barbican and the city centre, this
comfortable guest house provides a good base for leisure or business.
Bedrooms, including family rooms, are light and airy and furnished to
a consistent standard. Breakfast is served in the dining room, which
has an adjoining lounge area.

Rooms 9 rms (7 en suite) (2 pri facs) (2 fmly) ⊘ S £30-£35;
D £45-£50✱ **Facilities** TVB tea/coffee Cen ht TVL Wi-fi available
Parking 4

ENGLAND

PRINCETOWN MAP 02 SX57

►► The Plume of Feathers Inn *(SX592734)*

Plymouth PL20 6QQ

☎ 01822 890240

Dir: *Site accessed directly from B3212 rdbt (beside Plume of Feathers Inn) in centre of Princetown*

PETS: Stables on site **Public areas Exercise area** Dartmoor National Park adjacent disp bin **Facilities** dog chews cat treats washing facs walks info vet info **Resident Pets:** Bonnie (West Highland Terrier), Jeannie (Border Terrier)

Open all year Booking advisable all year Last arrival 23.30hrs Last departure 11.00hrs

Set amidst the rugged beauty of Dartmoor not far from the notorious prison, this campsite boasts new toilet facilities and all the amenities of the inn. The Plume of Feathers is Princetown's oldest building, and serves all day food in an atmospheric setting. The campsite is mainly for tents. A 3-acre site with 85 touring pitches.

Notes No caravans

ROCKBEARE MAP 03 SY09

★★ FARM HOUSE

Lower Allercombe Farm *(SY048946)*

EX5 2HD

☎ 01404 822519 📄 01404 822519 Ms S Holroyd

e-mail: susie@allercombe.fsnet.co

web: www.lowerallercombefarm.co.uk

Dir: *A30 at Daisy Mount onto B3180. After 200yds turn right to Allercombe. In 1m at Allercombe x-rds turn right, farm is 50yds on right*

PETS: Bedrooms Stables on site **Public areas Grounds** accessible on leads disp bin **Facilities** outdoor manège **Resident Pets:** Lizzie (Patterdale Terrier), Daisy (cat)

Lower Allercombe dates from the 17th century and offers comfortable accommodation. The rural location is handy for the A30 and Exeter Airport, and is convenient for visiting local attractions.

Rooms 3 rms (1 en suite) (1 pri facs) (1 fmly) S £30-£35; D £50-£60✳ **Facilities** TVB tea/coffee Cen ht TVL **Parking** 9 **Notes** 180 acres Horses Stud & cattle ⊛

SALCOMBE MAP 03 SX73

★★★★ 78% ◉◉ HOTEL

Soar Mill Cove

Soar Mill Cove, Malborough TQ7 3DS

☎ 01548 561566 📄 01548 561223

e-mail: info@soarmillcove.co.uk

web: www.soarmillcove.co.uk

Dir: *3m W of town off A381at Malborough. Follow 'Soar' signs*

PETS: Bedrooms (GF) **Grounds** accessible disp bin **Exercise area** on site **Facilities** cage storage walks info vet info **On Request** fridge access torch towels dog scoop/disp bags **Other** 2000 acres NT land & beach without restrictions for walking **Resident Pets:** Rosie (Bichon Frisé)

Situated amid spectacular scenery with dramatic sea views, this hotel is ideal for a relaxing stay. Family-run, with a committed team, keen standards of hospitality and service are upheld. Bedrooms are well equipped and many rooms have private terraces. There are different seating areas where impressive cream teas are served, or, for the more active, a choice of swimming pools. Local produce and seafood is used to good effect in the restaurant.

Rooms 22 en suite (5 fmly) (21 GF) ⊗ in all bedrooms S £70-£125; D £99-£249 (incl. bkfst)✳ **Facilities** ⊗ ⌇ ⌇ Putt green Wi-fi available Table tennis, Games room, 9 hole Pitch n putt ♫ Xmas New Year **Parking** 30 **Notes** LB Closed 2 Jan-8 Feb

★★★ 81% ◉ HOTEL

Tides Reach

South Sands TQ8 8LJ

☎ 01548 843466 📄 01548 843954

e-mail: enquire@tidesreach.com

web: www.tidesreach.com

Dir: *off A38 at Buckfastleigh to Totnes. Then take A381 to Salcombe, follow signs to South Sands*

PETS: Bedrooms unattended **Charges** £8.50 per night **Public areas** in one lounge only **Grounds** accessible disp bin **Facilities** bedding dog scoop/disp bags walks info vet info **On Request** fridge access torch towels

Superbly situated at the water's edge, this personally run, friendly hotel has splendid views of the estuary and beach. Bedrooms, many with balconies, are spacious and comfortable. In the bar and lounge, attentive service can be enjoyed along with the view, and the Garden Room restaurant serves appetising and accomplished cuisine.

Rooms 35 en suite (7 fmly) ⊗ in 14 bedrooms S £70-£143; D £124-£314 (incl. bkfst & dinner)✳ **Facilities** ☉ supervised Squash Gym Windsurfing Sailing Kayaking Scuba diving Hair & Beauty treatment ♫ **Services** Lift **Parking** 100 **Notes** LB No children 8yrs Closed Dec-early Feb

---

SAMPFORD PEVERELL   MAP 03 ST01

►►►► Minnows Touring Park *(SS042148)*

Holbrook Ln EX16 7EN

☎ 01884 821770 📄 01884 829199

web: www.ukparks.co.uk/minnows

Dir: *M5 junct 27, take A361 signed Tiverton & Barnstaple. In 600yds take 1st slip road, then right over bridge, site ahead*

PETS: Charges 2 dogs free, £1 per extra dog per night **Public areas** except buildings **Exercise area** canal towpath adjacent **Facilities** on site shop walks info vet info **Other** water at reception, dog ties by buildings

Open 10 Mar-3 Nov Booking advisable BH & Jun-Sep Last arrival 20.00hrs Last departure 11.30hrs

A small, well-sheltered park, peacefully located amidst fields and mature trees. The toilet facilities are of a high quality in keeping with the rest of the park, and there is a good laundry. The park has direct gated access to the canal towpath. A 5.5-acre site with 45 touring pitches, 43 hardstandings and 1 static.

Notes No cycling, no groundsheets on grass

SIDMOUTH   MAP 03 SY18

★★★★★ ⊛⊛ 🍴

RESTAURANT WITH ROOMS
The Salty Monk

Church St, Sidford EX10 9QP

☎ 01395 513174

e-mail: saltymonk@btconnect.com

web: www.saltymonk.biz

Dir: *On A3052 in Sidford opp church*

PETS: Bedrooms (GF) **Charges** £4 per night £15 per week charge for damage **Public areas** except restaurant on leads **Grounds** accessible on leads disp bin **Exercise area** 50yds **Facilities** food (pre-bookable) food bowl water bowl bedding dog chews dog scoop/disp bags leads washing facs cage storage walks info vet info **On Request** fridge access torch towels **Resident Pets:** Finn & Mardi (Irish Water Spaniels)

Set in the village of Sidford, this attractive property dates from the 16th century. Some of the well-presented bedrooms feature spa baths or special showers, and a ground-floor courtyard room has a king-size water bed. Meals are served in the restaurant, where the two owners both cook. They use fresh local produce to ensure that the food is of a high standard and thoroughly enjoyable.

Rooms 5 en suite (3 GF) ⊗ S £70-£95; D £100-£180✳ **Facilities** FTV TVB tea/coffee Cen ht Dinner Last d 9pm Wi-fi available **Parking** 20 **Notes** LB Closed 2wks Nov & 3wks Jan

---

►►►► Oakdown Touring & Holiday Caravan Park *(SY167902)*

Gatedown Ln, Weston EX10 0PD

☎ 01297 680387 📄 01297 680541

e-mail: enquiries@oakdown.co.uk

web: www.oakdown.co.uk

Dir: *Off A3052, 2.5m E of junct with A375*

PETS: Charges £2 per night **Public areas** except play area **Exercise area** field trails disp bin **Facilities** walks info vet info **Restrictions** Dogs must be kept on leads & exercised off park

Open Apr-Oct Booking advisable Spring bank hol & Jul-Aug Last arrival 22.00hrs Last departure 10.30hrs

Friendly, well-maintained park with good landscaping and plenty of maturing trees. Pitches are grouped in paddocks surrounded by shrubs, and the park is well screened from the A3502. The park's conservation areas with their natural flora and fauna offer attractive walks, and there is a hide by the Victorian reed bed for both casual and dedicated bird watchers. A 13-acre site with 100 touring pitches, 90 hardstandings and 62 statics.

Notes no bikes, no skateboards, no kite flying

SLAPTON   MAP 03 SX84

►►► Slapton Sands Camping & Caravanning Club Site *(SX825450)*

Middle Grounds TQ7 2QW

☎ 01548 580538

web: www.campingandcaravanningclub.co.uk/slaptonsands

Dir: *On A379 from Kingsbridge. Site entrance 0.25m from A379, beyond brow of hill approaching Slapton*

PETS: Public areas except buildings **Exercise area** on site disp bin **Facilities** walks info vet info **Other** prior notice required

Open 13 Mar-3 Nov Booking advisable BH & peak periods Last arrival 21.00hrs Last departure noon

A very attractive location and well-run site overlooking Start Bay, with extensive views from some pitches, and glimpses of the sea from others. The shingle beach of Slapton Sands, and the Blue Flag beach at Blackpool Sands are among attractions, along with a nearby freshwater lake and nature reserve. A 5.5-acre site with 115 touring pitches, 10 hardstandings.

Notes Members' touring caravans only. Site gates closed from 23.00-07.00.

SOURTON
MAP 03 SX59

★★ 78% COUNTRY HOUSE HOTEL
Collaven Manor
EX20 4HH

☎ 01837 861522 ▤ 01837 861614

e-mail: collavenmanor@supanet.com

Dir: *off A30 onto A386 to Tavistock, hotel 2m on right*

PETS: Bedrooms unattended **Charges** £5 per night
Grounds accessible **Exercise area** accessed directly from grounds
Facilities food water bowl **Resident Pets:** Willow, Jade, & Jack
(cats)

This delightful 15th-century manor house is quietly located in five acres
of well-tended grounds. The friendly proprietors provide attentive
service and ensure a relaxing environment. Charming public rooms
have old oak beams and granite fireplaces, and provide a range of
comfortable lounges and a well stocked bar. In the restaurant, a daily
changing menu offers interesting dishes.

Rooms 9 en suite (1 fmly) S £63; D £104-£142 (incl. bkfst)✲
Facilities ⌣ Bowls ch fac **Parking** 50 **Notes** LB

SOURTON CROSS
MAP 02 SX59

▶▶▶ Bundu Camping & Caravan Park

(SX546916)
EX20 4HT

☎ 01837 861611 ▤ 01837 861611

e-mail: frances@bunduplus.com

web: www.bundu.co.uk

Dir: *W on A30, past Okehampton. Take A386 to Tavistock. Take
1st left & left again*

PETS: Public areas Exercise area adjacent disp bin
Facilities washing facs walks info vet info **Resident Pets:** Sophie
(German Shepherd)

Open all year Booking advisable Jul & Aug Last arrival
23.30hrs Last departure 14.00hrs

Welcoming, friendly owners set the tone for this well-maintained site,
ideally positioned on the border of the Dartmoor National Park. Along
with fine views and level grassy pitches, the Granite Way cycle track
from Lydford to Okehampton along the old railway line, part of the
Devon Coast to Coast cycle trail, passes the edge of the park. A
4.5-acre site with 38 touring pitches, 8 hardstandings.

Notes 🖾

STOKE GABRIEL
MAP 03 SX85

▶▶▶ **Broadleigh Farm Park** (SX851587)

Coombe House Ln, Aish TQ9 6PU

☎ 01803 782309 & 782110

e-mail: enquiries@broadleighfarm.co.uk

web: www.broadleighfarm.co.uk

Dir: *From Exeter on A38 then A380 towards Tor Bay. Right onto
A385 for Totnes. After 0.5m at Parkers Arms left for Stoke Gabriel.
Right after Whitehill Country Park to site*

PETS: Exercise area field adjacent **Resident Pets:** 1 dog, 2 cats

Open Mar-Oct Booking advisable all times Last arrival
21.00hrs Last departure 11.30hrs

Set in a very rural location on a working farm which borders Paignton
and Stoke Gabriel. The large sloping field with a new timber-clad toilet
block in the centre is sheltered and peaceful, surrounded by rolling
countryside but handy for the beaches. A 3-acre site with 35 touring
pitches.

Notes 🖾

TAVISTOCK
MAP 02 SX47

★★★ GUEST ACCOMMODATION
Coach House
PL19 8NS

☎ 01822 617515 ▤ 01822 617515

e-mail: estevens255@aol.com

web: www.thecoachousehotel.co.uk

Dir: *2.5m NW of Tavistock. A390 from Tavistock to Gulworthy
Cross, at rdbt take 3rd exit towards Chipshop Inn turn right to
Ottery, 1st building in village*

PETS: Bedrooms Public areas bar only **Grounds** accessible
Exercise area 20yds

Dating from 1857, this building was constructed for the Duke of
Bedford and converted by the current owners. Some bedrooms are on
the ground floor and in an adjacent barn conversion. Dinner is
available in the cosy dining room or the restaurant, which leads onto
the south-facing garden.

Rooms 6 en suite 3 annexe en suite (4 GF) S £45; D £64✲
Facilities TVB tea/coffee Direct dial from bedrooms Cen ht Dinner Last
d 9pm **Parking** 24 **Notes** LB No children 5yrs

ENGLAND

★★★ BED & BREAKFAST
Sampford Manor
Sampford Spiney PL20 6LH
☎ 01822 853442 ▤ 01822 855691
e-mail: manor@sampford-spiney.fsnet.co.uk
web: www.sampford-spiney.fsnet.co.uk

Dir: *B3357 towards Princetown, right at 1st x-rds. Next x-rds Warren Cross left for Sampford Spiney. 2nd right, house below church*

PETS: Bedrooms Sep Accom Barn **Stables** on site **Charges** £2 per night **Grounds** accessible disp bin **Exercise area** 200yds **Facilities** feeding mat leads washing facs cage storage walks info vet info **On Request** fridge access torch towels
Restrictions Telephone for details **Resident Pets:** Spin (Terrier/Springer cross), Cleo (Springer collie/cross), Monty (cat)

Once owned by Sir Francis Drake, this manor house is tucked away in a tranquil corner of Dartmoor National Park. The family home is full of character, with exposed beams and slate floors, whilst outside, a herd of award winning alpaca's graze in the fields. Genuine hospitality is assured together with scrumptious breakfasts featuring home-produced eggs.

Rooms 3 rms (2 pri facs) (1 fmly) ⊗ S £27-£35; D £45-£65✳
Facilities TVB tea/coffee Cen ht Golf **Parking** 3 **Notes** Closed Xmas ⊚

►►►► Higher Longford Caravan & Camping Park *(SX520747)*
Moorshop PL19 9LQ
☎ 01822 613360 & 07717 507434 ▤ 01822 618722
e-mail: stay@higherlongford.co.uk
web: www.higherlongford.co.uk

Dir: *From A30 to Tavistock take B3357 towards Princetown. 2m on right before hill onto moors*

PETS: Stables nearby (5m) **Charges** £1-£1.80 per night **Public areas** on leads **Exercise area** on site nature walks & fenced area provided moors 0.5m disp bin **Facilities** on site shop food food bowl water bowl disp bags washing facs walks info vet info **Resident Pets:** 2 Labradors

Open all year Booking advisable Etr, Jun-Oct Last arrival 21.00hrs Last departure noon

A very pleasant park in Dartmoor National Park, with panoramic views of the moors. The mainly grassy pitches are sheltered, and some are secluded for extra peace and quiet. Higher Longford is surrounded by moorland parks, lanes and pretty rivers, yet Tavistock is only 2.5m away. The park is well served with a shop. A 7-acre site with 82 touring pitches, 20 hardstandings and 4 statics.

Notes No bikes, skateboards or scooters

►►►► Woodovis Park *(SX431745)*
Gulworthy PL19 8NY
☎ 01822 832968 ▤ 01822 832948
e-mail: info@woodovis.com
web: www.woodovis.com

Dir: *A390 from Tavistock signed Callington & Gunnislake. At top of hill turn right at rdbt signed Lamerton & 'Chipshop'. Park 1m on left*

PETS: Public areas except buildings on leads **Exercise area** on site dog walks & woods disp bin **Facilities** on site shop disp bags washing facs walks info vet info **Other** prior notice required
Resident Pets: Border Collie (and at times Springer cross & cat)

Open 15 Mar-1 Nov Booking advisable Jun-Aug Last arrival 22.00hrs Last departure noon

A well-kept park in a remote woodland setting on the edge of the Tamar Valley. This peacefully-located park is set at the end of a half-mile private tree-lined road, and has lots of on-site facilities. The toilets are excellent, and there is an indoor swimming pool, all in a friendly, purposeful atmosphere. A 14.5-acre site with 50 touring pitches, 18 hardstandings and 35 statics.

►►► Harford Bridge Holiday Park *(SX504767)*
Peter Tavy PL19 9LS
☎ 01822 810349 ▤ 01822 810028
e-mail: enquiry@harfordbridge.co.uk
web: www.harfordbridge.co.uk

Dir: *2m N of Tavistock, off A386 Okehampton Rd, take Peter Tavy turn, entrance 200yds on right*

PETS: Public areas on leads at all times **Exercise area** on site 4-acre fenced field provided disp bin **Facilities** walks info vet info
Resident Pets: horses, ducks

Open all year (rs Nov-Mar statics only & 5 hardstanding pitches) Booking advisable Aug, Etr, BHs Last arrival 21.00hrs Last departure noon

This beautiful spacious park is set beside the River Tavy in the Dartmoor National Park. Pitches are located beside the river and around the copses, and the park is very well equipped for the holidaymaker. An adventure playground and games room entertain children, and there is fly-fishing and a free tennis court. A 16-acre site with 120 touring pitches, 5 hardstandings and 80 statics.

Notes No large groups

TAVISTOCK CONTINUED

►►► Langstone Manor Camping & Caravan Park *(SX524738)*

Moortown PL19 9JZ

☎ 01822 613371 📠 01822 613371

e-mail: jane@langstone-manor.co.uk

web: www.langstone-manor.co.uk

Dir: *Take B3357 from Tavistock to Princetown. Approx 1.5m turn right at x-rds, follow signs*

PETS: Public areas Exercise area moors adjacent **Facilities** leads washing facs walks info vet info disp bin **Other** prior notice required space for loose box **Resident Pets:** Moo (Russian Blue cat)

Open 15 Mar-Oct (rs wkdAys in low season restricted hours in bar & restaurant) Booking advisable BH & Jul-Aug Last arrival 22.00hrs Last departure 11.00hrs

A secluded site set in the well-maintained grounds of a manor house in Dartmoor National Park. Many attractive mature trees provide a screen within the park, and there is a popular lounge bar with an excellent menu of reasonably priced evening meals. Plenty of activities and places of interest can be found within the surrounding moorland. A 5.5-acre site with 40 touring pitches, 5 hardstandings and 25 statics.

Notes No skateboards, scooters, cycles, ball games

THURLESTONE   MAP 03 SX64

★★★★ 79% ⊛ HOTEL
Thurlestone

TQ7 3NN

☎ 01548 560382 📠 01548 561069

e-mail: enquiries@thurlestone.co.uk

web: www.thurlestone.co.uk

Dir: *A38 take A384 into Totnes, A381 towards Kingsbridge, onto A379 towards Churchstow, onto B3197 turn into lane signed to Thurlestone*

PETS: Bedrooms unattended sign **Stables** nearby **Charges** £6 per night, charge for damage **Public areas** front foyer on leads **Grounds** accessible **Facilities** food (pre-bookable) pet sitting dog walking washing facs cage storage walks info vet info **On Request** fridge access torch towels

This perennially popular hotel has been in the same family-ownership since 1896 and continues to go from strength to strength. A vast range of facilities are available for all the family and include indoor and outdoor pools, golf course and beauty salon. Bedrooms are equipped to ensure a comfortable stay with many having wonderful views of the South Devon coast. A range of eating options includes the elegant and stylish restaurant with its stunning views.

Thurlestone

Rooms 64 en suite (23 fmly) S £87-£175; D £174-£350 (incl. bkfst)✳ **Facilities** STV ⊛ ↻ pool supervised ♨9 ♨ Squash Gym ↯ Putt green Wi-fi available Badminton courts Games room ♫ ch fac Xmas New Year **Services** Lift **Parking** 121 **Notes** LB Closed 1-2 wks Jan

TIVERTON   MAP 03 SS91

★★★ 72% HOTEL
Best Western Tiverton

Blundells Rd EX16 4DB

☎ 01884 256120 📠 01884 258101

e-mail: sales@tivertonhotel.co.uk

web: www.bw-tivertonhotel.co.uk

Dir: *A396 follow signs for town centre. Right at 2nd rdbt & immediately right into Blundells Rd. Hotel on right.*

PETS: Bedrooms unattended **Charges** £10 per night **Grounds** accessible **Exercise area** 200mtrs

Conveniently situated on the outskirts of the town, with easy access to the M5, this comfortable hotel has a relaxed atmosphere. The spacious bedrooms are well equipped and decorated in a contemporary style. A formal dining option is offered in the Gallery Restaurant, and lighter snacks are served in the bar area. Room service is extensive, as is the range of conference facilities.

Rooms 69 en suite (4 fmly) (30 GF) ⊘ in all bedrooms S £55-£95; D £75-£135 (incl. bkfst)✳ **Facilities** STV Fishing Wi-fi in bedrooms Xmas New Year **Services** Lift **Parking** 130 **Notes** LB

★★★★ 🏠 ➶ FARM HOUSE
Rhode Farm House *(SS967102)*

Exeter Hill EX16 4PL

☎ 01884 242853 📠 01884 242853 Mr & Mrs D Boulton

e-mail: david@rhodefarmhouse.com

web: www.rhodefarmhouse.com

Dir: *Signs to Grand Western Canal, right fork signed Exeter Hill, farmhouse 3m on left*

PETS: Stables on site **Charges** stabling £15 per night **Resident Pets:** Buster & Kitty (Fox Terriers), Fritz (cat), Miss Mouse & Tess (horses)

Guests receive a very warm welcome at Rhode Farm House. It stands in 5 acres with stables in the yard, a 30-minute drive from Exeter city centre. Bedrooms are finished with many considerate extras and there is an inviting lounge with a log fire for colder nights. A delicious breakfast, featuring local produce, is served around a communal table in the dining room. Carefully prepared and presented dinners are available by arrangement.

Rooms 2 en suite (2 fmly) ⊘ S £30-£38.50; D £55-£60✻ **Facilities** TVB tea/coffee Cen ht TVL Dinner Last d noon Riding **Parking** 5 **Notes** ⊗ No children 4yrs 4 acres

---

TORQUAY MAP 03 SX96

★★★ 74% HOTEL
Belgrave
Seafront TQ2 5HE
☎ 01803 296666 📠 01803 211308
e-mail: info@belgrave-hotel.co.uk
web: www.belgrave-hotel.co.uk

Dir: *on A380 into Torquay, continue to lights (Torre Station on right). Right into Avenue Road to Kings Drive. Left at seafront, hotel at lights*

PETS: Bedrooms (GF) unattended sign **Charges** £10 per night **Grounds** accessible disp bin **Exercise area** on site **Facilities** food (pre-bookable) dog scoop/disp bags washing facs cage storage walks info vet info **On Request** fridge access torch towels **Restrictions** dogs no larger than a standard poodle

Enjoying an impressive position overlooking Torbay, the Belgrave offers a range of spacious and well-appointed public rooms, including comfortable lounges, the elegant restaurant and outdoor pool and patio areas. The Dickens bar is particularly stylish, and offers an innovative menu, featuring local produce. A variety of bedroom styles is available and many have the advantage of stunning sea views.

Rooms 72 en suite (20 fmly) (18 GF) ⊘ in 61 bedrooms S fr £65; D £130-£174 (incl. bkfst) **Facilities** ↘ Wi-fi in bedrooms ♫ Xmas New Year **Services** Lift **Parking** 90

★★ 68% HOTEL
Red House Hotel & Maxton Lodge Apartments
Rousdown Rd, Chelston TQ2 6PB
☎ 01803 607811 📠 01803 200592
e-mail: stay@redhouse-hotel.co.uk
web: www.redhouse-hotel.co.uk

Dir: *towards seafront/Chelston, turn into Avenue Rd, 1st lights turn right. Past shops & church, take next left. Hotel on right*

PETS: Bedrooms (GF) unattended **Charges** £3 per night charge for damage **Public areas** except dining area & lounge on leads **Exercise area** 100yds **Facilities** vet info **Resident Pets:** Jemima (cat)

This friendly hotel enjoys pleasant views over Torbay in a quiet residential area of the town. Bedrooms vary in size but are generally spacious, comfortable and well appointed. Extensive leisure facilities are on offer including an outdoor and indoor pool, a gym and beauty treatment rooms.

Red House Hotel & Maxton Lodge Apartments

Rooms 9 en suite (3 fmly) S £55-£65; D £110-£130 (incl. bkfst & dinner) ✻ **Facilities** ↘ ↘ Gym Sun shower Beauty room Xmas New Year **Parking** 9 **Notes** LB

★★★ GUEST HOUSE
The Palms
537 Babbacombe Rd TQ1 1HQ
☎ 01803 293970 📠 01803 298573
e-mail: thepalmshotel@yahoo.co.uk
web: www.palmshoteltorquay.co.uk

Dir: *On A379, 300yds from Torquay Harbour opp Torwood Gardens*

PETS: Bedrooms Charges £5 per night (dogs only) **Public areas** except breakfast room on leads **Exercise area** 20yds **Facilities** food bowl water bowl cage storage walks info vet info **On Request** fridge access torch towels

The owners of Palms extend a very warm welcome. Family friendly, it offers comfortable accommodation, with books, games and videos available for children, and the cybercafé, well-stocked bar and bar meals are welcome facilities. Breakfast is served in the dining room overlooking Torwood Gardens.

Rooms 9 en suite (2 fmly) ⊘ S £25-£30; D £49-£65 **Facilities** FTV TVB tea/coffee Licensed Cen ht TVL Dinner Last d 6pm Wi-fi available **Parking** 2 **Notes** LB No coaches

---

★★★ GUEST ACCOMMODATION
Stover Lodge Hotel
29 Newton Rd TQ2 5DB
☎ 01803 297287 📠 01803 297287
e-mail: enquiries@stoverlodge.co.uk
web: www.stoverlodge.co.uk

Dir: *Signs to Torquay town centre, at station/Halfords left lane, Lodge on left after lights*

PETS: Bedrooms unattended

Located close to the town centre, the family-run Stover Lodge is relaxed and friendly. Children and babies are welcome, and a cot and high chair can be provided on request. Hearty breakfasts, with a vegetarian option, are served in the dining room. There is a garden to enjoy in summer.

Rooms 9 rms (8 en suite) (1 pri facs) (3 fmly) (2 GF) ⊘ S £22-£35; D £44-£50 **Facilities** FTV TVB tea/coffee Cen ht **Parking** 10 **Notes** LB ⊗

ENGLAND

▶▶▶▶ Widdicombe Farm Touring Park

(SX880650)

Marldon TQ3 1ST

☎ 01803 558325

e-mail: info@widdicombefarm.co.uk

web: www.widdicombefarm.co.uk

Dir: *On A380, midway between Torquay & Paignton ring road*

PETS: Charges £1.50-£2.50 per night £10.50-£16 per week
Public areas except buildings **Exercise area** on site small field
disp bin **Facilities** on site shop food bowl water bowl disp bags
walks info vet info **Restrictions** dogs on short leads only; certain
breeds not accepted **Resident Pets:** 2 Border Collies, 1 Jack
Russell, cat

Open mid Mar-mid Oct Booking advisable Whit & Jul-Aug Last
arrival 21.00hrs Last departure 10.00hrs

A friendly family-owned and run park on a working farm, with good
quality facilities and extensive views. The level pitches are terraced to
take advantage of the views towards the coast and Dartmoor. A quiet
but happy atmosphere pervades this park, encouraged by a large
children's play area. Other amenities include a well-stocked shop, a
restaurant, and a lounge bar. There is an adults-only field. An 8-acre
site with 196 touring pitches, 180 hardstandings and 3 statics.

Notes Families & couples only, 1 family field, 3 adults only fields

---

★★★★ GUEST ACCOMMODATION

The Red Slipper

Stoke Gabriel TQ9 6RU

☎ 01803 782315

e-mail: enquiries@redslipper.co.uk

web: www.redslipper.co.uk

Dir: *Off A385 S to Stoke Gabriel. Opp Church House Inn*

PETS: Bedrooms Public areas except dining room
Exercise area 10mtrs **Facilities** water bowl cat treats cage
storage walks info vet info **On Request** fridge access torch
towels **Resident Pets:** Tara & Tico (Siamese cats)

An ideal base for exploring the South Hams or just for a relaxing break,
this delightful 1920s house is hidden away in the picturesque village of
Stoke Gabriel. The bedrooms have many extra facilities. Well-cooked
dinners are served by arrangement, and feature local produce.

Rooms 3 en suite ⊘ **Facilities** TVB tea/coffee Cen ht TVL Dinner Last
d 9am **Parking** 4

★★ 83% ⚜ COUNTRY HOUSE HOTEL

Prince Hall

PL20 6SA

☎ 01822 890403 📠 01822 890676

e-mail: info@princehall.co.uk

web: www.princehall.co.uk

Dir: *on B3357 1m E of Two Bridges road junct*

PETS: Bedrooms Stables nearby (5m) **Public areas** except
restaurant **Grounds** accessible disp bin **Exercise area** adjacent
Facilities Water bowl dog chews dog scoop/disp bags leads
wash fac walks info vet info **On Request** fridge access torch
towels **Resident Pets:** Cello (Bouvier de Flandres)

Charm, peace and relaxed informality pervade at this small hotel,
which has a stunning location at the heart of Dartmoor. Bedrooms,
each named after a Dartmoor tor, have been equipped with thoughtful
extras. The history of the house and its location are reflected
throughout the public areas, which are very comfortable. The
accomplished cooking is memorable. Dogs are welcomed here as
warmly as their owners.

Rooms 8 en suite ⊘ in all bedrooms S £60-£95; D £170-£250 (incl. bkfst
& dinner)✳ **Facilities** Fishing Riding ⚒ Guided Dartmoor Walks Fly
fishing Garden tours arranged Art breaks Xmas New Year **Parking** 13
Notes No children 10yrs Closed 2 Jan-2 Feb

★★ 76% HOTEL

Two Bridges Hotel

PL20 6SW

☎ 01822 890581 📠 01822 892306

e-mail: enquiries@twobridges.co.uk

web: www.twobridges.co.uk

Dir: *junct of B3212 & B3357*

PETS: Bedrooms (GF) unattended **Public areas** except restaurant
on leads **Grounds** accessible on leads disp bin **Facilities** water
bowl dog chews washing facs cage storage walks info vet info
On Request fridge access torch towels

This wonderfully relaxing hotel is set in the heart of the Dartmoor
National Park, in a beautiful riverside location. Three standards of
comfortable rooms provide every modern convenience. There is a
choice of lounges and fine dining is available in the restaurant, with
menus featuring local game and seasonal produce.

Rooms 33 en suite (2 fmly) (6 GF) ⊘ in 11 bedrooms S £65-£90;
D £130-£180 (incl. bkfst)✳ **Facilities** STV Fishing Xmas New Year
Parking 100 **Notes** LB

ENGLAND

UMBERLEIGH — MAP 03 SS62

▶▶▶ Umberleigh Camping & Caravanning Club Site (SS604241)

Over Weir EX37 9DU

☎ 01769 560009

web: www.campingandcaravanningclub.co.uk/umberleigh

Dir: *On A377 from Barnstaple turn right at Umberleigh sign onto B3227. Site on right in 0.25m*

PETS: Public areas except buildings **Exercise area** on site disp bin **Facilities** walks info vet info **Other** prior notice required

Open 13 Mar-29 Sept Booking advisable BH & peak periods Last arrival 21.00hrs Last departure noon

There are fine country views from this compact site set on high ground. The site has the advantage of a games room with table tennis and skittle alley, and two quality tennis courts, with an adjacent wooded area for walks, and a nearby fishing pond. A 3-acre site with 60 touring pitches, 12 hardstandings.

Notes Site gates closed 23.00-07.00.

WESTWARD HO! — MAP 02 SS42

★★★ GUEST HOUSE

Culloden House

Fosketh Hill EX39 1UL

☎ 01237 479421

e-mail: enquiry@culloden-house.co.uk

web: www.culloden-house.co.uk

Dir: *S of town centre. Off B3236 Stanwell Hill onto Fosketh Hill*

PETS: Bedrooms (GF) **Public areas** except dining room on leads **Grounds** accessible on leads **Exercise area** short walk **Facilities** washing facs cage storage walks info vet info **On Request** fridge access torch towels **Resident Pets:** Pippa (Jack Russell cross)

This Victorian property stands on a wooded hillside with sweeping views over the beach and coast. A warm welcome is assured in this family friendly house. Guests can relax in the spacious lounge with its log-burning fire and enjoy the wonderful sea views.

Rooms 5 en suite (3 fmly) (1 GF) ⊗ S £35-£45; D £60-£70✱ **Facilities** TVB tea/coffee Cen ht TVL **Parking** available **Notes** No coaches Closed Xmas

WITHERIDGE — MAP 03 SS81

▶▶▶ West Middlewick Farm Caravan & Camping Site (SS826136)

Nomansland EX16 8NP

☎ 01884 861235 📠 01884 861235

e-mail: stay@westmiddlewick.co.uk

web: www.westmiddlewick.co.uk

Dir: *From M5 junct 27, A361 to Tiverton. Then B3137, follow Witheridge signs. Site 1m past Nomansland on right (8m from Tiverton)*

PETS: Stables nearby (loose box) **Charges** 50p per dog per night **Public areas** on leads **Exercise area** on site disp bin **Facilities** washing facs walks info vet info

Open all year Booking advisable Jul-Aug Last arrival 22.00hrs Last departure noon

A working dairy farm on a ridge west of the hamlet of Nomansland, with extensive rural views. This upgraded park offers campers a quiet and relaxing break, and is approximately one mile from the attractive and charming village of Witheridge which has a variety of amenities. A 3.5-acre site with 25 touring pitches, 16 hardstandings.

Notes ⊛ Children must be supervised

YELVERTON — MAP 02 SX56

★★★ 74% ⊛ HOTEL

Moorland Links

PL20 6DA

☎ 01822 852245 📠 01822 855004

e-mail: moorland.links@forestdale.com

web: www.forestdale.com

Dir: *A38 from Exeter to Plymouth, then A386 towards Tavistock. 5m onto open moorland, hotel 1m on left*

PETS: Bedrooms unattended **Charges** £7.50 per night **Public areas** except restaurant **Grounds** accessible

In Dartmoor National Park, set in nine acres of well-tended grounds, Moorland Links has spectacular views from many of the rooms across open moorland and the Tamar Valley. Bedrooms are well equipped and comfortably furnished, and some rooms have open balconies. A popular hotel for weddings, and a number of spacious meeting rooms are also available.

Rooms 44 en suite (4 fmly) (17 GF) ⊗ in 20 bedrooms **Facilities** STV ⊌ Wi-fi available **Parking** 120

DORSET

ALDERHOLT
MAP 04 SU11

▶▶▶▶ **Hill Cottage Farm Camping and Caravan Park** *(SU119133)*

Sandleheath Rd SP6 3EG

☎ 01425 650513 📠 01425 652339

Dir: *Take B3078 W of Fordingbridge. Turn off at Alderholt, site 0.25m on left after railway bridge*

PETS: Stables on site (loose box) **Charges** £1 per dog per night **Public areas** except fields **Exercise area** on site dog walks public footpath 100yds **Facilities** washing facs dog grooming walks info vet info **Other** prior notice required pet shop 0.25m

Open Mar-Oct Booking advisable BH & Jul-Aug Last arrival 19.00hrs Last departure 11.00hrs

Set within extensive grounds this rural, beautifully landscaped park has mainly full facility pitches set in individual hardstanding bays with mature hedges between giving adequate pitch privacy. A modern toilet block is kept immaculately clean, and there's a good range of leisure facilities. In high season there is an area available for tenting. 34 touring pitches, 34 hardstandings.

Notes ✆

BEAMINSTER
MAP 03 ST40

★★★ 78% ⊛ HOTEL
Bridge House

3 Prout Bridge DT8 3AY

☎ 01308 862200 📠 01308 863700

e-mail: enquiries@bridge-house.co.uk

web: www.bridge-house.co.uk

Dir: *off A3066, 100yds from Town Square*

PETS: Bedrooms (GF) **Charges** £15 pe stay **Grounds** accessible **Exercise area** country walks **Facilities** vet info

Dating back to the 13th century, this property offers friendly and attentive service. Bedrooms are tastefully furnished and decorated; those in the main house are generally more spacious than those in the adjacent coach house. Smartly presented public areas include the Georgian dining room, cosy bar and adjacent lounge, together with a breakfast room overlooking the attractive garden.

Rooms 9 en suite 5 annexe en suite (1 fmly) (5 GF) ⊗ in all bedrooms S £50-£90; D £116-£180✻ **Facilities** Wi-fi in bedrooms ch fac Xmas New Year **Parking** 20 **Notes** LB

BLANDFORD FORUM
MAP 03 ST80

★★★★ INN
The Anvil Inn

Salisbury Rd, Pimperne DT11 8UQ

☎ 01258 453431 📠 01258 480182

e-mail: theanvil.inn@btconnect.com

Dir: *2m NE of Blandford on A354 in Pimperne*

PETS:Bedrooms unattended **Charges** £10 per night **Public areas** Bar only **Exercise area** nearby

Located in a village near Blandford, this 16th-century thatched inn provides a traditional country welcome with plenty of character. Bedrooms have been refurbished to high standards. Dinner is a varied selection of home-made dishes with a tempting variety of hand-pulled ales and wines by the glass.

Rooms 13 en suite (1 GF) S £70-£75; D £95-£110✻ **Facilities** STV TVB tea/coffee Direct dial from bedrooms Cen ht Dinner Last d 9.30pm **Parking** 18 **Notes** LB No coaches

★★★★ 🍽 BED & BREAKFAST
St Martin's House

Whitecliff Mill St DT11 7BP

☎ 01258 451245 & 07748 887719

e-mail: info@stmartinshouse.co.uk

Dir: *Off Market Pl onto Salisbury St & left onto White Cliff Mill St, on right before traffic island*

PETS: Bedrooms **Charges** £5 per night charge for damage **Exercise area** nearby **Facilities** food bowl water bowl medium size dog beds, cage available walks info vet info **On Request** torch towels

Dating from 1866, this restored property was once part of the chorister's house for a local church. The bedrooms are comfortable and well equipped. The hosts offer warm hospitality and attentive service. Breakfast, which features local and home-made items, is enjoyed around a communal table. Carefully prepared dinners are available by arrangement.

Rooms 2 rms (2 pri facs) (1 fmly) ⊗ S fr £40; D fr £60✻ **Facilities** TVB tea/coffee Cen ht Dinner Last d 24hrs before **Parking** 3 **Notes** Closed 22 Dec-6 Jan ✆

▶▶▶▶ The Inside Park *(ST869046)*

Down House Estate DT11 9AD

☎ 01258 453719 📄 01258 459921

e-mail: inspark@aol.com

web: http://members.aol.com/inspark/inspark

Dir: *From town, over River Stour, follow Winterborne Stickland signs. Site in 1.5m*

PETS: Sep Accom day kennels **Charges** 60p-£1 per night
Public areas 50% of site **Exercise area** on site 6m private woods & farm walks disp bin **Facilities** on site shop food walks info vet info **Other** prior notice required

Open Etr-Oct Booking advisable BH & Jul-Aug Last arrival 22.00hrs Last departure noon

An attractive, well-sheltered and quiet park, 0.5m off a country lane in a wooded valley. Spacious pitches are divided by mature trees and shrubs, and amenities are housed in an 18th-century coach house and stables. There are some lovely woodland walks within the park. A 12-acre site with 125 touring pitches.

BOURNEMOUTH

MAP 04 SZ09

★★★ 75% HOTEL

Carrington House

31 Knyveton Rd BH1 3QQ

☎ 01202 369988 📄 01202 292221

e-mail: carrington.house@forestdale.com

web: www.forestdale.com

Dir: *A338 at St Paul's rdbt, continue 200mtrs & turn left into Knyveton Rd. Hotel 400mtrs on right*

PETS: Bedrooms unattended **Charges** £7.50 per night
Public areas except restaurant

This hotel occupies a prominent position on a tree-lined avenue and a short walk from the seafront. Bedrooms are generally spacious, comfortable and usefully equipped. In addition to the hotel's bar and restaurant there are extensive conference facilities and a leisure complex.

Rooms 145 en suite (42 fmly) ⊘ in 40 bedrooms **Facilities** STV ⊗ supervised Wi-fi in bedrooms Purpose built childrens play area **Services** Lift **Parking** 85

★★★ 75% HOTEL

Wessex

West Cliff Rd BH2 5EU

☎ 01202 551911 📄 01202 297354

e-mail: wessex@forestdale.com

web: www.forestdale.com

Dir: *Follow M27/A35 or A338 from Dorchester & A347 N. Hotel on West Cliff side of town*

PETS: Bedrooms unattended **Charges** £7.50 per night
Public areas except restaurant **Grounds** accessible

Centrally located and handy for the beach, the Wessex is a popular, relaxing hotel. Bedrooms vary in size and include premier rooms; all are comfortable, and equipped with a range of modern amenities. There are excellent leisure facilities, ample function rooms and an open-plan bar and lounge.

Rooms 109 en suite (32 fmly) (17 GF) ⊘ in 76 bedrooms **Facilities** STV ⊗ ⊸ supervised Gym Wi-fi in bedrooms Table tennis **Services** Lift **Parking** 160

★★★ 67% HOTEL

Burley Court

Bath Rd BH1 2NP

☎ 01202 552824 & 556704 📄 01202 298514

e-mail: info@burleycourthotel.co.uk

Dir: *leave A338 at St Pauls rdbt, take 3rd exit at next rdbt into Holdenhurst Rd. 3rd exit at next rdbt into Bath Rd, over crossing, 1st left*

PETS: Bedrooms (GF) unattended **Charges** £9 per night (dog), other pets rates on request charge for damage **Facilities** food (pre-bookable) cooked meat & vegetables (not tinned) can be provided walks info vet info **On Request** fridge access torch

Located on Bournemouth's West Cliff, this well-established hotel is easily located and convenient for the town and beaches. Bedrooms, many now refurbished, are pleasantly furnished and decorated in bright colours. A daily-changing menu is served in the spacious dining room.

Rooms 38 en suite (8 fmly) (4 GF) ⊘ in 20 bedrooms S £36-£50; D £72-£100 (incl. bkfst)✳ **Facilities** ⊸ Xmas **Services** Lift **Parking** 35 **Notes LB** Closed 30 Dec-14 Jan RS 15-31 Jan

ENGLAND

BOURNEMOUTH CONTINUED

⚘ 🐱 📻 🛏

★★★ 67% HOTEL
Heathlands Hotel
12 Grove Rd, East Cliff BH1 3AY
☎ 01202 553336 📠 01202 555937
e-mail: info@heathlandshotel.com
web: www.heathlandshotel.com
Dir: *A338 St Pauls rdbt 1st exit to East Cliff, 3rd exit at next rdbt to Holdenhurst Rd, 2nd exit off Lansdowne rdbt into Meyrick Rd. Left into Gervis Rd. Hotel on right*
PETS: Bedrooms (GF) **Charges** £5 (dogs) per night
Facilities cage storage vet info **On Request** fridge access torch towels

This is a large hotel on the East Cliff benefiting from an outdoor pool in summer and indoor fitness centre all year round. The Heathlands is popular with many groups and conferences, public areas are bright and spacious and the bedrooms offer a range of quality and comfort. Regular live entertainment is provided for guests.

Rooms 115 en suite (16 fmly) (11 GF) ⊗ in 15 bedrooms S £30-£60; D £50-£110 (incl. bkfst) **Facilities** STV ⊰ Gym Health suite Sauna ♫ Xmas New Year **Services** Lift **Parking** 100

★★ 71% HOTEL
Whitehall
Exeter Park Rd BH2 5AX
☎ 01202 554682 📠 01202 292637
e-mail: reservations@thewhitehallhotel.co.uk
web: www.thewhitehallhotel.co.uk
Dir: *follow BIC signs then turn into Exeter Park Rd off Exeter Rd*
PETS: Bedrooms unattended **Charges** £2 per night
Grounds accessible **Exercise area** green 50mtrs

This friendly hotel enjoys an elevated position overlooking the park and is also close to the town centre and seafront. The spacious public areas include a choice of lounges, a cosy bar and a well-presented restaurant. The bedrooms are spread over three floors and are inviting and well equipped.

Rooms 46 en suite (5 fmly) (3 GF) ⊗ in 20 bedrooms **Facilities** ♫ **Services** Lift **Parking** 25 **Notes** LB

BRIDPORT
MAP 03 SY49

⚘ 🐱 📻 🛏

★★ 67% HOTEL
Bridge House

115 East St DT6 3LB
☎ 01308 423371 📠 01308 459573
e-mail: info@bridgehousebridport.co.uk
Dir: *follow signs to town centre from A35 rdbt, hotel 200mtrs on right*
PETS: Bedrooms unattended **Public areas** except restaurant **Grounds** accessible disp bin **Exercise area** park adjacent **Charges** charge for damage **Facilities** vet info **On request** access to fridge

A short stroll from the town centre, this 18th-century Grade II listed property offers well-equipped bedrooms that vary in size. In addition to the main lounge, there is a small bar-lounge and a separate breakfast room. An interesting range of home-cooked meals is provided in the restaurant.

Rooms 10 en suite (3 fmly) ⊗ in all bedrooms S £59-£82; D £89-£122 (incl. bkfst) **Facilities** Wi-fi in bedrooms Complimentary membership to leisure park. New Year **Parking** 13 **Notes** LB

⚘ 📻 🛏

★★★★ GUEST ACCOMMODATION
Britmead House
West Bay Rd DT6 4EG
☎ 01308 422941 & 07973 725243
e-mail: britmead@talk21.com
web: www.britmeadhouse.co.uk
Dir: *1m S of town centre, off A35 onto West Bay Rd*
PETS: Bedrooms Public areas on leads **Grounds** accessible on leads **Exercise area** 100mtrs **Facilities** washing facs cage storage walks info vet info **On Request** fridge access towels

Britmead House is located south of Bridport, within easy reach of the town centre and West Bay harbour. Family-run, the atmosphere is friendly and the accommodation well-appointed and comfortable. Suitable for business and leisure, many guests return regularly. A choice of breakfast is served in the light and airy dining room.

Rooms 8 en suite (2 fmly) (2 GF) ⊗ S £40-£50; D £58-£74✳ **Facilities** TVB tea/coffee Cen ht TVL **Parking** 12 **Notes** LB

THE INDEPENDENTS
HOTEL ASSOCIATION

CASHMOOR MAP 03 ST91

★★★★ ≜ FARM HOUSE
Cashmoor House *(ST974136)*
DT11 8DN
☎ 01725 552339 Mrs M E Jones
e-mail: spencer@cashmoorhouse.co.uk
Dir: *On A354 Salisbury to Blandford, 3m S of Sixpenny Handley rdbt just past Inn on the Chase*
PETS: Bedrooms Public areas on leads **Exercise area Restrictions** small-medium size dogs only, 2 pets max no Rottweilers, German Shepherds **Resident Pets:** Holly & Daisy (Springer Spaniels), Grumpy (cat)
Situated halfway between Blandford and Salisbury, parts of Cashmoor House date from the 17th century. The attractive property retains much original character and has a warm and homely farmhouse ambience. Traditional Aga-cooked breakfasts, featuring home-made bread and preserves, and eggs laid by the owners' hens, are served in the beamed dining room.
Rooms 4 en suite (2 fmly) (2 GF) ⊘ S £30-£35; D £50✲ **Facilities** TVB tea/coffee Cen ht TVL **Parking** 8 **Notes** 8 acres pheasant rearing, hens, sheep ⊗

CERNE ABBAS MAP 03 ST60

▶▶ **Lyons Gate Caravan and Camping Park** *(ST660062)*
Lyons Gate DT2 7AZ
☎ 01300 345260
e-mail: info@lyons-gate.co.uk
web: www.lyons-gate.co.uk
Dir: *Signed with direct access from A352, 3m N of Cerne Abbas*
PETS: Charges 50p per night **Public areas Exercise area** on site disp bin **Facilities** on site shop walks info vet info **Other** prior notice required
Open all year Booking advisable peak times Last arrival 20.00hrs Last departure 11.30hrs
A peaceful park with pitches set out around the four attractive coarse fishing lakes. It is surrounded by mature woodland, with many footpaths and bridleways. Other easily accessible attractions include the Cerne Giant carved into the hills, the old market town of Dorchester, and the superb sandy beach at Weymouth. A 10-acre site with 90 touring pitches, 14 hardstandings.
Notes ⊗

▶▶ **Giant's Head Caravan & Camping Park** *(ST675029)*
Giants Head Farm, Old Sherborne Rd DT2 7TR
☎ 01300 341242
e-mail: holidays@giantshead.co.uk
web: www.giantshead.co.uk
Dir: *From Dorchester into town avoiding by-pass, at Top O'Town rdbt take Sherborne road, 500yds right fork at Esso (Loder's garage) site signed. From Sherborne take left hand fork at Middlemarsh off A352.*
PETS: Charges £1 per night **Public areas** only part of site **Exercise area** on site & adjacent disp bin **Facilities** vet info **Other** prior notice required
Open Etr-Oct (rs Etr shop & bar closed) Booking advisable Aug Last arrival anytime Last departure 13.00hrs
A pleasant though rather basic park set in Dorset downland near the Cerne Giant (the local landmark figure cut into the chalk) with stunning views. A good stopover site, ideal for tenters and backpackers on the Ridgeway route. A 4-acre site with 50 touring pitches.
Notes ⊗

CHARMOUTH MAP 03 SY39

▶▶▶▶▶ **Wood Farm Caravan & Camping Park** *(SY356940)*
Axminster Rd DT6 6BT
☎ 01297 560697 01297 561243
e-mail: holidays@woodfarm.co.uk
web: www.woodfarm.co.uk
Dir: *Park entered directly off A35 rdbt, on Axminster side of Charmouth*
PETS: Stables nearby (4m) **Charges** £2 per dog per night **Public areas** except play area & buildings **Exercise area** on site 2 acre dog walk 200mtrs **Facilities** on site shop food food bowl water bowl walks info vet info **Resident Pets:** dog, cats, sheep, chickens
Open Etr-Oct Booking advisable school hols Last arrival 19.00hrs Last departure noon
A pleasant, well-established and mature park overlooking Charmouth, the sea and the Dorset hills and valleys. It stands on a high spot, and the four camping fields are terraced, each with its own impressive toilet block. Convenient for Lyme Regis, Axminster, and the famous fossil coastline. A 13-acre site with 216 touring pitches, 175 hardstandings and 81 statics.
Notes No skateboards, scooters or roller skates

CHARMOUTH CONTINUED

►►►► Charmouth Camping & Caravanning Club Site *(SY330965)*

Monkton Wylde Farm DT6 6DB

☎ 01297 32965

web: www.campingandcaravanningclub.co.uk/charmouth

Dir: *From Dorchester on A35 turn right onto B3165 signed Hawkchurch, site on left in 0.25m*

PETS: Public areas except buildings **Exercise area** on site & Charmouth and Lyme Regis beaches disp bin **Facilities** walks info vet info **Other** prior notice required

Open 13 Mar-3 Mar Booking advisable BH & peak periods Last arrival 21.00hrs Last departure noon

Located in a rural setting almost on the Devon/Dorset border, this attractively terraced park with high quality toilet facilities is ideally placed for visiting the resorts of Charmouth, Lyme Regis and the Jurassic Coast. Friendly managers keep the whole park in tiptop condition. A 12-acre site with 125 touring pitches, 34 hardstandings.

Notes Site gates closed 23.00-07.00

►►►► Monkton Wyld Farm Caravan Park

(SY336964)

DT6 6DB

☎ 01297 34525 & 631131 (May-Sep) 🖳 01297 33594

e-mail: holidays@monktonwyld.co.uk

web: www.monktonwyld.co.uk

Dir: *From Charmouth on A35 towards Axminster, after approx 3m (ignore 1st sign to Monkton Wyld - road very steep) take next right signed Marshwood. Site 500mtrs on left*

PETS: Stables on site (loose box) **Public areas Exercise area** on site dog walk woods 100yds disp bin **Facilities** on site shop washing facs walks info vet info **Restrictions** no dangerous dogs (see page 7)

Open Etr-Oct Booking advisable school hols Last arrival 22.00hrs Last departure 11.00hrs

An attractive family park in a secluded location yet central for Charmouth, Lyme and the coast. It has been tastefully designed in a maturing landscape, with perimeter trees providing a screen, and every pitch backed by hedges or shrubs. A 20-acre site with 150 touring pitches, 79 hardstandings.

►►► Manor Farm Holiday Centre *(SY368937)*

DT6 6QL

☎ 01297 560226

e-mail: enq@manorfarmholidaycentre.co.uk

web: www.manorfarmholidaycentre.co.uk

Dir: *W on A35 to Charmouth, site 0.75m on right*

PETS: Charges £1-£3 per night **Public areas** except pool, bar, shop, restaurant **Exercise area** on site Open field available disp bin **Facilities** on site shop food vet info **Other** prior notice required

Open all year (rs End Oct-mid Mar statics only) Booking advisable high season Last arrival 20.00hrs Last departure 10.00hrs

Set just a short walk from the safe sand and shingle beach at Charmouth, this popular family park offers a good range of facilities. Children enjoy the activity area and outdoor swimming pool (so do their parents!), and the park also offers a lively programme in the extensive new bar and entertainment complex. A 15-acre site with 250 touring pitches, 80 hardstandings and 29 statics.

Notes No skateboards

CHRISTCHURCH MAP 04 SZ19

★★★ INN

Fishermans Haunt

Winkton BH23 7AS

☎ 01202 477283 🖳 01202 478883

e-mail: fishermanshaunt@accommodating-inns.co.uk

web: www.accommodating-inns.co.uk

Dir: *2m N of Christchurch. On B3347 in Winkton*

PETS: Bedrooms Public areas

Dating from 1673 and situated close to the River Avon, this characterful inn is poular with anglers and country-lovers alike. Bedrooms, some of which are suitable for families, offer comfortable accommodation with many added extras including satellite television. Real ales and wholesome cuisine can be enjoyed in the spacious restaurant and lounge bars, which have log fires in colder months.

Rooms 3 en suite 14 annexe en suite (2 fmly) (6 GF) **Facilities** TVB tea/coffee Direct dial from bedrooms Cen ht Dinner Last d 9pm Fishing **Parking** 70

DORCHESTER
MAP 03 SY69

★★★★★ ⟶ GUEST HOUSE
Yalbury Cottage Hotel & Restaurant
Lower Bockhampton DT2 8PZ

☎ 01305 262382

e-mail: yalburyemails@aol.com

Dir: *Off A35 past Thomas Hardys cottage, over x-rds, 400yds on left, past telephone box, opp village pump*

PETS: Bedrooms Charges £6 per night **Grounds** accessible **Exercise area** open countryside **Facilities** food

A fine country cottage with thatched roof and lots of character. The hosts are attentive and the atmosphere is friendly and relaxed. Bedrooms are comfortable and homely. Guests can enjoy a drink in the cosy lounge before feasting on freshly prepared dishes from the daily fixed-price menu. The beamed restaurant is open to the public for dinner.

Rooms 8 en suite (1 fmly) (6 GF) **Facilities** TVB tea/coffee Direct dial from bedrooms Licensed Cen ht Dinner Last d 9pm **Parking** 16 **Notes** No coaches

Nigel & Sarah wish you a warm welcome & invite you to try their extensive menu, fine wine list and real ales.

Sumptuous 21-room accommodation • 17th Century Restaurant • Riverside Garden

The Poachers Inn Piddletrenthide Dorchester Dorset DT2 7QX
tel: 01300 348358 info@thepoachersinn.co.uk www.thepoachersinn.co.uk

EVERSHOT
MAP 03 ST50

★★★★ ◉◉◉ COUNTRY HOUSE HOTEL
Summer Lodge Country House Hotel
DT2 0JR

☎ 01935 482000 ▤ 01935 482040

e-mail: summer@relaischateaux.com

Dir: *1m W of A37 halfway between Dorchester and Yeovil*

PETS: Bedrooms (GF) unattended sign **Stables** nearby (5m) **Charges** £10 per night £70 per week charge for damage **Public areas** except restaurant & drawing room **Grounds** accessible disp bin **Exercise area** 20yds **Facilities** food (pre-bookable) food bowl water bowl bedding dog chews feeding mat dog scoop/disp bags leads pet sitting dog walking washing facs dog grooming cage storage walks info vet info **On Request** fridge access torch towels **Resident Pets:** William (cat)

This picturesque hotel is situated in the heart of Dorset and is the ideal retreat for getting away from it all. It's worth arriving in time for afternoon tea. Bedrooms are appointed to a very high standard; they are individually designed with upholstered walls and come with a wealth of luxurious facilities. Delightful public areas include a sumptuous lounge complete with an open fire and the elegant restaurant where the cuisine continues to be the high point of any stay.

Rooms 10 en suite 14 annexe en suite (6 fmly) (2 GF) ⊘ in 10 bedrooms S £195-£465; D £225-£515 (incl. bkfst)✳ **Facilities** Spa STV ⊙ ⅌ Gym ⅃ Wi-fi in bedrooms Xmas New Year **Services** air con **Parking** 41 **Notes** LB

★★★★ ◉ ⟶ INN
The Acorn Inn
DT2 0JW

☎ 01935 83228 ▤ 01935 83707

e-mail: stay@acorn-inn.co.uk

web: www.acorn-inn.co.uk

Dir: *0.5m off A37 between Yeovil and Dorchester, signed Evershot, Holywell*

PETS: Bedrooms Charges £10 per night charge for damage **Public areas** except restaurant on leads **Grounds** accessible on leads **Facilities** water bowl walks info vet info **On Request** torch

This delightful 16th-century coaching inn is located at the heart of the village. Several of the bedrooms feature interesting four-poster beds, and all have been individually decorated and furnished. Public rooms retain many original features including oak panelling, open fires and stone-flagged floors. Fresh local produce is included on the varied menu.

Rooms 10 en suite (2 fmly) **Facilities** STV TVB tea/coffee Direct dial from bedrooms Cen ht TVL Dinner Last d 9pm Pool Table **Parking** 40

HOLTON HEATH MAP 03 SY99

Sandford Holiday Park *(SY939916)*
BH16 6JZ

☎ 0870 0667793 & 01202 622513 📄 01202 625678

e-mail: bookings@weststarholidays.co.uk

web: www.weststartouring.co.uk/aa

Dir: *A35 from Poole towards Dorchester, at lights onto A351 towards Wareham. Right at Holton Heath. Park 100yds on left*

PETS: Charges £5 per night **Public areas** except buildings on leads **Exercise area** on site large walking area woods nearby disp bin **Facilities** on site shop walks info vet info **Other** prior notice required **Restrictions** no dangerous dogs (see page 7)

Open Mar-Nov Booking advisable BH & Jul-Aug Last arrival 22.00hrs Last departure 10.00hrs

With touring pitches set individually in 20 acres surrounded by woodland, this park offers a full range of leisure activities and entertainment for the whole family. The touring area is neat and well maintained, and there are children's clubs in the daytime and nightly entertainment. A new reception area with lounge, bar, café and restaurant have created an excellent and attractive entrance, with a covered area outside with tables and chairs and newly landscaped gardens. A 64-acre site with 500 touring pitches and 305 statics.

Notes No unaccompanied minors

HORTON MAP 04 SU00

►►► Meadow View Caravan Park *(SU045070)*
Wigbeth BH21 7JH

☎ 01258 840040 📄 01258 840040

e-mail: mail@meadowviewcaravanpark.co.uk

web: www.meadowviewcaravanpark.co.uk

Dir: *Follow unclass road from Horton to site, 0.5m from Druscilla pub*

PETS: Charges £1 per night **Public areas** on leads **Exercise area** on site 2 acre paddock disp bin **Facilities** walks info vet info **Resident Pets:** Annie (Labrador), Meg (Terrier), Loops (cat)

Open all year Booking advisable Jul-Aug Last arrival 21.00hrs Last departure 11.00hrs

A small family-owned park, part of a specialised commercial turf farm, and set in a very rural area with its own lake and nature reserve. This very good park is always neatly trimmed and clean. A 1.5-acre site with 15 touring pitches, 7 hardstandings.

Notes 🐾

LYME REGIS MAP 03 SY39

►►► Hook Farm Caravan & Camping Park
(SY323930)

Gore Ln, Uplyme DT7 3UU

☎ 01297 442801 📄 01297 442801

e-mail: information@hookfarm-uplyme.co.uk

web: www.hookfarm-uplyme.co.uk

Dir: *From A35, take B3165 towards Lyme Regis & Uplyme at Hunters Lodge pub. 2m turn right into Gore Lane, site 400yds on right*

PETS: Charges £1 per night **Public areas** except shop & wash room **Exercise area** on site apple orchid available **Facilities** on site shop loose box space disp bags walks info vet info **Restrictions** No dangerous dogs (see page 7), no Rottweillers, Bull Mastifs or Dobermans

Open 15 Mar-Oct Shop closed in low season Booking advisable Etr, May BH, Jul & Aug Last arrival 21.30hrs Last departure 11.00hrs

Set in a peaceful and very rural location with views of Lym Valley and just a mile from the seaside at Lyme Regis. The modern toilet facilities are part of an upgrading programme, and there are good on-site amenities. Most pitches are level due to excellent terracing. A 5.5-acre site with 100 touring pitches and 17 statics.

Notes 🐾 No groups of 6 adults or more.

LYTCHETT MATRAVERS

►►► Huntick Farm Caravan Park *(SY955947)*
Huntick Rd BH16 6BB

☎ 01202 622222

Dir: *Between Lytchett Minster & Lytchett Matravers*

PETS: Charges Public areas Exercise area on site disp bin **Facilities** walks info vet info

Open Apr-Oct Booking advisable Last arrival 21.00hrs Last departure Noon

A really attractive little park nestling in rural surroundings edged by woodland, a mile from the village amenities of Lytchett Matravers. This neat grassy park is divided into three paddocks offering a peaceful location and yet close to the attractions of Poole and Bournemouth. A 4-acre site with 24 touring pitches.

LYTCHETT MINSTER

►►►► South Lytchett Manor *(SY954926)*

Dorchester Rd BH16 6JB

☎ 01202 622577

e-mail: info@southlytchettmanor.co.uk

web: www.southlytchettmanor.co.uk

Dir: On B3067, off A35, 1m E of Lytchett Minster

PETS: Charges Public areas Exercise area on site field & wood adjacent disp bin **Facilities** on site shop food bowl water bowl dog chews dog scoop/disp bags walks info vet info **Other** prior notice required **Resident Pets:** King Charles Spaniel

Open Etr-14 Oct Booking advisable Last arrival 21.00hrs Last departure Noon

A pleasant family-owned park set along the tree-lined driveway of the old manor house, with pitches enjoying open views of pastureland. Facilities are basic but clean and well cared for, and the park is only 3m from Poole. A 20-acre site with 150 touring pitches, 15 hardstandings.

MILTON ABBAS   MAP 03 ST80

★ ★ ★ FARM HOUSE

Fishmore Hill Farm *(ST799013)*

DT11 0DL

☎ 01258 881122 🖹 01258 881122 Mr & Mrs N Clarke

e-mail: neal.clarke@btinternet.com

Dir: Off A354 signed Milton Abbas, 3m left on sharp bend, up steep hill, 1st left

PETS: Sep Accom barn **Stables** on site **Charges** £10 per horse per night (stabling & bedding) **Grounds** accessible disp bin **Facilities** on site veterinary practice, paddock for horses cage storage walks info **On Request** torch **Resident Pets:** dogs, horses, sheep

This working sheep farm and family home is surrounded by beautiful Dorset countryside and is close to historic Milton Abbey and a short drive from the coast. Bedrooms, which vary in size, are comfortable and finished with considerate extras. The atmosphere is friendly and relaxed. Breakfast is served in the smart dining room around a communal table.

Rooms 3 en suite ⊘ **Facilities** TVB tea/coffee Cen ht **Parking** 4 **Notes** 50 acres Sheep and horses Closed Xmas & New Year ⊜

MORETON   MAP 03 SY88

►►► Moreton Camping & Caravanning Club Site *(SY782892)*

Station Rd DT2 8BB

☎ 01305 853801

web: www.campingandcaravanningclub.co.uk/moreton

Dir: From Poole on A35, past Bere Regis, left onto B3390 signed Alfpuddle. After approx 2m site on left before Moreton Station and next to public house

PETS: Public areas except buildings **Exercise area** on site **Facilities** walks info vet info **Other** prior notice required

Open 13 Mar-17 Nov Booking advisable BH & peak periods Last arrival 21.00hrs Last departure noon

Modern purpose-built site on level ground with good amenities. This tidy, well-maintained park offers electric hook-ups to most pitches, and there is a very good play area for children. A 7-acre site with 120 touring pitches, 10 hardstandings.

Notes Site gates closed 23.00-07.00.

OWERMOIGNE

►►► Sandyholme Caravan Park *(SY768863)*

Moreton Rd DT2 8HZ

☎ 01305 852677 🖹 01305 854677

e-mail: smeatons@sandyholme.co.uk

web: www.sandyholme.co.uk

Dir: From A352 (Wareham to Dorchester road) turn right to Owermoigne for 1m. Site on left

PETS: Charges £2 per night £12 per week **Public areas** on leads disp bin **Facilities** on site shop food dog scoop/disp bags dog tethers walks info vet info **Other** prior notice required Max 2 dogs per unit **Resident Pets:** dog & cat

Open Apr-Oct (rs Etr 2008) Booking advisable peak periods Last arrival 21.30hrs Last departure 10.30hrs

A quiet family-run site in a tree-lined rural setting within easy reach of the coast at Lulworth Cove, and handy for several seaside resorts. The facilities are very good, including a superb toilet block, and good food is available in the lounge/bar. A 6-acre site with 50 touring pitches and 30 statics.

ENGLAND

PIDDLETRENTHIDE — MAP 03 SY79

★★★★ INN
The Poachers
DT2 7QX

☎ 01300 348358 📄 01300 348153
e-mail: info@thepoachersinn.co.uk
web: www.thepoachersinn.co.uk

Dir: *N of Dorchester on B3143, inn on left*

PETS: **Bedrooms** (GF) **Stables** nearby (0.5m) **Charges** £2.50 per night charge for damage **Public areas** except restaurant on leads **Grounds** accessible on leads **Facilities** food bowl water bowl cage storage walks info vet info **On Request** fridge access torch towels

This friendly, owner-run inn combines original 16th-century character with contemporary style in the bar and dining areas. Home-cooked meals are a feature, and the smart, en suite bedrooms open onto a courtyard. In fine weather guests can lounge round the swimming pool or relax in the garden.

Rooms 21 en suite (3 fmly) (12 GF) ⊘ S £52-£60; D £74-£120✳
Facilities TVB tea/coffee Direct dial from bedrooms Cen ht Dinner Last d 9.30pm Wi-fi available ⌇ **Parking** 42 **Notes** LB

See advertisement under DORCHESTER

POOLE — MAP 04 SZ09

★★ 65% HOTEL
Antelope Inn
8 High St BH15 1BP

☎ 01202 672029 📄 01202 678286
e-mail: 6603@greeneking.co.uk
web: www.oldenglish.co.uk

PETS: **Bedrooms** unattended **Charges** £5 per night
Public areas Bar only **Grounds** accessible **Exercise area** 50mtrs

Close to Poole Quay, which is a one of the town's main attractions, this famous old coaching inn is the oldest licensed premises in Poole, and has long been a popular meeting point. All rooms are furnished to a high standard with modern facilities, and include some feature rooms. Public areas include a bar, a restaurant, and a quiet area.

Rooms 21 en suite (2 fmly) ⊘ in all bedrooms **Parking** 17 **Notes** LB

ST LEONARDS — MAP 04 SU10

►►►► **Back of Beyond Touring Park**
(SU103034)
234 Ringwood Rd BH24 2SB

☎ 01202 876968 📄 01202 876968
e-mail: melandsuepike@aol.com
web: www.backofbeyondtouringpark.co.uk

Dir: *From E: on A31 over Little Chef rdbt, pass St Leonard's Hotel, at next rdbt u-turn into lane immediately left to site at end of lane. From W: on A31 pass Texaco garage & Woodsman Inn, immediatley left to site*

PETS: **Charges** £1 per night **Exercise area** on site 18 acre wood & in 0.5m disp bin **Facilities** on site shop walks info vet info **Other** prior notice required **Resident Pets:** Holly, Dusty & Gabby (Dalmatians)

Open Mar-Oct Booking advisable summer Last arrival 19.00hrs Last departure noon

Set well off the beaten track in natural woodland surroundings, with its own river and lake yet close to many attractions. This tranquil park has been completely redeveloped by keen, friendly owners, and the quality facilities are for adults only. A 28-acre site with 80 touring pitches.

Notes Adults only, no commercial vehicles

►►►► Shamba Holidays *(SU105029)*

230 Ringwood Rd BH24 2SB

☎ 01202 873302 ▤ 01202 873392

e-mail: enquiries@shambaholidays.co.uk

web: www.shambaholidays.co.uk

Dir: *Off A31, from Poole turn left into Eastmoors Lane, 100yds past 2nd rdbt from Texaco garage. Park 0.25m on right (just past Woodman Inn)*

PETS: Charges £2.25 per night £15.75 per week **Public areas** except buildings **Exercise area** on site 12 acre field available woods 0.5m **Facilities** on site shop food walks info vet info

Open Mar-Oct (rs low season some facilities only open at wknds) Booking advisable BH & Jul-Aug Last arrival 22.00hrs Last departure 11.00hrs

A relaxed touring park in pleasant countryside between the New Forest and Bournemouth. The park is very well equipped for holidaymakers, with swimming pool, good playground, and bar, shop and takeaway. A 7-acre site with 150 touring pitches.

Notes No large groups, no commercial vehicles

►►► Forest Edge Touring Park *(SU104024)*

229 Ringwood Rd BH24 2SD

☎ 01590 648331 ▤ 01590 645610

e-mail: holidays@shorefield.co.uk

web: www.shorefield.co.uk

Dir: *From E: on A31 over 1st rdbt (Little Chef), pass St Leonards Hotel & left at next rdbt into Boundary Lane, site 100yds on left. From W: on A31 pass Texaco garage & Woodsman Inn, right at rdbt into Boundary Lane*

PETS: Charges £1.50-£3 per night £10.50-£21 per week **Exercise area** on site **Facilities** on site shop food disp bags walks info vet info **Other** prior notice required **Restrictions** 1 dog & 1 car per pitch, no Rottweilers or Staffordshire Bull Terriers

Open Feb-Dec (rs mid Jul-Aug pool/bar only open school & summer hols) Booking advisable at all times Last arrival 21.00hrs Last departure 10.00hrs

A tree-lined park set in grassland with plenty of excellent amenities for all the family, including an outdoor heated swimming pool and toddlers' pool, an adventure playground, and two launderettes. Visitors are invited to use the superb leisure club plus all amenities and entertainment at the sister site of Oakdene Forest Park less than a mile away. Some pitches may experience traffic noise from the nearby A31. A 9-acre site with 94 touring pitches and 28 statics.

★★★ 71% ◉ HOTEL

Best Western Royal Chase

Royal Chase Roundabout SP7 8DB

☎ 01747 853355 ▤ 01747 851969

e-mail: royalchasehotel@btinternet.com

web: www.theroyalchasehotel.co.uk

Dir: *A303 to A350 signed Blandford Forum. Avoid town centre, follow road to 3rd rdbt*

PETS: Bedrooms unattended **Charges** £6.50 per night **Grounds** accessible **Exercise area** many walks nearby

Equally suitable for both leisure and business guests, this well-known local landmark is situated close to the famous Gold Hill. Both Standard and Crown bedrooms offer good levels of comfort and quality. In addition to the fixed-price menu in the Byzant Restaurant, guests have the option of eating more informally in the convivial bar.

Rooms 33 en suite (13 fmly) (6 GF) ⊗ in all bedrooms **Facilities** STV ⊙ Wi-fi in bedrooms Turkish steam room **Parking** 100

►► Blackmore Vale Caravan & Camping Park *(ST835233)*

Sherborne Causeway SP7 9PX

☎ 01747 851523 & 852573 ▤ 01747 851671

e-mail: bmvgroup@ukf.net

web: www.ukcampsite.co.uk

Dir: *From Shaftesbury's Ivy Cross rdbt take A30 signed Sherborne. Site 2m on right*

PETS: Charges £1 per night **Public areas** on leads **Exercise area** on site large field adjacent disp bin **Facilities** vet info **Other** prior notice required **Restrictions** no Rottweilers, Pitt Bull Terriers or Dobenmans

Open all year Booking advisable BH Last arrival 21.00hrs

A comfortable touring park with spacious pitches and well-maintained facilities. Set behind a caravan sales showground and dealership, and about 2m from Shaftesbury. A 3-acre site with 26 touring pitches, 6 hardstandings.

ENGLAND

STURMINSTER NEWTON   MAP 03 ST71

STUDLAND   MAP 04 SZ08

★★ 78% HOTEL
Manor House
BH19 3AU
☎ 01929 450288 📠 01929 452255
e-mail: themanorhousehotel@lineone.net
web: www.themanorhousehotel.com
Dir: *A338 from Bournemouth, follow signs to Sandbanks ferry, cross on ferry, then 3m to Studland*
PETS: Bedrooms (GF) unattended **Stables** nearby (500yds) **Charges** £3.50 per night £24.50 per week charge for damage **Grounds** accessible on leads disp bin **Facilities** walks info vet info **On Request** fridge access torch **Resident Pets:** Fluffy (White German Shepherd), Minki (Blue Burmese cat)

Set in 20 acres of attractive grounds and with delightful views overlooking Studland Bay, this elegant hotel provides an impressive range of facilities. Bedrooms, many with excellent sea views, are all well equipped and many retain charming features of the original Gothic house. In the oak-panelled dining room, carefully prepared meals offer an interesting choice of dishes from the daily-changing menu.
Rooms 18 en suite 3 annexe en suite (9 fmly) (4 GF) S £118-£138; D £176-£268 (incl. bkfst & dinner)✱ **Facilities** ◈ ◈ Xmas New Year **Parking** 80 **Notes** LB No children 5yrs

STURMINSTER NEWTON   MAP 03 ST71

★★★ 🏠 FARM HOUSE
Honeysuckle House *(ST772102)*
1995 Fifehead St Quintin DT10 2AP
☎ 01258 817896 & 07980 085107 Mrs J Miller
Dir: *Off A357 up Glue Hill signed Hazelbury Bryan. Left after sharp bend, continue 2.5m*
PETS: Please telephone for details

The young proprietors of this 400-acre dairy farm offer a particularly friendly welcome and ensure all guests are very well looked after. The lovely rural setting is a delight with contented cows grazing in the fields awaiting milking time. Bedrooms are comfortable and include some welcome extras. Breakfasts are enormous, and be sure to book for dinner which is a real highlight.
Rooms 3 en suite (1 fmly) **Facilities** TVB tea/coffee Cen ht TVL Dinner Last d Previous day ↴ Fishing Riding ↴ Pony rides, farm tours, children's tractor rides **Parking** 6 **Notes** 400 acres Dairy Closed 22 Dec-2 Jan ◈

SWANAGE   MAP 04 SZ07

★★★ 71% HOTEL
The Pines
Burlington Rd BH19 1LT
☎ 01929 425211 📠 01929 422075
e-mail: reservations@pineshotel.co.uk
web: www.pineshotel.co.uk
Dir: *A351 to seafront, left then 2nd right. Hotel at end of road*
PETS: Bedrooms (GF) unattended **Stables** nearby (4m) **Grounds** accessible disp bin **Facilities** bowls must be pre arranged walks info vet info **On Request** torch towels
Enjoying a peaceful location with spectacular views over the cliffs and sea, The Pines is a pleasant place to stay. Many of the comfortable bedrooms have sea views. Guests can take tea in the lounge, enjoy appetising bar snacks in the attractive bar and interesting and accomplished cuisine in the restaurant.
Rooms 47 en suite (26 fmly) (6 GF) ◈ in all bedrooms S £61; D £122-£146 (incl. bkfst)✱ **Facilities** ♫ Xmas New Year **Services** Lift **Parking** 60 **Notes** LB

►►► Herston Caravan & Camping Park

(SZ018785)

Washpond Ln BH19 3DJ

☎ 01929 422932

Dir: *From Wareham on A351 towards Swanage. Washpond Lane on left just after 'Welcome to Swanage' sign.*

PETS: Public areas Exercise area on site disp bin **Facilities** on site shop food food bowl water bowl leads vet info **Other** prior notice required max 2 dogs per family

Open all year Booking advisable

Set in a rural area with extensive views of the Purbecks, this tree lined park has many full facility pitches and quality toilet facilities. Herston Halt is within walking distance, a stop for the famous Swanage steam railway between the town centre and Corfe Castle. A 10-acre site with 100 touring pitches, 71 hardstandings and 5 statics.

►►► Swanage Coastal Park *(SZ024797)*

Priestway BH19 2RS

☎ 01590 648331 📠 01590 645610

e-mail: holidays@shorefield.co.uk

web: www.shorefield.co.uk

Dir: *A351 from Wareham. 1m past 'Welcome to Swanage' sign, right into High St. 1st right into Bell Street Up hill, 1st left into Priests Road, 1st right into Priestway to site*

PETS: Charges £1.50-£3 per night £10.50-£21 per week **Exercise area** on site **Facilities** on site shop disp bags walks info vet info **Other** prior notice required **Restrictions** no Rottweilers, Staffordshire Bull Terriers

Open 24 Mar-Oct Booking advisable at all times Last arrival 22.00hrs Last departure 10.00hrs

A spacious site set in stunning countryside with views over Swanage Bay and the Purbeck Hills. The shops and beaches at Swanage are less than a mile away, and the adjacent holiday park offers day membership to its health and fitness club, including bar, indoor swimming pool, gym, sauna, solarium, shop and restaurant. A 15-acre site with 5 touring pitches, 5 hardstandings and 52 statics.

►►► Ulwell Cottage Caravan Park *(SZ019809)*

Ulwell Cottage, Ulwell BH19 3DG

☎ 01929 422823 📠 01929 421500

e-mail: enq@ulwellcottagepark.co.uk

web: www.ulwellcottagepark.co.uk

Dir: *From Swanage N for 2m on unclass road towards Studland*

PETS: Public areas on leads **Exercise area** 100yds disp bin **Facilities** on site shop food food bowl water bowl bedding dog chews litter dog scoop/disp bags leads walks info vet info

Open Mar-7 Jan (rs Mar-Spring bank hol & mid Sep-early Jan takeaway closed, shop open variable hrs) Booking advisable BH & Jul-Aug Last arrival 22.00hrs Last departure 11.00hrs

Nestling under the Purbeck Hills surrounded by scenic walks and only 2 miles from the beach. This family-run park caters well for families and couples, offering high quality facilities including an indoor heated swimming pool and village inn. A 13-acre site with 77 touring pitches, 19 hardstandings and 140 statics.

► Acton Field Camping Site *(SY991785)*

Acton Field, Langton Matravers BH19 3HS

☎ 01929 424184 & 439424 📠 01929 424184

e-mail: jojochisnoll@aol.com

Dir: *From A351 right after Corfe Castle onto B3069 to Langton Matravers, 2nd right after village sign (bridleway)*

PETS: Public areas on leads **Facilities** walks info vet info **Other** prior notice required

Open mid Jul-early Sep Booking advisable Last arrival 22.00hrs Last departure noon

An informal campsite bordered by farmland on the outskirts of Langton Maltravers. There are superb views of the Purbeck Hills and towards the Isle of Wight, and a footpath leads to the coastal path. The site was once a stone quarry, and rock pegs are required. A 7-acre site with 50 touring pitches.

Notes No open fires or noise after mdnt

ENGLAND

VERWOOD MAP 04 SU00

▶▶▶ Verwood Camping & Caravanning Club Site (SU069098)

Sutton Hill, Woodlands BH21 8NQ

☎ 01202 822763

web: www.campingandcaravanningclub.co.uk/verwood

Dir: *Turn left on A354 13m from Salisbury onto B3081, site is 1.5m W of Verwood*

PETS: Public areas except buildings Exercise area on site dog walks disp bin Facilities walks info vet info Other prior notice required

Open 13 Mar-3 Nov Booking advisable BH & peak periods Last arrival 21.00hrs Last departure noon

Set on rising ground between the woodland of the New Forest and the rolling downs of Cranborne Chase and Salisbury Plains. This comfortable site is well kept by very keen wardens. A 12.75-acre site with 150 touring pitches, 18 hardstandings.

Notes Sites gates closed 23.00-07.00

WAREHAM MAP 03 SY98

★★★ 73% HOTEL
Worgret Manor

Worgret Rd BH20 6AB

☎ 01929 552957 ⊟ 01929 554804

e-mail: admin@worgretmanorhotel.co.uk

web: www.worgretmanorhotel.co.uk

Dir: *on A352 (Wareham to Wool), 500mtrs from Wareham rdbt*

PETS: Bedrooms (GF) Public areas bar & lobby only Grounds accessible on leads Exercise area local walks Facilities vet info Resident Pets: Tammy (Retriever)

On the edge of Wareham, with easy access to major routes, this privately owned Georgian manor house offers a friendly, cheerful ambience. The bedrooms come in a variety of sizes. Public rooms are well presented and comprise a popular bar, a quiet lounge and an airy restaurant.

Rooms 12 en suite (1 fmly) (3 GF) ⊗ in all bedrooms S £65; D £110-£120 (incl. bkfst)✳ Facilities Free use of local sports centre Parking 25

▶▶▶▶ Wareham Forest Tourist Park

(SY894912)

North Trigon BH20 7NZ

☎ 01929 551393 ⊟ 01929 558321

e-mail: holiday@wareham-forest.co.uk

web: www.wareham-forest.co.uk

Dir: *Telephone for directions*

PETS: Charges 60p-£1.50 per night Public areas except buildings on leads Exercise area on site woodland walks forest nearby disp bin Facilities on site shop washing facs walks info vet info

Open all year (rs off-peak season limited services) Booking advisable Spring bank hol & Jul-Aug Last arrival 21.00hrs Last departure 10.30hrs

A woodland park within the tranquil Wareham Forest, with its many walks and proximity to Poole, Dorchester and the Purbeck coast. Two luxury blocks, with combined washbasin/WCs for total privacy, maintain a high standard of cleanliness. A heated outdoor swimming pool, off licence, shop and games room add to the pleasure of a stay here. A 42-acre site with 200 touring pitches, 70 hardstandings.

Notes Couples & families only, no group bookings

WEST BEXINGTON MAP 03 SY58

★★ 71% HOTEL
The Manor

Beach Rd DT2 9DF

☎ 01308 897616 ⊟ 01308 897704

e-mail: themanorhotel@btconnect.com

Dir: *B3157 to Burton Bradstock, continue to The Bull public house in Swire then turn immediately right to West Bexington.*

PETS: Bedrooms unattended Charges £15 per night Public areas except restaurant Grounds accessible Exercise area 5 mins

This hotel is something special. Surrounded by scenic splendour and just a short stroll from the magnificent sweep of Chesil Beach, the atmosphere is relaxed and welcoming with snug lounges and crackling wood fires. Bedrooms are individual in style, many with wonderful sea views and the sound of waves in the background. With an abundance of excellent local produce, dining here, in either the convivial Cellar Bar, or the elegant dining room is highly recommended.

Rooms 13 en suite (2 fmly) ⊗ in 1 bedroom Parking 80

WEST LULWORTH

MAP 03 SY88

★★ 74% HOTEL
Cromwell House

Lulworth Cove BH20 5RJ

☎ 01929 400253 & 400332 📠 01929 400566

e-mail: catriona@lulworthcove.co.uk

web: www.lulworthcove.co.uk

Dir: *200yds beyond end of West Lulworth village, left onto high slip road, hotel 100yds on left opposite beach car park*

PETS: Bedrooms (GF) unattended sign **Charges** £1 per night **Public areas** except dining room **Grounds** accessible disp bin **Exercise area** adjacent **Facilities** water bowl washing facs cage storage walks info vet info **On Request** fridge access torch towels **Resident Pets:** Jaldi (Springer Spaniel), Douglas (Bearded Collie cross), Lily (cat)

Built in 1881 by the Mayor of Weymouth, specifically as a guest house, this family-run hotel now provides visitors with an ideal base for touring the area and for exploring the beaches and coast. Cromwell House enjoys spectacular views across the sea and countryside. Bedrooms, many with sea views, are comfortable and some have been specifically designed for family use.

Rooms 17 en suite 1 annexe en suite (3 fmly) (2 GF) ⊘ in 17 bedrooms S £40-£67; D £80-£98 (incl. bkfst)✳ **Facilities** ⊰ Access to Dorset coastal footpath & Jurassic Coast **Parking** 17 **Notes LB** Closed 22 Dec-3 Jan

WEYMOUTH

MAP 03 SY67

★★ GUEST HOUSE
Charlotte Guest House

5 Commercial Rd DT4 7DW

☎ 01305 772942 & 07970 798433

e-mail: charlottegh1@aol.com

Dir: *On A353 Esplanade, at clock turn right onto Kings St. At rdbt take 1st left and then left again onto Commercial Rd*

PETS: Bedrooms Charges £5 per night £25 per week **Exercise area** 150yds

A warm welcome is offered at this small renovated guest house within easy walking distance of the town's amenities. The breakfast room is light and airy and bedrooms vary in size.

Rooms 12 rms (7 en suite) (3 fmly) (1 GF) ⊘ S £25-£40; D £50-£80✳ **Facilities** TVB tea/coffee Cen ht **Parking** 3 **Notes LB** ⊜

►►►► East Fleet Farm Touring Park

(SY640797)

Chickerell DT3 4DW

☎ 01305 785768

e-mail: enquiries@eastfleet.co.uk

web: www.eastfleet.co.uk

Dir: *On B3157 (Weymouth-Bridport road), 3m from Weymouth*

PETS: Charges 25p-£1 per night **Public areas** except play area **Exercise area** on site disp bin **Facilities** on site shop food food bowl water bowl dog chews cat treats dog scoop/disp bags leads washing facs walks info vet info **Resident Pets:** George & Clem (donkeys)

Open 16 Mar-Oct Booking advisable peak season Last arrival 22.00hrs Last departure 10.30hrs

Set on a working organic farm overlooking Fleet Lagoon and Chesil Beach, with a wide range of amenities and quality new toilet facilities in a Scandinavian log cabin. The friendly owners are welcoming and helpful, and their family bar serving meals and take-away food is open from Easter, with glorious views from the patio area. A 21-acre site with 400 touring pitches, 50 hardstandings.

►►► Bagwell Farm Touring Park *(SY627816)*

Knights in the Bottom, Chickerell DT3 4EA

☎ 01305 782575 📠 01305 780554

e-mail: aa@bagwellfarm.co.uk

web: www.bagwellfarm.co.uk

Dir: *4m W of Weymouth on B3157 (Weymouth-Bridport), past Chickerell, turn left into park 500yds after Victoria Inn*

PETS: Charges £1 per night **Public areas** on leads **Exercise area** on site field available & in 0.25m **Facilities** on site shop food food bowl water bowl dog chews cat treats dog scoop/disp bags leads walks info vet info **Other** prior notice required

Open all year (rs Winter bar closed) Booking advisable bank/school hols Last arrival 21.00hrs Last departure 11.00hrs

An idyllically-placed terraced site on a hillside and a valley overlooking Chesil Beach. The park is well equipped with mini-supermarket, children's play area and pets corner, and a bar and grill serving food in high season. A 14-acre site with 320 touring pitches, 10 hardstandings.

Notes Families only

WEYMOUTH CONTINUED

►► Sea Barn Farm *(SY625807)*

Fleet DT3 4ED

☎ 01305 782218 📠 01305 775396

e-mail: aa@seabarnfarm.co.uk

web: www.seabarnfarm.co.uk

Dir: *From Weymouth take B3157 towards Bridport for 3m. In Chickerell turn left at mini-rdbt towards Fleet. Site 1m on left*

PETS: Charges £2 per night **Public areas** dogs on leads at all times **Exercise area** nearby **Facilities** on site shop food dog scoop/disp bags leads walks info vet info **Other** prior notice required

Open 15 Mar-Oct Booking advisable Spring & Aug BH & school hols Last arrival 22.00hrs Last departure noon

A quiet site bordering the Fleet nature reserve, and close to the Dorset coastal path. Optional use of the clubhouse and swimming pool at West Fleet Holiday Farm is available. Pitches are sheltered by hedging, and there is plenty of space for games. A 12-acre site with 250 touring pitches and 1 static.

Notes Non-family groups by arrangement

WIMBORNE MINSTER   MAP 04 SZ09

►►►►► Merley Court *(SZ008984)*

Merley BH21 3AA

☎ 01590 648331 📠 01590 645610

e-mail: holidays@shorefield.co.uk

web: www.shorefield.co.uk

Dir: *Site signed on A31, Wimborne by-pass & Poole junct rdbt*

PETS: Charges £1.50-£3 per night £10.50-£21 per week **Exercise area** on site disp bin **Facilities** on site shop food disp bags walks info vet info **Other** prior notice required **Restrictions** No Rottweilers or Staffordshire Bull Terriers

Open Feb-7 Jan (rs low season pool closed & bar, shop open limited hrs) Booking advisable BH & Jun-Sep Last arrival 21.00hrs Last departure 11.00hrs

A superb site in a quiet rural position on the edge of Wimborne, with woodland on two sides and good access roads. The park is well landscaped, and offers generous individual pitches in sheltered grassland. There are plenty of amenities for all the family, including heated outdoor pool, tennis court and adventure playground. A 20-acre site with 160 touring pitches, 50 hardstandings.

Notes Couples & families only

►►► Charris Camping & Caravan Park

(SY992988)

Candy's Ln, Corfe Mullen BH21 3EF

☎ 01202 885970 📠 01202 881281

e-mail: bookings@charris.co.uk

web: www.charris.co.uk

Dir: *From E, exit Wimborne bypass (A31) W end. 300yds after Caravan Sales, follow brown sign. From W on A31, over A350 rdbt, take next turn after B3074, follow brown signs*

PETS: Public areas except shop & toilet block **Exercise area** 0.25m disp bin **Facilities** on site shop food bowl water bowl disp bags wash fac walks info vet info **Other** prior notice required **Resident Pets:** Spike (cat)

Open Mar-Jan Booking advisable at all times Last arrival 21.00hrs Last departure 11.00hrs

A sheltered park of grassland lined with trees, on the edge of the Stour Valley. The owners are friendly and welcoming, and they maintain the park facilities to a good standard. Barbecues are a popular occasional event. A 3.5-acre site with 45 touring pitches, 12 hardstandings.

Notes 🐾 Earliest arrival time 11.00hrs

CO DURHAM

BARNARD CASTLE   MAP 12 NZ01

►►►► Barnard Castle C&C Club Site

(NZ025168)

Dockenflatts Ln, Lartington DL12 9DG

☎ 01833 630228

web: www.campingandcaravanningclub.co.uk/
barnardcastle

Dir: *From Barnard Castle take B6277 to Middleton-in-Teesdale. After 1m turn left signed Raygill Riding Stables. Site 500mtrs on left*

PETS: Public areas except buildings **Exercise area** on site disp bin **Facilities** walks info vet info **Other** prior notice required

Open 13 Mar-3 Nov Booking advisable BH & peak periods Last arrival 21.00hrs Last departure noon

A peaceful site surrounded by mature woodland and meadowland, with first class facilities. This immaculately maintained park is set in the heart of the countryside. Pitches are well laid out and generous, on mainly level grass with some hardstandings. A 10-acre site with 90 touring pitches, 15 hardstandings.

Notes Site gates closed 23.00-07.00.

CONSETT MAP 12 NZ15

★★★ 73% HOTEL

Best Western Derwent Manor

OXFORD
HOTELS & INNS

Allensford DH8 9BB

☎ 01207 592000 ▤ 01207 502472

e-mail: gm@derwent-manor-hotel.com

web: www.oxfordhotelsandinns.com

Dir: *on A68 (Darlington to Corbridge road)*

PETS: Bedrooms Exercise area outside hotel

This hotel, built in the style of a manor house, is set in open grounds overlooking the River Derwent. Spacious bedrooms, including a number of suites, are comfortably equipped. A popular wedding venue, there are also extensive conference facilities and an impressive leisure suite. The Grouse & Claret bar serves a wide range of drinks and light meals, and Guinevere's restaurant offers the fine dining option.

Rooms 48 en suite (3 fmly) (26 GF) ⊘ in 26 bedrooms S £40-£102;
D £64-£122 (incl. bkfst)✳ **Facilities** STV FTV ⊙ supervised Gym Xmas
New Year **Services** Lift **Parking** 100 **Notes** LB

DARLINGTON MAP 08 NZ21

★★★ 73% ⊛ HOTEL

Hall Garth Hotel, Golf and Country Club

folio
Hotels

Coatham Mundeville DL1 3LU

☎ 0870 609 6131 ▤ 01325 310083

e-mail: hallgarth@foliohotels.com

web: www.foliohotels.com/hallgarth

Dir: *A1(M) junct 59, A167 towards Darlington. After 600yds left at top of hill, hotel on right*

PETS: Bedrooms unattended **Public areas** except restaurant
Grounds accessible **Exercise area** country lane walks

Peacefully situated in grounds that include a golf course, this hotel is just a few minutes from the motorway network. The well-equipped bedrooms come in various styles - its worth asking for the trendy, modern rooms. Public rooms include relaxing lounges, a fine-dining restaurant and a separate pub. The extensive leisure and conference facilities are an important focus here.

Rooms 40 en suite 11 annexe en suite ⊘ in all bedrooms **Facilities** STV
⊙ ♨9 Gym Putt green Wi-fi available Steam room Beauty Salon ♫
Parking 150

DURHAM MAP 12 NZ24

★★★★ 75% HOTEL

Durham Marriott Hotel, Royal County

Marriott.
HOTELS & RESORTS

Old Elvet DH1 3JN

☎ 0191 386 6821 ▤ 0191 386 0704

e-mail: mhrs.xvudm.frontdesk@marriotthotels.com

web: www.marriott.co.uk

Dir: *from A1(M) junct 62, then A690 to Durham, over 1st rdbt, left at 2nd rdbt left at lights, hotel on left*

PETS: Bedrooms (GF) **Facilities** vet info

In a wonderful position on the banks of the River Wear, the hotel's central location makes it ideal for visiting the attractions of this historic city. The building was developed from a series of Jacobean town houses. Today the hotel offers up-to-date, air-conditioned bedrooms, plus a choice of restaurants and lounge areas.

Rooms 142 en suite 8 annexe en suite (10 fmly) (15 GF) ⊘ in
111 bedrooms S £99-£185; D £99-£195 (incl. bkfst)✳ **Facilities** STV ⊙
supervised Gym Wi-fi available Turkish steam room Plunge pool,
sanarium, tropical fun shower **Services** Lift **Parking** 76

★★★ 66% HOTEL

Bowburn Hall

Bowburn DH6 5NH

☎ 0191 377 0311 ▤ 0191 377 3459

e-mail: onfo@bowburnhallhotel.co.uk

Dir: *towards Bowburn. Right at Cooperage Pub, then 0.5m to junct signed Durham. Hotel on left*

PETS: Bedrooms unattended **Grounds** accessible **Exercise area** playing field opposite **Facilities** vet info

A former country mansion, this hotel lies in five acres of grounds in a residential area, but within easy reach of the A1. The comfortable and spacious lounge bar and conservatory overlook the gardens, and offer both bar and restaurant meals. Bedrooms are not large but are very smartly presented and well equipped.

Rooms 19 en suite S £70; D £85 (incl. bkfst)✳ **Facilities** STV
Parking 100 **Notes** LB RS 24-26 Dec & 1 Jan

ENGLAND

MIDDLETON-IN-TEESDALE   MAP 12 NY92

★★ 65% HOTEL
The Teesdale Hotel
Market Place DL12 0QG
☎ 01833 640264 📄 01833 640651
e-mail: john@teesdalehotel.co.uk
web: www.teesdalehotel.com
Dir: *from Barnard Castle take B6278, follow signs for Middleton-in-Teesdale & Highforce. Hotel in town centre*
PETS: Bedrooms Public areas bar only **Exercise area** 50mtrs
Located in the heart of the popular village, this family-run hotel offers a relaxed and friendly atmosphere. Bedrooms and bathrooms are well equipped and offer a good standard of quality and comfort. Public areas include a residents' lounge on the first floor, a lounge bar which is popular with locals and a spacious restaurant.
Rooms 14 en suite (1 fmly) ⊘ in all bedrooms S fr £42.50; D fr £75 (incl. bkfst)✳ **Facilities** Xmas **Parking** 20 **Notes** LB

STOCKTON-ON-TEES   MAP 08 NZ41

★★★ GUEST ACCOMMODATION
The Parkwood
64-66 Darlington Rd, Hartburn TS18 5ER
☎ 01642 587933
e-mail: theparkwoodhotel@aol.com
web: www.theparkwoodhotel.com
Dir: *1.5m SW of town centre. A66 onto A137 signed Yarm & Stockton West, left at lights onto A1027, left onto Darlington Rd*
PETS: Bedrooms Public areas except dining areas
Grounds accessible **Exercise area** park nearby **Facilities** food
Resident Pets: Charlie (Yorkshire Terrier cross)
A very friendly welcome awaits you at this family-run establishment. The well-equipped en suite bedrooms come with many homely extras and a range of professionally prepared meals are served in the cosy bar lounge, conservatory, or the attractive dining room.
Rooms 6 en suite S £40; D £55 **Facilities** TVB tea/coffee Cen ht Dinner Last d 9.15pm **Parking** 36

BIRCHANGER GREEN   MAP 05 TL52
MOTORWAY SERVICE AREA (M11)

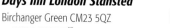

BUDGET HOTEL
Days Inn London Stansted

Birchanger Green CM23 5QZ
☎ 01279 656477 📄 01279 656590
e-mail: birchanger.hotel@welcomebreak.co.uk
web: www.daysinn.com
Dir: *M11 junct 8*
PETS: Bedrooms unattended **Public areas**
This modern building offers accommodation in smart, spacious and well-equipped bedrooms, suitable for families and business travellers, and all with en suite bathrooms. Continental breakfast is available and other refreshments may be taken at the nearby family restaurant. For further details see the Hotel Groups page.
Rooms 60 en suite

CANEWDON   MAP 05 TQ99

►►► Riverside Village Holiday Park
(TQ929951)
Creeksea Ferry Rd, Wallasea Island SS4 2EY
☎ 01702 258297 📄 01702 258555
Dir: *M25 junct 29, A127, towards Southend-on-Sea. Take B1013 towards Rochford. Follow signs for Wallsea Island & Baltic Wharf*
PETS: Charges £1 per night **Exercise area** on site dog walk area provided disp bin **Facilities** on site shop disp bags walks info vet info **Other** prior notice required, no dogs in tents
Open Mar-Oct Booking advisable Anytime
Next to a nature reserve beside the River Crouch, this holiday park is surrounded by wetlands but only eight miles from Southend. A new toilet block with disabled facilities has been provided for tourers. Several restaurants and pubs are within a short distance. A 25-acre site with 60 touring pitches and 162 statics.

KELVEDON HATCH

MAP 05 TQ59

►►► Kelvedon Hatch C&C Club Site

(TQ577976)

Warren Ln, Doddinghurst CM15 0JG

☎ 01277 372773

web: www.campingandcaravanningclub.co.uk/
kelvedonhatch

Dir: *M25 junct 28. Brentwood 2m left on A128 signed Ongar.
After 3m turn right. Site signed*

PETS: Public areas except buildings **Exercise area** on site
adjacent woodland disp bin **Facilities** walks info vet info
Other prior notice required

Open 13 Mar-3 Nov Booking advisable BH & peak periods
Last arrival 21.00hrs Last departure noon

A very pretty rural site with many separate areas amongst the trees,
and a secluded field for campers. This peaceful site has older-style
toilet facilities which are kept very clean, and smart laundry equipment.
A 12-acre site with 90 touring pitches, 23 hardstandings.

Notes Site gates will be closed from 23.00-07.00.

MERSEA ISLAND

MAP 05 TM01

Waldegraves Holiday Park *(TM033133)*

CO5 8SE

☎ 01206 382898 ☐ 01206 385359

e-mail: holidays@waldegraves.co.uk

web: www.waldegraves.co.uk

Dir: *B1025 to Mersea Island across the Strood. Left to East
Mersea, 2nd turn on right, follow tourist signs to park*

PETS: Charges £2 per night **Public areas** on leads
Exercise area on site field available beach disp bin **Facilities** on
site shop food food bowl water bowl walks info vet info
Other prior notice required

Open Mar-Nov Booking advisable all times Last arrival
22.00hrs Last departure noon

A spacious and pleasant site, located between farmland and its own
private beach on the Blackwater Estuary. Facilities include two
freshwater fishing lakes, heated swimming pool, club, amusements,
café and golf, and there is generally good provision for families. A
25-acre site with 60 touring pitches and 250 statics.

Notes No large groups

GLOUCESTERSHIRE

ALVESTON

MAP 03 ST68

★★★ 78% HOTEL

Alveston House

Davids Ln BS35 2LA

☎ 01454 415050 ☐ 01454 415425

e-mail: info@alvestonhousehotel.co.uk

web: www.alvestonhousehotel.co.uk

Dir: *M5 junct 14 from N or junct 16 from S, on A38*

PETS: Bedrooms (GF) unattended sign **Charges** charge for
damage **Grounds** accessible **Facilities** walks info vet info
On Request fridge access torch towels

In a quiet area with easy access to the city and a short drive from both
the M4 and M5, this smartly presented hotel provides an impressive
combination of good service, friendly hospitality and a relaxed
atmosphere. Bedrooms are well equipped and comfortable for
business or leisure use. The restaurant offers carefully prepared fresh
food, and the pleasant bar and conservatory area is perfect for
enjoying a pre-dinner drink.

Rooms 30 en suite (1 fmly) (6 GF) ⊘ in all bedrooms S £75-£104.50;
D £99.50-£114.50 (incl. bkfst)✳ **Facilities** STV Wi-fi available New Year
Parking 75 **Notes** LB

ENGLAND

BIBURY

MAP 04 SP10

★★★ 72% SMALL HOTEL
Swan

CLASSIC
BRITISH HOTELS

GL7 5NW

☎ 01285 740695 📄 01285 740473

e-mail: info@swanhotel.co.uk

web: www.cotswold-inns-hotels.co.uk

Dir: *9m S of Burford A40 on B4425, 6M N of Cirencester A4179 on B4425*

PETS: Bedrooms (GF) unattended **Charges** charge for damage **Public areas** except eating areas **Grounds** accessible **Facilities** cage storage walks info vet info **On Request** fridge access torch towels

The Swan Hotel, built in the 17th-century as a coaching inn, is set in peaceful, picturesque and beautiful surroundings. It now provides well-equipped and smartly presented accommodation, and public areas that are comfortable and elegant. There is a choice of dining options to suit all tastes.

Rooms 18 en suite (1 fmly) ⊘ in all bedrooms D £140-£180 (incl. bkfst) ✳ **Facilities** Fishing Wi-fi in bedrooms Xmas New Year **Services** Lift **Parking** 22 **Notes** ⊗

BLAKENEY

MAP 04 SO60

🐾 🐱

★★★ GUEST ACCOMMODATION
Old Nibley Farmhouse

Nibley Hill GL15 4DB

☎ 01594 516770 & 07989 575855

e-mail: enquiries@oldnibleyfarmhouse.co.uk

Dir: *On A48 S of Blakeney, opp T-junct, signed Parkend*

PETS: Bedrooms unattended **Charges** £5 per night max 2 dogs **Public areas** on leads **Grounds** accessible **Exercise area** forest 1m, path to fields adjacent **Other** Dog loo **Resident Pets:** Jasper, Albert, Charlie (cats)

Dating back some 200 years, this former farmhouse has been imaginatively refurbished to provide accommodation of quality and character. Bedrooms and bathrooms are individually styled, with original features cleverly incorporated with modern comforts to great effect. The spacious, beamed lounge features an impressive open fireplace. Breakfast (and dinner by arrangement) are served in the dining room with local produce used whenever possible.

Rooms 4 rms (2 en suite) (1 GF) ⊘ **Facilities** tea/coffee Cen ht TVL Dinner Last d 24hrs notice **Parking** 4 **Notes** No children 12yrs RS Nov-Dec

BOURTON-ON-THE-WATER

MAP 04 SP12

★★ 79% HOTEL
Chester House

Victoria St GL54 2BU

☎ 01451 820286 📄 01451 820471

e-mail: info@chesterhousehotel.com

Dir: *A429 between Northleach & Stow-on-Wold.*

PETS: Bedrooms (GF) unattended **Public areas** except lounge & bar **Grounds** accessible **Exercise area** 300mtrs **Facilities** cage storage walks info vet info **On Request** fridge access torch towels **Resident Pets:** Poppy (Patterdale Terrier)

This hotel occupies a secluded but central location in this delightful Cotswold village. Rooms, some at ground floor level, are situated in the main house and adjoining coach house. The public areas are stylish, light and airy. Breakfast is taken in the main building whereas dinner is served in the attractive restaurant just a few yards away.

Rooms 12 en suite 10 annexe en suite (8 fmly) (8 GF) ⊘ in all bedrooms D £70-£100 (incl. bkfst)✳ **Facilities** Beauty therapist New Year **Parking** 20

★★★ BED & BREAKFAST
Strathspey

Lansdowne GL54 2AR

☎ 01451 810321 & 07889 491993

e-mail: information@strathspey.org.uk

web: www.strathspey.org.uk

Dir: *Off A429 into Lansdowne, 200yds on right*

PETS: Bedrooms (GF) unattended **Charges** £5 per stay **Public areas** except eating areas **Grounds** accessible disp bin **Exercise area** nearby walks & fields **Facilities** vet info

This friendly Edwardian-style cottage is just a short riverside walk from the charming village centre, perfume factory and the famous model village. Bedrooms, one at ground floor level having its own front door, are well presented with many useful extras, and substantial breakfasts are part of the caring hospitality.

Rooms 2 en suite 1 annexe en suite (1 fmly) (1 GF) S fr £38; D fr £55 **Facilities** TVB tea/coffee Cen ht TVL **Parking** 4 **Notes** LB ⊗

CHELTENHAM  MAP 03 SO92

★★★★ 73% HOTEL
Paramount Cheltenham Park

Cirencester Rd, Charlton Kings GL53 8EA
PARAMOUNT
GROUP OF HOTELS
☎ 01242 222021 📄 01242 254880
e-mail: cheltenhamparkreservations@paramount-hotels.co.uk
web: www.paramount-hotels.co.uk
Dir: *on A435, 2m SE of Cheltenham near Lilley Brook Golf Course*
PETS: Bedrooms Charges £15 per night Grounds accessible
Exercise area on site

Located south of Cheltenham, this attractive Georgian hotel is set in its own landscaped gardens, adjacent to Lilley Brook Golf Course. All of the bedrooms are spacious and well equipped, and the hotel has an impressive leisure club and extensive meeting facilities. The Lakeside restaurant serves carefully prepared cuisine.

Rooms 33 en suite 119 annexe en suite (2 fmly) ⊘ in 67 bedrooms
S £59-£130✳ Facilities STV Gym Wi-fi available Beauty treatment
rooms Xmas New Year Parking 170

★★★ 83% HOTEL
The Greenway

Shurdington GL51 4UG
von Essen hotels
A PRIVATE COLLECTION
www.vonessenhotels.com
☎ 01242 862352 📄 01242 862780
e-mail: info@thegreenway.co.uk
web: www.vonessenhotels.co.uk
Dir: *2.5m SW on A46*
PETS: Bedrooms (GF) unattended Charges £5 per night
Grounds accessible On Request torch towels

This hotel, with a wealth of history, is peacefully located in a delightful setting close to the A46 and the M5. Within easy reach of the many attractions of the Cotswolds. The Greenway certainly offers something special. The attractive dining room overlooks the sunken garden and is the venue for exciting food, proudly served by dedicated and attentive staff.

Rooms 11 en suite 10 annexe en suite (1 fmly) (4 GF) ⊘ in 10 bedrooms
Facilities Wi-fi available Clay pigeon shooting, Horse riding, Mountain
biking, Beauty treatment Parking 50

★★ 69% HOTEL
Cotswold Grange
Pittville Circus Rd GL52 2QH
☎ 01242 515119 📄 01242 241537
e-mail: paul@cotswoldgrange.co.uk
Dir: *from town centre, follow Prestbury signs. Right at 1st rdbt, hotel 200yds on left*
PETS: Bedrooms Public areas except restaurant
Grounds accessible Exercise area adjacent Facilities walks info
vet info On Request fridge access torch

Built from Cotswold limestone, this attractive Georgian property retains many impressive architectural features. Situated conveniently close to the centre of Cheltenham, this long established, family-run hotel offers well-equipped and comfortable accommodation. The convivial bar is a popular venue, and additional facilities include a spacious restaurant, cosy lounge, pleasant rear garden and ample parking.

Rooms 25 en suite (4 fmly) Facilities ch fac Parking 20 Notes Closed
24 Dec-5 Jan RS Sat & Sun evening (food by arrangement)

★★★★ GUEST ACCOMMODATION
Butlers
Western Rd GL50 3RN
☎ 01242 570771 📄 01242 528724
e-mail: info@butlers-hotel.co.uk
Dir: *M5 junct 11, over 2 rdbts & 2 lights onto Landsdown Rd, left at next lights to end of Christchurch Rd, left at minirdbt onto Malvern Rd, Western Rd 2nd on the right*
PETS: Bedrooms (GF) unattended sign Charges £5 per night
Grounds accessible disp bin Facilities food bowl water bowl
feeding mat dog scoop/disp bags washing facs walks info vet
info On Request fridge access torch towels Other other pets by
arrangement

This elegant late Regency house has a quiet location yet is only a stroll from the Promenade, Montpellier and the town centre. Decor and furnishings are stylish, and the spacious, elegant bedrooms (named after butlers from literature and history) are extremely well equipped, and all have PCs. Public rooms include an inviting sitting room and a charming breakfast room that overlooks the delightful rear garden.

Rooms 6 en suite (2 fmly) (1 GF) ⊘ S £50-£65; D £75-£85✳
Facilities TVB tea/coffee Direct dial from bedrooms Cen ht TVL Wi-fi
available Parking 6 Notes No children 5yrs

CHELTENHAM CONTINUED

★★★★ GUEST ACCOMMODATION
White Lodge

Hatherley Ln GL51 6SH

☎ 01242 242347

e-mail: pamela@whitelodgebandb.wanadoo.co.uk

Dir: *M5 junct 11, A40 to Cheltenham, 1st rdbt 4th exit Hatherley Ln, White Lodge 1st on right*

PETS: Bedrooms (GF) unattended **Charges** £5 per night **Public areas** except dining room **Grounds** accessible disp bin

Built around 1900, this well cared for, smart and friendly establishment is convenient for access to and from the M5. Bedrooms, of varied size, offer quality and many extra facilities, including fridges and Wi-fi. The very comfortable dining room, where breakfast is served around a grand table, looks out across the extensive gardens, a pleasant backdrop to an enjoyable breakfast.

Rooms 3 en suite (1 GF) ⊘ S £35-£39; D £50-£55✳ **Facilities** FTV TVB tea/coffee Cen ht Wi-fi available **Parking** 6 **Notes** ☺

★★★ GUEST ACCOMMODATION
Hope Orchard

Gloucester Rd, Staverton GL51 0TF

☎ 01452 855556 📠 01452 530037

e-mail: info@hopeorchard.com

web: www.hopeorchard.com

Dir: *A40 onto B4063 at Arlecourt rdbt, Hope Orchard 1.25m on right*

PETS: Bedrooms (GF) unattended **Charges** charge for damage **Grounds** accessible disp bin **Exercise area** on site **Facilities** food bowl water bowl dog scoop/disp bags washing facs cage storage walks info vet info **On Request** fridge access torch towels **Resident Pets:** Bertie (Staffordshire Bull Terrier), Jessie, Jasper & Louis (cats)

Situated midway between Gloucester and Cheltenham, this is a good base for exploring the area. The comfortable bedrooms are next to the main house, all of which are on the ground floor and have their own separate entrances. There is a large garden and ample off-road parking is available.

Rooms 8 en suite (2 fmly) (8 GF) ⊘ **Facilities** FTV TVB tea/coffee Direct dial from bedrooms Cen ht Wi-fi available **Parking** 10

CHIPPING CAMPDEN   MAP 04 SP13

★★★★ HOTEL
Cotswold House

The Square GL55 6AN

☎ 01386 840330 📠 01386 840310

e-mail: reception@cotswoldhouse.com

web: www.cotswoldhouse.com

Dir: *A44 take B4081 to Chipping Campden. Right at T-junct into High St. House in The Square*

PETS: Bedrooms unattended **Exercise area** The Common

This is at the cutting edge of hotel keeping and relaxation is inevitable at this mellow Cotswold stone house, set in the centre of the town. Bedrooms, including spacious suites in the courtyard, are impressively individual and offer a beguiling blend of style, quality and comfort. The restaurant provides a stunning venue to sample accomplished and imaginative cuisine, with local produce at the heart of dishes on offer here. Alternatively, Hicks Brasserie and Bar provides a more informal dining experience. The AA Rosette award is currently under review, as there has been a recent change of chef

Rooms 29 en suite (1 fmly) (5 GF) ⊘ in 18 bedrooms S £150; D £150-£525 (incl. bkfst) **Facilities** STV ⌣ Wi-fi available Access to local Sports Centre Xmas New Year **Parking** 28 **Notes** LB

★★★ 80% ⚙ HOTEL
Three Ways House

Mickleton GL55 6SB

☎ 01386 438429 📠 01386 438118

e-mail: reception@puddingclub.com

web: www.puddingclub.com

Dir: *in centre of Mickleton, on B4632 (Stratford-upon-Avon to Broadway road*

PETS: Bedrooms unattended **Public areas** except restaurant **Grounds** accessible **Exercise area** 100mtrs

Built in 1870, this charming hotel has welcomed guests for over 100 years and is home to the world famous Pudding Club, formed in 1985 to promote traditional English puddings. Individuality is a hallmark here, as reflected in a number of bedrooms, which have been styled according to a pudding theme. Public areas are stylish and include the air-conditioned restaurant, lounges and meeting rooms.

Rooms 48 en suite (7 fmly) (14 GF) ⊘ in all bedrooms S £79-£102; D £130-£195 (incl. bkfst)✳ **Facilities** Wi-fi in bedrooms ♫ Xmas New Year **Services** Lift **Parking** 37 **Notes** LB

★★★ 73% HOTEL

Noel Arms

High St GL55 6AT

☎ 01386 840317 🖹 01386 841136

e-mail: reception@noelarmshotel.com

web: www.noelarmshotel.com

Dir: *off A44 onto B4081 to Chipping Campden, 1st right down hill into town. Hotel on right opposite Market Hall*

PETS: Bedrooms (GF) unattended Public areas bar only Grounds accessible Exercise area 100yds Facilities vet info Restrictions small-medium sized dogs only

This historic 14th-century hotel has a wealth of character and charm, and retains some of its original features. Bedrooms are very individual in style, but all have high levels of comfort and interesting interior design. Such distinctiveness is also evident throughout the public areas, which include the popular bar, conservatory lounge and attractive restaurant.

Rooms 26 en suite (1 fmly) (6 GF) ⊘ in all bedrooms S £95-£115; D £130-£220 (incl. bkfst)✳ Facilities Wi-fi available Xmas New Year Parking 26 Notes LB

★★★★ 🍴 GUEST ACCOMMODATION

The Kings

The Square GL55 6AW

☎ 01386 840256 🖹 01386 841598

e-mail: info@kingscampden.co.uk

Dir: *In centre of town square*

PETS: Bedrooms unattended sign Stables nearby Charges £5 per night Public areas except restaurant on leads Grounds accessible disp bin Exercise area 5 mins Resident Pets: Ceriad & Spoch (cats)

Located in the centre of historic Chipping Campden, this Grade II listed late Georgian inn is popular with visitors and locals alike, and the friendly and good-humoured staff contribute to the convivial buzz. Bedrooms offer ample comfort with period features and mod cons combining in stylish effect. The menus offer a range of flavour-packed dishes, complemented by a particularly good range of wines by the glass.

Rooms 14 en suite (2 fmly) S £75.50-£95; D £95-£165✳ Facilities FTV TVB tea/coffee Direct dial from bedrooms Cen ht Dinner Last d 9.30pm Wi-fi available Parking 8 Notes LB

★★★ 79% HOTEL

Best Western Stratton House

Gloucester Rd GL7 2LE

☎ 01285 651761 🖹 01285 640024

e-mail: stratton.house@forestdale.com

web: www.forestdale.com

Dir: *M4 junct 15, A419 to Cirencester. Hotel on left on A417 or M5 junct 11 to Cheltenham onto B4070 to A417. Hotel on right*

PETS: Bedrooms unattended Charges £7.50 per night Public areas

This attractive 17th-century manor house is quietly situated about half a mile from the town centre. Bedrooms are well presented, and spacious, stylish premier rooms are available. The comfortable drawing rooms and restaurant have views over well-tended gardens - the perfect place to enjoy pre-dinner drinks on a summer evening.

Rooms 39 en suite (9 GF) ⊘ in 19 bedrooms Facilities Wi-fi available Parking 100

★★★ 73% HOTEL

The Crown of Crucis

Ampney Crucis GL7 5RS

☎ 01285 851806 🖹 01285 851735

e-mail: info@thecrownofcrucis.co.uk

web: www.thecrownofcrucis.co.uk

Dir: *A417 to Fairford, hotel 2.5m on left*

PETS: Bedrooms (GF) unattended sign Charges £6 per night charge for damage Public areas bar only Grounds accessible disp bin Exercise area nearby over bridge Facilities food (pre-bookable) food bowl water bowl walks info vet info On Request fridge access torch

This delightful hotel consists of two buildings; one a 16th-century coaching inn, which now houses the bar and restaurant, and a more modern bedroom block which surrounds a courtyard. Rooms are attractively appointed and offer modern facilities; the restaurant serves a range of imaginative dishes.

Rooms 25 en suite (2 fmly) (13 GF) ⊘ in 21 bedrooms S £60-£72.50; D £75-£99 (incl. bkfst)✳ Facilities Wi-fi in bedrooms Free membership of local leisure centre Parking 82 Notes LB RS 25-26 Dec & 1 Jan

CIRCENCESTER CONTINUED

★★★ 70% HOTEL
Fleece Hotel

THE INDEPENDENTS
HOTEL ASSOCIATION

Market Place GL7 2NZ

☎ 01285 658507 📠 01285 651017

e-mail: relax@fleecehotel.co.uk

web: www.fleecehotel.co.uk

Dir: *A417/A419 Burford road junct, follow signs for town centre.
Right at lights into 'The Waterloo', car park 250yds on left*

PETS: Bedrooms (GF) unattended **Stables** nearby (1m)
Charges £8 per night charge for damage **Public areas** except
restaurant & bar on leads **Exercise area** 200yds **Facilities** water
bowl walks info vet info **On Request** fridge access

This old town centre coaching inn, which dates back to the Tudor
period, retains many original features such as flagstone floors and oak
beams. Well-equipped bedrooms vary in size and shape, but all offer
good levels of comfort and have plenty of character. The bar lounge is
a popular venue for morning coffee, and the stylish restaurant offers a
range of dishes in an informal and convivial atmosphere.

Rooms 28 en suite (3 fmly) (4 GF) ❷ in 24 bedrooms S £59-£119;
D £79-£129 (incl. bkfst)✴ **Facilities** Wi-fi available Xmas New Year
Parking 10

CLEARWELL   MAP 03 SO50

★★★ 72% ❀❀ HOTEL
Tudor Farmhouse Hotel & Restaurant

High St GL16 8JS

☎ 01594 833046 📠 01594 837093

e-mail: info@tudorfarmhousehotel.co.uk

web: www.tudorfarmhousehotel.co.uk

Dir: *off A4136 onto B4228, through Coleford, turn right into
Clearwell, hotel on right just before War Memorial Cross*

PETS: Bedrooms (GF) unattended **Charges** £5 per pet per night
charge for damage **Grounds** accessible **Facilities** walks info vet
info **On Request** torch towels

Dating from the 13th century, this idyllic former farmhouse retains a
host of original features including exposed stonework, oak beams, wall
panelling and wonderful inglenook fireplaces. Bedrooms have great

individuality and style and are located either within the main house, or
in converted buildings in the grounds. Creative menus offer quality
cuisine, served in the intimate, candlelit restaurant.

Tudor Farmhouse Hotel & Restaurant

Rooms 6 en suite 16 annexe en suite (3 fmly) (8 GF) ❷ in 20 bedrooms
S £60-£80; D £85-£160 (incl. bkfst)✴ **Facilities** STV Wi-fi in bedrooms
New Year **Parking** 30 **Notes LB** Closed 24-27 Dec

COLEFORD   MAP 03 SO51

[U]
Speech House

GL16 7EL

☎ 01594 822607 📠 01594 823658

e-mail: relax@thespeechhouse.co.uk

Dir: *M48 junct 2 to Chepstow follow A48 to Blakeney, turn left
signed Parkend, take right, hotel on right*

PETS: Bedrooms (GF) unattended **Stables** nearby (4m)
Public areas except dining room **Grounds** accessible
Facilities washing facs cage storage walks info vet info

At the time of going to press, the star classification for this hotel was
not confirmed. Please refer to the AA internet site www.theAA.com for
current information.

Rooms 15 en suite 22 annexe rms (11 en suite) (3 fmly) (18 GF) ❷ in
5 bedrooms S £65-£85; D £90-£150 (incl. bkfst)✴ **Facilities** Wi-fi in
bedrooms Xmas New Year

★★★★ FARM HOUSE
Dryslade Farm *(SO581147)*
English Bicknor GL16 7PA
☎ 01594 860259 🖹 01594 860259 Mrs D Gwilliam
e-mail: daphne@drysladefarm.co.uk
web: www.drysladefarm.co.uk
Dir: *3m N of Coleford. Off A4136 onto B4432, right towards English Bicknor, farm 1m*
PETS: Bedrooms Public areas except breakfast room
Grounds accessible **Facilities** dog scoop/disp bags washing facs
On Request fridge access torch towels **Resident Pets:** Kay & Milly (Spaniels)

You are warmly welcomed at this 184-acre working farm, which dates from 1780 and has been in the same family for almost 100 years. The en suite bedrooms are attractively furnished in natural pine and are well equipped. The lounge leads onto a conservatory where hearty breakfasts are served.

Rooms 3 en suite (1 GF) ⊘ S £40-£45; D £54-£70✱ **Facilities** TVB tea/coffee Cen ht TVL **Parking** 6 **Notes LB** 184 acres Beef 🐾

★★★ BED & BREAKFAST
Cor Unum
Monmouth Rd, Edge-End GL16 7HB
☎ 01594 837960
e-mail: antony@jones3649.freeserve.co.uk
Dir: *On A4136 in village of Edge End*
PETS: Bedrooms Charges charge for additional cleaning if necessary **Public areas Grounds** accessible disp bin
Exercise area 300yds **Facilities** food (pre-bookable) food bowl water bowl bedding dog chews cat treats all facilities available upon request at time of booking pet sitting dog walking washing facs cage storage vet info **On Request** fridge access torch towels **Other** all above facilities available on request at time of booking **Restrictions** small-medium dogs only

A genuine welcome is assured at this comfortably appointed bungalow which is located in the heart of the Forest of Dean. Bedrooms are neatly furnished, and the lounge has wonderful views across the garden of the Welsh mountains. Breakfast, served in the cosy dining room, is a tasty and fulfilling start to the day.

Rooms 3 rms (2 en suite) (3 GF) ⊘ S £27-£40; D £50-£80
Facilities TV2B tea/coffee Cen ht TVL Dinner Last d breakfast
Parking 1 **Notes LB** No children 🐾

★★★ 🏵🏵 HOTEL
Corse Lawn House
GL19 4LZ
☎ 01452 780771 🖹 01452 780840
e-mail: enquiries@corselawn.com
web: www.corselawn.com
Dir: *on B4211 5m SW of Tewkesbury*
PETS: Bedrooms (GF) unattended sign **Public areas** except restaurant on leads **Grounds** accessible disp bin
Exercise area 100yds **Facilities** food (pre-bookable) washing facs walks info vet info **On Request** fridge access torch
Resident Pets: Sugar & Spice (Black Labradors), Donna & Gigi (horses)

This gracious Grade II listed Queen Anne house has been home to the Hine family since 1978. Aided by an enthusiastic and committed team, the family still presides over all aspects, creating a relaxed and wonderfully comforting environment. Bedrooms offer a reassuring mix of comfort and quality. Impressive cuisine is based upon excellent produce, much of it locally sourced.

Rooms 19 en suite (2 fmly) (5 GF) ⊘ in all bedrooms S £90; D £145 (incl. bkfst)✱ **Facilities** STV 🕭 🏊 🏌 Wi-fi in bedrooms Badminton Table tennis New Year **Parking** 62 **Notes LB** Closed 24-26 Dec

DUMBLETON

MAP 04 SP03

★★★ 73% HOTEL

Dumbleton Hall

WR11 7TS

☎ 01386 881240 📄 01386 882142

e-mail: dh@pofr.co.uk

Dir: *M5 junct 9/A46. 2nd exit at rdbt signed Evesham. Through Beckford for 1m, turn right signed Dumbleton. Hotel at S end of village.*

PETS: Bedrooms unattended **Grounds** accessible

Originally constructed in the 16th century, and re-built in the mid-18th century this establishment is set in 19 acres of landscaped gardens and parkland. Spacious public rooms make this an ideal venue for weddings, conferences or a hideaway retreat - the location makes an ideal touring base. Panoramic views of the Vale of Evesham can be seen from every window.

Rooms 34 en suite (9 fmly) ⊘ in 25 bedrooms S £120; D £160-£260 (incl. bkfst)✳ **Facilities** FTV ⤹ Wi-fi available Xmas New Year **Services** Lift **Parking** 60 **Notes** LB

GLOUCESTER

MAP 03 SO81

★★★ 70% HOTEL

Macdonald Hatherley Manor

Down Hatherley Ln GL2 9QA

☎ 0870 1942126 & 01452 730217 📄 01452 731032

e-mail: hatherleymanor@macdonaldhotels.co.uk

web: www.macdonald-hotels.co.uk

Dir: *off A38 into Down Hatherley Lane, signed. Hotel 600yds on left*

PETS: Bedrooms (GF) unattended **Grounds** accessible

Within easy striking distance of the M5, Gloucester, Cheltenham and the Cotswolds, this stylish 17th-century manor remains popular with both business and leisure guests. Bedrooms all offer contemporary comforts. A range of meeting and function rooms is available.

Macdonald Hotels - AA Hotel Group of the Year 2007-8

Rooms 52 en suite ⊘ in all bedrooms **Facilities** STV Wi-fi in bedrooms **Parking** 250

★★★ 68% HOTEL

Ramada Hotel & Resort Gloucester

Matson Ln, Robinswood Hill GL4 6EA

☎ 01452 525653 📄 01452 307212

e-mail: sales.gloucester@ramadajarvis.co.uk

web: www.ramadajarvis.co.uk

Dir: *A40 towards Gloucester onto A38. Take 1st exit at 4th rdbt (Painswick Rd) and turn right onto Matson Ln*

PETS: Bedrooms Charges £5 per night **Grounds** accessible **Exercise area** adjacent

Conveniently located close to the M5, this large hotel is set in 240 acres of grounds. Bedrooms are comfortably appointed for both business and leisure guests.

Rooms 97 en suite (7 fmly) (20 GF) ⊘ in 59 bedrooms **Facilities** STV ☜ supervised ⅃ 18 ⌕ Squash Gym Putt green Wi-fi in bedrooms Dry ski slopes **Parking** 200 **Notes** Closed 24-26 Dec

---

►►► **Red Lion Camping & Caravan Park**

(SO849258)

Wainlode Hill, Norton GL2 9LW

☎ 01452 730251 📄 01452 730251

web: www.redlioninn-caravancampingpark.co.uk

Dir: *Turn off A38 at Norton and follow road to river*

PETS: Charges 1st dog free, 2nd dog £1.50 per night **Public areas** must be on short leads **Exercise area** river bank adjacent **Facilities** on site shop food dog chews cat treats walks info vet info **Other** prior notice required

Open all year Booking advisable Spring bank hol Last arrival 22.00hrs Last departure 11.00hrs

An attractive meadowland park, adjacent to a traditional pub, with the River Severn just across a country lane. This is an ideal touring and fishing base. A 13-acre site with 60 touring pitches, 10 hardstandings and 20 statics.

LONGHOPE

MAP 03 SO61

★★★★ BED & BREAKFAST

The Old Farm

Barrel Ln GL17 0LR

☎ 01452 830252

e-mail: lucy@the-old-farm.co.uk

Dir: *1m N of Longhope. Off A40 N onto Barrel Ln, B&B 300yds on right*

PETS: Bedrooms Exercise area paddock on farm **Facilities** vet info **Resident Pets:** Donna & Charlie (Golden Retrievers)

This former cider farm, just off the A40 between Gloucester and Ross-on-Wye, offers some bedrooms in the main house and self-catering cottages in adjacent converted barns. The house has lots of character and the friendly host gives a warm welcome. There is a lounge, and breakfast, featuring home-made items and daily specials, is served in the cosy dining area. There is a choice of pubs serving food within walking distance.

Rooms 3 en suite (1 GF) ⊗ **Facilities** TVB tea/coffee Cen ht **Parking** 6
Notes No children 12yrs Closed 20 Dec–4 Jan

MICHAEL WOOD MAP 03 ST79
MOTORWAY SERVICE AREA (M5)

BUDGET HOTEL
Days Inn Michaelwood

 **DAYS INN**

Michael Wood Service Area, Lower Wick
GL11 6DD
☎ 01454 261513 📠 01454 269150
e-mail: michaelwood.hotel@welcomebreak.co.uk
web: www.daysinn.com

Dir: *M5 northbound between junct 13 and 14*

PETS: Bedrooms (GF) unattended **Public areas** on leads
Grounds accessible on leads **Facilities** walks info vet info
Restrictions no dangerous breeds (see page 7)

This modern building offers accommodation in smart, spacious and well-equipped bedrooms, suitable for families and business travellers, and all with en suite bathrooms. Continental breakfast is available and other refreshments may be taken at the nearby family restaurant. For further details see the Hotel Groups page.

Rooms 38 en suite

MORETON-IN-MARSH MAP 04 SP23

★★★ 81% ◉◉ HOTEL
Manor House

CLASSIC
BRITISH HOTELS

High St GL56 0LJ
☎ 01608 650501 📠 01608 651481
e-mail: info@manorhousehotel.info
web: www.cotswold-inns-hotels.co.uk/manor

Dir: *off A429 at south end of town. Take East St off High St, hotel car park 3rd on right*

PETS: Bedrooms (GF) unattended **Charges** charge for damage
Public areas except eating areas **Grounds** accessible
Facilities cage storage walks info vet info **On Request** fridge access torch towels

Dating back to the 16th century, this charming Cotswold coaching inn retains much of its original character with stone walls, impressive fireplaces and a relaxed, country-house atmosphere. Bedrooms vary in size and reflect the individuality of the building; all are well equipped and some are particularly opulent. Comfortable public areas include the popular bar and stylish Mulberry Restaurant - dinner should not be missed here.

Rooms 35 en suite 3 annexe en suite (3 fmly) ⊗ in all bedrooms
D £135–£175 (incl. bkfst)✴ **Facilities** Wi-fi in bedrooms Xmas New Year
Services Lift **Parking** 24

NEWENT MAP 03 SO72

►►► **Pelerine Caravan and Camping**

(SO645183)

Ford House Rd GL18 1LQ
☎ 01531 822761
e-mail: pelerine@hotmail.com
web: www.newent.biz

Dir: *1m from Newent*

PETS: Charges 50p per night **Public areas**
Exercise area adjacent **Facilities** washing facs vet info
Other prior notice required **Resident Pets:** Bennie (Old English Sheepdog), Narla & Simba (Spaniels), Buttons (cat)

Open Mar–Nov Booking advisable Last arrival 22.00hrs Last departure 16.00hrs

A pleasant site divided into two areas, one of which is for adults only, with hardstandings and electric hook ups in each area. It is close to several vineyards, and well positioned in the north of the Forest of Dean with Tewkesbury and Cheltenham within easy reach. A 5-acre site with 35 touring pitches.

Notes 🐾

SLIMBRIDGE MAP 03 SO70

►►► **Tudor Caravan & Camping** (SO728040)

Shepherds Patch GL2 7BP
☎ 01453 890483
e-mail: aa@tudorcaravanpark.co.uk
web: www.tudorcaravanpark.com

Dir: *From M5 junct 13 follow signs for WWT Wetlands Wildlife Centre-Slimbridge. Site at rear of Tudor Arms pub*

PETS: Stables nearby (2m) **Charges** £1 per night
Public areas on leads **Exercise area** on site rally field available when not in use tow path adjacent **Facilities** on site shop food bowl water bowl walks info vet info **Other** prior notice required

Open all year Booking advisable bank & school hols Last arrival 20.00hrs Last departure noon

An orchard-style park sheltered by mature trees and shrubs, set in an attractive meadow beside a canal. This tidy site offers both level grass and gravel pitches complete with electric hook-ups, and there is a separate area for adults only. Slimbridge Wetlands Centre is close by, and there is much scope locally for bird-watching. An 8-acre site with 75 touring pitches, 48 hardstandings.

Notes 🐾

ENGLAND

STOW-ON-THE-WOLD
MAP 04 SP12

★★★ 75% HOTEL
The Unicorn
Sheep St GL54 1HQ
☎ 01451 830257 📠 01451 831090
e-mail: reception@birchhotels.co.uk
Dir: *at junct of A429 & A436*

PETS: Bedrooms unattended **Charges** £10 per night
Public areas bar only **Grounds** accessible **Exercise area** 1m
This attractive limestone hotel dates back to the 17th century.
Individually designed bedrooms include some delightful four-poster
rooms. Spacious public areas retain much character and include a
choice of inviting lounges and a traditional bar offering a good
selection of bar meals and ales. The restaurant provides a stylish venue
for impressive cuisine.
Rooms 20 en suite ⊘ in all bedrooms S £65-£90; D £85-£145 (incl. bkfst
& dinner)✳ **Facilities** Wi-fi available Xmas New Year **Parking** 40 **Notes**

★★ 71% SMALL HOTEL
Old Stocks
The Square GL54 1AF
☎ 01451 830666 📠 01451 870014
e-mail: aa@theoldstockshotel.co.uk
web: www.oldstockshotel.co.uk
Dir: *turn off A429 to town centre. Hotel facing village green*

PETS: Bedrooms (GF) unattended **Charges** £5 per stay
Public areas except restaurant on leads **Grounds** accessible on
leads disp bin **Exercise area** 500yds **Facilities** water bowl cage
storage walks info vet info **On Request** torch towels
Restrictions no noisy or dangerous breeds (see page 7)
Overlooking the old market square, this Grade II listed, mellow
Cotswold-stone building is a comfortable and friendly base from which
to explore this picturesque area. There is a lot of character and
atmosphere with bedrooms all offering individuality and charm.
Facilities include a guest lounge, restaurant and bar, whilst outside, the
patio is a popular summer venue for refreshing drinks and good food.
Rooms 15 en suite 3 annexe en suite (5 fmly) (4 GF) ⊘ in all bedrooms
S £35-£55; D £70-£130 (incl. bkfst) **Facilities** Xmas New Year **Parking** 12
Notes LB

★★★ GUEST ACCOMMODATION
Limes
Evesham Rd GL54 1EJ
☎ 01451 830034 📠 01451 830034
e-mail: thelimes@zoom.co.uk
Dir: *500yds from village centre on A424*

PETS: Bedrooms (GF) **Charges** charge for damage
Public areas except breakfast room on leads **Grounds** accessible
on leads disp bin **Facilities** water bowl dog chews leads walks
info vet info **On Request** fridge access torch towels
Resident Pets: Casey (Doberman)
Just a short walk from the village centre, this Victorian house provides a
comfortable base from which to explore this beautiful area. Bedroom
styles vary, with four-poster and ground-floor rooms offered. A warm
and genuine welcome is extended, and many guests return on a
regular basis. A spacious lounge is available and breakfast is served in
the light and airy dining room.
Rooms 4 en suite 1 annexe en suite (1 fmly) (1 GF) D £49-£52
Facilities STV TVB tea/coffee Cen ht TVL **Parking** 4 **Notes** Closed
Xmas ⊛

STROUD
MAP 03 SO80

★★★ 73% HOTEL
The Bear of Rodborough
Rodborough Common GL5 5DE
☎ 01453 878522 📠 01453 872523
e-mail: info@bearofrodborough.info
web: www.cotswold-inns-hotels.co.uk
Dir: *M5 junct 13, A419 to Stroud. Follow signs to Rodborough. Up
hill, left at top at T-junct. Hotel on right.*

CLASSIC
BRITISH HOTELS

PETS: Bedrooms (GF) unattended **Charges** charge for damage
Public areas except eating areas **Grounds** accessible
Facilities walks info vet info **On Request** fridge access torch
towels
This popular 17th-century coaching inn is situated high above Stroud
within acres of National Trust parkland. Character abounds in the
lounges, cocktail bar and Box Tree restaurant. Bedrooms offer equal
measures of comfort and style with plenty of extra touches. There is
also a traditional and well-patronised public bar. Cuisine is a feature
and local produce is frequently utilised.
Rooms 46 en suite (2 fmly) ⊘ in all bedrooms S fr £75; D £120-£130
(incl. bkfst)✳ **Facilities** ⌣ Putt green Wi-fi in bedrooms Xmas New Year
Parking 70 **Notes** LB

★★★★ BED & BREAKFAST
Hyde Crest

Cirencester Rd GL6 8PE

☎ 01453 731631

e-mail: anthea@hydecrest.demon.co.uk

web: www.hydecrest.co.uk

Dir: *Off A419, 5m E of Stroud, signed Minchinhampton & Aston Down, house 3rd right opp Ragged Cot pub*

PETS: Bedrooms (GF) unattended **Public areas**
Grounds accessible disp bin **Exercise area** local walks, 500-acre common within 1m **Facilities** washing facs walks info vet info **On Request** fridge access torch towels **Resident Pets:** Cocker Spaniel

Hyde Crest lies on the edge of the picturesque Cotswold village of Minchinhampton. Bedrooms are located at ground floor level, each with a private patio where welcome refreshments are enjoyed upon arrival (weather permitting). Guests are attentively cared for and scrumptious breakfasts are served in the small lounge-dining room around a communal table.

Rooms 3 en suite (3 GF) ⊗ D £60-£65 **Facilities** TVB tea/coffee Cen ht TVL Wi-fi available **Parking** 6 **Notes** No children 10yrs RS Xmas & New Year (no meals available) ⊗

TETBURY   MAP 03 ST89

★★★ 75% HOTEL
Best Western Hare & Hounds

Westonbirt GL8 8QL

☎ 01666 880233 & 881000 📄 01666 880241

e-mail: enquiries@hareandhoundshotel.com

web: www.hareandhoundshotel.com

Dir: *2.5m SW of Tetbury on A433*

PETS: Bedrooms (GF) unattended **Charges** £6.50 per night charge for damage **Public areas** except restaurant on leads **Grounds** accessible disp bin **Facilities** water bowl dog chews cage storage walks info vet info **On Request** fridge access

This popular hotel, set in extensive grounds, is situated close to Westonbirt Arboretum and has remained under the same ownership for over 50 years. Bedrooms are individual in style, with those in the main house more traditional and the stylish cottage rooms being contemporary in design. Public rooms include the informal bar and light, airy lounges, one with a log fire in colder months. Guests can dine either in the bar or attractive restaurant.

Best Western Hare & Hounds

Rooms 24 en suite 21 annexe en suite (8 fmly) (13 GF) ⊗ in all bedrooms S £80-£93; D £120-£175 (incl. bkfst)✳ **Facilities** STV ♨ ᕗ Putt green Wi-fi in bedrooms Xmas New Year **Parking** 85 **Notes** LB

★★ 64% HOTEL
Hunters Hall

Kingscote GL8 8XZ

☎ 01453 860393 📄 01453 860707

e-mail: huntershall.kingscote@greeneking.co.uk

web: www.oldenglish.co.uk

Dir: *M4 junct 18, take A46 towards Stroud. 10m turn left signed Kingscote, follow road to T-junct, turn left, hotel 0.5m on left.*

PETS: Bedrooms unattended **Charges** £5 per night **Public areas** except restaurant **Grounds** accessible **Exercise area** 5mtrs **Facilities** food **Resident Pets:** Biscuit (cat)

Situated close to Tetbury, this 16th-century inn has a wealth of charm and character, enhanced by beamed ceilings and open fires. There are three bars and a restaurant offering freshly prepared home cooked, traditional food from an extensive menu. There is a large garden and play area. The bedrooms, situated in the converted stable block, are comfortable with a good range of extras. One ground floor room has facilities for the disabled.

Rooms 12 annexe en suite (1 fmly) (8 GF) ⊗ in 8 bedrooms **Facilities** Pool table ch fac **Parking** 100 **Notes** LB

TEWKESBURY   MAP 03 SO83

★★ 60% HOTEL

Bell

52 Church St GL20 5SA

☎ 01684 293293 📠 01684 295938

e-mail: 6408@greeneking.co.uk

web: www.oldenglish.co.uk

Dir: *M5 junct 9, follow brown tourist signs for Tewkesbury Abbey, hotel directly opposite Abbey.*

PETS: Bedrooms Charges £5 per night **Public areas** except restaurant **Grounds** accessible **Exercise area** behind hotel

This 14th-century former coaching house is situated on the edge of the town, opposite the Norman abbey. The bar and lounge are the focal point of this atmospheric and friendly establishment, with a large open fire providing warmth. Bedrooms offer good levels of comfort and quality with many extra facilities provided, such as CD players.

Rooms 24 en suite (1 fmly) (4 GF) ⊘ in 7 bedrooms **Parking** 20
Notes LB

THORNBURY   MAP 04 ST69

★★★ ◉◉ HOTEL

Thornbury Castle

Castle St BS35 1HH   von Essen hotels
A PRIVATE COLLECTION
www.vonessenhotels.com

☎ 01454 281182 📠 01454 416188

e-mail: info@thornburycastle.co.uk

web: www.vonessenhotels.co.uk

Dir: *on A38 N'bound from Bristol take 1st turn to Thornbury. At end of High St left into Castle St, follow brown sign, entrance to Castle on left behind St Mary's Church*

PETS: Bedrooms (GF) **Charges** £10 per night £70 per week **Grounds** accessible **Exercise area** 0.5m **Facilities** washing facs cage storage walks info vet info **On Request** fridge access torch towels

Henry VIII ordered the first owner of this castle to be beheaded! Guests today have the opportunity of sleeping in historical surroundings fitted out with all modern amenities. Most rooms have four-poster or coronet beds and real fires. Tranquil lounges enjoy views over the

gardens, while elegant, wood-panelled dining rooms make a memorable setting for a leisurely award-winning meal.

Rooms 25 en suite (3 fmly) (3 GF) S £90-£110; D £155-£325 (incl. bkfst) ✳ **Facilities** ✨ Wi-fi available Archery Helicopter ride Clay pigeon shooting Massage treatment Xmas New Year **Parking** 40 **Notes** LB

TORMARTON   MAP 03 ST77

★★ 78% HOTEL

Best Western Compass Inn

GL9 1JB

☎ 01454 218242 & 218577 📠 01454 218741

e-mail: info@compass-inn.co.uk

web: www.compass-inn.co.uk

Dir: *0.5m from M4 junct 18*

PETS: Bedrooms (GF) unattended **Charges** £3 per night **Public areas** except restaurant **Grounds** accessible **Exercise area** countryside **Facilities** vet info **Resident Pets:** Basil & Harry (Black Standard Poodles), Chloe (cat)

Originally a coaching inn dating from the 18th century, this hostelry has grown considerably over the years. Bedrooms are spacious and well equipped, whilst public areas include a choice of bars and varied dining options. A range of conference rooms is also available, providing facilities for varied functions.

Rooms 26 en suite (5 fmly) (12 GF) ⊘ in 19 bedrooms S £88.50-£98.50; D £98.50-£108.50✳ **Facilities** Wi-fi in bedrooms French boules New Year **Parking** 160 **Notes** LB Closed 24-26 Dec

---

WINCHCOMBE   MAP 04 SP02

▶▶▶ **Winchcombe Camping & Caravanning Club Site** *(SP007324)*

Brooklands Farm, Alderton GL20 8NX

☎ 01242 620259

web: www.campingandcaravanningclub.co.uk/winchcombe

Dir: *M5 junct 9 onto A46, straight on at rdbt onto B4077 signed Stow-on-the-Wold. Site 3m on right*

PETS: Exercise area on site dog walk **Facilities** walks info vet info **Other** prior notice required

Open 16 Mar-15 Jan Booking advisable BHs & peak periods Last arrival 21.00hrs Last departure noon

A pleasant rural park with pitches spaced around two attractive lakes offering good fishing, and the benefit of a long season. This flower-filled park is in an area of historic buildings and picturesque villages between Cheltenham and Tewkesbury. A 20-acre site with 80 touring pitches, 63 hardstandings.

Notes Site gates will be closed from 23.00-07.00.

ENGLAND

GREATER LONDON

HEATHROW AIRPORT (LONDON)

MAP 04 TQ07

★★★ 75% HOTEL
Novotel London Heathrow

Cherry Ln UB7 9HB

NOVOTEL
ACCOR hotels

☎ 01895 431431 📠 01895 431221

e-mail: H1551gm@accor.com

web: www.novotel.com

Dir: *M4 junct 4, follow Uxbridge signs on A408. Keep left and take 2nd exit off traffic island into Cherry Ln signed West Drayton. Hotel on left*

PETS: Bedrooms unattended **Charges** £10 per night **Public areas**

Conveniently located for Heathrow and the motorway network, this modern hotel provides comfortable accommodation. The large, airy indoor atrium creates a sense of space to the public areas, which include an all-day restaurant and bar, meeting rooms, fitness centre and swimming pool. Ample secure parking is available.

Rooms 178 en suite (178 fmly) (10 GF) ⊗ in 140 bedrooms S £50-£145; D £50-£145✱ **Facilities** STV ⊗ Gym Wi-fi available **Services** Lift air con **Parking** 100 (charged)

★★★ GUEST ACCOMMODATION
Harmondsworth Hall

Summerhouse Ln, Harmondsworth Village UB7 0BG

☎ 020 8759 1824 & 07713 104229 📠 020 8897 6385

e-mail: elaine@harmondsworthhall.com

web: www.harmondsworthhall.com

Dir: *M4 junct 4, A3044 Holloway Ln onto Harmondsworth High St, left after Crown pub*

PETS: Bedrooms Charges £5 per night **Public areas** except breakfast room **Grounds** accessible **Exercise area** 2 mins walk **Resident Pets:** Connie (Golden Retriever)

Hidden away in the old part of the village, this delightful property has been restored and converted into a spacious guest house. It is well located for the airport and motorways. Breakfast is served in an attractive wood-panelled dining room overlooking the gardens and there is a spacious lounge. The well-equipped bedrooms are all individually furnished.

Rooms 10 en suite (4 fmly) (2 GF) ⊗ S £60-£70; D £70-£85✱ **Facilities** STV FTV TVB tea/coffee Direct dial from bedrooms Cen ht TVL Dinner Last d by arrangement Wi-fi available **Parking** 8 **Notes** LB

KINGSTON UPON THAMES

MAP 04 TQ16

★★★ GUEST ACCOMMODATION
Chase Lodge

10 Park Rd, Hampton Wick KT1 4AS

☎ 020 8943 1862 📠 020 8943 9363

e-mail: info@chaselodgehotel.com

web: www.chaselodgehotel.com

Dir: *A308 onto A310 signed Twickenham, 1st left onto Park Rd*

PETS: Bedrooms (GF) unattended **Charges** charge for damage **Exercise area** nearby **Facilities** pet sitting dog walking walks info vet info **Resident Pets:** Dibley (Jack Russell)

This delightful guest house is set in a quiet residential area, a short walk from Kingston Bridge. The individually decorated rooms vary in size and are all well-appointed and feature a range of useful extras. An attractive lounge-bar-restaurant is provided where breakfast, snacks and dinner by pre-arrangement are served. On-road parking is available.

Rooms 6 en suite 5 annexe en suite (2 fmly) (4 GF) ⊗ S £65-£79; D £79-£185✱ **Facilities** STV FTV TVB tea/coffee Direct dial from bedrooms Cen ht TVL Dinner Last d 8pm Wi-fi available **Notes** LB

GREATER MANCHESTER

ALTRINCHAM

MAP 07 SJ78

★★★ 75% HOTEL
Best Western Cresta Court

Church St WA14 4DP

Best Western

☎ 0161 927 7272 📠 0161 929 6548

e-mail: rooms@cresta-court.co.uk

web: www.cresta-court.co.uk

PETS: Bedrooms unattended **Charges** charge for damage **Public areas** except bar & restaurant on leads **Grounds** accessible on leads **Exercise area** nearby **On Request** towels

This modern hotel enjoys a prime location on the A56, close to the station, town centre shops and other amenities. Bedrooms vary in style from spacious four-posters to smaller, traditionally furnished rooms.

CONTINUED

ENGLAND

ALTRINCHAM CONTINUED

Public areas include a choice of bars and extensive function and conference facilities.

Best Western Cresta Court

Rooms 138 en suite (9 fmly) ⊗ in 127 bedrooms S £49-£89; D £59-£140
Facilities Gym Wi-fi in bedrooms **Services** Lift **Parking** 200 **Notes**

BOLTON   MAP 07 SD70

★★★ GUEST HOUSE
Broomfield House

33-35 Wigan Rd, Deane BL3 5PX
☎ 01204 61570 📠 01204 650932
e-mail: chris@broomfield.force9.net

Dir: M61 junct 5, A58 to 1st lights, onto A676, premises on right

PETS: Bedrooms unattended **Exercise area** across road
Facilities washing facs cage storage walks info vet info
On Request fridge access towels

A friendly relaxed atmosphere prevails at the Broomfield, close to the motorway and west of the town centre. The bedrooms, some suitable for families, have modern facilities, and public areas include a bar and a lounge. Hearty breakfasts are served in the separate dining room.

Rooms 20 en suite (2 fmly) (2 GF) ⊗ in 8 bedrooms S £38-£42; D £50✱ **Facilities** TVB tea/coffee Licensed Cen ht TVL **Parking** 12

DIGGLE   MAP 07 SE00

★★ GUEST HOUSE
Sunfield Accommodation

Diglea OL3 5LA
☎ 01457 874030
e-mail: sunfield.accom@lineone.net

Dir: Off A670 to Diggle village, off Huddersfield Rd onto Sam Rd to Diggle Hotel & signs for Diggle Ranges

PETS: Bedrooms (GF) unattended **Stables** on site **Exercise area** nearby **Facilities** food bowl water bowl leads cage storage walks info vet info **On Request** fridge access torch

This friendly, family-run operation is located within easy reach of Manchester and the M62, and affords wonderful views over the

Pennines; bedrooms are on the ground floor and pets are made welcome. Breakfast is served at one large table and a couple of good pubs serving food are located at the bottom of the lane.

Rooms 4 en suite (1 fmly) (4 GF) ⊗ S £35-£40; D £50-£60✱
Facilities FTV TVB tea/coffee Cen ht TVL **Parking** 11
Notes No coaches ⊗

MANCHESTER   MAP 07 SJ89

BUDGET HOTEL
Hotel Ibis Manchester City Centre

96 Portland St M1 4GY
☎ 0161 234 0600 📠 0161 234 0610
e-mail: H3142@accor-hotels.com
web: www.accorhotels.com

Dir: In city centre, between Princess St & Oxford St. 10min walk from Piccadilly

PETS: Bedrooms Public areas except restaurant on leads
Facilities vet info

Modern, budget hotel offering comfortable accommodation in bright and practical bedrooms. Breakfast is self-service and dinner is available in the restaurant. For further details, consult the Hotel Groups page.

Rooms 127 en suite

HAMPSHIRE

ALTON   MAP 04 SU73

★★★ 74% ⊛⊛ HOTEL
Alton Grange

London Rd GU34 4EG
☎ 01420 86565 📠 01420 541346
e-mail: info@altongrange.co.uk
web: www.altongrange.co.uk

Dir: from A31 right at rdbt signed Alton/Holybourne/Bordon B3004. Hotel 300yds on left

PETS: Bedrooms unattended **Charges** £5 per night
Public areas except restaurant **Grounds** accessible
Exercise area 100yds **Resident Pets:** Caramel, Barley, Smartie, Treacle, Honey, Saffron, Cracker (cats)

A friendly family owned hotel, conveniently located on the outskirts of this market town and set in two acres of lovingly tended gardens. The individually styled bedrooms, including three suites, are all thoughtfully equipped. Diners can choose between the more formal Truffles Restaurant or relaxed Muffins Brasserie. The attractive public areas include a function suite.

Rooms 26 en suite 4 annexe en suite (4 fmly) (7 GF) ⊗ in 11 bedrooms S £90; D £110 (incl. bkfst)✱ **Facilities** STV Wi-fi in bedrooms Hot air ballooning **Parking** 48 **Notes** LB No children 3yrs Closed 24 Dec-2 Jan

ANDOVER   MAP 04 SU34

★★★ 74% ◉ HOTEL
Esseborne Manor
Hurstbourne Tarrant SP11 0ER
☎ 01264 736444 🖷 01264 736725
e-mail: info@esseborne-manor.co.uk
web: www.esseborne-manor.co.uk
Dir: *halfway between Andover & Newbury on A343, just 1m N of Hurstbourne Tarrant*

PETS: Bedrooms (GF) unattended sign Charges charge for damage Grounds accessible disp bin Facilities water bowl washing facs cage storage walks info vet info On Request fridge access torch towels

Set in two acres of well-tended gardens, this attractive manor house is surrounded by the open countryside of the North Wessex Downs. Bedrooms are delightfully individual and are split between the main house, an adjoining courtyard and separate garden cottage. A wonderfully relaxed atmosphere pervades throughout, with public rooms combining elegance with comfort.

Rooms 11 en suite 9 annexe en suite (2 fmly) (6 GF) ⊘ in 6 bedrooms S £98-£130; D £125-£250 (incl. bkfst)✳ Facilities STV Ⓔ ✔ Wi-fi in bedrooms ch fac Parking 50 Notes LB

BEAULIEU   MAP 04 SU30

★★★ 73% ◉ HOTEL
Beaulieu
Beaulieu Rd SO42 7YQ
☎ 023 8029 3344 🖷 023 8029 2729
e-mail: beaulieu@newforesthotels.co.uk
web: www.newforesthotels.co.uk
Dir: *M27 junct 1/A337 towards Lyndhurst. Left at lights in Lyndhurst, through village, turn right onto B3056, continue for 3m.*

PETS: Bedrooms unattended Charges £5 per night Public areas except food areas Grounds accessible Exercise area adjacent

Conveniently located in the heart of the New Forest and close to Beaulieu Road railway station, this popular, small hotel provides an ideal base for exploring this lovely area. Facilities include an indoor swimming pool, an outdoor children's play area and an adjoining pub. A daily changing menu is offered in the restaurant.

Rooms 20 en suite 3 annexe en suite (2 fmly) (3 GF) Facilities ⓒ Steam room Services Lift Parking 60

BROCKENHURST   MAP 04 SU30

★★★ 83% ◉◉ HOTEL
New Park Manor

von Essen hotels
A PRIVATE COLLECTION
www.vonessenhotels.com

Lyndhurst Rd SO42 7QH
☎ 01590 623467 🖷 01590 622268
e-mail: info@newparkmanorhotel.co.uk
web: www.vonessenhotels.co.uk
Dir: *M27 junct 1, A337 to Lyndhurst & Brockenhurst. Hotel 1.5m on right*

PETS: Bedrooms unattended Stables nearby (2m) Charges £10 per night Public areas Grounds accessible Exercise area 100yds

Once the favoured hunting lodge of King Charles II, this well presented hotel enjoys a peaceful setting in the New Forest and comes complete with an equestrian centre. The bedrooms are divided between the old house and a purpose-built wing. The impressive spa offers a range of treatments.

Rooms 24 en suite (6 fmly) ⊘ in all bedrooms Facilities Spa ⓒ supervised ⤳ Ⓔ Riding Gym ✔ Wi-fi available Mountain biking Parking 70

★★★ 72% HOTEL
Forest Park
Rhinefield Rd SO42 7ZG
☎ 01590 622844 🖷 01590 623948
e-mail: forest.park@forestdale.com
web: www.forestdale.com
Dir: *A337 to Brockenhurst turn into Meerut Rd, follow road through Waters Green. Right at T-junct into Rhinefield Rd*

PETS: Bedrooms unattended Charges £7.50 per night Public areas except restaurant

A very friendly hotel offering good facilities for both adults and children. A heated pool, riding, children's meal times and a quiet location in the forest are just a few of the attractions here. The well-equipped, comfortable bedrooms vary in size and style, and a choice of lounge and bar areas is available.

Rooms 38 en suite (2 fmly) (7 GF) ⊘ in 2 bedrooms Facilities ⤳ Ⓔ Riding Wi-fi available Parking 80

BROCKENHURST CONTINUED

★★★ BED & BREAKFAST
Bridge House

Lyndhurst Rd SO42 7TR

☎ 01590 623135 & 624760 📄 01590 623916

e-mail: jmvb2@aol.com

Dir: *On A337 at N end of village*

PETS: Bedrooms sign **Stables** nearby (0.3m) **Charges** £3 per night charge for damage **Public areas** except dining room **Grounds** accessible disp bin **Exercise area** adjacent **Facilities** food bowl water bowl feeding mat dog scoop/disp bags leads pet sitting washing facs cage storage walks info vet info **On Request** fridge access torch

Located in the Waters Green conservation area, this 18th-century house is just off the Brockenhurst to Lyndhurst road. It is well positioned for easy access to the town and the surrounding New Forest, and the comfortably furnished bedrooms are equipped with thoughtful extra facilities. Breakfast is a hearty affair.

Rooms 3 rms (1 en suite) (1 fmly) ⊛ S £40-£55; D £50-£70✴ **Facilities** TVB tea/coffee Cen ht ⌣ **Parking** 5 **Notes** LB Closed Xmas 🐾

★★★ INN
White Buck Inn

Bisterne Close BH24 4AT

☎ 01425 402264 📄 01425 403588

e-mail: whitebuckinn@accommodating-inns.co.uk

web: www.accommodating-inns.co.uk

Dir: *Between A31 & A35, follow signs for Burley*

PETS: Bedrooms unattended **Charges** £10 per night charge for damage **Public areas** except restaurant on leads **Grounds** accessible on leads **Exercise area** adjacent to New Forest **Facilities** feeding mat leads wash fac cage storage walks info vet info **On Request** fridge access **Other** dogs in 1 bedroom only **Resident Pets:** Susie (Springer Spaniel), Millie (cat)

Set in three acres of parkland in the heart of the New Forest, this delightful inn offers comfortable accommodation in charming surroundings. Bedrooms, one of which offers a four-poster bed, provide many thoughtful extras. A substantial choice of home-cooked meals are available in the spacious bar and restaurant.

Rooms 9 en suite (3 fmly) **Facilities** TVB tea/coffee Direct dial from bedrooms Cen ht Dinner Last d 9pm Golf 18 Fishing Riding **Parking** 90 **Notes** Closed 24-26 Dec

---

BURLEY
MAP 04 SU20

★★★ 75% HOTEL
Burley Manor

Ringwood Rd BH24 4BS

☎ 01425 403522 📄 01425 403227

e-mail: burley.manor@forestdale.com

web: www.forestdale.com

Dir: *leave A31 at Burley sign, hotel 3m on left*

PETS: Bedrooms unattended **Stables** on site **Charges** £7.50 per night **Public areas** except restaurant

Set in extensive grounds, this 18th-century mansion house enjoys a relaxed ambience and a peaceful setting. Half of the well-equipped, comfortable bedrooms, including several with four-posters, are located in the main house. The remainder, many of which have balconies, are in the adjacent converted stable block overlooking the outdoor pool. Cosy public rooms benefit from log fires in winter.

Rooms 21 en suite 17 annexe en suite (2 fmly) (17 GF) ⊛ in 10 bedrooms **Facilities** ↘ supervised Riding Wi-fi available **Parking** 60

EAST TYTHERLEY
MAP 04 SU22

★★★★ ◉◉ INN
The Star Inn Tytherley

SO51 0LW

☎ 01794 340225

e-mail: info@starinn.co.uk

Dir: *1m S of East Tytherley*

PETS: Bedrooms (GF) unattended **Charges** charge for damage **Public areas** except restaurant on leads **Grounds** accessible on leads disp bin **Exercise area** adjoining **Facilities** food (pre-bookable) food bowl water bowl washing facs cage storage walks info vet info **On Request** fridge access torch towels

This charming coaching inn offers bedrooms in a purpose-built annexe, separate from the main pub. The spacious rooms have high levels of quality and comfort, and an outdoor children's play area is available. The inn has a loyal following of locals and visitors, drawn especially by the excellent food.

Rooms 3 annexe en suite (3 GF) ⊘ S £55-£70; D £90✳ **Facilities** FTV TVB tea/coffee Cen ht Dinner Last d 9pm Wi-fi available **Parking** 50 **Notes** RS Sun eve & Mon

---

FAREHAM
MAP 04 SU50

★★★ GUEST ACCOMMODATION
Travelrest - Solent Gateway

22 The Avenue PO14 1NS
☎ 01329 232175 📠 01329 232196
web: www.travelrest.co.uk
Dir: *0.5m from town centre on A27. 500yds from railway station*

PETS: Bedrooms (GF) unattended **Charges** £5 per night **Grounds** accessible **Exercise area** park **Facilities** food (pre-bookable) vet info **Other** pets in 2 rooms only

Situated just west of the town centre, this well-presented accommodation is convenient for the ferry terminals and naval heritage sites. The comfortable bedrooms are spacious and well equipped, and one has a four-poster bed. Breakfast is served in the cosy conservatory-dining room and conference rooms are available.

Rooms 19 en suite (3 fmly) (6 GF) ⊘ in 10 bedrooms S £49.50-£62.50; D £55-£75✳ (room only) **Facilities** FTV TVB tea/coffee Direct dial from bedrooms Cen ht Dinner Last d 10pm Wi-fi available **Parking** 27

FLEET MOTORWAY SERVICE AREA (M3)
MAP 04 SU75

BUDGET HOTEL
Days Inn Fleet

Fleet Services GU51 1AA
☎ 01252 815587 📠 01252 815587
e-mail: fleet.hotel@welcomebreak.co.uk
web: www.daysinn.com
Dir: *between junct 4a & 5 southbound on M3*

PETS: Bedrooms unattended **Grounds** accessible

This modern building offers accommodation in smart, spacious and well-equipped bedrooms, suitable for families and business travellers, and all with en suite bathrooms. Continental breakfast is available and other refreshments may be taken at the nearby family restaurant. For further details see the Hotel Groups page.

Rooms 58 en suite

FORDINGBRIDGE
MAP 04 SU11

 ### Sandy Balls Holiday Centre *(SU167148)*

Sandy Balls Estate Ltd, Godshill SP6 2JY
☎ 01425 653042 📠 01425 653067
e-mail: post@sandy-balls.co.uk
web: www.sandy-balls.co.uk
Dir: *M27 junct 1 onto B3078/B3079, W 8m to Godshill. Park 0.25m after cattle grid*

PETS: Charges £3 per night **Exercise area** on site 120 acres woods & parkland & The New Forest **Facilities** on site shop food food bowl water bowl dog chews washing facs walks info vet info **Other** max 2 dogs per booking

Open all year (rs Nov-Feb pitches reduced, no activities) Booking advisable bank & school hols & wknds Last arrival 21.00hrs Last departure 11.00hrs

A large, mostly wooded New Forest holiday complex with good provision of touring facilities on terraced, well-laid-out fields. Pitches are fully serviced with shingle bases, and groups can be sited beside the river and away from the main site. Excellent sport, leisure and entertainment facilities for the whole family, and now eight ready-erected tents for hire. A 120-acre site with 230 touring pitches, 230 hardstandings and 267 statics.

Notes Groups by arrangement, no gazebos

HAMBLE
MAP 04 SU40

►►► Riverside Holidays *(SU481081)*

Satchell Ln SO31 4HR
☎ 023 8045 3220 📠 023 8045 3611
e-mail: enquiries@riversideholidays.co.uk
web: www.riversideholidays.co.uk
Dir: *M27 junct 8, follow signs to Hamble B3397. Turn left into Satchell Lane, 1m down lane on left*

PETS: Charges £2 per night £14 per week **Public areas** except buildings **Exercise area** 0.5m **Facilities** walks info vet info

Open all year (rs Nov-Feb No camping or touring) Booking advisable BH, peak season & boat show wk Last arrival 22.00hrs Last departure 11.00hrs

A small, peaceful park next to the marina, and close to the pretty village of Hamble. The park is neatly kept, though the toilet facilities are dated. A pub and restaurant are very close by. A 6-acre site with 77 touring pitches and 45 statics.

HARTLEY WINTNEY
MAP 04 SU75

★★★ 79% HOTEL

Elvetham

RG27 8AR

☎ 01252 844871 📄 01252 844161

e-mail: enq@theelvetham.co.uk

web: www.theelvetham.co.uk

Dir: *M3 junct 4A W, junct 5 E (or M4 junct 11, A33, B3011). Hotel signed from A323 between Hartley Wintney & Fleet*

PETS: Bedrooms Charges £15 per night **Grounds** accessible **Exercise area** on site **Resident Pets:** Harvey (Golden Retriever)

A spectacular 19th-century mansion set in 35 acres of grounds with an arboretum. All bedrooms are individually styled and many have views of the manicured gardens. A popular venue for weddings and conferences, the hotel lends itself to team building events and outdoor pursuits.

Rooms 41 en suite 29 annexe en suite (7 GF) ⊘ in all bedrooms S £110; D £135-£200 (incl. bkfst)✳ **Facilities** STV 🏊 Gym 🏌 Putt green Wi-fi available Badminton Boules Volleyball **Parking** 200 **Notes** Closed 24 Dec-1 Jan

---

LINWOOD
MAP 04 SU10

▶▶▶ **Red Shoot Camping Park** *(SU187094)*

BH24 3QT

☎ 01425 473789 📄 01425 471558

e-mail: enquiries@redshoot-campingpark.com

web: www.redshoot-campingpark.com

Dir: *A31 onto A338 towards Fordingbridge & Salisbury. Right at brown signs for caravan park towards Linwood on unclassified roads, park signed*

PETS: Stables nearby (2m) **Charges** £1 per night £7 per week **Public areas** except shop & toilets on leads **Exercise area** New Forest adjacent **Facilities** on site shop food leads walks info vet info **Other** prior notice required

Open Mar-Oct Booking advisable Last arrival 20.30hrs Last departure 13.00hrs

Sitting behind the Red Shoot Inn in one of the most attractive parts of the New Forest, this park is in an ideal spot for nature lovers, walkers and tourers. It is personally supervised by friendly owners, and offers many amenities including a children's play area. A 3.5-acre site with 130 touring pitches.

Notes Quiet after 22.30

LYMINGTON
MAP 04 SZ39

★★★★ BED & BREAKFAST

Jevington

47 Waterford Ln SO41 3PT

☎ 01590 672148 📄 01590 672148

e-mail: jevingtonbb@lineone.net

Dir: *From High St at St Thomas's Church onto Church Ln, left fork onto Waterford Ln*

PETS: Bedrooms Exercise area nearby **Resident Pets:** Lady (Terrier cross)

Situated within walking distance of the town centre and marinas, Jevington offers attractive bedrooms furnished to a high standard with coordinated soft furnishings. An appetising breakfast is served at two tables in the dining room, and the friendly proprietors can suggest local places for dinner.

Rooms 3 en suite (1 fmly) ⊘ D £55-£60✳ **Facilities** FTV TVB tea/coffee Cen ht **Parking** 3 **Notes** No children 5yrs 🐾

★★★★ BED & BREAKFAST

1 Honeysuckle Gardens

Everton SO41 0EH

☎ 01590 641282

e-mail: mway286978@aol.com

web: www.newforest-uk.com/honeysucklebandb

Dir: *Off A337 Lymington to Christchurch onto Everton Rd, Honeysuckle Gardens 3rd left*

PETS: Bedrooms Charges £3 per night charge for damage **Exercise area** 100mtrs **Facilities** walks info vet info **On Request** fridge access towels **Restrictions** small dogs preferred

Located in a new residential development in the village of Everton, this charming house is a good base for visiting Lymington, New Milton and the New Forest. Bedrooms are well furnished and decorated, and a range of useful extra facilities is provided. Full English breakfasts are served around one large table.

The owner has won an award for green tourism by reducing his impact of his business on the environment.

Rooms 3 rms (2 en suite) (1 pri facs) (1 fmly) ⊘ S £35-£40; D £60 **Facilities** TVB tea/coffee Cen ht Wi-fi available **Parking** 3 **Notes** LB No children 3yrs 🐾

★★★ GUEST HOUSE
Gorse Meadow Country House Hotel

Sway Rd SO41 8LR

☎ 01590 673354 📄 01590 673336

e-mail: gorse.meadow.guesthouse@wildmushrooms.co.uk

web: www.wildmushrooms.co.uk

Dir: *Off A337 from Brockenhurst, right onto Sway Rd before Toll House pub, Gorse Meadow 1.5m on right*

PETS: Bedrooms Stables on site **Grounds** accessible **Exercise area** on site in garden under supervision **Facilities** food **Resident Pets:** Camilla & Igor (Great Danes), Otto (Black Labrador)

This imposing Edwardian house is situated within 14 acres of grounds and most bedrooms enjoy views across the gardens and paddocks. Situated just one mile from Lymington, this is an excellent base to enjoy the many leisure pursuits that the New Forest has to offer. Meals are also available here, and Mrs Tee often uses the local wild mushrooms in her dishes.

Rooms 5 en suite (2 fmly) (2 GF) **Facilities** TVB tea/coffee Licensed Cen ht Dinner Last d 6pm **Parking** 20 **Notes** No coaches

---

LYNDHURST
MAP 04 SU30

★★★ 71% HOTEL
Lyndhurst Park

High St SO43 7NL

☎ 023 8028 3923 📄 023 8028 3019

e-mail: lyndhurst.park@forestdale.com

web: www.forestdale.com

Dir: *M27 junct 1-3 to A35 to Lyndhurst. Hotel in High Street*

PETS: Bedrooms unattended **Charges** £7.50 per night **Public areas** except restaurant

Although it is just by the High Street, the hotel is afforded seclusion from the town due to its five acres of mature grounds. The comfortable bedrooms include home-from-home touches such as ducks in the bath! The bar offers a stylish setting for a snack whilst the restaurant provides a more formal dining venue.

Rooms 59 en suite (3 fmly) ⊘ in 10 bedrooms **Facilities** STV ⚲ 🏊 Wi-fi in bedrooms Sauna **Services** Lift **Parking** 100

★★ 67% HOTEL
Knightwood Lodge

THE INDEPENDENTS

Southampton Rd SO43 7BU

☎ 023 8028 2502 📄 023 8028 3730

e-mail: jackie4r@aol.com

web: www.knightwoodlodge.co.uk

Dir: *exit M27 junct 1 follow A337 to Lyndhurst. Left at traffic lights in village onto A35 towards Southampton. Hotel 0.25m on left*

PETS: Bedrooms unattended **Exercise area** nearby **Facilities** water bowl bedding washing facs walks info vet info **On Request** fridge access towels **Other** pets in cottages only

This friendly, family-run hotel is situated on the outskirts of Lyndhurst. Comfortable bedrooms are modern in style and well equipped with many useful extras. The hotel offers an excellent range of facilities including a swimming pool, a jacuzzi and a small gym area. Two separate cottages are available for families or larger groups, and dogs are also welcome to accompany their owners in these units.

Rooms 15 en suite 4 annexe en suite (2 fmly) (3 GF) ⊘ in all bedrooms S £35-£55; D £70-£110 (incl. bkfst)✷ **Facilities** STV 🏊 Gym Steam room **Parking** 15 **Notes** LB

MILFORD ON SEA
MAP 04 SZ29

[U] ⧄⧄
Westover Hall

Park Ln SO41 0PT

☎ 01590 643044 📄 01590 644490

e-mail: info@westoverhallhotel.com

Dir: *M3 & M27 W onto A337 to Lymington, follow signs to Milford-on-Sea onto B3058, hotel outside village towards cliff.*

PETS: Bedrooms unattended **Charges** £10 per night **Public areas** except restaurant & bar on leads **Grounds** accessible on leads **Exercise area** cliff top at end of garden **Facilities** washing facs walks info vet info **On Request** torch towels **Resident Pets:** Arthur (cat)

At the time of going to press, the star classification for this hotel was not confirmed. Please refer to the AA internet site www.theAA.com for current information.

Rooms 12 en suite (2 fmly) S £130-£220; D £190-£340 (incl. bkfst & dinner)✷ **Facilities** Fishing Wi-fi available Xmas New Year **Parking** 50 **Notes** LB

ENGLAND

MILFORD ON SEA CONTINUED

►►► Lytton Lawn Touring Park (SZ293937)

Lymore Ln SO41 0TX

☎ 01590 648331 📄 01590 645610

e-mail: holidays@shorefield.co.uk

web: www.shorefield.co.uk

Dir: *From Lymington A337 to Christchurch for 2.5m to Everton. Left onto B3058 to Milford on Sea. After 0.25m left*

PETS: Charges £1.50-£3 per night £10.50-£21 per week
Exercise area on site **Facilities** on site shop food disp bags
walks info vet info **Other** prior notice required
Restrictions no Rottweilers or Staffordshire Bull Terriers

Open Feb-2 Jan (rs Xmas/New year no grass pitches available)
Booking advisable at all times Last arrival 22.00hrs Last
departure 10.00hrs

A pleasant well-run park with good facilities, located near the coast.
The park is peaceful and quiet, but the facilities of a sister park 2.5
miles away are available to campers, including swimming pool, tennis
courts, bistro and bar/carvery, and large club with family
entertainment. Fully-serviced pitches provide good screening, and
standard pitches are on gently-sloping grass. A 5-acre site with 136
touring pitches, 48 hardstandings.

Notes Family only park

OWER   MAP 03 SU31

►►► Green Pastures Farm (SU321158)

SO51 6AJ

☎ 023 8081 4444

e-mail: enquiries@greenpasturesfarm.com

web: www.greenpasturesfarm.com

Dir: *M27 junct 2. Follow Salisbury signs for 0.5m. Then follow
brown tourist signs for Green Pastures. Also signed from A36 &
A3090 at Ower*

PETS: Sep Accom day kennels **Public areas Exercise area** on
site **Facilities** on site shop food walks info vet info space for
loose box **Other** prior notice required **Resident Pets:** Pudsey
(Collie), Molly (cat)

Open 15 Mar-Oct Booking advisable BH & peak periods Last
departure 11.00hrs

A pleasant site on a working farm, with good screening of trees and
shrubs around the perimeter. The touring area is divided by a border
of shrubs and, at times, colourful foxgloves. This peaceful location is
close to the M27 and New Forest. A 5-acre site with 45 touring pitches,
2 hardstandings.

Notes ⊛

PETERSFIELD   MAP 04 SU72

★★★ 81% ❀ HOTEL

Langrish House

Langrish GU32 1RN

☎ 01730 266941 📄 01730 260543

e-mail: frontdesk@langrishhouse.co.uk

web: www.langrishhouse.co.uk

Dir: *off A3 onto A272 towards Winchester. Hotel signed, 2.5m on
left*

PETS: Bedrooms unattended **Charges** £10 per night
Public areas except restaurant **Grounds** accessible
Exercise area surrounding area **Facilities** bedding dog scoop/
disp bags **On Request** towels **Other** Pet pack for dogs - welcome
letter, blanket, poop scoop, biscuits & towel **Resident Pets:** Tonga
(Black Labrador), Constansa & Bunji (cats), chicken, ducks,
guineafowl

Located in an idyllic country location just outside Petersfield, this family
home dates back to the 17th century. Rooms offer good levels of
comfort with beautiful views over the countryside. The public areas
consist of a small cosy restaurant, a bar in the vaults, and conference
and banqueting rooms that are popular for weddings. Staff throughout
are friendly and nothing is too much trouble.

Rooms 13 en suite (1 fmly) (3 GF) ⊗ in all bedrooms S £72-£90;
D £104.40-£155 (incl. bkfst)✳ **Facilities** Fishing Wi-fi available Xmas
New Year **Parking** 80 **Notes** LB

PORTSMOUTH   MAP 04 SU60

★★★★ 72% HOTEL

Portsmouth Marriott Hotel   **Marriott**
                                            HOTELS & RESORTS

Southampton Rd PO6 4SH

☎ 0870 400 7285 📄 0870 400 7385

web: www.marriott.co.uk

Dir: *M27 junct 12 keep left and hotel on left*

PETS: Bedrooms unattended **Grounds** accessible on leads
Exercise area park 0.5m **Facilities** vet info

Close to the motorway and ferry port, this hotel is well suited to
business trade. The comfortable and well-laid out bedrooms provide a
comprehensive range of facilities including up-to-date workstations.
The leisure club offers a pool, a gym, and a health and beauty salon.

Rooms 174 en suite (77 fmly) ⊗ in 149 bedrooms **Facilities** STV ✪
supervised Gym Exercise studio, Beauty salon **Services** Lift air con
Parking 250

★★★ 74% HOTEL

Best Western Royal Beach

South Pde, Southsea PO4 0RN

☎ 023 9273 1281 🖷 023 9281 7572

e-mail: enquiries@royalbeachhotel.co.uk

web: www.royalbeachhotel.co.uk

Dir: *M27 to M275, follow signs to seafront. Hotel on seafront*

PETS: Bedrooms Public areas except restaurant

Exercise area nearby park & green

This former Victorian seafront hotel is a smart and comfortable venue suitable for leisure and business guests alike. Bedrooms and public areas are well presented and generally spacious, and the smart Coast bar is an ideal venue for a relaxing drink.

Rooms 124 en suite (18 fmly) ⊘ in 72 bedrooms S £65-£115; D £75-£195 (incl. bkfst) **Facilities** STV Wi-fi in bedrooms ♫ Xmas New Year **Services** Lift **Parking** 50 **Notes** LB

RINGWOOD   MAP 04 SU10

★★★★ GUEST HOUSE

Little Forest Lodge

Poulner Hill BH24 3HS

☎ 01425 478848 🖷 01425 473564

Dir: *1.5m E of Ringwood on A31*

PETS: Bedrooms (GF) **Charges** £5 per night **Public areas** except dining room **Grounds** accessible disp bin **Facilities** dog chews feeding mat washing facs cage storage walks info vet info **On Request** fridge access torch towels **Resident Pets:** Jade (Retriever/Collie cross), Millie (Doberman/Whippet cross), Harry & Spike (cats), ducks, chickens

A warm welcome is given to you and your pets, at this charming Edwardian house set in two acres of woodland. Bedrooms are pleasantly decorated and equipped with thoughtful extras. Both the attractive wood-panelled dining room and the delightful lounge, with bar and wood-burning fire, overlook the gardens. Home-cooked evening meals by arrangement.

Rooms 6 en suite (3 fmly) (1 GF) ⊘ S £45-£50; D £70-£80 **Facilities** TVB tea/coffee Licensed Cen ht Dinner Last d 7.30pm ⅃ clock golf, badminton **Parking** 10 **Notes** No coaches

---

ROMSEY   MAP 03 SU32

►►►► **Hill Farm Caravan Park** *(SU287238)*

Branches Ln, Sherfield English SO51 6FH

☎ 01794 340402 🖷 01794 342358

e-mail: gjb@hillfarmpark.com

web: www.hillfarmpark.com

Dir: *Signed from A27 (Salisbury to Romsey road) in Sherfield English, 4m NW of Romsey & M27 junct 2*

PETS: Public areas Exercise area on site dog walks & in 2m **Facilities** on site shop disp bags leads washing facs dog grooming nearby walks info vet info

Open Mar-Oct Booking advisable bank & school hols & wknds Last arrival 20.00hrs Last departure noon

A small, well-sheltered park peacefully located amidst mature trees and meadows. The two toilet blocks offer smart unisex showers as well as a fully en suite family/disabled room and plenty of privacy in the wash rooms. The owners are continuing to develop this attractive park, and with its proximity to Salisbury and the New Forest, it makes an appealing holiday location. A 10.5-acre site with 70 touring pitches, 16 hardstandings and 6 statics.

Notes ⊗ Minimum noise at all times and no noise after 23.00hrs, one unit per pitch

---

SOUTHAMPTON   MAP 04 SU41

★★★ 71% HOTEL

Southampton Park

Cumberland Place SO15 2WY

☎ 023 8034 3343 🖷 023 8033 2538

e-mail: southampton.park@forestdale.com

web: www.forestdale.com

Dir: *at north end of Inner Ring Road, opposite Watts Park & Civic Centre*

PETS: Bedrooms unattended **Charges** £7.50 per night **Public areas** except restaurant

Located in the heart of the city opposite Watts Park, this modern hotel provides well-equipped, smartly appointed bedrooms with comfortable furnishings. The public areas include a good leisure centre, a spacious bar and lounge and the lively MJ's Brasserie. Parking is available in a multi-storey behind the hotel.

Rooms 72 en suite (10 fmly) ⊘ in 20 bedrooms **Facilities** Spa STV ⊛ supervised Gym Wi-fi available **Services** Lift **Notes** Closed 25 & 26 Dec nights

ENGLAND

SOUTHAMPTON *continued*

★★★ 70% HOTEL
The Woodlands Lodge

Bartley Rd, Woodlands SO40 7GN

☎ 023 8029 2257 📠 023 8029 3090

e-mail: reception@woodlands-lodge.co.uk

web: www.woodlands-lodge.co.uk

Dir: *M27 junct 2, A326 towards Fawley. 2nd rdbt turn right, left after 0.25m by White Horse PH. In 1.5m cross cattle grid, hotel is 70yds off on left*

PETS: Bedrooms unattended **Stables** on site **Charges** £5 per night **Grounds** accessible **Exercise area** 50yds
Resident Pets: Bentley (Dalmatian), Minty & Rambo (sheep), Christmas (goose), Napoleon (cockerel)

An 18th-century former hunting lodge, this hotel is set in four acres of impressive and well-tended grounds on the edge of the New Forest. Well-equipped bedrooms come in varying sizes and styles and all bathrooms have a jacuzzi bath. Public areas provide a pleasant lounge and intimate cocktail bar.

Rooms 16 en suite (1 fmly) (3 GF) ⊘ in 2 bedrooms S £72-£82; D £134-£222 (incl. bkfst)✴ **Facilities** 🦮 Wi-fi available Xmas New Year **Parking** 30 **Notes LB**

★★ 75% HOTEL
Elizabeth House

42-44 The Avenue SO17 1XP

☎ 023 8022 4327 📠 023 8022 4327

e-mail: mail@elizabethhousehotel.com

web: www.elizabethhousehotel.com

Dir: *on A33, on left towards city centre, after Southampton Common, before main lights*

PETS: Bedrooms (GF) unattended **Grounds** accessible **Exercise area** 200yds **Facilities** walks info **On Request** fridge access torch towels

This hotel is conveniently situated close to the city centre, so provides an ideal base for both business and leisure guests. The bedrooms are well equipped and are attractively furnished with comfort in mind. There is also a cosy and atmospheric bistro in the cellar where evening meals are served.

Rooms 20 en suite 7 annexe en suite (9 fmly) (8 GF) S £59.50; D £69.50 (incl. bkfst)✴ **Facilities** Wi-fi available **Parking** 31

STOCKBRIDGE
MAP 04 SU33

★★★★ 🛏 BED & BREAKFAST
York Lodge

Five Bells Ln, Nether Wallop SO20 8HE

☎ 01264 781313

e-mail: bradley@york-lodge.co.uk

web: www.york-lodge.co.uk

Dir: *3m W of Stockbridge in Nether Wallop*

PETS: Bedrooms (GF) **Charges** £5 per night **Public areas**
Grounds accessible disp bin **Exercise area** 5 mins walk
Facilities washing facs cage storage walks info vet info
On Request fridge access torch towels **Resident Pets:** Polly
(Black Labrador)

Located in the picturesque village famous for Agatha Christie's Miss Marple series, this charming house has comfortable accommodation in a self-contained wing. Bedrooms are stylishly presented with many thoughtful extra facilities. The dining room overlooks peaceful gardens, and delicious dinners are available by arrangement.

Rooms 2 en suite (2 GF) ⊘ S £35-£55; D £60-£70✴ **Facilities** TVB tea/coffee Cen ht Dinner Last d 24hrs prior **Parking** 4 **Notes** No children 8yrs ⊜

STRATFIELD TURGIS
MAP 04 SU65

★★★ 71% HOTEL
Wellington Arms

RG27 0AS

☎ 01256 882214 📠 01256 882934

e-mail: wellingtonarmsreception.basingstoke@
hall-woodhouse.co.uk

Dir: *A33 between Basingstoke & Reading*

PETS: Bedrooms unattended **Charges** £10 per night
Grounds accessible **Exercise area** on site

Situated at an entrance to the ancestral home of the Duke of Wellington. The majority of bedrooms are located in the modern Garden Wing; those in the original building have a period feel and unusual furniture. Public rooms include a brasserie and a comfortable lounge bar with log fire.

Rooms 28 en suite (3 fmly) (11 GF) ⊘ in all bedrooms S £65-£95; D £75-£130 (incl. bkfst)✴ **Facilities** FTV Wi-fi in bedrooms **Parking** 150

SWAY
MAP 04 SZ29

★★★ 72% HOTEL
Sway Manor Restaurant & Hotel
Station Rd SO41 6BA

☎ 01590 682754 📄 01590 682955

e-mail: info@swaymanor.com

web: www.swaymanor.com

Dir: *turn off B3055 Brockenhurst/New Milton road into Sway village centre*

PETS: Bedrooms unattended Charges £6 per night charge for damage Public areas except restaurant on leads
Grounds accessible on leads disp bin Facilities walks info vet info On Request fridge access Resident Pets: Bobby (Chocolate Labrador), Bernard (Golden Labrador)

Built at the turn of the 20th century, this attractive mansion is set in it own grounds, and conveniently located in the village centre. Bedrooms are well appointed and generously equipped; the bar and restaurant, both with views over the gardens, are popular with locals.

Rooms 15 en suite (3 fmly) ⊘ in 12 bedrooms S £57.50-£66.50; D £99-£115 (incl. bkfst)✱ Facilities FTV ⊰ ♫ Xmas Services Lift
Parking 40 Notes LB

★★★★ BED & BREAKFAST
Acorn Shetland Pony Stud
Meadows Cottage, Arnewood Bridge Rd SO41 6DA

☎ 01590 682000

e-mail: meadows.cottage@virgin.net

Dir: *M27 junct 1, A337 to Brockenhurst, B3055 to Sway, pass Birchy Hill Nursing Home, over x-rds, 2nd entrance left*

PETS: Bedrooms (GF) Stables on site Charges £3 per night
Grounds accessible on leads disp bin Facilities bedding leads washing facs cage storage walks info vet info On Request fridge access torch towels Restrictions more than 1 dog by arrangement only Resident Pets: Bill & Sir Bobby (cat), 10 Shetland ponies

Located on the outskirts of Sway, this comfortable establishment is set in over 6 acres of pony paddocks and a water garden. The ground-floor bedrooms are well furnished and have direct access onto patios. The enjoyable, freshly cooked breakfasts use a range of fine produce including delicious home-made bread.

Rooms 3 en suite (1 fmly) (3 GF) ⊘ D £58-£62✱ Facilities TVB tea/coffee Cen ht Carriage driving with Shetland ponies Parking 3
Notes LB ⊠

★★★ INN
The Forest Heath
Station Rd SO41 6BA

☎ 01590 682287 📄 01590 682626

e-mail: forestheathhotel@hotmail.co.uk

Dir: *M27 junct 1, A337 to Brockenhurst, B3055 to Sway, onto Church Ln & Station Rd*

PETS: Bedrooms unattended Stables nearby (5m) Charges £5 per night Public areas on leads Grounds accessible on leads disp bin Exercise area 1m Facilities washing facs cage storage walks info vet info On Request fridge access towels Resident Pets: Ollie (Patterdale cross), Crystal (Yorkshire Terrier), Bonnie (Black Labrador), Elvis, Tigger & Smudge (cats)

Located in a New Forest village, this late Victorian inn is a popular meeting place for the local community. Bedrooms are well equipped and comfortable, and a range of real ales and imaginative meals is offered in the bars and the conservatory dining room.

Rooms 4 en suite (2 fmly) S £45; D £65✱ Facilities TVB tea/coffee Cen ht Dinner Last d 8.45pm Wi-fi available Pool Table boules, petanque
Parking 20

WINCHESTER
MAP 04 SU42

★★★★ ◉◉◉ HOTEL
Lainston House
Sparsholt SO21 2LT

☎ 01962 863588 📄 01962 776672

e-mail: enquiries@lainstonhouse.com

web: www.exclusivehotels.co.uk

Dir: *2m NW off B3049 towards Stockbridge*

PETS: Bedrooms Charges £10 per night Public areas Other pet food by arrangement, dog menu

This graceful example of a William and Mary House enjoys a countryside location amidst mature grounds and gardens. Staff provide good levels of courtesy and care with a polished, professional service. Bedrooms are tastefully appointed and include some spectacular spacious rooms with stylish handmade beds and stunning bathrooms. Public rooms include a cocktail bar built entirely from a single cedar and stocked with an impressive range of rare drinks and cigars.

Rooms 50 en suite (6 fmly) (18 GF) S £125; D £225-£625✱
Facilities STV ⊜ Fishing Gym ⊰ Putt green Wi-fi available Archery Clay pigeon shooting Cycling Hot Air Ballooning Walking. ♫ Xmas New Year
Parking 150 Notes LB

WINCHESTER *CONTINUED*

★★★ 71% HOTEL
Marwell

"bespoke"

Thompsons Ln, Colden Common, Marwell
SO21 1JY
☎ 01962 777681 📠 01962 777625
e-mail: info@marwellhotel.co.uk
web: www.bespokehotels.com

Dir: *B3354 through Twyford. 1st exit at rdbt continue on B3354, then left onto B2177 signed Bishop Waltham. Turn left into Thomsons Ln after 1m, hotel on left*

PETS: Bedrooms (GF) unattended **Charges** £20 per night **Grounds** accessible **On Request** fridge access

Taking its theme from the adjacent zoo, this unusual hotel is based on the famous TreeTops safari lodge in Kenya. Bedrooms are well appointed and equipped, while the smart public areas include an airy lobby bar and an 'Out of Africa' style restaurant. There is also a selection of meeting and leisure facilities.

Rooms 66 en suite (10 fmly) (36 GF) ⊘ in 56 bedrooms S £79-£119; D £89-£129 (incl. bkfst)✳ **Facilities** STV ⑤ ♨ 18 Gym Wi-fi in bedrooms New Year **Parking** 120 **Notes LB**

HEREFORDSHIRE

HEREFORD
MAP 03 SO54

★★★★ FARM HOUSE
Sink Green *(SO542377)*

Rotherwas HR2 6LE
☎ 01432 870223 📠 01432 870223 Mr D E Jones
e-mail: enquiries@sinkgreenfarm.co.uk
web: www.sinkgreenfarm.co.uk

Dir: *3m SE of city centre. Off A49 onto B4399 for 2m*

PETS: Bedrooms Public areas Grounds accessible **Facilities** cage storage walks info **On Request** fridge access torch towels **Resident Pets:** Bob & Max (dogs)

This charming 16th-century farmhouse stands in attractive countryside and has many original features, including flagstone floors, exposed beams and open fireplaces. Bedrooms are traditionally furnished and one has a four-poster bed. The pleasant garden has a comfortable summer house, hot tub and barbecue. The friendly and relaxed atmosphere leaves a lasting impression.

Rooms 3 en suite ⊘ S £28-£35; D £56-£64✳ **Facilities** TVB tea/coffee Cen ht TVL Wi-fi available Fishing Hot Tub **Parking** 10 **Notes LB** 180 acres beef sheep 🐾

▶ **Ridge Hill Caravan and Campsite** *(SO509355)*
HR1 1UN
☎ 01432 351293
e-mail: ridgehill@fsmail.net
web: www.ridgehillcaravanandcampsite.co.uk

Dir: *From Hereford on A49, then B4399 signed Rotherwas. At 1st rdbt follow Dinedor/Little Dewchurch signs, in 1m signed Ridge Hill/Twyford, turn right, then right at phone box*

PETS: Public areas on leads **Facilities** walks info vet info

Open Mar-Oct Booking advisable Last departure noon

A simple, basic site set high on Ridge Hill 3 miles south of Hereford. This peaceful site offers outstanding views over the surrounding countryside. It does not have toilets or showers, and therefore own facilities are essential. A 1.5-acre site with 5 touring pitches.

Notes 🐾

LEDBURY
MAP 03 SO73

★★★★ FARM HOUSE
Church Farm *(SO718426)*

Coddington HR8 1JJ
☎ 01531 640271 Mrs West
web: www.dexta.co.uk

PETS: Bedrooms Stables nearby (1m) **Charges** £2 per night **Public areas Grounds** accessible disp bin **Facilities** food (pre-bookable) food bowl water bowl bedding dog chews feeding mat dog scoop/disp bags leads washing facs cage storage walks info vet info **On Request** fridge access torch towels **Other** all facilities are available on request only **Resident Pets:** Jackie (Jack Russell)

A warm welcome awaits you at Church Farm which provides comfortable accommodation in a Grade II-listed farm house. Aga-cooked breakfasts are served around the shared kitchen table or in the dining room. The farm house provides a peaceful and tranquil location set in the depths of rural Herefordshire. There is much to explore in the area, with numerous activities including golf, canoeing, cycling and various walks around the hamlet with the Malvern Hills only five miles away.

Rooms 3 rms (2 en suite) (1 pri facs) **Facilities** TV1B tea/coffee Cen ht TVL **Parking** 6 **Notes** 100 acres sheep/arable Closed 16 Dec-15 Jan 🐾

LEOMINSTER — MAP 03 SO45

★★★★★ 👜 GUEST ACCOMMODATION

Ford Abbey

Pudleston HR6 0RZ

☎ 01568 760700 🖹 01568 760264

e-mail: info@fordabbey.co.uk

web: www.fordabbey.co.uk

Dir: *A44 Leominster towards Worcester, turn left to Pudleston*

PETS: Bedrooms unattended **Charges** £15 per night
Public areas except dining room **Grounds** accessible
Exercise area adjacent **Other** Pet food on request
Resident Pets: Abbey (cat)

Attention to detail and a high level of hospitality are the hallmarks of this former property of Benedictine monks. Beams, old and new, and original features are everywhere, and there is a choice of lounges. The atmospheric restaurant serves excellent dinners featuring farm produce. Bedrooms are spacious and thoughtfully equipped, and there is also a leisure complex in the grounds.

Rooms 6 en suite (1 GF) D £130-£185✳ **Facilities** STV TVB tea/coffee Direct dial from bedrooms Cen ht TVL Dinner Last d 9.30pm 🐾 Solarium Gymnasium 🐾 **Parking** 20

MUCH BIRCH — MAP 03 SO53

★★★ 77% HOTEL

Pilgrim

THE INDEPENDENTS
HOTEL ASSOCIATION

Ross Rd HR2 8HJ

☎ 01981 540742 🖹 01981 540620

e-mail: stay@pilgrimhotel.co.uk

web: www.pilgrimhotel.co.uk

Dir: *on A49 6m from Ross-on-Wye, 5m from Hereford*

PETS: Bedrooms Charges £5 per night **Grounds** accessible
Exercise area 100yds

This much-extended former rectory is set back from the A49 and has sweeping views over the countryside. The extensive grounds contain a pitch and putt course. Privately owned and personally run, it provides accommodation that includes ground floor and four-poster rooms. Public areas include a restful lounge, a traditionally furnished restaurant and a pleasant bar.

Rooms 20 en suite (3 fmly) (8 GF) ⊘ in 17 bedrooms **Facilities** ♨ 3 🐾 🐾 Pitch & putt, Badminton **Parking** 42 **Notes** LB

PETERCHURCH — MAP 03 SO33

►►►►► Poston Mill Caravan & Camping Park *(SO355373)*

HR2 0SF

☎ 01981 550225 🖹 01981 550000

e-mail: enquiries@poston-mill.co.uk

web: www.bestparks.co.uk

Dir: *11m SW of Hereford on B4348*

PETS: Charges £1 per night **Public areas Exercise area** on site large field **Facilities** walks info vet info **Other** prior notice required

Open all year (rs Nov-Mar limited toilet facilities) Booking advisable bank & summer hols Last departure noon

Delightfully set in the Golden Valley and surrounded by hills, with beautiful views. This quality park has excellent facilities including sporting amenities which are to one side of the site. There is also an adjoining restaurant, The Mill, and a pleasant walk alongside the River Dore. A 33-acre site with 43 touring pitches, 33 hardstandings and 113 statics.

Notes No gazebo's, restricted use of scooters, bikes and skateboards

ROSS-ON-WYE — MAP 03 SO62

★★★ 80% HOTEL

Best Western Pengethley Manor

Best Western

Pengethley Park HR9 6LL

☎ 01989 730211 🖹 01989 730238

e-mail: reservations@pengethleymanor.co.uk

web: www.pengethleymanor.co.uk

Dir: *4m N on A49 Hereford road, from Ross-on-Wye*

PETS: Bedrooms (GF) unattended **Charges** £5 per night charge for damage **Public areas** except restaurant & bar on leads **Grounds** accessible on leads disp bin **Facilities** washing facs walks info vet info **On Request** fridge access torch towels
Resident Pets: Gem (Welsh Mountain pony), Dick-sy (Dalmatian), Ollie (Collie), Baxter (Springer Spaniel), Gypsy (cat)

This fine Georgian mansion is set in extensive grounds with two vineyards and glorious views. The accommodation is tastefully appointed and offers a wide variety of bedroom styles, all similarly well equipped. The elegant public rooms are furnished in a style sympathetic to the character of the house. Dinner provides a range of enjoyable options and is served in the comfortable, spacious restaurant.

Rooms 11 en suite 14 annexe en suite (3 fmly) (4 GF) S £79-£115; D £120-£160 (incl. bkfst)✳ **Facilities** ⊀ ♨ 9 🐾 Wi-fi available Golf improvement course ch fac Xmas New Year **Parking** 70 **Notes** LB

ROSS-ON-WYE CONTINUED

★★★ 77% ◉◉ HOTEL
Wilton Court Hotel
Wilton Ln HR9 6AQ
☎ 01989 562569 📄 01989 768460
e-mail: info@wiltoncourthotel.com
web: www.wiltoncourthotel.com
Dir: *M50 junct 4 onto A40 towards Monmouth at 3rd rdbt turn left signed Ross then take 1st right, hotel on right facing river*
PETS: Bedrooms unattended **Charges** £10 per night charge for damage **Public areas** (dogs only) except restaurant
Grounds accessible disp bin **Facilities** washing facs cage storage walks info vet info **On Request** fridge access torch towels **Restrictions** no very large dogs or long haired breeds
Dating back to the 16th century, this hotel has great charm and a wealth of character. Standing on the banks of the River Wye and just a short walk from the town centre, there is a genuinely relaxed, friendly and unhurried atmosphere here. Bedrooms are tastefully furnished and well equipped, while public areas include a comfortable lounge, traditional bar and pleasant restaurant with a conservatory extension overlooking the garden. High standards of food using fresh locally-sourced ingredients is offered.
Rooms 10 en suite (1 fmly) ⊗ in all bedrooms S £75-£110; D £100-£140 (incl. bkfst)✳ **Facilities** FTV Fishing Wi-fi in bedrooms Boule Xmas New Year **Parking** 24 **Notes** LB

★★★ 71% HOTEL
The Royal
Palace Pound HR9 5HZ
☎ 01989 565105 📄 01989 768058
e-mail: 6504@greeneking.co.uk
web: www.oldenglish.co.uk
Dir: *at end of M50 take A40 'Monmouth'. At 3rd rdbt, left to Ross, over bridge and take road signed 'The Royal Hotel' after left bend*
PETS: Bedrooms unattended **Charges** £10 per night charge for damage **Grounds** accessible on leads **Exercise area** 300yds **Facilities** vet info **Restrictions** small to medium sized dogs only
Close to the town centre, this imposing hotel enjoys panoramic views from its prominent hilltop position. Reputedly visited by Charles Dickens in 1867, the establishment has been sympathetically furnished to combine the ambience of a bygone era with the comforts of today. In addition to the lounge and elegant restaurant, there are function rooms and an attractive garden.
Rooms 42 en suite (1 fmly) ⊗ in all bedrooms **Parking** 44 **Notes** LB

★★★ 70% COUNTRY HOUSE HOTEL
Pencraig Court Country House Hotel
Pencraig HR9 6HR
☎ 01989 770306 📄 01989 770040
e-mail: info@pencraig-court.co.uk
web: www.pencraig-court.co.uk
Dir: *off A40, into Pencraig 4m S of Ross-on-Wye*
PETS: Bedrooms Charges £5-£20 per night **Public areas** except dining room **Grounds** accessible **Exercise area** on site & adjacent **Other** Pet food by prior arrangement **Resident Pets:** Sam (Sussex Spaniel), Fugley (Tibetan Spaniel), Ross (cat)
This former Georgian mansion commands impressive views of the River Wye to Ross-on-Wye beyond. Guests can be assured of a relaxing stay and the proprietors are on hand to ensure personal attention and service. The bedrooms have a traditional feel and include one room with a four-poster bed. The country-house atmosphere is carried through in the lounges and the elegant restaurant.
Rooms 11 en suite (1 fmly) ⊗ in all bedrooms **Facilities** ✔ **Parking** 20 **Notes** LB

★★ 69% SMALL HOTEL
Chasedale
Walford Rd HR9 5PQ
☎ 01989 562423 & 565801 📄 01989 567900
e-mail: chasedale@supanet.com
web: www.chasedale.co.uk
Dir: *from town centre, S on B4234, hotel 0.5m on left*
PETS: Bedrooms (GF) unattended **Public areas** except restaurant **Grounds** accessible disp bin **Exercise area** 300mtrs **Facilities** food bowl water bowl cage storage walks info vet info **On Request** fridge access towels **Resident Pets:** Marmite (Chocolate Labrador), Cassis (Black Labrador)
This large, mid-Victorian property is situated on the south-west outskirts of the town. Privately owned and personally run, it provides spacious, well-proportioned public areas and extensive grounds. The accommodation is well equipped and includes family rooms, whilst the restaurant offers a wide selection of wholesome food.
Rooms 10 en suite (2 fmly) (1 GF) ⊗ in 1 bedroom S £37.50-£40.50; D £75-£81 (incl. bkfst)✳ **Facilities** Wi-fi available Xmas **Parking** 14 **Notes** LB

★★ 67% HOTEL
King's Head
8 High St HR9 5HL
☎ 01989 763174 📠 01989 769578
e-mail: enquiries@kingshead.co.uk
web: www.kingshead.co.uk
Dir: *in town centre, turn right past Royal Hotel*
PETS: Bedrooms unattended **Public areas** bar only
Grounds accessible **Exercise area** 200yds **Facilities** food
The King's Head dates back to the 14th century and has a wealth of
charm and character. Bedrooms are well equipped and include both
four-poster and family rooms. The restaurant doubles as a coffee shop
during the day and is a popular venue with locals. There is also a very
pleasant bar and comfortable lounge.

Rooms 15 en suite (1 fmly) ⊘ in 7 bedrooms S £53.50; D £90 (incl.
bkfst)✻ **Facilities** Wi-fi available Xmas **Parking** 13 **Notes** LB

★★★★ 🏠 GUEST ACCOMMODATION
Lea House
Lea HR9 7JZ
☎ 01989 750652 📠 01989 750652
e-mail: enquiries@leahouse.co.uk
web: www.leahouse.co.uk
Dir: *4m SE of Ross on A40, in Lea village*
PETS: Bedrooms Charges £6 per stay **Public areas** except dining
room on leads **Grounds** accessible on leads disp bin
Exercise area 30yds **Facilities** washing facs cage storage walks
info vet info **On Request** torch towels **Resident Pets:** Cocoa
(Terrier), Cream (cat)

This former coaching inn is a good base for exploring the Forest of
Dean and the Wye Valley. The individually furnished bedrooms are
thoughtfully equipped with many extras and toiletries, and the
atmosphere is relaxed and homely. Breakfast in the oak-beamed dining
room is a tasty choice including freshly squeezed fruit juices, fish and
local sausages.

Rooms 3 rms (2 en suite) (1 pri facs) (1 fmly) ⊘ S £35-£45;
D £59-£68✻ **Facilities** TVB tea/coffee Cen ht TVL Dinner Last d by prior
arrangement **Parking** 4 **Notes** LB

★★★★ BED & BREAKFAST
Lumleys
Kern Bridge, Bishopswood HR9 5QT
☎ 01600 890040 📠 0870 706 2378
e-mail: helen@lumleys.force9.co.uk
web: www.lumleys.force9.co.uk
Dir: *Off A40 onto B4229 at Goodrich, over Kern Bridge, right at
Inn on the Wye, 400yds opp picnic ground*
PETS: Bedrooms unattended **Public areas** except dining room
Grounds accessible disp bin **Exercise area** 20yds **Facilities** most
facilities can be arranged washing facs cage storage walks info
vet info **On Request** fridge access torch towels
Resident Pets: Megan (Golden Cocker Spaniel)

This pleasant and friendly guest house overlooks the River Wye and
has been a hostelry since Victorian times. It offers the character of a
bygone era combined with modern comforts and facilities. Bedrooms
are individually and carefully furnished and one has a four-poster bed
and its own patio. Comfortable public areas include a choice of sitting
rooms.

Rooms 3 en suite ⊘ D £50-£70✻ **Facilities** STV FTV TVB tea/coffee
Direct dial from bedrooms Cen ht TVL Dinner Last d 7pm **Parking** 15
Notes ⊛

ROSS-ON-WYE CONTINUED

★★★★ GUEST ACCOMMODATION
Thatch Close

Llangrove HR9 6EL
☎ 01989 770300
e-mail: info@thatchclose.co.uk
web: www.thatchclose.com

Dir: Off A40 at Symonds Yat West/Whitchurch junct to Llangrove, right at x-rds after Post Office, Thatch Close 0.6m on left

PETS: Bedrooms Charges £2 per night £5 per week
Public areas Grounds accessible disp bin Facilities food bowl water bowl dog scoop/disp bags leads washing facs cage storage walks info vet info On Request fridge access torch towels
Resident Pets: Aku & Zippy (African Grey parrots), Oliver & Tilly (Spaniel Collie cross)

Standing in 13 acres, this sturdy farmhouse dating from 1760 is full of character. There is a wonderfully warm atmosphere here with a genuine welcome from your hosts. The homely bedrooms are equipped for comfort with many thoughtful extras. Breakfast and dinner are served in the elegant dining room, and a lounge is available. The extensive patios and gardens are popular in summer, providing plenty of space to find a quiet corner and relax with a good book.

Rooms 3 en suite ✆ Facilities TVB tea/coffee Cen ht TVL Dinner Last d 9am Parking 8 Notes ✆

STANFORD BISHOP   MAP 03 SO65

►►► Boyce Caravan Park (SO692528)

WR6 5UB
☎ 01886 884248 📠 01886 884187
e-mail: enquiries@boyceholidaypark.co.uk
web: www.boyceholidaypark.co.uk

Dir: From B4220 (Malvern road) take sharp turn opposite Herefordshire House pub, then right after 0.25m. Signed Linley Green, then 1st drive on right

PETS: Public areas except play area & buildings Exercise area on site dog walking area provided Facilities walks info vet info Other prior notice required Restrictions no Rottweilers, German Shepherds, Dobermans, Pitt Bull Terriers or similar breeds (see also page 7)

Open Feb-Dec (rs Mar-Oct Tourers) Booking advisable BH, wknds & Jun-Aug Last arrival 18.00hrs Last departure noon

A friendly and peaceful park with access allowed onto the 100 acres of farmland. Coarse fishing is also available in the grounds, and there are extensive views over the Malvern and Suckley Hills. Many walks available. A 10-acre site with 15 touring pitches and 150 statics.

SYMONDS YAT (WEST)   MAP 03 SO51

★★★★ 🛏 🍴 GUEST ACCOMMODATION
Norton House

Whitchurch HR9 6DJ
☎ 01600 890046 📠 01600 890045
e-mail: su@norton.wyenet.co.uk
web: www.norton-house.com

Dir: 0.5m N of Symonds Yat. Off A40 into Whitchurch village and left onto Old Monmouth Rd

PETS: Bedrooms Sep Accom large dog cage for loan Public areas on leads Grounds accessible disp bin Exercise area 0.25m Facilities food bowl water bowl dog chews cage storage feeding mat dog scoop/disp bags leads washing facs On Request fridge access torch towels Other welcome pack for dogs Resident Pets: Hector (Black Standard Poodle), Hamish (Brown Standard Poodle)

Built as a farmhouse, Norton House dates back 300 years and retains much character through features such as flagstone floors and beamed ceilings. The bedrooms, including a four-poster room, are individually styled and furnished for maximum comfort. Excellent local produce is used to create an imaginative range of breakfast and dinner options. The charming public areas include a snug lounge, with a wood-burning stove. Self-catering cottages are also available.

Rooms 3 en suite ✆ S £45-£50; D £64-£84 Facilities TVB tea/coffee Cen ht TVL Dinner Last d 9am Parking 5 Notes No children 12yrs Closed 25-26 Dec ✆

►►► Doward Park Camp Site (SO539167)

Great Doward HR9 6BP
☎ 01600 890438
e-mail: enquiries@dowardpark.co.uk
web: www.dowardpark.co.uk

Dir: 2m from A40 between Ross-on-Wye & Monmouth. Take Symonds Yat (West) turn, then Crockers Ash, follow signs to site

PETS: Charges £1 per night Public areas except play area on leads Facilities on site shop food bowl water bowl walks info vet info Other prior notice required Resident Pets: Fairy Sprinkle (cat)

Open Mar-Oct Booking advisable wknds, BH & Jul-Aug Last arrival 20.00hrs Last departure 11.30hrs

This delightful little park is set in peaceful woodlands on the hillside above the Wye Valley. It is ideal for campers and motor homes but not caravans due to the narrow approach roads. A warm welcome awaits and the facilities are spotless. A 1.5-acre site with 24 touring pitches.

Notes No caravans or fires, quiet after 22.00hrs

►► Symonds Yat Caravan & Camping Park

(SO554174)

HR9 6BY

☎ 01600 890883 & 891069

e-mail: enquiries@campingandcaravan.com

web: www.campingandcaravan.com

Dir: *On A40 between Ross-on-Wye & Monmouth, take Symonds Yat (West) exit. Follow signs*

PETS: Charges 50p per night **Public areas** on leads **Exercise area** 50yds **Facilities** vet info **Other** prior notice required

Open Mar-Oct Booking advisable BH & wknds Last departure noon

A popular little park next to the River Wye, with its own canoe hire and launching ramp. An amusement/leisure park next door can be very noisy, but this park is well suited to young tenters who enjoy canoeing. A 1.25-acre site with 35 touring pitches, 10 hardstandings.

Notes No cycling or ball games on site

YARKHILL

MAP 03 SO64

★★★★ FARM HOUSE

Garford Farm *(SO600435)*

HR1 3ST

☎ 01432 890226 📠 01432 890707 Mrs H Parker

e-mail: garfordfarm@lineone.net

Dir: *Off A417 at Newtown x-rds onto A4103 for Hereford, farm 1.5m on left*

PETS: Bedrooms Sep Accom kennels **Stables** on site **Charges** £4 per night (dogs) **Exercise area** on site on farm 25yds **Resident Pets:** Bertie, Millie & Berry (Black Labradors), Cokie & Soda (cats)

This black and white timber-framed farmhouse, set on a large arable holding, dates from the 17th century. Its character is enhanced by period furnishings, and fires burn in the comfortable lounge during colder weather. The traditionally furnished bedrooms, including a family room, have modern facilities.

Rooms 2 en suite (1 fmly) S fr £30; D fr £50✱ **Facilities** TVB tea/coffee Cen ht Fishing ⌣ **Parking** 6 **Notes** No children 2yrs 700 acres arable Closed 25-26 Dec 🐾

BISHOP'S STORTFORD

MAP 05 TL42

★★★★ 78% ◉◉ HOTEL

Down Hall Country House

Hatfield Heath CM22 7AS

☎ 01279 731441 📠 01279 730416

e-mail: reservations@downhall.co.uk

web: www.downhall.co.uk

Dir: *A1060, at Hatfield Heath keep left. Turn right into lane opposite Hunters Meet restaurant & left at end, follow sign*

PETS: Bedrooms (GF) unattended **Grounds** accessible disp bin **Facilities** food food bowl water bowl dog chews dog scoop/disp bags doggy pack on arrival cage storage vet info **On Request** fridge access torch **Resident Pets:** deer, peacocks

Imposing Victorian country-house hotel set amidst 100 acres of mature grounds in a peaceful location just a short drive from Stansted Airport. Bedrooms are generally quite spacious; each one is pleasantly decorated, tastefully furnished and equipped with modern facilities.

CONTINUED

ENGLAND

ENGLAND

BISHOP'S STORTFORD CONTINUED

Public rooms include a choice of restaurants, a cocktail bar, two lounges and leisure facilities.

Down Hall Country House

Rooms 99 en suite (20 GF) ⊗ in 93 bedrooms S £79-£99; D £89-£114 (incl. bkfst)✳ **Facilities** STV ⓣ ♨ ♨ Wi-fi in bedrooms Giant chess Whirlpool Sauna Xmas New Year **Services** Lift **Parking** 150 **Notes** LB

See advert on page 167

★★★ BED & BREAKFAST
Broadleaf Guest House

38 Broadleaf Av CM23 4JY

☎ 01279 835467

e-mail: b-tcannon@tiscali.co.uk

Dir: *1m SW of town centre. Off B1383 onto Whittinton Way & Friedburge Av, Broadleaf Av 6th left*

PETS: Bedrooms Exercise area countryside **Facilities** vet info

A delightful detached house situated in a peaceful residential area close to the town centre, and within easy striking distance of the M11 and Stansted Airport. The pleasantly decorated bedrooms are carefully furnished and equipped with many thoughtful touches. Breakfast is served in the smart dining room, which overlooks the pretty garden.

Rooms 2 rms (1 fmly) ⊗ S £30-£35; D £50-£60✳ **Facilities** TVB tea/coffee Cen ht **Parking** 2 **Notes** ⊗

HERTFORD   MAP 04 TL31

►►►► Hertford Camping & Caravanning Club Site *(TL334113)*

Mangrove Rd SG13 8QF

☎ 01992 586696

web: www.campingandcaravanningclub.co.uk/hertford

Dir: *From A10 follow A414/Hertford signs to next rdbt (Foxholes), straight over. In 200yds left signed Balls Park & Hertford University. Left at T-junct into Mangrove Road. Site on left*

PETS: Public areas except buildings **Exercise area** on site **Facilities** walks info vet info **Other** prior notice required

Open all year Booking advisable BH's & peak periods Last arrival 21.00hrs Last departure noon

A spacious, well-landscaped club site in a rural setting one mile south of Hertford, with immaculate modern toilet facilities. There are several hedged areas with good provision of hardstandings, and a cosy camping section in an old orchard. All kinds of wildlife flourish around the lake. A 32-acre site with 250 touring pitches, 54 hardstandings.

Notes Site gates closed 23.00-07.00

SOUTH MIMMS SERVICE AREA (M25)   MAP 04 TL20

BUDGET HOTEL
Days Inn South Mimms

Bignells Corner EN6 3QQ

☎ 01707 665440 📠 01707 660189

e-mail: south.mimms@welcomebreak.co.uk

web: www.daysinn.com

Dir: *M25 junct 23, at rdbt follow signs*

PETS: Bedrooms unattended **Grounds** accessible

This modern building offers accommodation in smart, spacious and well-equipped bedrooms, suitable for families and business travellers, and all with en suite bathrooms. Continental breakfast is available and other refreshments may be taken at the nearby family restaurant. For further details see the Hotel Groups page.

Rooms 74 en suite

WALTHAM CROSS   MAP 05 TL30

►► Theobalds Park C&C Club Site *(TL344005)*

Theobalds Park, Bulls Cross Ride EN7 5HS

☎ 01992 620604

web: www.campingandcaravanningclub.co.uk/theobaldspark

Dir: *M25 junct 25. A10 towards London keep in right lane. Right at 1st lights. Right at T-junct, right behind dog kennels. Site towards top of lane on right*

PETS: Public areas except buildings **Exercise area** on site **Facilities** walks info vet info **Other** prior notice required

Open 13 Mar-3 Nov Booking advisable BH & peak periods Last arrival 21.00hrs Last departure noon

A lovely open site surrounded by mature trees, and set in parkland at Theobalds Hall. The portacabin toilet facilities are freshly painted and extremely clean, and there are two separate glades for tents. A 14-acre site with 90 touring pitches.

Notes Site gates closed 23.00-07.00

WARE

MAP 05 TL31

★★★ 74% HOTEL
Roebuck

Baldock St SG12 9DR

☎ 01920 409955 📠 01920 468016

e-mail: roebuck@forestdale.com

web: www.forestdale.com

Dir: *A10 onto B1001, left at rdbt, 1st left behind fire station*

PETS: Bedrooms unattended **Charges** £7.50 per night
Public areas except restaurant

Close to the centre of this old market town, the hotel is convenient to major road networks connecting to major local towns and cities including Cambridge and Hertford; Stansted Airport is only a short drive away. The hotel has spacious bedrooms, a comfortable lounge, bar and conservatory restaurant. There is also a range of air-conditioned meeting rooms.

Rooms 50 en suite (1 fmly) (16 GF) ⊘ in 16 bedrooms **Facilities** STV Wi-fi available **Services** Lift **Parking** 64

KENT

ASHFORD

MAP 05 TR04

★★★★ GUEST ACCOMMODATION
Croft Hotel

Canterbury Rd, Kennington TN25 4DU

☎ 01233 622140 📠 01233 635271

e-mail: info@crofthotel.com

Dir: *M20 junct 10, 2m on A28 signed Canterbury*

PETS: Bedrooms unattended **Charges** £5-£7 per night
Grounds accessible **Exercise area** heath across road

An attractive red-brick house situated in 2 acres of landscaped grounds just a short drive from Ashford railway station. The generously proportioned bedrooms are in the main house and in pretty cottages; all are pleasantly decorated and thoughtfully equipped. Public rooms include a smart Italian restaurant, a bar, and a cosy lounge.

Rooms 27 en suite (6 fmly) (8 GF) ⊘ in 13 bedrooms **Facilities** TVB tea/coffee Direct dial from bedrooms Cen ht TVL Dinner Last d 9.30pm **Parking** 30

►►►► Broad Hembury Caravan & Camping Park *(TR009387)*

Steeds Ln, Kingsnorth TN26 1NQ

☎ 01233 620859 📠 01233 620918

e-mail: holidaypark@broadhembury.co.uk

web: www.broadhembury.co.uk

Dir: *From M20 junct 10 take A2070. Left at 2nd rdbt signed Kingsnorth, then left at 2nd x-roads in village*

PETS: Public areas except play area & toilets **Exercise area** on site 2 acre meadow public foot paths and woods adjacent **Facilities** on site shop food dog scoop/disp bags washing facs walks info vet info **Other** prior notice required **Resident Pets:** Bruce (German Shepherd), Henry (King Charles Spaniel), 4 chickens

Open all year Booking advisable BH & Jul-Aug Last arrival 23.00hrs Last departure noon

Well-run and maintained small family park surrounded by open pasture and neatly landscaped, with pitches sheltered by mature hedges. Some super pitches have proved a popular addition, and there is a well-equipped campers' kitchen. A 10-acre site with 60 touring pitches, 24 hardstandings and 25 statics.

CANTERBURY

MAP 05 TR15

★★★ 88% HOTEL
Best Western Abbots Barton

New Dover Rd CT1 3DU

☎ 01227 760341 📠 01227 785442

e-mail: sales@abbotsbartonhotel.com

Dir: *Turn off A2 onto A2050 at bridge, S of Canterbury. Hotel is 0.75m past Old Gate Inn on left*

PETS: Bedrooms (GF) **Charges** charge for damage **Public areas** except food areas on leads **Grounds** accessible on leads **Facilities** food bowl water bowl bedding feeding mat cage storage walks info vet info **On Request** torch

Delightful property with a country-house hotel feel set amid two acres of pretty landscaped gardens close to the city centre and major road networks. The spacious accommodation includes a range of stylish lounges, a smart bar and the Fountain Restaurant, which serves imaginative food. Conference and banqueting facilities are also available.

Rooms 50 en suite (2 fmly) (6 GF) ⊘ in 40 bedrooms S £60-£120; D £70-£220 **Facilities** STV Wi-fi in bedrooms Xmas New Year **Services** Lift air con **Parking** 80 **Notes LB**

CANTERBURY CONTINUED

★★★★ GUEST ACCOMMODATION
Yorke Lodge

50 London Rd CT2 8LF
☎ 01227 451243 📄 01227 462006
e-mail: enquiries@yorkelodge.com
web: www.yorkelodge.com
Dir: *750yds NW of city centre. A2 E onto A2050 to city, 1st rdbt left onto London Rd*

PETS: Bedrooms unattended **Exercise area** 100yds
Facilities walks info vet info **On Request** fridge access torch towels **Resident Pets:** Fleur (Dalmatian/Collie cross)

The charming Victorian property stands in a tree-lined road just ten minutes walk from the town centre and railway station. The spacious bedrooms are thoughtfully equipped and carefully decorated; some rooms have four-poster beds. The stylish dining room leads to a conservatory-lounge, which opens onto a superb terrace.

Rooms 8 en suite (1 fmly) ⊗ S £48-£60; D £85-£110 (incl. dinner)
Facilities TVB tea/coffee Cen ht Wi-fi available **Parking** 5 **Notes** LB

★★★ GUEST ACCOMMODATION
St Stephens Guest House

100 St Stephens Rd CT2 7JL
☎ 01227 767644 📄 01227 767644
Dir: *A290 from city Westgate & sharp right onto North Ln, 2nd rdbt left onto St Stephen's Rd, right onto Market Way, car park on right*

PETS: Bedrooms (GF) **Charges** £3 per night **Public areas** except dining room **Exercise area** nearby **Facilities** washing facs walks info vet info **On Request** fridge access torch towels **Resident Pets:** Jack & Molly (Springer Spaniels)

A large, privately-owned guest house situated close to the university and within easy walking distance of the city centre. The pleasant bedrooms are equipped with a good range of useful extras, and there is a cosy lounge. Breakfast is served at individual tables in the smart dining room.

Rooms 12 rms (11 en suite) (2 fmly) (3 GF) ⊗ S £38-£42; D £58-£65
Facilities TVB tea/coffee Cen ht TVL **Parking** 11 **Notes** No children 5yrs Closed 18 Dec-mid Jan 🐾

►►► **Canterbury Camping & Caravanning Club Site** *(TR172577)*

Bekesbourne Ln CT3 4AB
☎ 01227 463216
web: www.campingandcaravanningclub.co.uk/canterbury
Dir: *From Canterbury follow A257 signs (Sandwich), turn right opposite golf course*

PETS: Exercise area on site dog walks **Facilities** walks info vet info **Other** prior notice required

Open all year Booking advisable BH & peak periods Last arrival 21.00hrs Last departure noon

An attractive tree-screened site in pleasant rural surroundings yet within walking distance of the city centre. The park is well landscaped, and offers very smart toilet facilities in one block, with another older but well-kept building housing further facilities. A 20-acre site with 200 touring pitches, 21 hardstandings.

►► **Ashfield Farm** *(TR138508)*

Waddenhall, Petham CT4 5PX
☎ 01227 700624
e-mail: mpatterson@ashfieldfarm.freeserve.co.uk
Dir: *7m S of Canterbury on B2068*

PETS: Public areas Exercise area 100mtrs **Facilities** washing facs walks info vet info

Open Apr-Oct Booking advisable Jul & Aug Last arrival anytime Last departure noon

Small rural site with simple facilities and well-drained pitches, set in beautiful countryside and enjoying lovely open views. Located south of Canterbury, and with very security-conscious owners. A 4.5-acre site with 30 touring pitches and 1 static.

Notes 🐾

DARTFORD
MAP 05 TQ57

BUDGET HOTEL
Campanile

1 Clipper Boulevard West, Crossways Business Park DA2 6QN
☎ 01322 278925 📄 01322 278948
e-mail: dartford@campanile-hotels.com
web: www.envergure.fr
Dir: *follow signs for Ferry Terminal from Dartford Bridge*
PETS: Please telephone for details

This modern building offers accommodation in smart, well-equipped bedrooms, all with en suite bathrooms. Refreshments may be taken at the informal Bistro. For further details consult the Hotel Groups page.

Rooms 125 en suite

DEAL

MAP 05 TR35

★★★★★ 🍽 GUEST ACCOMMODATION

Sutherland House Hotel

186 London Rd CT14 9PT

☎ 01304 362853 📠 01304 381146

e-mail: info@sutherlandhouse.fsnet.co.uk

Dir: *0.5m W of town centre/seafront on A258*

PETS: Bedrooms (GF) unattended **Charges** charge for damage **Public areas Grounds** accessible **Facilities** water bowl washing facs walks info vet info **On Request** fridge access torch towels **Restrictions** small dogs only

This stylish accommodation offers impeccable taste with its charming, well-equipped bedrooms and a comfortable lounge. Fully stocked bar, books, magazines, Freeview TV and radio are some of the many amenities offered. The elegant dining room is the venue for home-cooked dinners and breakfasts.

Rooms 4 en suite (1 GF) ⊘ S £52-£57; D £65-£69 **Facilities** FTV TVB tea/coffee Direct dial from bedrooms Cen ht Dinner Last d 6.30pm Wi-fi available **Parking** 7 **Notes LB** No children 5yrs

---

DOVER

MAP 05 TR34

★★★★ GUEST ACCOMMODATION

Hubert House

9 Castle Hill Rd CT16 1QW

☎ 01304 202253 📠 01304 210142

e-mail: huberthouse@btinternet.com

web: www.huberthouse.co.uk

Dir: *On A258 by Dover Castle*

PETS: Bedrooms Charges £7.50 per night **Exercise area** 300mtrs **Other** Pet food on request **Resident Pets:** Lillie (Weimaraner)

This charming Georgian house is within walking distance of the ferry port and the town centre. Bedrooms are pleasantly decorated and furnished in a modern style. Breakfast, including full English and healthy options, is served in the smart coffee house, which is open all day. Families are especially welcome.

Rooms 7 en suite (4 fmly) ⊘ S £35-£50; D £50-£70✱ (room only) **Facilities** TVB tea/coffee Cen ht Dinner Last d 2pm Wi-fi available **Parking** 6 **Notes LB** Closed Jan-Feb

---

►►►► **Hawthorn Farm Caravan Park**

(TR342464)

Station Rd, Martin Mill CT15 5LA

☎ 01304 852658 & 852914 📠 01304 853417

e-mail: info@keatfarm.co.uk

web: www.keatfarm.co.uk/touringparks/hawthorn.htm

Dir: *Signed from A258*

PETS: Charges £1.50 per night **Public areas Exercise area** nearby **Facilities** on site shop food food bowl water bowl dog chews cat treats litter tray disp bags leads walks info vet info

Open Mar-Nov (rs winter water off if weather cold) Booking advisable BH & Jul-Aug Last arrival anytime Last departure noon

This pleasant rural park set in 28 acres of beautifully-landscaped gardens is screened by young trees and hedgerows, in grounds which include woods and a rose garden. The decent facilities include a shop and laundry. A 28-acre site with 147 touring pitches, 5 hardstandings and 176 statics.

FOLKESTONE

MAP 05 TR23

★★★ 70% HOTEL

Quality Hotel Burlington

Earls Av CT20 2HR

☎ 01303 255301 📠 01303 251301

e-mail: info@theburlingtonhotel.com

PETS: Bedrooms (GF) **Charges** £10 per night **Public areas** except restaurant on leads **Grounds** accessible on leads **Facilities** water bowl bedding cage storage walks info vet info

Resident Pets: Cherit (Golden Retriever), Misty (cat)

Situated close to the beach in a peaceful side road just a short walk from the town centre. The public rooms include a choice of lounges, the Bay Tree restaurant and a large cocktail bar. Bedrooms are pleasantly decorated and equipped with modern facilities; some rooms have superb sea views.

Rooms 50 en suite (6 fmly) (5 GF) ⊘ in 36 bedrooms S £60-£84; D £79-£119 (incl. bkfst)✱ **Facilities** FTV Putt green Wi-fi available Xmas New Year **Services** Lift **Parking** 20 **Notes LB**

FOLKESTONE CONTINUED

►►► Folkestone Camping & Caravanning Club Site (TR246376)

The Warren CT19 6NQ

☎ 01303 255093

web: www.campingandcaravanningclub.co.uk/folkestone

Dir: *From A2 or A20 onto A260, left at island into Folkestone. Continue straight over x-rds into Wear Bay Road, 2nd left past Martello Tower, site 0.5m on right*

PETS: Public areas except buildings **Exercise area** beach, 60mtrs **Facilities** walks info vet info **Other** prior notice required

Open 13 Mar-3 Nov Booking advisable BH & peak periods Last arrival 21.00hrs Last departure noon

This site commands marvellous views across the Strait of Dover, and is well located for the Channel ports. It nestles on the side of the cliff, and is tiered in some areas. The toilet facilities are modern and tasteful, with cubicled wash basins in both blocks. No caravans accepted. A 4-acre site with 80 touring pitches, 9 hardstandings.

Notes Site gates closed 23.00-07.00

►►► Little Satmar Holiday Park (TR260390)

Winehouse Ln, Capel Le Ferne CT18 7JF

☎ 01303 251188 ▤ 01303 251188

e-mail: info@keatfarm.co.uk

web: www.keatfarm.co.uk/touringparks/littlesatmar.htm

Dir: *Signed off B2011*

PETS: Charges £1.50 per night £9.45 per week **Public areas Exercise area** 100mtrs **Facilities** on site shop food food bowl water bowl dog chews cat treats dog scoop/disp bags washing facs walks info vet info

Open Mar-Nov Booking advisable BH & Jul-Aug Last arrival 23.00hrs Last departure 14.00hrs

A quiet, well-screened site well away from the road and statics, with clean and tidy facilities. A useful base for visiting Dover and Folkestone, and just a short walk from cliff paths with their views of the Channel, and sandy beaches below. A 5-acre site with 60 touring pitches and 80 statics.

►► Little Switzerland Camping & Caravan Site (TR248380)

Wear Bay Rd CT19 6PS

☎ 01303 252168

e-mail: btony328@aol.com

web: www.caravancampingsites.co.uk/kent/littleswitzerland.htm

Dir: *Signed from A20 E of Folkestone. Approaching from A259 or B2011 on E outskirts of Folkestone follow signs for Wear Bay/ Martello Tower, then tourist sign to site, follow signs to country park*

PETS: Stables nearby (1m) **Public areas Exercise area** on site dog walks 500mtrs **Facilities** washing facs walks info vet info **Resident Pets:** Fluffy (cat)

Open Mar-Oct Booking advisable from Mar Last arrival mdnt Last departure noon

Set on a narrow plateau below the white cliffs, this unusual site enjoys fine views across Wear Bay and the Strait of Dover. A licensed café with an alfresco area is popular; the basic toilet facilities are unsuitable for the disabled. A 3-acre site with 32 touring pitches and 13 statics.

Notes No open fires

MAIDSTONE MAP 05 TQ75

★★★★ INN

The Black Horse Inn

Pilgrims Way, Thurnham ME14 3LD

☎ 01622 737185 & 630830 ▤ 01622 739170

e-mail: info@wellieboot.net

web: www.wellieboot.net/home_blackhorse.htm

Dir: *M20 junct 7, N onto A249. Right into Detling, opp pub onto Pilgrims Way for 1m*

PETS: Bedrooms (GF) unattended **Charges** £6 per night **Public areas** except restaurant on leads **Grounds** accessible on leads disp bin **Facilities** dog scoop/disp bags washing facs cage storage walks info vet info **On Request** fridge access torch **Resident Pets:** Sam (Pointer), Jess (Collie), Donald, Howard, Percy, Dave (ducks)

This charming inn dates from the 17th century, and the public areas have a wealth of oak beams, exposed brickwork and open fireplaces.

The stylish bedrooms are in a series of cosy cabins behind the premises; each one is attractively furnished and thoughtfully equipped.

Rooms 16 annexe en suite (4 fmly) (11 GF) **Facilities** TV11B tea/coffee Cen ht Dinner Last d 10pm **Parking** 40 **Notes** No coaches

See advert on this page

MARGATE
MAP 05 TR37

★★★ GUEST ACCOMMODATION

The Greswolde

20 Surrey Rd, Cliftonville CT9 2LA

☎ 01843 223956 ▤ 01843 223956

e-mail: jbearl@freeuk.com

PETS: Bedrooms unattended **Public areas Exercise area** beach **Resident Pets:** Hatty, Daisy, Teddy, Timmy, Sam (cats)

An attractive Victorian house set in a peaceful area close to the seafront. The property has a lovely period atmosphere with interesting memorabilia and spacious bedrooms. The pleasant rooms are comfortably appointed and equipped. Breakfast is served in the elegant dining room, and there is a cosy lounge.

Rooms 5 en suite (2 fmly) **Facilities** TVB tea/coffee Cen ht

NEW ROMNEY
MAP 05 TR02

★★★ FARM HOUSE

Honeychild Manor Farmhouse *(TR062276)*

St Mary In The Marsh TN29 0DB

☎ 01797 366180 & 07951 237821 ▤ 01797 366925

Mrs V Furnival

e-mail: honeychild@farming.co.uk

Dir: *2m N of New Romney off A259. S of village centre*

PETS: Bedrooms Charges £10 per night for horses **Stables** on site **Grounds** accessible **Facilities** dog scoop/disp bags leads cage storage walks info vet info **On Request** fridge access torch towels **Resident Pets:** Georgie (Labrador), Molly (Collie), Buster & Charlie (horses)

This imposing Georgian farmhouse is part of a working dairy farm on Romney Marsh. Walkers and dreamers alike will enjoy the stunning views and can relax in the beautifully landscaped gardens or play tennis on the full-sized court. A hearty breakfast is served in the elegant dining room and features quality local produce. Bedrooms are pleasantly decorated, well furnished and thoughtfully equipped. This establishment is pet friendly.

Rooms 3 rms (1 fmly) ⊘ S fr £30; D fr £50✳ **Facilities** TVB tea/coffee Cen ht Dinner Last d 4pm ⚲ **Parking** 10 **Notes** 1500 acres Arable & Dairy ▣

The Black Horse Inn

Pilgrims Way
Thurnham
Kent ME14 3LD

Tel: 01622 737185
info@wellieboot.net
www.wellieboot.net

Individually furnished rooms set around a quiet courtyard in lovely countryside. Delightful views of the North Downs and some stunning scenery with walks on your doorstep – we provide maps and directions. Pet friendly rooms and our bar also accepts dogs on leads. We have a non-smoking restaurant renowned for its excellent, imaginative food using the very best local produce. Ideally situated for visiting Kent's many attractions including Leeds Castle just 5 minutes drive away.

SEVENOAKS MAP 05 TQ55

►►► **Oldbury Hill C&C Club Site** *(TQ577564)*

Styants Bottom, Seal TN15 0ET

☎ 01732 762728

web: www.campingandcaravanningclub.co.uk/oldburyhill

Dir: *Take A25 from Sevenoaks towards Borough Green. Left just after Crown Point Inn, on right, down narrow lane to Styants Bottom. Site on left*

PETS: Public areas except buildings **Exercise area** woods **Facilities** walks info vet info **Other** prior notice required

Open 13 Mar-3 Nov Booking advisable BH & peak periods Last arrival 21.00hrs Last departure noon

A remarkably tranquil site in the centre of National Trust woodland, with buildings blending well into the surroundings. Expect the usual high standard of customer care found at all Club sites. A 6-acre site with 60 touring pitches.

Notes Site gates closed 23.00-07.00

SITTINGBOURNE MAP 05 TQ96

★★★ 83% ◉ HOTEL

Hempstead House Country Hotel

London Rd, Bapchild ME9 9PP

☎ 01795 428020 🖨 01795 436362

e-mail: info@hempsteadhouse.co.uk

web: www.hempsteadhouse.co.uk

Dir: *1.5m from Sittingbourne town centre on A2 towards Canterbury*

PETS: Bedrooms (GF) unattended **Stables** nearby (2m) **Public areas Exercise area** nearby **Facilities** food bowl water bowl cage storage vet info **On Request** fridge access torch towels **Resident Pets:** Jade (Staffordshire Bull Terrier), cats

Expect a warm welcome at this charming detached Victorian property, situated amidst three acres of mature landscaped gardens. Bedrooms are attractively decorated with lovely co-ordinated fabrics, tastefully furnished and equipped with many thoughtful touches. Public rooms feature a choice of beautifully furnished lounges as well as a superb conservatory dining room.

Rooms 27 en suite (7 fmly) (1 GF) ⊗ in all bedrooms S £80-£110; D £90-£130 (incl. bkfst)✻ **Facilities** STV ⌇ ♨ Wi-fi in bedrooms Xmas New Year **Parking** 100 **Notes** LB

WHITSTABLE MAP 05 TR16

►►►► **Homing Park** *(TR095645)*

Church Ln, Seasalter CT5 4BU

☎ 01227 771777 🖨 01227 273512

e-mail: info@homingpark.co.uk

web: www.homingpark.co.uk

Dir: *Exit A299 for Whitstable & Canterbury, left at brown camping/caravan sign into Church Lane. Park entrance has 2 large flag poles*

PETS: Public areas Facilities walks info vet info

Open Mar-Oct Booking advisable Etr, BH & Aug Last arrival 20.00hrs Last departure 11.00hrs

A small touring park close to Seasalter Beach and Whitstable, which is famous for its oysters. All pitches are generously sized and fully serviced, and most are separated by hedging and shrubs. A clubhouse and swimming pool are available on the adjacent residential park at a small cost. A 12.75-acre site with 43 touring pitches and 195 statics.

Notes No commercial vehicles, no tents greater than 8 berth, no unaccompanied groups of under 18s

►►► **Seaview Holiday Village** *(TR145675)*

St John's Rd CT5 2RY

☎ 01227 792246 🖨 01227 792247

e-mail: info@parkholidaysuk.com

web: www.parkholidaysuk.com

Dir: *From A299 take A2990 then B2205 to Swalecliffe, site between Herne Bay & Whitstable*

PETS: Stables nearby (5m) **Charges** £2 per night **Public areas Exercise area** on site **Facilities** on site shop vet info **Other** prior notice required

Open Mar-Oct (rs Feb & Nov limited facilities) Booking advisable all times Last arrival 21.30hrs Last departure noon

A pleasant open site on the edge of Whitstable, set well away from the static area, with a smart, modern toilet block and both super and hardstanding pitches. A 12-acre site with 171 touring pitches, 41 hardstandings and 452 statics.

LANCASHIRE

BLACKPOOL
MAP 07 SD33

★★★★ 74% HOTEL
Paramount Imperial Hotel

PARAMOUNT
GROUP OF HOTELS

North Promenade FY1 2HB

☎ 01253 623971 📄 01253 751784

e-mail: imperialblackpool@paramount-hotels.co.uk

web: www.paramount-hotels.co.uk

Dir: *M55 junct 2, take A583 North Shore, follow signs to North Promenade. Hotel on seafront, north of tower.*

PETS: Please telephone for details

Enjoying a prime seafront location, this grand Victorian hotel offers smartly appointed, well-equipped bedrooms and spacious, elegant public areas. Facilities include a smart leisure club; a comfortable lounge, the No.10 bar and an attractive split-level restaurant that overlooks the seafront. Conferences and functions are extremely well catered for.

Rooms 180 en suite (9 fmly) ⊘ in 156 bedrooms S £59-£149✱
Facilities Spa STV ⊕ Gym Wi-fi available Xmas New Year **Services** Lift
Parking 150 (charged)

★★★ GUEST HOUSE
Windsor Park Hotel

96 Queens Promenade FY2 9NS

☎ 01253 357025

e-mail: info@windsorparkhotel.net

Dir: *Queens Promenade, North Shore*

PETS: Bedrooms unattended **Charges** £5 per night (may be charged) charge for damage **Public areas** on leads **Exercise area** nearby **Facilities** walks info vet info **On Request** fridge access **Restrictions** small & well behaved dogs only
Resident Pets: Molly (Yorkshire Terrier)

Having stunning views, this family-run guest house on the peaceful North Shore is just a tram ride from the attractions. Home-cooked meals and substantial breakfasts are served in the elegant dining room, and there is a pleasant bar area and a sun lounge. The bedrooms have modern amenities.

Rooms 9 en suite (1 fmly) **Facilities** TVB tea/coffee Licensed Cen ht TVL Dinner Last d 4pm Stair lift **Parking** 6 **Notes** No coaches Closed 8 Nov-Etr (ex Xmas/New Year)

BURNLEY
MAP 07 SD83

★★★ 78% HOTEL
Best Western Higher Trapp Country House

Best Western

Trapp Ln, Simonstone BB12 7QW

☎ 01282 772781 📄 01282 772782

e-mail: reception@highertrapphotel.co.uk

PETS: Bedrooms unattended **Public areas** except bar & lounge **Grounds** accessible on leads **Exercise area** local walks **Facilities** vet info

Set in beautifully maintained gardens with rolling countryside beyond, accommodation comprises spacious, comfortable bedrooms, some of which are located in the 'Lodge', a smart annexe building. Public areas include a comfortable lounge, spacious bar and conservatory restaurant where guests will find service friendly and attentive.

Rooms 19 en suite 10 annexe en suite (3 fmly) (4 GF) ⊘ in 10 bedrooms
Facilities STV **Parking** 100 **Notes**

CHARNOCK RICHARD
MAP 07 SD51
MOTORWAY SERVICE AREA (M6)

BUDGET HOTEL
Welcome Lodge Charnock Richard

Welcome Break Service Area PR7 5LR

☎ 01257 791746 📄 01257 793596

e-mail: charnockhotel@welcomebreak.co.uk

web: www.welcomebreak.co.uk

Dir: *between junct 27 & 28 of M6 northbound*

PETS: Bedrooms **Exercise area** on site

This modern building offers accommodation in smart, spacious and well-equipped bedrooms, suitable for families and business travellers, and all with en suite bathrooms. Refreshments may be taken at the nearby family restaurant. For further details see the Hotel Groups page.

Rooms 100 en suite

CLITHEROE
MAP 07 SD74

▶▶▶ **Clitheroe Camping & Caravanning Club Site** *(SD727413)*

Edisford Rd BB7 3LA

☎ 01200 425294

web: www.campingandcaravanningclub.co.uk/clithroe

Dir: *From W A671 to Clitheroe. Follow sign to Longridge/Sports Centre. Into Greenacre Rd to T-junct. Site 50mtrs*

PETS: Public areas except buildings **Facilities** walks info vet info **Other** prior notice required

Open Mar-Oct Booking advisable BH & peak periods Last arrival 21.00hrs Last departure noon

CONTINUED

CLITHEROE CONTINUED

Set on the banks of the River Ribble, this park is attractively landscaped with mature trees and shrubs. An ideal spot for walking and fishing, and the site is also adjacent to a park with a café, pitch and putt, leisure centre, swimming pool and miniature steam railway. The Ribble Country Way is nearby. A 6-acre site with 80 touring pitches, 30 hardstandings.

GARSTANG   MAP 07 SD44

►►►► Claylands Caravan Park (SD496485)

Cabus PR3 1AJ

☎ 01524 791242 ▤ 01524 792406

e-mail: alan@claylands.com

web: www.claylands.com

Dir: *From M6 junct 33 S to Garstang, approx 6m pass Little Chef, signed off A6 into private road on Lancaster side of Garstang*

PETS: Charges £1 per night Public areas on leads Exercise area on site on leads & nearby areas Facilities on site shop dog scoop/disp bags washing facs walks info vet info Restrictions Telephone for details

Open Mar-4 Jan (rs Jan & Feb holiday park only) Booking advisable BH & Jul-Aug Last arrival 23.00hrs Last departure 14.00hrs

A well-maintained site with lovely river and woodland walks and good views over the River Wyre towards the village of Scorton. This friendly park is set in delightful countryside. Guests can enjoy fishing, and the atmosphere is very relaxed. The quality facilities and amenities are of a high standard, and everything is immaculately maintained. A 14-acre site with 30 touring pitches, 30 hardstandings and 68 statics.

Notes no roller blades or skateboards

LANCASTER   MAP 07 SD46

★★★★ 73% ⊛ HOTEL
Lancaster House

Green Ln, Ellel LA1 4GJ

☎ 01524 844822 ▤ 01524 844766

e-mail: lancaster@elhmail.co.uk

web: www.elh.co.uk/hotels/lancaster

Dir: *M6 junct 33 N towards Lancaster. Through Galgate and into Green Ln. Hotel before university on right*

PETS: Bedrooms (GF) Charges £15 per night charge for damage Grounds accessible on leads disp bin Exercise area 500mtrs Facilities walks info vet info On Request fridge access towels

This modern hotel enjoys a rural setting south of the city and close to the university. The attractive open-plan reception and lounge boast a roaring log fire in colder months. Bedrooms are spacious, with 19 rooms being particularly well equipped for business guests. Public areas include leisure facilities with a hot tub and a function suite.

Rooms 99 en suite (29 fmly) (44 GF) ⊘ in 79 bedrooms S £72-£120; D £84-£140 (incl. bkfst)✳ Facilities Spa STV ⊙ supervised Gym Wi-fi available Beauty salon Outside hot tub ♫ Xmas New Year Parking 120 Notes LB

MORECAMBE   MAP 07 SD46

★★★ 68% HOTEL
Clarendon

76 Marine Rd West, West End Promenade LA4 4EP

☎ 01524 410180 ▤ 01524 421616

e-mail: clarendon@mitchellshotels.co.uk

Dir: *M6 junct 34 follow Morecambe signs. At rdbt with 'The Shrimp' on corner 1st exit to Westgate, follow to seafront. Right at traffic lights, hotel 3rd block along*

PETS: Bedrooms

This traditional seafront hotel offers modern facilities, and several long serving key staff ensure guests a home-from-home atmosphere. Well maintained throughout, it offers bright, cheerful public areas.

Rooms 29 en suite (4 fmly) ⊘ in 10 bedrooms S £40-£60; D £70-£90 (incl. bkfst)✳ Facilities STV Wi-fi in bedrooms Xmas New Year Services Lift Parking 22 Notes LB

►►► Venture Caravan Park (SD436633)

Langridge Way, Westgate LA4 4TQ

☎ 01524 412986 ▤ 01524 422029

e-mail: mark@venturecaravanpark.co.uk

web: www.venturecaravanpark.co.uk

Dir: *From M6 junct 34 follow Morecambe signs. At rdbt take road towards Westgate & follow park signs. 1st right after fire station*

PETS: Public areas on leads Exercise area nearby Facilities on site shop food litter tray disp bags vet info Other prior notice required

Open all year (rs 6 Jan-22 Feb touring vans only, one toilet block open) Booking advisable BH & peak periods Last arrival 22.00hrs Last departure noon

A large park with good modern facilities, including a small indoor heated pool, a licensed clubhouse and a family room with children's entertainment. The site has many statics, and is close to the town centre. A 17.5-acre site with 56 touring pitches, 40 hardstandings and 304 statics.

ORMSKIRK
MAP 07 SD40

►►►► Abbey Farm Caravan Park *(SD434098)*
Dark Ln L40 5TX

☎ 01695 572686 📠 01695 572686

e-mail: abbeyfarm@yahoo.com

web: www.abbeyfarmcaravanpark.co.uk

Dir: *M6 junct 27 onto A5209 to Burscough. 4m left onto B5240. Immediate right into Hobcross Ln. Park 1.5m on right*

PETS: Public areas on leads Exercise area on site field available local walks Facilities on site shop food walks info vet info

Open all year Booking advisable BHs & Jul-Aug Last arrival 21.00hrs Last departure 13.00hrs

Delightful hanging baskets and flower beds brighten this garden-like rural park which is sheltered by hedging and mature trees. Modern, very clean facilities include a family bathroom, and there are special pitches for the disabled near the toilets. A superb recreation field caters for children of all ages, and there is an indoor games room, large library, fishing lake and dog walk. Tents have their own area with BBQ and picnic tables. A 6-acre site with 56 touring pitches and 44 statics.

WREA GREEN
MAP 07 SD33

★★★ 74% HOTEL
Villa Country House
Moss Side Ln PR4 2PE

☎ 01772 684347 📠 01772 687647

e-mail: info@the-villahotel.co.uk

Dir: *M55 junct 3 follow signs to Kirkham at Wrea Green follow signs to Lytham*

PETS: Bedrooms (GF) Charges £5 per night charge for damage Public areas except restaurant Grounds accessible on leads disp bin Facilities food bowl water bowl walks info On Request fridge access towels

This 19th-century residence stands in a peaceful location close to the village of Wrea Green. There are extensive bars and a good range of quality food is served either in the bar or the many-roomed restaurant. The modern, air-conditioned bedrooms are very well designed. The staff are friendly and helpful.

Rooms 25 en suite (1 fmly) (10 GF) ⊘ in all bedrooms S £80-£110; D £80-£110 (incl. bkfst)✷ Facilities STV Xmas New Year Services Lift Parking 75 Notes LB

BUCKMINSTER
MAP 08 SK82

★★★★ ◉◉ ➡ GUEST ACCOMMODATION
The Tollemache Arms
48 Main St NG33 5SA

☎ 01476 860007

e-mail: enquiries@thetollemachearms.com

Dir: *Off A1 Colsterworth rdbt onto B676 to Buckminster*

PETS: Bedrooms Charges charge for damage Public areas except restaurant on leads Grounds accessible on leads Facilities pet sitting dog walking cage storage vet info On Request fridge access torch towels

This revamped village property has a minimalist decor of neutral colours, and strong shades in the pictures, brown leather chairs and crisp white table linen. Its busy restaurant serves high quality food.

Rooms 5 en suite (3 fmly) S £50; D £70✷ Facilities TVB tea/coffee Cen ht Dinner Last d 9.30pm Parking 21 Notes LB RS Sun-Mon

COALVILLE
MAP 08 SK41

★★★★ 🏠 GUEST HOUSE
Church Lane Farm House
Ravenstone LE67 2AE

☎ 01530 810536

e-mail: annthorne@ravenstone-guesthouse.co.uk

web: www.ravenstone-guesthouse.co.uk

Dir: *1.5m W of Coalville. Off A447 onto Church Ln for Ravenstone, 2nd house on left*

PETS: Bedrooms Stables may be possible by prior arrangement Charges donation to charity requested Public areas at proprietor's discretion Exercise area nearby Resident Pets: Faruska (Black Labrador), Saffron (Yellow Labrador)

Situated in the heart of Ravenstone village, this early 18th-century house is full of character. The bedrooms are individually decorated and feature period furniture, and local produce is used for dinner and in the extensive breakfast menu. The beamed dining room has an honesty bar and there is also a cosy lounge.

Rooms 3 en suite ⊘ Facilities TV available tea/coffee Licensed Cen ht TVL Dinner Last d noon Painting tuition Parking 6 Notes No children 18yrs No coaches Closed 23-30 Dec & 1 Jan

ENGLAND

KNIPTON — MAP 08 SK83

★★★★ ⊛ 🛏 GUEST ACCOMMODATION

The Manners Arms

Croxton Rd NG32 1RH

☎ 01476 879222 🖹 01476 879228

e-mail: info@mannersarms.com

web: www.mannersarms.com

Dir: *Off A607 into Knipton*

PETS: Bedrooms unattended **Stables** nearby (0.25m)
Charges £7 per night charge for damage **Grounds** accessible
Facilities food (pre-bookable) food bowl water bowl walks info
vet info **On Request** torch towels

Part of the Rutland Estate and built as a hunting lodge for the 6th
Duke, the Manners Arms has been renovated to provide thoughtfully
furnished bedrooms designed by the present Duchess. Public areas
include the intimate themed Beater's Bar and attractive Red Coats
Restaurant, popular for imaginative dining.

Rooms 10 en suite (1 fmly) S £55-£65; D £90-£130✲ **Facilities** TVB tea/
coffee Direct dial from bedrooms Cen ht TVL Dinner Last d 8.45pm
Parking 60 **Notes** LB

LEICESTER FOREST — MAP 04 SK50
MOTORWAY SERVICE AREA (M1)

BUDGET HOTEL

Days Inn Leicester Forest East

Leicester Forest East, Junction 21 M1
LE3 3GB

☎ 0116 239 0534 🖹 0116 239 0546

e-mail: leicester.hotel@welcomebreak.co.uk

web: www.daysinn.com

Dir: *on M1 northbound between junct 21 & 21A*

PETS: Bedrooms unattended

This modern building offers accommodation in smart, spacious and
well-equipped bedrooms, suitable for families and business travellers,
and all with en suite bathrooms. Continental breakfast is available and
other refreshments may be taken at the nearby family restaurant. For
further details see the Hotel Groups page.

Rooms 92 en suite

MARKFIELD — MAP 04 SK41

★★★ 70% HOTEL

Field Head

Markfield Ln LE6 9PS

☎ 01530 245454 🖹 01530 243740

e-mail: 9160@greeneking.co.uk

web: www.oldenglish.co.uk

Dir: *Exit M1 junct 22, towards Leicester. At rdbt turn left, then right*

PETS: Bedrooms unattended **Charges** £5 per night
Exercise area 10 min drive **Other** 2 pet friendly rooms

This conveniently situated hotel dates back to the 17th century when it
was a farmhouse. It has been considerably extended over the years.
Within the public areas, the bar and lounge are the focal point for
residents and non-residents alike, whilst meals can be taken either in
the bar or the dining room. Bedrooms are modern and well furnished
and offer good all round comforts and facilities. There are four large
feature bedrooms also available.

Rooms 28 en suite (1 fmly) (13 GF) ⊘ in all bedrooms **Facilities** 🎵
Parking 65

MELTON MOWBRAY — MAP 08 SK71

★★★★ ⊛⊛ HOTEL

Stapleford Park

Stapleford LE14 2EF

☎ 01572 787000 🖹 01572 787651

e-mail: reservations@stapleford.co.uk

web: www.staplefordpark.com

Dir: *1m SW of B676, 4m E of Melton Mowbray and 9m W of
Colsterworth*

PETS: Bedrooms Charges £15 per night charge for damage
Public areas except dining areas on leads **Grounds** accessible
except golf course on leads **Facilities** food bowl water bowl
bedding dog chews walks info vet info **On Request** fridge access

This stunning mansion, dating back to the 14th century, sits in over
500 acres of beautiful grounds. Spacious, sumptuous public rooms

include a choice of lounges and an elegant restaurant; an additional brasserie-style restaurant is located in the golf complex. The hotel also boasts a spa with health and beauty treatments and gym, a golf course, horse-riding and many other country pursuits. Bedrooms are individually styled and furnished to a high standard. Attentive service is delivered with a relaxed yet professional style. Dinner, in the impressive dining room, is a highlight of any stay.

Rooms 48 en suite 7 annexe en suite (10 fmly) ⊘ in all bedrooms **Facilities** Spa STV ⊗ ↧ 18 ♨ Fishing Riding Gym ✎ Putt green Archery, Croquet, Falconry, Horse Riding, Petanque, Shooting, Billiards **Services** Lift **Parking** 120

★★★ 75% HOTEL
Sysonby Knoll
Asfordby Rd LE13 0HP
☎ 01664 563563 🖨 01664 410364
e-mail: reception@sysonby.com
web: www.sysonby.com
Dir: *0.5m from town centre beside A6006*

PETS: Bedrooms (GF) **Charges** charge for damage **Public areas** except restaurant on leads **Grounds** accessible on leads disp bin **Facilities** bowls/food available on request washing facs cage storage walks info vet info **On Request** fridge access torch towels **Resident Pets:** Stalky (Miniature Dachshund)

This well-established hotel is on the edge of town and set in attractive gardens. A friendly and relaxed atmosphere prevails and the many returning guests have become friends. Bedrooms, including superior rooms in the annexe, are generally spacious and thoughtfully equipped. There is a choice of lounges, a cosy bar and a smart restaurant that offers carefully prepared meals.

Rooms 23 en suite 7 annexe en suite (1 fmly) (7 GF) ⊘ in 9 bedrooms S £64-£85; D £78-£110 (incl. bkfst)✱ **Facilities** STV FTV Fishing ✎ Wi-fi in bedrooms **Parking** 48 **Notes** LB Closed 25 Dec-1 Jan

★★★★ GUEST ACCOMMODATION
Bryn Barn
38 High St, Waltham-on-the-Wolds LE14 4AH
☎ 01664 464783 & 07791 215614
e-mail: glenarowlands@onetel.com
web: www.brynbarn.co.uk
Dir: *4.5m NE of Melton. Off A607 in Waltham village centre*

PETS: Bedrooms Charges £5 per night **Grounds** accessible **Other** Ground floor room with garden access

A warm welcome awaits you at this attractive, peacefully located cottage within easy reach of Melton Mowbray, Grantham, Rutland Water and Belvoir Castle. Bedrooms are smartly appointed and comfortably furnished, while public rooms include an inviting lounge overlooking a wonderful courtyard garden. Meals are available at one of the nearby village pubs.

Rooms 4 rms (3 en suite) (1 pri facs) (2 fmly) (1 GF) ⊘ S £30-£40; D £50-£60✱ **Facilities** FTV TVB tea/coffee Cen ht TVL **Parking** 4 **Notes** LB Closed 21 Dec-4 Jan RS wknds ⊜

LINCOLNSHIRE

ANCASTER   MAP 08 SK94

►►► **Woodland Waters** *(SK979435)*
Willoughby Rd NG32 3RT
☎ 01400 230888 🖨 01400 230888
e-mail: info@woodlandwaters.co.uk
web: www.woodlandwaters.co.uk
Dir: *On A153 W of x-roads with B6403*

PETS: Charges £1 per night £7 per week **Public areas** except bar & on leads at all times **Exercise area** on site lake and park walks adjacent **Facilities** dog bowls at outdoor eating areas upon request walks info vet info **Resident Pets:** 2 Black Labradors

Open all year Booking advisable BHs Last arrival 21.00hrs Last departure noon

Peacefully set around five impressive fishing lakes, with a few log cabins in a separate area, a pleasant open park. The access road is through mature woodland, and there is a very good heated toilet block, and a pub/club house with restaurant. A 5-acre site with 62 touring pitches.

Notes ⊜

CLEETHORPES — MAP 08 TA30

★★★★ GUEST HOUSE
Tudor Terrace
11 Bradford Av DN35 0BB
☎ 01472 600800 📠 01472 501395
e-mail: tudor.terrace@ntlworld.com
Dir: *Off seafront onto Bradford Av*
PETS: Bedrooms Public areas except dining room
Grounds accessible **Exercise area** 500yds

This guest house offers attractive bedrooms that are thoughtfully designed and furnished to a high standard. You can relax in the lounge, or outside on the patio in the well-maintained garden. Very caring and friendly service is provided, and the house is non-smoking except in the garden. Mobility scooter rental is available.

Rooms 6 en suite (1 GF) ⊘ **Facilities** TVB tea/coffee Cen ht TVL Dinner Last d 2pm **Parking** 3 **Notes** No children No coaches

---

GRANTHAM — MAP 08 SK93

★★★ 73% HOTEL
Best Western Kings
North Pde NG31 8AU
☎ 01476 590800 📠 01476 577072
e-mail: kings@bestwestern.co.uk
web: www.bw-kingshotel.co.uk
Dir: *S on A1, 1st exit to Grantham. Through Great Gonerby, 2m on left*
PETS: Bedrooms (GF) **Charges** charge for damage
Public areas except restaurant on leads **Exercise area** 200yds
Facilities cage storage walks info vet info **On Request** fridge access

Situated in this market town the Kings Hotel was originally a Victorian gentleman's residence. It provides comfortable bedrooms, including ground floor rooms, with all the expected facilities for the modern traveller. There are two eateries to choose from - the Orangery Restaurant is ideal for a quick snack or informal meal, and the Victorian Restaurant for more formal dining. Meeting and conference facilities are available.

Rooms 21 en suite (3 fmly) (3 GF) ⊘ in 14 bedrooms S £50-£84; D £60-£94 (incl. bkfst)✳ **Facilities** STV Wi-fi in bedrooms New Year **Parking** 40

GRIMSBY — MAP 08 TA21

★★★ 72% HOTEL
Hotel Elizabeth
Littlecoates Rd DN34 4LX
☎ 01472 240024 & 0870 1162716 📠 01472 241354
e-mail: elizabeth.grimsby@elizabethhotels.co.uk
web: www.elizabethhotels.co.uk
Dir: *A1136 signed Greatcoates, 1st rdbt left, 2nd rdbt right. Hotel 200mtrs on right*
PETS: Bedrooms Charges £5 per night **Exercise area** on site 200yds

Bedrooms at this pleasantly situated hotel are equipped with modern comforts and many have large windows and balconies overlooking the adjoining golf course. The popular restaurant shares the same tranquil view. There is a large banqueting suite, smaller meeting and conference rooms, and extensive parking which makes this an ideal business venue.

Rooms 52 en suite (4 fmly) ⊘ in 27 bedrooms S fr £45; D fr £60 (incl. bkfst)✳ **Facilities** STV Xmas **Services** Lift **Parking** 200

LINCOLN — MAP 08 SK97

★★ 79% HOTEL
Castle
Westgate LN1 3AS
☎ 01522 538801 📠 01522 575457
e-mail: aa@castlehotel.net
web: www.castlehotel.net
Dir: *follow signs for Historic Lincoln. Hotel at NE corner of castle*
PETS: Bedrooms Charges £5 per night **Exercise area** 10 mins walk

Located in the heart of historic Lincoln, this privately owned and run hotel has been carefully restored to offer comfortable, attractive, well-appointed accommodation. Bedrooms are thoughtfully equipped, particularly the deluxe rooms and the spacious Lincoln Suite. Specialising in traditional fayre, Knights Restaurant has an interesting medieval theme.

Rooms 16 en suite 3 annexe en suite (5 GF) ⊘ in 13 bedrooms S £60-£70; D £89-£99 (incl. bkfst)✳ **Parking** 20 **Notes** No children 8yrs RS Evening of Dec 25&26

★★ 74% HOTEL
Hillcrest

15 Lindum Ter LN2 5RT

☎ 01522 510182 📠 01522 538009

e-mail: reservations@hillcrest-hotel.com

web: www.hillcrest-hotel.com

Dir: *from A15 Wragby Rd and Lindum Rd, at bottom of Upper Lindum St turn left for hotel 200mtrs on right*

PETS: Bedrooms (GF) **Charges** charge for damage
Public areas except bar & restaurant on leads
Grounds accessible on leads disp bin **Exercise area** adjacent park **Facilities** cage storage walks info vet info
On Request fridge access towels

The hospitality offered by all the staff is one of the strengths of the Hillcrest, which sits in a quiet residential location just a seven minute' walk from the cathedral and city shops. Well-equipped bedrooms come in a variety of sizes, and the pleasant conservatory/dining room, with views over the park, offers a good range of freshly prepared food.

Rooms 14 en suite (6 fmly) (6 GF) ⊘ in all bedrooms S £58-£77; D £89-£98 (incl. bkfst) **Facilities** Wi-fi in bedrooms ch fac **Parking** 8 **Notes LB** Closed 23 Dec-3 Jan

★★★ GUEST HOUSE
Newport

26-28 Newport Rd LN1 3DF

☎ 01522 528590 📠 01522 542868

e-mail: info@newportguesthouse.co.uk

web: www.newportguesthouse.co.uk

Dir: *On A15 400yds N of cathedral*

PETS: Bedrooms (GF) **Charges** charge for damage
Exercise area 200mtrs **Facilities** walks info vet info
On Request fridge access

Situated in the quieter upper part of the city and just a few minutes' walk from the cathedral, this double fronted terrace house offers well-equipped and comfortable bedrooms with broadband access. The pleasing public areas include a very comfortable sitting room and a bright and attractive breakfast room.

Rooms 9 en suite (2 GF) ⊘ S £38-£40; D £58-£60 **Facilities** TVB tea/coffee Cen ht TVL **Parking** 4 **Notes** No coaches

★★ GUEST ACCOMMODATION
Jaymar

31 Newland St West LN1 1QQ

☎ 01522 532934 📠 01522 820182

e-mail: ward.jaymar4@ntlworld.com

Dir: *A46 onto A57 to city, 1st lights left onto Gresham St, then 2nd right, 500yds on left*

PETS: Bedrooms unattended **Public areas Grounds** accessible **Exercise area** 50yds **Facilities** food bowl water bowl feeding mat **Resident Pets:** Jessie (German Shepherd)

Situated within easy walking distance of the city, this small, friendly guest house has two well-equipped bedrooms. A full English breakfast, with vegetarian options, is served in the cosy dining room, and an early breakfast, from 5am onwards, is available on request. Children and pets are welcome, and you can be collected from the bus or railway stations if required.

Rooms 2 rms (1 fmly) ⊘ S £20; D £40 **Facilities** TVB tea/coffee **Notes** ⊛

LOUTH   **MAP 08 TF38**

★★★ 75% HOTEL
Best Western Kenwick Park

Kenwick Park Estate LN11 8NR

☎ 01507 608806 📠 01507 608027

e-mail: enquiries@kenwick-park.co.uk

web: www.kenwick-park.co.uk

Dir: *A16 from Grimsby, then A157 Mablethorpe/Manby Rd. Hotel 400mtrs down hill on right*

PETS: Please telephone for details

This elegant Georgian house is situated on the 320-acre Kenwick Park estate, overlooking its own golf course. Bedrooms are spacious, comfortable and provide modern facilities. Public areas include a restaurant and a conservatory bar that overlook the grounds. There is also an extensive leisure centre and state-of-the-art conference and banqueting facilities.

Rooms 29 en suite 5 annexe en suite (10 fmly) ⊘ in 11 bedrooms S £75-£109.50; D £100-£130 (incl. bkfst)✸ **Facilities Spa** STV ⊛ supervised ♪18 ⚐ Squash Gym Putt green Wi-fi available Health & beauty centre Xmas New Year **Parking** 100 **Notes LB**

181

ENGLAND

★★★ 70% HOTEL
Beaumont
66 Victoria Rd LN11 0BX
☎ 01507 605005 ▤ 01507 607768
e-mail: beaumonthotel@aol.com
PETS: Bedrooms (GF) unattended **Charges** £9 per night
Grounds accessible disp bin **Exercise area** 100yds
Facilities bowls & bedding available if required
Resident Pets: Dandy (Shih Tzu)

This smart, family-run hotel enjoys a quiet location, within easy reach of the town centre. Bedrooms are spacious and individually designed. Public areas include a smart restaurant with a strong Italian influence and an inviting lounge bar with comfortable deep sofas and open fires. Weddings and meetings are also catered for.

Rooms 16 en suite (2 fmly) (6 GF) S £60-£70; D £85-£95 (incl. bkfst)
Services Lift **Parking** 70 **Notes** RS Sun

MABLETHORPE
MAP 09 TF58

▶▶▶ **Mablethorpe Camping & Caravanning Club Site** *(TF499839)*
Highfield, 120 Church Ln LN12 2NU
☎ 01507 472374
web: www.campingandcaravanningclub.co.uk/
mablethorpe
Dir: *On outskirts of Mablethorpe, on A1104, just after the 'Welcome to Mablethorpe' sign turn right into Church Lane. 800yds to end of lane. Site on right*
PETS: Facilities walks info vet info **Other** prior notice required
Open Mar-Oct Booking advisable bank hol & peak periods Last arrival 21.00hrs Last departure noon
Located next to flat agricultural land one mile from the sea, and well away from the road. The camping area is in two hedged fields with rural views, and the modern toilet facilities and laundry are centrally sited. A 6-acre site with 105 touring pitches, 1 hardstanding.
Notes Site gates closed 23.00-07.00

MARTON (VILLAGE)
MAP 08 SK88

★★★★ GUEST ACCOMMODATION
Black Swan Guest House
21 High St DN21 5AH
☎ 01427 718878 ▤ 01427 718878
e-mail: info@blackswanguesthouse.co.uk
web: www.blackswanguesthouse.co.uk
Dir: *On A156 in village centre*
PETS: Bedrooms (GF) **Charges** charge for damage
Grounds accessible disp bin **Facilities** cage storage walks info vet info **On Request** fridge access torch **Resident Pets:** TC & Scooby (cats)

Centrally located in the village, this 18th-century former coaching inn retains many original features, and offers good hospitality and homely bedrooms with modern facilities. Tasty breakfasts are served in the cosy dining room and a comfortable lounge with Wi-fi internet access is available. Transport to nearby pubs and restaurants can be provided.

Rooms 6 en suite 4 annexe en suite (3 fmly) (4 GF) ⊘ S £45-£55; D £68-£78✳ **Facilities** TVB tea/coffee Cen ht TVL Wi-fi available **Parking** 10 **Notes** LB

OLD LEAKE
MAP 09 TF45

▶▶▶ **White Cat Caravan & Camping Park**
(TF415498)
Shaw Ln PE22 9LQ
☎ 01205 870121 ▤ 01205 870121
e-mail: kevin@klannen.freeserve.co.uk
web: www.whitecatpark.com
Dir: *Just off A52, 7m NE of Boston, opposite B1184*
PETS: Charges 50p per night £3 per week **Public areas** except toilets & shower facilities **Exercise area** 100yds **Facilities** on site shop dog chews cat treats dog scoop/disp bags washing facs walks info vet info **Other** prior notice required
Resident Pets: Sheepdog
Open Apr-Oct Booking advisable BH Last arrival 20.00hrs Last departure noon
A pleasant, well-maintained small touring park set down a rural lane just off the A52, surrounded by the typical quiet character of the

ENGLAND

Fenlands. It makes a peaceful base for exploring Boston and the Lincolnshire coast. A 2.5-acre site with 30 touring pitches, 4 hardstandings and 10 statics.

Notes ⊛

SALTFLEETBY ST PETER   MAP 09 TF48

►►► Saltfleetby Fisheries *(TF425892)*

Main Rd LN11 7SS

☎ 01507 338272

e-mail: saltfleetbyfish@btinternet.com

web: www.saltfleetbyfisheries.co.uk

Dir: *On B1200, 6m E of junct with A16; 3m W of A103*

PETS: Charges £1 per night **Public areas** on leads **Exercise area** on site **Facilities** on site shop food washing facs walks info vet info **Other** prior notice required

Open Mar-Nov Booking advisable BH Last arrival 18.00hrs Last departure noon

A pretty little site beside three well-stocked fishing lakes by the owner's house. An excellent toilet block offers quality facilities, and there are electric hook ups and spacious hardstandings. A 12-acre site with 18 touring pitches, 12 hardstandings and 1 static.

Notes ⊛ Adults only

SCUNTHORPE   MAP 08 SE81

★★★ 74% HOTEL

Wortley House

Rowland Rd DN16 1SU

☎ 01724 842223 📠 01724 280646

e-mail: reception@wortleyhousehotel.co.uk

web: www.wortleyhousehotel.co.uk

Dir: *M180 junct 3 take A18. Follow signs for Grimsby/Humberside airport, 2nd left into Brumby Wood Ln, over rdbt into Rowland Rd. Hotel 200yds on right*

PETS: Bedrooms Charges £10 deposit **Grounds** accessible **Exercise area** 2 mins walk

A friendly hotel with good facilities for conferences, meetings, banquets and other functions. Bedrooms offer modern comfort and facilities. An extensive range of dishes is available in both the formal restaurant and the more relaxed bar.

Rooms 38 en suite 4 annexe en suite (5 fmly) (4 GF) ⊘ in 28 bedrooms S £65-£75; D £75-£150 (incl. bkfst)✱ **Facilities** FTV Wi-fi in bedrooms Xmas New Year **Parking** 100 **Notes** LB

STAMFORD   MAP 04 TF00

★★★ 72% HOTEL

Garden House

High St, St Martins PE9 2LP

☎ 01780 763359 📠 01780 763339

e-mail: enquiries@gardenhousehotel.com

web: www.gardenhousehotel.com

Dir: *A1 to South Stamford, B1081, signed Stamford & Burghley House. Hotel on left on entering town*

PETS: Bedrooms Charges £10 per night **Public areas** except restaurant **Grounds** accessible **Exercise area** Burghley Park across road **Facilities** food **Resident Pets:** Oliver (Golden Retriever)

Situated within a few minutes' walk of the town centre, this transformed 18th-century town house provides pleasant accommodation. Bedroom styles vary; all are well equipped and comfortably furnished. Public rooms include a charming lounge bar, conservatory restaurant and a smart breakfast room. Service is attentive and friendly throughout.

Rooms 20 en suite (2 fmly) (4 GF) ⊘ in all bedrooms S £65-£90; D £90-£100 (incl. bkfst) **Facilities** STV Xmas **Parking** 22 **Notes** LB Closed 26-30 Dec RS 1-12 Jan

SUTTON ST JAMES   MAP 09 TF31

►►► Foremans Bridge Caravan Park

(TF409197)

Sutton Rd PE12 0HU

☎ 01945 440346

e-mail: foremansbridge@btconnect.com

web: www.foremans-bridge.co.uk

Dir: *2m from A17 on B1390*

PETS: Stables nearby (0.5m) (loose box) **Charges** £1 per night £7 per week **Public areas** on leads **Exercise area** on site river bank adjacent **Facilities** on site shop food dog chews disp bags walks info vet info **Other** prior notice required

Open Mar-Jan Booking advisable BH Last arrival 21.00hrs Last departure 10.00hrs

A small site set beside the South Holland Main Drain which flows past, and offers good fishing. This quiet park is mainly used by adults. A 2.5-acre site with 40 touring pitches, 22 hardstandings and 15 statics.

Notes ⊛ No cycling or ball gamesd

ENGLAND

WADDINGHAM   MAP 08 SK99

▶▶▶ **Brandy Wharf Leisure Park** *(TF014968)*
Brandy Wharf DN21 4RT
☎ 01673 818010 📄 01673 818010
e-mail: brandywharflp@freenetname.co.uk
web: www.brandywharfleisurepark.co.uk
Dir: *From A15 onto B1205 through Waddingham. Site 3m from Waddingham*

PETS: Stables nearby (5m) **Public areas Exercise area** on site river bank & in 50yds **Facilities** washing facs walks info vet info **Other** prior notice required **Resident Pets:** Bess, Fizz & Meg (Border Collies), Jabber (Clumber Spaniel), Ben (mongrel) & 12 cats. Pets' corner

Open Etr-Oct (rs Nov-Etr caravans only) Booking advisable Etr-Sep Last arrival dusk Last departure 17.00hrs

A simple, quiet site in a very rural area on the banks of the River Ancholme, where fishing is available. The basic unisex facilities are clean, and there are level grassy pitches, all with electricity, and a playing/picnic area. A 5-acre site with 30 touring pitches.

Notes @ no disposable BBQ's on grass, no music after 01.00

WINTERINGHAM   MAP 08 SE92

★ ★ ★ ★ ★ ★ ◉◉◉◉
RESTAURANT WITH ROOMS
Winteringham Fields
DN15 9PF
☎ 01724 733096 📄 01724 733898
e-mail: wintfields@aol.com
Dir: *In centre of village at x-rds*

PETS: Bedrooms Grounds accessible **Exercise area** 20mtrs **Other** courtyard bedrooms recommended **Resident Pets:** Juma & Peri (Labradors)

This highly regarded restaurant with rooms, located deep in the countryside in Winteringham village, is six miles west of the Humber Bridge. Chef Robert Thompson has a hand in every skilfully crafted dish, and diners will appreciate the expert service provided by a team of friendly staff. Public rooms and bedrooms, some of which are housed in renovated barns and cottages, are delightfully cosseting, but it is the inspired cooking that remains the main draw.

Rooms 4 en suite 6 annexe en suite (3 GF) @ S £105-£165; D £145-£215 **Facilities** TVB tea/coffee Direct dial from bedrooms Cen ht Dinner Last d 9pm **Parking** 14 **Notes LB** Closed 25 Dec for 2 wks, last wk Oct, 2 wks Aug

WOODHALL SPA   MAP 08 TF16

★ ★ ★ 74% HOTEL
Petwood
Stixwould Rd LN10 6QF
☎ 01526 352411 📄 01526 353473
e-mail: reception@petwood.co.uk
web: www.petwood.co.uk
Dir: *from Sleaford take A153 (signed Skegness). At Tattershall turn left on B1192. Hotel is signed from village*

PETS: Bedrooms (GF) unattended **Charges** £10 per night charge for damage **Exercise area** nearby **Facilities** washing facs walks info vet info **On Request** fridge access torch **Restrictions** Telephone for details

This lovely Edwardian house, set in 30 acres of gardens and woodlands, is adjacent to Woodhall Golf Course. Built in 1905, the house was used by 617 Squadron, the famous Dambusters, as an officers' mess during World War II. Bedrooms and public areas are spacious and comfortable, and retain many original features. Weddings and conferences are well catered for in modern facilities.

Rooms 53 en suite (3 GF) @ in all bedrooms S £95; D £140-£195 (incl. bkfst)✻ **Facilities** ♥ Putt green Complimentary pass to leisure centre ♫ Xmas New Year **Services** Lift **Parking** 140 **Notes LB**

★ ★ ★ 67% HOTEL
Golf Hotel
The Broadway LN10 6SG
☎ 01526 353535 📄 01526 353096
e-mail: reception@thegolf-hotel.com
web: www.thegolf-hotel.com
Dir: *from Lincoln take B1189 to Metheringham onto B1191 towards Woodhall Spa. Hotel on left approx 500yds along from rdbt*

PETS: Bedrooms certain rooms only **Charges** £10 per stay **Grounds** accessible **Exercise area** adjacent woodland **Facilities** vet info

Located near the centre of the village, this traditional hotel is ideally situated to explore the Lincolnshire countryside and coast. The adjacent golf course makes this a popular venue for golfers, and the hotels hydrotherapy suite uses the original spa water supplies. Bedrooms vary in size and include several recently refurbished rooms.

Rooms 50 en suite (4 fmly) (8 GF) @ in 21 bedrooms S £65-£105; D £85-£125 (incl. bkfst)✻ **Facilities** Spa STV Wi-fi available Guests have use of private leisure centre 1m from hotel Xmas New Year **Services** Lift **Parking** 100 **Notes LB**

▶▶▶ Woodhall Spa Camping & Caravanning Club Site *(TF225633)*

Wellsyke Ln, Kirkby-on-Bain LN10 6YU

☎ 01526 352911

web: www.campingandcaravanningclub.co.uk/woodhallspa

Dir: *From Sleaford or Horncastle take A153 to Haltham. At garage turn onto side road. Over bridge, left towards Kirkby-on-Bain. 1st turn right, signed.*

PETS: Public areas except buildings **Exercise area** on site small area **Facilities** walks info vet info **Other** prior notice required

Open 13 Mar-3 Oct Booking advisable BH & peak periods Last arrival 21.00hrs Last departure noon

A pleasant site in silver birch wood and moorland, with pitches laid out around a central lake (no fishing). Facilities include a family room, and a unisex room with en suite facilities. A 6-acre site with 90 touring pitches.

Notes site gates closed 23:00-07:00

WOOLSTHORPE   MAP 08 SK92

★★★★ ⊕ ☐ ☐ INN
The Chequers Inn

Main St NG32 1LU

☎ 01476 870701 📠 01476 870085

e-mail: justin@chequers-inn.net

Dir: *In village opp Post Office*

PETS: Bedrooms (GF) unattended **Stables** next door **Charges** £5 per stay charge for damage **Public areas** except restaurant **Grounds** accessible disp bin **Facilities** washing facs cage storage walks info vet info **On Request** fridge access torch towels **Resident Pets:** Hector (English Springer Spaniel)

A 17th-century coaching inn set in the lee of Belvoir Castle next to the village cricket pitch and having its own pétanque pitch (like boules). Exposed beams, open fireplaces and original stone and brickwork, with 24 wines by the glass, a gastro menu, and real ales. Comfortable bedrooms are in the former stable block.

Rooms 4 annexe en suite (1 fmly) (3 GF) S £49; D £59 **Facilities** TVB tea/coffee Cen ht TVL Dinner Last d 9.30pm **Parking** 40

E16

★★★★ 74% HOTEL
Novotel London ExCel

7 Western Gateway, Royal Victoria Docks
E16 1AA

☎ 020 7540 9700 & 0870 850 4560 📠 020 7540 9710

e-mail: H3656@accor.com

web: www.novotel.com

Dir: *M25 junct 30. A13 towards 'City', exit at Canning Town. Follow signs to 'ExCel West'. Hotel adjacent*

PETS: Bedrooms unattended **Charges** £12 per night charge for damage **Public areas** except restaurant on leads **Exercise area** 5mtrs **Facilities** food bowl water bowl cage storage walks info vet info **On Request** fridge access towels

This hotel is situated adjacent to the ExCel exhibition centre and overlooks the Royal Victoria Dock. Design throughout the hotel is contemporary and stylish. Public rooms include a range of meeting rooms, a modern coffee station, indoor leisure facilities and a smart bar and restaurant, both with a terrace overlooking the dock. Bedrooms feature modern decor, a bath and separate shower and an extensive range of extras.

Rooms 257 en suite (211 fmly) ⊘ in 183 bedrooms S £69-£175; D £89-£195✱ **Facilities** STV Gym Wi-fi available Steam room Relaxation room with massage bed **Services** Lift air con **Parking** 80 **Notes** LB

N9   MAP 04 TQ39

▶▶▶ Lee Valley Camping & Caravan Park
(TQ360945)

Meridian Way N9 0AS

☎ 020 8803 6900 📠 020 8884 4975

e-mail: leisurecomplex@leevalleypark.org.uk

web: www.leevalleypark.com

Dir: *From M25 junct 25, A10 S, 1st left on A1055, approx 5m to Leisure Centre. From A406 (North Circular), N on A1010, left after 0.25m, right (Pickets Lock Lane)*

PETS: Charges £1.65 per night £11.55 per week **Public areas** except shops, showers, toilets, laundry & kitchen **Exercise area** on site **Facilities** on site shop

Open all year Booking advisable Jul-Aug Last arrival 21.00hrs Last departure noon

A pleasant, open site within easy reach of London yet peacefully located close to two large reservoirs. The very good toilet facilities are beautifully kept by dedicated wardens, and the site has the advantage of being adjacent to a restaurant and bar, and a multi-screen cinema. A 4.5-acre site with 160 touring pitches, 41 hardstandings.

Notes No commercial vehicles

ENGLAND

SE1

★★★★ 75% HOTEL
Novotel London City South

Southwark Bridge Rd SE1 9HH
☎ 020 7089 0400 📄 020 7089 0410
e-mail: H3269@accor.com
web: www.novotel.com

Dir: *junct at Thrale St, off Southwark St*

PETS: Bedrooms Charges £8 per night **Public areas** except restaurant **Facilities** vet info

First of a new generation of Novotels, this hotel is contemporary in design with smart, modern bedrooms and spacious public rooms. There are a number of options for guests wanting to unwind, including treatments such as reflexology and immersion therapy, while a gym is available for the more energetic.

Rooms 182 en suite (139 fmly) ⊘ in 158 bedrooms S £79-£200; D £89-£220✱ **Facilities** STV FTV Gym Wi-fi available Steam Room Sauna **Services** Lift air con **Parking** 80(charged) **Notes LB**

★★★ 78% HOTEL
Mercure London City Bankside

PLAN 5 G5

71-79 Southwark St SE1 0JA
☎ 020 7902 0800 📄 020 7902 0810
e-mail: H2814@accor.com
web: www.mercure-uk.com

Dir: *A200 to London Bridge. Left into Southwark St. Hotel 2 mins by car from station*

PETS: Bedrooms (GF) unattended **Charges** £8 per night **Public areas** nearby **Grounds** accessible disp bin **Facilities** vet info

This smart, contemporary hotel forms part of the rejuvenation of the South Bank. With the City of London just over the river and a number of tourist attractions within easy reach, the hotel is well located for business and leisure visitors alike. Facilities include spacious air-cooled bedrooms, a modern bar and the stylish Loft Restaurant.

Rooms 144 en suite (15 fmly) (5 GF) ⊘ in 122 bedrooms S £79-£210; D £79-£210✱ **Facilities** STV Gym Wi-fi available 🎵 **Services** Lift air con **Parking** 6 **Notes LB** RS Xmas, Etr & BH's (restaurant closed)

SW1

MAP 05 TQ27

★★★★★ TOWN HOUSE HOTEL
No 41

41 Buckingham Palace Rd SW1W 0PS
☎ 020 7300 0041 📄 020 7300 0141
e-mail: book41@rchmail.com
web: www.redcarnationhotels.com

Dir: *opp Buckingham Palace Mews entrance.*

PETS: Bedrooms Charges deposit required **Public areas** assist dogs only **Facilities** food (pre-bookable) food bowl water bowl bedding dog chews cat treats feeding mat litter tray dog scoop/ disp bags leads pet menus, dedicated staff member for pets (pet sitting dog walking dog grooming by arrangement) cage storage walks info vet info **On Request** fridge access torch towels

Small, intimate and very private, this stunning town house is located opposite the Royal Mews. Decorated in stylish black and white, bedrooms successfully combine comfort with state-of-the-art technology. The large lounge is the focal point, food and drinks are available as is Internet access and magazines and newspapers from around the world. Attentive personal service and a host of thoughtful extra touches make "41" really special.

Rooms 28 en suite (2 fmly) ⊘ in all bedrooms S £345-£695; D £345-£695 (incl. bkfst)✱ **Facilities** STV Wi-fi in bedrooms Xmas New Year **Services** Lift air con **Notes LB**

★★★★ 85% ⊛ HOTEL
The Rubens at the Palace

39 Buckingham Palace Rd SW1W 0PS
☎ 020 7834 6600 📄 020 7233 6037
e-mail: bookrb@rchmail.com
web: www.redcarnationhotels.com

Dir: *opposite Royal Mews, 100mtrs away from Buckingham Palace*

PETS: Bedrooms Public areas Facilities food food bowl **Other** Dedicated staff member for pets. Pets by prior arrangements only

This hotel enjoys an enviable location next to Buckingham Palace. Stylish, air-conditioned bedrooms include the pinstripe-walled Saville Row rooms, which follow a tailoring theme, and the opulent Royal rooms, named after different monarchs. Public rooms include the Library fine dining restaurant and a comfortable stylish cocktail bar and lounge. The team here pride themselves on their warmth and friendliness.

Red Carnation Hotels - AA Small Hotel Group of the Year 2007-8

Rooms 161 en suite (13 fmly) ⊘ in 141 bedrooms S £180-£229; D £225-£255✱ **Facilities** STV Wi-fi available Health clubs locally 🎵 Xmas New Year **Services** Lift air con **Notes LB**

SW3   MAP 05 TQ27

★★★★★ 85% TOWN HOUSE HOTEL

Egerton House

Red Carnation HOTELS

17 Egerton Ter, Knightsbridge SW3 2BX

☎ 020 7589 2412 📠 020 7584 6540

e-mail: bookings@rchmail.com

web: www.redcarnationhotels.com

Dir: *Just off Brompton Rd, between Harrods and Victoria & Albert Museum, opposite Brompton Oratory.*

PETS: Bedrooms (GF) sign **Charges** charge for damage **Public areas** except dining room on leads **Exercise area** 10 mins walk Hyde Park **Facilities** food (pre-bookable) food bowl water bowl bedding dog chews dog scoop/disp bags leads walks info vet info all facilities are subject to request and availability **On Request** fridge access torch towels **Restrictions** small dogs only

This delightful town house enjoys a prestigious Knightsbridge location, a short walk from Harrods and close to the Victoria & Albert museum. Air-conditioned bedrooms and public rooms are appointed to the highest standards, with luxurious furnishings and quality antique pieces; an exceptional range of facilities include iPods, safes, mini bars and flat screen TVs. Staff offer the highest levels of personalised, attentive service.

Red Carnation Hotels - AA Small Hotel Group of the Year 2007-8.

Rooms 29 en suite (4 fmly) (3 GF) D £235-£395✱ **Facilities** STV Wi-fi in bedrooms Xmas New Year **Services** Lift air con **Notes LB**

★★★★★ 82% TOWN HOUSE HOTEL

The Draycott

26 Cadogan Gardens SW3 2RP

☎ 020 7730 6466 📠 020 7730 0236

e-mail: reservations@draycotthotel.com

web: www.draycotthotel.com

Dir: *From Sloane Sq station towards Peter Jones, keep to left. At Kings Rd. take first right Cadogan Gdns, 2nd right, hotel on left.*

PETS: Bedrooms (GF) unattended **Public areas** except breakfast room **Exercise area** 15 min walk to Hyde Park **Facilities** food bowl water bowl vet info will provide anything as required

Enjoying a prime location just yards from Sloane Square, this town house provides an ideal base in one of the most fashionable areas of London. Many regular guests regard this as their London residence and staff pride themselves on their hospitality. Beautifully appointed bedrooms include a number of very spacious suites and all are equipped to a high standard. Attractive day rooms, furnished with antique and period pieces, include a choice of lounges, one with access to a lovely sheltered garden.

Rooms 35 en suite (9 fmly) (2 GF) ⊗ in 30 bedrooms S £148-£160; D £207-£263✱ **Facilities** STV FTV Wi-fi in bedrooms Beauty treatment Massage **Services** Lift air con **Notes LB**

W1

★★★★★ ⊛ HOTEL   PLAN 4 G5

Four Seasons Hotel London

Hamilton Place, Park Ln W1A 1AZ

☎ 020 7499 0888 📠 020 7493 1895

e-mail: fsh.london@fourseasons.com

Dir: *from Piccadilly into Old Park Ln. Then Hamilton Place*

PETS: Bedrooms Public areas assist dogs only **Facilities** food bowl water bowl bedding walks info will assist with any requirements **Restrictions** small dogs only (15lbs or less)

This long-established popular hotel is discreetly located near Hyde Park Corner, in the heart of Mayfair. It successfully combines modern efficiencies with traditional luxury. Guest care is consistently of the highest order, even down to the smallest detail of the personalised wake-up call. The bedrooms are elegant and spacious, and the unique conservatory rooms are particularly special. Spacious public areas include extensive conference and banqueting facilities, Lane's bar and fine-dining restaurant and an elegant lounge where wonderful afternoon teas are served.

Rooms 219 en suite ⊗ in 96 bedrooms **Facilities** STV Gym Wi-fi available ♫ **Services** Lift air con **Parking** 72

★★★★★ 86% ⊛⊛⊛ HOTEL

The Metropolitan

Old Park Ln W1K 1LB

☎ 020 7447 1000 📠 020 7447 1100

e-mail: res.lon@metropolitan.como.bz

Dir: *on corner of Old Park Ln and Hertford St, within 200mtrs from Hyde Park corner*

PETS: Bedrooms Public areas Exercise areas Hyde Park opposite **Facilities** food (pre-bookable) vet info **Restrictions** small to medium sized dogs only

Overlooking Hyde Park on Park Lane, The Metropolitan is located within easy reach of the fashionable stores of Knightsbridge and Mayfair. The hotel's contemporary style allows freedom and space to relax. Understated luxury is the key here with bedrooms enjoying great natural light. There is also a Shambhala Spa, steam room and fully equipped gym. For those seeking a culinary experience, Nobu offers innovative Japanese cuisine with an upbeat atmosphere.

Rooms 150 en suite (53 fmly) ⊗ in 127 bedrooms **Facilities** STV Gym Treatments **Services** Lift air con **Parking** 15

ENGLAND

W1 CONTINUED

★★★★ 84% ® HOTEL

Chesterfield Mayfair

35 Charles St, Mayfair W1J 5EB

☎ 020 7491 2622 ▤ 020 7491 4793

e-mail: bookch@rchmail.com

web: www.redcarnationhotels.com

Red Carnation HOTELS

Dir: *From Hyde Park Corner along Piccadilly, left into Half Moon St. At end left and 1st right into Queens St, then right*

PETS: Bedrooms Charges deposit required charge for damage Public areas on leads Exercise area nearby Facilities food (pre-bookable) food bowl water bowl bedding dog chews cat treats feeding mat litter tray dog scoop/disp bags leads pet sitting dog walking washing facs cage storage walks info vet info all facilities available on request On Request fridge access torch towels dog grooming

Quiet elegance and an atmosphere of exclusivity characterise this stylish Mayfair hotel where attentive, friendly service is a highlight. Bedrooms have been decorated in a variety of contemporary styles, some with fabric walls; all are thoughtfully equipped and boast marble-clad bathrooms some boast heated floors and mirrors.

Red Carnation Hotels - AA Small Hotel Group of the Year 2007-8

Rooms 110 en suite (7 fmly) ⊗ in 100 bedrooms S £175-£225; D £195-£560✱ Facilities STV Wi-fi in bedrooms ♫ Xmas Services Lift air con Notes LB

W8

MAP 05 TQ27

★★★★★★ ®® HOTEL

Milestone Hotel & Apartments

1 Kensington Court W8 5DL

☎ 020 7917 1000 ▤ 020 7917 1010

e-mail: bookms@rchmail.com

web: www.redcarnationhotels.com

Red Carnation HOTELS

Dir: *M4 into Central London. Into Warwick Rd, then right into Kensington High St. Hotel 400yds past Kensington underground*

PETS: Bedrooms (GF) sign Charges deposit required charge for damage Public areas except food service areas Facilities food (pre-bookable) food bowl water bowl bedding dog chews cat treats feeding mat litter tray dog scoop/disp bags leads charge for dog walking service, pet menu & toys pet sitting cage storage walks info vet info On Request fridge access torch towels dog grooming Restrictions no larger breed than Golden Retriever

This delightful, stylish town house enjoys a wonderful location opposite Kensington Palace and is just a few minutes' walk from elegant shops. Individually themed bedrooms include a selection of stunning suites that are equipped with every conceivable extra. Public areas include the luxurious Park Lounge where afternoon tea is served, a delightful panelled bar and a sumptuous restaurant.

Red Carnation Hotels - AA Small Hotel Group of the Year 2007-8

Rooms 57 en suite (3 fmly) (2 GF) ⊗ in 40 bedrooms S £235-£295; D £265-£325✱ Facilities STV ᐃ Gym Wi-fi in bedrooms Health Club Resident Beauty ♫ Xmas New Year Services Lift air con Notes LB

WC1

★★★★ 73% ® HOTEL

PLAN 3 C4

The Montague on the Gardens

15 Montague St, Bloomsbury WC1B 5BJ

☎ 020 7637 1001 ▤ 020 7637 2516

e-mail: bookmt@rchmail.com

web: www.redcarnationhotels.com

Red Carnation HOTELS

Dir: *just off Russell Square*

PETS: Bedrooms (GF) Public areas Facilities vet info

This stylish hotel is situated next to the British Museum. A special feature is the al fresco terrace overlooking a delightful garden. Other public rooms include the Blue Door Bistro and Chef's Table, a bar, a lounge and a conservatory where traditional afternoon teas are served. The bedrooms are beautifully appointed and range from split-level suites to more compact rooms.

Red Carnation Hotels - AA Small Hotel Group of the Year 2007-8

Rooms 99 en suite (19 GF) ⊗ in 93 bedrooms S £165-£195; D £185-£245✱ Facilities STV Gym Wi-fi available ♫ ch fac Xmas New Year Services Lift air con Notes LB

LONDON GATEWAY
MOTORWAY SERVICE AREA (M1)

MAP 04 TQ29

BUDGET HOTEL

Days Hotel London North

Welcome Break Service Area NW7 3HU

☎ 020 8906 7000 ▤ 020 8906 7011

e-mail: lgw.hotel@welcomebreak.co.uk

web: www.daysinn.com

Dir: *on M1 between junct 2/4 northbound & southbound*

PETS: Bedrooms unattended Grounds accessible

This modern building offers accommodation in smart, spacious and well-equipped bedrooms, suitable for families and business travellers, and all with en suite bathrooms. Continental breakfast is available and other refreshments may be taken at the nearby family restaurant. For further details see the Hotel Groups page.

Rooms 200 en suite

ENGLAND

MERSEYSIDE

SOUTHPORT — MAP 07 SD31

★★ 65% HOTEL

Metropole

Portland St PR8 1LL

☎ 01704 536836 📠 01704 549041

e-mail: metropole.southport@btinternet.com

web: www.themetropolehotel.com

Dir: *after Prince of Wales Hotel left off Lord St. Metropole Hotel directly behind*

PETS: Bedrooms Charges £5 per night charge for damage **Public areas** on leads **Grounds** accessible on leads **Facilities** walks info vet info

This family-run hotel of long standing, popular with golfers, is ideally situated just 50 yards from the famous Lord Street. Accommodation is comfortably equipped with family rooms available. In addition to the restaurant that offers a selection of freshly prepared dishes, there is a choice of lounges including a popular bar-lounge.

Rooms 23 en suite (4 fmly) ⊘ in 6 bedrooms **Facilities** Golf can be arranged at 8 local courses **Parking** 12

★★★★ 🏛 GUEST ACCOMMODATION

Bay Tree House B & B

No1 Irving St, Marine Gate PR9 0HD

☎ 01704 510555 📠 0870 753 6318

e-mail: baytreehouseuk@aol.com

web: www.baytreehousesouthport.co.uk

Dir: *Off Leicester St*

PETS: Bedrooms Grounds accessible **Exercise area** promenade and park within a few minutes' walk **Resident Pets:** Sam (Jack Russell)

A warm welcome is assured at this immaculately maintained house, located a short walk from promenade and central attractions. Bedrooms are equipped with a wealth of thoughtful extras, and delicious imaginative breakfasts are served in an attractive dining room overlooking the pretty front patio garden.

Rooms 6 en suite ⊘ S £59.50-£79.50; D £75-£125 **Facilities** FTV TVB tea/coffee Direct dial from bedrooms Cen ht Dinner Last d 10am Wi-fi available **Parking** 2 **Notes LB** Closed 14 Dec-1 Feb

★★★★ GUEST ACCOMMODATION

Whitworth Falls

16 Lathom Rd PR9 0JH

☎ 01704 530074

e-mail: whitworthfalls@rapid.co.uk

Dir: *A565 N from town centre, over rdbt, 2nd left onto Alexandra Rd, 4th right*

PETS: Bedrooms Public areas
Exercise area nearby **Resident Pets:** Shelby (King Charles Spaniel), Zoe (Labrador), Sherbert (African Grey parrot), Minnie & Midge (cats)

Located on a mainly residential avenue within easy walking distance of seafront and Lord Street shops, this Victorian house has been renovated to provide a range of practical but homely bedrooms. Breakfasts and pre-theatre dinners are served in the attractive dining room, and a comfortable sitting room and lounge bar are also available.

Rooms 12 en suite (2 fmly) (1 GF) ⊘ in 7 bedrooms **Facilities** TVB tea/coffee Direct dial from bedrooms Cen ht TVL Dinner Last d noon **Parking** 8

NORFOLK

BARNEY — MAP 09 TF93

►►►► The Old Brick Kilns *(TG007328)*

Little Barney Ln NR21 0NL

☎ 01328 878305 📠 01328 878948

e-mail: enquiries@old-brick-kilns.co.uk

web: www.old-brick-kilns.co.uk

Dir: *From A148 (Fakenham-Cromer) follow brown tourist signs to Barney, then left into Little Barney Lane. Site at end of lane*

PETS: Charges 75p per night **Public areas Exercise area** on site dog walks & in 200yds **Facilities** on site shop food food bowl water bowl dog chews dog scoop/disp bags walks info vet info **Other** prior notice required

Open Mar-6 Jan (rs low season bar food/takeaway selected nights only) Booking advisable BH & Jul-Aug Last arrival 22.00hrs Last departure noon

A secluded and peaceful park approached via a quiet leafy country lane. The park is on two levels with its own boating and fishing pool and many mature trees. Excellent, well-planned toilet facilities can be found in two blocks, and there is a short dog walk. Due to a narrow access road, no arrivals until after 1pm. A 12.75-acre site with 65 touring pitches, 65 hardstandings.

BELTON MAP 05 TG40

►►►► Rose Farm Touring & Camping Park

(TG488033)

Stepshort NR31 9JS

☎ 01493 780896 📄 01493 780896

web: www.rosefarmtouringpark.co.uk

Dir: *Follow signs to Belton off A143, right at lane signed Stepshort, site 1st on right*

PETS: Public areas on leads **Exercise area** on site **Facilities** vet info **Other** prior notice required

Open all year Booking advisable Jul-Aug

A former railway line is the setting for this very peaceful site which enjoys rural views and is beautifully presented throughout. The ever-improving toilet facilities are spotlessly clean and inviting to use, and the park is brightened with many flower and herb beds. Customer care is truly exceptional. A 10-acre site with 80 touring pitches, 15 hardstandings.

Notes ☺

BLAKENEY MAP 09 TG04

★★★ ◉◉◉ HOTEL
Morston Hall

Morston, Holt NR25 7AA

☎ 01263 741041 📄 01263 740419

e-mail: reception@morstonhall.com

web: www.morstonhall.com

Dir: *1m W of Blakeney on A149 Kings Lynn/Cromer Rd coastal road*

PETS: Bedrooms unattended **Sep Accom** 2 kennels & small run **Charges** £5 per night charge for damage **Grounds** accessible on leads disp bin **Exercise area** 200yds, marshes **Facilities** walks info vet info **On Request** torch towels **Resident Pets:** Phyllis (cat - lives outside)

This delightful 17th-century country-house hotel enjoys a tranquil setting amid well-tended gardens. The comfortable public rooms offer a choice of attractive lounges and a sunny conservatory, while the elegant dining room is a perfect setting to enjoy Galton Blackiston's award-winning cuisine. The spacious bedrooms are individually decorated and stylishly furnished with modern opulence.

Rooms 7 en suite 6 annexe en suite (7 GF) ⊘ in all bedrooms S £150-£190; D £240-£260 (incl. bkfst & dinner)✳ **Facilities** New Year **Parking** 40 **Notes LB** Closed 1 Jan-2 Feb & 2 days Xmas

BRANCASTER STAITHE MAP 09 TF74

★★★ 75% ◉◉ HOTEL
White Horse

PE31 8BY

☎ 01485 210262 📄 01485 210930

e-mail: reception@whitehorsebrancaster.co.uk

web: www.whitehorsebrancaster.co.uk

Dir: *on A149 coast road midway between Hunstanton & Wells-next-the-Sea*

PETS: Bedrooms (GF) **Charges** £5 per night charge for damage **Public areas** except restaurant & 1st floor bedrooms **Grounds** accessible disp bin **Exercise area** Norfolk coastal path at end of garden **Facilities** washing facs walks info vet info **On Request** fridge access torch towels

Charming hotel situated on the north Norfolk coast with contemporary bedrooms in two wings, some featuring an interesting cobbled fascia. Each room is attractively decorated and thoughtfully equipped. There is a large bar and a lounge area leading through to the conservatory restaurant, with stunning tidal marshland views across to Scolt Head Island.

Rooms 7 en suite 8 annexe en suite (5 fmly) (8 GF) ⊘ in all bedrooms S £75-£100; D £100-£135 (incl. bkfst)✳ **Facilities** FTV Wi-fi in bedrooms Xmas New Year **Parking** 60 **Notes LB**

BURNHAM MARKET MAP 09 TF84

★★★ 80% ◉◉ HOTEL
Hoste Arms

The Green PE31 8HD

☎ 01328 738777 📄 01328 730103

e-mail: reception@hostearms.co.uk

web: www.hostearms.co.uk

Dir: *signed on B1155, 5m W of Wells-next-the-Sea*

PETS: Bedrooms (GF) unattended **Charges** £8.50 per stay **Public areas** bar & lounge only **Grounds** accessible on leads **Exercise area** green opposite **Facilities** vet info

Stylish, privately owned inn situated in the heart of this bustling village close to the north Norfolk coast. The extensive public rooms feature a range of dining areas that include a conservatory with plush furniture, a sunny patio and a traditional pub. The tastefully furnished, thoughtfully equipped bedrooms are generally very spacious and offer a high degree of comfort.

Rooms 35 en suite (7 GF) ⊘ in all bedrooms S £90-£165; D £122-£437 (incl. bkfst)✳ **Facilities** STV Wi-fi available Xmas New Year **Services** air con **Parking** 45

CLIPPESBY

MAP 09 TG41

►►►►► Clippesby Hall *(TG423147)*

Clippesby Hall NR29 3BL

☎ 01493 367800 📄 01493 367809

e-mail: holidays@clippesby.com

web: www.clippesby.com

Dir: *From A47 follow tourist signs for The Broads. At Acle rdbt take A1064, after 2m left onto B1152, 0.5m turn left opposite village sign, 400yds on right*

PETS: Charges £3.50 per night **Public areas** on leads **Exercise area** on site dog walk & adjacent **Facilities** on site shop food food bowl water bowl walks info vet info **Other** prior notice required

Open phone for details (rs Etr-23 May no swimming/tennis. Pub/cafe BH wknds) Booking advisable school hols Last arrival 17.30hrs Last departure 11.00hrs

A lovely country house estate with secluded pitches hidden among the trees or in sheltered sunny glades. The toilet facilities have been upgraded to a very good standard, providing a wide choice of cubicle. Amenities include a café, clubhouse and family crazy-golf. A 30-acre site with 120 touring pitches, 9 hardstandings.

CROMER

MAP 09 TG24

★★★ 71% HOTEL

The Cliftonville

NR27 9AS

☎ 01263 512543 📄 01263 515700

e-mail: reservations@cliftonvillehotel.co.uk

web: www.cliftonvillehotel.co.uk

Dir: *From A149 (coastal road), 500yds from town centre, northbound*

PETS: Bedrooms unattended **Stables** on site **Charges** £5 per night **Public areas** except restaurants **Exercise area** nearby **Facilities** cage storage walks info vet info

An imposing Edwardian hotel situated on the main coast road with stunning views of the sea. Public rooms feature a magnificent staircase, minstrels' gallery, coffee shop, lounge bar, a further residents' lounge, Boltons Bistro and an additional restaurant. The pleasantly decorated bedrooms are generally quite spacious and have lovely sea views.

Rooms 30 en suite (5 fmly) ⊗ in all bedrooms S £50-£67; D £100-£134 (incl. bkfst)✳ **Facilities** Wi-fi available Xmas New Year **Services** Lift **Parking** 20 **Notes** LB

★★★ GUEST HOUSE

Glendale

33 Macdonald Rd NR27 9AP

☎ 01263 513278

e-mail: glendalecromer@aol.com

Dir: *A149 coast road from Cromer centre, 4th left*

PETS: Bedrooms unattended **Public areas** except breakfast room on leads **Grounds** accessible on leads disp bin **Facilities** walks info vet info **On Request** fridge access torch towels **Resident Pets:** Daisy & Megan (Jack Russells), Jess (Collie/Springer Spaniel)

Victorian property situated in a peaceful side road adjacent to the seafront yet just a short walk from the town centre. Bedrooms are pleasantly decorated, well maintained and equipped with a good range of useful extras. Breakfast is served at individual tables in the smart dining room.

Rooms 5 rms (1 en suite) ⊗ S £21-£29; D £42-£58 **Facilities** TVB tea/ coffee **Parking** 2 **Notes** LB No coaches Closed 20 Oct-21 Mar

★★★ GUEST HOUSE

Sandcliff

Runton Rd NR27 9AS

☎ 01263 512888 📄 01263 512888

e-mail: admin@sandcliffhotel.co.uk

Dir: *500yds W of town centre on A149*

PETS: Bedrooms Charges £10 per stay **Exercise area** 100mtrs

Friendly family-run establishment situated on the seafront overlooking the promenade and beach, just a short walk from the town centre. The pleasant bedrooms are well maintained and thoughtfully equipped, and some have superb sea views. The spacious public rooms include a large lounge bar and a smart restaurant serving home-cooked food.

Rooms 22 rms (16 en suite) (10 fmly) (3 GF) **Facilities** TVB tea/coffee Licensed Dinner Last d 6pm **Parking** 10 **Notes** Closed 21 Dec-4 Jan

CROMER CONTINUED

▶▶▶ **Forest Park** (TG233405)

Northrepps Rd NR27 0JR

☎ 01263 513290 🖹 01263 511992

e-mail: info@forest-park.co.uk

web: www.forest-park.co.uk

Dir: *A140 from Norwich, left at T-junct signed Cromer, right signed Northrepps, right then immediate left, left at T-junct, site on right*

PETS: Stables nearby (0.75m) (loose box) **Charges** £2 per night **Public areas** on leads **Exercise area** on site large woods **Facilities** on site shop food food bowl water bowl dog chews disp bags walks info vet info **Other** prior notice required **Resident Pets:** Malacca (Black Labrador)

Open 15 Mar-15 Jan Booking advisable Etr, Spring bank hol & Jul-Aug Last arrival 21.00hrs Last departure 11.00hrs

Surrounded by forest, this gently sloping park offers a wide choice of pitches. Visitors have the use of a heated indoor swimming pool, and a large clubhouse with entertainment. A 100-acre site with 344 touring pitches and 372 statics.

▶▶▶ **Manor Farm Caravan & Campsite**

(TG198416)

East Runton NR27 9PR

☎ 01263 512858

e-mail: manor-farm@ukf.net

web: www.manorfarmcaravansite.co.uk

Dir: *1m W of Cromer, turn off A148 or A149 at Manor Farm sign*

PETS: Charges £1 per night **Public areas Exercise area** farmland & public footpaths adjacent **Facilities** walks info vet info space for loose box **Other** prior notice required specific area on site for pet owners **Resident Pets:** Mollie (Border Terrier/Lakeland cross), Titch & Gerbil (ponies)

Open Etr-Sep Booking advisable BH & all season for EHU points Last arrival 20.30hrs Last departure noon

A well-established family-run site on a working farm enjoying panoramic sea views. There are good modern facilities on the caravan-only area, and there is a well-maintained toilet block on the tenting field. A 17-acre site with 250 touring pitches.

Notes 🐾

FAKENHAM   MAP 09 TF92

★★★ FARM HOUSE

Abbott Farm (TF975390)

Walsingham Rd, Binham NR21 0AW

☎ 01328 830519 🖹 01328 830519 Mrs E Brown

e-mail: abbot.farm@btinternet.com

web: www.abbottfarm.co.uk

Dir: *6m NE of Fakenham. From Binham SW onto Walsingham Rd, farm 0.6m on left*

PETS: Bedrooms (GF) sign **Stables** nearby (1m) **Charges** charge for damage **Public areas Grounds** accessible disp bin **Facilities** food bowl water bowl bedding feeding mat litter tray leads dried pet food available washing facs cage storage walks info vet info **On Request** fridge access torch towels **Resident Pets:** Buster (Retriever/Labrador), Hecktor (cat)

A detached red-brick farmhouse set amidst 190 acres of arable farmland and surrounded by open countryside. The spacious bedrooms are pleasantly decorated and thoughtfully equipped; they include a ground-floor room with a large en suite shower. Breakfast is served in the attractive conservatory, which has superb views of the countryside.

Rooms 3 en suite (2 GF) ⊗ **Facilities** TVB tea/coffee Cen ht TVL **Parking** 20 **Notes** 190 acres arable 🐾

▶▶▶ **Caravan Club M.V.C. Site** (TF926288)

Fakenham Racecourse NR21 7NY

☎ 01328 862388 🖹 01328 855908

e-mail: caravan@fakenhamracecourse.co.uk

web: www.fakenhamracecourse.co.uk

Dir: *Towards Fakenham follow brown signs for 'racecourse' with tent & caravan symbols, directly to site entrance*

PETS: Stables on site (loose box) **Exercise area** on site **Facilities** on site shop dog chews walks info

Open all year (rs race days all caravans moved to centre of course) Booking advisable Jun-Sep Last arrival 21.00hrs Last departure noon

A very well laid out site set around the racecourse, with a grandstand offering smart modern toilet facilities. Tourers move to the centre of the course on race days, and enjoy free racing, and there's a wide range of sporting activities in the club house. An 11.5-acre site with 120 touring pitches, 25 hardstandings.

►► Crossways Caravan & Camping Park

(TF961321)

Crossways, Holt Rd, Little Snoring NR21 0AX

☎ 01328 878335

e-mail: hollands@mannasolutions.com

web: www.crosswayscaravan.co.uk

Dir: *From Fakenham take A148 towards Cromer. After 3m pass exit for Little Snoring. Site on A148 on left behind Post Office*

PETS: Charges 50p per night **Public areas** on leads
Exercise area 10mtrs **Facilities** on site shop food food bowl water bowl dog chews cat treats litter disp bags washing facs walks info vet info **Other** prior notice required

Open all year Booking advisable in high season, bank & school hols Last arrival 22:00hrs Last departure noon

Set on the edge of the peaceful hamlet of Little Snoring, this level site enjoys views across the fields towards the North Norfolk coast some seven miles away. Visitors can use the health suite for a small charge, and there is a shop on site, and a good village pub. A 2-acre site with 26 touring pitches, 10 hardstandings and 1 static.

GREAT YARMOUTH
MAP 05 TG50

★ ★ ★ ★ BED & BREAKFAST

Barnard House

2 Barnard Crescent NR30 4DR

☎ 01493 855139 🖹 01493 843143

e-mail: enquiries@barnardhouse.com

Dir: *0.5m N of town centre. Off A149 onto Barnard Crescent*

PETS: Bedrooms Public areas Exercise area nearby
Facilities walks info vet info **On Request** fridge access torch towels **Resident Pets:** Fergus & Flora (Field Spaniels)

Expect a warm welcome from the caring hosts at this friendly, family-run Bed & Breakfast, set in mature landscaped gardens in a residential area. The smartly decorated bedrooms have coordinated fabrics and many thoughtful touches. Breakfast is served in the stylish dining room and there is an elegant lounge with plush sofas.

Rooms 3 rms (2 en suite) (1 pri facs) ⊗ S £38-£40; D £58-£60
Facilities FTV TVB tea/coffee Cen ht TVL Wi-fi available **Parking** 3
Notes LB Closed Xmas & New Year

HUNSTANTON
MAP 09 TF64

★ ★ ★ 80% HOTEL

Caley Hall

Old Hunstanton Rd PE36 6HH

☎ 01485 533486 🖹 01485 533348

e-mail: mail@caleyhallhotel.co.uk

web: www.caleyhallhotel.co.uk

Dir: *1m from Hunstanton, on A149*

PETS: Bedrooms (GF) unattended **Charges** £3 per night
Public areas except bar & restaurant on leads
Grounds accessible on leads disp bin **Exercise area** 50mtrs
Facilities food bowl water bowl leads washing facs cage storage walks info vet info **On Request** fridge access torch towels
Resident Pets: Basil (Cocker Spaniel), Sox (cat)

Situated just off the A149 in Old Hunstanton and within easy walking distance of the seafront. The tastefully decorated bedrooms are in a series of converted outbuildings; each is smartly furnished and thoughtfully equipped. Public rooms feature a large open-plan lounge/bar with plush leather seating, and a restaurant offering an interesting choice of dishes.

Rooms 40 en suite (20 fmly) (30 GF) ⊗ in all bedrooms S £49-£99;
D £70-£150 (incl. bkfst) **Facilities** STV Wi-fi in bedrooms ch fac
Parking 80 **Notes** LB Closed 18 Dec-20 Jan

ENGLAND

Searles Leisure Resort *(TF671400)*

South Beach Rd PE36 5BB

☎ 01485 534211 📠 01485 533815

e-mail: bookings@searles.co.uk

web: www.searles.co.uk

Dir: *A149 from King's Lynn to Hunstanton. At rdbt follow signs for South Beach. Straight on at 2nd rdbt. Site on left*

PETS: Charges £2.50 per night **Public areas** except buildings **Exercise area** on site Field available for dogs on leads & in 500yds **Facilities** on site shop food food bowl water bowl bedding dog chews dog scoop/disp bags washing facs walks info vet info **Other** prior notice required **Restrictions** no Rottweilers, Pit Bulls, Staffordshire Bull Terriers, German Shepherds, Dobermans or half breeds of such breeds

Open all year (rs 25 Dec & Feb-May Limited Entertainment & restaurant) Booking advisable BH & Jul-Aug Last arrival 20.45hrs Last departure 11.00hrs

A large seaside holiday complex with well-managed facilities, adjacent to sea and beach. The tourers have their own areas, including two excellent toilet blocks, and pitches are individually marked by small maturing shrubs for privacy. The bars and entertainment, restaurant, bistro and takeaway, heated indoor and outdoor pools, golf, fishing and bowling green make this park popular throughout the year. A 50-acre site with 332 touring pitches, 100 hardstandings and 460 statics.

KING'S LYNN   MAP 09 TF62

★★★ GUEST HOUSE

Maranatha Guest House

115/117 Gaywood Rd PE30 2PU

☎ 01553 774596 📠 01553 763747

e-mail: maranathaguesthouse@yahoo.co.uk

Dir: *Signs to College of West Anglia, at junct in front of college onto Gaywood Rd, house opp school*

PETS: Bedrooms Charges £6 per night **Exercise area** 100yds **Resident Pets:** Goldie (Sheltie), Kim (Border Collie), Speedy (Siamese cat)

This large Victorian property is situated by the King Edward School, close to the hospital, and just a short walk from the town centre. The attractively decorated bedrooms are well equipped and have coordinated fabrics. Breakfast is served at individual tables in the lounge-dining room, which also has a pool table.

Rooms 10 rms (6 en suite) (2 fmly) ⊘ **Facilities** TVB tea/coffee Cen ht TVL **Parking** 12

NEATISHEAD   MAP 09 TG32

★★★★ GUEST ACCOMMODATION

Regency

The Street NR12 8AD

☎ 01692 630233 📠 01692 630233

e-mail: regencywrigley@btopenworld.com

Dir: *3m from Wroxham. Village 1m from A1151*

PETS: Bedrooms Sep Accom barn **Charges** £7 per night **Grounds** accessible on leads disp bin **Exercise area** adjacent **Facilities** water bowl feeding mat litter tray pet sitting dog walking cage storage vet info **On Request** torch towels **Restrictions** Telephone for details

Expect a warm welcome at this charming 17th-century property, situated in a picturesque village close to the Norfolk Broads. The attractive bedrooms have coordinated soft furnishings and many thoughtful touches. Breakfast is served in the smart dining room and there are two comfortable lounges with plush sofas.

Rooms 3 rms (2 en suite) (1 fmly) S fr £42; D £54-£62 **Facilities** TVB tea/coffee Dinner **Parking** 6 **Notes** LB ⊛

NORTH WALSHAM   MAP 09 TG23

★★★ ◉◉ HOTEL

Beechwood

Cromer Rd NR28 0HD

☎ 01692 403231 📠 01692 407284

e-mail: enquiries@beechwood-hotel.co.uk

web: www.beechwood-hotel.co.uk

Dir: *B1150 from Norwich. At North Walsham left at 1st lights, then right at next*

PETS: Bedrooms unattended **Charges** £8 per night **Public areas** except restaurant **Grounds** accessible **Exercise area** 400yds **Resident Pets:** Emily & Harry (Airedale Terriers)

Expect a warm welcome at this elegant 18th-century house, situated just a short walk from the town centre. The individually styled bedrooms are tastefully furnished with well-chosen antique pieces, attractive co-ordinated soft fabrics and many thoughtful touches. The spacious public areas include a lounge bar with plush furnishings, a further lounge and a smartly appointed restaurant.

Rooms 17 en suite (4 GF) ⊘ in all bedrooms S £72; D £90-£160 (incl. bkfst) **Facilities** FTV ◄ New Year **Parking** 20 **Notes** LB No children 10yrs

★★★★ BED & BREAKFAST
Green Ridges

104 Cromer Rd NR28 0HE
☎ 01692 402448 📄 01692 402448
e-mail: admin@greenridges.com
web: www.greenridges.com
Dir: *On A149 from North Walsham to Cromer, at junct of B1145 to Aylsham*

PETS: Bedrooms Public areas except breakfast room
Grounds accessible **Exercise area** on site lawns & surrounding countryside **Other** bowls, tinned/dry food available on request
Resident Pets: Chester (Great Dane/Black Labrador cross)

Green Ridges is an attractive detached property, situated on the edge of this busy market town. The smartly appointed, thoughtfully equipped bedrooms include two rooms with wheelchair access and superb wet rooms. Breakfast is served in the smart dining room, which overlooks the mature gardens.

Rooms 3 en suite (1 fmly) (3 GF) ⊘ S £25-£35; D £50-£60✳
Facilities TVB tea/coffee Cen ht Dinner Last d Previous day **Parking** 6
Notes ⊜

▶▶▶▶ **Two Mills Touring Park** *(TG291286)*

Yarmouth Rd NR28 9NA
☎ 01692 405829 📄 01692 405829
e-mail: enquiries@twomills.co.uk
web: www.twomills.co.uk
Dir: *1m S of North Walsham on Old Yarmouth road past police station & hospital on left*

PETS: Charges 75p per night **Public areas** except buildings
Exercise area on site dog walks & in 100yds **Facilities** on site shop food food bowl water bowl disp bags vet info

Open Mar-3 Jan Booking advisable Jul & Aug Last arrival 20.30hrs Last departure noon

Set in superb countryside in a peaceful spot which is also convenient for touring. Some fully-serviced pitches offer panoramic views over the site, and the layout of pitches and facilities is excellent. The very friendly and helpful owners keep the park in immaculate condition. This park does not accept children. A 5-acre site with 50 touring pitches, 50 hardstandings.

Notes Adults only, 2 dogs max per pitch

★★ 85% ⊛ HOTEL
Stower Grange

School Rd, Drayton NR8 6EF
☎ 01603 860210 📄 01603 860464
e-mail: enquiries@stowergrange.co.uk
web: www.stowergrange.co.uk

Dir: *Norwich ring road N to Asda supermarket. Take A1067 Fakenham Rd at Drayton village, right at traffic lights along School Rd. Hotel 150yds on right*

PETS: Bedrooms unattended **Public areas** except restaurant
Grounds accessible disp bin **Facilities** food (pre-bookable) pet sitting dog walking washing facs cage storage walks info vet info
On Request torch towels **Resident Pets:** Saffy (Staffordshire Bull Terrier)

Expect a warm welcome at this 17th-century, ivy-clad property situated in a peaceful residential area close to the city centre and airport. The individually decorated bedrooms are generally quite spacious; each one is tastefully furnished and equipped with many thoughtful touches. Public rooms include a smart open-plan lounge bar and an elegant restaurant.

Rooms 11 en suite (1 fmly) ⊘ in all bedrooms S fr £75; D £95-£150 (incl. bkfst)✳ **Facilities** ⅃ Wi-fi available New Year **Parking** 40
Notes LB

ENGLAND

★★★ GUEST ACCOMMODATION
Edmar Lodge
64 Earlham Rd NR2 3DF
☎ 01603 615599 📄 01603 495599
e-mail: mail@edmarlodge.co.uk
web: www.edmarlodge.co.uk
Dir: *Off A47 S bypass onto B1108 Earlham Rd, follow university and hospital signs*
PETS: Please telephone for details

Located just a ten minute walk from the city centre, this friendly family-run guest house offers a convenient location and ample private parking. Individually decorated bedrooms are smartly appointed and well equipped. Freshly prepared breakfasts are served within the cosy dining room; a microwave and a refrigerator are also available.

Rooms 5 en suite (1 fmly) ⊘ S £35-£45; D £40-£45✱ **Facilities** FTV TVB tea/coffee Cen ht Wi-fi available **Parking** 6

★★★ GUEST ACCOMMODATION
The Larches
345 Aylsham Rd NR3 2RU
☎ 01603 415420 📄 01603 465340
e-mail: lynda@thelarches.com
web: www.thelarches.com
Dir: *On A140 500yds past ring road, on left adjacent to Lloyds Bank*
PETS: Bedrooms (GF) **Exercise area** 50yds **Facilities** cage storage walks info vet info

Modern, detached property situated only a short drive from the city centre and airport. The spacious, well-equipped bedrooms are brightly decorated, pleasantly furnished and have coordinated soft fabrics. Breakfast is served at individual tables in the smart lounge-dining room.

Rooms 7 en suite (2 fmly) (1 GF) S fr £30; D fr £50✱ **Facilities** STV FTV TVB tea/coffee Cen ht TVL Wi-fi available **Parking** 10

►►► Norwich Camping & Caravanning Club Site *(TG237063)*
Martineau Ln NR1 2HX
☎ 01603 620060
web: www.campingandcaravanningclub.co.uk/norwich
Dir: *From A47 onto A146 towards city centre. Left at lights to next lights, under low bridge to Cock pub, turn left. Site 150yds on right*
PETS: Public areas except buildings **Exercise area** on site **Facilities** walks info vet info **Other** prior notice required

Open 13 Mar-3 Nov Booking advisable BH & peak periods
Last arrival 21.00hrs Last departure noon

A very pretty small site on the outskirts of the city, close to the River Yare. The park is built on two levels, with the lower meadow enjoying good rural views, and there is plenty of screening from nearby houses. The older-style toilet block is kept immaculately clean. A 2.5-acre site with 50 touring pitches.

Notes Gates closed 23:00-07:00

ST JOHN'S FEN END   MAP 09 TF51

►►►► Virginia Lake Caravan Park (TF538113)

Smeeth Rd PE14 8JF

☎ 01945 430332 & 430585

e-mail: louise@virginialake.co.uk

web: www.virginialake.co.uk

Dir: *From A47 E of Wisbech follow tourist signs to Terrington St John. Park on left*

PETS: Public areas except lakeside **Exercise area** on site dog walk & in 100mtrs **Facilities** on site shop food food bowl water bowl dog chews cat treats feeding mat litter tray disp bags leads washing facs walks info vet info **Other** prior notice required
Resident Pets: Labrador & 2 cats

Open all year Booking advisable BH Last arrival 23.00hrs Last departure noon

A well-established park beside a 2-acre fishing lake with good facilities for both anglers and tourers. The toilet facilities are very good, and security is carefully observed throughout the park. A clubhouse serves a selection of meals. A 5-acre site with 100 touring pitches, 20 hardstandings.

Notes ☺

SANDRINGHAM   MAP 09 TF62

►►►► Sandringham Camping & Caravanning Club Site (TF683274)

The Sandringham Estate, Double Lodges PE35 6EA

☎ 01485 542555

web: www.campingandcaravanningclub.co.uk/sandringham

Dir: *From A148 onto B1440 signed West Newton. Follow signs to site. Or take A149 turn left & follow site signs*

PETS: Public areas except buildings **Exercise area** adjacent area **Facilities** on site shop walks info vet info **Other** prior notice required

Open 14 Feb-24 Nov Booking advisable BH & peak periods Last arrival 21.00hrs Last departure noon

A prestige park, very well landscaped and laid out in mature woodland, with toilets and other buildings blending in with the scenery. There are plenty of walks from the site, and this is a good touring base for the rest of Norfolk. A 28-acre site with 275 touring pitches, 2 hardstandings.

Notes site gates will be closed 23:00-07:00

SWAFFHAM   MAP 05 TF80

►►► Breckland Meadows Touring Park (TF809094)

Lynn Rd PE37 7PT

☎ 01760 721246

e-mail: info@brecklandmeadows.co.uk

web: www.brecklandmeadows.co.uk

Dir: *1m W of Swaffham on old A47*

PETS: Charges 50p per night **Public areas** **Exercise area** on site **Facilities** washing facs walks info vet info space for loose box

Open all year Booking advisable BH Last arrival 21.00hrs Last departure 14:00hrs

An immaculate, well-landscaped little park on the edge of Swaffham. The impressive toilet block is well equipped, and there are hardstandings, full electricity and a laundry equipment. Plenty of planting is resulting in attractive screening. A 3-acre site with 45 touring pitches, 29 hardstandings.

Notes ☺ Adults only

SYDERSTONE   MAP 09 TF83

►►► The Garden Caravan Site (TF812337)

Barmer Hall Farm PE31 8SR

☎ 01485 578220 & 578178 🖷 01485 578178

e-mail: nigel@gardencaravansite.co.uk

web: www.gardencaravansite.co.uk

Dir: *Signed from B1454 at Barmer between A148 & Docking, 1m W of Syderstone*

PETS: Public areas **Exercise area** nearby **Facilities** walks info vet info **Other** max 2 dogs per pitch

Open Mar-Nov Booking advisable at all times Last departure noon

In the tranquil setting of a former walled garden beside a large farmhouse, with mature trees and shrubs, a secluded site surrounded by woodland. The site is run mainly on trust, with a daily notice indicating which pitches are available, and an honesty box for basic foods. An ideal site for the discerning camper, and well placed for touring north Norfolk. A 3.5-acre site with 30 touring pitches.

Notes ☺

THETFORD	MAP 05 TL88

★★★ 66% HOTEL

Bell

King St IP24 2AZ

☎ 01842 754455 📠 01842 755552

e-mail: bell.thetford@oldenglishinns.co.uk

web: www.oldenglish.co.uk

Dir: *From S exit A11 2m to 1st set of lights, turn right onto A134. 100yds turn left into Bridge St, 150 yds & over bridge*

PETS: Bedrooms Charges £10 per night **Public areas** except food areas on leads **Grounds** accessible on leads **Exercise area** river walks over bridge **Facilities** dog grooming (nearby) walks info vet info **On Request** fridge access towels

15th-century coaching inn situated in the heart of the old part of town. The historic charm permeates through much of the building and the oak beamed bar is full of character. The accommodation is split between the main building and the more modern bedroom wings. Public areas include a restaurant and conference facilities.

Rooms 46 en suite (1 fmly) ⊘ in 24 bedrooms **Parking** 55 **Notes** LB

★★ 68% HOTEL

The Thomas Paine Hotel

THE INDEPENDENTS
HOTEL ASSOCIATION

White Hart St IP24 1AA

☎ 01842 755631 📠 01842 766505

e-mail: bookings@thomaspainehotel.com

Dir: *N'bound on A11, at rdbt immediately before Thetford take A1075, hotel on right on approach to town*

PETS: Bedrooms unattended **Charges** £2.50 per night **Public areas** except bar & restaurant **Grounds** accessible **Exercise area** on site courtyard common nearby

This Grade II listed building is situated close to the town centre and Thetford Forest Park is just a short drive away. Public rooms include a large lounge bar, a pleasantly appointed restaurant and a meeting room. Bedrooms vary in size and style; each one is attractively decorated and thoughtfully equipped.

Rooms 13 en suite (2 fmly) ⊘ in 5 bedrooms **Parking** 30 **Notes** LB

THORNHAM	MAP 09 TF74

★★ 74% ⚜ HOTEL

Lifeboat Inn

Ship Ln PE36 6LT

☎ 01485 512236 📠 01485 512323

e-mail: reception@lifeboatinn.co.uk

web: www.lifeboatinn.co.uk

Dir: *follow coast road from Hunstanton A149 for approx 6m and take 1st left after Thornham sign*

PETS: Bedrooms (GF) unattended **Charges** £5 per stay **Public areas** except restaurant **Exercise area** nearby **Facilities** water bowl dog chews **On Request** torch towels

This popular 16th-century smugglers' alehouse enjoys superb views across open meadows to Thornham Harbour. The tastefully decorated bedrooms are furnished with pine pieces and have many thoughtful touches. The public rooms have a wealth of character and feature open fireplaces, exposed brickwork and oak beams.

Rooms 13 en suite (3 fmly) (1 GF) ⊘ in all bedrooms **Parking** 120 **Notes** LB

ENGLAND

TITCHWELL MAP 13 TF74

★★★ 82% ●● HOTEL

Titchwell Manor

PE31 8BB

☎ 01485 210221 ▤ 01485 210104

e-mail: margaret@titchwellmanor.com

web: www.titchwellmanor.com

Dir: *on A149 coast road between Brancaster and Thornham*

PETS: Bedrooms (GF) unattended sign **Sep Accom** kennels **Stables** nearby (2m) **Charges** £8 per night charge for damage **Public areas** except Conservatory restaurant **Grounds** accessible disp bin **Facilities** food bowl water bowl bedding dog chews cat treats feeding mat litter tray disp bags leads pet sitting washing facs cage storage walks info vet info **On Request** fridge access torch

Friendly family-run hotel ideally placed for touring the north Norfolk coastline. The tastefully appointed bedrooms are very comfortable; some in the adjacent annexe offer ground floor access. Smart public rooms include a lounge area, relaxed informal bar and a delightful conservatory restaurant, overlooking the walled garden. Imaginative menus feature quality local produce and fresh fish.

Rooms 8 en suite 18 annexe en suite (4 fmly) (16 GF) ✇ in all bedrooms S £45-£150; D £90-£200 (incl. bkfst) **Facilities** Xmas New Year **Parking** 50 **Notes** LB

WEST RUNTON MAP 09 TG14

▶▶▶▶ **West Runton Camping & Caravanning Club Site** *(TG189419)*

Holgate Ln NR27 9NW

☎ 01263 837544

e-mail: clibsitesguideentries@ campingandcaravanningclub.co.uk

web: www.campingandcaravanningclub.co.uk

Dir: *From King's Lynn on A148 towards West Runton. Left at Roman Camp Inn. Site track on right at crest of hill, 0.5m to site opposite National Trust sign*

PETS: Exercise area on site **Facilities** walks info vet info **Other** prior notice required

Open 13 Mar- 03 Nov Booking advisable BH & peak periods Last arrival 21.00hrs Last departure noon

A lovely, well-kept site with some gently sloping pitches on pleasantly undulating ground. This peaceful park is surrounded on three sides by woodland, with the fourth side open to fields and the coast beyond. The very well equipped family rooms and refurbished toilet blocks are excellent. A 15-acre site with 200 touring pitches, 3 hardstandings.

Notes Site gates will be closed 23:00-07:00

NORTHAMPTONSHIRE

WELLINGBOROUGH MAP 04 SP86

BUDGET HOTEL

Hotel Ibis Wellingborough

Enstone Court NN8 2DR

☎ 01933 228333 ▤ 01933 228444

e-mail: H3164@accor-hotels.com

web: www.ibishotel.com

Dir: *at junct of A45 & A509 towards Kettering*

PETS: Bedrooms (GF) **Public areas** except dining room & lounge **Grounds** accessible **Exercise area** nearby **Facilities** vet info

Modern, budget hotel offering comfortable accommodation in bright and practical bedrooms. Breakfast is self-service and dinner is available in the restaurant. For further details, consult the Hotel Groups page.

Rooms 78 en suite

NORTHUMBERLAND

BAMBURGH MAP 12 NU13

★★★ 78% COUNTRY HOUSE HOTEL

Waren House

Waren Mill NE70 7EE

☎ 01668 214581 ▤ 01668 214484

e-mail: enquiries@warenhousehotel.co.uk

web: www.warenhousehotel.co.uk

Dir: *2m E of A1 turn onto B1342 to Waren Mill, at T-junct turn right, hotel 100yds on right*

PETS: Bedrooms (GF) **Charges** charge for damage **Exercise area** 20mtrs **Facilities** vet info **On Request** fridge access torch

This delightful Georgian mansion is set in six acres of woodland and offers a welcoming atmosphere and views of the coastline. The individually themed bedrooms and suites include many with large bathrooms. Good, home-cooked food is served in the elegant dining room. A comfortable lounge and library are also available.

Rooms 13 en suite (1 GF) ✇ in all bedrooms D £145-£210 (incl. bkfst)✻ **Facilities** Xmas New Year **Parking** 20 **Notes** LB No children 14yrs

ENGLAND

BAMBURGH CONTINUED

►►►► Waren Caravan Park *(NU155343)*

Waren Mill NE70 7EE

☎ 01668 214366 📄 01668 214224

e-mail: waren@meadowhead.co.uk

web: www.meadowhead.co.uk

Dir: *2m E of town. From A1 onto B1342 signed Bamburgh. Take unclass road past Waren Mill, signed Budle*

PETS: **Charges** £1.60 per night **Public areas** except buildings **Exercise area** on site **Facilities** on site shop food dog scoop walks info vet info **Other** prior notice required

Open Apr-Oct (rs Nov-Feb Bar, shop & restaurant closed) Booking advisable Spring bank hol & Jul-Aug Last arrival 20.00hrs Last departure noon

Attractive seaside site with footpath access to the beach, surrounded by a slightly sloping grassy embankment giving shelter to caravans. The park offers excellent facilities including several family bathrooms. There is also a wigwam 'village'. A 4-acre site with 180 touring pitches, 24 hardstandings and 300 statics.

►►► Glororum Caravan Park *(NU166334)*

Glororum Farm NE69 7AW

☎ 01668 214457 📄 01688 214622

e-mail: info@glororum-caravanpark.co.uk

web: www.glororum-caravanpark.co.uk

Dir: *Exit A1 at junct with B1341 (Purdy's Lodge). In 3.5m left onto unclass road. Site 300yds on left*

PETS: **Stables** nearby (5m) (loose box) **Public areas** except play area **Exercise area** on site dog walks **Facilities** on site shop food disp bags washing facs walks info vet info **Other** prior notice required **Restrictions** No dangerous dogs (see page 7) Resident Pets: dogs, cats, budgies & horses

Open Apr-Oct Booking advisable BH & school hols Last arrival 22.00hrs Last departure noon

A pleasantly situated site where tourers have their own well-established facilities. The open countryside setting affords good views of Bamburgh Castle and surrounding farmland. A 6-acre site with 100 touring pitches and 150 statics.

BEADNELL

MAP 12 NU22

►► Beadnell Bay Camping & Caravanning Club Site *(NU231297)*

NE67 5BX

☎ 01665 720586

web: www.campingandcaravanningclub.co.uk/beadnellbay

Dir: *A1 onto B1430 signed Seahouses. At Beadnell ignore signs for Beadnell village. Site on left after village, just after left bend*

PETS: **Exercise area** on site dog walk **Facilities** walks info vet info **Other** prior notice required

Open 28 Apr-29 Sep Booking advisable BH & peak period Last arrival 21.00hrs Last departure noon

A level grassy site in a coastal area just across the road from the sea and sandy beach. Popular with divers, anglers, surfboarders and canoeists, and ideal for visiting many tourist attractions. Motorvans and tents only. A 6-acre site with 150 touring pitches.

Notes site gates will be closed 23:00-07:00

BELFORD

MAP 12 NU13

★★★ 63% HOTEL

Blue Bell

Market Place NE70 7NE

☎ 01668 213543 📄 01668 213787

e-mail: bluebel@globalnet.co.uk

web: www.bluebellhotel.com

Dir: *centre of village on left of St Mary's Church*

PETS: **Bedrooms** (GF) sign **Charges** charge for damage **Public areas** on leads (in lounge by prior arrangement) **Grounds** accessible on leads disp bin **Exercise area** nearby beaches **Facilities** water bowl disp bags wash facs cage storage walks info vet info **On Request** torch towel

Formerly a coaching inn, this popular and long established hotel is located in the village square. It offers a choice of superior and standard bedrooms all in classical style. Well-prepared meals can be enjoyed in the restaurant and in addition to the bar there is a comfortable lounge in which to relax.

Rooms 17 en suite (1 fmly) (1 GF) **Facilities** Riding ⅌ Putt green **Parking** 16 **Notes** LB

★★★★★ 🏨 GUEST ACCOMMODATION
Market Cross
1 Church St NE70 7LS
☎ 01668 213013
e-mail: info@marketcross.net
web: www.marketcross.net
Dir: *Off A1 into village, opp church*
PETS: Bedrooms Public areas Exercise area 200yds
Resident Pets: Ellie & Sophie (Dalmatians), Sylvie (cat)
Lying in the heart of the village, this Grade II listed building offers delightful, individually styled and thoughtfully equipped bedrooms. Breakfast is a real treat, an extensive and impressive range of delicious cooked dishes using local produce.
Rooms 3 en suite ⊘ S £35-£60; D £60-£80 **Facilities** FTV TVB tea/coffee Cen ht TVL **Parking** 3 **Notes** LB

★★★ 72% HOTEL
Marshall Meadows Country House
TD15 1UT
☎ 01289 331133 📠 01289 331438
e-mail: gm.marshallmeadows@classiclodges.co.uk
web: www.classiclodges.co.uk
Dir: *signed directly off A1, 300yds from Scottish border*
PETS: Bedrooms Charges £6 per night **Grounds** accessible **Exercise area** on site
This stylish Georgian mansion is set in wooded grounds flanked by farmland and has convenient access from the A1. A popular venue for weddings and conferences, it offers comfortable and well-equipped bedrooms. Public rooms include a cosy bar, a relaxing lounge and a two-tier restaurant, which serves imaginative dishes.
Rooms 19 en suite (1 fmly) ⊘ in 14 bedrooms D £90-£120 (incl. bkfst)✲ **Facilities** 🏊 Xmas New Year **Parking** 87 **Notes** LB ⊗

►►►►► Ord House Country Park *(NT982515)*
East Ord TD15 2NS
☎ 01289 305288 📠 01289 330832
e-mail: enquiries@ordhouse.co.uk
web: www.ordhouse.co.uk
Dir: *On A1, Berwick bypass, turn off at 2nd rdbt at East Ord, follow 'Caravan' signs*
PETS: Charges max £1.50 per night **Public areas** except club house **Exercise area** on site 2km walk **Facilities** walks info vet info **Other** prior notice required **Restrictions** max 1 large & 2 small breeds per family no dangerous breeds (see page 7) & no Rottweilers or Dobermans
Open all year Booking advisable BH & Jul-Aug Last arrival 23.00hrs Last departure noon

A very well run park set in the pleasant grounds of an 18th-century country house. Touring pitches are marked and well spaced, some of them fully-serviced. The very modern toilet facilities include family bath and shower suites, and first class disabled rooms. There is a six-hole golf course and an outdoor leisure shop with a good range of camping and caravanning spares, as well as clothing and equipment. A 42-acre site with 79 touring pitches, 46 hardstandings and 255 statics.

★★★ 83% ◉◉ HOTEL
Tillmouth Park Country House
TD12 4UU
☎ 01890 882255 📠 01890 882540
e-mail: reception@tillmouthpark.force9.co.uk
web: www.tillmouthpark.com
Dir: *off A1(M) at East Ord rdbt at Berwick-upon-Tweed. Take A698 to Cornhill and Coldstream. Hotel 9m on left*
PETS: Bedrooms unattended **Public areas** bar only **Grounds** accessible **Exercise area** on site **Resident Pets:** Carter & Teal (Black Labradors)
An imposing mansion set in landscaped grounds by the River Till. Gracious public rooms include a stunning galleried lounge with a drawing room adjacent. The quietly elegant dining room overlooks the gardens, whilst lunches and early dinners are available in the bistro. Bedrooms retain traditional character and include several magnificent master rooms.
Rooms 12 en suite 2 annexe en suite (1 fmly) S £52.50-£63; D £95-£190 (incl. bkfst)✲ **Facilities** FTV 🏌 Wi-fi available Game shooting Fishing New Year **Parking** 50 **Notes** LB

►►► Dunstan Hill Camping & Caravanning Club Site *(NU236214)*
Dunstan Hill, Dunstan NE66 3TQ
☎ 01665 576310
web: www.campingandcaravanningclub.co.uk/dunstanhill
Dir: *From A1, just N of Alnwick, take B1340 signed Seahouses. Continue to T-junct at Criston Bank, turn right. 2nd right signed Embleton. Right at x-rds then 1st left signed Craster*
PETS: Exercise area on site dog walk **Facilities** walks info vet info **Other** prior notice required
Open 13 Mar-03 Nov Booking advisable BHs & peak periods Last arrival 21.00hrs Last departure noon
An immaculately maintained site with pleasant landscaping, close to the beach and Craster harbour. The historic town of Alnwick is nearby, as is the ruined Dunstanburgh Castle. A 14-acre site with 150 touring pitches, 20 hardstandings.
Notes Site gates will be closed 23:00-07:00

EMBLETON — MAP 12 NU22

★★ 76% HOTEL
Dunstanburgh Castle Hotel
NE66 3UN
☎ 01665 576111 📠 01665 576203
e-mail: stay@dunstanburghcastlehotel.co.uk
web: www.dunstanburghcastlehotel.co.uk
Dir: *from A1, take B1340 to Denwick past Rennington & Masons Arms. Take next right signed Embleton, and into village*
PETS: **Bedrooms** unattended **Grounds** accessible disp bin
Exercise area 10mtrs **Facilities** dog scoop/disp bags walks info vet info **On Request** fridge access torch towels
Resident Pets: Uncle Bob (dog)

The focal point of the village, this friendly family-run hotel has a dining room and grill room offering different menus, plus a cosy bar and two lounges. In addition to the main bedrooms, a small courtyard conversion houses three stunning suites, each with a lounge and gallery bedroom above.
Rooms 20 en suite (4 fmly) ⊘ in all bedrooms S £34.50-£44.50; D £69-£89 (incl. bkfst)✴ **Parking** 16 **Notes** Closed Dec-Jan

HALTWHISTLE — MAP 12 NY76

▶▶▶ **Haltwhistle Camping & Caravanning Club Site** *(NY685621)*
Burnfoot Park Village NE49 0JP
☎ 01434 320106
web: www.campingandcaravanningclub.co.uk
Dir: *From A69 Haltwhistle bypass (NB do not enter town) take Alston Road S signed A689, then right signed Kellan*
PETS: **Exercise area** on site dog walk **Facilities** walks info vet info **Other** prior notice required
Open 13 Mar- 03 Nov Booking advisable BH & peak periods
Last arrival 21.00hrs Last departure noon
An attractive site on the banks of the River South Tyne amidst mature trees, on the Bellister Castle estate. This peaceful, relaxing site is a good cross country transit stop in excellent walking country. A 3.5-acre site with 50 touring pitches, 15 hardstandings.
Notes Site gates will be closed 23:00-07:00

OTTERBURN — MAP 21 NY89

★★★ 72% HOTEL
The Otterburn Tower Hotel
NE19 1NT
☎ 01830 520620 📠 01830 521504
e-mail: info@otterburntower.com
web: www.otterburntower.com
Dir: *in village, on A696 (Newcastle to Edinburgh road)*
PETS: **Bedrooms Sep Accom** kennel **Stables** at adjacent stud farm **Charges** £10 per night **Public areas** except restaurant **Grounds** accessible **Exercise area** on site **Resident Pets:** Pete (Jack Russell)
Built by the cousin of William the Conqueror, this mansion is set in its own grounds. The hotel is steeped in history - Sir Walter Scott stayed here in 1812. Bedrooms come in a variety of sizes and some have huge ornamental fireplaces. Though furnished in period style, they are equipped with all modern amenities. The restaurant features 16th-century oak panelling.
Rooms 18 en suite (2 fmly) (2 GF) ⊘ in all bedrooms S £65; D £130-£190 (incl. bkfst)✴ **Facilities** STV Fishing ⚓ Wi-fi in bedrooms ch fac Xmas New Year **Parking** 70 **Notes** LB

SEAHOUSES — MAP 12 NU23

★★★ 74% HOTEL
Bamburgh Castle
NE68 7SQ
☎ 01665 720283
e-mail: bamburghcastlehotel@btinternet.com
web: www.bamburghcastlehotel.co.uk
Dir: *A1 to Seahouses, car park opposite Barclays Bank*
PETS: **Bedrooms** (GF) unattended **Charges** £8.95 per night **Exercise area** nearby **Facilities** walks info vet info **On Request** torch towels **Restrictions** Telephone for details
This family-run hotel enjoys a seafront location overlooking the harbour. There is a relaxed and friendly atmosphere with professional, friendly staff providing attentive service. The bedrooms vary in size and style, with superior rooms being more spacious. Front-facing rooms, plus the main lounge and restaurant all take advantage of the panoramic views out to sea.
Rooms 20 en suite (2 fmly) (2 GF) ⊘ in all bedrooms S £48.95-£58.95; D £87.90-£110.90 (incl. bkfst) **Facilities** Wi-fi available New Year **Parking** 30 **Notes** LB Closed 24-26 Dec & 2wks mid Jan

NOTTINGHAMSHIRE

FARNSFIELD MAP 08 SK65

★★★ GUEST ACCOMMODATION
Grange Cottage
Main St NG22 8EA
☎ 01623 882259
e-mail: bedandbreakfast@grange-cottage.co.uk
web: www.grange-cottage.co.uk
Dir: *In village opp Plough Inn car park*

PETS: **Bedrooms Sep Accom** run **Charges** £5 per week
Public areas except dining room on leads **Grounds** accessible
Exercise area 150yds **Facilities** dried dog food walks info vet
info **On Request** torch towels **Resident Pets:** Ellie (Pointer),
Major (Belgian Shepherd)

Grange Cottage is a charming 18th-century Georgian building set in
2 acres of delightful gardens and grounds behind security gates. The
bedrooms are comfortable and homely, each individually furnished
with lots of family touches. A freshly-cooked breakfast is served at one
large table in the elegant dining room.

Rooms 4 rms (1 en suite) (1 pri facs) 1 annexe en suite (1 GF) ⊘
S £25-£30; D £50-£60✱ **Facilities** TVB tea/coffee Cen ht **Parking** 6
Notes LB ⊛

HOLME PIERREPONT MAP 08 SK63

★★★ GUEST ACCOMMODATION
Holme Grange Cottage
Adbolton Ln NG12 2LU
☎ 0115 981 0413
e-mail: jean.colinwightman@talk21.com
Dir: *Off A52 SE of Nottingham, opp National Water Sports Centre*

PETS: **Bedrooms Public areas Grounds** accessible disp bin
Facilities cage storage walks info vet info **On Request** fridge
access torch **Restrictions** only 1 large dog at one time
Resident Pets: Peggy (Cavalier King Charles Spaniel)

A stone's throw from the National Water Sports Centre, this
establishment with its own all-weather tennis court is ideal for the
active guest. Indeed, when not providing warm hospitality and freshly
cooked breakfasts, the proprietor is usually on the golf course.

Rooms 3 rms (1 en suite) (1 fmly) ⊘ S £28-£32; D £48-£52✱
Facilities TVB tea/coffee Cen ht TVL ≊ **Parking** 6 **Notes** Closed Xmas
⊛

NOTTINGHAM MAP 08 SK54

★★★★ 82% ◉◉ HOTEL
Hart's
Standard Hill, Park Row NG1 6FN
☎ 0115 988 1900 ▤ 0115 947 7600
e-mail: ask@hartshotel.co.uk
web: www.hartsnottingham.co.uk
Dir: *at junct of Park Row & Rope Walk, close to city centre*

PETS: **Bedroomss** (GF) **Charges** £5 per night **Exercise area** local
walks **Facilities** food (pre-bookable) **Restrictions** some breeds
may not be accepted

This outstanding modern building stands on the site of the ramparts of
the medieval castle, overlooking the city. Many of the bedrooms enjoy
splendid views. Rooms are well appointed and stylish, while the Park
Bar is the focal point of the public areas; service is professional and
caring. Fine dining is offered at nearby Hart's Restaurant. Secure
parking and private gardens are an added bonus.

Rooms 32 en suite (1 fmly) (7 GF) ⊘ in all bedrooms D £120-£260✱
Facilities STV Gym Wi-fi in bedrooms Small, unsupervised exercise room
Xmas **Services** Lift **Parking** 19(charged) **Notes** LB

★★★★ 75% ◉ TOWN HOUSE HOTEL
Lace Market
29-31 High Pavement NG1 1HE
☎ 0115 852 3232 ▤ 0115 852 3223
e-mail: stay@lacemarkethotel.co.uk
web: www.lacemarkethotel.co.uk
Dir: *follow tourist signs for Galleries of Justice. Hotel opposite*

PETS: **Bedrooms Charges** £15 **Public areas** in gastro pub
on leads **Exercise area** 100mtrs **Restrictions** small dogs only

This smart town house, a conversion of two Georgian houses, is
located in the trendy Lace Market area. Smart public areas, including
the stylish and very popular Merchants Restaurant and Saints Bar, are
complemented by the 'Cock and Hoop', a traditional pub offering real
ales and fine wines. Accommodation is stylish and contemporary and
includes spacious superior rooms and suites; are all thoughtfully
equipped with a host of extras including CD players and mini bars.

Rooms 42 en suite ⊘ in all bedrooms **Facilities** STV Wi-fi in bedrooms
Complimentary use of nearby health club ♫ **Services** Lift

NOTTINGHAM CONTINUED

★★★ 70% HOTEL
Best Western Bestwood Lodge

Bestwood Country Park, Arnold NG5 8NE

☎ 0115 920 3011 📠 0115 964 9678

e-mail: bestwoodlodge@btconnect.com

web: www.bw-bestwoodlodge.co.uk

Dir: *3m N off A60. Left at lights into Oxclose Ln, right at next lights into Queens Bower Rd. 1st right. Keep right at fork in road*

PETS: Please telephone for details

A Victorian hunting lodge in 700 acres of parkland, the stunning architecture includes Gothic features and high vaulted ceilings. Bedrooms include all modern comforts, suitable for both business and leisure guests, and a popular restaurant serves an extensive menu.

Rooms 39 en suite (5 fmly) ⊗ in 5 bedrooms **Facilities** ☺ Riding Wi-fi in bedrooms Guided walks **Parking** 120 **Notes** RS 25 Dec & 1 Jan

★★★ 70% HOTEL
Rutland Square Hotel

St James St NG1 6FJ

☎ 0115 941 1114 📠 0115 941 0014

e-mail: rutland.square@forestdale.com

web: www.forestdale.com

Dir: *follow signs to castle. Hotel on right 50yds beyond castle*

PETS: Bedrooms **Charges** £7.50 per night

In an enviable location in the heart of the city adjacent to the castle makes this hotel a popular choice with both leisure and business travellers. Behind its mock Regency façade the hotel is modern and comfortable with good business facilities. Bedrooms come in a variety of styles with the Premier rooms offering a host of thoughtful extras. Public rooms include Woods Restaurant.

Rooms 87 en suite (3 fmly) ⊗ in 38 bedrooms **Facilities** STV Wi-fi in bedrooms Discounted day passes to nearby gym **Services** Lift **Parking** 30 (charged)

★★★ 68% HOTEL
Nottingham Gateway

Nuthall Rd, Cinderhill NG8 6AZ

☎ 0115 979 4949 📠 0115 979 4744

e-mail: sales@nottinghamgatewayhotel.co.uk

web: www.nottinghamgatewayhotel.co.uk

Dir: *M1 junct 26, A610, hotel on 3rd rdbt on left*

PETS: Bedrooms unattended **Exercise area** nearby
Facilities cage storage walks info vet info **On Request** fridge access torch towels

Located approximately three miles from the city centre, with easy access to the M1. This modern hotel provides spacious public areas, with popular restaurant and lounge bar, and the contemporary accommodation is suitably well equipped. Ample car parking is a bonus.

Rooms 108 en suite (18 fmly) ⊗ in 30 bedrooms S £47-£80; D £52-£90 (incl. bkfst)✱ **Facilities** Xmas **Services** Lift **Parking** 250 **Notes** LB

RADCLIFFE ON TRENT   MAP 08 SK63

►►► Thornton's Holt Camping Park

(SK638377)

Stragglethorpe Rd, Stragglethorpe NG12 2JZ

☎ 0115 933 2125 & 933 4204 📠 0115 933 3318

e-mail: camping@thorntons-holt.co.uk

web: www.thorntons-holt.co.uk

Dir: *Take A52, 3m E of Nottingham. Turn S at lights towards Cropwell Bishop. Park 0.5m on left. Or A46 SE of Nottingham. N at lights. Park 2.5m on right*

PETS: Public areas except pool, play area & toilet block
Exercise area on site public footpaths country park 0.5m
Facilities on site shop washing facs walks info vet info
Resident Pets: Pickle (Border Terrier), Sprocket, Perkins & Scrabble (cats) Eric (horse)

Open all year (rs 2 Nov-24 Mar no pool, shop or games room) Booking advisable BH & wknds mid May-Oct Last arrival 21.00hrs Last departure 13.00hrs

A well-run family site in former meadowland, with pitches located among young trees and bushes for a rural atmosphere and outlook. The toilets are housed in converted farm buildings, and an indoor swimming pool is a popular attraction. A 13-acre site with 155 touring pitches, 35 hardstandings.

Notes noise curfew at 22.00hrs

RETFORD (EAST) MAP 08 SK78

★★★ 74% HOTEL

Best Western West Retford

24 North Rd DN22 7XG

☎ 01777 706333 & 0870 609 6162

▤ 01777 709951

e-mail: reservations@westretfordhotel.co.uk

web: www.westfordhotel.co.uk

Dir: *From A1 take A620 to Ranby/Retford. Left at rdbt into North Rd (A638). Hotel on right*

PETS: Bedrooms (GF) unattended **Stables** nearby (3m) **Charges** £10 per night charge for damage **Grounds** accessible on leads disp bin **Exercise area** adjacent **Facilities** walks info vet info **Restrictions** dogs accepted at managers discretion

Stylishly appointed throughout, and set in very attractive gardens close to the town centre, this 18th-century manor house offers a good range of well-equipped meeting facilities. The spacious, well-laid out bedrooms and suites are located in separate buildings and all offer modern facilities and comforts.

Rooms 63 en suite (32 GF) ⊘ in 37 bedrooms **Parking** 100 **Notes** LB

TEVERSAL MAP 08 SK46

►►►► Teversal Camping & Caravanning Club Site *(SK472615)*

Silverhill Ln NG17 3JJ

☎ 01623 551838

web: www.campingandcaravanningclub.co.uk/teversal

Dir: *M1 junct 28 onto A38 towards Mansfield. Left at lights onto B6027. At top of hill straight over at lights & left at Peacock Hotel. Right onto B6014, left at Craven Arms, site on left*

PETS: Facilities on site shop walks info vet info **Other** prior notice required

Open all year Booking advisable BH Last arrival 21.00hrs Last departure noon

A top notch park with excellent purpose-built facilities, set in a rural former mining area. Each pitch is spacious, and there are views of and access to the surrounding countryside and nearby Silverhill Community Woods. The attention to detail and all-round quality are truly exceptional. A 6-acre site with 126 touring pitches, 96 hardstandings and 1 static.

Notes Site gates closed 23:00-07:00

WORKSOP MAP 08 SK57

★★★ 70% HOTEL

Clumber Park

Clumber Park S80 3PA

☎ 01623 835333 ▤ 01623 835525

e-mail: reservations@clumberparkhotel.com

web: www.clumberparkhotel.com

Dir: *M1 junct 30/31 follow signs to A57 and A1. From A1 take A614 towards Nottingham. Hotel is 2m on the left*

PETS: Bedrooms (GF) unattended **Charges** £5 per night charge for damage **Public areas** except restaurant & bar on leads **Grounds** accessible on leads disp bin **Facilities** food bowl water bowl dog walking cage storage walks info vet info **On Request** fridge access torch towels

Beside the A614, this hotel is situated in open countryside, edging on to Sherwood Forest and Clumber Park. Bedrooms are comfortably furnished and well-equipped and public areas include a choice of formal and informal eating options. Dukes Tavern is lively and casual, while the restaurant offers a more traditional style of service.

Rooms 48 en suite (5 fmly) (8 GF) ⊘ in 30 bedrooms S £90-£140; D £99-£140 (incl. bkfst) **Facilities** STV Wi-fi in bedrooms Xmas New Year **Parking** 100 **Notes** LB

►►► Riverside Caravan Park *(SK582790)*

Central Av S80 1ER

☎ 01909 474118

Dir: *From A57 E of town follow international camping sign to site.*

PETS: Public areas on leads **Exercise area** 0.25m

Open all year Booking advisable BH & wknds Last arrival 20.00hrs Last departure 14.00hrs

A very well maintained park within the attractive market town of Worksop and next door to the cricket/bowls club where Riverside customers are made welcome. This is an ideal park for those wishing to be within walking distance of all amenities yet within a 10 minute car journey of the extensive Clumber Park and numerous good garden centres. The towpath of the adjacent Chesterfield Canal provides excellent walking opportunities. A 4-acre site with 60 touring pitches, 59 hardstandings.

Notes ☺

OXFORDSHIRE

BANBURY
MAP 04 SP44

★★★ 71% HOTEL

Best Western Wroxton House

Wroxton St Mary OX15 6QB

☎ 01295 730777 📄 01295 730800

e-mail: reservations@wroxtonhousehotel.com

Dir: *A422 from Banbury, 2.5m to Wroxton, hotel on right entering village*

PETS: Bedrooms (GF) unattended Charges £5 per night
Public areas except restaurant on leads Grounds accessible on leads Facilities walks info vet info On Request fridge access torch towels Resident Pets: Cocoa (Chocolate Labrador)

Dating in parts from 1647, this partially thatched hotel is set just off the main road. Bedrooms, which have either been created out of converted cottages or are situated in a more modern wing, are comfortable and well equipped. The public areas are open plan and consist of a reception lounge and a bar, and the low-beamed Inglenook Restaurant has a peaceful atmosphere for dining.

Rooms 32 en suite (1 fmly) (7 GF) ⊘ in 15 bedrooms S £60-£99; D £80-£125 (incl. bkfst) Facilities STV Wi-fi available Xmas New Year Parking 50 Notes LB

▶▶▶▶ Bo Peep Farm Caravan Park

(SP481348)

Bo Peep Farm, Aynho Rd, Adderbury OX17 3NP

☎ 01295 810605 📄 01295 810605

e-mail: warden@bo-peep.co.uk

web: www.bo-peep.co.uk

Dir: *1m E of Adderbury & A4260, on B4100 (Aynho road)*

PETS: Charges £1 per dog per stay Public areas
Exercise area on site & extensive walks nearby Facilities on site shop food food bowl water bowl dog chews cat treats dog scoop/disp bags leads washing facs walks info vet info space for loose box Resident Pets: 3 cats

Open Mar-Oct Booking advisable BH, British Grand Prix Last arrival 20.00hrs Last departure noon

A delightful park with good views and a spacious feel. Four well laid out camping areas including two with hardstandings and a separate tent field are all planted with maturing shrubs and trees. The two facility blocks are in attractive Cotswold stone. Unusually there is a bay in which you can clean your caravan or motorhome. A 13-acre site with 98 touring pitches.

Notes ⊛

BURFORD
MAP 04 SP21

★★★ 79% ⊛ HOTEL

The Bay Tree Hotel

Sheep St OX18 4LW

☎ 01993 822791 📄 01993 823008

e-mail: info@baytreehotel.info

web: www.cotswold-inns-hotels.co.uk/bay-tree

Dir: *M40 junct 8 or M5 junct 11, then follow A40 to Burford. Or M4 junct 15, then A419 then A361 to Burford. From High St turn into Sheep St, next to the old market square. Hotel is on right.*

PETS: Bedrooms (GF) Charges charge for damage
Public areas except eating areas Grounds accessible
Facilities cage storage walks info vet info On Request fridge access torch towels

History and modern flair sit happily side by side at this delightful old inn, situated near the town centre. Bedrooms are tastefully furnished using the original features to good effect and some have four-poster and half-tester beds. Public areas consist of a character bar, a sophisticated airy restaurant, a selection of meeting rooms and an attractive walled garden.

Rooms 8 en suite 13 annexe en suite (2 fmly) ⊘ in all bedrooms S £119-£129; D £145-£175 (incl. bkfst)✳ Facilities ᐧ Wi-fi available Xmas New Year Parking 50

★★★ 78% ⊛⊛ HOTEL

The Lamb Inn

Sheep St OX18 4LR

☎ 01993 823155 📄 01993 822228

e-mail: info@lambinn-burford.co.uk

web: www.cotswold-inns-hotels.co.uk

Dir: *Turn off A40 into Burford, downhill, take 1st left into Sheep St, hotel last on right*

PETS: Bedrooms (GF) Charges charge for damage
Public areas except eating areas Grounds accessible
Facilities cage storage walks info vet info On Request fridge access torch towels

This enchanting old inn is just a short walk from the centre of a delightful Cotswold village. An abundance of character and charm is found inside with a cosy lounge and log fire, and in intimate bar with flagged floors. An elegant restaurant offers locally sourced produce in carefully prepared dishes. Bedrooms, some with original features are comfortable and well appointed.

Rooms 17 en suite (1 fmly) (4 GF) ⊘ in all bedrooms D £145-£165 (incl. bkfst)✳ Facilities Wi-fi in bedrooms Xmas New Year

★★ 74% HOTEL

The Inn For All Seasons

 THE INDEPENDENTS

The Barringtons OX18 4TN

☎ 01451 844324 📠 01451 844375

e-mail: sharp@innforallseasons.com

web: www.innforallseasons.com

Dir: 3m W of Burford on A40 towards Cheltenham

PETS: Bedrooms Charges £5 per night

This 16th-century coaching inn is conveniently near Burford. Bedrooms are comfortable; public areas retain a feeling of period charm with original fireplaces and oak beams. A good selection of bar meals is available at lunchtime, while the evening menu includes an appetising selection of fresh fish.

Rooms 9 en suite 1 annexe en suite (2 fmly) (1 GF) ⊘ in 5 bedrooms S £59.50-£69; D £90-£110 (incl. bkfst)✲ **Facilities** STV Xmas New Year **Parking** 62 **Notes** LB

CHARLBURY   MAP 04 SP31

★★ 68% ⚽ HOTEL

The Bell

Church St OX7 3PP

☎ 01608 810278 📠 01608 811447

e-mail: info@bellhotel-charlbury.com

web: www.bellhotel-charlbury.co.uk

Dir: turn off A44 onto B4437. Once in Charlbury, 2nd left (signed Centre). Past church, hotel top of hill on right

PETS: Bedrooms unattended **Charges** £10 per night charge for damage **Public areas** except restaurant on leads **Grounds** accessible **Facilities** food bowl water bowl pet sitting dog walking washing facs dog grooming cage storage walks info vet info **On Request** fridge access torch

This mellow Cotswold-stone inn dates back to the 16th century, when it was home to Customs & Excise, and sits close to the town centre. Popular with locals, the bar has an enjoyable and relaxed atmosphere and comes complete with flagstone floors and log fires. The well-equipped bedrooms are situated in the main building and the adjacent converted barn.

Rooms 8 en suite 4 annexe en suite (6 fmly) ⊘ in all bedrooms S £50-£80; D £60-£95 (incl. bkfst)✲ **Facilities** Wi-fi in bedrooms Xmas New Year **Parking** 25 **Notes** RS 25 Dec

---

CHIPPING NORTON   MAP 04 SP32

▶▶▶ Chipping Norton C&C Club Site

(SP315244)

Chipping Norton Rd, Chadlington OX7 3PE

☎ 01608 641993

web: www.campingandcaravanningclub.co.uk/ chippingnorton

Dir: Take A44 to Chipping Norton onto A361 Burford road. After 1.5m bear left at fork signed Chadlington

PETS: Facilities walks info vet info **Other** prior notice required

Open 13 Mar-03 Nov Booking advisable BH & peak periods Last arrival 21.00hrs Last departure noon

A hilltop site surrounded by trees but close to a busy main road. The toilets are very clean and visitors are given the usual warm Club welcome. A 4-acre site with 105 touring pitches.

Notes site gates will be closed 23:00-07:00

KINGHAM

MAP 04 SP22

★★★ 81% ◎◎ HOTEL
Mill House Hotel & Restaurant

OX7 6UH

☎ 01608 658188 📠 01608 658492

e-mail: stay@millhousehotel.co.uk

web: www.millhousehotel.co.uk

Dir: *off A44 onto B4450. Hotel indicated by tourist sign*

PETS: Bedrooms (GF) unattended **Stables** nearby (4m) **Charges** charge for damage **Grounds** accessible disp bin **Facilities** food (pre-bookable) food bowl water bowl dog chews dog scoop/disp bags cage storage walks info vet info **On Request** fridge access torch towels **Resident Pets:** Ben (Labrador)

This Cotswold-stone, former mill house has been carefully converted into a comfortable and attractive hotel. It is set in well-kept grounds bordered by its own trout stream. Bedrooms are comfortable and provide thoughtfully equipped accommodation. There is a peaceful lounge and bar, plus an atmospheric restaurant where the imaginative, skilfully cooked dishes are a highlight of any stay.

Rooms 21 en suite 2 annexe en suite (1 fmly) (7 GF) ⊗ in all bedrooms S £90-£100; D £130-£150 (incl. bkfst) **Facilities** STV Fishing Wi-fi available Xmas New Year **Parking** 62 **Notes** LB

★★★★ 🍴 INN
The Tollgate Inn & Restaurant

Church St OX7 6YA

☎ 01608 658389

e-mail: info@thetollgate.com

PETS: Please telephone for details

Situated in the idyllic Cotswold village of Kingham, this Grade II-listed Georgian building has been lovingly restored to provide a complete home-from-home among some of the most beautiful and historic countryside in Britain. The Tollgate provides comfortable, well equipped accommodation in pleasant surroundings. A good choice of menu for lunch and dinner is available with good use made of fresh and local produce. You can also be sure of a hearty breakfast provided in the modern, well-equipped dining room.

Rooms 5 en suite 4 annexe en suite (1 fmly) (4 GF) **Facilities** TVB tea/coffee Cen ht Dinner Last d 9/9.30pm Fri/Sat **Parking** 12

OXFORD

MAP 04 SP50

★★★★ 76% HOTEL
Paramount Oxford

Godstow Rd, Wolvercote Roundabout OX2 8AL

☎ 01865 489988 📠 01865 489952

e-mail: oxford@paramount-hotels.co.uk

web: www.paramount-hotels.co.uk

Dir: *adjacent to A34/A40, 2m from city centre*

PETS: Bedrooms (GF) unattended sign **Charges** £15 per night charge for damage **Grounds** accessible on leads **Exercise area** at rear of hotel **Facilities** walks info vet info

Conveniently located on the northern edge of the city centre, this purpose-built hotel offers bedrooms that are bright, modern and well equipped. Guests can eat in the 'Medio' restaurant or try the Cappuccino bar menu. The hotel offers impressive conference, business and leisure facilities.

Rooms 168 en suite (13 fmly) (89 GF) ⊗ in 140 bedrooms S £69-£145✳ **Facilities** STV ⍰ supervised Squash Gym Wi-fi available Steam room New Year **Parking** 250 (charged)

►►► Oxford Camping & Caravanning Club Site *(SP519039)*

426 Abingdon Rd OX1 4XG

☎ 01865 244088

web: www.campingandcaravanningclub.co.uk/oxford

Dir: *From M40 onto A34, exit at A423 for Oxford. Turn left immediately after junct into Abingdon Road, site on left behind Touchwood Sports*

PETS: Facilities walks info vet info **Other** prior notice required

Open all year Booking advisable BH & peak periods Last arrival 21.00hrs Last departure noon

A very busy town site with handy park-and-ride into Oxford. All pitches are on grass, and most offer electric hook-ups. A 5-acre site with 85 touring pitches.

Notes site gates will be closed 23:00-07:00

OXFORD MOTORWAY SERVICE AREA (M40) MAP 04 SP60

BUDGET HOTEL

Days Inn Oxford

M40 junction 8A, Waterstock OX33 1LJ

☎ 01865 877000 📄 01865 877016

e-mail: oxford.hotel@welcomebreak.co.uk

web: www.daysinn.com

Dir: *M40 junct 8a, Welcome Break service area.*

PETS: Bedrooms unattended **Grounds** accessible

This modern building offers accommodation in smart, spacious and well-equipped bedrooms, suitable for families and business travellers, and all with en suite bathrooms. Continental breakfast is available and other refreshments may be taken at the nearby family restaurant. For further details see the Hotel Groups page.

Rooms 59 en suite

STANDLAKE

►►►►► Lincoln Farm Park Oxfordshire *(SP395028)*

High St OX29 7RH

☎ 01865 300239 📄 01865 300127

e-mail: lincolnfarmpark@btconnect.com

web: www.lincolnfarmpark.co.uk

Dir: *In village off A415 between Abingdon & Witney, 5m SE of Witney*

PETS: Charges £1.25 per night **Public areas** except play area **Exercise area** on site 2 small dog runs **Facilities** on site shop food food bowl water bowl bedding dog chews cat treats litter tray dog scoop/disp bags leads walks info vet info **Resident Pets:** Chance (Border Collie)

Open Feb-Nov Booking advisable BH, Jul-Aug & most wknds Last arrival 21.00hrs Last departure noon

An attractively landscaped park in a quiet village setting, with superb facilities and a high standard of maintenance. Family rooms, fully-serviced pitches, two indoor swimming pools and a fully-equipped gym are part of the comprehensive amenities. A 9-acre site with 90 touring pitches, 75 hardstandings and 19 statics.

Notes No gazebos

WALLINGFORD MAP 04 SU68

★★★ 78% ◉ HOTEL

The Springs Hotel & Golf Club

Wallingford Rd, North Stoke OX10 6BE

☎ 01491 836687 📄 01491 836877

e-mail: info@thespringshotel.com

web: www.thespringshotel.com

Dir: *off A4074 (Oxford-Reading road) onto B4009 (Goring). Hotel approx 1m on right*

PETS: Bedrooms (GF) unattended **Charges** £15 per night charge for damage **Grounds** accessible on leads disp bin **Facilities** food bowl water bowl **Restrictions** only 1 bedroom allocated for dogs, therefore only 1 dog is permitted at any time vet info

Set on its own golf course, this Victorian mansion has a timeless and peaceful atmosphere. The generously equipped bedrooms vary in size but many are spacious. The elegant restaurant enjoys splendid views over the spring-fed lake where a variety of wildfowl enjoy the natural surroundings. There is also a comfortable lounge with original features, and a cosy bar to relax in.

Rooms 32 en suite (4 fmly) (8 GF) ⊗ in 20 bedrooms S £95-£120; D £110-£135 (incl. bkfst) **Facilities** STV ʒ ⅃ 18 Fishing ↘ Putt green Wi-fi in bedrooms Clay pigeon shooting nearby ♫ Xmas New Year **Parking** 150 **Notes** LB

WALLINGFORD CONTINUED

★★★ 74% HOTEL

Shillingford Bridge

Shillingford OX10 8LZ

☎ 01865 858567 🖹 01865 858636

e-mail: shillingford.bridge@forestdale.com

web: www.forestdale.com

Dir: *M4 junct 10, A329 through Wallingford towards Thame, then B4009 through Watlington. Right on A4074 at Benson, then left at Shillingford rdbt (unclass road) Wallingford Road*

PETS: Bedrooms (GF) unattended sign **Charges** £7.50 per night charge for damage **Public areas** except restaurant on leads **Grounds** accessible on leads disp bin **Facilities** food (pre-bookable) food bowl water bowl washing facs cage storage walks info vet info **On Request** fridge access torch towels

This hotel enjoys a superb position right on the banks of the River Thames, and benefits from private moorings and a waterside open-air swimming pool. Public areas are stylish with a contemporary feel and have large picture windows making the best use of the view. Bedrooms are well equipped and furnished with guest comfort in mind.

Rooms 32 en suite 8 annexe en suite (6 fmly) (9 GF) ⊘ in 23 bedrooms **Facilities** STV ↳ supervised Fishing Wi-fi available Table tennis ♫ **Parking** 100

WOODSTOCK   MAP 04 SP41

★★★ 83% ⚫⚫ HOTEL

Feathers

bespoke

Market St OX20 1SX

☎ 01993 812291 🖹 01993 813158

e-mail: enquiries@feathers.co.uk

web: www.bespokehotels.com

Dir: *from Oxford take A44 to Woodstock, 1st left after lights. Hotel on left*

PETS: Bedrooms (GF) unattended **Stables** nearby (1m) **Charges** £10 per night **Public areas** except restaurant & bar on leads **Grounds** accessible on leads disp bin **Exercise area** 0.5m **Facilities** food (pre-bookable) food bowl water bowl bedding dog chews washing facs cage storage walks info vet info **On Request** fridge access torch towels **Resident Pets:** Johann (African Grey parrot)

This intimate, individual hotel enjoys a town centre location with easy access to nearby Blenheim Palace. Public areas are elegant and full of traditional character from the cosy drawing room to the atmospheric restaurant. Individually styled bedrooms are appointed to a high standard and are furnished with attractive period furniture.

Feathers

Rooms 20 en suite (4 fmly) (2 GF) ⊘ in all bedrooms **Facilities** FTV Wi-fi in bedrooms 1 suite has steam room

RUTLAND

EMPINGHAM   MAP 04 SK90

★★ 74% HOTEL

The White Horse Inn

Main St LE15 8PS

☎ 01780 460221 🖹 01780 460521

e-mail: info@whitehorserutland.co.uk

web: www.whitehorserutland.co.uk

Dir: *on A606, Oakham to Stamford road*

PETS: Bedrooms (GF) unattended **Charges** £5 per night **Grounds** accessible **Facilities** walks info vet info

This attractive stone-built inn, offering bright, comfortable accommodation, is conveniently located just minutes from the A1. Bedrooms in the main building are spacious and include a number of family rooms. Public areas include a well-stocked bar, a bistro and restaurant where a wide range of meals is served.

Rooms 4 en suite 9 annexe en suite (3 fmly) (5 GF) ⊘ in 4 bedrooms S £50; D £65-£80 (incl. bkfst)✻ **Parking** 60 **Notes** Closed 25 Dec

OAKHAM MAP 04 SK80

★★★★ ◉◉◉◉ COUNTRY HOUSE HOTEL

Hambleton Hall

RELAIS & CHATEAUX

Hambleton LE15 8TH

☎ 01572 756991 📠 01572 724721

e-mail: hotel@hambletonhall.com

web: www.hambletonhall.com

Dir: *3m E off A606*

PETS: Bedrooms sign **Stables** nearby (15mins) **Charges** £10 per night £70 per week **Grounds** accessible on leads **Facilities** vet info

Established over 25 years ago by Tim and Stefa Hart this delightful country house enjoys tranquil and spectacular views over Rutland Water. The beautifully manicured grounds are a delight to walk in. The bedrooms in the main house are stylish, individually decorated and equipped with a range of thoughtful extras. A two-bedroom folly, with its own sitting and breakfast room, is only a short walk away. Day rooms include a cosy bar and a sumptuous drawing room, both featuring open fires. The elegant restaurant serves skilfully prepared, award-winning cuisine with menus highlighting locally sourced, seasonal produce - some grown in the hotel's own grounds.

Rooms 15 en suite 2 annexe en suite ⊘ in all bedrooms S £165-£195; D £195-£600✳ **Facilities** STV ⤳ supervised ⌣ ⤳ Wi-fi available Private access to lake Xmas New Year **Services** Lift **Parking** 40 **Notes** LB

★★★ 77% ◉ HOTEL

Barnsdale Lodge

The Avenue, Rutland Water, North Shore LE15 8AH

☎ 01572 724678 📠 01572 724961

e-mail: enquiries@barnsdalelodge.co.uk

web: www.barnsdalelodge.co.uk

Dir: *off A1 onto A606. Hotel 5m on right, 2m E of Oakham*

PETS: Bedrooms (GF) unattended **Charges** £10 per night **Public areas** bar only **Grounds** accessible disp bin **Facilities** food bowl water bowl walks info vet info **On Request** fridge access torch towels **Resident Pets:** Coco (dog)

A popular and interesting hotel converted from a farmstead overlooking Rutland Water. The public areas are dominated by a very successful food operation with a good range of appealing meals on offer for either formal or informal dining. Bedrooms are comfortably appointed with excellent beds enhanced by contemporary soft furnishings and thoughtful extras.

Barnsdale Lodge

Rooms 44 en suite (2 fmly) (15 GF) ⊘ in all bedrooms S £75-£85; D £105-£125 (incl. bkfst)✳ **Facilities** STV Fishing ⤳ Archery Beauty treatments Golf Shooting Xmas New Year **Parking** 200 **Notes** LB

UPPINGHAM MAP 04 SP89

★★★ 66% HOTEL

Falcon

The Market Place LE15 9PY

☎ 01572 823535 📠 01572 821620

e-mail: sales@thefalconhotel.com

web: www.thefalconhotel.com

Dir: *A47 onto A6003, left at lights, hotel on right*

PETS: Bedrooms (GF) unattended **Charges** charge for damage **Public areas** on leads **Grounds** accessible **Exercise area** nearby **Facilities** food vet info

An attractive, 16th-century coaching inn situated in the heart of this bustling market town. Public areas feature an open-plan lounge bar, with a relaxing atmosphere and comfortable sofas. The brasserie area offers a cosmopolitan-style snack menu, while more formal meals are provided in the Garden Terrace Restaurant.

Rooms 25 en suite (4 fmly) (3 GF) S fr £60; D £95-£130 (incl. bkfst)✳ **Facilities** FTV Wi-fi in bedrooms Xmas New Year **Parking** 33 **Notes** LB

SHROPSHIRE

BRIDGNORTH — MAP 07 SO79

►►►► Stanmore Hall Touring Park

(SO742923)

Stourbridge Rd WV15 6DT

☎ 01746 761761 📄 01746 768069

e-mail: stanmore@morris-leisure.co.uk

web: www.morris-leisure.co.uk

Dir: *2m E of Bridgnorth on A458*

PETS: **Charges** £1 per night **Public areas** **Exercise area** on site 2 dog walks & in 100mtrs **Facilities** on site shop food food bowl water bowl dog chews cat treats dog scoop/disp bags leads washing facs walks info vet info **Other** max 2 dogs per pitch

Open all year Booking advisable BH, school hols & Jul-Aug Last arrival 20.00hrs Last departure noon

An excellent park in peaceful surroundings offering outstanding facilities. The pitches, many of them fully serviced, are arranged around the lake in Stanmore Hall, home of the Midland Motor Museum. Handy for touring Ironbridge and the Severn Valley Railway, while Bridgnorth itself is an attractive old market town. A 12.5-acre site with 131 touring pitches, 44 hardstandings.

BROOME — MAP 07 SO48

►► Engine & Tender Inn (SO399812)

SY7 0NT

☎ 01588 660275

Dir: *W from Craven Arms on B4368, fork left to B4367, site in village, 2m on right*

PETS: **Public areas** **Other** prior notice required

Open all year Booking advisable BH Last arrival 21.00hrs Last departure 14.00hrs

A rural site in a pleasant setting adjacent to the country pub, and accessible through the pub car park. The site has clean but fairly basic facilities. A 1-acre site with 20 touring pitches and 2 statics.

CHURCH STRETTON — MAP 07 SO49

★★★★ BED & BREAKFAST
North Hill Farm

Cardington SY6 7LL

☎ 01694 771532

e-mail: cbrandon@btinternet.com

Dir: *From Cardington village S onto Church Stretton road, right signed Cardington Moor, farm at top of hill on left*

PETS: **Bedrooms** (GF) **Sep Accom** kennels, barn **Stables** on site **Charges** £2 per night charge for damage **Public areas** except dining room **Grounds** accessible disp bin **Facilities** food bowl water bowl dog scoop/disp bags leads washing facs cage storage walks info vet info **On Request** fridge access torch towels **Restrictions** pets must not be fed in rooms, large breeds must stay in kennels, no Rottweilers or American Pit Bull Terriers **Resident Pets:** Saffron, Connie & Bryony (Gordon Setters), Bonnie & Millie (English Springer Spaniels), Sam (cat), Sonny & Opal (horses)

This delightful house has been modernised to provide comfortable accommodation. It is located on a fairly remote 20-acre sheep-rearing holding amid the scenery of the Shropshire hills. The lounge, with exposed beams, has log fires in cold weather. Guests share one large table in the breakfast room.

Rooms 2 rms (2 pri facs) 1 annexe en suite (1 GF) ⊗ S £30; D £50-£60✳ **Facilities** TVB tea/coffee Cen ht **Parking** 6 **Notes** LB No children 10yrs Closed Xmas 🐾

CRAVEN ARMS — MAP 07 SO48

★★★★ BED & BREAKFAST
Castle View
Stokesay SY7 9AL
☎ 01588 673712
e-mail: castleviewb_b@btinternet.com
Dir: *On A49 S of Craven Arms opp turning to Stokesay Castle*
PETS: Bedrooms unattended **Public areas** except dining room
(except assist dogs) **Grounds** accessible disp bin **Facilities** food
bowl water bowl feeding mat walks info vet info
On Request fridge access torch towels **Resident Pets:** Cindy
(Bearded Collie)

The Victorian cottage, extended about 20 years ago, stands in delightful
gardens on the southern outskirts of Craven Arms, close to Stokesay
Castle. Bedrooms are thoughtfully furnished, and breakfasts, featuring
local produce, are served in the cosy, traditionally-furnished dining
room.

Rooms 3 rms (1 en suite) (2 pri facs) ✆ S £35-£40; D £55-£60
Facilities TVB tea/coffee Cen ht **Parking** 4 **Notes** LB No children 3yrs

---

HAUGHTON — MAP 07 SJ51

▶ **Ebury Hill Camping & Caravanning Club**
Site *(SJ546164)*
Ebury Hill, Ring Bank SY4 4GB
☎ 01743 709334
web: www.campingandcaravanningclub.co.uk/eburyhill
Dir: *2.5m through Shrewsbury on A53. Turn right signed
Haughton & Upton Magna. Continue 1.5m site on right*
PETS: Exercise area on site dog walk **Facilities** walks info vet
info **Other** prior notice required

Open 13 Mar-03 Nov Booking advisable BH & peak periods
Last arrival 21.00hrs Last departure noon

A wooded hill fort with a central lake overlooking the countryside. The
site is well screened by mature trees, and there is good fishing in a
disused quarry. Though there are no toilet or shower facilities, this
lovely park is very popular with discerning visitors. An 18-acre site with
100 touring pitches, 21 hardstandings.

Notes Site gates will be closed 23:00-07:00

IRONBRIDGE — MAP 07 SJ60

★★★★ BED & BREAKFAST
Woodlands Farm Guest House
Beech Rd TF8 7PA
☎ 01952 432741 🖷 01952 432741
e-mail: woodlandsfarm@ironbridge68.fsnet.co.uk
web: www.woodlandsfarmguesthouse.co.uk
Dir: *Off B4373 rdbt in Ironbridge onto Church Hill & Beech Rd,
house on private lane 0.5m on right*
PETS: Bedrooms (GF) sign **Charges** £2 per night charge for
damage **Public areas** except dining room on leads
Grounds accessible on leads disp bin **Exercise area** 10yds
Facilities cage storage walks info vet info **On Request** fridge
access torch

This extended Victorian bungalow has been thoughtfully renovated
and provides a range of well-equipped and homely bedrooms all of
which benefit from a private sitting room. A comprehensive breakfast is
served in the cosy pine-furnished dining room, which overlooks the
pretty garden.

Rooms 3 en suite (1 fmly) (3 GF) ✆ S £35-£70; D £60-£70
Facilities STV FTV TVB tea/coffee Cen ht TVL **Parking** 8 **Notes** LB
No children 5 yrs Closed 24 Dec-1 Jan

KNOCKIN — MAP 07 SJ32

★★★★ 🏨 GUEST HOUSE
Top Farm House
SY10 8HN
☎ 01691 682582 🖷 01691 682070
e-mail: p.a.m@knockin.freeserve.co.uk
web: www.topfarmknockin.co.uk
Dir: *Off B4396 in village centre*
PETS: Bedrooms Public areas except dining rooms
Grounds accessible

This impressive half-timbered Tudor house, set amid pretty gardens,
retains many original features including a wealth of exposed beams
and open fires. Bedrooms are equipped with many thoughtful extras,
and the open-plan ground-floor area includes a comfortable sitting
room and elegant dining section, where imaginative comprehensive
breakfasts are served.

Rooms 3 en suite (1 fmly) S £35-£40; D £65-£75✳ **Facilities** TVB tea/
coffee Cen ht TVL **Parking** 6 **Notes** LB No coaches

ENGLAND

LUDLOW
MAP 07 SO57

★★★ 78% ◎◎ HOTEL

Dinham Hall

By the Castle SY8 1EJ

☎ 01584 876464 📄 01584 876019

e-mail: info@dinhamhall.co.uk

web: www.dinhamhall.co.uk

Dir: *opposite the castle*

PETS: Bedrooms (GF) unattended **Charges** £9 per night
Grounds accessible **Exercise area** woods nearby **Facilities** vet info

Built in 1792, this lovely old house stands in attractive gardens immediately opposite Ludlow Castle. It has a well-deserved reputation for warm hospitality and fine cuisine. Well-equipped bedrooms include two in a converted cottage and some with four-poster beds. The comfortable public rooms are elegantly appointed.

Rooms 11 en suite 2 annexe en suite (3 fmly) (1 GF) S £95-£140;
D £140-£240 (incl. bkfst)✳ **Facilities** Wi-fi available Xmas New Year
Parking 16 **Notes** LB

★★ 68% HOTEL

Cliffe

Dinham SY8 2JE

☎ 01584 872063 📄 01584 873991

e-mail: thecliffehotel@hotmail.com

Dir: *in town centre turn left at castle gates to Dinham, follow over bridge. Take right fork, hotel 200yds on left*

PETS: Bedrooms Charges £5 per night **Exercise area** nearby
Resident Pets: 2 Labradors

Built in the 19th century and standing in extensive grounds and gardens, this privately owned and personally run hotel is quietly located close to the castle and the river. It provides well-equipped accommodation, and facilities include a lounge bar, a pleasant restaurant and a patio overlooking the garden.

Rooms 9 en suite (2 fmly) ⊘ in all bedrooms S £50-£60; D £80-£100
(incl. bkfst) **Parking** 22 **Notes** LB

★★★★ BED & BREAKFAST

Bromley Court B & B

Lower Broad St SY8 1PH

☎ 01584 876996 📄 01584 873666

e-mail: phil@ludlowhotels.com

Dir: *Off B4361 at bridge into town centre*

PETS: Bedrooms unattended **Stables** nearby (1m)
Charges charge for damage **Public areas Grounds** accessible
disp bin **Exercise area** 300mtrs **Facilities** washing facs walks info
vet info **On Request** fridge access torch towels

Located close to the river and attractions of this historic town, this award-winning renovation of Georgian cottages provides split-level suites. All have with comfortable sitting areas and kitchenettes, the carefully furnished bedrooms are filled with thoughtful extras and a peaceful patio garden is also available. Comprehensive continental breakfasts are available within each suite and cooked English breakfasts are available at town centre Bull Hotel, which is under the same ownership.

Rooms 3 en suite ⊘ S £90-£115; D £100-£120✳ **Facilities** TVB tea/coffee Cen ht TVL **Notes** LB

★★★★ INN

Church Inn

The Buttercross SY8 1AW

☎ 01584 872174 📄 01584 877146

web: www.thechurchinn.com

Dir: *In town centre at top of Broad St*

PETS: Bedrooms unattended **Public areas Other** must bring dog's own bedding

Set right in the heart of the historic town, this Grade II listed inn has been renovated to provide quality accommodation with smart modern bathrooms, some with spa baths. Other areas include a small lounge, a well-equipped meeting room, and cosy bar areas where imaginative food and real ales are served.

Rooms 8 en suite (3 fmly) S £35-£80; D £70-£80✳ **Facilities** TVB tea/coffee Direct dial from bedrooms Cen ht TVL Dinner Last d 9pm **Notes** No coaches

★★★★ GUEST HOUSE

Moor Hall

Cleedownton SY8 3EG

☎ 01584 823209 📠 08715 041324

e-mail: enquiries@moorhall.co.uk

Dir: *A4117 Ludlow to Kidderminster, left to Brignorth. B4364, follow for 3.5m, Moor Hall on right*

PETS: Bedrooms Public areas except dining room
Grounds accessible Exercise area fields Facilities vet info

This impressive Georgian house, once the home of Lord Boyne, is surrounded by extensive gardens and farmland. Bedrooms are richly decorated, well equipped, and one room has a sitting area. Public areas are spacious and comfortably furnished. There is a choice of sitting rooms and a library bar. Guests dine family-style in an elegant dining room.

Rooms 3 en suite (1 fmly) S £35-£38; D £50-£56❉ Facilities TVB tea/coffee Licensed Cen ht Dinner Last d day before Fishing Parking 7
Notes LB No coaches Closed 25-26 Dec 🐾

Ⓤ

Angel House

Bitterley SY8 3HT

☎ 01584 📠 891377

e-mail: lockett1956@yahoo.co.uk

web: www.angelhousecleehill.co.uk

Dir: *On A4117 towards Kidderminster*

PETS: Bedrooms Charges £5 per stay Public areas Grounds
Exercise area local walks Facilities water bowl food bowl

At the time of going to press the rating for this establishment had not been confirmed. Please check the AA website www.theAA.com for up-to-date information.

Rooms 2 en suite (1 fmly) ❷ S £40-£65; D £65 Facilities TVB tea/coffee Cen ht Dinner Parking 30 Notes No children 5yrs 🐾

►►►► **Fernwood Caravan Park** *(SJ445346)*

SY12 0QF

☎ 01948 710221 📠 01948 710324

e-mail: enquiries@fernwoodpark.co.uk

web: www.fernwoodpark.co.uk

Dir: *From A495 in Welshampton take B5063, over canal bridge, turn right as signed*

PETS: Public areas Exercise area on site adjacent woods
Facilities on site shop food dog scoop/disp bags walks info vet info Other Prior notice required Resident Pets: Poppy (Border Collie)

Open Mar-Nov Booking advisable BH & summer hols Last arrival 21.00hrs Last departure 17.00hrs

A peaceful park set in wooded countryside, with a screened, tree-lined touring area and coarse fishing lake. The approach is past flower beds, and the static area which is tastefully arranged around an attractive children's playing area. There is a small child-free touring area for those wanting complete relaxation, and the park has 20 acres of woodland walks. A 26-acre site with 60 touring pitches, 8 hardstandings and 165 statics.

★★★★ FARM HOUSE

Yew Tree *(SO543958)*

Longville in the Dale TF13 6EB

☎ 01694 771866 📠 01694 771867 Mr & Mrs A Hilbery

e-mail: hilbery@tiscali.co.uk

Dir: *5m SW of Much Wenlock. N off B4371 at Longville, left at pub, right at x-rds, farm 1.2m on right*

PETS: Bedrooms Sep Accom Stables nearby (6m)
Charges charge for damage Grounds accessible disp bin
Exercise area adjacent Facilities food bowl water bowl feeding mat dog scoop/disp bags leads pet sitting washing facs cage storage vet info On Request fridge access torch towels Restrictions no giant breeds Resident Pets: Inyanga, Saffie & Tuli (Norfolk Terriers), sheep, chickens

Peacefully located between Much Wenlock and Church Stretton in ten acres of unspoiled countryside, where rare breed pigs, sheep and chickens are reared and own produce is a feature on the comprehensive breakfast menu. Bedrooms are equipped with thoughtful extras and a warm welcome is assured.

Rooms 2 rms (1 en suite) (1 pri facs) ❷ S fr £30; D £60❉
Facilities TVB tea/coffee Cen ht TVL Parking 4 Notes LB 10 acres small holding 🐾

NEWPORT
MAP 07 SJ71

★★★ FARM HOUSE
Moreton Hall Farm *(SJ789174)*
Moreton TF10 9DY
☎ 01952 691544 📄 01952 691544 Mrs S Bloor
e-mail: sarabloor@hotmail.co.uk

Dir: *Exit M54 junct 3, A41 Chester. Turn right Stockton, Moreton, Church Eaton 1.5m, turn left to farm*

PETS: Bedrooms unattended **Charges** at owner's discretion **Public areas** on leads **Grounds** accessible on leads disp bin **Exercise area** countryside adjacent **Facilities** food food bowl water bowl bedding leads wash facs walks info vet info **On Request** access to fridge torch towels **Other** pets must be kept in transportation cages in bedrooms **Resident Pets:** Maizy (Borderr Terrier), Molly (German Shepherd), Blue (cat), 10 rare breed chickens

Peacefully located close to major road links, a warm welcome is assured at this 18th-century farmhouse, which stands in pretty mature gardens and benefits from a swimming pool. Bedrooms are equipped with lots of homely extras and locally-sourced produce is featured on the breakfast selection.

Rooms 3 rms (2 en suite) (1 pri facs) (1 fmly) ⊘ S £24-£25; D £48-£55 **Facilities** TVB tea/coffee Cen ht ⤞ **Parking** 6 **Notes** 200 acres Dairy ✪

OSWESTRY
MAP 07 SJ22

★★★ 82% ◉◉ HOTEL
Pen-y-Dyffryn Country Hotel
Rhydycroesau SY10 7JD
☎ 01691 653700 📄 01978 211004
e-mail: stay@peny.co.uk
web: www.peny.co.uk

WELSH RAREBITS

Dir: *from A5 into Oswestry town centre. Follow signs to Llansilin on B4580, hotel 3m W of Oswestry before Rhydycroesau village*

PETS: Bedrooms (GF) unattended **Stables** on site **Public areas** not after 6pm **Grounds** accessible disp bin **Exercise area** excellent dog walks in area **Facilities** food bowl water bowl dog scoop/disp bags leads washing facs cage storage walks info vet info **On Request** fridge access torch towels

Peacefully situated in five acres of grounds, this charming old house dates back to around 1840, when it was built as a rectory. The tastefully

appointed public rooms have real fires during cold weather, and the accommodation includes several mini-cottages, each with its own patio. This hotel attracts many guests for its food and for its attentive, friendly service.

Pen-y-Dyffryn Hall Country Hotel

Rooms 8 en suite 4 annexe en suite (1 fmly) (1 GF) ⊘ in all bedrooms S £84-£86; D £108-£155 (incl. bkfst) **Facilities** STV Riding Wi-fi in bedrooms Guided walks Xmas New Year **Parking** 18 **Notes LB** No children 3yrs Closed 18 Dec-19 Jan

SHIFNAL
MAP 07 SJ70

★★★★ 75% HOTEL
Park House
Park St TF11 9BA
☎ 01952 460128 📄 01952 461658
e-mail: reception@parkhousehotel.net

Dir: *M54 junct 4 follow A464 Wolverhampton Rd for approx 2m, under railway bridge and hotel is 100yds on left*

PETS: Bedrooms (GF) unattended **Charges** £20 per night **Public areas** except restaurant & bar **Grounds** accessible **Facilities** walks info vet info **On Request** fridge access

This hotel was created from what were originally two country houses of very different architectural styles. Located on the edge of the historic market town, it offers guests easy access to motorway networks, a choice of banqueting and meeting rooms, and leisure facilities.

CONTINUED

Park House

Rooms 38 en suite 16 annexe en suite (4 fmly) (8 GF) ⊘ in 16 bedrooms
S £75-£120; D £100-£250 (incl. bkfst)✷ **Facilities** STV Gym Wi-fi
available Xmas New Year **Services** Lift **Parking** 90 **Notes** LB

SHREWSBURY   MAP 07 SJ41

★★★★ 71% @ HOTEL
Albright Hussey Manor Hotel & Restaurant
Ellesmere Rd SY4 3AF
☎ 01939 290571 & 290523 ▤ 01939 291143
e-mail: info@albrighthussey.co.uk
web: www.albrighthussey.co.uk
Dir: *2.5m N of Shrewsbury on A528, follow signs for Ellesmere*
PETS: Bedrooms unattended **Charges** £10 per night
First mentioned in the Domesday Book, this enchanting medieval
manor house is complete with a moat. Bedrooms are situated in either
the sumptuously appointed main house or in the more modern wing.
The intimate restaurant displays an abundance of original features and
there is also a comfortable cocktail bar and lounge.

Rooms 26 en suite (4 fmly) (8 GF) ⊘ in 16 bedrooms S £85-£110;
D £120-£190 **Facilities** ✍ Wi-fi in bedrooms Xmas New Year
Parking 100 **Notes** LB

★★★ 75% @@ HOTEL
Mytton & Mermaid
Atcham SY5 6QG
☎ 01743 761220 ▤ 01743 761292
e-mail: admin@myttonandmermaid.co.uk
web: www.myttonandmermaid.co.uk
Dir: *from Shrewsbury over old bridge in Atcham. Hotel opposite
main entrance to Attingham Park*
PETS: Bedrooms (GF) unattended **Charges** £10 per night
Grounds accessible disp bin **Facilities** food bowl water bowl
cage storage walks info vet info **On Request** fridge access
Convenient for Shrewsbury, this ivy-clad former coaching inn enjoys a
pleasant location beside the River Severn. Some bedrooms, including
family suites, are in a converted stable block adjacent to the hotel.

There is a large lounge bar, a comfortable lounge, and a brasserie that
has gained a well-deserved local reputation for the quality of its food.

Rooms 11 en suite 7 annexe en suite (1 fmly) ⊘ in all bedrooms
S £80-£85; D £100-£160 (incl. bkfst)✷ **Facilities** Fishing Wi-fi in
bedrooms ♫ New Year **Parking** 50 **Notes** Closed 25 Dec

★★ 64% HOTEL
Lion & Pheasant
49-50 Wyle Cop SY1 1XJ
☎ 01743 236288 ▤ 01743 244475
e-mail: lionandpheasant@aol.com
PETS: Bedrooms unattended **Charges** £5 per night
Located close to The English Bridge and within easy walking distance of
historic centre, this traditional coaching hotel provides a range of
bedrooms some of which are situated in a new extension. Public areas
include a cottage style restaurant, a café bar and a cosy foyer lounge.

Rooms 27 rms (25 en suite) S £35-£45; D £60-£70 (incl. bkfst)✷
Parking 22 **Notes** Closed Xmas

▶▶▶▶ **Oxon Hall Touring Park** *(SJ455138)*
Welshpool Rd SY3 5FB
☎ 01743 340868 ▤ 01743 340869
e-mail: oxon@morris-leisure.co.uk
web: www.morris-leisure.co.uk
Dir: *Leave A5 ring road at junct with A458. Park shares entrance
with 'Oxon Park & Ride'*
PETS: Charges £1 per night **Public areas Exercise area** on site 2
dog walks & in 100mtrs **Facilities** on site shop food food bowl
water bowl dog chews cat treats dog scoop/disp bags leads
washing facs walks info vet info **Other** prior notice required max
2 dogs per pitch
Open all year Booking advisable high season Last arrival
21.00hrs
A delightful park with quality facilities, and a choice of grass and
fully-serviced pitches. An adults-only section is very popular with those
wanting a peaceful holiday, and there is an inviting patio area next to
reception and the shop, overlooking a small lake. This site is ideally
located for visiting Shrewsbury and the surrounding countryside, and
there is always a warm welcome here. A 15-acre site with 124 touring
pitches, 72 hardstandings and 42 statics.

ENGLAND

TELFORD

MAP 07 SJ60

★★★★ BED & BREAKFAST
Avenue Farm
Uppington TF6 5HW
☎ 01952 740253 & 07711 219453 📄 01952 740401
e-mail: jones@avenuefarm.fsnet.co.uk
web: www.virtual-shropshire.co.uk/avenuefarm
Dir: *M54 junct 7, B5061 for Atcham, 2nd left signed Uppington.
Right after sawmill, farm 400yds on right*

PETS: **Bedrooms Sep Accom** kennels **Stables** on site
Charges £5 per night **Grounds** accessible on leads
Exercise area 200yds **Facilities** washing facs vet info
On Request fridge access torch **Resident Pets:** Baloo (Labrador),
Spike (Lucas Terrier), Rosie (cat)

This impressive, well-proportioned house stands within immaculate
mature gardens in the hamlet of Uppington. Quality furnishings and
décor highlight the many original features, and the bedrooms are
homely. A comfortable sitting room is also available.

Rooms 3 en suite (1 fmly) ⊗ S £30-£35; D £55-£60✳ **Facilities** TV2B
tea/coffee TVL Riding **Parking** 4 **Notes** ⊗ Closed Xmas ☺

★★★★ BED & BREAKFAST
Church Farm
Wrockwardine Village, Wellington TF6 5DG
☎ 01952 244917 📄 01952 244917
e-mail: jo@churchfarm.freeserve.co.uk
Dir: *In village centre opp church.*

PETS: **Bedrooms** (GF) **Charges** £5 per night charge for damage
Public areas except dining room on leads **Grounds** accessible
on leads **Facilities** walks info vet info **On Request** fridge access
torch towels **Restrictions** Telephone for details
Resident Pets: Heidi & Lottie (Miniature Schnauzers), Ginger Bits
(cat)

This impressive Grade II listed house is opposite the village church in
the pretty rural community of Wrockwardine. Original features include
exposed beams, flagstone floors and open fireplaces. Bedrooms are
homely and thoughtfully furnished, a spacious lounge is available, and
the elegant dining room is the setting for memorable breakfasts.

Rooms 4 rms (3 en suite) 1 annexe en suite (1 fmly) (2 GF) S £32-£45;
D £52-£60✳ **Facilities** TVB tea/coffee Cen ht TVL **Parking** 10
Notes LB No children 10yrs

TELFORD SERVICE
AREA (M54)

MAP 07 SJ70

BUDGET HOTEL
Days Inn Telford
Telford Services, Priorslee Rd TF11 8TG
☎ 01952 238400 📄 01952 238410
e-mail: telford.hotel@welcomebreak.co.uk
web: www.daysinn.com
Dir: *M54 junct 4*

PETS: **Bedrooms Grounds** accessible

This modern building offers accommodation in smart, spacious and
well-equipped bedrooms, suitable for families and business travellers,
and all with en suite bathrooms. Continental breakfast is available and
other refreshments may be taken at the nearby family restaurant. For
further details see the Hotel Groups page.

Rooms 48 en suite

WENTNOR

MAP 07 SO39

►►► **The Green Caravan Park** *(SO380932)*
SY9 5EF
☎ 01588 650605
e-mail: info@greencaravanpark.co.uk
web: www.greencaravanpark.co.uk
Dir: *1m NE of Bishop's Castle on A489. Turn right at brown
tourist sign*

PETS: **Stables** nearby (1.5m) (loose box) **Charges** £1 per dog per
night £6.30 per week **Public areas** on leads at all times
Exercise area on site **Facilities** on site shop food pet scoops
provided free walks info vet info **Resident Pets:** Englebert,
Ronnie, Reggie (Pygmy goats), Sophie & Lily (cats)

Open Etr-Oct Booking advisable BH & wknds Last arrival
21.00hrs Last departure 13.00hrs

A pleasant site in a peaceful setting convenient for visiting Ludlow or
Shrewsbury. The grassy pitches are mainly level. A 15-acre site with 140
touring pitches, 4 hardstandings and 20 statics.

WORFIELD

MAP 07 SO79

★★★ ◉◉◉ HOTEL

Old Vicarage Hotel and Restaurant

Worfield WV15 5JZ

☎ 01746 716497 🖹 01746 716552

e-mail: admin@the-old-vicarage.demon.co.uk

web: www.oldvicarageworfield.com

Dir: *off A454 between Bridgnorth & Wolverhampton, 5m S of Telford's southern business area*

PETS: Bedrooms unattended **Sep Accom** kennel **Charges** £10 per night **Grounds** accessible **Resident Pets:** Oscar (Golden Labrador), Bertie (West Highland Terrier), Smudge (cat)

This delightful property is set in acres of wooded farmland in a quiet and peaceful area of Shropshire. Service is friendly and helpful, and customer care is one the many strengths of this charming small hotel. The well-equipped bedrooms are individually appointed, and thoughtfully and luxuriously furnished. The lounge and conservatory are the perfect places to enjoy a pre-dinner drink or the complimentary afternoon tea. The restaurant is a joy, serving award-winning modern British cuisine in elegant surroundings.

Rooms 10 en suite 4 annexe en suite (1 fmly) (2 GF) ⊘ in all bedrooms S £85-£115; D £99.50-£180 (incl. bkfst) **Facilities** 🏊 Wi-fi available New Year **Parking** 30 **Notes** LB

SOMERSET

BATH

MAP 03 ST76

★★★ 85% ◉ HOTEL

Best Western Cliffe

Cliffe Dr, Crowe Hill, Limpley Stoke BA2 7FY

☎ 01225 723226 🖹 01225 723871

e-mail: cliffe@bestwestern.co.uk

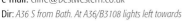

Dir: *A36 S from Bath. At A36/B3108 lights left towards Bradford-on-Avon, 0.5m. Right before bridge through village, hotel on right*

PETS: Bedrooms (GF) **Charges** £8 per night charge for damage **Public areas** except food areas on leads **Grounds** accessible on leads **Facilities** water bowl walks info vet info **On Request** fridge access torch towels

With stunning countryside views, this attractive country house is just a short drive from the City of Bath. Bedrooms vary in size and style but are well equipped; several are particularly spacious and a number of rooms are on the ground floor. The restaurant overlooks the well-tended garden and offers a tempting selection of carefully prepared dishes. Wi-fi is available throughout.

Rooms 8 en suite 3 annexe en suite (2 fmly) (4 GF) ⊘ in 5 bedrooms **Facilities** STV ⌇ Wi-fi available Xmas New Year **Parking** 20

★★★ 73% HOTEL

Pratts

South Pde BA2 4AB

☎ 01225 460441 🖹 01225 448807

e-mail: pratts@forestdale.com

web: www.forestdale.com

Dir: *A46 into city centre. Left at 1st lights (Curfew Pub), right at next lights. 2nd exit at next rdbt, right at lights, left at next lights, 1st left into South Pde*

PETS: Bedrooms Charges £7.50 per night

Part of a Georgian terrace, this long-established and popular hotel is situated close to the city centre. Public rooms and bedrooms retain original features to complement the Georgian surroundings. The ground-floor day rooms include two lounges, a writing room and a popular bar and restaurant.

Rooms 46 en suite (2 fmly) ⊘ in 15 bedrooms **Facilities** STV Wi-fi available **Services** Lift

★★★★ GUEST ACCOMMODATION

Eagle House

Church St, Bathford BA1 7RS

☎ 01225 859946 🖹 01225 859430

e-mail: jonap@eagleho.demon.co.uk

web: www.eaglehouse.co.uk

Dir: *Off A363 onto Church St*

PETS: Bedrooms Stables nearby (2m) **Charges** £3.50 per dog per night **Public areas Grounds** accessible disp bin **Exercise area** 300yds **Facilities** water bowl cage storage walks info vet info **On Request** fridge access torch towels **Resident Pets:** Aquilla (Labrador), Inka (cat), Twitch (rabbit)

Set in attractive gardens, this delightful Georgian guest house is pleasantly located on the outskirts of the city. Bedrooms are individually styled, and each has a thoughtful range of extra facilities. The impressive lounge is adorned with attractive pictures, and the dining room has views of the grounds and tennis court.

Rooms 5 en suite 2 annexe en suite (2 fmly) (2 GF) S £44-£68; D £62-£104✳ **Facilities** TV8B tea/coffee Direct dial from bedrooms Cen ht 🕉 🏊 **Parking** 10 **Notes** LB Closed 12 Dec-8 Jan

ENGLAND

BATH CONTINUED

★★★★ GUEST ACCOMMODATION
Marlborough House
1 Marlborough Ln BA1 2NQ
☎ 01225 318175 📠 01225 466127
e-mail: mars@manque.dircon.co.uk
web: www.marlborough-house.net
Dir: *450yds W of city centre, on junct A4*
PETS: Bedrooms Charges £5 per night **Public areas**
Exercise area 2 min walk **Facilities** water bowl walks info vet
info

This elegant house, situated opposite Royal Victoria Park, is convenient
for the city centre and close to the Royal Crescent. Some original
features remain and the establishment is filled with period furniture.
The atmosphere is relaxed, and service is attentive and friendly.
Bedrooms offer a range of considerate extras. Food here is totally
vegetarian and organic; the breakfast menu features house specialities,
ensuring that breakfast is interesting and memorable.
Rooms 6 en suite (2 fmly) (1 GF) ⊗ S £85-£95; D £95-£130
Facilities TVB tea/coffee Direct dial from bedrooms Cen ht Wi-fi available
Parking 3 **Notes** LB Closed 24-25 Dec

►►►► Newton Mill Caravan and Camping
Park *(ST715649)*
Newton Rd BA2 9JF
☎ 01225 333909
e-mail: newtonmill@hotmail.com
web: www.campinginbath.co.uk
Dir: *From Bath W on A4 to A39 rdbt, immediate left, site 1m on
left*
PETS: Charges Public areas except restaurant, bar & shop
Exercise area on site **Facilities** on site shop food vet info
Other prior notice required
Open all year Booking advisable BHs & Jul-Aug Last arrival
21.00hrs Last departure noon
An attractive, high quality park set in a sheltered valley and surrounded
by woodland, with a stream running through. It offers excellent toilet
facilities with private cubicles and rooms, and there is an appealing

restaurant and bar offering a wide choice of menus throughout the
year. The city is easily accessible by bus or via the Bristol to Bath cycle
path. A 42-acre site with 195 touring pitches, 85 hardstandings.

BAWDRIP MAP 03 ST33

►►► The Fairways International
Touring C & C Park *(ST349402)*
Bath Rd TA7 8PP
☎ 01278 685569 📠 01278 685569
e-mail: fairwaysint@btinternet.com
web: www.fairwaysint.btinternet.co.uk
Dir: *A39 onto B3141, 100yds on right*
PETS: Charges £1 per night £6 per week **Public areas**
Exercise area on site **Facilities** on site shop disp bags washing
facs walks info vet info
Open Mar-mid Nov Booking advisable Etr, Mayday, Whitsun,
summer hols & Nov Last arrival 22.00hrs Last departure
22.00hrs
This family orientated site is well positioned for visiting the many
attractions in the area including Burnham-on-Sea, Weston-Super-Mare
and Glastonbury. The park also makes a convenient overnight stop off
the M5. A 5.75-acre site with 200 touring pitches.

BREAN MAP 03 ST25

Warren Farm Holiday Centre
(ST297564)
Brean Sands TA8 2RP
☎ 01278 751227
e-mail: enquiries@warren-farm.co.uk
web: www.warren-farm.co.uk
Dir: *M5 junct 22 onto B3140 through Burnham-on-Sea to Berrow
and Brean. Centre 1.5m past Brean Leisure Park*
PETS: Public areas except Field 6, Sunnyside & buildings
Exercise area on site farm walk beach 100mtrs **Facilities** on site
shop food food bowl water bowl litter tray etc dog scoop/disp
bags walks info vet info **Other** prior notice required
Open Apr-Oct Booking advisable BH's & school hols Last
arrival 20.00hrs Last departure noon
A large family-run holiday park close to the beach, divided into several
fields each with its own designated facilities. Pitches are spacious and
level, and enjoy panoramic views of the Mendip Hills and Brean Down.
A bar and restaurant are part of the complex, which provide
entertainment for all the family, and there is also separate
entertainment for children. A 100-acre site with 575 touring pitches and
800 statics.

Notes No commerical vehicles

►►►► Northam Farm Caravan & Touring Park *(ST299556)*

TA8 2SE

☎ 01278 751244 📄 01278 751150

e-mail: enquiries@northamfarm.co.uk

web: www.northamfarm.co.uk

Dir: *From M5 junct 22 to Burnham-on-Sea. In Brean, Northam Farm on right 0.5m past Brean leisure park*

PETS: Public areas on leads **Exercise area** on site beach 600yds **Facilities** on site shop food food bowl water bowl dog chews disp bags washing facs walks info vet info **Other** prior notice required

Open Mar-Oct (rs Mar & Oct shop/cafe/takeaway open limited hours) Booking advisable bank & school hols Last arrival 21.00hrs Last departure 10.30hrs

An attractive site a short walk from the sea with game, coarse fishing and sea fishing close by. The quality park also has lots of children's play areas, and is near a long sandy beach. It also runs the Seagull Inn about 600yds away, which includes a restaurant and entertainment. A 30-acre site with 350 touring pitches, 156 hardstandings and 112 statics.

Notes Families & couples only, no motorcycles or commercial vans

---

BRIDGETOWN   MAP 03 SS93

►►► Exe Valley Caravan Site *(SS923333)*

Mill House TA22 9JR

☎ 01643 851432

e-mail: paul@paulmatt.fsnet.co.uk

web: www.exevalleycamping.co.uk

Dir: *Take A396 (Tiverton to Minehead road). Turn W in centre of Bridgetown, site 40yds on right*

PETS: Stables nearby (3m) **Charges** £1 per night £6 per week **Public areas Exercise area** on site riverside walks & nearby bridleway **Facilities** on site shop food free disposal bags walks info vet info space for loose box **Restrictions** Telephone for details

Open 14 Mar-13 Oct Booking advisable at all times Last arrival 22.00hrs

Set in the Exmoor National Park, this 'adults only' park occupies an enchanting, peaceful spot in a wooded valley alongside the River Exe. There is free fly fishing, and an abundance of wildlife, with excellent walks directly from the park. The inn opposite serves lunchtime and evening meals. A 4-acre site with 50 touring pitches, 10 hardstandings.

Notes Adults only

BURTLE   MAP 03 ST34

► Orchard Camping *(ST397434)*

Ye Olde Burtle Inn, Catcott Rd TA7 8NG

☎ 01278 722269 & 722123 📄 01278 722269

e-mail: food@theinn.eu

web: www.theinn.eu

Dir: *From M5 junct 23 onto A39, approx 4m turn left onto unclass road to Burtle, site by pub in village centre*

PETS: Stables adjacent (loose box) **Public areas** except restaurant **Exercise area** surrounding open countryside **Facilities** food bowl if required water bowl washing facs walks info vet info **Other** prior notice required

Open all year Booking advisable BH & peak season Last arrival anytime

A simple campsite set in an orchard at the rear of a lovely 17th-century family inn in the heart of the Somerset Levels. The restaurant offers a wide range of meals, and breakfast can be pre-ordered by campers. A shower and disabled toilet have been added and these facilities are available to campers outside pub opening hours. A 0.75-acre site with 30 touring pitches.

Notes no cars by tents

CHARD   MAP 03 ST30

★ ★ ★ GUEST HOUSE

Watermead

83 High St TA20 1QT

☎ 01460 62834 📄 01460 67448

e-mail: trudy@watermeadguesthouse.co.uk

web: www.watermeadguesthouse.co.uk

Dir: *On A30 in town centre*

PETS: Bedrooms Charges £5 per night charge for damage **Public areas** except dining room on leads **Grounds** accessible disp bin **Exercise area** 100mtrs **Facilities** water bowl dog scoop/disp bags leads washing facs cage storage walks info vet info **On Request** torch towels **Resident Pets:** Jasper (Black Labrador), Charlie (cat)

You will feel at home at this family-run house, a smart accommodation in a convenient location. Hearty breakfasts are served in the dining room overlooking the garden. Bedrooms are neat, and the spacious, self-contained suite is popular with families. Free Wi-fi access is available.

Rooms 9 rms (6 en suite) 1 annexe en suite (1 fmly) S £29; D £56 **Facilities** TVB tea/coffee Cen ht TVL Wi-fi available **Parking** 10 **Notes** LB No coaches

ENGLAND

CHARD CONTINUED

▶▶▶ 84% **Alpine Grove Touring Park**

(ST342071)

Forton TA20 4HD

☎ 01460 63479 📠 01460 63479

e-mail: stay@alpinegrovetouringpark.com

web: www.alpinegrovetouringpark.com

Dir: *Turn off A30 between Chard & Crewkerne towards Cricket St Thomas, follow signs. Park 2m on right*

PETS: Sep Accom single kennel for dog sitting **Stables** adjacent (loose box) **Charges** £3 per night £21 per week **Public areas** on leads except play area **Exercise area** on site woodland trail bridleway **Facilities** on site shop dog scoop/disp bags washing facs walks info vet info **Other** prior notice required
Resident Pets: Freddie (American Cocker Spaniel), Murphy (Springer/Collie cross)

Open 1 wk before Etr-Sep Booking advisable BH & Jul-Aug Last arrival 21.00hrs Last departure 11.00hrs

A warm welcome awaits at this attractive, quiet wooded park with both hardstandings and grass pitches, close to Cricket St Thomas Wildlife Park. The newly refurbished facilities are kept spotlessly clean. Families particularly enjoy the small swimming pool and terrace in summer. Log cabins are also available for hire on this park. An 8.5-acre site with 40 touring pitches, 15 hardstandings.

Notes no open fires

CHEDDAR MAP 03 ST45

▶▶▶▶▶ **Broadway House Holiday Caravan & Camping Park**

(ST448547)

Axbridge Rd BS27 3DB

☎ 01934 742610 📠 01934 744950

e-mail: info@broadwayhouse.uk.com

web: www.broadwayhouse.uk.com

Dir: *From M5 junct 22 follow signs to Cheddar Gorge & Caves (8m). Park midway between Cheddar & Axbridge on A371*

PETS: Charges £1 per night **Public areas** except pool **Exercise area** on site woods **Facilities** on site shop food food bowl water bowl dog chews cat treats dog scoop/disp bags leads walks info vet info **Other** prior notice required **Restrictions** no Rottweilers, Pit Bulls, Rhodesian Ridgeback or Akitas

Open Mar-mid Nov (rs Mar-end May & Oct-Nov bar & pool closed, limited shop hours) Booking advisable BH & end Jul-Aug Last arrival 23.00hrs Last departure noon

A well-equipped family park on the slopes of the Mendips with an exceptional range of activities for all ages. This is a busy and lively park in the main holiday periods, but can be quiet and peaceful off-peak. Broadway has its own activity centre based on the site, providing archery, shooting, climbing, caving, ballooning and much more. The slightly-terraced pitches face south, and are backed by the Mendips. A 30-acre site with 200 touring pitches, 60 hardstandings and 37 statics.

Notes Children to be supervised at all times

CLEVEDON MAP 03 ST47

★★★ 73% HOTEL

Best Western Walton Park

Wellington Ter BS21 7BL

☎ 01275 874253 📠 01275 343577

e-mail: waltonpark@aol.com

Dir: *M5 junct 20, signs for seafront. Stay on coast road, past pier into Wellington Terrace, hotel on left*

PETS: Bedrooms Charges £7 per night **Grounds** accessible on leads **Facilities** pet sitting dog walking walks info vet info **On Request** torch towels **Resident Pets:** Charlie (cat)

Quietly located with spectacular views across the Bristol Channel to Wales, this popular Victorian hotel offers a relaxed atmosphere. Bedrooms are well decorated and equipped to meet the demands of both business and leisure guests. A high standard of home-cooked food is served in the comfortable restaurant, and lighter meals are available in the convivial bar at lunchtime.

Rooms 40 en suite (4 fmly) ⊗ in 23 bedrooms S £55-£92; D £92-£115 (incl. bkfst)✳ **Facilities** STV Wi-fi in bedrooms **Services** Lift **Parking** 50 **Notes** LB

CREWKERNE MAP 03 ST40

★★★ GUEST ACCOMMODATION

Manor Farm

Wayford TA18 8QL

☎ 01460 78865 & 0776 7620031 📠 01460 78865

web: www.manorfarm.biz

Dir: *B3165 from Crewkerne to Lyme Regis, 3m in Clapton right onto Dunsham Ln, Manor Farm 0.5m up hill on right*

PETS: Sep Accom kennels **Stables** on site **Public areas Grounds** accessible **Other** pet food on request
Resident Pets: Charlie & Ginger (cats)

Located off the beaten track, this fine Victorian country house has extensive views over Clapton towards the Axe Valley. The comfortably furnished bedrooms are well equipped; front-facing rooms enjoy splendid views. Breakfast is served at separate tables in the dining room, and a spacious lounge is also provided.

Rooms 4 en suite 1 annexe en suite ⊗ S £40; D £65-£70✳ **Facilities** STV TV4B tea/coffee Cen ht TVL Fishing Riding **Parking** 14 **Notes** ⊗

DULVERTON   MAP 03 SS92

★★ 65% HOTEL
Lion
Bank Square TA22 9BU

☎ 01398 324437 📄 01398 323980

e-mail: info@lionhoteldulverton.com

Dir: M5 junct 27, A361, then A396 to Dulverton

PETS: Bedrooms sign **Stables** nearby (3m) **Charges** £5 per dog per night £15 per dog per week charge for damage
Public areas except dining room **Exercise area** 10yds
Facilities food (pre-bookable) food bowl water bowl bedding dog chews cat treats feeding mat litter tray leads cage storage walks info vet info **On Request** fridge access torch towels
Resident Pets: Charlie (Labrador), Tilly (Tibetan Terrier), 4 cats

This long established inn has been welcoming guests for many years with old-fashioned hospitality always on offer. Located in the centre of Dulverton, this is an ideal base from which to explore Exmoor National Park. The traditional bar is popular with locals and visitors alike, offering a variety of local real ales and quality meals. Bedrooms are soundly appointed with both four-poster and family rooms available.

Rooms 14 en suite (1 fmly) ⊗ in all bedrooms S fr £50; D fr £78 (incl. bkfst)☀ **Facilities** Xmas New Year **Parking** 6

★★★★ GUEST ACCOMMODATION
Threadneedle
EX16 9JH

☎ 01398 341598

e-mail: info@threadneedlecottage.co.uk

web: www.threadneedlecottage.co.uk

Dir: On Devon/Somerset border just off B3227 between Oldways End & East Anstey

PETS: Bedrooms Stables on site **Charges** charge for damage
Public areas on leads **Grounds** accessible disp bin
Exercise area 40yds **Facilities** food (pre-bookable) food bowl water bowl bedding dog chews dog scoop/disp bags leads washing facs cage storage walks info vet info **On Request** fridge access torch towels **Resident Pets:** Scamp & Charlie (Shetland Sheepdogs), Jack (horse)

Situated on the edge of Exmoor near Dulverton, Threadneedle is built in the style of a Devon longhouse. The spacious, well-appointed family home offers comfortable, en suite accommodation. The light airy dining room overlooks the garden and surrounding countryside.

Rooms 2 en suite (1 fmly) S fr £37; D £60-£70☀ **Facilities** TVB tea/coffee Cen ht **Parking** 12 **Notes** LB ⊗

DUNSTER   MAP 03 SS94

★★★ 73% ⑩ HOTEL
The Luttrell Arms Hotel
High St TA24 6SG

☎ 01643 821555 📄 01643 821567

e-mail: info@luttrellarms.fsnet.co.uk

web: www.luttrellarms.co.uk/main.htm

Dir: A39/A396 S toward Tiverton. Hotel on left opposite Yarn Market

PETS: Bedrooms unattended **Charges** £5 for dogs per night
Public areas Exercise area nearby

Occupying an enviable position on the high street, this 15th-century hotel looks up to the town's famous castle. Beautifully renovated and decorated, high levels of comfort can be found throughout. Some of the spacious bedrooms have four-poster beds. The warm and friendly staff provide attentive service within a relaxed atmosphere.

Rooms 28 en suite (3 fmly) ⊗ in all bedrooms S £65-£115; D £126-£160 (incl. bkfst) **Facilities** Exmoor safaris, Historic tours, Walking tours New Year **Notes** LB

EXFORD   MAP 03 SS83

★★★ 74% ⑩⑩ HOTEL
Crown
TA24 7PP

☎ 01643 831554 📄 01643 831665

e-mail: info@crownhotelexmoor.co.uk

web: www.crownhotelexmoor.co.uk

Dir: M5 junct 25, follow Taunton signs. Take A358 out of Taunton, then B3224 via Wheddon Cross into Exford

PETS: Bedrooms unattended **Sep Accom** stables for dogs
Stables on site **Charges** £7.50 up to 5 days £15 over 5 days charge for damage **Public areas** except restaurant
Grounds accessible **Exercise area** 25mtrs **Facilities** water bowl dog chews washing facs walks info vet info **On Request** fridge access torch towels **Resident Pets:** Benson & Oscar (Patterdale Terriers)

Guest comfort is certainly the hallmark here. Afternoon tea is served in the lounge beside a roaring fire and tempting menus in the bar and

CONTINUED

EXFORD CONTINUED

restaurant are all part of the charm of this delightful old coaching inn that specialises in breaks for shooting and other country sports. Bedrooms retain a traditional style yet offer a range of modern comforts and facilities, many with views of this pretty moorland village.

Crown

Rooms 17 en suite (3 fmly) ⊘ in 6 bedrooms S £67.50; D £105-£135 (incl. bkfst)✳ **Facilities** Riding Xmas New Year **Parking** 30 **Notes** LB

►► Westermill Farm *(SS825398)*

TA24 7NJ

☎ 01643 831238 📄 01643 831216

e-mail: aa@westermill.com

web: www.westermill.com

Dir: *Leave Exford on Porlock road. After 0.25m fork left, continue along valley until 'Westermill' sign on tree. Take left fork*

PETS: Stables on site **Charges** £2 dogs per night (horses by arrangment) **Public areas Exercise area** on site farmland walks **Facilities** on site shop walks info vet info **Restrictions** Telephone for details **Resident Pets:** Terriers, Labradors, Sheepdogs, cat. Cattle, sheep, pigs, chickens on farm

Open all year (rs Nov-May larger toilet block & shop closed) Booking advisable Spring bank hol & Jul-Aug

An idyllic site for peace and quiet, in a sheltered valley in the heart of Exmoor, which has won awards for conservation. Four waymarked walks over 500 acre working farm. Only approach from Exford (other approaches difficult). A 6-acre site with 60 touring pitches.

Notes ☺

GLASTONBURY MAP 03 ST53

►►►► Isle of Avalon Touring Caravan Park *(ST494397)*

Godney Rd BA6 9AF

☎ 01458 833618 📄 01458 833618

Dir: *M5 junct 23, A39 to outskirts of Glastonbury, 2nd exit signed Wells at B&Q rdbt, straight over next rdbt, 1st exit at 3rd rdbt (B3151), 200yds right*

PETS: Charges £1.50 per night **Public areas Exercise area** on site **Facilities** on site shop food food bowl water bowl dog chews cat treats disp bags leads washing facs walks info vet info **Other** prior notice required

Open all year Booking advisable mid Jul-mid Aug Last arrival 21.00hrs Last departure 11.00hrs

A popular site on the south side of this historic town and within easy walking distance of the town centre. This level park offers a quiet environment in which to stay and explore the many local attractions including the Tor, Wells, Wookey Hole and Clark's Village. An 8-acre site with 120 touring pitches, 70 hardstandings.

GORDANO SERVICE AREA MAP 03 ST57
(M5)

BUDGET HOTEL

Days Inn Bristol West

BS20 7XJ

☎ 01275 373709 & 373624 📄 01275 374104

e-mail: gordano.hotel@welcomebreak.co.uk

web: www.daysinn.com

Dir: *M5 junct 19, follow signs for Gordano services*

PETS: Bedrooms

This modern building offers accommodation in smart, spacious and well-equipped bedrooms, suitable for families and business travellers, and all with en suite bathrooms. Continental breakfast is available and other refreshments may be taken at the nearby family restaurant. For further details see the Hotel Groups page.

Rooms 60 en suite

HIGHBRIDGE MAP 03 ST34

★★ 68% SMALL HOTEL
Sundowner
74 Main Rd, West Huntspill TA9 3QU
☎ 01278 784766 📄 01278 794133
e-mail: runnalls@msn.com
Dir: *from M5 junct 23, 3m N on A38*
PETS: Bedrooms Public areas except restaurant on leads
Grounds accessible on leads **Exercise area** adjacent bridle path
Restrictions small dogs only

Friendly service and an informal atmosphere are just two of the
highlights of this small hotel. The open-plan lounge/bar is a
comfortable, homely area in which to relax after a busy day exploring
the area or working in the locality. An extensive menu, featuring freshly
cooked, imaginative dishes, is offered in the popular restaurant.

Rooms 8 en suite (1 fmly) S £55-£60; D £70-£75 (incl. bkfst) **Parking** 18
Notes Closed 26-31 Dec & 1 Jan RS 25-Dec

HOLCOMBE MAP 03 ST64

★★ 74% HOTEL
The Ring O' Roses
Stratton Rd BA3 5EB
☎ 01761 232478 📄 01761 233737
e-mail: ringorosesholcombe@tesco.net
Dir: *A367 to Stratton on The Fosse, take hidden left turn opposite
Downside Abbey, signed Holcombe. Next right, hotel 1.5m on left*
PETS: Please telephone for details

With views of Downside Abbey in the distance, this inn dates back to
the 16th century. The attentive owners and pleasant staff create a
friendly and relaxed atmosphere. Bedrooms are individually furnished
and very comfortable. Real ales are served in the bar, which is
open-plan with the attractive split-level restaurant.

Rooms 8 en suite ⊘ in all bedrooms **Parking** 35 **Notes** LB

HOLFORD MAP 03 ST14

★★ 79% ⊛ HOTEL
Combe House
TA5 1RZ
☎ 01278 741382 📄 01278 741322
e-mail: enquiries@combehouse.co.uk
web: www.combehouse.co.uk
Dir: *from A39 W left in Holford then left at T-junct. Left at fork,
0.25m to Holford Combe*
PETS: Bedrooms (GF) unattended **Charges** £3 per night charge
for damage **Public areas** bar only **Grounds** accessible disp bin
Facilities food (pre-bookable) food bowl water bowl leads
washing facs cage storage walks info vet info **On Request** fridge
access torch towels **Resident Pets:** Roger & Flo (Springer
Spaniel/Collie cross)

Once a tannery, this 17th-century longhouse is peacefully situated in
lovely grounds, and provides an ideal retreat for walking in the
Quantock Hills. Bedrooms are traditional in style and the public rooms
include a choice of sitting areas. There is a focus on home cooking in
the dining room.

Rooms 17 en suite 1 annexe en suite (3 fmly) (1 GF) ⊘ in all bedrooms
S £70-£75; D £115-£140 (incl. bkfst) **Facilities** STV 🕙 ⅃ Gym 🏊 Wi-fi
available Sauna Xmas **Parking** 43 **Notes** LB

HUNSTRETE — MAP 03 ST66

★★★ 82% ◉◉ COUNTRY HOUSE HOTEL

Hunstrete House

von Essen hotels
A PRIVATE COLLECTION
www.vonessenhotels.com

BS39 4NS

☎ 01761 490490 📠 01761 490732

e-mail: reception@hunstretehouse.co.uk

web: www.vonessenhotels.co.uk

Dir: from Bath take A4 to Bristol. At Globe Inn rdbt 2nd left onto A368 to Wells. 1m after Marksbury turn right for Hunstrete village. Hotel next left

PETS: Bedrooms (GF) Charges £10 per night charge for damage Grounds accessible Exercise area adjacent Facilities walks info vet info

This delightful Georgian house enjoys a stunning setting in 92 acres of deer park and woodland on the edge of the Mendip Hills. Elegant bedrooms in the main building and coach house are both spacious and comfortable. Public areas feature antiques, paintings and fine china. The restaurant enjoys a well-deserved reputation for fine food and utilises much home-grown produce.

Rooms 25 en suite (2 fmly) (8 GF) ⊘ in all bedrooms S £135; D £205-£300 (incl. bkfst)✳ Facilities STV ↘ ♨ ♨ Xmas New Year Parking 50 Notes LB

ILMINSTER — MAP 03 ST31

★★★ 77% HOTEL

Best Western Shrubbery

Best Western

TA19 9AR

☎ 01460 52108 📠 01460 53660

e-mail: stuart@shrubberyhotel.com

web: www.shrubberyhotel.com

Dir: 0.5m from A303 towards Ilminster town centre

PETS: Bedrooms (GF) unattended Public areas except restaurant on leads Grounds accessible on leads Facilities food bowl water bowl food by prior arrangement & chargeable walks info vet info On Request fridge access Resident Pets: Oscar (Collie)

Set in attractive terraced gardens, the Shrubbery is a well established hotel in this small town. Bedrooms are well equipped and bright, they include three ground-floor rooms and impressive executive rooms. Bar meals or full meals are available in the bar, lounges and restaurant. Additional facilities include a range of function rooms.

Rooms 21 en suite (3 fmly) S £75-£90; D £80-£130 (incl. bkfst)✳ Facilities STV ↘ ♨ Wi-fi available ♪ Xmas New Year Parking 100 Notes LB

LANGPORT — MAP 03 ST42

▶▶▶ **Thorney Lakes Caravan Park** *(ST430237)*

Thorney Lakes, Muchelney TA10 0DW

☎ 01458 250811

web: www.thorneylakes.co.uk

Dir: From A303 at Podimore rdbt take A372 to Langport. At Huish Episcopi Church turn left for Muchelney. In 100yds left (signed Muchelney & Crewkerne). Site 300yds after John Leach Pottery

PETS: Stables on site (loose box) Public areas Exercise area on site 2 miles around farm and site Facilities vet info

Open Apr-Oct Booking advisable

A small, basic but very attractive park set in a cider apple orchard, with coarse fishing in the three well-stocked on-site lakes. The famous John Leach pottery shop is nearby. A 6-acre site with 36 touring pitches.

Notes ⊛

MINEHEAD — MAP 03 SS94

▶▶▶ **Minehead & Exmoor Caravan & Camping Site** *(SS950457)*

Porlock Rd TA24 8SW

☎ 01643 703074

Dir: 1m W of Minehead centre, close to A39

PETS: Public areas Facilities walks info vet info Other on-site vet certain days.

Open all year (rs Nov-Feb reduced no. of pitches) Booking advisable BH & Jul-Aug Last arrival 22.00hrs Last departure noon

A small terraced park on the edge of Exmoor, spread over five paddocks and screened by the mature trees that surround it. The level pitches provide a comfortable space for each unit on this family-run park. There is a laundrette in nearby Minehead. A 3-acre site with 50 touring pitches, 8 hardstandings.

Notes ⊛

▶▶▶ **Minehead Camping & Caravanning Club Site** *(SS958471)*

Hill Rd, North Hill TA24 5LB

☎ 01643 704138

web: www.campingandcaravanningclub.co.uk/minehead

Dir: From A39 towards town centre. In main street turn opposite W H Smith to Blenheim Rd. Left in 50yds (by pub) into Martlet Rd. Up hill, site on right

PETS: Public areas except buildings Facilities walks info vet info Other prior notice required

Open 28 Apr-29 Sep Booking advisable BH & peak periods Last arrival 21.00hrs Last departure noon

A secluded site on a hilltop with glorious views of the Bristol Channel and the Quantocks. Good clean facilities plus a laundry and information room make this a popular choice for those seeking an isolated holiday. A 3.75-acre site with 60 touring pitches, 10 hardstandings.

Notes site gates will be closed 23:00-07:00

MUCHELNEY   MAP 03 ST42

►►► Muchelney Caravan & Camping Site

(ST429249)

Abbey Farm TA10 0DQ

☎ 01458 250112 & 07881 524426 📄 01458 250112

Dir: *From A303 at Podimore rdbt take A372 towards Langport. At church in Huish Episcopi follow Muchelney Abbey sign. In Muchelney left at village cross. Site in 50mtrs*

PETS: Facilities space for loose box **Charges** £1.50 for dogs per night **Public areas Exercise area** on site dog walk & in 400yds **Facilities** washing facs vet info **Other** prior notice required **Restrictions** Dogs & cats must be kept on leads

Open all year Booking advisable bank & school hols

This small developing site is situated opposite Muchelney Abbey, an English Heritage property. This quiet and peaceful site will appeal to all lovers of the countryside, and is well positioned for visiting the Somerset Levels. A 3-acre site with 40 touring pitches, 5 hardstandings.

Notes 🐾

NETHER STOWEY   MAP 03 ST13

★★★★★ 🛏 GUEST ACCOMMODATION

Castle of Comfort Country House

TA5 1LE

☎ 01278 741264 📄 01278 741144

e-mail: reception@castle-of-comfort.co.uk

web: www.castle-of-comfort.co.uk

Dir: *On A39 1.3m W of Nether Stowey on left*

PETS: Bedrooms unattended **Sep Accom** kennels **Stables** on site **Public areas** except lounge & restaurant **Grounds** accessible **Exercise area** on site **Resident Pets:** Humbug & Treacle (cats)

Dating in part from the 16th century, this former inn is situated beside the A39 on the northern slopes of the Quantock Hills in an Area of Outstanding Natural Beauty. Bedrooms and bathrooms are well equipped while the public rooms are smart and comfortable. The delightful gardens and a heated swimming pool are available in summer. An imaginative choice of dishes is offered at dinner which makes use of good local produce.

Rooms 5 en suite 1 annexe en suite (1 fmly) (1 GF) ✆ S £40-£88; D £99-£135✱ **Facilities** TVB tea/coffee Direct dial from bedrooms Cen ht Dinner Last d 8pm ⚓ Stabling with access to bridle paths **Parking** 10 **Notes LB** Closed 24 Dec-2 Jan

PORLOCK   MAP 03 SS84

►►►► Porlock Caravan Park *(SS882469)*

TA24 8ND

☎ 01643 862269 📄 01643 862269

e-mail: info@porlockcaravanpark.co.uk

web: www.porlockcaravanpark.co.uk

Dir: *Through village fork right signed Porlock Weir, site on right*

PETS: Charges £1 per night £7 per week **Public areas** except buildings & mature gardens **Exercise area** on site enclosed dog walk & in 100yds **Facilities** walks info vet info **Other** prior notice required organised walks with dogs **Resident Pets:** Sid & Alfie (cats)

Open 15 Mar-Oct Booking advisable Etr, Whit & Jul-Aug Last arrival 22.00hrs Last departure noon

A sheltered touring park in the centre of lovely countryside on the edge of the village, with Exmoor right on the doorstep. The toilet facilities are superb, and there's a popular kitchen area with microwave and freezer. A 3-acre site with 40 touring pitches, 14 hardstandings and 56 statics.

Notes 🔥 no open fires

►►► Burrowhayes Farm Caravan & Camping Site *(SS897460)*

West Luccombe TA24 8HT

☎ 01643 862463

e-mail: info@burrowhayes.co.uk

web: www.burrowhayes.co.uk

Dir: *A39 from Minehead towards Porlock for 5m. Left at Red Post to Horner & West Lucombe, site 0.25m on right, immediately before humpback bridge*

PETS: Stables nearby (2m) **Public areas Exercise area** adjacent woods **Facilities** on site shop food dog scoop/disp bags leads balls walks info vet info **Other** prior notice required

Open 15 Mar-Oct shop closed until Sat before Etr Booking advisable Etr, Spring bank hol & Jul-Aug Last arrival 22.00hrs Last departure noon

A delightful site on the edge of Exmoor, sloping gently down to Horner Water. The farm buildings have been converted into riding stables which offers escorted rides on the moors, and the excellent toilet facilities are housed in timber-clad buildings. There are many walks directly into the countryside. An 8-acre site with 120 touring pitches, 3 hardstandings and 20 statics.

ENGLAND

PRIDDY
MAP 03 ST55

►►►► Cheddar, Mendip Heights C&C Club Site (ST522519)
Townsend BA5 3BP
☎ 01749 870241
web: www.campingandcaravanningclub.co.uk/chedder
Dir: *From A39 take B3135 to Cheddar. After 4.5m turn left. Site 200yds on right*
PETS: **Exercise area** on site dog walk **Facilities** on site shop walks info vet info **Other** prior notice required
Open 06 Mar-15 Nov Booking advisable BH Last arrival 21.00hrs Last departure noon
A gently sloping site set high on the Mendip Hills and surrounded by trees. This excellent site offers good self-catered facilities especially for families, and fresh bread is baked daily. The site is well positioned for visiting local attractions like Cheddar, Wookey Hole, Wells and Glastonbury, and is popular with walkers. A 3.5-acre site with 90 touring pitches, 30 hardstandings and 2 statics.
Notes Site gates will be closed 23:00-07:00

RUDGE
MAP 03 ST85

★★★★ INN
The Full Moon Inn
BA11 2QF
☎ 01373 830936 📠 01373 831366
e-mail: info@thefullmoon.co.uk
Dir: *Off A36 into village centre*
PETS: **Bedrooms** unattended **Charges** £5 per night
Public areas except restaurant **Grounds** accessible on leads disp bin **Exercise area** local walks **Facilities** vet info
This quaint village inn is very popular for its extensive range of food. Most of the modern, well-equipped accommodation is on the ground and first floors of two purpose-built annexes, each having its own lounge for guest use; two rooms have easier access. Other rooms are located in the main house. Facilities include a swimming pool, a function room and skittle alley.
Rooms 16 en suite (2 fmly) (4 GF) **Facilities** STV TVB tea/coffee Direct dial from bedrooms Cen ht TVL Dinner Last d 9.30pm ⓧ Gymnasium
Parking 50

SEDGEMOOR MOTORWAY SERVICE AREA (M5)
MAP 03 ST35

BUDGET HOTEL
Days Inn Sedgemoor

DAYS INN

Sedgemoor BS24 0JL
☎ 01934 750831 📠 01934 750808
e-mail: sedgemoor.hotel@welcomebreak.co.uk
web: www.daysinn.com
Dir: *M5 northbound junct 21/22*
PETS: **Bedrooms** **Grounds** accessible
This modern building offers accommodation in smart, spacious and well-equipped bedrooms, suitable for families and business travellers, and all with en suite bathrooms. Continental breakfast is available and other refreshments may be taken at the nearby family restaurant. For further details see the Hotel Groups page.
Rooms 40 en suite

STANTON DREW
MAP 03 ST56

★★★★ FARM HOUSE
Greenlands (ST597636)
BS39 4ES
☎ 01275 333487 📠 01275 331211 Mrs J Cleverley
Dir: *A37 onto B3130, on right before Stanton Drew Garage*
PETS: **Bedrooms** **Grounds** accessible disp bin
Exercise area adjacent **Facilities** washing facs cage storage walks info vet info **On request** fridge access torch
Resident Pets: Spoof & Magic (Labradors)

Situated near the ancient village of Stanton Drew in the heart of the Chew Valley, Greenlands is convenient for Bristol Airport and Bath, Bristol and Wells. There are comfortable, well-equipped bedrooms and a downstairs lounge, though breakfast is the highlight of any stay here.
Rooms 4 en suite **Facilities** STV TVB tea/coffee Cen ht TVL **Parking** 8
Notes No children 12yrs ⊛

STON EASTON

Ston Easton Park

von Essen hotels
A PRIVATE COLLECTION
www.vonessenhotels.co.uk

BA3 4DF

☎ 01761 241631 📠 01761 241377

e-mail: info@stoneaston.co.uk

web: www.vonessenhotels.co.uk

Dir: *on A37*

PETS: Bedrooms Charges £10 per night **Public areas** except restaurant **Grounds** accessible **Exercise area** on site

Resident Pets: Sorrel (Springer Spaniel), Sweep (Cocker Spaniel)

At the time of going to press, the star classification for this hotel was not confirmed. Please refer to the AA internet site www.theAA.com for current information.

Rooms 19 en suite 3 annexe en suite (2 fmly) (2 GF) ⊘ in all bedrooms **Facilities** ⌣ Fishing ↳ By prior arrangement Archery Clay pigeon shooting Quad bikes Hot air balloon **Parking** 120

TAUNTON

★★★ 71% SMALL HOTEL

Farthings Country House Hotel and Restaurant

Village Rd, Hatch Beauchamp TA3 6SG

☎ 01823 480664 0785 6688 128 📠 01823 481118

e-mail: info@farthingshotel.co.uk

web: www.farthingshotel.com

Dir: *from A358, between Taunton and Ilminster turn into Hatch Beauchamp for hotel in village centre*

PETS: Bedrooms (GF) **Public areas** on leads **Grounds** accessible on leads disp bin **Facilities** food (pre-bookable) food bowl water bowl dog chews dog scoop/disp bags leads washing facs cage storage walks info vet info **On Request** fridge access torch towels **Resident Pets:** Xzina (dog), chickens, geese, ducks

This delightful hotel, set in its own extensive gardens in a peaceful village location, offers comfortable accommodation, combined with all the character and charm of a building dating back over 200 years. The calm atmosphere makes this a great place to relax and unwind. Dinner service is attentive, and menus feature best quality local ingredients prepared and presented with care.

Rooms 11 en suite (1 fmly) (2 GF) ⊘ in all bedrooms S £50-£155; D £60-£175 (incl. bkfst) **Facilities** ↳ Wi-fi available Xmas New Year **Parking** 20 **Notes** LB

★★★★ INN

The Hatch Inn

Village Rd, Hatch Beauchamp TA3 6SG

☎ 01823 480245 📠 01823 481104

e-mail: bagleyjag@aol.com

Dir: *6m SE of Taunton. Off A358 into Hatch Beauchamp*

PETS: Bedrooms unattended **Public areas** except lounge bar **Exercise area** nearby country walks **Facilities** food on request vet info

This village inn caters well for locals and leisure or business guests. The majority of bedrooms are particularly spacious and come with a number of useful extras. Relaxed and friendly service continues through dinner and breakfast, which both use a good selection of carefully prepared ingredients.

Rooms 7 en suite (1 fmly) **Facilities** TVB tea/coffee Cen ht Dinner Last d 8.30pm Pool Table **Parking** 15 **Notes** No coaches

★★★ GUEST ACCOMMODATION

Blorenge House

57 Staple Grove Rd TA1 1DG

☎ 01823 283005 📠 01823 283005

e-mail: enquiries@blorengehouse.co.uk

Dir: *M5 junct 25, towards cricket ground & Morrisons on left, left at lights, right at 2nd lights, house 150yds on left*

PETS: Bedrooms Public areas except dining rooms **Grounds** accessible **Exercise area** 150yds

This fine Victorian property offers spacious accommodation within walking distance of the town centre. The bedrooms (some at ground floor level and some with four-poster beds) are individually furnished and vary in size. A lounge is available, and the garden with outdoor swimming pool is open to guests during daytime hours most days of the week. There is also ample parking.

Rooms 25 rms (20 en suite) (4 fmly) (3 GF) ⊘ in 23 bedrooms **Facilities** TVB tea/coffee Cen ht TVL ↳ **Parking** 25

▶▶▶▶ Cornish Farm Touring Park *(ST235217)*

Shoreditch TA3 7BS

☎ 01823 327746 📠 01823 354946

e-mail: warden@cornishfarm.com

web: www.cornishfarm.com

Dir: *M5 junct 25 towards Taunton. At lights left. 3rd left in Ilminster Road (follow Corfe signs). Right at rdbt, left at next. Right at T-junct, left into Killams Drive, 2nd left into Killams Ave. Follow road over motorway bridge. Site on left, take 2nd entrance*

PETS: Charges 50p per night £3.50 per week **Public areas Exercise area** public footpath adjacent **Facilities** walks info vet info

Open all year Booking advisable BHs & race days Last arrival anytime Last departure noon

CONTINUED

ENGLAND

TAUNTON CONTINUED

This smart park provides really top quality facilities throughout. Although only two miles from Taunton, the park is set in open countryside and is a very convenient base for visiting the many attractions of the area such as Clarks Village, Glastonbury and Cheddar Gorge. A 3.5-acre site with 50 touring pitches, 25 hardstandings.

►►► Holly Bush Park *(ST220162)*

Culmhead TA3 7EA

☎ 01823 421515

e-mail: info@hollybushpark.com

web: www.hollybushpark.com

Dir: *M5 junct 25 towards Taunton. At 1st lights turn left signed Corfe/Taunton Racecourse. 3.5m past Corfe on B3170 turn right at x-rds at top of hill on unclass road towards Wellington. Right at next junct, site 150yds on left*

PETS: Public areas except toilet block, reception **Exercise area** woods 50yds **Facilities** on site shop food bowl water bowl disp bags washing facs walks info vet info **Other** prior notice required **Restrictions** Telephone for details **Resident Pets:** Vada, Leila, Tie (Lurchers), Star, Lucas, Holly (Whippets), rabbits

Open all year Booking advisable BH & high season Last arrival 21.00hrs Last departure 11.00hrs

An immaculate little park set in an orchard in attractive countryside, with easy access to Wellington and Taunton. The friendly owners are welcoming and keen to help, and keep the facilities in good order. A 2-acre site with 40 touring pitches, 5 hardstandings.

WELLINGTON

MAP 03 ST12

★★★ ◉◉ COUNTRY HOUSE HOTEL

Bindon Country House Hotel & Restaurant

PRIDE OF BRITAIN HOTELS

Langford Budville TA21 0RU

☎ 01823 400070 ▤ 01823 400071

e-mail: stay@bindon.com

web: www.bindon.com

Dir: *from Wellington B3187 to Langford Budville, through village, right towards Wiveliscombe, right at junct, pass Bindon Farm, right after 450yds*

PETS: Bedrooms unattended **Stables** nearby **Grounds** accessible **Exercise area** on site **Resident Pets:** Ziggy & Indie (Schnauzers)

This delightful country-house hotel is set in seven acres of formal woodland gardens. Mentioned in the Domesday Book, this tranquil retreat is the perfect antidote to stress. Bedrooms are named after battles fought by the Duke of Wellington and each is individually decorated with sumptuous fabrics and equipped with useful extras. Public rooms are elegant and stylish, and the dining room is the venue for impressive and accomplished cuisine.

Rooms 12 en suite (2 fmly) (1 GF) ⊘ in all bedrooms S £95-£145; D £115-£215 (incl. bkfst)✳ **Facilities** ↘ ♨ ⋓ Wi-fi in bedrooms ♫ Xmas **Parking** 30 **Notes** LB

★★★ 67% HOTEL

The Cleve Hotel & Country Club

Mantle St TA21 8SN

☎ 01823 662033 ▤ 01823 660874

e-mail: reception@clevehotel.com

web: www.clevehotel.com

Dir: *M5 junct 26 follow signs to Wellington. Left before Total petrol station*

PETS: Bedrooms Charges £15 per night charge for damage **Public areas** except restaurant & bar on leads **Grounds** accessible on leads **Facilities** food bowl water bowl vet info **Resident Pets:** Mitzi (Boxer)

Offering comfortable bedrooms and public areas, this hotel is quietly located in an elevated position above the town. The atmosphere is relaxed and guests can enjoy Mediterranean influenced cuisine in the stylish restaurant. Extensive leisure facilities are available, including a heated indoor pool, a well-equipped gym, sauna and snooker table.

Rooms 20 en suite (5 fmly) (3 GF) ⊘ in all bedrooms✳ **Facilities** ⓢ supervised Gym **Parking** 100

►►► Gamlins Farm Caravan Park *(ST083195)*

Gamlins Farm House, Greenham TA21 0LZ

☎ 01823 672859 & 07986 832516 ▤ 01823 673391

Dir: *M5 junct 26, A38 towards Tiverton. 4m turn right for Greenham, site 1m on right*

PETS: Stables on site (loose box) **Charges** cats & dogs 50p, horses £10 per night **Public areas** except wash room, laundry room on leads **Exercise area** on site field available **Facilities** washing facs walks info vet info **Other** sand school (80 x 20mtrs) available

Open Etr-Sep Booking advisable BH Last arrival 20.00hrs

A well-planned site in a secluded position with panoramic views. The friendly owners keep the toilet facilities to a good standard of cleanliness. A 3-acre site with 25 touring pitches, 3 hardstandings and 1 static.

Notes ⊗ no loud noise after 22.00

WELLS   MAP 03 ST54

★★ 77% HOTEL
White Hart
Sadler St BA5 2EH
☎ 01749 672056 📄 01749 671074
e-mail: info@whitehart-wells.co.uk
web: www.whitehart-wells.co.uk
Dir: *Sadler St at start of one-way system. Hotel opposite cathedral*
PETS: Bedrooms (GF) unattended **Exercise area** 300yds
Facilities food bowl water bowl washing facs cage storage walks info vet info **On Request** fridge access torch towels

A former coaching inn dating back to the 15th century, this hotel offers comfortable, modern accommodation. Some bedrooms are in an adjoining former stable block and some are at ground floor level. Public areas include a guest lounge, a popular restaurant and bar. The restaurant serves a good choice of fish, meat, vegetarian dishes and daily specials.
Rooms 15 en suite (3 fmly) (2 GF) ⊘ in 5 bedrooms S £80-£85; D £99-£110 (incl. bkfst)✶ **Facilities** Wi-fi in bedrooms Xmas **Parking** 17 **Notes** LB

★★ 76% HOTEL
Crown at Wells
Market Place BA5 2RP
☎ 01749 673457 📄 01749 679792
e-mail: stay@crownatwells.co.uk
web: www.crownatwells.co.uk
Dir: *on entering Wells follow signs for Hotels/Deliveries. Hotel in Market Place*
PETS: Bedrooms Charges £5 per night **Grounds** courtyard accessible **Exercise area** local walks (2 mins) **Facilities** vet info
Retaining its original features and period charm, this historic old inn is situated in the heart of the city, just a short stroll from the cathedral. The building's frontage has even been used for film sets. Bedrooms, all with modern facilities, vary in size and style. Public areas focus around

Anton's, the popular bistro, which offers a light and airy environment and relaxed atmosphere. The Penn Bar offers an alternative eating option and real ales.
Rooms 15 en suite (2 fmly) ⊘ in all bedrooms S £60-£90; D £90-£110 (incl. bkfst)✶ **Parking** 15 **Notes** LB RS 25 Dec food not available in evening

★★ 67% HOTEL
Ancient Gate House
20 Sadler St BA5 2SE
☎ 01749 672029 📄 01749 670319
e-mail: info@ancientgatehouse.co.uk
Dir: *1st hotel on left on Cathedral Green*
PETS: Bedrooms Public areas except restaurant **Grounds** accessible **Exercise area** nearby **Facilities** vet info
Guests are treated to good old-fashioned hospitality in a friendly informal atmosphere at this charming hotel. Bedrooms, many of which boast unrivalled cathedral views and four-poster beds, are well equipped and furnished in keeping with the age and character of the building. The hotel's Rugantino Restaurant remains popular, offering typically Italian specialities and traditional English dishes.
Rooms 8 en suite ⊘ in 2 bedrooms S £76; D £91 (incl. bkfst)✶ **Facilities** Wi-fi in bedrooms Xmas New Year **Notes** LB Closed 27-29 Dec

ENGLAND

WELLS CONTINUED

★★★★ BED & BREAKFAST
Infield House

36 Portway BA5 2BN

☎ 01749 670989 📠 01749 679093

e-mail: infield@talk21.com

web: www.infieldhouse.co.uk

Dir: *500yds W of city centre on A371 Portway*

PETS: Bedrooms Grounds accessible on leads disp bin
Exercise area 0.5m **Facilities** food (pre-bookable) leads washing
facs walks info vet info **On Request** fridge access torch towels
Restrictions no dogs under 1yr **Resident Pets:** Pepper (Pembroke
Corgi)

This charming Victorian house offers comfortable, spacious rooms of
elegance and style. The friendly hosts are very welcoming and provide
a relaxing home from home. Guests may bring their pets, by
arrangement. Dinners, also by arrangement, are served in the pleasant
dining room where good home cooking ensures an enjoyable and
varied range of options.

Rooms 3 en suite ⊘ D £56-£58✳ **Facilities** TVB tea/coffee Cen ht TVL
Dinner Last d 10.30am **Parking** 3 **Notes** No children 12yrs

★★★ GUEST ACCOMMODATION
Birdwood House

Birdwood, Bath Rd BA5 3EW

☎ 01749 679250

e-mail: info@birdwood-bandb.co.uk

web: www.birdwood-bandb.co.uk

Dir: *1.5m NE of city centre. On B3139 between South & West
Horrington*

PETS: Bedrooms Sep Accom large pen with run **Stables** nearby
(4m) **Public areas** except dining room on leads
Grounds accessible disp bin **Exercise area** 100mtrs
Facilities food (pre-bookable) food bowl water bowl bedding
dog chews feeding mat dog scoop/disp bags leads dog walking
washing facs cage storage walks info vet info **On Request** fridge
access towels **Restrictions** No Pitt Bull Terriers
Resident Pets: Florrie (Springer Spaniel), Daisy (cat), cows,
peahen

Set in extensive grounds and gardens just a short drive from the town
centre, this imposing detached house dates from the 1850s. The

bedrooms are comfortable and equipped with a number of extra
facilities. Breakfast is served around a communal table in the pleasant
dining room or conservatory, which is also available for guest use and
enjoyment throughout the day.

Rooms 3 rms (2 en suite) (1 pri facs) (1 fmly) ⊗ S £25-£30;
D £50-£60✳ **Facilities** TVB tea/coffee Cen ht TVL 🐾 **Parking** 12
Notes LB ⊛

►► 80% **Homestead Park** *(ST532474)*

Wookey Hole BA5 1BW

☎ 01749 673022 📠 01749 673022

e-mail: enquiries@homesteadpark.co.uk

web: www.homesteadpark.co.uk

Dir: *0.5m NW off A371 (Wells to Cheddar road) (weight limit on
bridge into touring area now 1 tonne)*

PETS: Charges 50p per night **Public areas Exercise area** nearby
Facilities on site shop food vet info **Restrictions** Telephone for
details **Resident Pets:** Jasper (Golden Retriever)

Open Etr-Sep Booking advisable BH Last arrival 20.00hrs Last
departure noon

This attractive, small site for tents only is by a stream and has mature
trees. Set in hilly woods and meadowland with access to the river and
Wookey Hole. This park is for adults only. A 2-acre site with 30 touring
pitches and 28 statics.

Notes ⊛ Adults only, tents only

WESTON-SUPER-MARE   MAP 03 ST36

★★★★ BED & BREAKFAST
Camellia Lodge

76 Walliscote Rd BS23 1ED

☎ 01934 613534 📠 01934 613534

e-mail: dachefscamellia@aol.com

Dir: *200yds from seafront*

PETS: Bedrooms unattended **Charges** charge for damage
Public areas except food areas on leads **Exercise area** 200mtrs
Facilities walks info vet info **On Request** torch
Resident Pets: Jack (dog), Rosie & Riley (cats)

Guests return regularly for the warm welcome they receive at this
immaculate Victorian family home, which is just off the seafront and
within walking distance of the town centre. Bedrooms have a range of
thoughtful touches, and carefully prepared breakfasts are served in the
relaxing dining room. Home cooked dinners are also available by prior
arrangement.

Rooms 5 en suite (2 fmly) ⊗ S £27.50-£30; D £55-£65 **Facilities** TVB
tea/coffee Cen ht Dinner Last d 10.30am

★★★★ GUEST ACCOMMODATION
Rookery Manor
Edingworth Rd, Edingworth BS24 0JB
☎ 01934 750200 📠 01934 750014
e-mail: enquiries@rookery-manor.co.uk
web: www.rookery-manor.co.uk
Dir: *M5 junct 22, A370 towards Weston, 2m right to Rookery Manor*

PETS: Bedrooms Grounds accessible **Excercise area** Countryside **Facilities** vet info

Situated in its own delightful gardens and grounds within easy reach of the M5 and all the resort attractions of Weston-Super-Mare, this 16th-century manor house is best known for its extensive wedding and conference facilities. Bedrooms, each with its own access to the garden, are modern and bright. A carte menu is offered in Truffles Restaurant.

Rooms 22 en suite (2 fmly) (10 GF) S £50-£65; D £75-£95✻
Facilities TVB tea/coffee Direct dial from bedrooms Cen ht TVL Dinner Last d 9pm Golf 9 ⛳ Riding Snooker Pool Table ⚒ ⚓ **Parking** 460
Notes LB

►►► Country View Caravan Park *(ST335647)*
Sand Rd, Sand Bay BS22 9UJ
☎ 01934 627595
web: www.cvhp.co.uk
Dir: *M5 junct 21, A370 towards Weston-Super-Mare. Immediately take left lane, follow Kewstoke/Sand Bay signs. Straight over 3 rdbts onto Lower Norton Ln. At Sand Bay right into Sand Rd, site on right*

PETS: Stables nearby (1m) **Charges** £1 per night £7 per week **Public areas** except bar & restaurant **Exercise area** 200yds **Facilities** on site shop walks info vet info **Other** prior notice required

Open Mar-Jan Booking advisable BH, wknds & peak periods Last arrival 20.00hrs Last departure noon

A pleasant open site in a rural area a few hundred yards from Sandy Bay and beach. The park is also well placed for energetic walks along the coast at either end of the beach. The toilet facilities are excellent and well maintained. An 8-acre site with 120 touring pitches, 90 hardstandings and 65 statics.

Notes 🖥

WHEDDON CROSS   MAP 03 SS94

★★★★★ 🛏 🍴 FARM HOUSE
North Wheddon Farm *(SS923385)*
TA24 7EX
☎ 01643 841791 & 07891 294775 Mrs R Abraham
e-mail: northwheddonfarm@aol.com
web: www.go-exmoor.co.uk
Dir: *500yds S of village x-rds on A396. Pass Moorland Hall on left, driveway next right*

PETS: Bedrooms Stables on site **Charges** dogs £5 per night charge for damage **Public areas** except dining areas on leads **Grounds** accessible disp bin **Exercise area** 0.25m **Facilities** washing facs cage storage walks info vet info **On Request** torch **Resident Pets:** Poppy & Mingming (Border/ Lakeland Terrier cross), sheep, pigs, chickens, ducks

The farm is a delightfully friendly and comfortable environment with great views. The tranquil grounds include a pleasant garden, and the memorable dinners and breakfasts feature local and the farm's own fresh produce. The bedrooms are thoughtfully equipped and beds are most comfortable.

Rooms 3 rms (2 en suite) (1 pri facs) ⊘ S £27.50-£30; D £60 **Facilities** TVB tea/coffee Licensed Cen ht Dinner Last d 10am Wi-fi available Riding **Parking** 5 **Notes** LB 17 acres Mixed

WINSFORD　　　　　　　MAP 03 SS93

★★★★ ◉ ⇔ GUEST HOUSE
Karslake House
Halse Ln TA24 7JE
☎ 01643 851242 📠 01643 851242
e-mail: enquiries@karslakehouse.co.uk
web: www.karslakehouse.co.uk
Dir: *In village centre, past the pub and up the hill*
PETS: Bedrooms (GF) unattended Stables nearby (0.25m)
Charges £5 per night charge for damage Public areas
Exercise area 50yds Facilities washing facs cage storage vet info
On Request fridge access torch towels Resident Pets: Sally
(Staffordshire cross), Timmy & Molly (cats)

The 15th-century Karslake House stands in a peaceful Exmoor village.
Its public rooms feature original beams and fireplaces, and an
interesting menu of delicious meals is available in the dining room.
Bedrooms are thoughtfully furnished and have a number of extra
touches.

Rooms 6 rms (5 en suite) (1 pri facs) (1 GF) ⊘ S £55-£75; D £80-£115✱
Facilities TVB tea/coffee Licensed Cen ht Dinner Last d 8.15pm
Aroma-therapist & Masseuse Parking 15 Notes No children 12yrs
No coaches Closed Feb & Mar RS Nov-Jan

►►► Halse Farm Caravan & Camping Park
(SS894344)
TA24 7JL
☎ 01643 851259 📠 01643 851592
e-mail: enquiries@halsefarm.co.uk
web: www.halsefarm.co.uk
Dir: *Signed from A396 at Bridgetown. In Winsford turn left and
bear left past pub. 1m up hill, entrance on left immediately after
cattle grid*
PETS: Stables nearby (2m) (loose box) Charges charge for
horses by arrangement Public areas Exercise area extensive
walks on Exmoor Facilities vet info
Open 22 Mar-Oct Booking advisable BH & mid Jul-Aug Last
arrival 22.00hrs Last departure noon
A peaceful little site on Exmoor overlooking a wooded valley with
glorious views. This moorland site is quite remote, but it provides good

modern toilet facilities which are kept immaculately clean. A 3-acre site
with 44 touring pitches, 11 hardstandings.

WITHYPOOL　　　　　　MAP 03 SS83

★★★★★ 🛏 BED & BREAKFAST
Kings Farm
TA24 7RE
☎ 01643 831381 📠 01643 831381
e-mail: info@kingsfarmexmoor.co.uk
Dir: *Off B3223 to Withypool, over bridge & sharp left to farm*
PETS: Stables on site Charges horses £10 per night
Grounds accessible Facilities cage storage walks info vet info
On Request torch Resident Pets: 4 dogs & 6 horses
Over two acres of landscaped gardens beside the river form the
backdrop of this delightful farmhouse, set in an idyllic valley beside the
Barle. It combines all the character and charm of its 19th-century
origins with every modern comfort. From the carefully planned
bedrooms to the sumptuously furnished sitting room, delicious
home-cooked breakfasts and the warmest of welcomes, top quality is
most definitely the hallmark of Kings Farm. Stabling and fishing
available.

Rooms 2 rms (1 en suite) (1 pri facs) ⊘ S £55; D £79-£89✱
Facilities STV TVB tea/coffee Cen ht Wi-fi available Fishing Parking 3
Notes No children 14yrs

WIVELISCOMBE　　　　　MAP 03 ST02

►►►► Waterrow Touring Park *(ST053251)*
TA4 2AZ
☎ 01984 623464 📠 01984 624280
web: www.waterrowpark.co.uk
Dir: *From M5 junct 25 take A358 (signed Minehead) around
Taunton, then B3227 through Wiveliscombe. Site after 3m at
Waterrow, 0.25m past Rock Inn*
PETS: Sep Accom day kennels Charges £1 per night £7 per week
Public areas Exercise area on site dog exercise field & river
walks adjacent Facilities walks info vet info Other prior notice
required max 2 dogs per unit Resident Pets: Labrador
Open all year Booking advisable BH & Jul-Aug Last arrival
20.30hrs Last departure 11.30hrs
A pretty park for adults only with individual pitches and plenty of
hardstandings. The River Tone runs along a valley beneath the park,
accessed by steps to a nature area created by the owners, where fly
fishing is permitted. Painting workshops and other activities are
available, and the local pub is a short walk away. A 6-acre site with 45
touring pitches, 27 hardstandings and 1 static.

Notes Adults only

YEOVILTON

MAP 03 ST52

★★★★ FARM HOUSE
Cary Fitzpaine Farm (ST549270)

BA22 8JB

☎ 01458 223250 & 07967 476531 📄 01458 223372

Mrs S Crang

e-mail: acrang@aol.com

web: www.caryfitzpaine.com

Dir: *A303 at Podimore onto A37 N for 1m, 1st right to farm*

PETS: Bedrooms Sep Accom downstairs utility room stables on site **Charges** £3 per night **Public areas** except dining room **Grounds** accessible disp bin **Exercise area** farmland **Facilities** vet info **Resident Pets:** Muffin & Toffy (Golden Retrievers), Cookie & Tessa (Jack Russells), guinea pigs, horses & chickens

Surrounded by 600 acres of mixed farmland, this charming farmhouse dates from Georgian times. The comfortable bedrooms are well equipped and fitted with modern facilities. Breakfast is served at a communal or separate table in the spacious dining room, or on sunny mornings can be enjoyed on the veranda.

Rooms 3 en suite (1 fmly) ⊗ **Facilities** TVB tea/coffee Cen ht TVL Fishing **Parking** 6 **Notes** 600 acres sheep horses chicken Closed 23-26 Dec

STAFFORDSHIRE

BURTON UPON TRENT

MAP 08 SK22

★★ 72% HOTEL
Riverside

Riverside Dr, Branston DE14 3EP

☎ 01283 511234 📄 01283 511441

e-mail: riverside.branston@oldenglishinns.co.uk

web: www.oldenglish.co.uk

Dir: *on A5121 follow signs for Branston over small humped-backed bridge and turn right into Warren Lane. 2nd left into Riverside Drive*

PETS: Bedrooms (GF) unattended **Stables** nearby (1m) **Charges** £10 per night charge for damage **Grounds** accessible on leads **Facilities** water bowl cage storage walks info vet info **Resident Pets:** Lily & Pearl (Staffordshire Bull Terriers)

With its quiet residential location and well-kept terraced garden stretching down to the River Trent, this hotel has all the ingredients for

a relaxing stay. Many of the tables in the Garden Room restaurant have views over the garden. Bedrooms are tastefully furnished and decorated and provide a good range of extras.

Rooms 22 en suite (10 GF) ⊗ in all bedrooms **Facilities** STV Fishing **Parking** 200 **Notes** LB

CANNOCK

MAP 07 SJ91

►►► Cannock Chase Camping & Caravanning Club Site (SK039145)

Old Youth Hostel, Wandon WS15 1QW

☎ 01889 582166

web: www.campingandcaravanningclub.co.uk

Dir: *on A460 to Hednesford, right at Rawnsley/Hazelslade sign, then 1st left. Site 0.5m past golf club*

PETS: Public areas except buildings **Exercise area** on site adjacent to site **Facilities** walks info vet info **Other** prior notice required

Open Mar-Oct Booking advisable BH & Jul-Aug Last arrival 21.00hrs Last departure noon

Very popular and attractive site in an excellent location in the heart of the Chase, with gently sloping ground and timber-built facilities. Walks from the site into this Area of Outstanding Natural Beauty are a pleasant feature of this park, just 2.5 miles from Rugeley. A 5-acre site with 60 touring pitches, 6 hardstandings.

LEEK

MAP 07 SJ95

►►► Leek Camping & Caravanning Club Site (SK004591)

Blackshaw Grange, Blackshaw Moor ST13 8TL

☎ 01538 300285

web: www.campingandcaravanningclub.co.uk/leek

Dir: *2m from Leek on A53 Leek to Buxton road. Site 200yds past sign for 'Blackshaw Moor' on left*

PETS: Public areas except buildings **Exercise area** on site dog walks **Facilities** walks info vet info **Other** prior notice required

Open all year Booking advisable BH & peak periods Last arrival 21.00hrs Last departure noon

A beautifully located club site with well-screened pitches. The very good facilities are kept in pristine condition, and children will enjoy the enclosed play area. A 6-acre site with 70 touring pitches, 39 hardstandings.

Notes Site gates closed 23.00-07.00

LONGNOR **MAP 07 SK06**

▶▶▶▶ **Longnor Wood Caravan & Camping Park** (SK072640)

SK17 0NG

☎ 01298 83648 📠 01298 83648

e-mail: info@longnorwood.co.uk

web: www.longnorwood.co.uk

Dir: *1.25m from Longnor (off Longnor to Leek road), signed from village*

PETS: Public areas except toilet, shop/reception **Exercise area** on site 4 acre field **Facilities** on site shop food bowl water bowl dog scoop/disp bags leads walks info vet info

Open Mar-10 Jan Booking advisable BH, wknds & Jun-Aug Last arrival 21.00hrs Last departure noon

This spacious adult only park enjoys a secluded setting in the Peak National Park, an Area of Outstanding Natural Beauty. It is surrounded by beautiful rolling countryside and sheltered by woodland, with wildlife encouraged. The friendly new owners are already making their mark, and plan to upgrade the toilet block. The nearby village of Longnor offers pub food, restaurants and shops. A 10.5-acre site with 47 touring pitches, 26 hardstandings and 14 statics.

Notes Adults only

STOKE-ON-TRENT **MAP 07 SJ84**

★★★ 70% ⊕ HOTEL

Haydon House

Haydon St, Basford ST4 6JD

☎ 01782 711311 & 01782 753690 📠 01782 717470

e-mail: enquiries@haydon-house-hotel.co.uk

Dir: *A500/A53 (Hanley/Newcastle) turn left at rdbt, 2nd left at brow of hill, 2nd left into Haydon St. Hotel on left*

PETS: Bedrooms Charges charge for damage **Public areas Facilities** water bowl

A Victorian property, within easy reach of Newcastle-under-Lyme. The public rooms are furnished in a style befitting the age and character of the house and bedrooms have modern furnishings; several rooms are located in a separate house across the road. The hotel has a good reputation for its food and is popular with locals.

Rooms 17 en suite 6 annexe en suite (4 fmly) S £50-£75; D £60-£85 (incl. bkfst)✶ **Parking** 52 **Notes** LB

TAMWORTH **MAP 07 SK20**

★★★★ BED & BREAKFAST

The Old Rectory

Churchside, Harlaston B79 9HE

☎ 01827 383583 & 07973 756367 📠 01827 383583

e-mail: dandcking@talktalk.net

web: www.harlastonoldrectory.co.uk

Dir: *4.5m N, off A513 into Harlaston village. Turn right at White Lion pub. House on right past church*

PETS: Bedrooms Charges £2.50 per night **Public areas Grounds** accessible disp bin **Facilities** food bowl water bowl feeding mat dog scoop/disp bags leads walks info vet info **On Request** fridge access torch towels **Resident Pets:** Jake (Jack Russell)

This former Victorian rectory stands in the heart of this pretty, award-winning village. A range of bedrooms, furnished in quality pine with pretty co-ordinating fabrics, offer thoughtful extras, and imaginative breakfasts are served in a spacious sunny kitchen-dining room overlooking the immaculate garden.

Rooms 4 rms (3 en suite) (1 fmly) ⊗ S £27-£30; D £48 **Facilities** TVB tea/coffee Cen ht ⌣ **Parking** 7 **Notes** ⊛

UTTOXETER **MAP 07 SK03**

★★★ GUEST HOUSE

Oldroyd Guest House & Motel

18-22 Bridge St ST14 8AP

☎ 01889 562763 📠 01889 568916

e-mail: enquiries@oldroyd-guesthouse.com

Dir: *On A518 near racecourse*

PETS: Bedrooms Grounds accessible **Exercise area** on site 2 mins walk **Resident Pets:** Romy (Labrador)

This privately-owned and personally-run guest house is close to the town centre and 8 miles from Alton Towers. Bedrooms have modern facilities, and some family and ground-floor rooms are available. Breakfast is served at separate tables in the bright and pleasant breakfast room.

Rooms 12 rms (10 en suite) 3 annexe en suite (7 fmly) (5 GF) ⊗ **Facilities** TVB tea/coffee Cen ht TVL **Parking** 20

SUFFOLK

ALDEBURGH MAP 05 TM45

★★★ 86% ●● HOTEL
The Brudenell
The Parade IP15 5BU
☎ 01728 452071 📄 01728 454082
e-mail: info@brudenellhotel.co.uk
Dir: *A12/A1094, on reaching town, turn right at junct into High St. Hotel on seafront adjoining Fort Green car park*
PETS: **Bedrooms** unattended **Charges** £7.50 per night charge for damage **Public areas** except bar & restaurant on leads
Exercise area nearby **Facilities** food (pre-bookable) food bowl water bowl dog chews vet info **On Request** fridge access torch
Situated at the far end of the town centre just a step away from the beach, this hotel has a contemporary appearance, enhanced by subtle lighting and quality soft furnishings. Many of the bedrooms have superb sea views; they include deluxe rooms with king-sized beds and superior rooms suitable for families.
Rooms 42 en suite (15 fmly) ⊗ in all bedrooms S £62-£108; D £100-£224 (incl. bkfst)✳ **Facilities** STV Wi-fi in bedrooms Xmas New Year **Services** Lift **Parking** 20 **Notes** LB

★★★ 86% ●● HOTEL
Wentworth
Wentworth Rd IP15 5BD
☎ 01728 452312 📄 01728 454343
e-mail: stay@wentworth-aldeburgh.co.uk
web: www.wentworth-aldeburgh.com
Dir: *off A12 onto A1094, 6m to Aldeburgh, with church on left and left at bottom of hill*
PETS: **Bedrooms** (GF) unattended **Charges** £2 per night **Public areas Grounds** accessible **Exercise area** 300mtrs **Facilities** walks info vet info **On Request** fridge access torch **Restrictions** no breeds larger than Labrador

A delightful privately owned hotel overlooking the beach and sea beyond. The attractive, well-maintained public rooms include three stylish lounges as well as a cocktail bar and elegant restaurant. Bedrooms are smartly decorated with co-ordinated fabrics and have

many thoughtful touches; some rooms have superb sea views. Several very spacious Mediterranean-style rooms are located across the road.
Rooms 28 en suite 7 annexe en suite (5 GF) ⊗ in all bedrooms S £65-£99; D £136-£234 (incl. bkfst & dinner)✳ **Facilities** Wi-fi available Xmas New Year **Parking** 30 **Notes** LB

BARNINGHAM MAP 05 TL97

★★★★ BED & BREAKFAST
College House Farm
Bardwell Rd IP31 1DF
☎ 01359 221512 📄 01359 221512
e-mail: jackie.brightwell@talk21.com
Dir: *Off B1111 to village x-rds & onto Bardwell Rd*
PETS: **Bedrooms Stables** on site **Charges** £5 per night **Grounds** accessible **Exercise area** on site **Resident Pets:** Luther, Bliss, Lenny, Jude & Seamus (cats), Ocre, Cat, Ryan, Dillon & Woody (horses)
Expect a warm welcome at this charming Grade II-listed Jacobean property, which stands in a peaceful location close to Bury St Edmunds. Its abundant original character is complemented by fine period furnishings. Bedrooms are generally quite spacious and thoughtfully equipped. Public rooms include an elegant dining room and a cosy lounge.
Rooms 4 rms (1 en suite) 2 annexe en suite (4 fmly) ⊗ S £35; D £60-£70✳ **Facilities** TVB tea/coffee Cen ht Dinner ⌁ **Parking** 8 **Notes** LB No children 5yrs ⊛

BECCLES MAP 05 TM48

▶▶ **Beulah Hall Caravan Park** *(TM478892)*
Dairy Ln, Mutford NR34 7QJ
☎ 01502 476609
e-mail: beulah.hall@btinternet.com
Dir: *0.5m from A146, midway between Beccles & Lowestoft. At Barnby exit A146 into New Road, right at T-junct, park 2nd on right (300yds)*
PETS: **Public areas Exercise area** on site adjacent **Facilities** walks info vet info **Other** prior notice required **Resident Pets:** Newfoundland dogs
Open Apr-Oct Booking advisable Jul-Aug Last arrival 22.00hrs Last departure noon
Small secluded site in well kept grounds with mature trees and hedging. The neat pitches and pleasant tent area are beneath large trees opposite the swimming pool, and there are clean and well maintained portaloo toilets. This park is now for adults only. A 2.5-acre site with 30 touring pitches.
Notes ⊛ Adults only

ENGLAND

BILDESTON

MAP 05 TL94

★★★ 85% ◉◉ HOTEL

Bildeston Crown

104 High St IP7 7EB

☎ 01449 740510 📄 01449 741843

e-mail: hayley@thebildestoncrown.co.uk

web: www.thebildestoncrown.co.uk

Dir: *A12 junct 31, turn right onto B1070 & follow signs to Hadleigh. At t-junct turn left onto A1141, then immediately right onto B1115. Hotel 0.5m*

PETS: **Bedrooms** unattended **Stables** on site **Charges** £10 per stay per night **Public areas** except restaurant **Grounds** accessible

Charming inn situated in a peaceful village close to the historic town of Lavenham. Public areas feature beams, exposed brickwork and oak floors, with contemporary style decor; they include a choice of bars, a lounge and a restaurant. The tastefully decorated bedrooms have lovely co-ordinated fabrics and modern facilities that include a Yamaha music system and LCD TVs. Food here is a real focus and draw, guests can expect fresh, high-quality local produce and accomplished technical skills in both modern and classic dishes.

Rooms 10 en suite ⊘ in all bedrooms S £60-£90; D £110-£170 (incl. bkfst)✳ **Facilities** STV Riding Wi-fi in bedrooms Xmas New Year **Services** Lift **Parking** 30

BUNGAY

MAP 05 TM38

★★★★ 🏠 FARM HOUSE

Earsham Park Farm *(TM304883)*

Old Railway Rd, Earsham NR35 2AQ

☎ 01986 892180 📄 01986 894796 Mrs B Watchorn

e-mail: aa@earsham-parkfarm.co.uk

web: www.earsham-parkfarm.co.uk

Dir: *3m SW of Bungay on A143*

PETS: **Bedrooms Stables** on site **Charges** £5 per night charge for damage **Grounds** accessible on leads disp bin **Exercise area** 100mtrs **Facilities** feeding mat dog scoop/disp bags leads washing facs cage storage walks info vet info **On Request** fridge access torch towels **Resident Pets:** Widget (Jack Russell), Woggle (Weimaraner), George & Pedro (horses)

A superb detached Victorian property overlooking open countryside and forming part of a working farm. The property has been restored by the enthusiastic owners and retains many original features. Bedrooms and public areas are attractively furnished, and the excellent breakfasts feature home-made produce including sausages and bacon from the organically reared pigs.

Rooms 3 en suite ⊘ S £48-£60; D £68-£90 **Facilities** TVB tea/coffee Cen ht Wi-fi available **Parking** 11 **Notes** 589 acres arable, pigs (outdoor)

▶▶▶ **Outney Meadow Caravan Park**

(TM333905)

Outney Meadow NR35 1HG

☎ 01986 892338 📄 01986 896627

e-mail: c.r.hancy@ukgateway.net

web: www.outneymeadow.co.uk

Dir: *At Bungay park signed from rdbt junction of A143 & A144*

PETS: **Public areas** on leads some areas restricted **Exercise area** on site dog walks adjacent **Facilities** walks info vet info **Other** prior notice required

Open Mar-Oct Booking advisable BH Last arrival 21.00hrs Last departure 16.00hrs

Three pleasant grassy areas beside the River Waveney, with screened pitches. The central toilet block offers good modern facilities, especially in the ladies, and is open at all times. The views from the site across the wide flood plain could be straight out of a Constable painting. Canoeing and boating, coarse fishing and cycling are all available here. A 6-acre site with 45 touring pitches, 5 hardstandings and 30 statics.

Notes ⊛

BURY ST EDMUNDS MAP 05 TL86

★★★ 87% ◉◉ COUNTRY HOUSE HOTEL

Ravenwood Hall

Rougham IP30 9JA

☎ 01359 270345 📠 01359 270788

e-mail: enquiries@ravenwoodhall.co.uk

web: www.ravenwoodhall.co.uk

Dir: *3m E off A14, junct 45. Hotel on left*

PETS: Bedrooms (GF) Stables paddock Charges charge for damage Public areas except restaurant on leads Grounds accessible on leads disp bin Exercise area adjacent Facilities water bowl food by arrangement, special dog area & pet loo walks info vet info On Request fridge access torch Resident Pets: Mackerson (Black Labrador), pygmy goats, geese

Delightful 15th-century property set in seven acres of woodland and landscaped gardens. The building has many original features including carved timbers and inglenook fireplaces. The spacious bedrooms are attractively decorated, tastefully furnished with well-chosen pieces and equipped with many thoughtful touches. Public rooms include an elegant restaurant and a smart lounge bar with an open fire.

Rooms 7 en suite 7 annexe en suite (5 GF) ⊘ in all bedrooms S £97.50-£130; D £120-£195 (incl. bkfst)✱ Facilities ⬎ ⬐ Shooting & fishing Hunting can be arranged ch fac Xmas New Year Parking 150 Notes LB

DUNWICH MAP 05 TM47

►► *Haw Wood Farm Caravan Park*

(TM421717)

Hinton IP17 3QT

☎ 01986 784248

Dir: *Turn right off A12, 1.5m N of Darsham level crossing at Little Chef. Park 0.5m on right*

PETS: Public areas on leads Exercise area on site large field Facilities on site shop food food bowl water bowl dog chews disp bags leads washing facs walks info vet info Other prior notice required Resident Pets: a cat & a dog

Open Mar-Oct Booking advisable BH & Jul-Aug Last arrival 21.00hrs Last departure noon

An unpretentious family-orientated park set in two large fields surrounded by low hedges. The toilets are clean and functional, and

there is plenty of space for children to play. An 8-acre site with 65 touring pitches and 25 statics.

Notes ⌨

ELMSWELL MAP 05 TL96

★★★★ GUEST HOUSE

Kiln Farm

Kiln Ln IP30 9QR

☎ 01359 240442

e-mail: davejankilnfarm@btinternet.com

Dir: *Exit A14 junct 47, just off A1088*

PETS: Bedrooms (GF) Charges charge for damage Public areas Grounds accessible Exercise area 10mtrs Facilities feeding mat cage storage vet info On Request fridge access torch towels Other owners are expected to fully provide for their pets Resident Pets: Barney & MummaPuss (cats)

Delightful Victorian farmhouse set in a peaceful rural location amid 3 acres of landscaped grounds with lovely views. Bedrooms are housed in a converted barn; each is pleasantly decorated and furnished in country style. Breakfast is served in the bar-dining room and there is a cosy lounge.

Rooms 2 en suite 6 annexe en suite (2 fmly) (6 GF) ⊘ Facilities TVB tea/coffee Licensed Cen ht TVL Dinner Last d 6pm Parking 20 Notes No coaches ⌨

FELIXSTOWE MAP 05 TM33

►►► Peewit Caravan Park (TM290338)

Walton Av IP11 2HB

☎ 01394 284511

web: www.peewitcaravanpark.co.uk

Dir: *Signed from A14 in Felixstowe, 100mtrs past dock gate 1, 1st on left*

PETS: Public areas except shower/toilet block Exercise area on site & in 500mtrs grass walkway disp bin Facilities walks info vet info

Open Apr or Etr-Oct Booking advisable BH & school hols Last arrival 21.00hrs Last departure 11.00hrs

A grass touring area fringed by trees, with well-maintained grounds and a colourful floral display. This handy urban site is not overlooked by houses, and the toilet facilities are clean and well cared for. A function room contains a TV and library. The beach is a few minutes away by car. A 13-acre site with 45 touring pitches, 4 hardstandings and 200 statics.

Notes ⌨ Only foam footballs permitted

FRAMLINGHAM   MAP 05 TM26

★★★ GUEST ACCOMMODATION
Church Farm

Church Rd, Kettleburgh IP13 7LF

☎ 01728 723532

e-mail: jbater@suffolkonline.net

Dir: *Off A12 to Wickham Market, signs to Easton Farm Park & Kettleburgh 1.25m, house behind church*

PETS: Bedrooms (GF) **Public areas** on leads **Grounds** accessible on leads **Facilities** feeding mat leads cage storage walks info vet info **On Request** fridge access torch towels
Resident Pets: Minnie (Jack Russell), Jessie (Labrador), Boots (Border/Jack Russell)

A charming 300-year-old farmhouse situated close to the village church amid superb grounds with a duck pond, mature shrubs and sweeping lawns. The converted property retains exposed beams and open fireplaces. Bedrooms are pleasantly decorated and equipped with useful extras, and a ground-floor bedroom is available.

Rooms 3 rms (1 en suite) (1 GF) ⊗ S £28-£32; D £56-£64
Facilities tea/coffee Cen ht TVL Dinner Last d 7.30pm Fishing Clay pigeon shooting **Parking** 10 **Notes** ⊛

HORRINGER   MAP 05 TL86

★★★★ 81% ⊛⊛ HOTEL
The Ickworth Hotel & Apartments

IP29 5QE

von Essen hotels
A PRIVATE COLLECTION
www.vonessenhotels.com

☎ 01284 735350 📠 01284 736300

e-mail: ickworth@ickworthhotel.com

web: www.vonessenhotels.co.uk

Dir: *A14 exit for Bury St Edmunds, follow brown signs for Ickworth House, 4th exit at rdbt, to staggered x-rds. Then onto T-junct, left into village, almost immediately right into Ickworth Estate*

PETS: Bedrooms unattended **Stables** on site **Charges** £7 per night **Public areas** except food areas **Grounds** accessible **Exercise area** on site **Resident Pets:** Truffle (Black Labrador) Saffron (Golden Labrador)

Gifted to the National Trust in 1956 this stunning property is in part a luxurious hotel that combines the glorious design and atmosphere of the past with a reputation for making children very welcome. The staff

are friendly and easy going, there is a children's play area, crèche, horses and bikes to ride, and wonderful 'Capability' Brown gardens to roam in. Plus tennis, swimming, beauty treatments and two dining rooms.

Rooms 27 en suite 11 annexe en suite (35 fmly) (4 GF) ⊗ in all bedrooms **Facilities** STV ⓢ ♨ Riding ♣ Childrens creche Massage Manicures Aromatherapy **Services** Lift **Parking** 40

IPSWICH   MAP 05 TM14

★★★ 72% HOTEL
Novotel Ipswich Centre

Greyfriars Rd IP1 1UP

☎ 01473 232400 📠 01473 232414

e-mail: h0995@accor.com

web: www.novotel.com

NOVOTEL
Accor Hotels

Dir: *from A14 towards Felixstowe. Left onto A137, follow for 2m into town centre. Hotel on double rdbt by Stoke Bridge*

PETS: Bedrooms unattended sign **Charges** £7.50 per night charge for damage **Public areas** except restaurant on leads **Grounds** accessible on leads **Facilities** cage storage walks info vet info

Modern red brick hotel perfectly placed in the centre of town close to shops, bars and restaurants. The open-plan public areas include a Mediterranean-style restaurant and a bar with a small games area. The bedrooms are smartly appointed and have many thoughtful touches; three rooms are suitable for less mobile guests.

Rooms 101 en suite (8 fmly) ⊗ in all bedrooms **Facilities** STV Gym Wi-fi in bedrooms Pool table, sauna **Services** Lift air con **Parking** 53 (charged)

▶▶▶▶ Priory Park *(TM198409)*

IP10 0JT

☎ 01473 727393 & 726373 📠 01473 278372

e-mail: jwl@priory-park.com

web: www.priory-park.com

Dir: *Exit A14 at Ipswich southern by-pass towards town centre. 300mtrs left towards Priory Park. Follow single track road into park*

PETS: Charges £1 per night £7 per week **Public areas** except bar & restaurant **Exercise area** on site woodland & river walks adjacent **Facilities** walks info vet info

Open Apr-Oct (rs Apr-Jun & Sep-Oct limited pitches,club & pool closed) Booking advisable at all times Last arrival 18.00hrs Last departure 14.00hrs

A well-screened and very peaceful south-facing park set close to the banks of the tidal River Orwell, and with panoramic views out over the water. The park is attractively landscaped, and offers superb toilet facilities with smartly-tiled, fully-serviced cubicles. A 100-acre site with 75 touring pitches, 59 hardstandings and 260 statics.

Notes ⊛ No commercial vehicles, pup tents or group bookings

KESSINGLAND   MAP 05 TM58

▶▶▶▶ **Kessingland Camping & Caravanning Club Site** *(TM520860)*

Suffolk Wildlife Park, Whites Ln NR33 7TF

☎ 01502 742040

web: www.campingandcaravanningclub.co.uk/kessingland

Dir: *On A12 from Lowestoft at Kessingland rdbt, follow Wildlife Park signs, turn right through park entrance*

PETS: Public areas except buildings **Exercise area** on site
Facilities walks info vet info **Other** prior notice required

Open 13 Mar-3 Nov Booking advisable BH & peak periods
Last arrival 21.00hrs Last departure noon

A well screened open site next to Suffolk Wildlife Park, where concessions are available for visitors. An extensive renovation has created superb facilities, including three family rooms, a disabled unit, and smart reception. A well-equipped laundry and covered dishwashing sinks add to the quality amenities. A 5-acre site with 90 touring pitches.

Notes Site gates closed 23.00hrs-7.00hrs

LAVENHAM   MAP 05 TL94

★★★★ 81% ◉◉ HOTEL

The Swan

High St CO10 9QA

☎ 01787 247477 🖨 01787 248286

e-mail: info@theswanatlavenham.co.uk

web: www.bespokehotels.com

Dir: *from A12 or A14 onto A134, then B1071 to Lavenham*

PETS: Bedrooms (GF) unattended **Charges** £10 per night
Public areas except food areas on leads **Grounds** accessible
Exercise area 400yds **Facilities** water bowl walks info vet info
On Request fridge access torch towels

A delightful collection of listed buildings dating back to the 14th century, lovingly restored to retain their original charm. Public rooms include comfortable lounge areas, a charming rustic bar, an informal brasserie and a fine-dining restaurant. Bedrooms are tastefully furnished and equipped with many thoughtful touches. The friendly staff are helpful, attentive and offer professional service.

Rooms 51 en suite (4 fmly) (12 GF) ⊘ in all bedrooms S £60-£80;
D £120-£200 (incl. bkfst)✳ **Facilities** STV Xmas **Parking** 62 **Notes** LB

★★★★★ ◉◉🖥🛏
RESTAURANT WITH ROOMS

Lavenham Great House 5 Star Restaurant with Rooms

Market Place CO10 9QZ

☎ 01787 247431 🖨 01787 248007

e-mail: info@greathouse.co.uk

web: www.greathouse.co.uk

Dir: *Off A1141 onto Market Ln, behind cross on Market Place*

PETS: Bedrooms Charges charge for damage
Exercise area 200mtrs **Facilities** water bowl walks info vet info
On Request fridge access

The 18th-century front on Market Place conceals a 15th-century timber-framed building that houses a restaurant with rooms. The restaurant is a pocket of France and offers high-quality rural cuisine served by French staff. The spacious bedrooms are individually decorated and thoughtfully equipped with many useful extras; some rooms have a separate lounge area.

Rooms 5 en suite (2 fmly) ⊘ S £65-£165; D £70-£165✳ (room only)
Facilities FTV TVB tea/coffee Direct dial from bedrooms Cen ht Dinner
Last d 9.30pm Wi-fi available **Notes** LB Closed Jan RS Sun eve & Mon

LEISTON   MAP 05 TM46

▶▶▶ **Cakes & Ale** *(TM432637)*

Abbey Ln, Theberton IP16 4TE

☎ 01728 831655 🖨 01728 831998

e-mail: info@cakesandale.f2s.com

web: www.cakesandale.net

Dir: *From Saxmundham E on B1119. 3m follow minor road over level crossing, turn right, in 0.5m straight on at x-rds, entrance 0.5m on left*

PETS: Charges £1 per night £7 per week **Public areas**
Exercise area on site small wooded area **Facilities** on site shop
washing facs walks info vet info **Other** prior notice required
Resident Pets: Jasper (Blue Merle Border Collie)

Open Apr-Oct (rs low season club, shop & reception limited hours) Booking advisable public & school hols Last arrival 20.00hrs Last departure 13.00hrs

A large, well spread out site with many trees and bushes on a former Second World War airfield. The spacious touring area includes plenty of hardstandings and super pitches, and there is a good bar and a well-maintained toilet block. Wireless internet access is available on site. A 5-acre site with 50 touring pitches, 50 hardstandings and 200 statics.

Notes No group bookings, no noise between 21.00hrs-08.00hrs

ENGLAND

LONG MELFORD
MAP 05 TL84

★★★ 81% ⑱ HOTEL

The Black Lion

Church Walk, The Green CO10 9DN

☎ 01787 312356 📄 01787 374557

e-mail: enquiries@blacklionhotel.net

web: www.blacklionhotel.net

Dir: *at junct of A134 & A1092*

PETS: Bedrooms Charges charge for damage **Public areas** except restaurant on leads **Grounds** accessible on leads **Exercise area** opposite **Facilities** water bowl food by prior arrangement & chargeable walks info vet info **On Request** fridge access torch **Resident Pets:** Mackerson (Black Labrador)

This charming 15th-century hotel is situated on the edge of this bustling town overlooking the green. Bedrooms are generally spacious and each is attractively decorated, tastefully furnished and equipped with useful extras. An interesting range of dishes is served in the lounge bar or guests may choose to dine from the same innovative menu in the more formal restaurant.

Rooms 10 en suite (1 fmly) ⊘ in all bedrooms S £97.50-£135; D £150-£195 (incl. bkfst)✳ **Facilities** ch fac Xmas New Year **Parking** 10 **Notes** LB

LOWESTOFT
MAP 05 TM59

★★★ 82% ⑱⑱ HOTEL

Ivy House Country Hotel

Ivy Ln, Beccles Rd, Oulton Broad NR33 8HY

☎ 01502 501353 & 588144 📄 01502 501539

e-mail: aa@ivyhousecountryhotel.co.uk

web: www.ivyhousecountryhotel.co.uk

Dir: *on A146 SW of Oulton Broad turn into Ivy Ln beside Esso petrol station. Over railway bridge and follow private driveway*

PETS: Bedrooms (GF) unattended sign **Charges** £15 per stay **Public areas Grounds** accessible on leads disp bin **Facilities** water bowl bedding dog chews dog scoop/disp bags leads washing facs walks info vet info **On Request** fridge access torch towels **Resident Pets:** Tammie (Jack Russell), Patch (Labrador)

Peacefully located, family-run hotel set in three acres of mature landscaped grounds just a short walk from Oulton Broad. Public rooms include an 18th-century thatched barn restaurant where an interesting choice of dishes is served. The attractively decorated bedrooms are housed in garden wings, and many have lovely views of the grounds to the countryside beyond.

Rooms 20 annexe en suite (1 fmly) (17 GF) ⊘ in all bedrooms S £95-£112; D £125-£162 (incl. bkfst)✳ **Facilities** FTV **Parking** 50 **Notes** LB Closed 23 Dec-6 Jan

★★★★ GUEST ACCOMMODATION
Somerton House
7 Kirkley Cliff NR33 0BY
☎ 01502 565665 📠 01502 501176
e-mail: somerton@screaming.net
Dir: *On the old A12, 100yds from Claremont Pier*
PETS: Bedrooms (GF) **Charges** £5 per stay **Public areas** except dining room **Exercise area** beach opposite **Facilities** vet info
Grade II Victorian terrace situated in a peaceful area of town overlooking the sea. Bedrooms are smartly furnished in a period style and have many thoughtful touches; some rooms have four poster or half-tester beds. Breakfast is served in the smart dining room and guests have the use of a cosy lounge.
Rooms 7 rms (5 en suite) (2 pri facs) (1 fmly) (1 GF) ◎ S £35-£45; D £55-£60✴ **Facilities** STV FTV TVB tea/coffee Cen ht TVL Dinner Last d noon **Notes LB** Closed 25-26 Dec

★★★ GUEST HOUSE
Fairways
398 London Rd South NR33 0BQ
☎ 01502 572659
e-mail: amontali@netmatters.co.uk
Dir: *S of town centre on A12, 1m from railway and bus station*
PETS: Bedrooms Stables nearby (1m) **Charges** charge for damage **Facilities** vet info
Expect a friendly welcome at this family-run guest house, which is located at the southern end of the town. Bedrooms come in a variety of sizes and styles; each room is pleasantly decorated and thoughtfully equipped. Breakfast is served in the smart dining room and there is also a cosy lounge.
Rooms 7 rms (4 en suite) (2 fmly) ◎ **Facilities** TVB tea/coffee Licensed Cen ht TVL

NEWMARKET   MAP 12 TL66

★★★ 78% HOTEL
Best Western Heath Court
Moulton Rd CB8 8DY
☎ 01638 667171 📠 01638 666533
e-mail: quality@heathcourthotel.com
Dir: *leave A14 at Newmarket & Ely exit onto A142. Follow town centre signs over mini rdbt. At clocktower left into Moulton Rd*
PETS: Bedrooms unattended sign **Stables** nearby (3m) **Charges** charge for damage **Exercise area** 100yds **Facilities** food bowl water bowl pet sitting dog walking washing facs cage storage walks info vet info **On Request** fridge access torch towels
Modern red-brick hotel situated close to Newmarket Heath and perfectly placed for the town centre. Public rooms include a choice of dining options - informal meals can be taken in the lounge bar or a modern carte menu is offered in the restaurant. The smartly presented bedrooms are mostly spacious and some have air conditioning.
Rooms 41 en suite (2 fmly) ◎ in all bedrooms S £78-£100; D £120-£290 (incl. bkfst)✴ **Facilities** STV Wi-fi in bedrooms Health & beauty salon New Year **Services** Lift **Parking** 60 **Notes LB**

ORFORD   MAP 05 TM45

★★ 85% ◉◉ HOTEL
The Crown & Castle
IP12 2LJ
☎ 01394 450205
e-mail: info@crownandcastle.co.uk
web: www.crownandcastle.co.uk
Dir: *turn right from B1084 on entering village, towards castle*
PETS: Bedrooms (GF) unattended **Charges** £10 per dog, per stay charge for damage **Public areas** bar only & table 30 on leads **Grounds** accessible on leads disp bin **Exercise area** 100yds **Facilities** food (pre-bookable) dog chews dog scoop/disp bags doggy bag on arrival washing facs walks info vet info **On Request** fridge access torch towels **Restrictions** very large dogs not permitted, no more than 2 dogs per room **Resident Pets:** Jack & Annie (Wire-Haired Fox Terrier), Chloe (cat)

Delightful inn situated adjacent to the Norman castle keep. Contemporary style bedrooms are spilt between the main house and the garden wing; the latter are more spacious and have patios with access to the garden. The restaurant has an informal atmosphere with polished tables and local artwork; the menu features quality, locally sourced produce.
Rooms 7 en suite 11 annexe en suite (1 fmly) (11 GF) ◎ in all bedrooms S £100.50-£230; D £145-£230 (incl. bkfst & dinner)✴ **Facilities** Wi-fi available Xmas New Year **Parking** 20 **Notes LB** Closed 7-11 Jan

ENGLAND

SAXMUNDHAM MAP 05 TM36

★★★★ BED & BREAKFAST
Sandpit Farm

Bruisyard IP17 2EB

☎ 01728 663445

e-mail: smarshall@aldevalleybreaks.co.uk

web: www.aldevalleybreaks.co.uk

Dir: *4m W of Saxmundham. A1120 onto B1120, 1st left for Bruisyard, house 1.5m on left*

PETS: Bedrooms sign one bedroom allocated for pet stay **Sep Accom** outbuildings by barn **Stables** on site **Charges** charge for damage **Grounds** accessible on leads disp bin **Facilities** cage storage walks info vet info **On Request** fridge access **Resident Pets:** Twiggy & Inca (Black Labradors), chickens, guinea fowl

A warm welcome awaits you at this delightful Grade II listed farmhouse set in 20 acres of grounds. Bedrooms have many thoughtful touches and lovely country views, and there are two cosy lounges to enjoy. Breakfast features quality local produce and freshly laid free-range eggs.

Rooms 2 en suite ⊘ **Facilities** tea/coffee Cen ht TVL ♨ Riding ♨ **Parking** 4 **Notes** ⊗ Closed 24-26 Dec ▨

WESTLETON MAP 05 TM46

★★★ 77% ◉◉ HOTEL
Westleton Crown

The Street IP17 3AD

☎ 01728 648777 📠 01728 648239

e-mail: reception@westletoncrown.co.uk

web: www.westletoncrown.co.uk

Dir: *A12 N, turn right for Westleton just after Yoxford. Hotel opposite on entering Westleton*

PETS: Bedrooms Charges £5 per night **Public areas** except main dining room **Grounds** accessible **Exercise area** outside hotel **Facilities** food bowl water bowl treats for dogs **Resident Pets:** Stopit (Lurcher)

Charming coaching inn situated in a peaceful village location just a few minutes from the A12. Public rooms include a smart, award-winning restaurant, comfortable lounge, and busy bar with exposed beams and

open fireplaces. The stylish bedrooms are tastefully decorated and equipped with many thoughtful little extras.

Rooms 22 en suite 3 annexe en suite (2 fmly) (8 GF) ⊘ in all bedrooms **Parking** 26 **Notes** LB Closed 25-26 Dec

SURREY

CHERTSEY MAP 04 TQ06

►►►► Chertsey Camping & Caravanning Club Site *(TQ052667)*

Bridge Rd KT16 8JX

☎ 01932 562405

web: www.campingandcaravanningclub.co.uk/chertsey

Dir: *M25 junct 11, follow A317 to Chertsey. At rdbt take 1st exit to lights. Straight over at next lights. Turn right 400yds, turn left into site*

PETS: Exercise area on site dog walk **Facilities** walks info vet info **Other** prior notice required

Open all year Booking advisable BH & peak periods Last arrival 21.00hrs Last departure noon

A pretty Thames-side site set amongst trees and shrubs in well-tended grounds, ideally placed for the M3/M25 and for visiting London. Some attractive riverside pitches are very popular, and fishing and boating is allowed from the site on the river. The toilet facilities are very good. A 12-acre site with 200 touring pitches, 50 hardstandings.

Notes site gates closed 23.00hrs-7.00hrs

CHOBHAM MAP 04 SU96

★★★★ GUEST ACCOMMODATION
Pembroke House

Valley End Rd GU24 8TB

☎ 01276 857654 📠 01276 858445

e-mail: pembroke_house@btinternet.com

Dir: *A30 onto B383 signed Chobham, 3m right onto Valley End Rd, B&B 1m on left*

PETS: Bedrooms Public areas except dining room **Grounds** accessible disp bin **Facilities** food bowl water bowl bedding leads pet sitting washing facs cage storage walks info vet info **On Request** fridge access torch towels **Resident Pets:** Puzzle, Carrie, Pandora (Jack Russells)

Proprietor Julia Holland takes obvious pleasure in treating you as a friend at her beautifully appointed and spacious home. The elegantly proportioned public areas include an imposing entrance hall and dining room with views over the surrounding countryside. Bedrooms are restful and filled with thoughtful extras.

Rooms 4 rms (2 en suite) (2 pri facs) ⊘ S £40-£50; D £80-£130✳ **Facilities** STV TVB tea/coffee Cen ht ♨ **Parking** 10 **Notes** No children 6yrs ▨

EAST HORSLEY
MAP 04 TQ05

►►► Horsley Camping & Caravanning Club Site *(TQ083552)*
Ockham Rd North KT24 6PE

☎ 01483 283273

web: www.campingandcaravanningclub.co.uk/horsley

Dir: *M25 junct 10. S & take 1st major turn signed Ockham/ Southend/Ripley. Left & site 2.5m on right. From S take A3 past Guildford & take B2215 towards Ripley*

PETS: Public areas except buildings **Exercise area** on site **Facilities** walks info vet info **Other** prior notice required

Open 13 Mar-3 Nov Booking advisable BH & peak periods Last arrival 21.00hrs Last departure noon

A beautiful lakeside site with plenty of trees and shrubs and separate camping fields, providing a tranquil base within easy reach of London. Toilet facilities are well maintained and clean. A 9.5-acre site with 130 touring pitches, 41 hardstandings.

Notes Site gates closed 23.00hrs-7.00hrs

PEASLAKE
MAP 04 TQ04

★★ 68% HOTEL
Hurtwood Inn Hotel
Walking Bottom GU5 9RR

☎ 01306 730851 📄 01306 731390

e-mail: sales@hurtwoodinnhotel.com

web: www.hurtwoodinnhotel.com

Dir: *off A25 at Gomshall opposite petrol station towards Peaslake. After 2.5m turn right at village shop, hotel in village centre*

PETS: Bedrooms unattended **Public areas** except restaurant **Grounds** accessible **Exercise area** on site

With its tranquil location this hotel makes an ideal base for exploring the attractions of the area. The brightly decorated bedrooms are well appointed, and some have views over the gardens. Public areas include the restaurant, a private dining room and a bar/bistro where drinks by the open fire can be enjoyed.

Rooms 15 en suite 6 annexe en suite (6 fmly) (6 GF) ⊗ in 5 bedrooms S £65; D £75-£100 (incl. bkfst)✳ **Facilities** Wi-fi in bedrooms **Parking** 22 **Notes** LB

ALFRISTON
MAP 05 TQ50

★★★ 81% ⊛ HOTEL
Deans Place
Seaford Rd BN26 5TW

☎ 01323 870248 📄 01323 870918

e-mail: mail@deansplacehotel.co.uk

web: www.deansplacehotel.co.uk

Dir: *off A27, signed Alfriston & Drusillas Zoo Park. Continue south through village*

PETS: Bedrooms (GF) unattended **Charges** £5 per night **Public areas** except restaurant & function rooms on leads **Grounds** accessible **Facilities** bowls are subject to prior arrangment washing facs cage storage walks info vet info **On Request** fridge access torch towels

Situated on the southern fringe of the village, this friendly hotel is set in attractive gardens. Bedrooms vary in size and are well appointed with good facilities. A wide range of food is offered including an extensive bar menu and a fine dining option in Harcourt's Restaurant.

Rooms 36 en suite (4 fmly) (8 GF) ⊗ in 17 bedrooms S £74-£120; D £95-£168 (incl. bkfst) **Facilities** STV ↘ ⤴ Putt green Wi-fi in bedrooms Boules Xmas New Year **Parking** 100 **Notes** LB

★★★ 70% HOTEL
The Star Inn
BN26 5TA

☎ 01323 870495 📄 01323 870922

e-mail: bookings@star-inn-alfriston.com

web: www.star-inn-alfriston.com

Dir: *2m off A27, at Drusillas rdbt follow Alfriston signs. Hotel on right in centre of High Street*

PETS: Bedrooms Charges £25 per stay **Public areas** except restaurant **Grounds** accessible **Exercise area** 100yds

Located in a sleepy town on the edge of the South Downs this 14th-century inn provides smart accommodation. Whilst some rooms retain original features, the majority are contemporary in style and design. Public areas maintain the original charm and character of the house including open fires and flagstones.

Rooms 37 en suite (12 GF) ⊗ in all bedrooms S £44-£84; D £88-£158 (incl. bkfst)✳ **Facilities** Xmas New Year **Parking** 40 **Notes** LB

BATTLE MAP 05 TQ71

★★★ 79% <20> HOTEL
Powder Mills
Powdermill Ln TN33 0SP
☎ 01424 775511 📠 01424 774540
e-mail: powdc@aol.com
web: www.powdermillshotel.com
Dir: *pass Abbey on A2100. 1st right, hotel 1m on right*
PETS: Bedrooms (GF) unattended sign Stables on site
Charges charge for damage Public areas except restaurant
Grounds accessible disp bin Facilities leads washing facs cage
storage walks info vet info On Request torch towels
Resident Pets: Jessica, Holly & Jenny (Springer Spaniels)
A delightful 18th-century country house hotel set amidst 150 acres of
landscaped grounds with lakes and woodland. The individually
decorated bedrooms are tastefully furnished and thoughtfully
equipped, some rooms have sun terraces with lovely views over the
lake. Public rooms include a cosy lounge bar, music room, drawing
room, library, restaurant and conservatory.
Rooms 30 en suite 10 annexe en suite (3 GF) ⊗ in all bedrooms
S £95-£105; D £120-£350 (incl. bkfst)✳ Facilities STV ⚓ ♨ Fishing
Wi-fi in bedrooms Xmas New Year Parking 101 Notes LB

★★★★ 🏠 FARM HOUSE
Fox Hole Farm *(TQ694166)*
Kane Hythe Rd TN33 9QU
☎ 01424 772053 📠 01424 772053 Mr & Mrs P Collins
e-mail: foxholefarm@kanehythe.orangehome.co.uk
Dir: *Off A271 onto B2096 farm 0.75m from junct on right*
PETS: Bedrooms (GF) Public areas except dining room
Grounds accessible Facilities water bowl bedding feeding mat
leads cage storage walks info vet info On Request fridge access
torch towels Resident Pets: Foxy (Border Terrier), Lucy (Golden
Retriever)

A delightful 18th-century woodcutter's cottage set in forty acres of
grounds a short drive from historic Battle. The spacious bedrooms are
individually decorated and thoughtfully equipped. Breakfast includes
home-baked bread and is served in the charming dining room. The
cosy sitting room has exposed beams and an inglenook fireplace.

Rooms 3 en suite (1 GF) ⊗ S £39-£49; D £56-£65✳ Facilities TVB tea/
coffee Cen ht Parking 6 Notes 40 acres ducks sheep chickens Closed
Jan

►►► 74% **Brakes Coppice Park** *(TQ765134)*
Forewood Ln TN33 9AB
☎ 01424 830322
e-mail: brakesco@btinternet.com
web: www.brakescoppicepark.co.uk
Dir: *From Battle on A2100 towards Hastings. After 2m turn right
for Crowhurst. Site 1m on left*
PETS: Stables nearby (2m) (loose box) Charges 25p per night
£1.75 per week Public areas on leads Exercise area on site
woods & in 1m Facilities on site shop walks info vet info
Other prior notice required
Open Mar-Oct Booking advisable BH & Jul-Aug Last arrival
21.00hrs Last departure noon
Secluded farm site in meadow surrounded by woodland with small
stream and fishing lake, and a raised garden in the centre. Pitches are
neatly laid out on a terrace, and tents are pitched on grass edged by
woodland. A 3-acre site with 30 touring pitches, 10 hardstandings.
Notes no fires, footballs or kite flying

BRIGHTON & HOVE MAP 04 TQ30

★★★ 72% HOTEL
The Granville
124 King's Rd BN1 2FA
☎ 01273 326302 📠 01273 728294
e-mail: granville@brighton.co.uk
web: www.granvillehotel.co.uk
Dir: *opposite West Pier next to Hilton Metropole*
PETS: Bedrooms (GF) unattended Charges charge for damage
Public areas bar only on leads On Request fridge access torch
Resident Pets: Mai-Mai (Jack Russell), Nan-Nan (West Highland
Terrier)

This stylish hotel is located on Brighton's busy seafront. Bedrooms are
carefully furnished and decorated with great style. A trendy cocktail bar
and restaurant is located in the cellar with street access and a cosy
terrace for warmer months. Tasty traditional breakfasts are also
available.

Rooms 24 en suite (2 fmly) (2 GF) ⊗ in all bedrooms S £55-£125; D £88-£185 (incl. bkfst)✳ **Facilities** Wi-fi in bedrooms **Services** Lift **Notes** LB

★★★★ GUEST ACCOMMODATION

Brighton Pavilions

7 Charlotte St BN2 1AG

☎ 01273 621750 📄 01273 622477

e-mail: sanchez-crespo@lineone.net

web: www.brightonpavilions.com

Dir: *A23 to Brighton Pier, left onto A259 Marine Parade, Charlotte St 15th left*

PETS: Bedrooms (GF) unattended **Charges** £10 per night charge for damage **Public areas** except dining room on leads **Exercise area** 5 mins walk **Facilities** walks info vet info **On Request** fridge access **Restrictions** very large breeds not permitted **Resident Pets:** Fluffy (budgie)

This well-run operation is in one of Brighton's Regency streets, a short walk from the seafront and town centre. Bedrooms have style themes such as Mikado or Pompeii, and are very smartly presented with many thoughtful extras. The bright breakfast room is styled after a Titanic garden restaurant.

Rooms 10 rms (7 en suite) (1 fmly) (1 GF) ⊗ S £40-£75; D £80-£150✳ **Facilities** TVB tea/coffee Direct dial from bedrooms Cen ht **Notes** LB

★★★★ GUEST ACCOMMODATION

Ambassador Brighton

22-23 New Steine, Marine Pde BN2 1PD

☎ 01273 676869 📄 01273 689988

e-mail: info@ambassadorbrighton.co.uk

web: www.ambassadorbrighton.co.uk

Dir: *A23 to Brighton Pier, left onto A259, 9th left, onto Garden Sq, 1st left*

PETS: Bedrooms Charges charge for damage **Public areas** bar only **Facilities** feeding mat dog walking walks info **On Request** fridge access torch

At the heart of bustling Kemp Town, overlooking the attractive garden square next to the seaside, this well established property has a friendly and relaxing atmosphere. Bedrooms are well equipped and vary in size with the largest having the best views. A small lounge with a separate bar is available.

Rooms 24 en suite (9 fmly) (3 GF) ⊗ in 12 bedrooms **Facilities** TVB tea/coffee Direct dial from bedrooms Cen ht

CROWBOROUGH MAP 05 TQ53

►►► Crowborough Camping & Caravanning Club Site *(TQ520315)*

Goldsmith Recreation Ground TN6 2TN

☎ 01892 664827

web: www.campingandcaravanningclub.co.uk/ crowborough

Dir: *Turn off A26 into entrance to 'Goldsmiths Ground', signed Leisure Centre. At top of road right onto site lane*

PETS: Public areas except buildings **Exercise area** on site **Facilities** walks info vet info **Other** prior notice required

Open Mar-Dec Booking advisable BH & peak periods Last arrival 21.00hrs Last departure noon

A spacious terraced site with stunning views across the Weald to the North Downs in Kent. This good quality site has clean, modern toilets, a kitchen and eating area for campers, a recreation room, and good provision of hardstandings. An excellent leisure centre is adjacent to the park. A 13-acre site with 90 touring pitches, 26 hardstandings.

Notes site gates closed 23.00hrs-7.00hrs

EASTBOURNE MAP 05 TV69

★★★★★ 85% ◉◉ HOTEL

Grand

King Edward's Pde BN21 4EQ

☎ 01323 412345 📄 01323 412233

e-mail: reservations@grandeastbourne.com

web: www.grandeastbourne.com

Dir: *on seafront W of Eastbourne, 1m from railway station*

PETS: Bedrooms Charges £7 per night **Exercise area** park adjacent

This famous Victorian hotel offers high standards of service and hospitality. The extensive public rooms feature a magnificent Great Hall, with marble columns and high ceilings, where guests can relax and enjoy afternoon tea. The spacious bedrooms provide high levels of comfort and some rooms have balconies with stunning sea views. There is a choice of restaurants and bars as well as superb leisure facilities.

Rooms 152 en suite (20 fmly) S £150-£480; D £180-£510 (incl. bkfst)✳ **Facilities** STV ⊗ ⊰ supervised Gym Putt green Hairdressing Beauty therapy ♫ ch fac Xmas New Year **Services** Lift **Parking** 60 **Notes** LB

EASTBOURNE CONTINUED

★★★ 75% HOTEL
Best Western Lansdowne
King Edward's Pde BN21 4EE

☎ 01323 725174 📄 01323 739721
e-mail: reception@lansdowne-hotel.co.uk
web: www.bw-lansdownehotel.co.uk
Dir: *hotel at W end of seafront opposite Western Lawns*
PETS: Bedrooms unattended **Charges** £5 per night charge for damage **Facilities** vet info

Enjoying an enviable position at the quieter end of the parade, this hotel overlooks the Western Lawns and Wish Tower and is just a few minutes' walk from many of the town's attractions. Public rooms include a variety of lounges, a range of meeting rooms and games rooms. Bedrooms are attractively decorated and many offer sea views.
Rooms 101 en suite (10 fmly) ⊘ in 56 bedrooms S £52-£78; D £95-£173 (incl. bkfst) **Facilities** STV FTV Wi-fi in bedrooms Table tennis, Pool table Xmas New Year **Services** Lift **Parking** 22 **Notes** LB Closed 2-17 Jan

★★ 69% HOTEL
Courtlands
3-5 Wilmington Gardens BN21 4JN
☎ 01323 723737 📄 01323 732902
e-mail: bookings@courtlandseastbourne.com
Dir: *Turn off Grand Parade at Carlisle Rd, hotel is opposite Congress Theatre*
PETS: Bedrooms Charges £4.99 per night
Situated opposite the Congress Theatre, this hotel is just a short walk from both the seafront and Devonshire Park. Bedrooms are comfortably furnished and pleasantly decorated. Public areas are smartly appointed and include a cosy bar, a separate lounge and an attractive downstairs dining room.
Rooms 46 en suite (4 fmly) (3 GF) ⊘ in all bedrooms **Facilities** STV ♨ ♫ **Services** Lift **Parking** 36

★★★★ GUEST ACCOMMODATION
The Gladwyn
16 Blackwater Rd BN21 4JD
☎ 01323 733142
e-mail: gladwynhotel@aol.com
web: www.gladwynhotel.com
Dir: *250yds S of town centre. Off A259 South St onto Hardwick Rd & 1st right*
PETS: Bedrooms (GF) unattended sign **Charges** charge for damage **Public areas** except bkfst room on leads **Grounds** accessible disp bin **Exercise area** 500yds **Facilities** walks info vet info **On Request** fridge access torch towels **Resident Pets:** Saffe & Tasha (Staffordshire cross), Billy (Staffordshire Bull Terrier)

A warm welcome is guaranteed at this delightful guest house located opposite the famous tennis courts. Art work and interesting collectables feature throughout the property, including public areas and bedrooms. Freshly prepared breakfasts are served in the cosy dining room overlooking the attractive garden, which is available during the summer.

Rooms 10 en suite (1 fmly) (2 GF) ⊘ S £30-£32; D £60-£64✳ **Facilities** TVB tea/coffee TVL Wi-fi available **Notes** LB

FURNER'S GREEN   MAP 05 TQ42

►► **Heaven Farm** *(TQ403264)*

TN22 3RG

☎ 01825 790226 🖺 01825 790881

web: www.heavenfarm.co.uk

Dir: *On A275 between Lewes & East Grinstead, 1m N of Sheffield Park Gardens*

PETS: Public areas except toilets **Exercise area** on site meadows adjacent **Facilities** tea shop vet info **Other** prior notice required **Restrictions** dogs must not worry resident poultry & ducks; no young labradors or spaniels **Resident Pets:** 3 cats

Open Apr-Oct (rs Nov-Mar caravans only allowed on concrete area) Booking advisable Last arrival 21.00hrs Last departure noon

Delightful small rural site on a popular farm complex incorporating a farm museum, craft shop, tea room and nature trail. Good clean facilities in well-converted outbuildings. A 1.5-acre site with 25 touring pitches.

Notes 🐾 Prefer no children between 6-18yrs

HAILSHAM   MAP 05 TQ50

★★ 75% HOTEL

The Olde Forge Hotel & Restaurant

Magham Down BN27 1PN

☎ 01323 842893 🖺 01323 842893

e-mail: theoldeforgehotel@tesco.net

web: www.theoldeforgehotel.co.uk

Dir: *off Boship rdbt on A271 to Bexhill & Herstmonceux. 3m on left*

PETS: Please telephone for further information

In the heart of the countryside, this family-run hotel offers a friendly welcome and an informal atmosphere. The bedrooms are attractively decorated with thoughtful extras. The restaurant, with its timbered beams and log fires, was a forge in the 16th century; today it has a good local reputation for both its cuisine and service.

Rooms 7 en suite ⊘ in all bedrooms S £48; D £78 (incl. bkfst)✱ **Parking** 11

NEWICK   MAP 05 TQ42

★★★ ◎◎ HOTEL

Newick Park Hotel & Country Estate

BN8 4SB

☎ 01825 723633 🖺 01825 723969

e-mail: bookings@newickpark.co.uk

web: www.newickpark.co.uk

Dir: *Turn off A272 at Newick Green continue 1m pass church and pub. Turn left, hotel 0.25m on the right.*

PETS: Bedrooms (GF) sign **Grounds** accessible **Facilities** all facilities can be arrange with prior notice washing facs cage storage walks info vet info **On Request** fridge access torch towels **Resident Pets:** Ellie & Maddy (Black Labradors)

Delightful Grade II listed Georgian country house set amid 250 acres of Sussex parkland and landscaped gardens. The spacious, individually decorated bedrooms are tastefully furnished, thoughtfully equipped and have superb views of the grounds; many rooms have huge American king-size beds. The comfortable public rooms include a study, a sitting room, lounge bar and an elegant restaurant.

Rooms 13 en suite 3 annexe en suite (5 fmly) (1 GF) ⊘ in all bedrooms S fr £125; D £165-£285 (incl. bkfst)✱ **Facilities** STV ⊁ 🎣 Fishing 🏌 Wi-fi available Badminton Clay pigeon shooting Helicopter rides Quad biking Tank driving ch fac Xmas **Parking** 52 **Notes** LB

NORMAN'S BAY   MAP 05 TQ60

►►► **Norman's Bay Camping & Caravanning Club Site** *(TQ682055)*

BN24 6PR

☎ 01323 761190

web: www.campingandcaravanningclub.co.uk/normansbay

Dir: *From rdbt junct of A27/A259 follow A259 signed Eastbourne. In Pevensey Bay village take 1st left signed Beachlands only. 1.25m site on site*

PETS: Public areas except buildings **Exercise area** on site **Facilities** on site shop walks info vet info **Other** prior notice required

Open 13 Mar-3 Nov Booking advisable BH & peak periods Last arrival 21.00hrs Last departure noon

A well kept site with immaculate toilet block, right beside the sea. This popular family park enjoys good rural views towards Rye and Pevensey. A 13-acre site with 200 touring pitches, 5 hardstandings.

Notes site gates closed 23.00hrs-7.00hrs

PEASMARSH — MAP 05 TQ82

★★★ 78% HOTEL

Best Western Flackley Ash

TN31 6YH

☎ 01797 230651 📠 01797 230510

e-mail: enquiries@flackleyashhotel.co.uk

web: www.flackleyashhotel.co.uk

Dir: *exit A21 onto A268 to Newenden, next left A268 to Rye. Hotel on left on entering Peasmarsh*

PETS: Bedrooms (GF) unattended **Charges** £8.50 per night **Public areas** except restaurant, leisure centre on leads **Grounds** accessible disp bin **Exercise area** 10mtrs **Facilities** walks info vet info **On Request** torch

Five acres of beautifully kept grounds are the lovely backdrop to this elegant Georgian country house. The hotel is superbly situated for exploring the many local attractions, including the ancient Cinque Port of Rye, just a short drive away. The pleasantly decorated bedrooms have co-ordinated fabrics and many thoughtful touches.

Rooms 45 en suite (5 fmly) (19 GF) S £89-£129; D £148-£198 (incl. bkfst)✶ **Facilities** Spa STV ③ supervised Gym ↝ Putt green Wi-fi in bedrooms Beauty salon Steam room Sauna Xmas New Year **Parking** 80 **Notes** LB

RYE — MAP 05 TQ92

★★★ 75% HOTEL

Rye Lodge

Hilders Cliff TN31 7LD

☎ 01797 223838 📠 01797 223585

e-mail: info@ryelodge.co.uk

web: www.ryelodge.co.uk

Dir: *one-way system in Rye, follow signs for town centre, through Landgate arch, hotel 100yds on right*

PETS: Bedrooms unattended **Charges** £8 per night **Public areas** except restaurant **Exercise area** 150yds **Facilities** food

Standing in an elevated position, Rye Lodge has panoramic views across Romney Marshes and the Rother Estuary. Bedrooms come in a variety of sizes and styles; they are attractively decorated, tastefully furnished and thoughtfully equipped. Public rooms feature indoor leisure facilities, and The Terrace Room Restaurant where an interesting choice of home-made dishes is offered.

Rooms 18 en suite (5 GF) ⊘ in 4 bedrooms S £70-£100; D £100-£200 (incl. bkfst)✶ **Facilities** STV ③ Aromatherapy Steam cabinet Xmas **Parking** 20 **Notes** LB

★★★★★ GUEST ACCOMMODATION

Jeake's House

Mermaid St TN31 7ET

☎ 01797 222828 📠 01797 222623

e-mail: stay@jeakeshouse.com

web: www.jeakeshouse.com

Dir: *Approach from High St or The Strand*

PETS: Bedrooms Charges £5 per night **Public areas** except dining room **Exercise area** 5-10 mins walk **Facilities** walks info vet info **On Request** fridge access torch towels **Resident Pets:** Princess Yum Yum & Monte (Tonkinese cats)

Previously a 17th-century wool store and then a 19th-century Baptist school, this delightful house stands on a cobbled street in one of the most beautiful parts of this small, bustling town. The individually decorated bedrooms combine elegance and comfort with modern facilities. Breakfast is served at separate tables in the galleried dining room, and there is an oak-beamed lounge as well as a stylish book-lined bar with old pews.

Rooms 11 rms (10 en suite) (1 pri facs) (2 fmly) ⊘ in 9 bedrooms S £79; D £90-£124 **Facilities** TVB tea/coffee Direct dial from bedrooms Cen ht **Parking** 21 **Notes** No children 8yrs

★★★★ GUEST ACCOMMODATION
Little Saltcote
22 Military Rd TN31 7NY
☎ 01797 223210 🖨 01797 224474
e-mail: info@littlesaltcote.co.uk
web: www.littlesaltcote.co.uk
Dir: *0.5m N of town centre. Off A268 onto Military Rd signed Appledore, house 300yds on left*

PETS: Bedrooms (GF) **Charges** £5 per night charge for damage **Exercise area** 0.5m **Facilities** cage storage walks info vet info **On Request** fridge access torch towels **Resident Pets:** Bajan (cat)

This delightful family-run guest house stands in quiet surroundings within walking distance of Rye town centre. The bright and airy en suite bedrooms are equipped with modern facilities including Wi-fi, and you can enjoy afternoon tea in the garden conservatory. A hearty breakfast is served at individual tables in the dining room.

Rooms 4 en suite (2 fmly) (1 GF) ⊘ S £31.50-£63; D £63-£74
Facilities TVB tea/coffee Cen ht Wi-fi available **Parking** 5 **Notes** LB

★★★★ GUEST ACCOMMODATION
Silverdale
21 Sutton Park Rd BN25 1RH
☎ 01323 491849 🖨 01323 890854
e-mail: silverdale@mistral.co.uk
web: www.silverdale.mistral.co.uk
Dir: *On A259 in the centre of Seaford, close to memorial*

PETS: Bedrooms (GF) **Charges** charge for damage **Public areas**
Facilities food bowl water bowl dog chews cat treats feeding mat litter tray disp bags leads pet sitting dog walking dog grooming with prior notice cage storage walks info (map available) vet info **On Request** fridge access torch towels **Other** information on dog friendly pubs available **Restrictions** Telephone for details **Resident Pets:** Bertie & Bessie (American Cocker Spaniels)

A warm welcome is assured at this family-run establishment, which is well situated for the town centre and the seafront. The pleasant bedrooms have many useful extras, and breakfast and dinner are served in the dining room. The cosy well-stocked lounge bar specialises in English wines and malt whiskies.

Silverdale

Rooms 7 en suite (2 fmly) (1 GF) ⊘ D £40-£70✳ **Facilities** TVB tea/coffee Direct dial from bedrooms Cen ht Dinner Last d 2pm **Parking** 3 **Notes** LB

SUSSEX, WEST

★★★ 71% HOTEL
Norfolk Arms
High St BN18 9AB
☎ 01903 882101 🖨 01903 884275
e-mail: norfolk.arms@forestdale.com
web: www.forestdale.com
Dir: *on High St in city centre*

PETS: Bedrooms unattended **Charges** £7.50 per night
Public areas except restaurant

Built by the 10th Duke of Norfolk, this Georgian coaching inn enjoys a superb setting beneath the battlements of Arundel Castle. Bedrooms come in a variety of sizes and styles, all are well equipped. Public areas include two bars, a comfortable lounge, a traditional English restaurant and a range of meeting rooms.

Rooms 21 en suite 13 annexe en suite (4 fmly) (8 GF) ⊘ in 11 bedrooms **Facilities** Wi-fi available Xmas New Year **Parking** 34

ENGLAND

ARUNDEL CONTINUED

►► Ship & Anchor Marina *(TQ002040)*

Station Rd, Ford BN18 0BJ

☎ 01243 551262 ▤ 01243 555256

e-mail: ysm36@dial.pipex.com

Dir: *From A27 at Arundel take road S signed Ford. Site 2m from Arundel on left after level crossing*

PETS: Public areas Exercise area on site riverside walks
Facilities on site shop food dog chews cat treats walks info vet info space for loose box **Resident Pets:** 2 dogs & 5 cats

Open Mar-Oct Booking advisable during Goodwood Motor Festival Last arrival 21.00hrs Last departure noon

A neat and tidy site in a pleasant position beside the Ship & Anchor pub and the tidal River Arun. There are good walks from the site both to Arundel and to the coast. A 12-acre site with 120 touring pitches, 11 hardstandings and 40 statics.

Notes ☺

BARNS GREEN   MAP 04 TQ12

►►► Sumners Ponds Fishery & Campsite

(TQ125268)

Chapel Rd RH13 0PR

☎ 01403 732539

e-mail: sumnersponds@dsl.co.uk

web: www.sumnersponds.co.uk

Dir: *From A272 at Coolham x-rds, N towards Barns Green. In 1.5m take 1st left at small x-rds. 1m, over level crossing. Site on left just after right bend*

PETS: Stables nearby (2m) **Public areas Exercise area** on site
Facilities on site shop food water bowl walks info vet info

Open all year Booking advisable all year Last arrival 20.00hrs Last departure 17.00hrs

A touring area on a working farm on the edge of the quiet village of Barnes Green, with purpose built facilities of a high standard. There are three well-stocked fishing lakes set in attractive surroundings, and a woodland walk with direct access to miles of footpaths. Horsham and Brighton are within easy reach. A 40-acre site with 61 touring pitches, 31 hardstandings.

Notes Only one car per pitch - all other cars must be left in car park

BILLINGSHURST   MAP 04 TQ02

►► Limeburners Arms Camp Site *(TQ072255)*

Lordings Rd, Newbridge RH14 9JA

☎ 01403 782311

e-mail: chippy.sawyer@virgin.net

Dir: *From A29 turn W onto A272 for 1m, then left onto B2133. Site 300yds on left*

PETS: Public areas Exercise area adjacent walks **Facilities** vet info

Open Apr-Oct Booking advisable BH & Jul-Aug Last arrival 22.00hrs Last departure 14.00hrs

A secluded site in rural West Sussex, at the rear of the Limeburners Arms public house, and surrounded by fields. It makes a pleasant base for touring the South Downs and the Arun Valley. The toilets are basic but very clean. A 2.75-acre site with 40 touring pitches.

BOGNOR REGIS   MAP 04 SZ99

★★★ 71% HOTEL

Royal Norfolk

The Esplanade PO21 2LH

☎ 01243 826222 ▤ 01243 826325

e-mail: accommodation@royalnorfolkhotel.com

web: www.royalnorfolkhotel.com

Dir: *from A259 follow Longford Rd through lights to Canada Grove to T-junct. Right, take 2nd exit at rdbt. Hotel on right*

PETS: Bedrooms Charges £20 per stay **Public areas** except restaurant **Exercise area** nearby **Restrictions** Telephone for details

On the Esplanade, but set back behind its own lawns and gardens, this fine-looking hotel has been welcoming guests since Regency times. Today the traditionally furnished bedrooms, four with four-poster beds, are well provided with all the modern comforts. Public areas offer sea views from the elegant restaurant and comfortable lobby lounge.

Rooms 41 en suite (6 fmly) ⊘ in all bedrooms S £35-£60; D £70-£120 (incl. bkfst)✴ **Facilities** ♫ Xmas **Services** Lift **Parking** 60

CHICHESTER MAP 04 SU80

★★★★ BED & BREAKFAST
Old Chapel Forge

Lower Bognor Rd, Lagness PO20 1LR

☎ 01243 264380

e-mail: info@oldchapelforge.co.uk

Dir: *4m SE of Chichester. Off A27 Chichester bypass at Bognor rdbt signed Pagham/Runcton, onto B2166 Pagham Rd & Lower Bognor Rd, Old Chapel Forge on right*

PETS: Bedrooms (GF) **Stables** nearby (0.25m)
Charges donation to local nature reserve (min £5) charge for damage **Public areas** except bkfst area on leads
Grounds accessible on leads **Exercise area** 80 acres adjacent walks info vet info **On Request** fridge access torch towels
Other all pets by prior arrangement only **Resident Pets:** Eddie and Ellie (geese), Jade (Labrador), 4 donkeys

Great local produce features in the hearty breakfasts at this comfortable, eco-friendly property, an idyllic 17th-century house and chapel set in mature gardens with panoramic views of the South Downs. Old Chapel Forge is a short drive from Chichester, Goodwood, Pagham Harbour Nature Reserve and the beach. Bedrooms, including suites in the chapel, are luxurious, and all have Internet access.

Rooms 4 annexe en suite (2 fmly) (4 GF) ⊘ S £45-£55; D £50-£110✱
Facilities TVB tea/coffee Cen ht Dinner Last d Breakfast Wi-fi available
Parking 6 **Notes** LB

►►► Ellscott Park *(SU829995)*

Sidlesham Ln, Birdham PO20 7QL

☎ 01243 512003 📄 01243 512003

e-mail: camping@ellscottpark.co.uk

web: www.ellscottpark.co.uk

Dir: *Take A286 (Chichester/Wittering road) for approx 4m, left at Butterfly Farm sign, site 500yds right*

PETS: Public areas on leads **Exercise area** on site **Facilities** vet info **Resident Pets:** Tigger (Scottish Terrier)

Open Mar-Oct Booking advisable BH & Aug

A well-kept park set in meadowland behind the owners' nursery and van storage area. The park attracts a peace-loving clientele, and is handy for the beach and other local attractions. Home-grown produce and eggs are for sale. A 2.5-acre site with 50 touring pitches.

Notes 🐾

CHILGROVE

★★★★ 🔵🔵 ☕ RESTAURANT WITH ROOMS
The Chilgrove White Horse

PO18 9HX

☎ 01243 535219 📄 01243 535301

e-mail: info@whitehorsechilgrove.co.uk

web: www.whitehorsechilgrove.co.uk

Dir: *Off A286 onto B2141 to village*

PETS: Bedrooms (GF) **Charges** charge for damage
Public areas except restaurant on leads **Grounds** accessible on leads **Exercise area** 30yds **Facilities** washing facs cage storage vet info **On Request** fridge access torch towels
Resident Pets: Beth & Holly (working Cocker Spaniels)

Dating in part from the 17th century, this homely inn retains much original charm with its beams and stone floors. Food and service however are completely up to date and memorable, while the smart bedrooms are situated in a nearby annexe and are well equipped and furnished.

Rooms 9 en suite (5 GF) ⊘ S £75-£95; D £95-£160✱ **Facilities** TVB tea/coffee Direct dial from bedrooms Cen ht Dinner Last d 9pm Massage can be arranged with prior notice **Parking** 60 **Notes** LB Closed Sun evening & all day Mon

CLIMPING
MAP 04 SU90

★★★ 83% HOTEL

Bailiffscourt Hotel & Spa

Climping St BN17 5RW

☎ 01903 723511 📠 01903 718987

e-mail: bailiffscourt@hshotels.co.uk

web: www.hshotels.co.uk

Dir: *A259, follow Climping Beach signs. Hotel 0.5m on right*

PETS: Bedrooms (GF) unattended **Charges** £12 per night
Public areas Grounds accessible disp bin **Exercise area** 200mtrs
Facilities food (pre-bookable) food bowl water bowl dog chews
feeding mat disp bags washing facs cage storage walks info vet
info room service **On Request** fridge access torch towels

This delightful 'medieval manor' dating back only to the 1920s has the
appearance of having been in existence for centuries. Bedrooms vary
from atmospheric feature rooms with log fires, oak beams and
four-poster beds to spacious, stylish, and contemporary rooms located
in the grounds. Classic European cooking is a highlight, and a stylish
spa plus a choice of cosy lounges completes the package.

Rooms 9 en suite 30 annexe en suite (25 fmly) (16 GF) S £185-£455;
D £205-£510 (incl. bkfst)✳ **Facilities** Spa STV ⊗ ↻ pool supervised ⊗
Gym ♨ Wi-fi available Xmas New Year **Parking** 100 **Notes** LB

CUCKFIELD
MAP 04 TQ32

★★★ HOTEL

Ockenden Manor

Ockenden Ln RH17 5LD

☎ 01444 416111 📠 01444 415549

e-mail: reservations@ockenden-manor.com

web: www.hshotels.co.uk

Dir: *A23 towards Brighton. 4.5m left onto B2115 towards
Haywards Heath. Cuckfield 3m. Ockendon Lane off High St. Hotel
at end*

PETS: Bedrooms (GF) unattended **Charges** £10 per night charge
for damage **Grounds** accessible **Facilities** cage storage

This charming 16th-century hotel enjoys fine views of the South
Downs. Bedrooms offer high standards of accommodation, some with
historic features. Public rooms, retaining much original character,
include an elegant sitting room with all the elements for a relaxing

afternoon in front of the fire. Imaginative, noteworthy cuisine is a
highlight to any stay.

Rooms 22 en suite (4 fmly) (4 GF) ⊗ in all bedrooms S £105-£185;
D £170-£350 (incl. bkfst)✳ **Facilities** STV ♨ Wi-fi available Xmas New
Year **Parking** 43 **Notes** LB

GATWICK AIRPORT (LONDON)
MAP 04 TQ24

★★★★ GUEST HOUSE

The Lawn Guest House

30 Massetts Rd RH6 7DF

☎ 01293 775751 📠 01293 821803

e-mail: info@lawnguesthouse.co.uk

web: www.lawnguesthouse.co.uk

Dir: *M23 junct 9, signs to A23 (Redhill), 3rd exit at rdbt by Esso
station, 300yds right at lights*

PETS: Bedrooms Grounds accessible **Exercise area** 0.5m

Convenient for Gatwick Airport, this fine detached Victorian house
offers comfortable bedrooms, equipped with many thoughtful extras.
The atmosphere is relaxed, the welcome friendly, and an Internet
facility is available. A choice of breakfast is served in an attractive dining
room. Holiday parking and airport transfer is a real bonus.

Rooms 12 en suite (4 fmly) ⊗ S £45-£50; D £60-£65✳ **Facilities** TVB
tea/coffee Direct dial from bedrooms Cen ht **Parking** 15
Notes No coaches

GRAFFHAM
MAP 04 SU91

▶▶▶ **Graffham Camping & Caravanning
Club Site** (*SU941187*)

Great Bury GU28 0QJ

☎ 01798 867476

web: www.campingandcaravanningclub.co.uk/graffham

Dir: *From Petworth on A285 pass Badgers pub on left & BP
garage on right. Next right signed Selham Graffham. Follow sign
to site*

PETS: Public areas except buildings **Exercise area** on site dog
walks **Facilities** walks info vet info **Other** prior notice required

Open 13 Mar-3 Nov Booking advisable BH & peak periods
Last arrival 21.00hrs Last departure noon

A superb woodland site with some pitches occupying their own private,
naturally-screened areas. A peaceful retreat, or base for touring the
South Downs, Chichester and the south coast. A 20-acre site with 90
touring pitches.

Notes Site gates will be closed 23.00hrs-07.00hrs

LITTLEHAMPTON MAP 04 TQ00

▶▶▶ White Rose Touring Park *(TQ029039)*

Mill Ln, Wick BN17 7PH

☎ 01903 716176 📄 01903 732671

e-mail: snowdondavid@hotmail.com

web: www.whiterosetouringpark.co.uk

Dir: *From A27 take A284, turn left into Mill Lane, after approx 1.5m just after Six Bells Pub*

PETS: Charges £1 per night **Public areas** except shower block **Exercise area** on site fenced area beach & countryside nearby **Facilities** on site shop food vet info **Resident Pets:** Holly (Springer Spaniel)

Open 15 Mar-14 Dec Booking advisable BH & Jul-Aug Last arrival 22.00hrs Last departure noon

Farmland surrounds this carefully maintained site located on well-drained ground close to Arundel and Littlehampton. The family-run site offers a choice of super pitches and mini pitches for tents, and there is good hedging and landscaping. A 7-acre site with 127 touring pitches and 13 statics.

MIDHURST MAP 04 SU82

★★★ 80% ⊕⊕ HOTEL
Spread Eagle Hotel and Spa

South St GU29 9NH

☎ 01730 816911 📄 01730 815668

e-mail: spreadeagle@hshotels.co.uk

web: www.hshotels.co.uk/spread/spreadeagle-main.htm

Dir: *from M25 junct 10 follow A3 S, exit A3 at Milford and follow A286 to Midhurst. Hotel adjacent to Market Square on South Street*

PETS: Bedrooms unattended **Stables** nearby **Charges** £15 per night charge for damage **Public areas** except restaurant **Grounds** accessible **Facilities** food (pre-bookable) food bowl water bowl bedding walks info vet info **On Request** fridge access torch

Offering accommodation since 1430, this historic property is full of character, evident in its sloping floors and inglenook fireplaces. Individually styled bedrooms provide modern comforts; those in the main house have oak panelling and include some spacious feature rooms. The hotel also boasts a well-equipped spa and offers noteworthy food in the oak beamed restaurant.

Rooms 35 en suite 4 annexe en suite (8 GF) ⊗ in all bedrooms S £90-£400; D £99-£400 (incl. bkfst) **Facilities** Spa STV ⊕ Gym Wi-fi available Health & beauty treatment rooms Steam room Fitness trainer Xmas New Year **Parking** 75 **Notes** LB

★★★★ BED & BREAKFAST
Redford Cottage

Redford GU29 0QF

☎ 01428 741242

Dir: *Off A272 1m W of Midhurst signed Redford, Redford Cottage 400yds past Redford village sign on left*

PETS: Sep Accom boot room utility room for pets **Stables** nearby (1m) **Charges** £5 per night **Public areas** **Grounds** accessible **Exercise area** adjacent **Facilities** washing facs cage storage walks info vet info **On Request** fridge access torch

This delightful farmhouse stands in an Area of Outstanding Natural Beauty. Bedroom styles vary, with a traditional cottage room in the main house and a garden suite of stylish Swedish design; each room has access to a private sitting room. The new timber-framed lounge opens onto the attractive mature gardens, and breakfasts are served family-style in a separate dining room.

Rooms 1 en suite 2 annexe en suite (1 GF) ⊗ S £65-£70; D £95-£105 **Facilities** TVB tea/coffee Cen ht TVL **Parking** 10 **Notes** Closed Xmas & New Year ⊕

SELSEY MAP 04 SZ89

★★★★ GUEST ACCOMMODATION
St Andrews Lodge

Chichester Rd PO20 0LX

☎ 01243 606899 📄 01243 607826

e-mail: info@standrewslodge.co.uk

web: www.standrewslodge.co.uk

Dir: *B2145 into Selsey, on right just before the church*

PETS: Bedrooms (GF) unattended **Charges** £3 per stay **Public areas** except restaurant lounge **Grounds** accessible disp bin **Exercise area** 200yds **Facilities** food bowl water bowl cage storage walks info vet info **On Request** fridge access torch towels **Resident Pets:** Pepper (cat)

This friendly lodge is just half a mile from the seafront. The refurbished bedrooms are bright and spacious, and have a range of useful extras. Five ground-floor rooms, one with easier access, overlook the large south-facing garden, which is perfect for a drink on a summer evening.

Rooms 5 en suite 5 annexe en suite (3 fmly) (5 GF) ⊗ S £36-£50; D £62.50-£85 **Facilities** TVB tea/coffee Direct dial from bedrooms Cen ht TVL **Parking** 14 **Notes** LB Closed 21 Dec-11 Jan

SLINDON — MAP 04 SU90

▶ Slindon Camping & Caravanning Club Site (SU958084)

Slindon Park BN18 0RG

☎ 01243 814387

web: www.campingandcaravanningclub.co.uk/slindon

Dir: *From A27 Fontwell to Chichester turn right at sign for Brittons Lane & 2nd right to Slindon. Site on this road*

PETS: **Public areas** except buildings **Exercise area** on site interesting walks around camp site **Facilities** walks info vet info **Other** prior notice required

Open 13 Mar-29 Sep Booking advisable BH & peak periods Last arrival 21.00hrs Last departure noon

A beautiful former orchard, completely screened by National Trust trees, and very quiet. It is ideal for the self-contained camper, and own sanitary facilities are essential. The entrance gate is narrow and on a bend, and touring units are advised to take a wide sweep on approach from private gravel roadway. A 2-acre site with 40 touring pitches.

Notes Site gates will be closed 23.00hrs-7.00hrs

SOUTHBOURNE — MAP 04 SU70

▶▶▶ Chichester Camping & Caravanning Club Site (SU774056)

Main Rd PO10 8JH

☎ 01243 373202

web: www.campingandcaravanningclub.co.uk/chichester

Dir: *From Chichester take A259 to Southampton, site on right past Inlands Road*

PETS: **Facilities** walks info vet info **Other** prior notice required

Open 7 Feb-17 Nov Booking advisable BH & peak periods Last arrival 21.00hrs Last departure noon

Situated in open meadow and orchard, a very pleasant, popular site with well looked after, clean facilities. Well placed for Chichester, South Downs and the ferry ports. A 3-acre site with 58 touring pitches, 42 hardstandings.

Notes site gates closed 23.00hrs-7.00hrs

WORTHING — MAP 04 TQ10

★★ 62% HOTEL

Cavendish

THE INDEPENDENTS
HOTEL ASSOCIATION

115 Marine Pde BN11 3QG

☎ 01903 236767 🖷 01903 823840

e-mail: reservations@cavendishworthing.co.uk

web: www.cavendishworthing.co.uk

Dir: *on seafront, 600yds W of pier*

PETS: **Bedrooms** (GF) unattended **Public areas** except restaurant on leads **Facilities** walks info vet info **On Request** fridge access towels **Exercise area** nearby

This popular, family-run hotel enjoys a prominent seafront location. Bedrooms are well equipped and soundly decorated. Guests have an extensive choice of meal options, with a varied bar menu, and carte and daily menus offered in the restaurant. Limited parking is available at the rear of the hotel.

Rooms 17 en suite (4 fmly) ⊘ in 3 bedrooms S £45-£49; D £69.50-£85 (incl. bkfst)✳ **Facilities** STV Wi-fi available **Services** air con **Parking** 5 **Notes** LB

TYNE & WEAR

NEWCASTLE UPON TYNE MAP 12 NZ26

★★★★ 76% ⊛ HOTEL
Newcastle Marriott Hotel Gosforth Park

High Gosforth Park, Gosforth NE3 5HN
☎ 0191 236 4111 ▤ 0191 236 8192
web: www.marriott.co.uk
Dir: *onto A1056 to Killingworth & Wideopen. 3rd exit to Gosforth Park, hotel ahead*

PETS: Bedrooms Grounds accessible on leads **Facilities** vet info
Set within its own grounds, this modern hotel offers extensive conference and banqueting facilities, along with indoor and outdoor leisure and a choice of formal and informal dining. Many of the air-conditioned bedrooms have views over the park; executive rooms feature extras such as CD players. The hotel is conveniently located for the by-pass, airport and racecourse.

Rooms 178 en suite ⊘ in 145 bedrooms **Facilities** Spa STV ⊗ supervised ⚲ Squash Gym Wi-fi available Trim & jogging trail in hotel grounds ♫ New Year **Services** Lift air con **Parking** 340 **Notes** RS Xmas & New Year

WHICKHAM MAP 12 NZ26

★★★ 70% HOTEL
Gibside
Front St NE16 4JG
☎ 0191 488 9292 ▤ 0191 488 8000
e-mail: reception@gibside-hotel.co.uk
web: www.gibside-hotel.co.uk
Dir: *off A1(M) towards Whickham on B6317, onto Front St, 2m on right*

PETS: Bedrooms unattended **Grounds** accessible **Exercise area** opposite
Conveniently located in the village centre, this hotel is close to the Newcastle by-pass and its elevated position affords views over the Tyne Valley. Bedrooms come in two styles, classical and contemporary. Public rooms include the Egyptian-themed Sphinx bar and a more formal restaurant. Secure garage parking is available.

Rooms 45 en suite (2 fmly) (13 GF) ⊘ in all bedrooms S £62.50-£75; D £72.50-£85✻ **Facilities** STV Wi-fi in bedrooms Golf Academy at The Beamish Park ♫ New Year **Services** Lift **Parking** 28

WARWICKSHIRE

BAGINTON MAP 04 SP37

★★★ INN
The Oak
Coventry Rd CV8 3AU
☎ 02476 518855 ▤ 02476 518866
e-mail: thebagintonoak@aol.com
web: www.theoak.greatpubs.net

PETS: Bedrooms (GF) unattended **Stables** nearby (0.5m) **Charges** £5 per night charge for damage **Public areas** on leads **Grounds** accessible disp bin **Exercise area** adjacent **Facilities** walks info vet info

Located close to major road links and Coventry Airport, this popular inn provides a wide range of value food throughout themed open plan public areas and families are especially welcome. Modern well equipped bedrooms are situated within a separate accommodation building.

Rooms 13 annexe en suite (1 fmly) (6 GF) D £40-£60✻ **Facilities** FTV TVB tea/coffee Cen ht Dinner Last d 9pm Wi-fi available **Parking** 110

GREAT WOLFORD MAP 04 SP23

★★★★ ⊜ INN
The Fox & Hounds Inn
CV36 5NQ
☎ 01608 674220 ▤ 01608 674160
e-mail: info@thefoxandhoundsinn.com
Dir: *Off A3400, 1.5m to Great Wolford*

PETS: Bedrooms unattended **Public areas Grounds** accessible **Exercise area** 50yds
Very much a focal point of the local community, this 16th-century inn retains many original features, which are enhanced by rustic furniture and memorabilia. The thoughtfully furnished bedrooms are in converted outbuildings, and a warm welcome is assured.

Rooms 3 annexe en suite S £50; D £80✻ **Facilities** TVB tea/coffee Cen ht Dinner Last d 9pm **Parking** 12 **Notes** RS Sun & Mon

ENGLAND

KENILWORTH — MAP 04 SP27

★★★★ 71% HOTEL

Chesford Grange

 QHOTELS

Chesford Bridge CV8 2LD

☎ 01926 859331 📠 01926 859272

e-mail: chesfordgrangereservations@qhotels.co.uk
web: www.qhotels.co.uk

Dir: *0.5m SE of junct A46/A452. At rdbt turn right signed Leamington Spa the follow signs to hotel*

PETS: Bedrooms unattended **Charges** £10 per night
Grounds accessible large grounds available **Other** Well behaved dogs only

This much-extended hotel set in 17 acres of private grounds is well situated for Birmingham International Airport, the NEC and major routes. Bedrooms range from traditional style to contemporary rooms featuring state-of-the-art technology. Public areas include a leisure club and extensive conference and banqueting facilities.

Rooms 209 en suite (20 fmly) (43 GF) S £60-£150; D £70-£160 (incl. bkfst)✳ **Facilities Spa** STV ☜ supervised **Gym** Wi-fi in bedrooms Steam room Xmas New Year **Services** Lift **Parking** 650 **Notes LB**

KINGSBURY — MAP 04 SP29

►►►► Kingsbury Water Park C&C Club Site *(SP202968)*

Kingsbury Water Park, Bodymoor, Heath Ln B76 0DY

☎ 01827 874101

web: www.campingandcaravanningclub.co.uk/
kingsburywaterpark

Dir: *From M42 junct 9 take B4097 Kingsbury road. Left at rdbt, past main entrance to water park, over motorway, take next right. Follow lane for 0.5m to site*

PETS: Public areas except buildings **Facilities** walks info vet info
Other prior notice required

Open all year Booking advisable BH & peak periods Last arrival 21.00hrs Last departure noon

A very upmarket site providing high standards in every area. Along with private washing facilities in the quality toilets, there is good security on this attractive former gravel pit, with its complex of lakes, canals, woods and marshland, with good access roads. An 18-acre site with 150 touring pitches, 75 hardstandings.

Notes site gates closed 23.00hrs-7.00hrs

LEAMINGTON SPA (ROYAL) — MAP 04 SP36

★★★ 72% HOTEL

Best Western Falstaff

 Best Western

16-20 Warwick New Rd CV32 5JQ

☎ 01926 312044 📠 01926 450574

e-mail: falstaff@meridianleisure.com
web: www.meridianleisure.com

Dir: *M40 junct 13 or 14 follow signs for Leamington Spa. Over 4 rdbts then under bridge. Left into Princes Drive, then right at mini rdbt*

PETS: Bedrooms (GF) unattended **Charges** £10 per night
Grounds accessible on leads **Facilities** vet info
On Request fridge access towels

Bedrooms at this hotel come in a variety of sizes and styles but are well equipped, with many thoughtful extras. Snacks can be taken in the relaxing lounge bar, and an interesting selection of English and continental dishes is offered in the restaurant; 24-hour room service is also available. Conference and banqueting facilities are extensive.

Rooms 63 en suite (2 fmly) (16 GF) ⊗ in all bedrooms **Facilities** FTV Wi-fi in bedrooms Arrangement with local health club **Parking** 50

★★★★ GUEST ACCOMMODATION

Bubbenhall House

Paget's Ln CV8 3BJ

☎ 024 7630 2409 & 07746 282541 📠 024 7630 2409

e-mail: wharrison@bubbenhallhouse.freeserve.co.uk

Dir: *5m NE of Leamington. Off A445 at Bubbenhall S onto Pagets Ln, 1m on single-track lane (over 4 speed humps)*

PETS: Bedrooms Public areas except dining room on leads
Grounds accessible disp bin **Facilities** food (pre-bookable) food bowl water bowl dog chews pet sitting washing facs cage storage walks info vet info **On Request** fridge access torch towels **Resident Pets:** Zippy (Black Labrador), Budweiser (Jack Russell), Kitty (cat)

Located between Leamington Spa and Coventry in extensive mature grounds with an abundance of wildlife, this impressive late Edwardian house was once the home of the Alexander Issigonis, designer of the Mini. It contains many interesting features including a Jacobean-style staircase. Thoughtful extras are provided in the bedrooms and public areas include an elegant dining room and choice of sumptuous lounges.

Rooms 3 en suite S £47-£49; D £67-£69✳ **Facilities** TVB tea/coffee Cen ht TVL Dinner Last d 7.30pm ☕ 🍴 **Parking** 12 **Notes LB** 🐾

NUNEATON   MAP 04 SP39

★★★ 72% HOTEL
Best Western Weston Hall

Weston Ln, Bulkington CV12 9RU
☎ 024 7631 2989 🖷 024 7664 0846
e-mail: info@westonhallhotel.co.uk
Dir: *M6 junct 2 follow B4065 through Ansty. Left in Shilton, follow Nuneaton signs out of Bulkington, turn into Weston Ln at 30mph sign*
PETS: Bedrooms (GF) **Charges** £10 per dog per night
Public areas except at meal times **Grounds** accessible
Facilities food (pre-bookable) food bowl water bowl bedding dog chews cat treats washing facs cage storage walks info vet info **On Request** fridge access torch towels
Resident Pets: Charlie & Snowy (cats)

This Grade II listed hotel, whose origins date back to the reign of Elizabeth I, sits within seven acres of peaceful grounds. The original three-gabled building retains many original features, such as the carved wooden fireplace situated in the library. Friendly service is provided; and bedrooms, that vary in size, are thoughtfully equipped.
Rooms 40 en suite (1 fmly) (14 GF) ⊘ in 26 bedrooms **Facilities** ⤵ Steam room **Parking** 300 **Notes** LB

RUGBY   MAP 04 SP57

▶▶ Lodge Farm Campsite *(SP476748)*

Bilton Ln, Long Lawford CV23 9DU
☎ 01788 560193 🖷 01788 550603
e-mail: alec@lodgefarm.com
web: www.lodgefarm.com
Dir: *From Rugby take A428 (Lawford Road) 1.5m towards Coventry. At Sheaf & Sickle pub left into Bilton Lane, site 500yds*
PETS: Stables nearby (3m) (loose box) **Exercise area** 200yds
Facilities washing facs walks info vet info **Resident Pets:** a Collie, 2 cats
Open Etr-Nov Booking advisable BH Last arrival 22.00hrs
A small, simple farm site set behind the friendly owner's home and self-catering cottages, with converted stables housing the toilet facilities. Rugby is only a short drive away, and the site is tucked well away from the main road. A 2.5-acre site with 35 touring pitches, 3 hardstandings and 10 statics.

STRATFORD-UPON-AVON   MAP 04 SP25

★★★ 62% HOTEL
Charlecote Pheasant Hotel

folio Hotels

Charlecote CV35 9EW
☎ 0870 609 6159 🖷 01789 470222
e-mail: charlecote@foliohotels.com
web: www.foliohotels.com/charlcotepheasant
Dir: *M40 junct 15, A429 towards Cirencester through Barford. In 2m turn right into Charlecote, hotel opposite Charlecote Manor Park*
PETS: Bedrooms unattended **Charges** £10 per night
Exercise area on site adjacent field
Located just outside Stratford, this hotel is set in extensive grounds and is a popular conference venue. Various bedroom styles are available within the annexe wings, ranging from standard rooms to executive suites. The main building houses the restaurant and a lounge bar area.
Rooms 70 en suite (39 fmly) ⊘ in 48 bedrooms **Facilities** STV ⤽ ⤸ Wi-fi available Children's Play area **Parking** 100

★★★ GUEST ACCOMMODATION
Avon Lodge

Ryon Hill, Warwick Rd CV37 0NZ
☎ 01789 295196
PETS: Bedrooms Exercise area 2 acres on site **Facilities** walks info vet info **Resident Pets:** Jacko (German Shephard)
Located in immaculate mature gardens on the outskirts of town, this former Victorian cottage has been carefully modernised and extended to provide cosy bedrooms. Imaginative breakfasts are served in the attractive cottage-style dining room.
Rooms 6 en suite (1 fmly) ⊘ **Facilities** TV5B tea/coffee Cen ht TVL Golf **Parking** 7 **Notes** ✉

WARWICK   MAP 04 SP26

★★★★ GUEST ACCOMMODATION
Croft

Haseley Knob CV35 7NL
☎ 01926 484447 🖷 01926 484447
e-mail: david@croftguesthouse.co.uk
web: www.croftguesthouse.co.uk
Dir: *4.5m NW of Warwick. Off A4177 into Haseley Knob, follow B&B signs*
PETS: Bedrooms (GF) **Charges** £3 per night **Grounds** accessible on leads **Facilities** feeding mat cage storage walks info vet info **On Request** fridge access torch
Friendly proprietors provide homely accommodation at this modern detached house, set in peaceful countryside and convenient for Warwick and the NEC, Birmingham. The conservatory dining room

CONTINUED

ENGLAND

WARWICK CONTINUED

overlooks large well-kept gardens. Fresh eggs from home-reared chickens are used for memorable English breakfasts.

Rooms 7 rms (5 en suite) (2 pri facs) 2 annexe rms (1 en suite) (1 annexe pri facs) (2 fmly) (4 GF) ◎ S fr £40; D fr £60 **Facilities** TVB tea/coffee Cen ht TVL **Parking** 9 **Notes** Closed Xmas wk

WARWICK MOTORWAY SERVICE AREA (M40)
MAP 04 SP35

BUDGET HOTEL
Days Inn Stratford upon Avon

Warwick Services, M40 Northbound junction 12-13, Banbury Rd CV35 0AA

☎ 01926 651681 📠 01926 651634

e-mail: warwick.north.hotel@welcomebreak.co.uk

web: www.daysinn.com

Dir: *M40 northbound between junct 12 & 13*

PETS: Bedrooms (GF) sign **Public areas** on leads **Grounds** accessible on leads disp bin **Exercise area** nearby

This modern building offers accommodation in smart, spacious and well-equipped bedrooms, suitable for families and business travellers, and all with en suite bathrooms. Continental breakfast is available and other refreshments may be taken at the nearby family restaurant. For further details see the Hotel Groups page.

Rooms 54 en suite

BUDGET HOTEL
Days Inn Warwick South

Warwick Services, M40 Southbound, Banbury Rd CV35 0AA

☎ 01926 650168 📠 01926 651601

e-mail: warwick.south.hotel@welcomebreak.co.uk

web: www.daysinn.com

Dir: *M40 southbound between junct 14 & 12*

PETS: Bedrooms (GF) sign **Public areas** on leads **Grounds** accessible on leads disp bin **Exercise area** on site

This modern building offers accommodation in smart, spacious and well-equipped bedrooms, suitable for families and business travellers, and all with en suite bathrooms. Continental breakfast is available and other refreshments may be taken at the nearby family restaurant. For further details see the Hotel Groups page.

Rooms 40 en suite

WOLVEY
MAP 04 SP48

►►► Wolvey Villa Farm Caravan & Camping Site *(SP428869)*

LE10 3HF

☎ 01455 220493 & 220630

web: www.wolveycaravan park.itgo.com

Dir: *From M6 junct 2 take B4065 follow Wolvey signs. Or M69 junct 1 & follow Wolvey signs*

PETS: Charges 50p per dog per night **Public areas** **Exercise area** on site grass field **Facilities** on site shop food vet info

Open all year Booking advisable Spring BH-mid Aug Last arrival 22.00hrs Last departure noon

A level grass site surrounded by trees and shrubs, on the borders of Warwickshire and Leicestershire. This quiet country site has its own popular fishing lake, and is convenient for visiting the major cities of Coventry and Leicester. A 7-acre site with 110 touring pitches, 24 hardstandings.

Notes ◎ No twin axles

WEST MIDLANDS

BIRMINGHAM
MAP 07 SP08

★★★★ 71% HOTEL
Novotel Birmingham Centre

70 Broad St B1 2HT

☎ 0121 643 2000 📠 0121 643 9796

e-mail: h1077@accor.com

web: www.novotel.com

Dir: *A38/A456, hotel on right beyond International Convention Centre*

PETS: Other Please telephone for details

This large, modern, purpose-built hotel benefits from an excellent city centre location, with the bonus of secure parking. Bedrooms are spacious, modern and well equipped especially for business users; four rooms have facilities for less able guests. Public areas include the Garden Brasserie, function rooms and a fitness room.

Rooms 148 en suite (148 fmly) ◎ in 113 bedrooms S £59-£165; D £59-£175✳ **Facilities** STV Gym Wi-fi in bedrooms **Services** Lift air con **Parking** 53 **Notes** LB

★★ 75% HOTEL

Copperfield House

60 Upland Rd, Selly Park B29 7JS

☎ 0121 472 8344 📄 0121 415 5655

e-mail: info@copperfieldhousehotel.fsnet.co.uk

Dir: *M6 junct 6/A38 through city centre. After tunnels, right at lights into Belgrave Middleway. Right at rdbt onto A441. At Selly Park Tavern, right into Upland Rd*

PETS: Bedrooms (GF) **Charges** £5 per night **Grounds** accessible disp bin **Exercise area** 0.25m **Facilities** walks info vet info **On Request** torch towels

A delightful Victorian hotel, situated in a leafy suburb, close to the BBC's Pebble Mill Studios and within easy reach of the centre. Accommodation is smartly presented and well equipped, and the executive rooms are particularly spacious. There is a lounge with an honesty bar and the restaurant offers carefully prepared, seasonally-inspired food accompanied by a well-chosen wine list.

Rooms 17 en suite (1 fmly) (2 GF) S £50-£90; D £70-£100 (incl. bkfst)✳ **Facilities** FTV Wi-fi available **Parking** 11 **Notes** LB Closed 24 Dec - 2 Jan

★★ 68% HOTEL

Fountain Court

THE INDEPENDENTS
HOTEL ASSOCIATION

339-343 Hagley Rd B17 8NH

☎ 0121 429 1754 📄 0121 429 1209

e-mail: info@fountain-court.co.uk

Dir: *on A456, towards Birmingham, 3m from M5 junct 3*

PETS: Bedrooms Grounds accessible **Exercise area** approx 200yds **Resident Pets:** Lucky & Pebbles (Jack Russells)

This family-owned hotel is on the A456, near to the M5 and a short drive from the city centre. A warm welcome is assured and day rooms include comfortable lounges and a cottage-style dining room, the setting for home-cooked dinners and comprehensive breakfasts.

Rooms 23 en suite (4 fmly) (3 GF) S £39.50-£50; D £60-£75 (incl. bkfst) ✳ **Parking** 20

★★ GUEST ACCOMMODATION

Rollason Wood

130 Wood End Rd, Erdington B24 8BJ

☎ 0121 373 1230 📄 0121 382 2578

e-mail: rollwood@globalnet.co.uk

Dir: *M6 junct 6, A5127 to Erdington, right onto A4040, 0.25m on left*

PETS: Bedrooms Exercise area 200yds **Facilities** cage storage walks info vet info **On Request** torch

Well situated for routes and the city centre, this owner-managed establishment is popular with contractors. The choice of three different bedroom styles suits most budgets, and rates include full English breakfasts. Ground-floor areas include a popular bar, cosy television lounge and a dining room.

Rooms 35 rms (11 en suite) (5 fmly) ⊘ in 14 bedrooms S £21.50-£39.95; D £40-£49.50✳ **Facilities** TVB tea/coffee Cen ht TVL Dinner Last d 8.30pm Pool Table **Parking** 35

BIRMINGHAM AIRPORT   MAP 07 SP18

★★★ 74% HOTEL

Novotel Birmingham Airport

B26 3QL

☎ 0121 782 7000 & 782 4111 📄 0121 782 0445

e-mail: H1158@accor.com

web: www.novotel.com

Dir: *M42 junct 6/A45 to Birmingham, signed to airport. Hotel opposite main terminal*

PETS: Please telephone for details

This large, purpose-built hotel is located opposite the main passenger terminal. Bedrooms are spacious, modern in style and well equipped, including Playstations to keep the children busy. Several rooms have facilities for less able guests. The Garden Brasserie is open from noon until midnight, the bar is open 24 hours and a full room service is available.

Rooms 195 en suite (36 fmly) ⊘ in 156 bedrooms S £65-£155; D £65-£155✳ **Facilities** STV Wi-fi in bedrooms **Services** Lift **Notes** LB

BIRMINGHAM   MAP 07 SP18
(NATIONAL EXHIBITION CENTRE)

★★★ 71% HOTEL

Arden Hotel & Leisure Club

Coventry Rd, Bickenhill B92 0EH

☎ 01675 443221 📄 01675 445604

e-mail: enquiries@ardenhotel.co.uk

Dir: *M42 junct 6/A45 towards Birmingham. Hotel 0.25m on right, just off Birmingham International railway island*

PETS: Bedrooms Charges £10 per stay **Grounds** accessible

This smart hotel neighbouring the NEC offers modern rooms and well-equipped leisure facilities. After dinner in the formal restaurant, the place to relax is the spacious lounge area. A buffet breakfast is served in the bright and airy Meeting Place.

Rooms 216 en suite (6 fmly) (6 GF) ⊘ in 155 bedrooms S £65-£120; D £89-£170✳ **Facilities** Spa STV ⊠ supervised Gym Wi-fi in bedrooms Sports therapy Beautician ♫ Xmas New Year **Services** Lift **Parking** 300 **Notes** LB RS 25-28 Dec

BIRMINGHAM (NATIONAL EXHIBITION CENTRE) *CONTINUED*

★★ 68% HOTEL

Heath Lodge

117 Coleshill Rd, Marston Green B37 7HT

☎ 0121 779 2218 📄 0121 770 5648

e-mail: reception@heathlodgehotel.freeserve.co.uk

Dir: *1m N of NEC or Birmingham International Airport & station. From M6 take A446, then A452 junct 4*

PETS: Bedrooms unattended **Sep Accom** kennels **Charges** minimum £5 per night **Public areas** except dining room **Grounds** accessible **Other** cats must be kept in own cages if taken to bedrooms

This privately owned and personally run hotel is ideally located for visitors to the NEC and Birmingham Airport. Hospitality and service standards are high and while some bedrooms are compact, all are well equipped and comfortable. Public areas include a bar, a lounge and dining room which overlooks the pretty garden.

Rooms 17 rms (16 en suite) (1 fmly) (1 GF) ✆ in 6 bedrooms **Facilities** ch fac **Parking** 24 **Notes** LB Closed 25-26 Dec, 1 Jan

---

HAMPTON-IN-ARDEN MAP 04 SP28

★★★★ GUEST HOUSE

The Cottage Guest House

Kenilworth Rd B92 0LW

☎ 01675 442323 📄 01675 443323

e-mail: cottage.roger88@virgin.net

web: www.cottageguesthouse.net

Dir: *2m SE of Hampton on A452*

PETS: Bedrooms Charges £1 per night charge for damage **Resident Pets:** North & South (Longhaired German Shepherds)

A fine collection of antique memorabilia adorns the public areas of this delightful cottage, which is convenient for visiting the NEC, Birmingham, or exploring the area. Many guests return for the friendly and relaxing atmosphere and the attentive service. Freshly cooked traditional breakfasts, served in the cottage dining room, provide a good start to the day.

Rooms 9 en suite (2 GF) ✆ in 5 bedrooms S £30-£45; D £48-£60✹ **Facilities** TVB tea/coffee Cen ht TVL **Parking** 14 **Notes** Closed Xmas

MERIDEN MAP 04 SP28

★★★ 81% ◉ HOTEL

Manor

Main Rd CV7 7NH

☎ 01676 522735 📄 01676 522186

e-mail: reservations@manorhotelmeriden.co.uk

web: www.manorhotelmeriden.co.uk

Dir: *M42 junct 6, A45 towards Coventry then A452 signed Leamington. At rdbt take B4102 signed Meriden, hotel on left*

PETS: Bedrooms (GF) unattended **Grounds** accessible on leads disp bin **Facilities** vet info

A sympathetically extended Georgian manor in the heart of a sleepy village is just a few minutes away from the M6, M42 and National Exhibition Centre. The Regency Restaurant offers modern dishes, while the Triumph Buttery serves lighter meals and snacks. The bedrooms are smart and well equipped bedrooms.

Rooms 110 en suite (20 GF) ✆ in all bedrooms S £70-£140; D £88-£180 (incl. bkfst)✹ **Facilities** Wi-fi in bedrooms **Services** Lift **Parking** 200 **Notes** LB RS 24 Dec-2 Jan

►►►► **Somers Wood Caravan Park**

(SP225824)

Somers Rd CV7 7PL

☎ 01676 522978 📄 01676 522978

e-mail: somerswoodcpk@aol.com

web: www.somerswood.co.uk

Dir: *M42 junct 6, A45 signed Coventry. Keep left (do not take flyover). Then right onto A452 signed Meriden/Leamington. At next rdbt left onto B4102, Hampton Lane. Site in 0.5m on left*

PETS: Public areas Exercise area adjacent **Facilities** walks info vet info **Other** prior notice required **Resident Pets:** Jodie (dog), Tiddles (cat)

Open Feb-12 Dec Booking advisable NEC exhibitions & BH

A peaceful adults-only park set in the heart of England with spotless facilities. The park is well positioned for visiting the National Exhibition Centre (NEC) or the NEC Arena and National Indoor Arena (NIA), and Birminghan is only 12 miles away. The park also makes and ideal touring base for Warwick, Coventry and Stratford-on-Avon just 22 miles away. A 4-acre site with 48 touring pitches, 48 hardstandings.

Notes No children, no tents

SOLIHULL — MAP 07 SP17

★★★ 70% HOTEL
Corus hotel Solihull

Stratford Rd, Shirley B90 4EB

☎ 0870 609 6133 📠 0121 733 3801

e-mail: solihull@corushotels.com

web: www.corushotels.com

Dir: *M42 junct 4 onto A34 for Shirley, cross 1st 3 rdbts, then double back along dual carriageway, hotel on left*

PETS: Bedrooms (GF) **Charges** £5 per night
Public areas reception only **Facilities** walks info vet info

A large friendly hotel attracting both the corporate and leisure markets. Ideally located within minutes of all major transportation links and benefiting from its own leisure centre that includes, amongst its many facilities, a lagoon pool, sauna and gym.

Rooms 111 en suite (11 fmly) (13 GF) ⊘ in 64 bedrooms **Facilities** STV ⊙ Gym Wi-fi available Steam room Plunge pool New Year **Services** Lift **Parking** 275 **Notes** RS over Xmas

WOLVERHAMPTON — MAP 07 SO99

★★★ 75% HOTEL
Novotel Wolverhampton

Union St WV1 3JN

☎ 01902 871100 📠 01902 870054

e-mail: H1188@accor.com

web: www.novotel.com

Dir: *6m from M6 junct 10. A454 to Wolverhampton. Hotel on main ring road*

PETS: Bedrooms unattended **Charges** £5 per night charge for damage **Public areas** bar/lounge only on leads
Exercise area canal walk **Facilities** walks info vet info
On Request towels

This large, modern, purpose-built hotel stands close to the town centre. It provides spacious, smartly presented and well-equipped bedrooms, all of which contain convertible bed settees for family occupancy. In addition to the open-plan lounge and bar area, there is an attractive brasserie-style restaurant, which overlooks the small outdoor swimming pool.

Rooms 132 en suite (9 fmly) ⊘ in 114 bedrooms **Facilities** STV ⊙ Wi-fi available **Services** Lift **Parking** 120 **Notes** RS 23 Dec -4 Jan

COWES — MAP 04 SZ49

★★★ 72% HOTEL
Best Western New Holmwood

Queens Rd, Egypt Point PO31 8BW

☎ 01983 292508 📠 01983 295020

e-mail: reception@newholmwoodhotel.co.uk

Dir: *from A3020 at Northwood Garage lights, left & follow road to rdbt. 1st left then sharp right into Baring Rd, 4th left into Egypt Hill. At bottom turn right, hotel on right*

PETS: Bedrooms unattended **Public areas** except restaurant **Grounds** accessible **Exercise area** 2 mins walk to beach

Just by the Esplanade, this hotel has an enviable outlook. Bedrooms are comfortable and very well equipped, and the light and airy, glass-fronted restaurant looks out to sea and serves a range of interesting meals. The sun terrace is delightful in the summer and there is a small pool area.

Rooms 26 en suite (1 fmly) (9 GF) ⊘ in all bedrooms S £81-£125; D £97-£125 (incl. bkfst)✱ **Facilities** STV ⊙ Wi-fi in bedrooms Xmas New Year **Parking** 20 **Notes** LB

★★★★ BED & BREAKFAST
1 Lammas Close

PO31 8DT

☎ 01983 282541 📠 01983 282541

Dir: *0.5m W of town centre. Off The Parade onto Castle Hill & Baring Rd, 3rd right into Lammas Cl, 1st house on left*

PETS: Bedrooms Public areas Exercise area nearby
Resident Pets: Weasley (cat), Classy (Golden Retriever)

Looking across the Solent and situated one mile from central Cowes. Yachts-people will find kindred spirits in the very friendly Mr and Mrs Rising. A hearty and enjoyable breakfast in the elegant dining room completes the picture. Guest can be met on arrival in Cowes and also taken in daily if required, free of charge.

Rooms 1 rms (1 pri facs) S £35-£40; D £70-£80✱ **Facilities** FTV TVB tea/coffee Cen ht Golf 9 **Parking** 2 **Notes** No children 12yrs 🐾

ENGLAND

COWES CONTINUED

★★★ GUEST ACCOMMODATION
Windward House

69 Mill Hill Rd PO31 7EQ

☎ 01983 280940 & 07771 573580 📠 01983 280940

e-mail: sueogston1@tiscali.co.uk

Dir: *A320 Cowes-Newport, halfway up Mill Hill Rd on right from floating bridge from E Cowes (Red Funnel Ferries*

PETS: Bedrooms Public areas except dining room
Grounds accessible **Exercise area** on site garden & in 0.25m
Other Pet food by request **Resident Pets:** Gem (German Shepherd)

A friendly atmosphere prevails at this comfortable Victorian house, located close to the centre of Cowes. Bedrooms are bright and neat, and downstairs there is a spacious lounge equipped with satellite television, video and music systems. Breakfast is served in a separate dining room around a shared table.

Rooms 6 rms (3 en suite) (2 fmly) (1 GF) ⊘ S £25-£30; D £60-£80✱
Facilities TVB tea/coffee Cen ht TVL ↘ **Parking** 4 **Notes** ⊜

FRESHWATER   MAP 04 SZ38

★★★ 76% ⊛ HOTEL
Farringford

Bedbury Ln PO40 9PE

☎ 01983 752500 📠 01983 756515

e-mail: enquiries@farringford.co.uk

web: www.farringford.co.uk

Dir: *A3054, left to Norton Green down Pixlie Hill. Left to Freshwater Bay. At bay turn right into Bedbury Lane, hotel on left*

PETS: Bedrooms unattended **Charges** £7 per night charge for damage **Grounds** accessible on leads disp bin **Facilities** water bowl walks info vet info **On Request** fridge access torch towels **Resident Pets:** Woodie (Irish Setter)

Upon seeing Farringford, Alfred Lord Tennyson is said to have remarked "we will go no further, this must be our home" and so it was for some forty years. One hundred and fifty years later, the hotel provides bedrooms ranging in style and size, from large rooms in the main house to adjoining chalet-style rooms. The atmosphere is relaxed and dinner features fresh local produce.

Farringford

Rooms 14 en suite 4 annexe en suite (5 fmly) (4 GF) **Facilities** ↘ ↕9 ⊜ ↕ Putt green Beauty treatment room Bowling Green ♫ **Parking** 55

►►► Heathfield Farm Camping (SZ335879)

Heathfield Rd PO40 9SH

☎ 01983 756756

e-mail: web@heathfieldcamping.co.uk

web: www.heathfieldcamping.co.uk

Dir: *2m W from Yarmouth ferry port on A3054, left to Heathfield Rd, entrance 200yds on right*

PETS: Charges £1.50 per night **Exercise area** on site adjacent meadow adjacent walks **Facilities** vet info

Open May-Sep Booking advisable BHs & Jul-Aug Last arrival 22.00hrs Last departure 22.00hrs

A good quality park with friendly owners and lovely views across the Solent to Hurst Castle. The toilet facilities, amenities and grounds are very well maintained, and this park is constantly improving to meet the needs of campers and caravanners. A 10-acre site with 60 touring pitches.

Notes ⊜ Family camping only

NEWBRIDGE   MAP 04 SZ48

►►►►► Orchards Holiday Caravan Park
(SZ411881)

PO41 0TS

☎ 01983 531331 & 531350 📠 01983 531666

e-mail: info@orchards-holiday-park.co.uk

web: www.orchards-holiday-park.co.uk

Dir: *4m E of Yarmouth; 6m W of Newport on B3401*

PETS: Charges £1.50-£2.50 per night **Exercise area** on site fenced field **Facilities** on site shop food food bowl water bowl dog chews leads washing facs walks info vet info **Other** prior notice required

Open 11 Feb-2 Jan (rs Nov-Jan & Feb-mid Mar shop/takeaway closed/pool closed Sep-May) Booking advisable Etr, Spring BH, Jun-Aug, Oct half term Last arrival 23.00hrs Last departure 11.00hrs

A really excellent, well-managed park set in a peaceful village location amid downs and meadowland, with glorious downland views. Pitches are terraced, and offer a good provision of hardstandings, including super pitches. The toilet facilities are immaculate, and the park has indoor and outdoor swimming pools. There is excellent provision for families, and disabled access to all facilities on site, plus disabled toilets. A 15-acre site with 171 touring pitches, 74 hardstandings and 65 statics.

NEWCHURCH

MAP 04 SZ58

▶▶▶▶▶ Southland Camping Park (SZ557847)

PO36 0LZ

☎ 01983 865385 📠 01983 867663

e-mail: info@southland.co.uk

web: www.southland.co.uk

Dir: *A3056 towards Sandown. 2nd left after Fighting Cocks pub towards Newchurch. Site 1m on left*

PETS: **Charges** dogs £1.15 per night (cat free) **Public areas** except buildings **Exercise area** on site various country walks **Facilities** on site shop disp bags dog tethers walks info vet info **Restrictions** no dangerous dogs (see page 7), no Rottweilers or Pitt Bulls

Open Apr-Sep Booking advisable Jun-Aug Last arrival 21.30hrs Last departure 11.00hrs

Beautifully maintained site, peacefully located and impressively laid out on the outskirts of the village in the Arreton Valley. Spotless sanitary facilities including spacious family rooms enhance the park. Pitches are well screened by lovely trees and shrubs. A 9-acre site with 120 touring pitches.

RYDE

MAP 04 SZ59

★★★ 72% HOTEL
Yelf's

Union St PO33 2LG

☎ 01983 564062 📠 01983 563937

e-mail: manager@yelfshotel.com

web: www.yelfshotel.com

Dir: *from Ryde Esplanade turn into Union Street. Hotel on right*

PETS: **Bedrooms** unattended **Charges** £10 per night **Public areas** guide dogs only **Grounds** accessible on leads disp bin **Facilities** washing facs cage storage walks info vet info **On Request** fridge access torch towels

This former coaching inn has smart public areas including a busy bar, a separate lounge and an attractive dining room. Bedrooms are comfortably furnished and well equipped and some are located in an adjoining wing and some in an annexe. A conservatory lounge bar and stylish terrace are ideal for relaxing.

Rooms 31 en suite 9 annexe en suite (5 fmly) (3 GF) ⊘ in 5 bedrooms S £74; D £89 (incl. bkfst) **Facilities** STV **Services** Lift **Parking** 23 Notes LB

▶▶▶▶ Whitefield Forest Touring Park

(SZ604893)

Brading Rd PO33 1QL

☎ 01983 617069 & 407778

Dir: *On A3055 (Brading road), approx 2.5m from Ryde*

PETS: **Charges** £1-£1.50 per night **Public areas** except toilets **Other** prior notice required **Facilities** walks info vet info **Resident Pets:** Izzy (West Highland White Terrier), Scooby (Black Labrador)

This newly developed park is beautifully laid out in Whitefield Forest, and offers a wide variety of pitches, all of which have electricity. It offers excellent modern facilities which are spotlessly clean. The park takes great care in retaining the natural beauty of the forest, and is a haven for wildlife, including the red squirrel. 100 touring pitches.

SANDOWN

MAP 04 SZ58

★★ 72% HOTEL
The Wight Montrene

11 Avenue Rd PO36 8BN

☎ 01983 403722 📠 01983 405553

e-mail: enquiries@wighthotel.co.uk

web: www.wighthotel.co.uk

Dir: *100yds after mini-rdbt between High St and Avenue Rd*

PETS: **Bedrooms** (GF) unattended sign **Stables** (8m) **Charges** charge for damage **Grounds** accessible on leads disp bin **Exercise area** 300yds **Facilities** cage storage walks info vet info **Resident Pets:** Magnum (Great Pyrenian Mountain Dog)

A family hotel set in secluded grounds that is only a short walk from Sandown's beach and high street shops. Bedrooms provide comfort and are either on the ground or first floor. Guests can relax in the heated swimming pool or enjoy evening entertainment in the bar. The dinner menu changes nightly, and a plentiful breakfast is served in the colourful dining room.

Rooms 41 en suite (18 fmly) (21 GF) ⊘ in all bedrooms S £32-£48; D £64-£96 (incl. bkfst) **Facilities** ⊕ supervised Gym Wi-fi in bedrooms Pool table Steam room Table tennis ♫ ch fac Xmas New Year **Parking** 40 Notes LB

See advert on page 266

ENGLAND

SANDOWN CONTINUED

The Wight Montrene Hotel

Avenue Road, Sandown, Isle of Wight PO36 8BN
Tel: 01983 403722 Fax: 01983 405553
enquiries@wighthotel.co.uk www.wighthotel.co.uk

A 2 star AA (72% merit score) hotel for a holiday out of the ordinary – whatever the weather! Set in its own grounds just 150 yards from the sea we have 41 comfortable ensuite bedrooms, all with TV, hospitality tray, hair-dryer and digital safe. Outstanding food – visit our web site for example menus. Large bar, entertainment several nights each week, superb indoor pool with jacuzzi, sauna, steam room and solarium, games room, dedicated snooker room, trimnasium, large car park – the list goes on and on.

★★ 68% HOTEL
Riviera

2 Royal St PO36 8LP
☎ 01983 406532 📠 01983 402518
e-mail: enquiries@rivierahotel.org.uk
web: www.rivierahotel.org.uk
Dir: *Top of Sandown High St, turning past main Post Office.*
PETS: Bedrooms unattended Public areas except dining room
Exercise area nearby

Regular guests return year after year to this friendly and welcoming family-run hotel. It is located near to the High Street and just a short stroll from the beach, pier and shops. Bedrooms, including several at ground floor level, are very well furnished and comfortably equipped. Enjoyable home-cooked meals are served in the spacious dining room.

Rooms 43 en suite (6 fmly) (11 GF) ⊘ in 25 bedrooms D £70-£90 (incl. bkfst) Facilities ♫ Xmas New Year Parking 30 Notes LB

★★★★ GUEST HOUSE
Carisbrooke House

11 Beachfield Rd PO36 8NA
☎ 01983 402257 📠 01983 402257
e-mail: wmch583@aol.com
Dir: *2 minutes from Sandown town, beach and leisure centre, opposite Ferncliffs Gardens*
PETS: Bedrooms Charges £5 per stay Public areas except dining areas Grounds accessible Exercise area across road

Expect a friendly welcome at this family run guest-house situated opposite Ferncliff Gardens and within walking distance of the town centre and seafront. A full English breakfast is served in the dining room overlooking the sun terrace. Enjoy a drink in the bar/lounge. Dinner by arrangement

Rooms 10 rms (8 en suite) (2 pri facs) (4 fmly) (2 GF) ⊘ S £26-£38; D £54-£60✳ Facilities TVB tea/coffee Licensed Cen ht TVL Dinner Last d breakfast same day Notes LB

▶▶▶▶ Adgestone Camping & Caravanning Club Site (*SZ590855*)

Lower Adgestone Rd PO36 0HL
☎ 01983 403432
web: www.campingandcaravanningclub.co.uk
Dir: *Turn off A3055 (Sandown/Shanklin road) at Manor House pub, in Lake. Past school & golf course on left, turn right at T-junct, park 200yds on right*
PETS: Exercise area on site dog walk Facilities on site shop walks info vet info Other prior notice required

Open Apr-Oct Booking advisable BH & peak periods Last arrival 21.00hrs Last departure noon

A popular, well-managed park in a quiet, rural location not far from Sandown. The level pitches are imaginatively laid out, and surrounded by beautiful flower beds and trees set close to a small river. This planting offers good screening as well as enhancing the appearance of the park. There is excellent provision for families in general. A 22-acre site with 270 touring pitches.

SEAVIEW   MAP 04 SZ69

★★★ 82% ®® HOTEL
The Seaview

High St PO34 5EX
☎ 01983 612711 📠 01983 613729
e-mail: reception@seaviewhotel.co.uk
Dir: *from B3330, turn left via Puckpool along seafront*
PETS: Bedrooms (GF) unattended Public areas except restaurant on leads Exercise area 50yds Facilities water bowl walks info vet info On Request fridge access

This relaxed and charming hotel, in a quiet location just a stroll away from the seafront, has undergone a complete transformation. The contemporary bedrooms, including the new Seafront Modern rooms, are designer led in their fittings and furnishings - crisp white linen, intimate lighting, flat screen satellite TVs, DVD/CD players set the style. The same menu can be enjoyed in the traditional Victorian dining room or the Sunshine conservatory restaurant.

Rooms 24 en suite (7 fmly) (4 GF) ⌀ in all bedrooms S £100-£199; D £120-£199 (incl. bkfst)✳ **Facilities** FTV Wi-fi available Beauty therapy Xmas New Year **Services** Lift **Parking Notes** LB

SHANKLIN   MAP 04 SZ58

★★ 76% HOTEL
Melbourne Ardenlea

4-6 Queens Rd PO37 6AP

☎ 01983 862283 ▤ 01983 862865

e-mail: reservations@melbourneardenlea.co.uk

Dir: *A3055 to Shanklin. Then follow signs to Ventnor via B3328 (Queens Rd). Hotel just before end of road on right*

PETS: Bedrooms (GF) unattended sign **Charges** £3.50 per night **Public areas** except dining room on leads **Grounds** accessible disp bin **Exercise area** 500mtrs **Facilities** food (pre-bookable) water bowl cage storage walks info vet info **On Request** torch towels

This quietly located hotel is within easy walking distance of the town centre and the lift down to the promenade and successfully caters for the needs of holidaymakers. Bedrooms are traditionally furnished and guests can enjoy the various spacious public areas including a welcoming bar and a large heated indoor swimming pool.

Rooms 54 en suite (5 fmly) (6 GF) S £25-£55; D £50-£100 (incl. bkfst)✳ **Facilities** ⌀ Wi-fi available ♫ New Year **Services** Lift **Parking** 26 **Notes** LB Closed 27 Dec-3 Jan

★★ 71% HOTEL
Curraghmore Hotel

22 Hope Rd PO37 6EA

☎ 01983 862605 ▤ 01983 863342

e-mail: curraghmorehotel@aol.com

Dir: *Turn off A3055 signed Esplanade, hotel is 100mtrs left.*

PETS: Bedrooms **Charges** £10 per stay **Public areas** except dining room **Grounds** accessible **Exercise area** beach 100yds

This hotel has a pleasant location, close to the beach and just a short stroll from the shops and Shanklin village. Bedrooms include several with sea views. Entertainment is provided three or four nights of the week with dancing in the lounge and a separate adjoining bar.

Rooms 23 en suite (7 fmly) (6 GF) ⌀ in 15 bedrooms **Facilities** ♫ **Parking** 20

★★★★ ➡ GUEST ACCOMMODATION
Hayes Barton

7 Highfield Rd PO37 6PP

☎ 01983 867747 ▤ 01983 862104

e-mail: williams.2000@virgin.net

web: www.hayesbarton.co.uk

Dir: *A3055 onto A3020 Victoria Av, 3rd left*

PETS: Bedrooms (6GF) unattended **Charges** £3.50 per night £22 per week charge for damage **Public areas** except dining room **Grounds** accessible disp bin **Exercise area** 200yds **Facilities** feeding mat dog scoop/disp bags pet sitting washing facs cage storage walks info vet info **On Request** fridge access torch towels **Resident Pets:** Samantha (Labrador cross)

Hayes Barton has the relaxed atmosphere of a family home and provides well-equipped bedrooms and a range of comfortable public areas. Dinner is available from a short selection of home-cooked dishes and there is a cosy bar lounge. The old village, beach and promenade are all within walking distance.

Rooms 9 en suite (4 fmly) (2 GF) **Facilities** TVB tea/coffee Cen ht TVL Dinner Last d noon **Parking** 8 **Notes** LB Closed Nov-Mar

TOTLAND BAY   MAP 04 SZ38

★★★ 72% HOTEL
Sentry Mead

Madeira Rd PO39 0BJ

☎ 01983 753212 ▤ 01983 754710

e-mail: info@sentrymead.co.uk

web: www.sentrymead.co.uk

Dir: *off A3054 onto B3322. At 1st rdbt turn right into Madeira Rd. Hotel is 250mtrs on right*

PETS: Bedrooms unattended sign **Charges** £3 per night **Public areas** except dining room on leads **Grounds** accessible disp bin **Exercise area** 50yds **Facilities** food bowl water bowl bedding dog scoop/disp bags washing facs cage storage walks info vet info **On Request** fridge access torch towels

Just two minutes' walk from the sea at Totland Bay, this well-kept Victorian villa has a comfortable lounge and separate bar, as well as a conservatory that looks out over the delightful garden. Bedrooms

CONTINUED

TOTLAND BAY CONTINUED

feature co-ordinated soft furnishings and welcome extras such as mineral water and biscuits.

Rooms 13 en suite (1 fmly) ⊛ in all bedrooms S £50-£65; D £100-£130 (incl. bkfst)✳ **Facilities** Wi-fi in bedrooms **Parking** 9 **Notes** LB

▶▶ Stoats Farm Caravan & Camping

(SZ324865)

PO39 0HE

☎ 01983 755258 & 753416 📠 01983 755258

e-mail: david@stoats-farm.co.uk

web: www.stoats-farm.co.uk

Dir: On Alum Bay road, 1.5m from Freshwater

PETS: Public areas Exercise area on site non-camping field **Facilities** on site shop food food bowl water bowl dog chews cat treats litter tray etc dog scoop/disp bags leads dog grooming walks info vet info (all facilities available on request) **Resident Pets:** Spud, Bridie & Alfie (Lurchers)

Open Mar-Oct Booking advisable Aug

A friendly, personally run site in a quiet country setting close to Alum Bay, Tennyson Down and The Needles. It has good laundry and shower facilities, and the shop, though small, is well stocked. Popular with families, walkers and cyclists. A 10-acre site with 100 touring pitches.

VENTNOR   MAP 04 SZ57

★★★ 68% HOTEL
Eversley

Park Av PO38 1LB

☎ 01983 852244 & 852462 📠 01983 856534

e-mail: eversleyhotel@yahoo.co.uk

web: www.eversleyhotel.com

Dir: on A3055 W of Ventnor, next to Ventnor Park

PETS: Please telephone for details

Located west of Ventnor, this hotel enjoys a quiet location and has some rooms offering garden and pool views. The spacious restaurant is sometimes used for local functions, and there is a bar, television

room, lounge area and a card room as well as a jacuzzi and gym. Bedrooms are generally a good size.

Rooms 30 en suite (8 fmly) (2 GF) **Facilities** ⌇ Gym Pool table **Parking** 23 **Notes** Closed 30 Nov-22 Dec & 2 Jan-8 Feb

See advert on opposite page

★★★★ GUEST ACCOMMODATION
The Lake

Shore Rd, Bonchurch PO38 1RF

☎ 01983 852613

e-mail: enquiries@lakehotel.co.uk

Dir: 0.5m E of Ventnor. Off A3055 to Bonchurch, opp village pond

PETS: Bedrooms Charges £5 per night **Grounds** accessible **Exercise area** 400yds **Other** Pet food on request

A warm welcome is assured at this friendly, family-run property set in 2 acres of well-tended gardens close to the sea. Bedrooms are equipped with modern facilities and the elegant public rooms offer a high standard of comfort. A choice of menus is offered at dinner and breakfast.

Rooms 11 en suite 9 annexe en suite (7 fmly) (4 GF) **Facilities** TVB tea/coffee Cen ht TVL Dinner Last d 6.30pm **Parking** 20 **Notes** No children 3yrs RS Nov-Feb ⊛

★★★★ GUEST ACCOMMODATION
The Hillside

Mitchell Av PO38 1DR

☎ 01983 852271 📠 01983 852271

e-mail: aa@hillside-hotel.co.uk

web: www.hillside-hotel.co.uk

Dir: exit A3055 onto B3327, premises 600 yards on right

PETS: Please telephone for details

Hospitality is an important factor at this friendly establishment run by Brenda and Peter Hart. Built originally as an Inn, this charming thatched house dates back to 1801 and has beautiful views of the sea. Bedrooms are well furnished and equipped with en suite facilities. Guests can relax in the cosy bar, the elegant lounge and the charming plant-filled conservatory. There is a bright dining room where Brenda's home-cooked dinners are served, always with good vegetarian options (the Harts are themselves vegetarian).

Rooms 12 en suite (1 fmly) (1 GF)✳ **Facilities** TVB tea/coffee Cen ht ⌇ **Parking** 12 **Notes** LB No children 5yrs Closed Xmas

WHITECLIFF BAY   MAP 04 SZ68

Whitecliff Bay Holiday Park (SZ637862)

Hillway Rd, Bembridge PO35 5PL

☎ 01983 872671 📄 01983 872941

e-mail: holiday@whitecliff-bay.com

web: www.whitecliff-bay.com

Dir: *1m S of Bembridge, signed off B3395 in village*

PETS: Charges £1 per night £7 per week **Exercise area** on site dog field & walkway through park **Facilities** on site shop food dog chews cat treats dog scoop/disp bags vet info **Other** prior notice required **Restrictions** no pets in high season

Open Mar-Oct Booking advisable Jul-Aug Last arrival 21.00hrs Last departure 10.30hrs

A large seaside complex on two sites, with tourers and tents on one, and tourers and statics on the other. There is an indoor and outdoor swimming pool, a leisure centre, and plenty of traditional on-site entertainment, plus easy access to a lovely sandy beach. A 49-acre site with 400 touring pitches, 50 hardstandings and 227 statics.

Notes Adults and families only

WOOTTON BRIDGE   MAP 04 SZ59

►►► Kite Hill Farm Caravan Park (SZ549906)

Firestone Copse Rd PO33 4LE

☎ 01983 882543 & 883261 📄 01983 883883

e-mail: barry@kitehillfarm.freeserve.co.uk

web: www.campingparkisleofwight.com

Dir: *Signed off A3054 at Wootton Bridge, between Ryde & Newport*

PETS: Public areas Exercise area on site 2 acre area woods adjacent **Facilities** walks info vet info

Open all year Booking advisable Jun-Aug

The park, on a gently sloping field, is tucked away behind the owners' farm, just a short walk from the village and attractive river estuary. Facilities are well maintained and the atmosphere pleasantly relaxing. A 12.5-acre site with 50 touring pitches, 10 hardstandings.

WILTSHIRE

BRADFORD-ON-AVON   MAP 03 ST86

★★★ 82% ◉◉ HOTEL

Woolley Grange

Woolley Green BA15 1TX

☎ 01225 864705 📄 01225 864059

e-mail: info@woolleygrangehotel.co.uk

web: www.vonessenhotels.co.uk

von Essen hotels
A PRIVATE COLLECTION
www.vonessenhotels.com

Dir: *Turn off A4 onto B3109. Bradford Leigh, left at crossroads, hotel 0.5m on right at Woolley Green*

PETS: Bedrooms (GF) unattended **Charges** £7-£25 per stay depending on room type **Public areas** except dining areas **Grounds** accessible disp bin **Facilities** food bowl water bowl bedding dog chews dog scoop/disp bags leads walks info vet info **On Request** fridge access torch towels **Restrictions** dog owners are advised to keep dogs on leads due to children staying at establishment **Resident Pets:** Peanut (Cocker Spaniel), Chunky (cat)

This splendid Cotswold manor house is set in beautiful countryside. Children are made especially welcome; there is a trained nanny on duty in the nursery. Bedrooms and public areas are charmingly furnished and decorated in true country-house style, with many thoughtful touches and luxurious extras. The hotel offers a varied and well-balanced menu selection, including ingredients from the hotel's own garden.

Rooms 14 en suite 12 annexe en suite (8 fmly) ⊗ in all bedrooms D £180-£240 (incl. bkfst & dinner)✱ **Facilities** ↘ ⅃ Putt green Wi-fi available Badminton, Beauty treatments, Football, Games room, Table Tennis ch fac Xmas New Year **Parking** 40 **Notes** LB

BRADFORD-ON-AVON CONTINUED

★★★ 78% COUNTRY HOUSE HOTEL

Best Western Leigh Park Hotel

Leigh Park West BA15 2RA

☎ 01225 864885 📠 01225 862315

e-mail: inof@leighparkhotel.eclipse.co.uk

Dir: *A363 Bath/Frome road. Take B3105 signed Holt/Woolley Green. Hotel 0.25m on right on x-roads of B3105/B3109. N side of Bradford-on-Avon*

PETS: Bedrooms (GF) **Charges** £10 per night **Other** ground floor rooms only

Enjoying splendid countryside views, this relaxing Georgian hotel is set in five acres of well-tended grounds, complete with a vineyard. Combining charm and character with modern facilities, the hotel is equally well suited to business and leisure travellers. The restaurant serves dishes cooked to order, using home-grown fruit and vegetables, and wine from the vineyard.

Rooms 22 en suite (4 fmly) (7 GF) ⊘ in 14 bedrooms
Facilities Vineyard **Parking** 80 **Notes** LB

CALNE   MAP 03 ST97

►►► **Blackland Lakes Holiday & Leisure Centre** *(ST973687)*

Stockley Ln SN11 0NQ

☎ 01249 813672 📠 01249 811346

e-mail: info@blacklandlakes.co.uk

web: www.blacklandlakes.co.uk

Dir: *From Calne take A4 E for 1.5m, right at camp sign. Site 1m on left*

PETS: Stables nearby (1m) (loose box) **Charges** £1.47 per night £10.29 per week **Public areas Exercise area** on site dog walks & in 1.5m **Facilities** on site shop food dog scoop/disp bags washing facs walks info vet info **Other** prior notice required

Open all year (rs Nov-mid Mar bookings only (pre paid))
Booking advisable all year Last arrival 22.00hrs Last departure noon

A rural site surrounded by the North and West Downs. The park is divided into several paddocks separated by hedges, trees and fences, and there are two well-stocked carp fisheries for the angling enthusiast. Some excellent walks close by, and the interesting market town of Devizes is a few miles away. A 15-acre site with 180 touring pitches, 25 hardstandings.

CASTLE COMBE   MAP 03 ST87

★★★★ ⊛⊛⊛ COUNTRY HOUSE HOTEL

Manor House

SN14 7HR

☎ 01249 782206 📠 01249 782159

e-mail: enquiries@manor-housecc.co.uk

web: www.exclusivehotels.co.uk

Dir: *M4 junct 17 follow Chippenham signs onto A420 Bristol, then right onto B4039. Through village, right after bridge*

PETS: Bedrooms (GF) unattended **Charges** £75 for duration of stay **Public areas** except dining areas **Grounds** accessible on leads **Exercise area** on site **Facilities** cage storage walks info vet info **On Request** fridge access **Restrictions** Telephone for details **Resident Pets:** 1 cat, 6 chickens, 4 geese

This delightful hotel is situated in a secluded valley adjacent to a picturesque village, where there have been no new buildings for 300 years. There are 365 acres of grounds to enjoy, complete with an Italian garden and an 18-hole golf course. Bedrooms, some in the main house and some in a row of stone cottages, have been superbly furnished, and public rooms include a number of cosy lounges with roaring fires. Service is a pleasing blend of professionalism and friendliness. The food offered utilises top quality local produce.

Rooms 22 en suite 26 annexe en suite (8 fmly) (12 GF) ⊘ in all bedrooms S £185-£800; D £185-£800 (incl. bkfst)✳ **Facilities** STV ♨ 18 ♨ Fishing ⛳ Putt green Wi-fi available Jogging track Xmas New Year **Parking** 100 **Notes** LB

DEVIZES   MAP 04 SU06

►►►► **Devizes Camping & Caravanning Club Site** *(ST951619)*

Spout Ln, Nr Seend, Melksham SN12 6RN

☎ 01380 828839

web: www.campingandcaravanningclub.co.uk/devises

Dir: *From Devizes on A361 turn right onto A365, over canal, next left down lane beside 3 Magpies pub. Site on right*

PETS: Public areas except buildings **Exercise area** on site **Facilities** walks info vet info **Other** prior notice required

Open all year Booking advisable BHs & peak periods Last arrival 21.00hrs Last departure noon

An excellent club site with well designed, quality facilities and a high level of staff commitment. This popular park is set beside the Kennet and Avon Canal, with a gate to the towpath for walking and cycling, and with fishing available in the canal. Well situated for exploring Salisbury Plain and the Marlborough Downs. A 13.5-acre site with 90 touring pitches, 70 hardstandings.

Notes site gates closed 23.00-07.00

LANDFORD MAP 04 SU21

►►► Greenhill Farm Camping & Caravan Park (SU266183)

Greenhill Farm, New Rd SP5 2AZ

☎ 01794 324117 & 023 8081 1506 📄 023 8081 3209

e-mail: greenhillcamping@btconnect.com

web: www.newforest-uk.com/greenhill.htm

Dir: *M27 junct 2, A36 towards Salisbury, approx 3m after Hants/ Wilts border, (Shoe Inn pub on right, BP garage on left) take next left into New Rd, signed Nomansland, 2nd site on left*

PETS: Charges 1st dog free, £1 per additional dog per night **Public areas** on leads **Exercise area** on site & in 250yds **Facilities** vet info **Restrictions** except near fish breeding lakes

Open 16 Jan-21 Dec Booking advisable BH & Jul-Aug Last arrival 21.30hrs Last departure 10.30hrs

A tranquil, well-landscaped park hidden away in unspoilt countryside on the edge of the New Forest. Pitches overlooking the fishing lake include hardstandings. Facilities are housed in portable type buildings. This park is for adults only. A 13-acre site with 80 touring pitches, 30 hardstandings.

Notes Adults only, no kites/flags

LOWER CHICKSGROVE MAP 03 ST92

★★★★ 🌑 🍺 INN
Compasses Inn

SP3 6NB

☎ 01722 714318 📄 01722 714318

e-mail: thecompasses@aol.com

web: www.thecompassesinn.com

Dir: *Off A30 signed Lower Chicksgrove, 1st left onto Lagpond Ln, single-track lane to village*

PETS: Bedrooms unattended **Public areas Grounds** accessible disp bin **Exercise area** adjacent **Facilities** food bowl water bowl cage storage walks info vet info **On Request** fridge access torch towels

This charming 17th-century inn, within easy reach of the Bath, Salisbury, Glastonbury and the Dorset coast, offers comfortable accommodation in a peaceful setting. Carefully prepared dinners are enjoyed in the warm atmosphere of the bar-restaurant, while breakfast is served in a separate dining room.

Rooms 5 en suite (1 fmly) S £65-£90; D £85-£120 **Facilities** FTV TVB tea/coffee Cen ht Dinner Last d 9.30pm **Parking** 40 **Notes** LB Closed 25-26 Dec

MALMESBURY MAP 03 ST98

★★★★★ 🌑🌑🌑 HOTEL
Whatley Manor

Easton Grey SN16 0RB

☎ 01666 822888 📄 01666 826120

e-mail: reservations@whatleymanor.com

web: www.whatleymanor.com

RELAIS & CHATEAUX

Dir: *M4 junct17, follow signs to Malmesbury continue over 2 rdbts. Follow B4040 & signs fort Sherston, hotel 2m on left*

PETS: Bedrooms unattended **Charges** £25 per night **Grounds** accessible on leads disp bin **Facilities** food (pre-bookable) food bowl water bowl bedding dog scoop/disp bags welcome letter & guidelines, luxury dog basket, treats, walk routes, maps and more **On Request** towels

Sitting in 12 acres of beautiful countryside, this impressive country house provides the most luxurious surroundings. Spacious bedrooms, most with views over the attractive gardens, are individually decorated with splendid features. Several eating options are available: Le Mazot, a Swiss-style brasserie, The Dining Room that serves classical French cuisine with a contemporary twist, plus the Kitchen Garden Terrace for alfresco breakfasts, lunches and dinners. The old Loggia Barn is ideal for wedding ceremonies, and the Aquarius Spa is magnificent.

Rooms 23 en suite (4 GF) ⊘ in 6 bedrooms D £285-£850 (incl. bkfst)✳ **Facilities** Spa STV Fishing Gym Wi-fi available Cinema, Hydro pool Xmas New Year **Services** Lift **Parking** 100 **Notes** LB No children 12yrs

MELKSHAM — MAP 03 ST96

★★ 74% HOTEL

Shaw Country

Bath Rd, Shaw SN12 8EF

☎ 01225 702836 & 790321 📠 01225 790275

e-mail: info@shawcountryhotel.com

web: www.shawcountryhotel.com

Dir: *1m from Melksham, 9m from Bath on A365*

PETS: Bedrooms Exercise area nearby

Located within easy reach of both Bath and the M4, this relaxed and friendly hotel sits in its own gardens, that has a patio area ideal for enjoying a cool drink during warm summer months. The house boasts some very well-appointed bedrooms, a comfortable lounge and bar and the Mulberry Restaurant, where a wide selection of innovative dishes make up both carte and set menus. A spacious function room is a useful addition.

Rooms 13 en suite (2 fmly) ⊘ in all bedrooms S £56; D £76-£96 (incl. bkfst)✳ **Facilities** Wi-fi in bedrooms **Parking** 30 **Notes LB** RS 26-27 Dec & 1 Jan

NETTLETON — MAP 03 ST87

★★★★ 🍴 BED & BREAKFAST

Fosse Farmhouse Chambre d'Hote

Nettleton Shrub SN14 7NJ

☎ 01249 782286 📠 01249 783066

e-mail: caroncooper@compuserve.com

web: www.fossefarmhouse.com

Dir: *1.5m N from Castle Combe on B4039, left at Gib, farm 1m on right*

PETS: Bedrooms Grounds accessible **Facilities** food on request only **Other** Certain bedrooms only available for pets

Set in quiet Wiltshire countryside close to Castle Combe, this guest house has well-equipped bedrooms decorated in keeping with its 18th-century origins. Excellent dinners are served in the farmhouse, and cream teas can be enjoyed in the old stables or the delightful garden.

Rooms 3 en suite (1 fmly) S £55-£65; D £90-£130✳ **Facilities** TVB tea/coffee Cen ht Dinner Last d 8.30pm Golf 18 **Parking** 12 **Notes LB**

ORCHESTON — MAP 04 SU04

►►► **Stonehenge Touring Park** *(SU061456)*

SP3 4SH

☎ 01980 620304

e-mail: stay@stonehengetouringpark.com

web: www.stonehengetouringpark.com

Dir: *Off A360*

PETS: Public areas except facilities block & shop **Exercise area** 50mtrs **Facilities** on site shop food disp bags walks info vet info **Other** prior notice required

Open all year Booking advisable BH & Jul-Aug Last arrival 21.00hrs Last departure 11.00hrs

A quiet site adjacent to the small village of Orcheston near the centre of Salisbury Plain and 4m from Stonehenge. A 2-acre site with 30 touring pitches, 12 hardstandings.

PURTON — MAP 04 SU08

★★★ 80% ⚛⚛ HOTEL

The Pear Tree at Purton

Church End SN5 4ED

☎ 01793 772100 📠 01793 772369

e-mail: stay@peartreepurton.co.uk

Dir: *M4 junct 16 follow signs to Purton, at Spar shop turn right. Hotel 0.25m on left*

PETS: Bedrooms Public areas except restaurant **Grounds** accessible disp bin **Exercise area** adjacent **Facilities** food bowl water bowl dog chews cat treats dog scoop/disp bags leads welcome pack washing facs walks info vet info **On Request** fridge access torch towels **Resident Pets:** Smudge (dog), Poppy, Buzz & Raz (cats)

A charming 15th-century, former vicarage set amidst fully landscaped gardens in a peaceful location. The resident proprietors and staff provide efficient, dedicated service and friendly hospitality. The spacious bedrooms are individually decorated and have a good range of thoughtful extras such as fresh flowers and sherry. Fresh ingredients feature on the menus at both lunch and dinner.

The Pear Tree at Purton

Rooms 17 en suite (2 fmly) (6 GF) S £120-£180; D £120-£180 (incl. bkfst) **Facilities** STV ⚓ Wi-fi in bedrooms Outdoor giant chess, Vineyard **Parking** 60 **Notes** LB Closed 26-30 Dec

---

SALISBURY

MAP 04 SU12

★★★ 68% HOTEL

Grasmere House Hotel

Harnham Rd SP2 8JN

☎ 01722 338388 🖨 01722 333710

e-mail: info@grasmerehotel.com

web: www.grasmerehotel.com

Dir: on A3094 on S side of Salisbury next to All Saints Church in Harnham

PETS: Please telephone for details

This popular hotel dates from 1896 and has gardens overlooking the water meadows and the cathedral. The attractive bedrooms vary in size, some offer excellent quality and comfort, and some rooms are specially equipped for less mobile guests. In summer, guests have the option of dining on the pleasant outdoor terrace.

Rooms 7 en suite 31 annexe en suite (16 fmly) (9 GF) ⊘ in 30 bedrooms S £95.50-£115.50; D £115.50-£145.50 (incl. bkfst) **Facilities** STV Fishing ⚓ Wi-fi in bedrooms Xmas New Year **Parking** 64 **Notes** LB

★★★ GUEST ACCOMMODATION

Byways Guest House

31 Fowlers Rd SP1 2QP

☎ 01722 328364 🖨 01722 322146

e-mail: info@bywayshouse.co.uk

web: www.bywayshouse.co.uk

Dir: A30 onto A36 signed Southampton, follow Youth Hostel signs to hostel

PETS: Bedrooms (GF) **Exercise area** nearby **Facilities** vet info **On Request** fridge access torch towels

Located in a quiet street with off-road parking, Byways is within walking distance of the town centre. Several bedrooms have been decorated in a Victorian style and another two have four-poster beds. All rooms offer good levels of comfort, with one adapted for easier access.

Rooms 23 en suite (6 fmly) (13 GF) ⊘ S £38-£60; D £50-£75✲ **Facilities** TVB tea/coffee Cen ht Wi-fi available **Parking** 15 **Notes** Closed Xmas & New Year

►►►► **Coombe Touring Park** *(SU099282)*

Race Plain, Netherhampton SP2 8PN

☎ 01722 328451 🖨 01722 328451

Dir: A3094, then 2m SW, adjacent to Salisbury racecourse

PETS: Charges 20p per night **Public areas** except shower & toilet block & laundry **Exercise area** nearby **Facilities** on site shop washing facs walks info vet info **Residents pets** Alfie (Labrador/Collie cross), Tigger & Blackie (cats)

Open all year (rs Oct-Apr shop closed Oct-May) Booking advisable BH Last arrival 21.00hrs Last dep noon

A very neat and attractive site adjacent to the racecourse with views over the downs. The park is well landscaped with shrubs and maturing trees, and the very colourful beds are stocked from the owner's greenhouse. A comfortable park with a superb luxury toilet block. A 3-acre site with 50 touring pitches.

Notes ⌖ no disposable BBQs or fires, no mini motorbikes

►►►► **Salisbury Camping & Caravanning Club Site** *(SU140320)*

Hudsons Field, Castle Rd SP1 3RR

☎ 01722 320713

web: www.campingandcaravanningclub.co.uk/saiisbury

Dir: 1.5m from Salisbury on A345.

PETS: Public areas Exercise area adjacent **Facilities** walks info vet info **Other** prior notice required

Open 13 Mar-3 Nov Booking advisable BH & peak periods Last arrival 21.00hrs Last departure noon

Well placed within walking distance of Salisbury, this tidy site has friendly and helpful wardens, and immaculate toilet facilities with cubicled wash basins. A 4.5-acre site with 150 touring pitches, 16 hardstandings.

SWINDON MAP 04 SU18

★★★ 70% HOTEL
Goddard Arms
High St, Old Town SN1 3EG
☎ 01793 692313 📠 01793 512984
e-mail: goddard.arms@forestdale.com
web: www.forestdale.com
Dir: *M4 junct 15, A4259 towards Swindon, onto B4006 to Old Town follow signs for PM Hospital. Hotel in High St opp Wood St next to Lloyds Bank*
PETS: **Bedrooms** unattended **Charges** £7.50 per night
Public areas except restaurant **Grounds** accessible

Situated in the attractive Old Town area, this ivy-clad coaching inn offers bedrooms in either the main building or in a modern annexe to the rear of the property. Public areas are tastefully decorated in a traditional style; there is a lounge, Vaults bar and the popular Buccleuch Grill, with its modern approach to food. The conference rooms are extensive and the car park secure.

Rooms 18 en suite 47 annexe en suite (3 fmly) (24 GF) ⊘ in 33 bedrooms **Facilities** STV Wi-fi available ch fac **Parking** 90

★★★ GUEST ACCOMMODATION
Portquin
Broadbush, Broad Blunsdon SN26 7DH
☎ 01793 721261
e-mail: portquin@msn.com
Dir: *A419 onto B4019 at Blunsdon signed Highworth, continue 0.5m*
PETS: **Bedrooms** (GF) **Charges** charge for damage
Public areas except dining room **Grounds** accessible disp bin
Facilities walks info vet info **On Request** fridge access torch
Restrictions no dogs of similar size to Great Danes
Resident Pets: Basil & Diva (horses)

This friendly guest house near Swindon provides a warm welcome and views of the Lambourn Downs. The rooms vary in shape and size, with six in the main house and three in an adjacent annexe. Full English breakfasts are served at two large tables in the kitchen-dining area.

Rooms 6 en suite 3 annexe en suite (2 fmly) (4 GF) ⊘ S £35-£45; D £50-£70✱ **Facilities** TVB tea/coffee Direct dial from bedrooms Cen ht Wi-fi available **Parking** 12

WARMINSTER MAP 03 ST84

★★★★ 79% ◉◉ HOTEL
Bishopstrow House
BA12 9HH
☎ 01985 212312 📠 01985 216769
e-mail: info@bishopstrow.co.uk
web: www.vonessenhotels.co.uk

Dir: *A303, A36, B3414, hotel 2m on right*
PETS: **Bedrooms** unattended **Charges** £10 per pet per night
Public areas except restaurant, conservatory & pool area
Facilities food

This is a fine example of a Georgian country home, situated in 27 acres of grounds. Public areas are traditional in style and feature antiques and open fires. Most bedrooms offer DVD players. A spa, a tennis court and several country walks ensure there is something for all guests. The restaurant serves quality contemporary cuisine.

Rooms 32 en suite (2 fmly) (7 GF) ⊘ in all bedrooms S £79-£330; D £160-£330 (incl. bkfst)✱ **Facilities** Spa STV FTV ⊗ ↘ ⌣ Fishing Gym ⅃ Wi-fi available Clay pigeon, Shooting, Archery, Cycling Xmas New Year **Parking** 100 **Notes** LB

★★★ 🚢 INN

The Dove Inn

Corton BA12 0SZ

☎ 01985 850109 📄 01985 851041

e-mail: info@thedove.co.uk

Dir: *5m SE of Warminster. Off A36 to Corton village*

PETS: Bedrooms unattended **Charges** £10 per night
Public areas except restaurant **Grounds** accessible
Exercise area across road **Facilities** food (pre-bookable) water
bowl **Other** chocolates and dog biscuits **Resident Pets:** Pepper
(Alsatian/Collie cross)

This relaxing inn stands in the heart of a peaceful village. There are
carefully furnished courtyard rooms and a conservatory, and in cooler
months a roaring log fire accompanies the imaginative bar menu.
Home cooked dishes and a selection of real ales are highlights of any
stay here.

Rooms 5 annexe en suite (1 fmly) (4 GF) **Facilities** TVB tea/coffee
Cen ht Dinner Last d 9pm **Parking** 24

WESTBURY   MAP 03 ST85

►►► **Brokerswood Country Park** *(ST836523)*

Brokerswood BA13 4EH

☎ 01373 822238 📄 01373 858474

e-mail: woodland.park@virgin.net

web: www.brokerswood.co.uk

Dir: *From M4 junct 17 south on A350. Right at Yarnbrook to
Rising Sun pub at North Bradley, then left at rdbt. Left on bend
approaching Southwick, follow lane for 2.5m, site on right*

PETS: Charges £1 per dog per night **Public areas** except café,
shop, toilet/shower facilities **Exercise area** on site 80 acre country
park **Facilities** on site shop food bowl water bowl dog scoop/
disp bags leads walks info vet info **Other** prior notice required

Open all year Booking advisable BH & peak season Last arrival
21.30hrs Last departure 11.00hrs

A pleasant site on the edge of an 80-acre woodland park with nature
trails and fishing lakes. An adventure playground offers plenty of fun
for all ages, and there is a miniature railway of one-third of a mile, an
indoor play centre, and a licensed café. A 5-acre site with 69 touring
pitches, 21 hardstandings.

Notes Families only, no cycling, no disposable BBQs

BROADWAY   MAP 04 SP03

★★★★ 85% ◉◉ HOTEL

Lygon Arms

High St WR12 7DU

☎ 01386 852255 📄 01386 854470

e-mail: info@thelygonarms.co.uk

web: www.paramount-thelygonarms.co.uk

PARAMOUNT
GROUP OF HOTELS

Dir: *From Evesham take A44 signed for Oxford, 5m. Follow
Broadway signs. Hotel on left*

PETS: Bedrooms (GF) unattended **Stables** nearby (3m)
Charges £15 per night £105 per week charge for damage
Public areas except dining room on leads **Grounds** accessible on
leads disp bin **Facilities** food bowl water bowl bedding walks
info vet info **On Request** fridge access towels

A hotel with a wealth of historic charm and character, the Lygon Arms
dates back to the 16th century. There is a choice of restaurants, a stylish
cosy bar, an array of lounges and a smart spa and leisure club.
Bedrooms vary in size and style, but all are thoughtfully equipped and
include a number of stylish contemporary rooms as well as a cottage in
the grounds.

Rooms 69 en suite (8 fmly) (9 GF) **Facilities** Spa STV ☒ supervised
🛁 Gym 🏌 **Parking** 200

★★★ 77% HOTEL

Broadway

The Green, High St WR12 7AA

☎ 01386 852401 📄 01386 853879

e-mail: info@broadwayhotel.info

web: www.cotswold-inns-hotels.co.uk

CLASSIC
BRITISH HOTELS

Dir: *Follow signs to Evesham, then Broadway*

PETS: Bedrooms (GF) unattended **Public areas** except eating
areas **Grounds** accessible **Facilities** cage storage walks info vet
info **On Request** fridge access torch towels

A half-timbered Cotswold stone property, built in the 15th century as a
retreat for the Abbots of Pershore. The hotel now combines modern,
attractive decor with original charm and character. Bedrooms are
tastefully furnished and well equipped while public rooms include a
relaxing lounge, cosy bar and charming restaurant; alfresco all day
dining in summer months proves popular.

Rooms 19 en suite (1 fmly) ⊘ in all bedrooms D £135-£155 (incl. bkfst)
✳ **Facilities** Wi-fi available Xmas New Year **Parking** 20

ENGLAND

★★★★ 🍺 INN
Horse & Hound

54 High St WR12 7DT
☎ 01386 852287 📄 01386 853784
e-mail: k2mtk@aol.com
Dir: *Off A46 to Evesham*
PETS: Bedrooms unattended **Charges** £10 per stay
Public areas except restaurants **Other** small dogs only
Resident Pets: Talisker (Springer Spaniel)

The Horse & Hounds is at the heart of this beautiful Cotswold village. A warm welcome is guaranteed whether dining in the inviting pub or staying overnight in the attractive and well-appointed bedrooms. Breakfast and dinner should not to be missed both using carefully prepared local produce.

Rooms 5 en suite (1 fmly) D £70-£80✻ **Facilities** TVB tea/coffee Cen ht Dinner Last d 9pm **Parking** 15 **Notes LB**

EVESHAM
MAP 04 SP04

★★★ 79% 🏵 HOTEL
The Evesham

Coopers Ln, Off Waterside WR11 1DA
☎ 01386 765566 & 0800 716969 (Res) 📄 01386 765443
e-mail: reception@eveshamhotel.com
web: www.eveshamhotel.com
Dir: *Coopers Lane is off road by River Avon*
PETS: Bedrooms (GF) unattended **Grounds** accessible

Dating from 1540 and set in extensive grounds, this delightful hotel has well-equipped accommodation that includes a selection of quirkily themed rooms - Alice in Wonderland, Egyptian, and Aquarium (which has a tropical fish tank in the bathroom). A reputation for food is well deserved, with a particularly strong choice for vegetarians. Children are welcome and toys are always available.

Rooms 39 en suite 1 annexe en suite (3 fmly) (11 GF) ⊘ in 30 bedrooms S £76-£89; D £126 (incl. bkfst)✻ **Facilities** 🏓 ≽ Putt green New Year **Parking** 50 **Notes LB** Closed 25-26 Dec

---

HANLEY SWAN
MAP 03 SO84

►►►► **Blackmore Camping & Caravanning Club Site** *(SO812440)*

Blackmore Camp Site No 2 WR8 0EE
☎ 01684 310280
web: www.campingandcaravanningclub.co.uk/blackmore
Dir: *A38 to Upton on Severn. Turn N over river bridge. 2nd left, then 1st left signed Hanley Swan. Site 1m on right*
PETS: Public areas except buildings **Exercise area** on site
Facilities walks info vet info **Other** prior notice required

Open all year Booking advisable BH & peak periods Last arrival 21.00hrs Last departure noon

Blackmore is a well-established, level wooded park, ideally located for exploring the Malvern Hills and Worcester. The excellent toilet facilities are spotlessly maintained. A 17-acre site with 200 touring pitches, 66 hardstandings.

MALVERN
MAP 03 SO74

★★★ 83% 🏵🏵 HOTEL
The Cottage in the Wood Hotel and Restaurant

Holywell Rd, Malvern Wells WR14 4LG
☎ 01684 575859 📄 01684 560662
e-mail: reception@cottageinthewood.co.uk
web: www.cottageinthewood.co.uk
Dir: *3m S of Great Malvern off A449, 500yds N of B4209, on opposite side of road*
PETS: Bedrooms (GF) unattended **Charges** £5 per night
Grounds accessible disp bin **Exercise area** adjacent
Facilities food bowl water bowl bedding vet info
On Request fridge access torch

Sitting high up on a wooded hillside, this delightful, family-run hotel boasts lovely views over the Severn Valley. The bedrooms are divided between the main house, Beech Cottage and the Pinnacles. The public areas are very stylishly decorated and imaginative food is served in an elegant dining room, overlooking the immaculate grounds.

CONTINUED

ENGLAND

The Cottage in the Wood Hotel and Restaurant

Rooms 8 en suite 23 annexe en suite (9 GF) ⊘ in 26 bedrooms
S £79-£115; D £99-£189 (incl. bkfst)☀ **Facilities** STV FTV Wi-fi available
Direct access to Malvern Hills Xmas New Year **Parking** 40 **Notes** LB

★★ 80% ⊛ HOTEL
Holdfast Cottage
Marlbank Rd, Welland WR13 6NA
☎ 01684 310288 📄 01684 311117
e-mail: enquiries@holdfast-cottage.co.uk
web: www.holdfast-cottage.co.uk
Dir: *A438 to Tewkesbury, at War Memorial rdbt turn right signed A438, at mini rdbt left for Ledbury*

PETS: Bedrooms Charges £5 per night **Public areas** except
lounge & restaurant **Grounds** accessible on leads
Exercise area 200yds

At the base of the Malvern Hills this delightful wisteria-covered hotel sits in attractive manicured grounds. Charming public areas include an intimate bar, a log fire enhanced lounge and an elegant dining room. Bedrooms vary in size but all are comfortable and well appointed. Fresh local and seasonal produce are the basis for award-winning cuisine.

Rooms 8 en suite (3 fmly) ⊘ in all bedrooms S £55; D £94-£98 (incl. bkfst)☀ **Facilities** ❦ Xmas New Year **Parking** 15 **Notes** LB

★★★ BED & BREAKFAST
Four Hedges
The Rhydd, Hanley Castle WR8 0AD
☎ 01684 310405
e-mail: fredgies@aol.com
Dir: *4m E of Malvern at junct of B4211 & B4424*

PETS: Bedrooms unattended **Public areas Grounds** accessible
disp bin **Exercise area** adjoining **Facilities** food bowl water bowl
leads pet sitting washing facs cage storage walks info vet info
On Request fridge access torch towels **Resident Pets:** Machu &
Pichu (cats)

Situated in a rural location, this detached house stands in mature grounds with wild birds in abundance. The bedrooms are equipped with thoughtful extras. Tasty English breakfasts, using free-range eggs, are served in a cosy dining room at a table made from a 300-year-old elm tree.

Rooms 4 rms (2 en suite) ⊘ S £20; D £40 **Facilities** TV1B tea/coffee
Cen ht TVL Fishing ❦ **Parking** 5 **Notes** Closed Xmas ⊛

▶▶▶▶ **Clent Hills Camping & Caravanning
Club Site** *(SO955795)*
Fieldhouse Ln B62 0NH
☎ 01562 710015
web: www.campingandcaravanningclub.co.uk/clenthills
Dir: *From M5 junct 3 take A456. Left on B4551 to Romsley. Turn right past Sun Hotel, take 5th left, then next left. Site 330yds on left*

PETS: Public areas except buildings **Exercise area** on site
Facilities walks info vet info **Other** prior notice required
Open 13 Mar-3 Nov Booking advisable BH & peak periods
Last arrival 21.00hrs Last departure noon

A very pretty, well tended park surrounded by wooded hills. The site offers excellent facilities, including hardstandings to provide flat pitches for motorhomes. Lovely views of the Clent Hills can be enjoyed from this park, and there are plenty of local scenic walks. A 7.5-acre site with 95 touring pitches, 27 hardstandings.

Notes site gates closed 23.00-07.00

★★★ 74% ⊛ HOTEL
White Lion
21 High St WR8 0HJ
☎ 01684 592551 📄 01684 593333
e-mail: reservations@whitelionhotel.biz
Dir: *A422, A38 towards Tewkesbury. In 8m take B4104, after 1m cross bridge, turn left to hotel, past bend on left*

PETS: Bedrooms (GF) unattended **Charges** £5 per night
Public areas except restaurant **Exercise area** local walks
Facilities vet info

Famed for being the inn depicted in Henry Fielding's novel 'Tom Jones', this 16th-century hotel is a reminder of old England with its exposed beams, wall timbers etc. The quality furnishing and decor schemes throughout the public areas all enhance its character. The hotel has a good reputation for its food, which is complemented by friendly, attentive service.

Rooms 11 en suite 2 annexe en suite (2 fmly) (2 GF) S £70; D £99 (incl. bkfst)☀ **Parking** 18 **Notes** Closed 1 Jan RS 25 Dec

ENGLAND

WOLVERLEY
MAP 07 SO87

▶▶▶ Wolverley Camping & Caravanning Club Site *(SO833792)*

Brown Westhead Park DY10 3PX

☎ 01562 850909

web: www.campingandcaravanningclub.co.uk/wolverley

Dir: *From Kidderminster A449 to Wolverhampton, turn left at lights onto B4189 signed Wolverley. Follow brown camping signs, turn right. Site on left*

PETS: Public areas except buildings **Exercise area** on site
Facilities walks info vet info **Other** prior notice required

Open 13 Mar-3 Nov Booking advisable BH & peak periods
Last arrival 21.00hrs Last departure noon

A very pleasant grassy site on the edge of the village, with the canal lock and towpath close to the entrance, and a pub overlooking the water. The site has good access to and from nearby motorways. A 12-acre site with 120 touring pitches.

Notes site gates closed 23.00-07.00

YORKSHIRE, EAST RIDING OF

BEVERLEY
MAP 08 TA03

★★ 76% ◉◉ HOTEL
Manor House

Northlands, Walkington HU17 8RT

☎ 01482 881645 ▤ 01482 866501

e-mail: info@walkingtonmanorhouse.co.uk

web: www.walkingtonmanorhouse.co.uk

Dir: *from M62 junct 38 follow 'Walkington' signs. 4m SW off B1230. Through Walkington, left at lights. Left at 1st x-roads. Approx 400yds hotel on left*

PETS: Bedrooms (GF) **Charges** charge for damage
Grounds accessible **Facilities** vet info **On Request** fridge access towels **Resident Pets:** Arthur (Great Dane)

This delightful country-house hotel is set in open country amid well-tended gardens. The spacious bedrooms have been attractively decorated and thoughtfully equipped. Public rooms include a conservatory restaurant and a very inviting lounge. A good range of dishes is available from two menus, with an emphasis on fresh, local produce.

Rooms 6 en suite 1 annexe en suite (1 fmly) (1 GF) ⊘ in 5 bedrooms S £75-£85; D £105-£145 (incl. bkfst)✳ **Parking** 40 **Notes** LB Closed 26 Dec-4 Jan RS Sun

BRIDLINGTON
MAP 17 TA16

★★★★★ GUEST ACCOMMODATION
Marton Grange

Flamborough Rd, Marton cum Sewerby YO15 1DU

☎ 01262 602034 ▤ 01262 602034

e-mail: martongrange@talk21.com

web: www.marton-grange.co.uk

Dir: *2m NE of Bridlington. On B1255, 600yds W of Links golf club*

PETS: Bedrooms (GF) **Charges** £5 per night charge for damage
Public areas conservatory only on leads **Grounds** accessible on leads disp bin **Facilities** cage storage walks info vet info
On Request fridge access torch **Resident Pets:** chickens

There is a welcoming atmosphere at this country guest house and the bedrooms are all of high quality, with a range of extra facilities; ground-floor rooms are available. There are attractive lounges with views over the immaculate gardens while substantial breakfasts are served in the delightful dining room.

Rooms 11 en suite (3 GF) ⊘ S £42-£49.50; D £67-£79✳ **Facilities** TVB tea/coffee Lift Cen ht **Parking** 11 **Notes** No children 12yrs Closed Dec-Feb

★★★ GUEST HOUSE
Shearwater

22 Vernon Rd YO15 2HE

☎ 01262 679883

e-mail: shearwaterhotel@amserve.com

Dir: *In town centre. Off B1254 Promenade onto Trinity Rd & Vernon Rd*

PETS: Bedrooms Charges £5 per stay **Public areas** except dining room & lounge **Exercise area** 5 mins to sea, 20 mins to park
Facilities food bedding

A friendly welcome awaits you at this well-furnished house in a residential area near the seafront. Bedrooms are very comfortably furnished and equipped. There is a cosy lounge, and quality home-cooked meals are provided in the modern dining room.

Rooms 7 en suite (3 fmly) (1 GF) ⊘ D £35-£50✳ **Facilities** TVB tea/coffee Cen ht Dinner Last d 4.30pm **Notes** LB ⊛

▶▶ Poplars Touring Park *(TA194701)*

45 Jewison Ln, Sewerby YO15 1DX

☎ 01262 677251

web: www.the-poplars.co.uk

Dir: *B1255 towards Flamborough, at 2nd bend off Z-bend, 1st left after Marton Hall, site 0.33m on left*

PETS: Charges dogs 50p per night **Public areas** on leads
Exercise area 1m **Facilities** walks info vet info

Open Mar-Oct Booking advisable BH & school summer hols
Last arrival 21.00hrs Last departure noon

A small, peaceful park with immaculate facilities including a well-appointed toilet block. The friendly owners also run a B&B next door, and there is a good pub close by. A 1.25-acre site with 30 touring pitches, 10 hardstandings.

Notes ⊗ No large groups

KINGSTON UPON HULL MAP 08 TA02

★★★ 75% HOTEL
Portland

Paragon St HU1 3JP

☎ 01482 326462 📠 01482 213460

e-mail: info@portland-hotel.co.uk

web: www.portland-hull.com

Dir: *M62 onto A63, to 1st main rdbt. Left at 2nd lights and over x-rds. Right at next junct onto Carr Ln, follow one-way system*

PETS: Bedrooms Facilities vet info **On Request** fridge access torch

A modern hotel situated next to the City Hall providing a good range of accommodation. Most of the public rooms are on the first floor and all offer wireless internet. In addition, the Bay Tree Café, at street level, is open during the day and evening. Staff are friendly and helpful and take care of car parking for hotel guests.

Rooms 126 en suite (4 fmly) ⊗ in 70 bedrooms **Facilities** STV Complimentary use of nearby health & fitness centre Xmas **Services** Lift **Parking** 12

MARKET WEIGHTON MAP 08 SE84

★★★ GUEST ACCOMMODATION
Robeanne House

Driffield Ln, Shiptonthorpe YO43 3PW

☎ 01430 873312 📠 01430 873312

e-mail: enquires@robeannehouse.co.uk

web: www.robeannehouse.co.uk

Dir: *1.5m NW on A614*

PETS: Bedrooms (GF) **Stables** on site **Charges** £5 (dogs) £15 (horses) per night charge for damage **Public areas** except dining room on leads **Grounds** accessible on leads disp bin **Exercise area** 400yds **Facilities** food (pre-bookable) food bowl water bowl bedding dog chews cat treats feeding mat litter tray etc dog scoop/disp bags leads all weather horse exercise area & paddocks pet sitting dog walking washing facs cage storage walks info vet info **On Request** fridge access torch towels **Resident Pets:** Beatty & Josie, Nina (horses), Megan & Dylan (ponies), Moulder (cat), (Jack & Guinness - visiting Labradors)

Set back off the A614 in a quiet location, this delightful modern family home was built as a farmhouse. York, the coast, and the Yorkshire Moors and Dales are within easy driving distance. All bedrooms have country views and include a large family room. A charming wooden chalet is available in the garden.

Rooms 2 en suite 3 annexe en suite (2 fmly) (2 GF) ⊗ in 1 bedrooms S £25-£35; D £50-£60❋ **Facilities** TVB tea/coffee Cen ht Dinner Last d 24hrs prior Outdoor hot-tub **Parking** 10 **Notes** LB

RUDSTON MAP 08 TA06

►►► Thorpe Hall Caravan & Camping Site

(TA108677)

Thorpe Hall YO25 4JE

☎ 01262 420393 & 420574 📠 01262 420588

e-mail: caravansite@thorpehall.co.uk

web: www.thorpehall.co.uk

Dir: *5m from Bridlington on B1253*

PETS: Public areas except games room & toilets **Exercise area** on site several dog walks **Facilities** on site shop food food bowl water bowl disp bags walks info vet info

Open Mar-Oct reception & shop limited opening hours Booking advisable BH & peak periods Last arrival 22.00hrs Last departure noon

A delightful, peaceful small park within the walled gardens of Thorpe Hall yet within a few miles of the bustling seaside resort of Bridlington. The site offers a games field, its own coarse fishery, pitch & putt, and a games and TV lounge, and there are numerous walks locally. A 4.5-acre site with 90 touring pitches.

YORKSHIRE, NORTH

ALLERSTON MAP 08 SE88

►►►► Vale of Pickering Caravan Park

(SE879808)

Carr House Farm YO18 7PQ

☎ 01723 859280 📠 01723 850060

e-mail: tony@valeofpickering.co.uk

web: www.valeofpickering.co.uk

Dir: *On B1415, 1.75m off A170 (Pickering-Scarborough road)*

PETS: Charges 50p per dog per night **Public areas** on leads **Exercise area** on site large dog walk **Facilities** on site shop food disp bags leads walks info vet info **Other** prior notice required

Open Mar-Jan (rs Mar) Booking advisable BHs Last arrival 21.00hrs Last departure noon

A well-maintained, spacious family park with excellent facilities including a well-stocked shop. Younger children will enjoy the attractive play area, while the large ball sports area will attract older ones. The park is set in open countryside bounded by hedges, and is handy for the North Yorkshire Moors and the attractions of Scarborough. A 13-acre site with 120 touring pitches, 80 hardstandings.

ASKRIGG — MAP 07 SD99

★★★★ BED & BREAKFAST
Whitfield

Helm DL8 3JF

☎ 01969 650565 ▤ 01969 650565

e-mail: empsall@askrigg-cottages.co.uk

web: www.askrigg-cottages.co.uk

Dir: *Off A684 at Bainbridge signed Askrigg, right at T-junct, 150yds to No Through Rd sign, left up hill 0.5m*

PETS: Bedrooms Charges £10 per stay **Public areas Grounds** accessible **Exercise area** adjacent **Facilities** leads washing facs cage storage walks info vet info **On Request** fridge access torch towels **Restrictions** no dogs of similar size or larger to St.Bernards/Afghan Hounds, or any breed that has to be muzzled **Resident Pets:** Molly & Sally (Border Collies)

Set high in the fells, this smart accommodation is in a carefully converted barn, built of Yorkshire limestone. Both bedrooms are homely, and have stunning views of the Wensleydale countryside. Hearty breakfasts are served around a communal table in the inviting lounge-dining room.

Rooms 2 en suite ⊗ S £42-£45; D £54-£64 **Facilities** TVB tea/coffee Cen ht TVL **Parking** 1 **Notes LB** Closed 23 Dec-2 Jan

BISHOP MONKTON — MAP 08 SE36

►►► Church Farm Caravan Park *(SE328660)*

Knaresborough Rd HG3 3QQ

☎ 01765 677668 & 07932 158924 ▤ 01765 677668

e-mail: churchfarmcaravans@uwelub.net

Dir: *Left at Boroughbridge (A1), right off A61. Park opposite church*

PETS: Stables nearby (1m) (loose box) **Public areas** on leads **Exercise area** adjacent **Facilities** washing facs walks info vet info **Other** prior notice required **Resident Pets:** Cocker Spaniel, cat, 3 horses

Open Mar-Oct Booking advisable BH Last arrival 22.30hrs Last departure 15.30hrs

A very pleasant rural site on a working farm, on the edge of the attractive village of Bishop Monkton with its well-stocked shop and pubs. Whilst very much a place to relax, there are many attractions close by including Fountains Abbey, Newby Hall, Ripon and Harrogate. A 4-acre site with 45 touring pitches and 3 statics.

Notes 🐾 No ball games

BOLTON ABBEY — MAP 07 SE05

★★★★ ◉◉◉◉ HOTEL
Devonshire Arms Country House Hotel & Spa

BD23 6AJ

☎ 01756 710441 & 718111 ▤ 01756 710564

e-mail: res@thedevonshirehotels.co.uk

web: www.devonshirehotels.co.uk

Dir: *on B6160, 250yds N of junct with A59*

PETS: Bedrooms (GF) unattended sign **Stables** nearby (1m) **Public areas** except restaurant & health spa **Grounds** accessible disp bin **Exercise area** adjacent **Facilities** food bowl & water bowl on request bedding dog chews cat treats feeding mat dog scoop/disp bags leads dog goodie bag dogs greeted by name! dog walking washing facs cage storage walks info vet info **On Request** fridge access torch towels **Resident Pets:** Pip (Lurcher), Poppy (Black Labrador), Cindy (Yorkshire Terrier)

With stunning views of the Wharfedale countryside, this beautiful hotel, owned by the Duke and Duchess of Devonshire, dates back to the 17th century. Bedrooms are elegantly furnished; those in the old part of the house are particularly spacious, complete with four-posters and fine antiques. The sitting rooms are delightfully cosy with log fires, and the dedicated staff deliver service with a blend of friendliness and professionalism. The Burlington Restaurant offers award-winning, highly accomplished cuisine, while the brasserie provides a lighter alternative.

Rooms 40 en suite (1 fmly) (17 GF) ⊗ in 30 bedrooms S £175-£395; D £220-£405 (incl. bkfst)✻ **Facilities** Spa STV ⓒ supervised ⌇ Fishing Gym ⌇ Wi-fi in bedrooms Classic cars Falconry Laser pigeon shooting Flyfishing Cricket Xmas New Year **Parking** 150 **Notes LB**

ENGLAND

BOROUGHBRIDGE   MAP 08 SE36

►►►► Boroughbridge Camping & Caravanning Club Site (SE384662)

Bar Ln, Roecliffe YO51 9LS

☎ 01423 322683

web: www.campingandcaravanningclub.co.uk/boroughbridge

Dir: *From A1(M) junct 48 follow signs for Bar Lane Ind Est & Roecliffe. Site 0.25m from rdbt*

PETS: Public areas except buildings **Exercise area** on site **Facilities** walks info vet info **Other** prior notice required

Open all year Booking advisable BH & peak periods Last arrival 21.00hrs Last departure noon

A quiet riverside site with direct access onto the River Ure, with fishing and boating available. Close enough to the A1(M) but far enough away to hear little traffic noise, this site is a perfect stopover for longer journeys. Ripon, Knaresborough, Harrogate and York are within easy reach, and Boroughbridge offers plenty of facilities just a short walk away. A 5-acre site with 85 touring pitches, 13 hardstandings.

Notes site gates closed 23.00-07.00

FILEY   MAP 08 TA18

★★★★ GUEST HOUSE

Gables

2A Rutland St YO14 9JB

☎ 01723 514750

e-mail: thegablesfiley@aol.com

Dir: *Off A165 signs for town centre, right onto West Av, 2nd left onto Rutland St, the Gables opp church*

PETS: Bedrooms Charges Public areas except dining room **Grounds** accessible **Exercise area** on site opposite **Resident Pets:** Boots (Old English Sheepdog), Psycho & Smokey (cats)

Located in a quiet residential area, just a stroll from the centre and promenade, this smart Edwardian house extends a warm welcome. Bedrooms are brightly decorated and well equipped and some are suitable for families. Breakfasts are substantial and a varied evening menu is available.

Rooms 5 en suite (3 fmly) ⊗ **Facilities** TVB tea/coffee Cen ht Dinner Last d noon Golf 18 ♨ **Parking** 2 **Notes** No coaches

GREAT AYTON   MAP 08 NZ51

★★★ INN

Royal Oak Hotel

123 High St TS9 6BW

☎ 01642 722361 & 723270 📄 01642 724047

e-mail: info@royaloak-hotel.co.uk

PETS: Bedrooms Grounds accessible on leads **Exercise area** nearby walks **Facilities** food on request vet info

This 18th-century former coaching inn is very popular with locals and visitors to the village. Bedrooms are all comfortably equipped. The restaurant and public bar retain many original features and offer a good selection of fine ales; an extensive range of food is available all day and is served in the bar or the dining room.

Rooms 5 en suite **Facilities** TVB tea/coffee Direct dial from bedrooms Cen ht Dinner Last d 9.30pm

HARROGATE   MAP 08 SE35

★★★★ 75% HOTEL

Paramount Majestic

Ripon Rd HG1 2HU

☎ 01423 700300 📄 01423 521332

e-mail: majestic@paramount-hotels.co.uk

web: www.paramount-hotels.co.uk

PARAMOUNT
GROUP OF HOTELS

Dir: *from M1 onto A1(M) at Wetherby. Take A661 to Harrogate. Hotel in town centre adjacent to Royal Hall*

PETS: Bedrooms unattended **Charges** £15 per night **Exercise area** on site

Popular for conferences and functions, this grand Victorian hotel is set in 12 acres of landscaped grounds that is within walking distance of the town centre. It benefits from spacious public areas, and the comfortable bedrooms, including some spacious suites, come in a variety of sizes.

Rooms 168 en suite (9 fmly) ⊗ in 86 bedrooms S £69-£140✷ **Facilities Spa** STV ⊛ supervised ♨ Gym Wi-fi available Golf practice net Xmas New Year **Services** Lift **Parking** 250 (charged) **Notes** LB

ENGLAND

HARROGATE CONTINUED

★★★ 83% ⊛⊛ HOTEL
The Boar's Head Hotel
Ripley Castle Estate HG3 3AY
☎ 01423 771888 📇 01423 771509
e-mail: reservations@boarsheadripley.co.uk
Dir: *on A61 (Harrogate to Ripon road). Hotel in town centre*
PETS: Bedrooms unattended **Charges** £10 per night
Public areas except all food areas **Grounds** accessible
Part of the Ripley Castle estate, this delightful and popular hotel is
renowned for its warm hospitality and as a dining destination.
Bedrooms offer many comforts, and the luxurious day rooms feature
works of art from the nearby castle. The banqueting suites in the castle
are very impressive.
Rooms 19 en suite 6 annexe en suite (2 fmly) ⊛ in all bedrooms
S £105-£125; D £125-£150 (incl. bkfst)※ **Facilities** ♨ Fishing Clay pigeon
shooting, Tennis, Fishing 🎵 Xmas **Parking** 50 **Notes** LB

★★ 78% HOTEL
Ascot House
53 Kings Rd HG1 5HJ
☎ 01423 531005 📇 01423 503523
e-mail: admin@ascothouse.com
web: www.ascothouse.com
Dir: *follow signs for town centre/Conference & Exhibition Centre
into Kings Rd, hotel on left after park*
PETS: Bedrooms (GF) **Charges** £10 per week **Grounds** accessible
on leads disp bin **Exercise area** 20yds **Facilities** cage storage
walks info vet info **On Request** fridge access torch towels
This late-Victorian house is situated a short distance from the
International Conference Centre and provides comfortable, well
equipped bedrooms and smartly presented bathrooms. The attractive
public areas include an inviting lounge, bar, elegant dining room and
beautiful stained glass window on the main staircase.
Rooms 18 en suite (2 fmly) (4 GF) ⊛ in 19 bedrooms S £65-£79;
D £105-£119 (incl. bkfst) **Facilities** Wi-fi in bedrooms Xmas **Parking** 14
Notes LB Closed New Year & 27 Jan-10 Feb

★★★★ ⇔ GUEST HOUSE
Alexa House & Stable Cottages
26 Ripon Rd HG1 2JJ
☎ 01423 501988 📇 01423 504086
e-mail: enquiries@alexa-house.co.uk
web: www.alexa-house.co.uk
Dir: *On A61, 0.25m from junct A59*
PETS: Bedrooms (GF) **Charges** charge for damage
Grounds accessible on leads **Facilities** walks info vet info
On Request fridge access torch
This popular establishment has stylish, well-equipped bedrooms split
between the main house and cottage rooms. All rooms come with
homely extras. Light meals are available and dinners are available for
groups by arrangement. The opulent day rooms include an elegant
lounge with honesty bar, and a bright dining room. The hands-on
proprietors ensure high levels of customer care.
Rooms 9 en suite 4 annexe en suite (2 fmly) (4 GF) ⊛ S £50-£60;
D £80-£100 **Facilities** TVB tea/coffee Direct dial from bedrooms Licensed
Cen ht **Parking** 10 **Notes** No coaches Closed 23-26 Dec

►► **Bilton Park** *(SE317577)*
Village Farm, Bilton Ln HG1 4DH
☎ 01423 863121
Dir: *Turn E off A59 at Skipton Inn into Bilton Lane. Site approx
1m*
PETS: Public areas Exercise area on site 8 acre fields & walks
adjacent **Facilities** on site shop food bowl water bowl vet info
Other kennels within 100yds
Open Apr-Oct Booking advisable
An established family-owned park in open countryside yet only two
miles from the shops and tearooms of Harrogate. The spacious grass
pitches are complemented by a well appointed toilet block with private
facilities. The Nidd Gorge right on the doorstep. A 4-acre site with 50
touring pitches.
Notes ⊛

HAWNBY MAP 08 SE58

★★★★ ▣ GUEST ACCOMMODATION
Laskill Grange
YO62 5NB
☎ 01439 798268 📄 01439 798498
e-mail: suesmith@laskillfarm.fsnet.co.uk
web: www.laskillgrange.co.uk
Dir: *6m N of Helmsley on B1257*

PETS: Bedrooms Public areas except dining room & lounge **Grounds** accessible disp bin **Exercise area** adjacent **Facilities** food bowl water bowl feeding mat washing facs cage storage walks info vet info **On Request** fridge access torch towels **Resident Pets:** ducks, peacocks & chickens

Country lovers will enjoy this charming 19th-century farmhouse. Guests can take a walk in the surrounding countryside, fish the River Seph which runs through the grounds, or visit nearby Rievaulx Abbey. Comfortable bedrooms are in the main house and are well furnished and supplied with many thoughtful extras.

Rooms 4 annexe en suite (4 GF) ⊗ **Facilities** TVB tea/coffee Cen ht TVL Fishing Riding **Parking** 20

HELMSLEY MAP 08 SE68

★★★ 78% SMALL HOTEL
Pheasant
Harome YO62 5JG
☎ 01439 771241 📄 01439 771744
e-mail: reservations@thepheasanthotel.com
web: www.thepheasanthotel.com
Dir: *2.5m SE, leave A170 after 0.25m. Right signed Harome for further 2m. Hotel opposite church*

PETS: Bedrooms (GF) **Exercise area** 200yds **Facilities** water bowl washing facs cage storage walks info vet info **On Request** fridge access torch towels

Guests can expect a family welcome at this hotel, which has spacious, comfortable bedrooms and enjoys a delightful setting next to the village pond. The beamed, flagstoned bar leads into the charming lounge and conservatory dining room, where very enjoyable English food is served. A separate building contains the swimming pool. The hotel offers dinner-inclusive tariffs, and has many regulars.

Rooms 12 en suite 2 annexe en suite (1 GF) ⊗ in all bedrooms S £82-£88; D £164-£176 (incl. bkfst & dinner) **Facilities** STV ☺ **Parking** 20 **Notes** LB No children 12yrs Closed Xmas & Jan-Feb

▶▶▶ **Foxholme Caravan Park** *(SE658828)*
Harome YO62 5JG
☎ 01439 771241 📄 01439 771744
Dir: *A170 from Helmsley towards Scarborough, right signed Harome, left at church, through village, follow signs*

PETS: Public areas on leads **Exercise area** on site dog walk area **Facilities** on site shop washing facs vet info

Open Etr-Oct Booking advisable bank & school hols Last arrival 23.00hrs Last departure noon

A quiet park set in secluded wooded countryside, with well-shaded pitches in individual clearings divided by mature trees. The facilities are well maintained, and the site is ideal as a touring base or a place to relax. Caravans are prohibited on the A170 at Sutton Bank between Thirsk and Helmsley. A 6-acre site with 60 touring pitches.

Notes ⊗ Adults only

HIGH BENTHAM MAP 07 SD66

▶ **Lowther Hill Caravan Park** *(SD696695)*
LA2 7AN
☎ 01524 261657
web: www.caravancampingsites.co.uk/northyorkshire/lowtherhill
Dir: *From A65 at Clapham onto B6480 signed Bentham. 3m to site on right*

PETS: Public areas Facilities vet info

Open Mar-Nov Booking advisable Last arrival 21.00hrs Last departure 14.00hrs

A simple site with stunning panoramic views from every pitch. Peace reigns on this little park, though the tourist villages of Ingleton, Clapham and Settle are not far away. All pitches have electricity, and there is a heated toilet/washroom. A 1-acre site with 9 touring pitches, 4 hardstandings and 1 static.

Notes ⊗

HINDERWELL

MAP 08 NZ71

►►► 76% Serenity Touring and Camping Park (NZ792167)

26A High St TS13 5JH

☎ 01947 841122

e-mail: patandni@aol.com

web: www.serenitycaravanpark.co.uk

Dir: *Off A174 in village of Hinderwell*

PETS: Charges 50p per night **Public areas** on leads
Exercise area cliff walks 0.5m **Facilities** vet info
Resident Pets: DJ (Black Labrador)

Open Mar-Oct Booking advisable peak periods Last arrival 21.00hrs Last departure noon

A charming park mainly for adults, being developed by enthusiastic owners. It lies behind the village of Hinderwell with its two pubs and store, and is handy for backpackers on the Cleveland Way. The sandy Runswick Bay and old fishing port of Staithes are close by, whilst Whitby is a short drive away. A 5.5-acre site with 20 touring pitches, 2 hardstandings.

Notes Mainly adult site, no ball games, kites or frisbees

HOVINGHAM

MAP 08 SE67

★★★ 71% ⚙ HOTEL
Worsley Arms

High St YO62 4LA

☎ 01653 628234 🖹 01653 628130

e-mail: worsleyarms@aol.com

Dir: *A64, signed York, towards Malton. At dual carriageway left to Hovingham. At Slingsby left, then 2m*

PETS: Bedrooms Exercise area nearby **Charges** £5 per night
Public areas except restaurant **Grounds** accessible
Resident Pets: Badger (Black Labrador)

Overlooking the village green, this hotel has relaxing and attractive lounges with welcoming open fires. Bedrooms are also comfortable and several are contained in cottages across the green. The restaurant provides interesting quality cooking, with less formal dining in the Cricketers' Bar and Bistro to the rear.

Rooms 12 en suite 8 annexe en suite (2 fmly) (4 GF) ⊘ in all bedrooms
Facilities ⌣ Shooting **Parking** 25

KNARESBOROUGH

MAP 08 SE35

★★★★ 🏨 ➾ GUEST HOUSE
Gallon House

47 Kirkgate HG5 8BZ

☎ 01423 862102

e-mail: gallon-house@ntlworld.com

web: www.gallon-house.co.uk

Dir: *Next to railway station, in the centre of town*

PETS: Bedrooms Public areas Grounds accessible
Exercise area 100mtrs **Facilities** food Dog welcome pack inc water bowl, towel, dog biscuits **Resident Pets:** Lucy (Springer Spaniel)

This delightful Tudor-style building has spectacular views over the River Nidd, and offers very stylish accommodation and a homely atmosphere. The bedrooms are all individual with many homely extras. Rick's culinary delights are not too be missed: dinner (by arrangement) features quality local and home-made produce.

Rooms 3 en suite S £85; D £110 **Facilities** TVB tea/coffee Licensed Cen ht Dinner Last d noon Wi-fi available **Notes** LB No coaches ⊗

★★★★ 🏨 GUEST ACCOMMODATION
Newton House

5-7 York Place HG5 0AD

☎ 01423 863539 🖹 01423 869748

e-mail: newtonhouse@btinternet.com

web: www.newtonhouseyorkshire.com

Dir: *On A59 in Knaresborough, 500yds from town centre*

PETS: Bedrooms (GF) **Public areas** except bkfst room
Exercise area 150mtrs **Facilities** food bowl water bowl bedding dog chews feeding mat washing facs cage storage walks info vet info **On Request** fridge access torch towels
Resident Pets: Keema (dog)

The delightful 18th-century former coaching inn is only a short walk from the river, castle and market square. The property is entered by an archway into a courtyard. The attractive, very well-equipped bedrooms include some four-posters and also king-size doubles. There is a comfortable lounge, and memorable breakfasts are served in the attractive dining room.

Newton House

Rooms 9 rms (8 en suite) (1 pri facs) 2 annexe en suite (3 fmly) (3 GF) ⊘ S £50-£85; D £75-£100✳ **Facilities** TVB tea/coffee Direct dial from bedrooms Cen ht TVL Wi-fi available **Parking** 10 **Notes** LB Closed 1wk Xmas

See advert on this page

LEYBURN   MAP 07 SE19

★ 68% HOTEL
Golden Lion
Market Place DL8 5AS
☎ 01969 622161 📠 01969 623836
e-mail: annegoldenlion@aol.com
web: www.thegoldenlion.co.uk
Dir: *on A684 in market square*

PETS: Bedrooms sign **Stables** nearby (3m) **Charges** charge for damage **Public areas Exercise area** 100yds **Facilities** washing facs cage storage walks info vet info **On Request** fridge access torch towels

Dating back to 1765, this traditional inn overlooks the cobbled market square where weekly markets still take place. Bedrooms, including some family rooms, offer appropriate levels of comfort. The restaurant, with murals depicting scenes of the Dales, offers a good range of meals. Food can also be enjoyed in the cosy bar which is a popular meeting place for local people.

Rooms 14 rms (13 en suite) (5 fmly) S £30-£38; D £60-£76 (incl. bkfst)✳ **Facilities** Wi-fi available New Year **Services** Lift **Notes** LB Closed 25 & 26 Dec

---

LONG PRESTON   MAP 07 SD85

▶▶▶▶ **Gallaber Park** *(SD840570)*
BD23 4QF
☎ 01729 851397 📠 01729 851398
e-mail: info@gallaberpark.co.uk
web: www.gallaberpark.com
Dir: *On A682 between Long Preston & Gisburn*

PETS: Public areas Exercise area on site dog walk area & nearby villages **Facilities** disp bags walks info vet info **Other** prior notice required max 2 pets per caravan

Open mid Mar-Oct Booking advisable BH Last arrival 20.00hrs Last departure 13.00hrs

Set in the picturesque Ribble Valley, this park enjoys lovely views across the Dales. A stone barn houses excellent toilets and a family bathroom, and there are various types of pitches including some fully serviced ones. The emphasis is on quiet relaxation, and the spacious grounds and plentiful young shrubs and trees support this impression. 63 touring pitches, 27 hardstandings and 21 statics.

LUMBY
MAP 08 SE43

★★★ 72% HOTEL

Quality Hotel Leeds Selby Fork

LS25 5LF

☎ 01977 682761 🖷 01977 685462

e-mail: enquiries@hotels-leeds-selby.com

Dir: *A1M junct 42/A63 signposted Selby, hotel on A63 on left*

PETS: Bedrooms Public areas except restaurant **Grounds** accessible

A modern hotel situated in extensive grounds near the A1/A63 junction. Attractive day rooms include the Woodlands Restaurant and the Leisure Club includes outdoor tennis and golf. Service, provided by friendly staff, includes an all-day lounge menu and 24-hour room service.

Rooms 97 en suite (18 fmly) (56 GF) ⊘ in 57 bedrooms S £45-£105; D £45-£105✳ **Facilities** STV 🐧 🏊 Gym Putt green Wi-fi available Xmas New Year **Parking** 230 **Notes LB**

MALHAM
MAP 07 SD96

★★★ GUEST HOUSE

Beck Hall

Cove Rd BD23 4DJ

☎ 01729 830332

e-mail: alice@beckhallmalham.com

web: www.beckhallmalham.com

Dir: *A65 to Gargrave, turn right to Malham. B&B 100yds on right after mini-rdbt*

PETS: Bedrooms (GF) unattended sign **Stables** nearby (100yds) **Public areas Grounds** accessible disp bin **Exercise area** 10yds **Facilities** water bowl pet sitting dog walking washing facs walks info vet info **On Request** fridge access torch towels
Resident Pets: Harvey (cat)

A small stone bridge over Malham Beck leads to this delightful property. Dating from 1710, the house has true character, with bedrooms carefully furnished with four-poster beds. Delicious afternoon teas are available in the colourful garden in warmer months, while roaring log fires welcome you in the winter.

Rooms 10 rms (9 en suite) (1 pri facs) 7 annexe en suite (4 fmly) (4 GF) ⊘ S £22-£60; D £40-£80 **Facilities** STV TV15B tea/coffee Licensed Cen ht Dinner Last d 5.30pm Wi-fi available Fishing Riding **Parking** 40 **Notes LB** ch fac

MARKINGTON
MAP 08 SE26

★★★ 82% COUNTRY HOUSE HOTEL

Hob Green

HG3 3PJ

☎ 01423 770031 🖷 01423 771589

e-mail: info@hobgreen.com

web: www.hobgreen.com

Dir: *from A61, 4m N of Harrogate, left at Wormald Green, follow hotel signs*

PETS: Please telephone for details

This hospitable country house is set in delightful gardens amidst rolling countryside midway between Harrogate and Ripon. The inviting lounges boast open fires in season and there is an elegant restaurant with a small private dining room. The individual bedrooms are very comfortable and come with a host of thoughtful extras.

Rooms 12 en suite (1 fmly) ⊘ in all bedrooms S £98-£118; D £115-£135 (incl. bkfst) **Facilities** FTV 🦮 Xmas New Year **Parking** 40 **Notes LB**

MASHAM
MAP 08 SE28

★★★★ ⑨⑨⑨ HOTEL

Swinton Park

HG4 4JH

☎ 01765 680900 🖷 01765 680901

e-mail: enquiries@swintonpark.com

web: www.swintonpark.com

Dir: *A1 onto B6267/8 to Masham. Follow signs through town centre & turn right into Swinton Terrace. 1m past golf course, over bridge, up hill. Hotel on right*

PETS: Bedrooms Stables on site **Charges** £10 per night **Grounds** accessible disp bin **Facilities** food (pre-bookable) food bowl water bowl bedding dog chews disp bags dog walking washing facs cage storage walks info vet info **On Request** fridge access torch towels

Extended during the Victorian and Edwardian eras, the original part of this welcoming castle dates from the 17th century. Bedrooms are luxuriously furnished and come with a host of thoughtful extras. Samuel's restaurant (built by the current owner's great-great-great grandfather) is very elegant and serves imaginative dishes using local produce, much being sourced from the Swinton estate itself.

Rooms 30 en suite (4 fmly) ⊗ in all bedrooms D £150-£350 (incl. bkfst) ✳ **Facilities** Spa FTV ♨9 Fishing Riding Gym ⤣ Putt green Wi-fi in bedrooms Shooting Falconry Pony trekking Cookery school Off-road driving ch fac Xmas New Year **Services** Lift **Parking** 50 **Notes** LB

►►► Old Station Caravan Park *(SE232812)*

Old Station Yard, Low Burton HG4 4DF

☎ 01765 689569 📄 01765 689569

e-mail: oldstation@tiscali.co.uk

web: www.oldstation-masham.co.uk

Dir: *Exit A1 onto B6267 signed Masham & Thirsk. In 8m left onto A6108. In 100yds left into site*

PETS: Stables (loose box) **Public areas Exercise area** on site **Facilities** on site shop walks info vet info space for loose box

Open Mar-Nov Booking advisable Last arrival 20.00hrs Last departure noon

An interesting site on a former station. The enthusiastic and caring family owners have maintained the railway theme in creating a park with high quality facilities. The small town of Masham with its Theakston and Black Sheep breweries are within easy walking distance of the park. The reception/café in a carefully restored wagon shed is the latest feature of this park. A 3.75-acre site with 50 touring pitches and 12 statics.

Notes ☺

MONK FRYSTON   MAP 08 SE52

★★★ 80% COUNTRY HOUSE HOTEL
Monk Fryston Hall

LS25 5DU

☎ 01977 682369 📄 01977 683544

e-mail: reception@monkfrystonhallhotel.co.uk

web: www.monkfrystonhallhotel.co.uk

Dir: *A1M junct 42/A63 towards Selby. Monk Fryston village in 2m, hotel on left*

PETS: Bedrooms unattended **Charges** £5 per night **Public areas** except restaurant **Grounds** accessible **Exercise area** on site

This delightful 16th-century mansion house enjoys a peaceful location in 30 acres of grounds, yet is only minutes' drive from the A1. Many original features have been retained and the public rooms are furnished with antique and period pieces. Bedrooms are individually styled and thoughtfully equipped for both business and leisure guests.

Rooms 29 en suite (2 fmly) (5 GF) ⊗ in 20 bedrooms S £75-£105; D £110-£175 (incl. bkfst)✳ **Facilities** STV ⤣ Wi-fi available Xmas New Year **Parking** 80 **Notes** LB

NORTHALLERTON   MAP 08 SE39

★★★ 70% HOTEL
Solberge Hall

Newby Wiske DL7 9ER

☎ 01609 779191 📄 01609 780472

e-mail: reservations@solbergehall.co.uk

web: www.solbergehall.co.uk

Dir: *Exit A1 at Leeming Bar, follow A684, turn right at x-rds, hotel in 2m on right*

PETS: Bedrooms (GF) **Charges** £10 per stay charge for damage **Grounds** accessible on leads disp bin **Facilities** food bowl water bowl washing facs cage storage walks info vet info **On Request** fridge access torch towels

This Grade II listed Georgian country house is set in 16 acres of parkland and commands panoramic views over open countryside. Spacious bedrooms, some with four-poster beds, vary in style. Public areas include a comfortable lounge bar and an elegant drawing room. The restaurant offers an interesting range of carefully prepared dishes.

Rooms 24 en suite (2 fmly) (5 GF) ⊗ in 20 bedrooms S £75-£90; D £110-£140 (incl. bkfst) **Facilities** STV ⤣ Wi-fi in bedrooms Xmas **Parking** 100 **Notes** LB

NORTH STAINLEY   MAP 08 SE27

►►► Sleningford Water Mill Caravan Camping Park *(SE280783)*

HG4 3HQ

☎ 01765 635201

e-mail: sleningford@hotmail.co.uk

web: www.ukparks.co.uk/sleningford

Dir: *Adjacent to A6108. 4m N of Ripon & 1m N of North Stainley*

PETS: Charges £1 per night **Public areas** except buildings on leads **Facilities** on site shop food bowl water bowl disp bags walks info vet info **Other** prior notice required

Resident Pets: Poppy (Springer Spaniel/Border Collie cross) Murphy & Rosie (Cats)

Open Etr & Apr-Oct Booking advisable bank, school hols & wknds Last arrival 21.00hrs Last departure 12.30hrs

The old watermill and the River Ure make an attractive setting for this touring park which is laid out in two areas. Pitches are placed in meadowland and close to mature woodland, and the park has two enthusiastic managers. Popular place with canoeists. A 14-acre site with 80 touring pitches.

Notes Youth groups by prior arrangement only

ENGLAND

OSMOTHERLEY MAP 08 SE49

▶▶▶▶ Cote Ghyll Caravan & Camping Park

(SE459979)

DL6 3AH

☎ 01609 883425

e-mail: hills@coteghyll.com

web: www.coteghyll.com

Dir: *Exit A19 dual carriageway at A684 (Northallerton junct). Follow signs to Osmotherley. Left in village centre. Site entrance 0.5m on right*

PETS: Public areas on leads at all times **Exercise area** on site dog walk adjacent **Facilities** on site shop washing facs walks info vet info

Open Mar-Oct Booking advisable bank & school hols Last arrival 23.00hrs Last departure noon

Quiet, peaceful site in a pleasant valley on the edge of moors, close to the village. The park is divided into terraces bordered by woodland, and the well-appointed newly built amenity block is a welcome addition to this attractive park. There are pubs and shops nearby. A 7-acre site with 77 touring pitches, 5 hardstandings and 18 statics.

Notes ⊛ Family park

PICKERING MAP 08 SE78

★★★ 81% ⊛ HOTEL

The White Swan Inn

Market Place YO18 7AA

☎ 01751 472288 ▤ 01751 475554

e-mail: welcome@white-swan.co.uk

web: www.white-swan.co.uk

Dir: *in town, between church & steam railway station*

PETS: Bedrooms (GF) unattended **Stables** nearby **Charges** £12.50 per stay **Public areas** except restaurant **Grounds** accessible disp bin **Exercise area** 200mtrs **Facilities** food bowl water bowl disp bags washing facs cage storage walks info vet info **On Request** torch

This 16th-century coaching inn offers well-equipped, comfortable bedrooms, including suites, either of a more traditional style in the main building or modern rooms in the annexe. Service is friendly and attentive and the standard of cuisine high, in both the attractive restaurant and the cosy bar and lounge where log fires burn in the cooler months. A comprehensive wine list specialises in many fine vintages. A private dining room is also available.

Rooms 12 en suite 9 annexe en suite (3 fmly) (8 GF) ⊘ in all bedrooms D £130-£245 (incl. bkfst)✳ **Facilities** Spa FTV Wi-fi available Xmas New Year **Parking** 45 **Notes** LB

RICHMOND MAP 07 NZ10

▶▶▶▶ Brompton Caravan Park *(NZ199002)*

Brompton-on-Swale DL10 7EZ

☎ 01748 824629 ▤ 01748 826383

e-mail: brompton.caravanpark@btinternet.com

web: www.bromptoncaravanpark.co.uk

Dir: *Take B6271 off A1 signed Richmond, site 1m on left*

PETS: Charges 50p per night **Public areas Exercise area** on site **Facilities** on site shop food dog chews disp bags walks info vet info **Other** prior notice required, pet shop adjacent **Restrictions** No Pitt Bull Terriers **Resident Pets:** Poppy (Jack Russell) Griff (cross) Marmie, Scatcat & Fluff (cats)

Open all year (rs Oct-Jan closed to tourers) Booking advisable summer & wknds Last arrival 20.00hrs Last departure noon

A family riverside park which has recently been acquired by enthusiastic young owners with local connections. Fishing is available on the River Swale which flows through the park, and there is a good children's playground. A 14.5-acre site with 177 touring pitches, 6 hardstandings and 22 statics.

Notes Family park

RIPON MAP 08 SE37

★★★ 79% HOTEL

Best Western Ripon Spa

Park St HG4 2BU

Best Western

☎ 01765 602172 ▤ 01765 690770

e-mail: spahotel@bronco.co.uk

web: www.bw-riponspa.com

Dir: *From A61 take to Ripon then follow signs towards Fountains Abbey. Hotel on left after hospital. Or from A1(M) junct 48 take B6265 to Ripon, straight on at 2 rdbts. Right at lights towards city centre. Left at top of hill. Bear left at Give Way sign. Hotel on left*

PETS: Bedrooms (GF) unattended **Public areas** except food areas **Grounds** accessible on leads disp bin **Exercise area** 25yds **Facilities** cage storage walks info vet info **On Request** torch towels

This privately owned hotel is set in extensive and attractive gardens just a short walk from the city centre. The bedrooms are well equipped to meet the needs of leisure and business travellers alike, while the comfortable lounges are complemented by the convivial atmosphere of the Turf Bar.

Rooms 40 en suite (5 fmly) (4 GF) ⊘ in all bedrooms S £85-£98; D £110 (incl. bkfst)✳ **Facilities** FTV ⅋ Wi-fi in bedrooms Free use of gym (approx 1m) Xmas New Year **Services** Lift **Parking** 60 **Notes** LB

ROSEDALE ABBEY   MAP 08 SE79

★★★ 71% HOTEL
Blacksmith's Country Inn

Hartoft End YO18 8EN

☎ 01751 417331 📠 01751 417167

e-mail: info@hartoft-bci.co.uk

Dir: *off A170 in village of Wrelton, N to Hartoft*

PETS: Bedrooms (GF) unattended **Stables** nearby (5m)
Charges £5 per night charge for damage **Public areas**
Grounds accessible disp bin **Facilities** dog chews cat treats
walks info vet info **On Request** fridge access torch

Set amongst the wooded valleys and hillsides of the Yorkshire Moors,
this charming hotel offers a choice of popular bars and intimate, cosy
lounges, and retains the friendly atmosphere of a country inn. Food is
available either in the bars or the spacious restaurant, while bedrooms
vary in size all equipped to comfortable modern standards.

Rooms 19 en suite (2 fmly) (4 GF) ⊗ in all bedrooms S £30-£35;
D £80-£100 (incl. bkfst)✳ **Facilities** Fishing Xmas New Year **Parking** 100
Notes LB RS Oct-Mar

★★ 72% HOTEL
Milburn Arms

YO18 8RA

☎ 01751 417312 📠 01751 417541

e-mail: info@milburnarms.co.uk

web: www.milburnarms.co.uk

Dir: *Leave A64 at Malton turning, towards Pickering, Rosedale
Abbey 10m*

PETS: Please telephone for details

This attractive inn dates back to the 16th century and enjoys an idyllic,
peaceful location in this scenic village. Bedrooms, some of which are
located in an adjacent stone block, are spacious, comfortable and
smartly appointed. Guests can enjoy carefully prepared food either in
the traditional bar or in the elegant restaurant.

CONTINUED

Milburn Arms

Rooms 5 en suite 8 annexe en suite (3 fmly) (4 GF) ⊗ in all bedrooms
S £38-£60; D £76-£120 (incl. bkfst) **Facilities** Xmas New Year **Parking** 10
Notes LB

SALTBURN-BY-THE-SEA   MAP 08 NZ62

★★★ 73% HOTEL
Rushpool Hall Hotel

Saltburn Ln TS12 1HD

☎ 01287 624111 📠 01287 625255

web: www.rushpoolhallhotel.co.uk

Dir: *A174 Redcar & Whitby, straight over 5 rdbts, at 6th rdbt take
3rd exit for Skelton, left at next 2 rdbts, hotel 0.5m on left*

PETS: Bedrooms unattended chalets only **Public areas** on leads
Grounds accessible **Exercise area** 90-acre estate & beach nearby

A grand Victorian mansion located in its own grounds and woodlands.
Stylish, elegant bedrooms are well equipped and spacious; many enjoy
excellent sea views. The interesting public rooms are filled with charm
and character, and roaring fires welcome guests in cooler months. The
hotel boasts an excellent reputation as a wedding venue thanks to its
superb location and experienced event management.

Rooms 21 en suite S £55-£90; D £115-£165 (incl. bkfst)✳ **Facilities** STV
Fishing 🚣 Bird watching Walking Jogging track ch fac Xmas New Year
Parking 120 **Notes** LB ⊗

SCARBOROUGH   MAP 08 TA08

★★★ 73% HOTEL
Ox Pasture Hall

Lady Edith's Dr, Raincliffe Woods YO12 5TD

☎ 01723 365295 📠 01723 355156

e-mail: oxpasturehall@btconnect.com

web: www.oxpasturehall.com

Dir: *from A171 (Scarborough to Scalby road) turn into Lady
Edith's Drive*

PETS: Bedrooms (GF) unattended **Stables** nearby **Charges** £10
per stay charge for damage **Public areas** bar only
Grounds accessible disp bin **Facilities** vet info
Resident Pets: Homee (Border Collie cross), Buster & Boxer
(Welsh Cobb horses)

This delightful family-run, country hotel is set in the quiet North Riding

CONTINUED

ENGLAND

SCARBOROUGH CONTINUED

Forest Park and has a very friendly atmosphere. Bedrooms, split between the main house, townhouse and the delightful courtyard, are individual, stylish and comfortably equipped. Public areas include a split-level bar, quiet lounge, and attractive restaurant. There is also an extensive banqueting area licensed for civil weddings.

Ox Pasture Hall

Rooms 16 en suite 6 annexe en suite (1 fmly) (14 GF) ⊘ in all bedrooms S £60; D £120-£160 (incl. bkfst)✳ **Facilities** FTV Fishing Xmas New Year **Parking** 100 (charged) **Notes** LB

★★★ 68% HOTEL
East Ayton Lodge Country House
Moor Ln, Forge Valley YO13 9EW
☎ 01723 864227 🖹 01723 862680
e-mail: ealodgehtl@cix.co.uk
Dir: *400yds off A170*
PETS: Bedrooms (GF) **Charges** £5 per night **Public areas** except restaurant/bar **Grounds** accessible on leads disp bin **Facilities** cage storage walks info vet info **On Request** fridge access towels

Set in three acres of grounds close to the River Derwent and discreetly situated in a quiet lane on the edge of the forest, this hotel is constructed around two cottages, the original buildings on the site. Bedrooms are well equipped and those on the courtyard are particularly spacious; public rooms include a large conservatory. A good range of food is available.

Rooms 12 en suite 14 annexe en suite (5 fmly) (7 GF) ⊘ in 12 bedrooms S £55; D £65-£95 (incl. bkfst)✳ **Facilities** STV ch fac Xmas New Year **Parking** 70

►►►► Jacobs Mount Caravan Park
(TA021868)
Jacobs Mount, Stepney Rd YO12 5NL
☎ 01723 361178 🖹 01723 361178
e-mail: jacobsmount@yahoo.co.uk
web: www.jacobsmount.co.uk
Dir: *Direct access from A170*
PETS: Stables nearby (1.5m) (loose box) **Charges** £2.50 per night £17.50 per week **Public areas** except toilets on leads **Exercise area** on site wooded and field walks 0.5m **Facilities** on site shop food food bowl water bowl dog chews cat treats disp bags dog walking washing facs walks info vet info **Resident Pets:** 2 working dogs (Dobermans)

Open Mar-Nov (rs Mar-May & Oct limited hours at shop/bar) Booking advisable BH & late Jun-early Sep Last arrival 21.00hrs Last departure noon

An elevated family-run park surrounded by woodland and open countryside, yet only two miles from the beach. Touring pitches are terraced gravel stands with individual services. A licensed bar and family room provide meals and snacks, and there is a separate well-equipped games room for teenagers. An 18-acre site with 156 touring pitches, 131 hardstandings and 60 statics.

►►►► Scarborough Camping & Caravanning Club Site *(TA025911)*
Field Ln, Burniston Rd YO13 0DA
☎ 01723 366212
web: www.campingandcaravanningclub.co.uk
Dir: *On W side of A165, 1m N of Scarborough*
PETS: Exercise area on site dog walk & North Yorkshire Moors **Facilities** walks info vet info **Other** prior notice required

Open Apr-Oct Booking advisable BH & peak period Last arrival 21.00hrs Last departure noon

This spacious site is of a high standard. The majority of pitches are hardstandings of plastic webbing which allow the grass to grow through naturally. This is an excellent family-orientated park with its own shop and takeaway, within easy reach of the resort of Scarborough. A 20-acre site with 300 touring pitches, 100 hardstandings.

►►► Killerby Old Hall *(TA063829)*

Killerby YO11 3TW

☎ 01723 583799 📄 01723 583799

Dir: Direct access via B1261 at Killerby, near Cayton

PETS: Charges £1 per night **Public areas Exercise area** on site adjacent field open countryside nearby **Facilities** vet info

Open Mar-Oct Booking advisable BHs & school hols Last departure noon

A small secluded park, well sheltered by mature trees and shrubs, located at the rear of the old hall. Use of the small indoor swimming pool is shared by visitors to the hall's holiday accommodation. A 2-acre site with 20 touring pitches, 20 hardstandings.

SCOTCH CORNER   MAP 08 NZ20

►►► Scotch Corner Caravan Park *(NZ210054)*

DL10 6NS

☎ 01748 822530 📄 01748 822530

e-mail: marshallleisure@aol.com

web: www.scotchcornercaravanpark.co.uk

Dir: From Scotch Corner junct of A1 & A66 take A6108 towards Richmond. 250mtrs, cross central reservation, return 200mtrs to site

PETS: Public areas Charges Exercise area on site 3 acre dog walk **Facilities** on site shop disp bags vet info **Other** prior notice required **Resident Pets:** Labrador

Open Etr-Oct Booking advisable public hols & Jul-Aug Last arrival 22.30hrs Last departure noon

A well-maintained site with good facilities, ideally situated as a stopover, and an equally good location for touring. The Vintage Hotel which serves food can be accessed from the rear of the site. A 7-acre site with 96 touring pitches, 4 hardstandings.

SHERIFF HUTTON   MAP 08 SE66

►►► Sheriff Hutton C&C Club Site *(SE638652)*

Bracken Hill YO60 6QG

☎ 01347 878660

web: www.campingandcaravanningclub.co.uk

Dir: From York follow 'Earswick Strensall' signs. Keep left at filling station & Ship Inn. Follow signs for Sheriff Hutton. Turn left in village of Strensall, site 2nd on right

PETS: Exercise area on site dog walk **Facilities** walks info vet info **Other** prior notice required

Open Mar-Oct Booking advisable BH & peak periods Last arrival 21.00hrs Last departure noon

A quiet rural site in open meadowland within easy reach of York. This well-established park is friendly and welcoming, and the landscaping is attractive and mature. A 10-acre site with 90 touring pitches, 16 hardstandings.

SKIPTON   MAP 07 SD95

★★★ 79% HOTEL

The Coniston

Coniston Cold BD23 4EB

☎ 01756 748080 📄 01756 749487

e-mail: info@theconistonhotel.com

Dir: on A65, 6m NW of Skipton

PETS: Bedrooms (GF) unattended **Charges** £10 per stay **Public areas** except restaurant areas **Grounds** accessible **Facilities** food bowl water bowl cage storage walks info vet info **On Request** fridge access towels

Privately owned and situated on a 1,400 acre estate centred around a beautiful 24-acre lake, this hotel offers guests many exciting outdoor activities. The modern bedrooms are comfortable and most have king-size beds. Macleod's Bar and the main restaurant serve all-day meals, and fine dining is available in the evening from both carte and fixed-price menus. Staff are very friendly and nothing is too much trouble.

Rooms 50 en suite (13 fmly) (25 GF) ⊘ in 42 bedrooms S £75-£125; D £87-£149 **Facilities** STV Fishing Wi-fi available Clay pigeon shooting Falconry Fishing Off road Land Rover driving Xmas New Year **Parking** 120 **Notes LB**

SKIPTON CONTINUED

★★★ GUEST ACCOMMODATION
Craven House

56 Keighley Rd BD23 2NB

☎ 01756 794657 ◻ 01756 794657

e-mail: info@craven-house.co.uk

web: www.craven-house.co.uk

Dir: *500yds S of town centre on A6131, S of canal bridge*

PETS: Bedrooms unattended **Charges** £5 per night
Exercise area 200yds **Resident Pets:** Wallace (Labrador), Monty
(Springer Spaniel)

A warm welcome awaits you at this centrally located guest house which
has been renovated to provide comfortable accommodation.
Bedrooms vary in size, and feature homely extras and wi-fi facilities.

Rooms 5 rms (3 en suite) (2 pri facs) ⊘ **Facilities** TVB tea/coffee
Cen ht

SLINGSBY   MAP 08 SE67

►►► Slingsby Camping & Caravanning
Club Site *(SE699755)*

Railway St YO62 4AA

☎ 01653 628335

web: www.campingandcaravanningclub.co.uk

Dir: *0.25m N of Slingsby. Also signed from Helmsley/Malton on
B1257*

PETS: Facilities walks info vet info **Other** prior notice required

Open Mar-Oct Booking advisable BH & peak periods Last
arrival 21.00hrs Last departure noon

A well cared for park in a traditional North Yorkshire village. Pitches are
a mixture of grass and hardstanding, and there is a well-appointed
toilet block with cubicled facilities. The village pub serving food is a few
minutes walk away. Caravans are prohibited on the A170 at Sutton
Bank between Thirsk and Helmsley. A 3-acre site with 60 touring
pitches, 7 hardstandings.

STAINFORTH   MAP 07 SD86

►►►► Knight Stainforth Hall Caravan &
Campsite *(SD816672)*

BD24 0DP

☎ 01729 822200 ◻ 01729 823387

e-mail: info@knightstainforth.co.uk

web: www.knightstainforth.co.uk

Dir: *From W, on A65 take B6480 for Settle, left before swimming
pool signed Little Stainforth. From E, through Settle on B6480,
over bridge to swimming pool, then turn right*

PETS: Public areas Stables (0.5m) **Exercise area** on site dog
walks public footpaths adjacent **Facilities** on site shop food disp
bags walks info vet info

Open May-Oct Booking advisable BH & Jul-Aug Last arrival
22.00hrs Last departure noon

Located near Settle and the River Ribble in the Yorkshire Dales National
Park, this well-maintained family site is sheltered by mature woodland.
It is an ideal base for walking or touring in the beautiful surrounding
areas. The toilet block is appointed to a very high standard. A 6-acre
site with 100 touring pitches and 60 statics.

Notes No groups of young people

STILLINGFLEET   MAP 08 SE54

►►► Home Farm Caravan & Camping

(SE595427)

Moreby YO19 6HN

☎ 01904 728263 ◻ 01904 720059

e-mail: home_farm@hotmail.co.uk

Dir: *6m from York on B1222, 1.5m N of Stillingfleet*

PETS: Public areas on leads **Exercise area** on site fields &
woodland **Facilities** washing facs walks info vet info **Other** prior
notice required **Resident Pets:** cats

Open Feb-Dec Booking advisable BH Last arrival 22.00hrs

A traditional meadowland site on a working farm bordered by parkland
on one side and the River Ouse on another. Facilities are in converted
farm buildings, and the family owners extend a friendly welcome to
tourers. An excellent site for relaxing and unwinding in, yet only a short
distance from the attractions of York. A 5-acre site with 25 touring
pitches and 2 statics.

Notes ⊚

THIRSK
MAP 08 SE48

►►► Sowerby Caravan Park *(SE437801)*

Sowerby YO7 3AG

☎ 01845 522753 📠 01845 574520

Dir: *From A19 approx 3m S of Thirsk, turn W for Sowerby. Turn right at junct. Site 1m on left*

PETS: Public areas except play area **Exercise area** adjacent **Facilities** on site shop vet info

Open Mar-Oct Booking advisable BH Last arrival 22.00hrs

A grassy site beside a tree-lined river bank, with basic but functional toilet facilities. Tourers enjoy a separate grassed area with an open outlook, away from the statics. A 1-acre site with 25 touring pitches, 5 hardstandings and 85 statics.

Notes ⊜

►► Thirkleby Hall Caravan Park *(SE472794)*

Thirkleby YO7 3AR

☎ 01845 501360 & 07799 641815

e-mail: greenwood.parks@virgin.net

web: www.greenwoodparks.com

Dir: *3m S of Thirsk on A19. Turn E through arched gatehouse into park*

PETS: Public areas on leads **Exercise area** on site adjacent wood and field **Facilities** washing facs walks info vet info space for loose box **Restrictions** Telephone for details

Open Mar-Oct Booking advisable BHs & Aug wknds Last arrival 20.00hrs Last departure 16.30hrs

A long-established site in the grounds of the old hall, with statics in wooded areas around a fishing lake and tourers based on slightly sloping grassy pitches. Toilet facilities are basic but clean and functional, and this well-screened park has superb views of the Hambledon Hills. A 53-acre site with 50 touring pitches and 185 statics.

Notes ⊜

THORNTON WATLASS
MAP 08 SE28

★★★ INN
Buck Inn

HG4 4AH

☎ 01677 422461 📠 01677 422447

e-mail: innwatlass1@btconnect.com

Dir: *From A1 at Leeming Bar take A684 towards Bedale, B6268 towards Masham 2m, turn right at x-rds to Thornton Watlass*

PETS: Bedrooms unattended **Charges** £5 per night **Public areas** residents' lounge only **Grounds** accessible **Resident Pets:** Tess (Border Collie)

This traditional country inn is situated on the edge of the village green overlooking the cricket pitch. Cricket prints and old photographs are found throughout and an open fire in the bar adds to the warm and intimate atmosphere. Wholesome lunches and dinners, from an extensive menu, are served in the bar or dining room. Bedrooms are brightly decorated and well equipped.

Rooms 7 rms (5 en suite) (1 fmly) (1 GF) S £50-£65; D £65-£75✱ **Facilities** TVB tea/coffee Cen ht TVL Dinner Last d 9.15pm Wi-fi available Fishing Pool Table Quoits **Parking** 10 **Notes** LB Closed 24-25 Dec

TOLLERTON
MAP 08 SE56

►►► Tollerton Holiday Park *(SE513643)*

Station Rd YO61 1RD

☎ 01347 838313 📠 01347 838313

e-mail: greenwood.parks@virgin.net

web: www.greenwoodparks.com

Dir: *From York take A19 towards Thirsk. At x-rds left towards Tollerton. 1m to Chinese restaurant just before rail bridge. Site entrance through restaurant car park*

PETS: Public areas on leads **Exercise area** on site adjacent field & lane **Facilities** washing facs walks info vet info space for loose box **Restrictions** No Pitt Bull Terriers

Open Mar-Oct Booking advisable BH Last arrival 20.00hrs Last departure 16.00hrs

A small park within a few minutes walk of Tollerton village. It is set in open countryside a short drive from the Park & Ride for York. There is little disturbance from the East Coast mainline which passes near to the park. 50 touring pitches and 25 statics.

Notes ⊜ No groups

WEST KNAPTON
MAP 08 SE87

►►► Wolds Way Caravan and Camping
(SE896743)

West Farm YO17 8JE

☎ 01944 728463 & 728180

e-mail: knapton.wold.farms@farming.co.uk

web: www.rydalesbest.co.uk

Dir: *Signed between Rillington & West Heslerton on A64 (Malton to Scarborough road). Site 1.5m*

PETS: Stables on site loose box **Charges** for horses only **Public areas Exercise area** on site adjacent **Facilities** on site shop dog chews cat treats dog scoop/disp bags leads walks info vet info **Other** prior notice required

Open Mar-Oct Booking advisable

A park on a working farm in a peaceful, high position on the Yorkshire Wolds, with magnificent views over the Vale of Pickering. This is an excellent walking area, with the Wolds Way passing the entrance to the park. A pleasant 1.5 mile path leads to a lavender farm, with its first-class coffee shop. A 7.5-acre site with 70 touring pitches, 30 hardstandings.

Notes ⊜

ENGLAND

WHITBY

MAP 08 NZ81

★★ 68% HOTEL
Cliffemount

Bank Top Ln, Runswick Bay TS13 5HU

☎ 01947 840103 📄 01947 841025

e-mail: info@cliffemounthotel.co.uk

Dir: *turn off A174 8m N of Whitby, follow road 1m to end*

PETS: Bedrooms (GF) **Charges** £7.50 per night charge for damage **Public areas** bar only on leads **Grounds** accessible on leads disp bin **Exercise area** 10ft **Facilities** walks info vet info **On Request** towels **Restrictions** small dogs only

Enjoying an elevated position above the cliff-side village and with splendid views across the bay, this hotel offers a warm welcome. The cosy bar leads to the restaurant where locally caught fish features on the extensive menus. The bedrooms, many with sea-view balconies, are well equipped with both practical and homely extras.

Rooms 20 en suite (4 fmly) (5 GF) ⊗ in all bedrooms S £50-£80; D £88-£130 (incl. bkfst)✳ **Facilities** Wi-fi available Xmas New Year **Parking** 25 **Notes** LB

★★★★ GUEST HOUSE
Chiltern Guest House

13 Normanby Ter, West Cliff YO21 3ES

☎ 01947 604981

e-mail: Jjchiltern@aol.com

Dir: *Whalebones next to Harbour, sea on right. Royal Hotel on left, 200yds. Royal Gardens turn left, 2nd road on left 6th House on right*

PETS: Bedrooms Charges £2 per stay **Resident Pets:** 2 dogs, 1 parrot, tropical fish

The Victorian terrace house offers a warm welcome and comfortable accommodation within walking distance of the town centre and seafront. Public areas include a smartly decorated lounge and a bright, attractive dining room. Bedrooms are thoughtfully equipped and many have small, modern en suites.

Rooms 8 rms (7 en suite) (3 fmly) ⊗ S £25-£35; D £50-£70✳ **Facilities** TVB tea/coffee Cen ht TVL Golf 18 **Notes** ⊛

▶▶▶ **Ladycross Plantation Caravan Park**

(NZ821080)

Egton YO21 1UA

☎ 01947 895502

e-mail: enquiries@ladycrossplantation.co.uk

web: www.ladycrossplantation.co.uk

Dir: *On unclassified road (signed) off A171 (Whitby-Teeside road)*

PETS: Public areas except toilets & showers **Exercise area** on site **Facilities** on site shop food bowl water bowl walks info vet info **Other** prior notice required

Open end Mar-Oct Booking advisable BH & Aug Last arrival 20.30hrs Last departure noon

A delightful woodland setting with pitches sited in small groups in clearings around an amenities block. The site is well placed for Whitby and the Moors. Children will enjoy exploring the woodland around the site. A 12-acre site with 130 touring pitches, 18 hardstandings.

▶▶▶ **Rigg Farm Caravan Park** *(NZ915061)*

Stainsacre YO22 4LP

☎ 01947 880430 📄 01947 880430

Dir: *From A171 Scarborough road left onto B1416 signed Ruswarp. Right in 3.25m onto unclass road signed Hawsker. Left in 1.25m. Site in 0.5m*

PETS: Public areas Facilities washing facs walks info vet info **Other** prior notice required

Open Mar-Oct Booking advisable BH & Jul-Aug Last arrival 22.00hrs Last departure noon

A neat rural site with distant views of the coast and Whitby Abbey, set in peaceful surroundings. The former farm buildings are used to house reception and a small games room. A 3-acre site with 14 touring pitches, 14 hardstandings and 15 statics.

Notes No ball games, cycling, skateboards, roller skating or kite flying

ENGLAND

WYKEHAM MAP 08 SE98

►►►► St Helens Caravan Park (SE967836)

St Helens in the Park YO13 9QD

☎ 01723 862771 🖹 01723 866613

e-mail: caravans@wykeham.co.uk

web: www.wykeham.co.uk

Dir: *On A170 in village, 150yds on left beyond Downe Arms Hotel towards Scarborough*

PETS: Charges £1.50 per night £10.50 per week
Public areas except play park **Exercise area** on site 3 acre field & 50yds **Facilities** on site shop food washing facs dog grooming walks info vet info **Other** local creche for pets also does dog grooming **Restrictions** Telephone for details
Resident Pets: Alpacas, Jacob Sheep

Open Feb-Jan (rs Nov-Jan shop/laundry closed) Booking advisable BH & Jul-Aug Last arrival 22.00hrs Last departure 17.00hrs

Set on the edge of the North York Moors National Park this delightfully landscaped park is well-maintained and thoughtfully laid out with top quality facilities. The site is divided into terraces with tree-screening creating smaller areas, including an adults' zone. A cycle route leads through the surrounding Wykeham Estate, and there is a short pathway to the adjoining Downe Arms country pub. A 25-acre site with 250 touring pitches, 2 hardstandings.

YORK MAP 08 SE65

★★★★ 73% HOTEL

Royal York Hotel & Events Centre

Station Rd YO24 2AA

☎ 01904 653681 🖹 01904 623503

e-mail: sales.york@principal-hotels.com

web: www.principal-hotels.com

Dir: *adjacent to railway station*

PETS: Bedrooms Public areas Exercise area on site

Situated in three acres of landscaped grounds in the very heart of the city, this Victorian railway hotel has views over the city and York Minster. Contemporary bedrooms are divided between those in the main hotel and the air-conditioned garden mews. There is also a leisure complex and state-of-the-art conference centre.

Rooms 167 en suite (8 fmly) ⊘ in 123 bedrooms **Facilities** STV ⊗ supervised Gym Wi-fi available Steam room **Services** Lift **Parking** 80 (charged)

★★★ ◉◉ HOTEL

The Grange

1 Clifton YO30 6AA

☎ 01904 644744 🖹 01904 612453

e-mail: info@grangehotel.co.uk

web: www.grangehotel.co.uk

Dir: *on A19 York/Thirsk road, approx 500yds from city centre*

PETS: Bedrooms (GF) unattended **Charges** charge for damage **Exercise area** 5 mins walk **Facilities** cage storage walks info vet info **On Request** fridge access torch towels

This bustling Regency town house is just a few minutes' walk from the centre of York. A professional service is efficiently delivered by caring staff in a very friendly and helpful manner. Public rooms are comfortable and have been stylishly furnished; these include three dining options, the popular and informal cellar brasserie, seafood bar and The Ivy, which offers fine dining in a lavishly decorated environment. The individually designed bedrooms are comfortably appointed and have been thoughtfully equipped.

Rooms 30 en suite (6 GF) S £115-£265; D £139-£265 (incl. bkfst)✳
Facilities STV Wi-fi in bedrooms Discount at local health spa Xmas New Year **Parking** 26 **Notes LB**

★★★ 79% HOTEL

Best Western Monkbar

Monkbar YO31 7JA

☎ 01904 638086 🖹 01904 629195

e-mail: june@monkbarhotel.co.uk

Dir: *A64 onto A1079 to city, turn right at city walls, take middle lane at lights. Hotel on right*

PETS: Bedrooms (GF) unattended sign **Charges** £7.50 per night charge for damage **Public areas** except bar/restaurant on leads **Grounds** accessible on leads disp bin **Exercise area** 100yds **Facilities** food (pre-bookable) food bowl water bowl bedding dog chews cat treats dog scoop/disp bags leads pet sitting dog walking cage storage walks info vet info **On Request** fridge access torch towels **Resident Pets:** Bonnie (Black Labrador)

This smart hotel enjoys a prominent position adjacent to the city walls, and just a few minutes' walk from the cathedral. Individually styled bedrooms are well equipped for both business and leisure guests. Spacious public areas include comfortable lounges, an

CONTINUED

YORK CONTINUED

American-style bar, an airy restaurant and impressive meeting and training facilities.

Rooms 99 en suite (8 fmly) (2 GF) ⊘ in 97 bedrooms S £110-£125; D £150-£180 (incl. bkfst) **Facilities** STV FTV Wi-fi in bedrooms Xmas New Year **Services** Lift **Parking** 70 **Notes** LB

★★★ 72% HOTEL
Novotel York

Fishergate YO10 4FD
☎ 01904 611660 📠 01904 610925
e-mail: H0949@accor.com
web: www.novotel.com

Dir: *A19 north to city centre, hotel set back on left*
PETS: Please telephone for details

Set just outside the ancient city walls, this modern, family-friendly hotel is conveniently located for visitors to the city. Bedrooms feature bathrooms with separate toilet room, plus excellent desk space and sofa beds. Four rooms are equipped for less able guests. The hotel's facilities include indoor and outdoor children's play areas and an indoor pool.

Rooms 124 en suite (124 fmly) ⊘ in 91 bedrooms S £118-£128; D £118-£128 **Facilities** STV 🎱 Wi-fi available Xmas New Year **Services** Lift **Parking** 150 **Notes** LB

★★★★ GUEST ACCOMMODATION
Ascot House

80 East Pde YO31 7YH
☎ 01904 426826 📠 01904 431077
e-mail: admin@ascothouseyork.com
web: www.ascothouseyork.com

Dir: *0.5m NE of city centre. Off A1036 Heworth Green onto Mill Ln, 2nd left*
PETS: **Bedrooms** (GF) unattended **Public areas** except dining room **Grounds** accessible disp bin **Exercise area** 300yds **Facilities** dog chews feeding mat leads pet sitting washing facs cage storage walks info vet info **On Request** fridge access torch towels **Resident Pets:** Gemma & Millie (Black Labradors)

June and Keith Wood provide friendly service at the 1869 Ascot House, a 15-minute walk from the town centre. Bedrooms are thoughtfully

equipped, many with four-poster or canopy beds and other period furniture. Reception rooms include a cosy lounge that also retains its original features.

Ascot House

Rooms 15 rms (12 en suite) (1 pri facs) (3 fmly) (2 GF) S £30-£70; D £60-£76 **Facilities** TVB tea/coffee Cen ht TVL Sauna wi-fi available **Parking** 14 **Notes** LB Closed 21-28 Dec

★★★ GUEST HOUSE
Greenside

124 Clifton YO30 6BQ
☎ 01904 623631 📠 01904 623631
e-mail: greenside@surfree.co.uk
web: www.greensideguesthouse.co.uk

Dir: *A19 N towards city centre, over lights for Greenside, on left opp Clifton Green*
PETS: **Bedrooms** unattended **Facilities** food bowl water bowl

Overlooking Clifton Green, this detached house is just within walking distance of the city centre. Accommodation consists of simply furnished bedrooms and there is a cosy lounge and a dining room, where dinners by arrangement and traditional breakfasts are served. It is a family home, and other families are welcome.

Rooms 6 rms (3 en suite) (2 fmly) (3 GF) ⊘ S fr £28; D fr £46⊹ **Facilities** TVB tea/coffee Cen ht TVL Last d 6pm wi-fi available **Parking** 6 **Notes** LB No coaches Closed Xmas & New Year ⊛

★★★ GUEST ACCOMMODATION
St Georges

6 St Georges Place, Tadcaster Rd YO24 1DR
☎ 01904 625056 📠 01904 625009
e-mail: sixstgeorge@aol.com
web: www.stgeorgesyork.com

Dir: *A64 onto A1036 N to city centre, as racecourse ends, St Georges Place on left*
PETS: **Bedrooms** **Public areas** except dining areas **Grounds** accessible **Exercise area** 50yds **Resident Pets:** George, Ebony, Bob, Coral & Leo (dogs), Kitson (cat)

Located near the racecourse, this family-run establishment is within walking distance of the city. The attractive bedrooms are equipped with modern facilities, and some rooms have four-poster beds and others can accommodate families. A cosy lounge is available and hearty breakfasts are served in the delightful dining room.

Rooms 10 en suite (5 fmly) (1 GF) ⊘ S £35-£50; D £50-£65
Facilities TVB tea/coffee Cen ht Dinner Last d 11am **Parking** 7
Notes LB Closed 20 Dec-2 Jan

►►► Riverside Caravan & Camping Park

(SE598477)

Ferry Ln, Bishopthorpe YO23 2SB

☎ 01904 705812 & 704442 ⓘ 01904 705824

e-mail: info@yorkmarine.co.uk

web: www.yorkmarine.co.uk

Dir: *From A64 take A1036. Right at lights signed Bishopthorpe, left into main street at T-junct. At end of road right into Ancaster Lane, left in 150yds*

PETS: Charges 1st pet free, £1 per extra pet per night
Public areas on leads **Exercise area** on site river walk public walks adjacent **Facilities** on site shop food bowl water bowl disp bags washing facs vet info **Other** prior notice required

Open Apr-Oct Booking advisable BH & Jul-Sep Last arrival 22.00hrs Last departure noon

A small level grassy park in a hedged field on the banks of the River Ouse, on the outskirts of York. This is a popular site with those who enjoy messing about on the river. A 1-acre site with 25 touring pitches.

YORKSHIRE, SOUTH

BARNSLEY   MAP 08 SE30

★★★ 78% HOTEL
Ardsley House

Doncaster Rd, Ardsley S71 5EH

☎ 01226 309955 ⓘ 01226 205374

e-mail: ardsley.house@forestdale.com

web: www.forestdale.com

Dir: *on A635, 0.75m from Stairfoot rdbt*

PETS: Bedrooms unattended **Charges** £7.50 per night
Public areas except restaurant

Quietly situated on the Barnsley to Doncaster road, this hotel has many regular customers. Comfortable and well-equipped bedrooms, excellent leisure facilities including a gym and pool, and good conference facilities are just some of the attractions here. Public rooms include a choice of bars and a busy restaurant.

Rooms 75 en suite (12 fmly) (14 GF) ⊘ in 50 bedrooms **Facilities Spa**
STV ⓒ supervised Gym Wi-fi in bedrooms Beauty spa, 3 treatment rooms ♫ **Parking** 200

DONCASTER   MAP 08 SE50

★★★ 74% HOTEL
Regent

Regent Square DN1 2DS

☎ 01302 364180 ⓘ 01302 322331

e-mail: reservations@theregenthotel.co.uk

web: www.theregenthotel.co.uk

Dir: *on corner of A630 & A638, 1m from racecourse*

PETS: Bedrooms (GF) **Charges** charge for damage
Exercise area opposite **Facilities** vet info **On Request** fridge access torch towels

This town centre hotel overlooks a delightful small square. Public rooms include the modern bar and delightful restaurant, where an interesting range of dishes is offered. Service is friendly and attentive. Modern bedrooms have been furnished in a contemporary style and offer high levels of comfort.

Rooms 52 en suite (6 fmly) (8 GF) ⊘ in all bedrooms S £65-£100;
D £75-£110 (incl. bkfst)✳ **Facilities** STV FTV Wi-fi available ♫
Services Lift **Parking** 20 **Notes** Closed 25 Dec & 1 Jan RS Bank Hols

★★★ 70% HOTEL
Danum

High St DN1 1DN

☎ 01302 342261 ⓘ 01302 329034

e-mail: info@danumhotel.com

Dir: *M18 junct 3, A6182 to Doncaster. Over rdbt, right at next. Right at 'give way' sign, left at mini rdbt, hotel ahead*

PETS: Bedrooms unattended **Public areas** except restaurant
Exercise area 10 mins walk

Situated in the centre of the town, this Edwardian hotel offers well equipped conference rooms together with comfortable bedrooms. A contemporary lounge area provides modern dining and especially negotiated rates at a local leisure centre are offered.

Rooms 64 en suite (5 fmly) ⊘ in 12 bedrooms S £55-£90; D £65-£110
(incl. bkfst)✳ **Facilities** STV Wi-fi in bedrooms Special rates at Cannons Health Club ♫ Xmas New Year **Services** Lift **Parking** 36 **Notes** LB
RS 26-30 Dec

ENGLAND

ROTHERHAM MAP 08 SK49

★★★ 77% HOTEL
Best Western Elton

Main St, Bramley S66 2SF

☎ 01709 545681 ▤ 01709 549100

e-mail: bestwestern.eltonhotel@btinternet.com

web: www.bw-eltonhotel.co.uk

Dir: *M18 junct 1 follow A631 Rotherham, turn right to Ravenfield, hotel at end of Bramley village, follow brown signs*

PETS: Bedrooms (GF) unattended **Grounds** accessible on leads **Facilities** food (pre-bookable) cage storage walks info vet info **On Request** fridge access

Within easy reach of the M18, this welcoming, stone-built hotel is set in well-tended gardens. The Elton offers good modern accommodation, with larger rooms in the extension that are particularly comfortable and well equipped. A civil licence is held for wedding ceremonies and conference rooms are available.

Rooms 13 en suite 16 annexe en suite (4 fmly) (11 GF) ⊘ in 11 bedrooms S £55-£90; D £78-£99 (incl. bkfst) **Facilities** STV Wi-fi in bedrooms **Parking** 48 **Notes** LB

SHEFFIELD MAP 08 SK38

★★★ 72% HOTEL
The Beauchief Hotel

161 Abbeydale Rd South S7 2QW

☎ 0114 262 0500 ▤ 0114 235 0197

e-mail: beauchief@corushotels.com

web: www.corushotels.com

Dir: *from city centre 2m on A621 signed Bakewell*

PETS: Grounds accessible **Exercise area** park nearby **Restrictions** small dogs only

On the southern outskirts of the city, this busy property attracts both resident and local business. The popular restaurant and Merchant's bar have an excellent reputation in the area for good food and hospitality. The well-equipped bedrooms come in various styles and sizes. Ample parking is also a bonus.

Rooms 50 en suite (2 fmly) (19 GF) ⊘ in 39 bedrooms **Facilities** STV **Parking** 200 **Notes** LB

★★★ 71% HOTEL
Novotel Sheffield

50 Arundel Gate S1 2PR

☎ 0114 278 1781 ▤ 0114 278 7744

e-mail: h1348-re@accor.com

web: www.novotel.com

Dir: *between Registry Office and Crucible/Lyceum Theatres, follow signs to Town Hall/Theatres & Hallam University*

PETS: Please telephone for details

In the heart of the city centre, this "new generation" Novotel has stylish public areas including a very modern restaurant, indoor swimming pool and a range of meeting rooms. Spacious bedrooms are suitable for family occupation and "Novation" rooms are ideal for business users.

Rooms 144 en suite (40 fmly) ⊘ in 108 bedrooms S £58-£110; D £58-£110✳ **Facilities** STV ☉ Local gym facilities free for residents use Xmas **Services** Lift air con **Parking** 60 **Notes** LB

WOODALL MOTORWAY MAP 08 SK48
SERVICE AREA (M1)

BUDGET HOTEL
Days Inn Sheffield

Woodall Service Area S26 7XR

☎ 0114 248 7992 ▤ 0114 248 5634

e-mail: woodall.hotel@welcomebreak.co.uk

web: www.daysinn.com

Dir: *M1southbound, at Woodall Services, between juncts 30/31*

PETS: Bedrooms unattended **Grounds** accessible

This modern building offers accommodation in smart, spacious and well-equipped bedrooms, suitable for families and business travellers, and all with en suite bathrooms. Continental breakfast is available and other refreshments may be taken at the nearby family restaurant. For further details see the Hotel Groups page.

Rooms 38 en suite

WORSBROUGH MAP 08 SE30

►► Greensprings Touring Park *(SE330020)*

Rockley Abbey Farm, Rockley Ln S75 3DS

☎ 01226 288298 ▤ 01226 288298

Dir: *M1 junct 36, A61 to Barnsley. Turn left after 0.25m onto road signed Pilley. Site 1m at bottom of hill*

PETS: Stables nearby (0.25m) (loose box) **Exercise area** on site dog walk area **Facilities** walks info vet info **Other** prior notice required **Restrictions** no more that 2 dogs per caravan

Open Apr-Oct Booking advisable when hook up is required Last arrival 21.00hrs Last departure noon

A secluded and attractive farm site set amidst woods and farmland, with access to the river and several good local walks. There are two touring areas, one gently sloping and each with its own toilet block. Although not far from the M1, there is almost no traffic noise, and this site is convenient for exploring the area's industrial heritage, as well as the Peak District. A 4-acre site with 65 touring pitches, 13 hardstandings.

Notes ✉

YORKSHIRE, WEST

BARDSEY   MAP 08 SE34

►►► Glenfield Caravan Park *(SE351421)*

120 Blackmoor Ln LS17 9DZ

☎ 01937 574657 📄 01937 579529

e-mail: glenfielddcp@aol.com

web: www.ukparks.co.uk/glenfielddcp

Dir: *From A58 at Bardsey turn into Church Lane, past church, up hill. Continue 0.5m, site on right*

PETS: Charges £1 per night **Public areas** on leads **Exercise area** 2m **Facilities** vet info

Open all year Booking advisable Last arrival 23.00hrs Last departure noon

A quiet family-owned rural site in a well-screened, tree-lined meadow. The site has an excellent toilet block complete with family room. A convenient touring base for Leeds and the surrounding area. Discounted golf, and food are both available at the local golf club. A 4-acre site with 30 touring pitches, 30 hardstandings and 1 static.

Notes ✉

BINGLEY   MAP 07 SE13

★★ 74% SMALL HOTEL

Five Rise Locks Hotel & Restaurant

Beck Ln BD16 4DD

☎ 01274 565296 📄 01274 568828

e-mail: info@five-rise-locks.co.uk

Dir: *Off Main St onto Park Rd, 0.5m left onto Beck Ln*

PETS: Bedrooms unattended **Charges** £5 per night **Grounds** accessible **Resident Pets:** Charlie (Border Collie)

This small hotel, an impressive Victorian building, offers a warm welcome and comfortable accommodation. Bedrooms are of a good size and feature homely extras. The restaurant serves imaginative dishes, and the bright breakfast room overlooks open countryside.

Rooms 9 en suite (2 fmly) (2 GF) ⊘ in all bedrooms S £50-£60; D £72✲ **Parking** 20

BRADFORD   MAP 07 SE13

★★★ 79% HOTEL

Midland Hotel

Forster Square BD1 4HU

☎ 01274 735735 📄 01274 720003

e-mail: info@midland-hotel-bradford.com

web: www.peelhotel.com

Dir: *M62 junct 26, then M606 towards Bradford. Left opp Asda, left at rdbt onto A650. Through 2 rdbts & 2 lights, follow A6181/ Haworth signs.*

PETS: Bedrooms

Ideally situated in the heart of the city, this grand Victorian hotel provides modern, very well equipped accommodation and comfortable, spacious day rooms. Ample parking is available in what used to be the city's railway station, and a preserved walkway dating from Victorian times linking the hotel to the old platform can still be used today.

Rooms 90 en suite (4 fmly) ⊘ in 40 bedrooms S £65-£110; D £75-£135✲ **Facilities** STV Wi-fi in bedrooms ♫ Xmas New Year **Services** Lift **Parking** 50 **Notes** LB

★★★ 73% HOTEL

Best Western Guide Post Hotel

Common Rd, Low Moor BD12 0ST

☎ 01274 607866 📄 01274 671085

e-mail: sales@guideposthotel.net

web: www.guideposthotel.net

Dir: *from M606 rdbt take 3rd exit (Little Chef on right). At next rdbt take 1st exit (Cleckheaton Road). 0.5m, turn right at bollard into Common Road*

PETS: Bedrooms (GF) unattended **Public areas Facilities** walks info vet info **On Request** towels **Resident Pets:** William (Springer Spaniel)

Situated south of the city, this hotel offers attractively styled, modern, comfortable bedrooms. The restaurant offers an extensive range of food using fresh, local produce; lighter snack meals are served in the bar. There is also a choice of well-equipped meeting and function rooms.

Rooms 41 en suite (4 fmly) (14 GF) ⊘ in 20 bedrooms S £59.50-£67.50; D £59.50-£67.50 (incl. bkfst) **Facilities** STV Wi-fi in bedrooms **Parking** 100

ENGLAND

BRADFORD CONTINUED

★★★ 70% HOTEL
Novotel Bradford

6 Roydsdale Way BD4 6SA

☎ 01274 683683 🖹 01274 651342

e-mail: h0510@accor.com

web: www.novotel.com

Dir: *M606 junct 2, exit to Euroway Trading Estate turn right at lights at bottom of slip road, then 2nd right onto Roydsdale Way*

PETS: Please telephone for details

This purpose-built hotel stands in a handy location for access to the motorway. It provides spacious bedrooms that are comfortably equipped. Open-plan day rooms include a stylish bar, and a lounge that leads into the Garden Brasserie. Several function rooms are also available.

Rooms 119 en suite (37 fmly) (9 GF) ⊘ in 69 bedrooms S £49-£69; D £49-£69✱ **Facilities** STV Wi-fi available Xmas **Services** Lift **Parking** 200 **Notes** LB

HARTSHEAD MOOR MOTORWAY SERVICE AREA (M62)
MAP 08 SE12

BUDGET HOTEL
Days Inn Bradford

Hartshead Moor Service Area, Clifton HD6 4JX

☎ 01274 851706 🖹 01274 855169

e-mail: hartshead.hotel@welcomebreak.co.uk

web: www.daysinn.com

Dir: *M62 between junct 25 and 26*

PETS: Bedrooms unattended **Public areas** on leads **Grounds** accessible disp bin **Facilities** vet info **On Request** fridge access

This modern building offers accommodation in smart, spacious and well-equipped bedrooms, suitable for families and business travellers, and all with en suite bathrooms. Continental breakfast is available and other refreshments may be taken at the nearby family restaurant. For further details see the Hotel Groups page.

Rooms 38 en suite

HORSFORTH
MAP 08 SE23

►►► **St Helena's Caravan Park** *(SE240421)*

Otley Old Rd LS18 5HZ

☎ 0113 284 1142

Dir: *From A658 follow signs for Leeds/Bradford Airport. Then follow site signs*

PETS: Public areas except toilet block **Exercise area** on site wooded dog walks Otley Chevin nearby **Facilities** on site shop vet info **Other** prior notice required

Open Apr-Oct Booking advisable Last arrival 19.30hrs Last departure 14.00hrs

A well-maintained parkland setting surrounded by woodland yet within easy reach of Leeds with its excellent shopping and cultural opportunities, Ilkley, and the attractive Wharfedale town of Otley. Some visitors may just want to relax in this adults-only park's spacious and pleasant surroundings. A 12-acre site with 60 touring pitches and 40 statics.

Notes ⊘ Adults only

HUDDERSFIELD
MAP 07 SE11

★★★★ 68% HOTEL
Cedar Court

Ainley Top HD3 3RH

☎ 01422 375431 🖹 01422 314050

e-mail: huddersfield@cedarcourthotels.co.uk

web: www.cedarcourthotels.co.uk

Dir: *500yds from M62 junct 24*

PETS: Bedrooms unattended **Charges** charge for damage **Grounds** accessible on leads disp bin **Facilities** cage storage vet info **On Request** fridge access torch towels

Sitting adjacent to the M62, this hotel is an ideal location for business travellers or for those touring West Yorkshire. Bedrooms are spacious and comfortable and there is a busy lounge with snacks available all day, as well as a modern restaurant and a fully equipped leisure centre. There are extensive meeting and banqueting facilities.

Rooms 114 en suite (6 fmly) (10 GF) ⊘ in 70 bedrooms S £65-£144.50; D £75-£159 (incl. bkfst)✱ **Facilities** STV ⊗ supervised Gym Steam room **Services** Lift **Parking** 250 **Notes** LB

ENGLAND

ILKLEY
MAP 07 SE14

★★★ 82% HOTEL

Best Western Rombalds Hotel & Restaurant

11 West View, Wells Rd LS29 9JG

☎ 01943 603201 📄 01943 816586

e-mail: reception@rombalds.demon.co.uk

web: www.rombalds.co.uk

Dir: *A65 from Leeds. Left at 3rd main lights, follow Ilkley Moor signs. Right at HSBC Bank onto Wells Rd. Hotel 600yds on left*

PETS: Bedrooms Grounds accessible **Exercise area** adjacent

This elegantly furnished Georgian townhouse is located in a peaceful terrace between the town and the moors. Delightful day rooms include a choice of comfortable lounges and an attractive restaurant which provides a relaxed venue in which to sample the skilfully prepared, imaginative meals. The bedrooms are tastefully furnished, well-equipped and include several spacious suites.

Rooms 15 en suite (4 fmly) ⊘ in all bedrooms S £75-£109; D £95-£128 (incl. bkfst)✱ **Facilities** STV Wi-fi in bedrooms Xmas **Parking** 28 **Notes** LB Closed 28 Dec-2 Jan

---

KEIGHLEY
MAP 07 SE04

★★ 70% HOTEL

Dalesgate

406 Skipton Rd, Utley BD20 6HP

☎ 01535 664930 📄 01535 611253

e-mail: stephen.e.atha@btinternet.com

Dir: *In town centre follow A629 over rdbt onto B6265. Right after 0.75m into St. John's Rd. 1st right into hotel car park*

PETS: Bedrooms (GF) unattended **Charges** charge for damage **Public areas** except bar & restaurant **Exercise area** 300yds **Facilities** leads washing facs cage storage **On Request** fridge access torch towels **Resident Pets:** Max (German Shepherd cross)

Originally the residence of a local chapel minister, this modern, well-established hotel provides well-equipped, comfortable bedrooms. It also boasts a cosy bar and pleasant restaurant, serving an imaginative range of dishes. A large car park is provided to the rear.

Rooms 20 en suite (2 fmly) (3 GF) S £40-£45; D £55-£65 (incl. bkfst)✱ **Parking** 25 **Notes** RS 22 Dec-4 Jan

LEEDS
MAP 08 SE33

★★★ 80% HOTEL

Novotel Leeds Centre

4 Whitehall, Whitehall Quay LS1 4HR

☎ 0113 242 6446 📄 0113 242 6445

e-mail: H3270@accor.com

web: www.novotel.com

Dir: *M621 junct 3, follow signs to train station. Turn into Aire Street & left at lights*

PETS: Please telephone for details

With a minimalist style, this contemporary hotel provides a quality, value-for-money experience close to the city centre. Spacious, climate-controlled bedrooms are provided, whilst public areas offer deep leather sofas and an eye-catching water feature in reception. Light snacks are provided in the airy bar and the restaurant doubles as a bistro. Staff are committed to guest care and nothing is too much trouble.

Rooms 195 en suite (50 fmly) ⊘ in 159 bedrooms **Facilities** STV Gym Playstation in rooms, play area, steam room **Services** Lift air con **Parking** 90 (charged)

★★★ 72% HOTEL

Golden Lion

2 Lower Briggate LS1 4AE

☎ 0113 243 6454 📄 0113 243 4241

e-mail: info@goldenlion-hotel-leeds.com

web: www.peelhotel.com

Dir: *M621 junct 3. Keep in right lane. Follow until road splits into 4 lanes. Keep right & right at lights. (Asda House on left). Left at lights. Over bridge, turn left, hotel opposite. Parking 150mtrs further on*

PETS: Bedrooms unattended **Charges** charge for damage **Facilities** vet info **On Request** fridge access torch towels **Restrictions** no large dogs

This smartly presented hotel is set in a Victorian building on the south side of the city. The well-equipped bedrooms offer a choice of standard or executive grades. Staff are friendly and helpful, ensuring a warm and welcoming atmosphere. Free overnight parking is provided in a 24-hour car park close-by the hotel.

Rooms 89 en suite (5 fmly) ⊘ in 46 bedrooms S £49-£105; D £59-£140✱ **Facilities** STV Wi-fi in bedrooms Xmas **Services** Lift **Notes** LB

ENGLAND

WAKEFIELD — MAP 08 SE32

★★★★ 72% HOTEL
Cedar Court

Denby Dale Rd WF4 3QZ
☎ 01924 276310 📠 01924 280221
e-mail: sales@cedarcourthotels.co.uk
web: www.cedarcourthotels.co.uk
Dir: *adjacent to M1 junct 39*
PETS: Bedrooms Public areas except food areas
Grounds accessible **Exercise area** on site

This hotel enjoys a convenient location just off the M1. Traditionally styled bedrooms offer a good range of facilities while open-plan public areas include a busy bar and restaurant operation. Conferences and functions are extremely well catered for and a modern leisure club completes the picture.

Rooms 149 en suite (2 fmly) (74 GF) ⊘ in 100 bedrooms S £80-£120; D £80-£140✳ **Facilities** STV 📺 supervised Gym Wi-fi in bedrooms Xmas New Year **Services** Lift air con **Parking** 350 **Notes LB**

★★★ GUEST HOUSE
Stanley View

226-230 Stanley Rd WF1 4AE
☎ 01924 376803 📠 01924 369123
e-mail: enquiries@stanleyviewguesthouse.co.uk
Dir: *M62 junct 30, Follow Aberford Road for appox 3m then take the m1 junkt 41. Follow signs for City Centre Approx 1 mile from town centre, Nr Pinderfields Hospital*
PETS: Bedrooms (GF) **Public areas** except dining area
Other ground floor bedrooms only

Part of an attractive terrace, this well established guest house is just 0.5m from the city centre and has private parking at the rear. The well equipped bedrooms are brightly decorated, and there is a licensed bar and comfortable lounge. Hearty home cooked meals are served in the attractive dining room.

Rooms 13 en suite (6 fmly) (7 GF) ⊘ **Facilities** STV TV17B tea/coffee Direct dial from bedrooms Licensed Cen ht TVL Dinner Last d 8.30pm **Parking** 10

CHANNEL ISLANDS
Guernsey

CASTEL — MAP 16

►►► Fauxquets Valley Farm

GY5 7QA
☎ 01481 255460 📠 01481 251797
e-mail: info@fauxquets.co.uk
web: www.fauxquets.co.uk
Dir: *Off pier. 2nd exit off rdbt. Top of hill left onto Queens Rd. Continue for 2m. Turn right onto Candie Rd. Opposite sign for German Occupation Museum*
PETS: Public areas on leads **Exercise area** fields adjacent
Facilities on site shop food washing facs walks info vet info space for loose box **Other** prior notice required
Resident Pets: Bracken (Jack Russell), Morley (Chocolate Labrador), Blackie (Black Labrador)

Open mid Jun-Aug (rs May-mid Jun & 1-15 Sep Haybarn restaurant & bar closed) Booking advisable last 2 wks Jul-1st 3 wks Aug

A beautiful, quiet farm site in a hidden valley close to the sea. Friendly helpful owners, who understand campers' needs, offer good quality facilities and amenities, including an outdoor swimming pool, bar/restaurant, nature trail and sports areas. A 3-acre site with 100 touring pitches.

Jersey

GROUVILLE — MAP 16

★★★ 71% HOTEL
Beausite

Les Rue des Pres, Grouville Bay JE3 9DJ
☎ 01534 857577 📠 01534 857211
e-mail: beausite@jerseymail.co.uk
web: www.southernhotels.com
Dir: *Opposite the Royal Jersey Golf Course*
PETS: Bedrooms Exercise area 200mtrs

Within 300 metres of the Royal Jersey Golf Club, this hotel is situated on the south-east side of the island; a short distance from the picturesque harbour at Gorey. With parts dating back to 1636, the public rooms retain original character and charm; bedrooms are generally spacious and modern in design. The indoor swimming pool, fitness room, saunas and spa bath are an added bonus.

Rooms 75 en suite (5 fmly) (18 GF) S £44-£99.75; D £88-£114 (incl. bkfst)✳ **Facilities** STV 📺 Gym **Parking** 60 **Notes** Closed Nov-Mar

ST BRELADE — MAP 16

★★ 72% HOTEL
Hotel Miramar

Mont Gras D'Eau JE3 8ED

☎ 01534 743831 📠 01534 745009

e-mail: miramarjsy@localdial.com

Dir: From airport take B36 at lights, turn left onto A13, take 1st turning on right down Mont Gras D'Eau

PETS: Bedrooms (GF) unattended **Facilities** cage storage walks info vet info

A friendly welcome awaits at this family-run hotel set in delightful sheltered gardens, overlooking the beautiful bay. Accommodation is comfortable with well appointed bedrooms; some are on the ground floor, and there are two on the lower ground with their own terrace overlooking the outdoor heated pool. The restaurant offers a varied set menu.

Rooms 38 en suite (2 fmly) (14 GF) S £30-£40; D £60-£80 (incl. bkfst)✶ **Facilities** FTV ⚒ **Parking** 30 **Notes** Closed Oct-mid Apr

ST MARTIN — MAP 16

►►►►► Beuvelande Camp Site

Beuvelande JE3 6EZ

☎ 01534 853575 📠 01534 857788

e-mail: info@campingjersey.com

web: www.campingjersey.com

Dir: Take A6 from St Helier to St Martin & follow signs to campsite before St Martins church

PETS: Charges £2 per dog per night **Public areas**
Exercise area on site **Facilities** on site shop food food bowl water bowl dog scoop/disp bags vet info **Other** prior notice required

Open Apr-Sep (rs Apr-May & Sep restaurant closed, shop hours limited) Booking advisable

A well-established site with excellent toilet facilities, accessed via narrow lanes in peaceful countryside close to St Martin. An attractive bar/restaurant is the focal point of the park, especially in the evenings, and there is a small swimming pool and playground. Motorhomes and towed caravans will be met at the ferry and escorted to the site if requested when booking. A 6-acre site with 150 touring pitches and 75 statics.

ST OUEN — MAP 16

►►►► Bleu Soleil Campsite

La Route de Vinchelez, Leoville JE3 2DB

☎ 01534 481007 📠 01534 481525

e-mail: info@bleusoleilcamping.com

web: www.bleusoleilcamping.com

Dir: From St Helier ferry port take A2 towards St Aubin then turn right onto A12 passing airport to Leoville. Site on right of La Route de Vinchelez

PETS: Public areas except café, shop, TV lounge
Exercise area beach nearby **Facilities** on site shop vet info
Resident Pets: cats

Open 28 Apr-Sep Booking advisable Jul-Aug Last arrival 23.00hrs Last departure 10.00hrs

A compact tent park set in the NW corner of the island and surrounded by beautiful countryside. Greve-de-Lacq beach is close by, and the golden beaches at St Ouen's Bay and St Brelade's Bay are only a short drive away. There are 45 ready-erected tents for hire. A 1.5-acre site with 55 touring pitches, 8 hardstandings and 45 statics.

ISLE OF MAN

PORT ERIN — MAP 06 SC16

★★ 69% HOTEL
Falcon's Nest

The Promenade IM9 6AF

☎ 01624 834077 📠 01624 835370

e-mail: falconsnest@enterprise.net

web: www.falconsnesthotel.co.uk

Dir: follow coastal road, S from airport or ferry. Hotel on seafront, immediately after steam railway station

PETS: Bedrooms Exercise area 50mtrs to beach/park

Situated overlooking the bay and harbour, this Victorian hotel offers generally spacious bedrooms. There is a choice of bars, one of which attracts many locals. Meals can be taken in the lounge bar, conservatory or in the attractively decorated main restaurant.

Rooms 35 en suite (9 fmly) ⊗ in 3 bedrooms S £35-£42.50; D £70-£85 (incl. bkfst)✶ **Facilities** STV Wi-fi available Xmas New Year **Parking** 40 **Notes** LB

Scotland

CITY OF ABERDEEN

ABERDEEN　　　　　　　MAP 15 NJ90

★★★★ 77% HOTEL
Aberdeen Patio

Beach Boulevard AB24 5EF

☎ 01224 633339 & 380000 📄 01224 638833

e-mail: info@patiohotels.com

web: www.patiohotels.com

Dir: *from A90 follow signs for city centre, then for sea. On Beach Blvd, turn left at lights, hotel on right*

PETS: Bedrooms unattended Exercise area 100yds

This modern, purpose-built hotel lies close to the seafront. Bedrooms come in two different styles - the retro-style Class ics and spacious Premiers. A new building, the Platinum Club, offers a unique experience of 44 superb high spec bedrooms that have their own reception and bar/lounge/dinner/breakfast room. The restaurant and striking Atrium bar is housed in the main building.

Rooms 124 en suite 44 annexe en suite (8 fmly) (22 GF) ⊘ in 127 bedrooms S £66-£285; D £76-£300 (incl. bkfst)✳ Facilities Spa STV ⓩ supervised Gym Wi-fi available Steam room, Treatment Room New Year Services Lift Parking 172

ABERDEENSHIRE

ABOYNE　　　　　　　MAP 15 NO59

►►► Aboyne Loch Caravan Park *(NO538998)*

AB34 5BR

☎ 013398 86244 & 01330 811351 📄 01330 811669

Dir: *On A93, 1m E of Aboyne*

PETS: Exercise area on site dog walks Facilities walks info vet info

Open 31 Mar-Oct Booking advisable Jul-Aug Last arrival 20.00hrs Last departure 11.00hrs

Attractively-sited caravan park set amidst woodland on the shores of the lovely Aboyne Loch in scenic Deeside. The facilities are modern and immaculately maintained, and amenities include boat-launching, boating and fishing. An ideally-situated park for touring Royal Deeside and the Aberdeenshire uplands. A 6-acre site with 35 touring pitches, 25 hardstandings and 80 statics.

FORDOUN　　　　　　　MAP 15 NO77

►►► Brownmuir Caravan Park *(NO740772)*

AB30 1SJ

☎ 01561 320786 📄 01561 320786

e-mail: brownmuircaravanpark@talk21.com

web: www.brownmuircaravanpark.co.uk

Dir: *From N on A90 take B966 signed Fettercairn & site 1.5m on left. From S take A90, turn off 4m N of Laurencekirk signed Fordoun, site 1m on right*

PETS: Public areas except play area Exercise area on site Facilities walks info vet info

Open Apr-Oct Booking advisable Last arrival 23.00hrs Last departure noon

A mainly static site set in a rural location with level pitches and good touring facilities. The area is ideal for cyclists, walkers and golfers, as well as those wanting to visit Aberdeen, Banchory, Ballater, Balmoral, Glamis and Dundee. A 7-acre site with 9 touring pitches and 51 statics.

Notes ☺

HUNTLY　　　　　　　MAP 15 NJ53

★★ 65% HOTEL
Gordon Arms Hotel

The Square AB54 8AF

☎ 01466 792288 📄 01466 794556

e-mail: reception@gordonarms.demon.co.uk

Dir: *off A96 Aberdeen to Inverness road at Huntly. Hotel immediately on left after entering town square*

PETS: Bedrooms Charges £5 per night

This friendly family-run hotel is located in the town square and offers a good selection of tasty, well-portioned dishes served in the bar (or in the restaurant at weekends or midweek by appointment). Bedrooms come in a variety of sizes, and all come with a good range of accessories.

Rooms 13 en suite (3 fmly) ⊘ in all bedrooms Facilities STV ♫

MACDUFF   MAP 15 NJ76

►► Wester Bonnyton Farm Site *(NJ741638)*

Gamrie AB45 3EP

☎ 01261 832470 📄 01261 831853

e-mail: taylor@westerbonnyton.freeserve.co.uk

Dir: *From A98 (1m S of Macduff) take B9031 signed Rosehearty. Site 1.25m on right*

PETS: Stables nearby (3m) **Public areas** except play barn, toilet block **Exercise area** on site woods surrounding park & 2m **Facilities** on site shop food food bowl water bowl dog chews cat treats litter dog scoop/disp bags leads washing facs walks info vet info **Other** prior notice required **Resident Pets:** Lady (Collie), Sam, Chestnut & Panda (Shetland Ponies), cats, chickens

Open Mar-Oct Booking advisable Jul-Aug

A spacious farm site in a screened meadow, with level touring pitches enjoying views across Moray Firth. The site is continually improving, and offers some electric hook-ups and a laundry. A 4-acre site with 10 touring pitches, 5 hardstandings and 45 statics.

Notes ⊛

NORTH WATER BRIDGE   MAP 15 NO66

►►► Dovecot Caravan Park *(NO648663)*

AB30 1QL

☎ 01674 840630 📄 01674 840630

e-mail: dovecotcaravanpark@tinyworld.co.uk

web: www.dovecotcaravanpark.com

Dir: *Take A90, 5m S of Laurencekirk. At Edzell Woods sign turn left. Site 500yds on left*

PETS: Public areas Exercise area on site riverside dog walk woodland 500mtrs **Facilities** walks info vet info

Open Apr-Oct Booking advisable Jul & Aug for hook ups Last arrival 20.00hrs Last departure noon

A level grassy site in a country area close to the A90, with mature trees screening one side and the River North Esk on the other. The immaculate toilet facilities make this a handy overnight stop in a good touring area. A 6-acre site with 25 touring pitches, 8 hardstandings and 44 statics.

Notes ⊛

TARLAND   MAP 15 NJ40

►►► Tarland Camping & Caravanning Club Site *(NJ477044)*

AB34 4UP

☎ 013398 81388

web: www.campingandcaravanningclub.co.uk

Dir: *A93 from Aberdeen turn right in Aboyne at Struan Hotel onto B9094. After 6m take next right, then fork left before bridge, 600yds site on left*

PETS: Public areas except buildings **Exercise area** on site **Facilities** walks info vet info **Other** prior notice required

Open Apr-Oct Booking advisable BH & peak periods Last arrival 21.00hrs Last departure noon

A pretty park on the edge of the village, laid out on two levels. The upper area has hardstandings and electric hook-ups, and views over hills and moorland, while the lower level is well screened with mature trees and grassy. An 8-acre site with 90 touring pitches, 32 hardstandings.

ANGUS

MONIFIETH   MAP 12 NO43

►►►► Riverview Caravan Park *(NO502322)*

Marine Rd DD5 4NN

☎ 01382 535471 📄 01382 535375

e-mail: riverviewcaravan@btinternet.com

web: www.ukparks.co.uk/riverview

Dir: *Signed in both directions from A930 in centre of Monifieth*

PETS: Stables nearby (3m) (loose box) **Public areas Exercise area** on site park & beach 20yds **Facilities** washing facs **Other** prior notice required pet grooming kennels nearby (booking required)

Open Apr-Oct (rs Nov-Mar holiday homes open) Booking advisable Jul-Aug Last arrival 22.00hrs Last departure 12.30hrs

A well-landscaped seaside site with individual hedged pitches, and direct access to the beach. The modernised toilet block has excellent facilities which are immaculately maintained. Amenities include a multi-gym, sauna and steam rooms. A 5.5-acre site with 60 touring pitches, 40 hardstandings and 25 statics.

SCOTLAND

ARGYLL & BUTE

ARDUAINE MAP 10 NM71

★★★ 82% ◉◉ HOTEL
Loch Melfort
PA34 4XG
☎ 01852 200233 📄 01852 200214
e-mail: reception@lochmelfort.co.uk
web: www.lochmelfort.co.uk
Dir: on A816, midway between Oban and Lochgilphead
PETS: Bedrooms (GF) unattended **Stables** on site
Charges charge for damage **Grounds** accessible **Facilities** food
(pre-bookable) food bowl water bowl washing facs cage storage
walks info vet info **On Request** torch towels **Other** dogs in
certain bedrooms only **Pets:** Rosie (Beagle), Evie & Bethan
(horses)

Enjoying one of the finest locations on the West Coast, this popular,
family-run hotel has outstanding views across Asknish Bay towards the
Islands of Jura, Scarba and Shuna. Accommodation is provided in
either the balconied rooms of the Cedar wing or the more traditional
rooms in the main hotel. Skilfully cooked dinners remain the highlight
of any visit.

Rooms 5 en suite 20 annexe en suite (2 fmly) (10 GF) ⊘ in all bedrooms
S £54-£89; D £85-£138 (incl. bkfst)✳ **Facilities** Xmas New Year
Parking 65 **Notes LB** Closed 3 Jan-15 Feb

BARCALDINE MAP 10 NM94

▶▶▶ **Oban Camping & Caravanning Club Site** (NM966420)
PA37 1SG
☎ 01631 720348
web: www.campingandcaravanningclub.co.uk
Dir: N on A828, 7m from Connel Bridge, turn into site at Club
sign on right (opposite Marine Resource Centre)
PETS: **Public areas** except buildings **Exercise area** on site ajacent
woodland **Facilities** walks info vet info **Other** prior notice
required

Open Apr-Oct Booking advisable BH & peak periods Last
arrival 21.00hrs Last departure noon
A sheltered site within a walled garden, bordered by Barcaldine Forest,
close to Loch Creran. Tourers are arranged against the old garden
walls, with some located outside in quiet grassed areas. There are
pleasant woodland walks from the park, including the Sutherland
memorial woods close by. A 4.5-acre site with 75 touring pitches, 27
hardstandings.

CAIRNDOW MAP 10 NN11

★★ 66% HOTEL
Cairndow Stagecoach Inn
PA26 8BN
☎ 01499 600286 & 600252 📄 01499 600220
e-mail: cairndowinn@aol.com
Dir: from North, either A82 to Tarbet, then A83 to Cairndow or
A85 to Palmally, A819 to Inveraray and A83 to Cairndow.
PETS: **Bedrooms** unattended **Grounds** accessible **Facilities** water
bowl

A relaxed, friendly atmosphere prevails at this 18th-century inn,
overlooking the beautiful Loch Fyne. Bedrooms offer individual décor
and thoughtful extras. Traditional public areas include a comfortable
beamed lounge, a well-stocked bar where food is served throughout
the day, and a spacious restaurant with conservatory extension.

Rooms 13 en suite (2 fmly) ⊘ in 3 bedrooms **Facilities** Gym
Parking 32 **Notes LB**

CARRADALE MAP 10 NR83

►►► Carradale Bay Caravan Park (NR815385)
PA28 6QG
☎ 01583 431665
e-mail: info@carradalebay.com
web: www.carradalebay.com

Dir: *A83 from Tarbert towards Campbeltown, left onto B842 (Carradale road), right onto B879. Site 0.5m*

PETS: Charges 1st pet free, 2nd pet £1 per night **Public areas Exercise area** on site walks & beach **Facilities** washing facs walks info vet info

Open Apr-Sep Booking advisable BH & Jul-Aug Last arrival 22.00hrs Last departure noon

A beautiful, natural site on the sea's edge with superb views over Kilbrannan Sound to the Isle of Arran. Pitches are landscaped into small bays broken up by shrubs and bushes, and backed by dunes close to the long sandy beach. An 8-acre site with 75 touring pitches and 12 statics.

CLACHAN-SEIL MAP 10 NM71

★★ 85% ◉◉ SMALL HOTEL
Willowburn
PA34 4TJ
☎ 01852 300276
e-mail: willowburn.hotel@virgin.net
web: www.willowburn.co.uk

Dir: *0.5m from Atlantic Bridge, on left*

PETS: Bedrooms (GF) unattended **Charges** charge for damage **Public areas** bar only on leads **Grounds** accessible disp bin **Exercise area** 0.5m **Facilities** food bowl water bowl dog scoop/disp bags leads washing facs walks info vet info **On Request** fridge access torch towels **Resident Pets:** Sisko (Black Labrador), Tussock (Hovawart), Odo (cat)

This welcoming small hotel enjoys a peaceful setting, with grounds stretching down to the shores of Clachan Sound. Friendly unassuming service, a relaxed atmosphere and fine food are keys to its success. Bedrooms are bright, cheerful and thoughtfully equipped. Guests can watch the wildlife from the dining room, lounge or cosy bar.

Rooms 7 en suite (1 GF) ⊘ in all bedrooms S £82; D £164 (incl. bkfst & dinner)✳ **Facilities** Wi-fi in bedrooms **Parking** 20 **Notes** LB No children 8yrs Closed Nov-Mar

CONNEL MAP 10 NM93

★★★ 75% HOTEL
Falls of Lora
PA37 1PB
☎ 01631 710483 📠 01631 710694
e-mail: enquiries@fallsoflora.com
web: www.fallsoflora.com

Dir: *hotel set back from A85 from Glasgow, 0.5m past Connel sign, 5m before Oban*

PETS: Bedrooms (GF) **Charges** charge for damage **Public areas** except restaurant/lounge on leads **Grounds** accessible disp bin **Exercise area** 100mtrs **Facilities** washing facs cage storage vet info **On Request** fridge access torch towels

Personally run and welcoming, this long-established and thriving holiday hotel enjoys inspiring views over Loch Etive. The spacious ground floor takes in a comfortable, traditional lounge and a cocktail bar with over a hundred whiskies and an open log fire. Guests can eat in the popular, informal bistro, which is open all day. Bedrooms come in a variety of styles, ranging from the cosy standard rooms to high quality luxury rooms.

Rooms 30 en suite (4 fmly) (4 GF) S £41.50-£59.50; D £49-£131 (incl. bkfst)✳ **Parking** 40 **Notes** LB Closed mid Dec & Jan

GLENDARUEL MAP 10 NR98

►►► Glendaruel Caravan Park (NR005865)
PA22 3AB
☎ 01369 820267 📠 01369 820367
e-mail: mail@glendaruelcaravanpark.co.uk
web: www.glendaruelcaravanpark.co.uk

Dir: *From A83 take A815 to Strathur, then 13m to park on A886. By ferry from Gourock to Dunoon then B836, then A886 for approx 4m N. (NB this route not recommended for towing vehicles - 1:5 uphill gradient on B836)*

PETS: Public areas except games room, shop & toilets on leads at all times **Exercise area** on site woodland walk several public woodland walks nearby **Facilities** on site shop food food bowl water bowl disp bags walks info vet info

Open Apr-Oct Booking advisable spring bank hol & mid Jul-Aug Last arrival 22.00hrs Last departure noon

A very pleasant, well-established site in the beautiful Victorian gardens of Glendaruel House. The level grass and hardstanding pitches are set in 23 acres of wooded parkland in a valley surrounded by mountains, with many rare specimen trees. The owners are hospitable and friendly. A 3-acre site with 35 touring pitches, 24 hardstandings and 30 statics.

INVERARAY
MAP 10 NN00

★★★ 81% HOTEL

Loch Fyne Hotel & Leisure Club
CRERAR HOTELS

PA32 8XT

☎ 0870 950 6270 📄 01499 302348

e-mail: lochfyne@crerarhotels.com

web: www.crerarhotels.com

Dir: *from A83 Loch Lomond, through town centre on A80 to Lochgilphead. Hotel in 0.5m*

PETS: Bedrooms unattended **Stables** with prior notice
Charges £10 per night **Public areas Grounds** accessible
Exercise area 0.5m

This popular holiday hotel overlooks Loch Fyne. Bedrooms are mainly spacious and offer comfortable modern appointments. Guests can relax in the well-stocked bar and enjoy views over the Loch, or enjoy a meal in the delightful restaurant. There is also a well-equipped leisure centre.

Rooms 74 en suite ⊗ in 4 bedrooms **Facilities** ⊗ supervised Steam Room ♫ **Services** Lift **Parking** 50 **Notes** LB

INVERUGLAS
MAP 10 NN30

▶▶▶ **Loch Lomond Holiday Park** (NN320092)

G83 7DW

☎ 01301 704224 📄 01301 704206

e-mail: enquiries@lochlomond-caravans.co.uk

web: www.lochlomond-lodges.co.uk

Dir: *On A82 3.5m N of Tarbet*

PETS: Public areas except play area & beach **Exercise area** on site dog walks in forest **Facilities** on site shop food food bowl water bowl dog chews cat treats disp bags washing facs dog grooming walks info vet info

Open Mar-Oct (rs Dec-Jan main amenity building restricted hours) Booking advisable May-Aug Last arrival 20.00hrs Last departure 11.45hrs

A lovely setting on the shores of Loch Lomond with views of forests and mountains, and boat hire available. The small touring area is beautifully situated overlooking the loch, and handily placed for the toilets and clubhouse. A 6-acre site with 18 touring pitches and 72 statics.

LUSS
MAP 10 NS39

▶▶▶ **Luss Camping & Caravanning Club Site** (NS360936)

G83 8NT

☎ 01436 860658

web: www.campingandcaravanningclub.co.uk

Dir: *From Erkside bridge take A82 N towards Tarbet. (NB ignore 1st sign for Luss). After workshops take next right at Lodge of Loch Lomond & International Camping sign. Site 200yds*

PETS: Public areas except buildings **Exercise area** on site
Facilities walks info vet info **Other** prior notice required

Open Mar-Oct Booking advisable BH & peak periods Last arrival 21.00hrs Last departure noon

A lovely tenting site on the grassy western shore of Loch Lomond. The site has two superbly equipped toilet blocks, including a parent and child facility, and a good laundry. Club members' caravans and motorvans only permitted. A 12-acre site with 90 touring pitches, 30 hardstandings.

Notes Caravan pitches for members only

OBAN
MAP 10 NM83

★★★ 72% HOTEL

Oban Bay Hotel and Spa
CRERAR HOTELS

The Esplanade PA34 5AG

☎ 0870 950 6273 📄 01631 564006

e-mail: obanbay@crerarhotels.com

web: www.crerarhotels.com

Dir: *Follow A85 into Oban. Straight at 1st rdbt & right at 2nd, hotel 200yds on right.*

PETS: Bedrooms (GF) **Charges** £5 per night
Exercise area 250yds **Facilities** walks info vet info
On Request fridge access torch

Situated on the esplanade, this hotel enjoys splendid views across the bay to nearby islands. Smart and comfortable lounges set the scene, along with the stylish bedrooms. There are also two very impressive suites. A small spa includes an outside hot tub.

Rooms 80 en suite (3 GF) ⊗ in all bedrooms S £75-£95; D £110-£190 (incl. bkfst) ✳ **Facilities** FTV Wi-fi in bedrooms Steam room Sauna ♫ Xmas New Year **Services** Lift **Parking** 20 (charged) **Notes** LB

PORT APPIN
MAP 14 NM94

★★★★ ◉◉◉ HOTEL

Airds
PA38 4DF
☎ 01631 730236 ▤ 01631 730535
e-mail: airds@airds-hotel.com
web: www.airds-hotel.com

Dir: *from A828 Oban to Fort William road, turn at Appin signed Port Appin. Hotel 2.5m on left*

PETS: **Bedrooms** (GF) unattended **Charges** £10 per night charge for damage **Grounds** accessible **Exercise area** surrounding area **Facilities** bedding walks info vet info **On Request** torch towels

The views are stunning from this small, luxury hotel on the shores of Loch Linnhe where the staff are delightful and nothing is too much trouble. The well-equipped bedrooms provide style and luxury whilst many bathrooms are furnished in marble and have power showers. Expertly prepared dishes utilising the finest of ingredients are served in the elegant dining room. Comfortable lounges with deep sofas and roaring fires provide the ideal retreat for relaxation. A real get-away-from-it-all experience.

Rooms 11 en suite (3 fmly) (2 GF) ⊗ in all bedrooms S £180-£330; D £245-£395 (incl. bkfst & dinner)✴ **Facilities** STV FTV 🥢 Putt green Wi-fi in bedrooms Xmas New Year **Parking** 21 **Notes** LB Closed 8-30 Jan RS Nov-Feb

TIGHNABRUAICH
MAP 10 NR97

★★★ ◉◉ SMALL HOTEL

An Lochan
Shore Rd PA21 2BE
☎ 01700 811239 ▤ 01700 811300
e-mail: info@anlochan.co.uk
web: www.anlochan.co.uk

Dir: *from Strachur on A886 right onto A8003 to Tighnabruaich. Hotel on right at bottom of hill*

PETS: **Bedrooms** **Charges** charge for damage **Public areas** except restaurants **Grounds** accessible & beach 100yds **Facilities** cage storage dog walking walks info vet info **On request** fridge access torch towels

This outstanding family-run hotel provides high levels of personal care from the proprietors and their locally recruited staff. Set just yards from the loch shore, stunning views are guaranteed from many rooms, including the elegant Crustacean Restaurant, and the more informal Deck Restaurant. Seafood and game, sourced on the doorstep, feature strongly on the menus. Guest can expect to find Egyptian cotton sheets, fluffy towels and local produced toiletries in the individually-styled, luxuriously appointed bedrooms.

Rooms 11 en suite ⊗ in all bedrooms S £100-£180; D £100-£180 (incl. bkfst)✴ **Facilities** Wi-fi available sailing, fishing, windsurfing, riding, Xmas New Year **Parking** 20 **Notes** LB Closed 4 days Xmas

---

CLACKMANNANSHIRE

DOLLAR
MAP 11 NS99

★★ 75% SMALL HOTEL

Castle Campbell Hotel
11 Bridge St FK14 7DE
☎ 01259 742519 ▤ 01259 743742
e-mail: bookings@castle-campbell.co.uk
web: www.castle-campbell.co.uk

Dir: *on A91 Stirling to St Andrews Rd, in the centre of Dollar, by bridge overlooking Dollar Burn & Clock Tower*

PETS: **Bedrooms** **Charges** £5 per night charge for damage **Public areas** except restaurant **Exercise area** nearby **Facilities** walks info vet info **Restrictions** Telephone for details **Resident Pets:** Jasper (Cocker Spaniel)

Set in the centre of a delightful country town, this hotel is popular with both local people and tourists. Accommodation ranges in size, though all rooms are thoughtfully equipped. Inviting public rooms feature a delightful lounge with real fire, a well-stocked whisky bar and a stylish restaurant.

Rooms 9 en suite (2 fmly) ⊗ in all bedrooms S £65; D £97.50 (incl. bkfst)✴ **Facilities** Wi-fi available Xmas New Year **Parking** 8 **Notes** LB

TILLICOULTRY
MAP 11 NS99

★★★★ BED & BREAKFAST

Westbourne House
10 Dollar Rd FK13 6PA
☎ 01259 750314
e-mail: info@westbournehouse.co.uk
web:
Dir: *A91 to St Andrews. Establishment on left just past minirdbt*

PETS: **Bedrooms** (GF) **Grounds** accessible **Resident Pets:** Brock (Border Collie)

This former mill-owner's home, set in wooded gardens on the edge of the village, is adorned with memorabilia gathered by the owners during their travels abroad. They offer a friendly welcome and an excellent choice is offered at breakfast.

Rooms 3 rms (2 en suite) (1 pri facs) (1 fmly) (1 GF) ⊗ S £35-£40; D £54-£60✴ **Facilities** TVB tea/coffee Cen ht TVL 🥢 **Parking** 3 **Notes** Closed Xmas-New Year

SCOTLAND

DUMFRIES & GALLOWAY

AUCHENCAIRN   MAP 11 NX75

★★★ 85% ◉◉ HOTEL

Balcary Bay

DG7 1QZ

☎ 01556 640217 & 640311 📠 01556 640272

e-mail: reservations@balcary-bay-hotel.co.uk

web: www.balcary-bay-hotel.co.uk

Dir: *on the A711 between Dalbeattie and Kirkcudbright, hotel on Shore road, 2m from village*

PETS: Bedrooms (GF) unattended **Grounds** accessible disp bin **Exercise area** beach adjacent **Facilities** food bowl water bowl dog scoop/disp bags leads washing facs cage storage walks info vet info **On Request** fridge access torch towels

Resident Pets: Rusty (Irish Red Setter)

Taking its name from the bay on which it lies, this hotel has lawns running down to the shore. The larger bedrooms enjoy stunning views over the bay, whilst others overlook the gardens. Comfortable public areas invite relaxation. Imaginative dishes feature at dinner, accompanied by a good wine list.

Rooms 20 en suite (1 fmly) (3 GF) ⊗ in all bedrooms S £69; D £124-£154 (incl. bkfst) **Facilities** FTV **Parking** 50 **Notes** LB

BALMINNOCH   MAP 10 NX26

►►►► **Three Lochs Holiday Park** *(NX272655)*

DG8 0EP

☎ 01671 830304 📠 01671 830335

e-mail: info@3lochs.co.uk

web: www.3lochs.co.uk

Dir: *Follow A75 W towards Stranraer. Approx 10km from Newton Stewart rdbt turn right at small x-roads, follow signs to site, park 4m on right*

PETS: Charges £1 per night **Public areas** except buildings **Exercise area** on site country surrounding site **Facilities** on site shop food vet info **Other** prior notice required

Open Mar-Oct Booking advisable BH & Jul-Aug Last arrival 22.00hrs Last departure 11.00hrs

A remote and very peaceful park set in beautiful moorland on the banks of Loch Heron, with further lochs and woodland nearby. This spacious grass park offers some fully-serviced pitches in a stunning location, and as well as being an ideal holiday spot for walkers and anglers, it provides heated indoor swimming pool and well-equipped games room. A 22.5-acre site with 45 touring pitches, 20 hardstandings and 90 statics.

Notes ✆

BEATTOCK   MAP 11 NT00

►►► **Craigielands Country Park** *(NY079023)*

DG10 9RE

☎ 01683 300591 📠 01683 300105

e-mail: admin@craigielandsleisure.com

web: www.craigielands.co.uk

Dir: *A74(M) junct 15 follow Beattock. Site in 350yds*

PETS: Stables nearby (2m) (loose box) **Charges** £5 per night **Public areas** except bar on leads **Exercise area** on site & large field **Facilities** washing facs walks info vet info **Other** prior notice required **Restrictions** no dangerous breeds (see page 7)

Open Mar-6 Jan (pub open wknds only) Booking advisable Last arrival 23.00hrs Last departure 14.00hrs

A relaxed park in part of a former country estate on the edge of the village of Beattock. A very large coarse fishing lake is available free to campers, stocked with trout, tench and carp. A bar and restaurant serve home cooking, and there is some entertainment at weekends during the high season. A 56-acre site with 125 touring pitches, 6 hardstandings and 104 statics.

SCOTLAND

CASTLE DOUGLAS MAP 11 NX76

★★ 68% HOTEL

Imperial

35 King St DG7 1AA

☎ 01556 502086 ▤ 01556 503009

e-mail: david@thegolfhotel.co.uk

web: www.thegolfhotel.co.uk

Dir: *exit A75 at sign for Castle Douglas, hotel opposite library*

PETS: Bedrooms unattended **Public areas** except eating areas **Grounds** accessible disp bin **Facilities** food bowl water bowl washing facs cage storage walks info vet info **On Request** fridge access torch towels

Situated in the main street, this former coaching inn, popular with golfers, offers guests well-equipped and cheerfully decorated bedrooms. There is a choice of bars and good-value meals are served either in the foyer bar or the upstairs dining room.

Rooms 12 en suite (1 fmly) ⊘ in all bedrooms S £47-£59; D £75-£80 (incl. bkfst)✳ **Facilities** STV **Parking** 29 **Notes** LB Closed 23-26 Dec & 1-3 Jan

★★★★ 🛏 ⇔ GUEST HOUSE

Craigadam

Craigadam DG7 3HU

☎ 01556 650233 & 650100 ▤ 01556 650233

e-mail: inquiry@craigadam.com

web: www.craigadam.com

Dir: *From Castle Douglas E on A75 to Crocketford. In Crocketford turn left on A712 for 2m. House on hill*

PETS: Bedrooms unattended **Sep Accom** kennel **Grounds** accessible **Exercise area** field adjacent **Resident Pets:** Craig (Collie), Ted & Jet (Black Labradors), Highland cattle

Set on a farm, this elegant country house offers gracious living in a relaxed environment. The large bedrooms, most set around a courtyard, are strikingly individual in style. Public areas include a billiard room with comprehensive honesty bar and the panelled dining room features a magnificent 15-seater table, the setting for Celia Pickup's delightful meals.

Rooms 10 en suite (2 fmly) (7 GF) ⊘ S £42-£84; D £84✳ **Facilities** TVB tea/coffee Licensed Cen ht Dinner Last d 8am Fishing Snooker ⌣ **Parking** 12 **Notes** LB No coaches Closed Xmas & New Year

▶▶▶ **Lochside Caravan & Camping Site**

(NX766618)

Lochside Park DG7 1EZ

☎ 01556 502949 & 503806 ▤ 01556 503806

e-mail: scottg2@dumgal.gov.uk

web: www.dumgal.gov.uk/lochsidecs

Dir: *Off A75 towards Castle Douglas by Carlingwark Loch*

PETS: Public areas on leads **Facilities** on site shop vet info

Open Etr-Oct Booking advisable Last arrival 19.30hrs Last departure noon

Well-managed municipal touring site in a pleasant location adjacent to Carlingwark Loch and parkland but close to the town. A 5.5-acre site with 161 touring pitches, 74 hardstandings.

Notes ⊛ Height restriction barrier

CREETOWN MAP 11 NX46

▶▶▶▶▶ **Castle Cary Holiday Park** *(NX475576)*

DG8 7DQ

☎ 01671 820264 ▤ 01671 820670

e-mail: enquiries@castlecarypark.f9.co.uk

web: www.castlecary-caravans.com

Dir: *Signed with direct access off A75, 0.5m S of village*

PETS: Stables nearby (3m) **Charges** 70p per night £4.90 per week **Public areas** on leads at all times **Exercise area** on site field and woodland walk & 0.25m **Facilities** on site shop food food bowl water bowl dog chews cat treats litter dog scoop/disp bags leads walks info vet info **Restrictions** no dangerous dogs (see page 7); no Rottweilers, Pit or Staffordshire Bull Terriers **Resident Pets:** Golden Retriever, Yorkshire Terrier, cats, donkeys, geese, swans, ducks

Open all year (rs Oct-Mar reception/shop, no heated outdoor pool) Booking advisable BHs & Jul-Aug Last arrival anytime Last departure noon

This attractive site in the grounds of Cassencarie House is sheltered by woodlands, and faces south towards Wigtown Bay. The park is in a secluded location with beautiful landscaping and excellent facilities. The bar/restaurant is housed in part of an old castle, and enjoys extensive views over the River Cree estuary. A 12-acre site with 50 touring pitches, 50 hardstandings and 26 statics.

CROCKETFORD   MAP 11 NX87

▶▶▶▶ **Park of Brandedleys** *(NX830725)*

DG2 8RG

☎ 0845 4561760 📄 01556 690681

e-mail: brandedleys@holgates.com

web: www.holgates.com

Dir: *In village on A75, from Dumfries towards Stranraer site on left up minor road, entrance 200yds on right*

PETS: Stables nearby (2km) (loose box) **Charges** £2 per night £14 per week **Public areas** except buildings **Exercise area** on site dog trail around park **Facilities** walks info vet info **Restrictions** no dangerous breeds (see page 7)

Open all year (rs Nov-Mar bar/restaurant open Fri-Sun afternoon) Booking advisable public hols & Jul-Aug Last arrival 22.00hrs Last departure noon

A well-maintained site in an elevated position off the A75, with fine views of Auchenreoch Loch and beyond. This comfortable park offers a wide range of amenities, including a fine games room and a tastefully-designed bar with adjoining bistro. Well placed for enjoying walking, fishing, sailing and golf. A 24-acre site with 80 touring pitches, 40 hardstandings and 63 statics.

Notes Guidelines issued on arrival

ECCLEFECHAN   MAP 11 NY17

▶▶▶▶▶ **Hoddom Castle Caravan Park**

(NY154729)

Hoddom DG11 1AS

☎ 01576 300251 📄 01576 300757

e-mail: hoddomcastle@aol.com

web: www.hoddomcastle.co.uk

Dir: *M74 junct 19, follow signs to site. From A75 W of Annan take B723 for 5m, follow signs to site*

PETS: Charges £1.50 per night **Public areas**
Exercise area adjacent **Facilities** on site shop food food bowl water bowl disp bags walks info vet info **Other** prior notice required

Open Etr or Apr-Oct (rs early season cafeteria closed) Booking advisable BH & Jul-Aug Last arrival 21.00hrs Last departure 14.00hrs

The peaceful, well-equipped park can be found on the banks of the River Annan, and offers a good mix of grassy and hard pitches, beautifully landscaped and blending into the surroundings. There are signed nature trails, maintained by the park's countryside ranger, a 9-hole golf course, trout and salmon fishing, and plenty of activity ideas for children. A 28-acre site with 200 touring pitches, 150 hardstandings and 44 statics.

GATEHOUSE OF FLEET   MAP 11 NX55

★★★ 73% HOTEL

Murray Arms

DG7 2HY

☎ 01557 814207 📄 01557 814370

e-mail: info@murrayarmshotel.co.uk

web: www.murrayarmshotel.co.uk

Dir: *off A75, hotel at edge of town, near clock tower*

PETS: Bedrooms unattended **Charges** £7.50 per stay
Grounds accessible **Facilities** food bowl water bowl dog chews dog scoop/disp bags walks info vet info **On Request** fridge access torch towels **Resident Pets:** Daisy (Jack Russell)

A relaxed and welcoming atmosphere prevails at this historic coaching inn that has associations with Robert Burns. Public areas retain a comfortable, traditional feel and include a choice of sitting areas, a snug bar and an all-day restaurant serving honest and popular dishes. Bedrooms are comfortable and well presented.

Rooms 12 en suite (3 fmly) ⊘ in 10 bedrooms S £48-£67.50; D £96-£135 (incl. bkfst)✻ **Facilities** 🎱 Fishing 🏌 Wi-fi in bedrooms Xmas New Year **Parking** 50 **Notes** LB

▶▶▶ **Mossyard Caravan & Camping Park**

(NX546518)

Mossyard DG7 2ET

☎ 01557 840226 📄 01557 840226

e-mail: enquiry@mossyard.co.uk

web: www.mossyard.co.uk

Dir: *0.75m off A75 on private tarmaced farm road, 4.5m W of Gatehouse of Fleet*

PETS: Stables nearby (1.5m) (loose box) **Public areas**
Exercise area on site beach walks woodland & parks adjacent **Facilities** washing facs walks info vet info **Resident Pets:** Sophie (Black Labrador), Jay & Pip (working Collies), Archie & Alice (cats), sheep & cows

Open Etr/Apr-Oct Booking advisable Spring BH, Jul-Aug, wknds

A grassy park with its own beach, located on a working farm, and offering an air of peace and tranquillity. Stunning sea and coastal views from touring pitches, and the tenting field is almost on the beach. A 6.5-acre site with 35 touring pitches and 15 statics.

Notes ☻

GRETNA
MAP 11 NY36

▶▶▶ Bruce's Cave Caravan & Camping Park *(NY266705)*

Cove Estate, Kirkpatrick Fleming DG11 3AT

☎ 01461 800285 📄 01461 800269

e-mail: enquiries@brucescave.co.uk

web: www.brucescave.co.uk

Dir: *Exit A74(M) junct 21 for Kirkpatrick Fleming follow N through village, pass Station Inn, at Bruce's Court turn left. Over rail crossing to site entrance.*

PETS: Public areas except toilets, shop & play area on leads **Exercise area** on site river walk **Facilities** on site shop food disp bags washing facs walks info vet info space for loose box **Resident Pets:** Scamp, Cally, Bruce & Bruno (dogs), Silver & Buttercup (cats), Daisy (Shetland Pony), Silver & Prince (horses), ducks

Open all year (rs Nov-Mar Shop closed, water restriction) Booking advisable Last arrival 23.00hrs Last departure 19.00hrs

The lovely wooded grounds of an old castle and mansion are the setting for this pleasant park. The mature woodland is a haven for wildlife, and there is a riverside walk to Robert the Bruce's Cave. A toilet block with en suite facilities is of special appeal to families. An 80-acre site with 75 touring pitches, 60 hardstandings and 35 statics.

Notes 🐾

GRETNA SERVICE AREA (A74(M))
MAP 11 NY36

BUDGET HOTEL
Days Inn Gretna Green

Welcome Break Service Area DG16 5HQ

☎ 01461 337566 📄 01461 337823

e-mail: gretna.hotel@welcomebreak.co.uk

web: www.daysinn.com

Dir: *between junct 21/22 on M74 - accessible from both N'bound & S'bound carriageway*

PETS: Bedrooms (GF) **Grounds** accessible on leads disp bin **Exercise area** 20yds **Facilities** walks info vet info **On Request** torch

This modern building offers accommodation in smart, spacious and well-equipped bedrooms, suitable for families and business travellers, and all with en suite bathrooms. Continental breakfast is available and other refreshments may be taken at the nearby family restaurant. For further details see the Hotel Groups page.

Rooms 64 en suite

KIRKBEAN
MAP 11 NX95

★★ 85% ⑩ COUNTRY HOUSE HOTEL
Cavens

DG2 8AA

☎ 01387 880234 📄 01387 880467

e-mail: enquiries@cavens.com

web: www.cavens.com

Dir: *on entering Kirkbean on A710, hotel signed*

PETS: Bedrooms Charges £10 per stay **Exercise area** nearby **Resident Pets:** Rosco (Border Terrier), Hamish (Labrador)

Set in parkland gardens, Cavens encapsulates all the virtues of an intimate country-house hotel. Quality is the keynote, and the proprietors have spared no effort in completing a fine renovation of the house. Bedrooms are delightfully individual and very comfortably equipped, and a choice of lounges invites peaceful relaxation. A set dinner offers the best of local and home-made produce.

Rooms 6 en suite ⊘ in all bedrooms S £80-£150; D £80-£220 (incl. bkfst)✲ **Facilities** FTV ⤵ Shooting, Fishing, Horse riding New Year **Parking** 12 **Notes LB** No children 12yrs

---

KIRKCUDBRIGHT
MAP 11 NX65

★★ 67% HOTEL
Arden House Hotel

Tongland Rd DG6 4UU

☎ 01557 330544 📄 01557 330742

Dir: *off A57 Euro route (Stranraer), 4m W of Castle Douglas onto A711. Signed for Kirkcudbright, crossing Telford Bridge. Hotel 400mtrs on left*

PETS: Bedrooms unattended **Public areas** except restaurant **Grounds** accessible disp bin **Exercise area** country walks **Facilities** vet info bowls on request

Set well back from the main road in extensive grounds on the northeast side of town, this spotlessly maintained hotel offers attractive bedrooms, a lounge bar and adjoining conservatory serving a range of popular dishes, which are also available in the dining room. It boasts an impressive function suite in its grounds.

Rooms 9 rms (8 en suite) (7 fmly) S £45-£50; D £70-£75 (incl. bkfst)✲ **Parking** 70 **Notes** 🐾

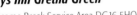

SCOTLAND

KIRKCUDBRIGHT CONTINUED

►►► Silvercraigs Caravan & Camping Site

(NX686508)

Silvercraigs Rd DG6 4BT

☎ 01557 330123 & 01556 503806 ▤ 01557 330123

e-mail: scottg2@dumgal.gov.uk

web: www.dumgal.gov.uk/silvercraigscs

Dir: *In Kirkcudbright off Silvercraigs Rd. Access via A711, follow signs to site*

PETS: Public areas on leads **Exercise area** woods adjacent **Facilities** vet info

Open Etr-Oct Last departure noon

A well-maintained municipal park in an elevated position with extensive views overlooking the picturesque, unspoilt town and harbour to the countryside beyond. Toilet facilities are of a very good standard, and the town centre is just a short stroll away. A 6-acre site with 50 touring pitches.

Notes ☺

LOCHMABEN   MAP 11 NY08

►► Kirk Loch Caravan & Camping Site

(NY082825)

DG11 1PZ

☎ 01556 503806 & 07746 123783 ▤ 01556 503806

e-mail: scottg2@dumgal.gov.uk

web: www.dumgal.gov.uk/kirklochcs

Dir: *In Lochmaben enter via Kirkloch Brae*

PETS: Public areas on leads **Facilities** vet info

Open Etr-Oct Last departure noon

A grassy lochside site with superb views and well-maintained facilities. Some hard pitches are available at this municipal park, which is adjacent to a golf club, and close to three lochs. A 1.5-acre site with 30 touring pitches, 14 hardstandings.

Notes ☺

LOCKERBIE   MAP 11 NY18

★★★ 79% ◉ HOTEL

Dryfesdale

Dryfebridge DG11 2SF

☎ 01576 202427 ▤ 01576 204187

e-mail: reception@dryfesdalehotel.co.uk

web: www.dryfesdalehotel.co.uk

Dir: *from M74 junct 17 take 'Lockerbie North', 3rd left at 1st rdbt, 1st exit left at 2nd rdbt, hotel is 200yds on left*

PETS: Bedrooms (GF) unattended **Charges** £5 per night **Grounds** accessible disp bin **Facilities** food (pre-bookable) food bowl bedding dog chews feeding mat dog scoop/disp bags welcome pack for dogs cage storage walks info vet info **On Request** fridge access torch towels

Conveniently situated for the M74, yet discreetly screened from it, this friendly hotel provides attentive service. Bedrooms, some with access to patio areas, vary in size and style, offer good levels of comfort and are well equipped. Creative, good value dinners make use of local produce and are served in the airy restaurant overlooking the manicured gardens and rolling countryside.

Rooms 16 en suite (4 fmly) (6 GF) ⊘ in 8 bedrooms **Facilities** STV ⓢ Putt green Clay pigeon shooting, Fishing ♫ **Parking** 60

★★ 67% HOTEL

Ravenshill House

12 Dumfries Rd DG11 2EF

☎ 01576 202882 ▤ 01576 202882

e-mail: aaenquiries@ravenshillhotellockerbie.co.uk

web: www.ravenshillhotellockerbie.co.uk

Dir: *from A74(M) Lockerbie junct onto A709. Hotel 0.5m on right*

PETS: Bedrooms Grounds accessible on leads disp bin **Exercise area** 100yds **Facilities** water bowl walks info vet info **On Request** fridge access

Set in spacious gardens on the fringe of the town, this friendly, family-run hotel offers cheerful service and good value, home-cooked meals. Bedrooms are generally spacious and comfortably equipped, including an ideal two-room family unit.

Rooms 8 rms (7 en suite) (2 fmly) ⊘ in all bedrooms S £45-£65; D £70-£75 (incl. bkfst)✳ **Facilities** New Year **Parking** 35 **Notes** LB

MOFFAT   MAP 11 NT00

★★★★ GUEST HOUSE

Hartfell House

Hartfell Crescent DG10 9AL

☎ 01683 220153

e-mail: enquiries@hartfellhouse.co.uk

Dir: *Off High St at war memorial onto Well St & Old Well Rd, Hartfell Crescent on right*

PETS: Bedrooms (GF) **Grounds** accessible disp bin
Exercise area 300mtrs **Facilities** walks info vet info
On Request fridge access torch

Built in 1850, this impressive Victorian house is in a peaceful terrace high above the town, having lovely views of the surrounding countryside. Beautifully maintained, its bedrooms offer high quality and comfort. There is an inviting first-floor lounge and attractive dining room, where delicious breakfasts are served. A computer with broadband and Wi-fi is now also available for guests use.

Rooms 8 rms (7 en suite) (1 pri facs) (2 fmly) (2 GF) ⊘ S £35; D £60
Facilities TVB tea/coffee Licensed Cen ht Wi-fi available **Parking** 6
Notes LB No coaches Closed Xmas

★★★★ GUEST ACCOMMODATION

Limetree House

Eastgate DG10 9AE

☎ 01683 220001

e-mail: info@limetreehouse.co.uk

web: www.limetreehouse.co.uk

Dir: *Off High St onto Well St, left onto Eastgate, house 100yds*

PETS: Bedrooms (GF) **Charges** charge for damage
Public areas on leads **Facilities** food bowl water bowl cage storage walks info vet info **On Request** fridge access torch
towels **Restrictions** no large breeds **Resident Pets:** Mike, Sully & Beatrice (cats)

A warm welcome is assured at this well-maintained guest house, quietly situated behind the main high street. Recognisable by its colourful flower baskets in season, it provides an inviting lounge and bright cheerful breakfast room. Bedrooms are smartly furnished in pine and include a large family room.

Rooms 6 en suite (1 fmly) (1 GF) ⊘ S £37.50; D £60-£70 **Facilities** FTV
TVB tea/coffee Cen ht Dinner Last d 5pm **Parking** 3 **Notes** LB
No children 5yrs RS Xmas & New Year

★★ GUEST ACCOMMODATION

Barnhill Springs Country

DG10 9QS

☎ 01683 220580

Dir: *A74(M) junct 15, A701 towards Moffat, Barnhill Rd 50yds on right*

PETS: Bedrooms unattended **Public areas** except dining room
Grounds accessible (1.5 acres) disp bin **Facilities** food bowl
water bowl dog chews dog scoop/disp bags leads washing facs
cage storage walks info vet info **On Request** fridge access torch
towels **Restrictions** Telephone for details **Resident Pets:** Kim
(Collie cross)

This former farmhouse has a quiet rural location south of the town and within easy reach of the M74. Bedrooms are well proportioned; one having a bathroom en suite. There is a comfortable lounge and separate dining room.

Rooms 5 rms (1 en suite) (1 fmly) (1 GF) ⊘ S £29; D £56
Facilities tea/coffee Cen ht TVL Dinner Last d 9am **Parking** 10
Notes ⊠

▶▶▶ **Moffat Camping & Caravanning Club Site** *(NT085050)*

Hammerlands Farm DG10 9QL

☎ 01683 220436

web: www.campingandcaravanningclub.co.uk

Dir: *From A74 follow Moffat sign. After 1m turn right by Bank of Scotland, right again in 200yds. Sign for site on right*

PETS: Public areas except buildings **Exercise area** on site dog
walk adjacent countryside **Facilities** vet info

Open Mar-Oct Booking advisable BH & peak periods Last arrival 21.00hrs Last departure noon

Well-maintained level grass touring site, with extensive views of the surrounding hilly countryside from many parts of the park. This busy stopover site is always well maintained, and looks bright and cheerful thanks to meticulous wardens. A 10-acre site with 180 touring pitches, 42 hardstandings.

SCOTLAND

SCOTLAND

PARTON MAP 11 NX67

►►► Loch Ken Holiday Park (NX687702)

DG7 3NE

☎ 01644 470282 📄 01644 470297

e-mail: penny@lochkenholidaypark.co.uk

web: www.lochkenholidaypark.co.uk

Dir: *On A713, N of Parton*

PETS: Charges £2 per night **Public areas** except shop on leads **Exercise area** on site field provided farm walk 300yds **Facilities** on site shop food food bowl water bowl dog scoop/disp bags leads walks vet info **Other** prior notice required **Restrictions** Telephone for details **Resident Pets:** 12 ducks

Open Mar-mid Nov (rs Mar/Apr (ex Etr) & late Sep-Nov restricted shop hours) Booking advisable Etr, Spring bank hol & Jun-Aug Last departure noon

A busy and popular park with a natural emphasis on water activities set, on the eastern shores of Loch Ken, with superb views. Family owned and run, it is in a peaceful and beautiful spot opposite the RSPB reserve, with direct access to the loch for boat launching. The park offers a variety of water sports, as well as farm visits and nature trails. Showers are charged for at £1 a time. A 7-acre site with 52 touring pitches, 4 hardstandings and 35 statics.

Notes 📵

PORTPATRICK MAP 10 NW95

★★★ ◉◉◉ HOTEL

Knockinaam Lodge

DG9 9AD

☎ 01776 810471 📄 01776 810435

e-mail: reservations@knockinaamlodge.com

web: www.knockinaamlodge.com

Dir: *from A77 or A75 follow signs to Portpatrick. Through Lochans. After 2m left at signs for hotel*

PETS: Bedrooms certain rooms only **Charges** £15 per stay

Any tour of Dumfries & Galloway would not be complete without a night or two at this haven of tranquillity and relaxation. Knockinaam Lodge is an extended Victorian house, set in an idyllic cove with its own pebble beach and sheltered by majestic cliffs and woodlands. A warm welcome is assured from the proprietors and their committed team, and much emphasis is placed on providing a sophisticated but intimate home-from-home experience. The cooking at all meals is a real treat and showcases superb local produce. Dinner is a set meal, but choices can be discussed in advance.

Rooms 9 en suite ⊘ in all bedrooms S £165-£300; D £190-£400 (incl. bkfst & dinner)✻ **Facilities** Fishing ⛵ Wi-fi in bedrooms Shooting, Walking, Sea fishing, Clay pigeon shooting ch fac Xmas New Year **Parking** 20 **Notes** LB

★★★ 80% ◉ HOTEL

Fernhill

Heugh Rd DG9 8TD

☎ 01776 810220 📄 01776 810596

e-mail: info@fernhillhotel.co.uk

web: www.fernhillhotel.co.uk

Dir: *from Stranraer A77 to Portpatrick, 100yds past Portpatrick village sign, turn right before war memorial. Hotel 1st on left*

PETS: Bedrooms Grounds accessible **Exercise area** wooded area

Set high above the village, this hotel looks out over the harbour and Irish Sea. Many of the bedrooms take advantage of the views. A modern wing offers particularly spacious and well-appointed rooms - some have balconies. The smart conservatory restaurant offers interesting dishes.

Rooms 27 en suite 9 annexe en suite (3 fmly) (8 GF) ⊘ in all bedrooms S £60-£83; D £70-£110 (incl. bkfst)✻ **Facilities** STV Xmas New Year **Parking** 45 **Notes** LB Closed mid Jan-mid Feb

PORT WILLIAM MAP 10 NX34

►►► Kings Green Caravan Site (NX340430)

32 South St DG8 9SG

☎ 01988 700880

web: www.portwilliam.com

Dir: *Direct access from A747 at junct with B7085, towards Whithorn*

PETS: Public areas except toilet/shower block **Exercise area** beach **Facilities** vet info

Open Etr-Oct Booking advisable Last departure noon

Set beside the unspoilt village with all its amenities and the attractive harbour, this level grassy park is community owned and run. Approached via the coast road, the park has views reaching as far as the Isle of Man. A 3-acre site with 30 touring pitches.

Notes 📵

SHAWHEAD MAP 11 NX87

►►► Barnsoul Farm (NX876778)

DG2 9SQ

☎ 01387 730249 & 730453 📠 01387 730453

e-mail: barnsouldg@aol.com

web: www.barnsoulfarm.co.uk

Dir: *Exit A75 between Dumfries & Crocketford at site sign onto unclass road signed Shawhead. At T-junct turn right & immediate left. Site 1m on left, follow Barnsoul signs*

PETS: Charges Public areas on leads **Exercise area** on site **Other** max 2 dogs space for loose box **Restrictions** no breeds larger than an Alsatian, no Matiffs or similar breeds

Open Apr-Oct (rs Feb-Mar chalets & bothies by appointment only) Booking advisable Jul & Aug Last arrival 23.00hrs Last departure noon

A very spacious, peaceful and scenic farm site with views across open countryside in all directions. Set in 250 acres of woodland, parkland and farmland, and an ideal centre for touring the surrounding unspoilt countryside. It offers excellent kitchen facilities and a dining area for lightweight campers. A 10-acre site with 30 touring pitches, 12 hardstandings and 6 statics.

Notes ⊕ No unbooked groups, no loud noise after 23.00hrs

STRANRAER MAP 10 NX06

★★★ 75% ⊛ HOTEL

Corsewall Lighthouse Hotel

Corsewall Point, Kirkcolm DG9 0QG

☎ 01776 853220 📠 01776 854231

e-mail: lighthousehotel@btinternet.com

web: www.lighthousehotel.co.uk

Dir: *A718 from Stranraer to Kirkcolm (approx 8m) then follow signs to hotel for further 4m*

PETS: Bedrooms unattended **Charges** £5 small dog, £10 large dog per night **Public areas** except restaurant **Grounds** accessible **Exercise area** adjacent **Facilities** food **Other** pets in 3 cottage suites only **Resident Pets:** Highland cattle

Looking for something completely different? A unique hotel converted from buildings that adjoin a listed 19th-century lighthouse set on a rocky coastline. Bedrooms come in a variety of sizes, some reached by a spiral staircase, and as with the public areas, are cosy and atmospheric. Three cottage suites in the grounds offer greater space.

Rooms 6 en suite 4 annexe en suite (4 fmly) (6 GF) ⊘ in 8 bedrooms
S £120-£230; D £140-£250 (incl. bkfst & dinner)✱ **Facilities** FTV Xmas
New Year **Parking** 20 **Notes** LB

►►►► Aird Donald Caravan Park (NX075605)

London Rd DG9 8RN

☎ 01776 702025

e-mail: enquiries@aird-donald.co.uk

web: www.aird-donald.co.uk

Dir: *Turn left off A75 on entering Stranraer, (signed). Opposite school, site 300yds*

PETS: Public areas Exercise area on site wooded area **Facilities** vet info

Open all year Booking advisable Last departure 16.00hrs

A spacious touring site, mainly grass but with tarmac hardstanding area, with pitches large enough to accommodate a car and caravan overnight without unhitching. On the fringe of town screened by mature shrubs and trees. Ideal stopover en route to Northern Irish ferry ports. A 12-acre site with 100 touring pitches.

Notes ⊕

WIGTOWN MAP 10 NX45

►►► Drumroamin Farm Camping & Touring Site (NX445507)

1 South Balfern DG8 9DB

☎ 01988 840613

e-mail: enquiry@drumroamin.co.uk

web: www.drumroamin.co.uk

Dir: *A75 towards Newton Stewart, turn onto A714 for Wigtown. Left on B7005 through Bladnock, A746 through Kirkinner. Take B7004 Garlieston, 2nd left opposite Kilsture Forest, site 0.75m at end of lane*

PETS: Public areas play room & toilet block **Exercise area** on site field perimiter walk woodland walk 0.5m **Facilities** washing facs walks info vet info **Resident Pets:** Maggie (Chocolate Labrador)

Open all year Booking advisable Last arrival 21.00hrs Last departure noon

An open, spacious park in a quiet spot a mile from the main road, and close to Wigton Bay. A superb toilet block offers spacious showers, and there's a lounge/games room and plenty of room for children to play. A 5-acre site with 48 touring pitches and 2 statics.

Notes ⊕ No fires

EAST LOTHIAN

DUNBAR — MAP 12 NT67

►►►►► Thurston Manor Holiday Home Park (NT712745)

Innerwick EH42 1SA

☎ 01368 840643 📠 01368 840261

e-mail: mail@thurstonmanor.co.uk

web: www.thurstonmanor.co.uk

Dir: *4m S of Dunbar, signed off A1*

PETS: Public areas except play area and buildings
Exercise area on site **Facilities** on site shop food food bowl water bowl dog chews cat treats litter disp bags leads vet info **Other** prior notice required max 2 dogs per unit

Open Mar-8 Jan (rs 1-23 Dec wknds only) Booking advisable BH, Etr & high season Last arrival 23.00hrs Last departure noon

A pleasant park set in 250 acres of unspoilt countryside. The touring and static areas of this large park are in separate areas. The main touring area occupies an open, level position, and the toilet facilities are modern and exceptionally well maintained. The park boasts a well-stocked fishing loch, a heated indoor swimming pool, steam room, sauna, jacuzzi, mini-gym and fitness room and seasonal entertainment. A 250-acre site with 100 touring pitches, 45 hardstandings and 420 statics.

►►► Barns Ness Camping & Caravanning Club Site (NT723773)

Barns Ness EH42 1QP

☎ 01368 863536

web: www.campingandcaravanningclub.co.uk

Dir: *On A1, 6m S of Dunbar (near power station). Sign for Barns Ness & Skateraw 1m down road. Turn right at site sign towards lighthouse*

PETS: Exercise area on site dog walk **Facilities** walks info vet info **Other** prior notice required

Open Mar-Oct Booking advisable BH & peak periods Last arrival 21.00hrs Last departure noon

A grassy, landscaped site close to the foreshore and lighthouse on a coastline noted for its natural and geological history. A 10-acre site with 80 touring pitches.

►►► Belhaven Bay Caravan & Camping Park (NT661781)

Belhaven Bay EH42 1TU

☎ 01368 865956 📠 01368 865022

e-mail: belhaven@meadowhead.co.uk

web: www.meadowhead.co.uk

Dir: *From A1 onto A1087 towards Dunbar. Site (1m) in John Muir Park*

PETS: Public areas except play area on leads **Exercise area** on site lakeside grass area beaches, woodland & fields nearby **Facilities** food bowl water bowl washing facs walks info vet info space for loose box **Other** prior notice required **Restrictions** no dangerous dogs (see page 7)

Open Mar-Oct Booking advisable Last arrival 20.00hrs Last departure noon

Small, well-maintained park in a sheltered location and within walking distance of the beach. This is an excellent spot for seabird watching, and there is a good rail connection with Edinburgh from Dunbar. A 40-acre site with 52 touring pitches, 11 hardstandings and 64 statics.

GULLANE
MAP 12 NT48

★★★ ◉◉◉ HOTEL

Greywalls
Muirfield EH31 2EG
☎ 01620 842144 📄 01620 842241
e-mail: hotel@greywalls.co.uk
web: www.greywalls.co.uk

Dir: *A198, hotel signed at E end of village*

PETS: Bedrooms Grounds accessible **Exercise area** adjacent
Other A very warm welcome to well behaved dogs!

A dignified but relaxing Edwardian country house designed by Sir
Edwin Lutyens; Greywalls overlooks the famous Muirfield Golf Course
and is ideally placed just a half hours' drive from Edinburgh. Delightful
public rooms look onto beautiful gardens and freshly prepared cuisine
may be enjoyed in the restaurant. Stylish bedrooms, whether cosy
singles or spacious master rooms, are thoughtfully equipped and many
command views of the course. A gatehouse lodge is ideal for golfing
parties.

Rooms 17 en suite 6 annexe en suite (9 GF) S £140-£285; D £240-£300
(incl. bkfst)✳ **Facilities** STV ⬦ ⬦ Putt green Wi-fi available **Parking** 40
Notes LB Closed Jan-Feb

MUSSELBURGH
MAP 11 NT37

▶▶▶▶ **Drum Mohr Caravan Park** *(NT373734)*
Levenhall EH21 8JS
☎ 0131 665 6867 📄 0131 653 6859
e-mail: bookings@drummohr.org
web: www.drummohr.org

Dir: *Leave A1 at junct with A199 towards Musselburgh, at rdbt
turn right onto B1361 signed Prestonpans, take 1st left & site
400yds*

PETS: Stables nearby (1km) **Charges** £1 per night
Public areas except play area **Exercise area** on site perimeter
walk **Facilities** on site shop food vet info **Other** max 2 dogs per
pitch

Open Mar-Oct Booking advisable Jul-Aug Last arrival 20.00hrs
Last departure noon

This attractive park is sheltered by mature trees on all sides, and
carefully landscaped within. The park is divided into separate areas by
mature hedging and planting of trees and ornamental shrubs. Pitches
are generous in size, and there are a number of fully serviced pitches
plus first-class amenities. A 9-acre site with 120 touring pitches, 50
hardstandings and 12 statics.

CITY OF EDINBURGH

EDINBURGH
MAP 11 NT27

★★★★ 72% HOTEL

Novotel Edinburgh Centre
Lauriston Place, Lady Lawson St EH3 9DE
☎ 0131 656 3500 📄 0131 656 3510
e-mail: H3271@accor.com
web: www.novotel.com

Dir: *from Edinburgh Castle right onto George IV Bridge from
Royal Mile. Follow to junct, then right onto Lauriston Pl for hotel
700mtrs on right.*

PETS: Bedrooms unattended **Charges** £10 per night charge for
damage **Public areas** only in lobby **Facilities** walks info vet info

One of the new generations of Novotels, this modern hotel is located
in the centre of the city, close to Edinburgh Castle. Smart and stylish
public areas include a cosmopolitan bar, brasserie style restaurant and
indoor leisure facilities. The air-conditioned bedrooms feature a
comprehensive range of extras and bathrooms with baths and separate
shower cabinets.

Rooms 180 en suite (146 fmly) ⊛ in 135 bedrooms S £69-£219;
D £69-£219✳ **Facilities** STV ☼ Gym Wi-fi available Xmas **Services** Lift
air con **Parking** 15 **Notes** LB

★★★ 78% HOTEL

Best Western Kings Manor
100 Milton Rd East EH15 2NP
☎ 0131 669 0444 & 468 8003 📄 0131 669 6650
e-mail: reservations@kingsmanor.com
web: www.kingsmanor.com

Dir: *A720 E to Old Craighall junct, left into city, right att A1/A199
junct, hotel 400mtrs on right*

PETS: Bedrooms Public areas except dining area
Grounds accessible **Exercise area** on site **Other** Guide Dogs for
the Blind Association use this hotel as residential training centre

Lying on the eastern side of the city and convenient for the by-pass,
this hotel is popular with business guests, tour groups and for
conferences. It boasts a fine leisure complex and a bright modern
bistro, which complements the quality, creative cooking in the main
restaurant.

Rooms 95 en suite (8 fmly) (13 GF) ⊛ in all bedrooms S £75-£112;
D £120-£180 (incl. bkfst) **Facilities** STV FTV ☼ ⬦ Gym Wi-fi in
bedrooms Health & beauty salon Steam room Xmas New Year
Services Lift **Parking** 120 **Notes** LB

SCOTLAND

EDINBURGH CONTINUED

★★★ GUEST HOUSE
Galloway
22 Dean Park Crescent EH4 1PH
☎ 0131 332 3672 📠 0131 332 3672
e-mail: galloway_theclarks@hotmail.com
Dir: *0.5m NW of castle & Princes St. Off A90 onto Comely Bank Av & Dean Park Cres*
PETS: Bedrooms unattended **Public areas** except dining room **Exercise area** 0.5km

Located in a peaceful residential area, conveniently situated for both the shops and bistros north of the city centre, this guest house provides smart, thoughtfully equipped bedrooms. Breakfasts featuring a comprehensive selection of starters and hot dishes are served in the ground floor dining room.

Rooms 10 rms (6 en suite) (1 pri facs) (6 fmly) (1 GF) ⊗ in 3 bedrooms S £35-£70; D £45-£75 **Facilities** TVB tea/coffee Cen ht **Notes LB**

★★★ GUEST HOUSE
Garfield Guest House
264 Ferry Rd EH5 3AN
☎ 0131 552 2369
e-mail: enquiries@garfieldguesthouse.co.uk
PETS: Bedrooms Exercise area 50mtrs

Friendly hospitality and good value, no-frills accommodation offering modern comfortable bedrooms. Well situated within easy striking distance of the centre of Edinburgh and well serviced by a regular bus service.

Rooms 7 rms (6 en suite) (1 pri facs) (1 GF) ⊗ **Facilities** TVB tea/coffee Cen ht

FIFE

ABERDOUR   MAP 11 NT18

★★ 69% HOTEL
The Aberdour Hotel
38 High St KY3 0SW
☎ 01383 860325 📠 01383 860808
e-mail: reception@aberdourhotel.co.uk
web: www.aberdourhotel.co.uk
Dir: *M90 junct 1, E on A921 for 5m. Hotel in centre of village opp post office*
PETS: Bedrooms (GF) unattended **Charges** £10 per night **Public areas** except restaurant on leads **Exercise area** 500yds **Facilities** walks info vet info **On Request** fridge access torch

This small hotel has a relaxed and welcoming atmosphere. Real ale is featured in the cosy bar where good-value, home-cooked meals are available, as they are in the cosy dining room with its nautical theme. Bedrooms vary in size and style but all are well equipped, and those in the stable block are particularly comfortable.

Rooms 12 en suite 4 annexe en suite (4 fmly) (2 GF) ⊗ in 14 bedrooms S £45-£55; D £60-£75 (incl. bkfst)✳ **Facilities** STV Wi-fi available **Parking** 8 **Notes LB**

ANSTRUTHER   MAP 12 NO50

★★★★ 🖴 GUEST ACCOMMODATION
The Spindrift
Pittenweem Rd KY10 3DT
☎ 01333 310573 📠 01333 310573
e-mail: info@thespindrift.co.uk
web: www.thespindrift.co.uk
Dir: *Entering town from W on A917, 1st building on left*
PETS: Bedrooms Exercise area 2 mins **Facilities** water bowl bedding towels on request vet info

This immaculate Victorian villa stands on the western edge of the village. The attractive bedrooms offer a wide range of extra touches; the Captain's Room, a replica of a wood-panelled cabin, is a particular feature. The inviting lounge has an honesty bar, while imaginative breakfasts, and enjoyable home-cooked meals by arrangement, are served in the cheerful dining room.

CONTINUED

SCOTLAND

Rooms 8 rms (7 en suite) (1 pri facs) (2 fmly) ⊘ S £38.50-£48.50;
D £57-£76 **Facilities** FTV TVB tea/coffee Direct dial from bedrooms
Cen ht Dinner Last d noon Wi-fi available **Parking** 12 **Notes** LB
No children 10yrs Closed Xmas-late Jan

DUNFERMLINE   MAP 11 NT08

★★★ 75% HOTEL
Pitbauchlie House

Aberdour Rd KY11 4PB

☎ 01383 722282 📠 01383 620738

e-mail: info@pitbauchlie.com

web: www.pitbauchlie.com

Dir: M90 junct 2, onto A823, then B916. Hotel 0.5m on right

PETS: Bedrooms

This hotel is set in landscaped gardens a mile south of the town centre.
A stylish foyer and cocktail lounge catch the eye; the latter overlooking
the garden, as does the restaurant and separate bar/bistro. The
modern bedrooms are well equipped, the deluxe rooms having CD
players and videos.

Rooms 50 en suite (3 fmly) (19 GF) ⊘ in 31 bedrooms S £90-£100;
D £108-£118 (incl. bkfst)✳ **Facilities** STV Gym Wi-fi in bedrooms
Parking 80 **Notes** LB

LADYBANK   MAP 11 NO30

★★★ 74% HOTEL
Fernie Castle

Letham KY15 7RU

☎ 01337 810381 📠 01337 810422

e-mail: mail@ferniecastle.demon.co.uk

Dir: M90 junct 8 take A91 E (Tay Bridge/St Andrews) to Melville
Lodges rdbt. Left onto A92 signed Tay Bridge. Hotel 1.2m on right

PETS: Bedrooms (GF) unattended sign **Stables** nearby (3m)
Charges charge for damage **Public areas** on leads
Grounds accessible on leads disp bin **Exercise area** 50yds
Facilities food (pre-bookable) food bowl water bowl dog chews
cat treats leads washing facs cage storage walks info vet info
On Request fridge access torch towels **Resident Pets:** Cinderella
(Great Dane), Buttons (Chihuahua), Apollo (Dalmatian), Heather
(Highland cow), Hamish (Highland bull)

An historic, turreted castle set in 17 acres of wooded grounds in the
heart of Fife, that is an extremely popular venue for weddings.

Bedrooms range from King and Queen rooms, to the more
standard-sized Squire and Lady rooms. The elegant Auld Alliance
Restaurant presents a formal setting for dining, but guests can also eat
in the bar which has impressive vaulted stone walls and ceiling.

Rooms 20 en suite (2 fmly) ⊘ in 15 bedrooms S £50-£75; D £110-£180
(incl. bkfst)✳ **Facilities** ☞ Wi-fi available Xmas New Year **Parking** 80

LUNDIN LINKS   MAP 12 NO40

▶▶▶ **Woodland Gardens Caravan &
Camping Site** (NO418031)

Blindwell Rd KY8 5QG

☎ 01333 360319

e-mail: woodlandgardens@lineone.net

web: www.woodland-gardens.co.uk

Dir: Off A915 (coast road) at Largo. At E end of Lundin Links,
turn N off A915, 0.5m signed

PETS: Charges £5 per stay **Exercise area** 100yds **Facilities** disp
bags walks info vet info **Other** prior notice required
Restrictions 1 dog per unit, no dangerous breeds (see page 7)
Resident Pets: Bramble (Golden Retriever)

Open Apr-Oct Booking advisable Jul-Aug Last arrival 21.00hrs
Last departure noon

A secluded and sheltered 'little jewel' of a site in a small orchard under
the hill called Largo Law. This very attractive site is family owned and
run to an immaculate standard, and pitches are grouped in twos and
threes by low hedging and gorse. A 1-acre site with 20 touring pitches,
3 hardstandings and 4 statics.

Notes ⊗ Children over 14yrs only

NEWBURGH   MAP 11 NO21

★★★ INN
The Abbey Inn

East Port KY14 6EZ

☎ 01337 840761 📠 01337 842220

e-mail: drew@lindoresabbey.co.uk

web: www.theabbeyinn.com

Dir: On A913 High St

PETS: Bedrooms unattended **Public areas** lounge only
Grounds accessible

Situated at the east end of the village, the Abbey Inn offers comfortable
good value accommodation. The bright, well-appointed bedrooms are
on the first floor and are all en suite. There is a popular public bar and
home-made meals are served in the lounge bar.

Rooms 3 en suite ⊘ **Facilities** TVB tea/coffee Cen ht Dinner Last d
9pm Pool Table **Notes** No coaches

ST ANDREWS
MAP 12 NO51

★★★★★ ◎◎◎ HOTEL
The Old Course Hotel, Golf Resort & Spa
KY16 9SP

☎ 01334 474371 📠 01334 477668

e-mail: reservations@oldcoursehotel.co.uk

Dir: *M90 junct 8 then A91 to St Andrews*

PETS: Bedrooms (GF) unattended sign Stables nearby (2m) Charges £20 (2 nights), £30 thereafter Public areas except restaurants & bars on leads Grounds accessible on leads disp bin Exercise area 0.5m beach Facilities food (pre-bookable) food bowl water bowl bedding dog chews feeding mat map of dog walks available, pet sitting/dog walking charged at £10 per hour walks info vet info On Request fridge access torch towels

A haven for golfers, this internationally renowned hotel sits adjacent to the 17th hole of the championship course. Bedrooms vary in size and style but all provide decadent levels of luxury. Day rooms include intimate lounges, a bright conservatory, a spa and a range of pro golf shops. The fine dining 'Grill', the seafood bar 'Sands' and the informal Jigger pub are all popular eating venues. Staff throughout are friendly whilst services are impeccably delivered.

Rooms 144 en suite (5 fmly) (1 GF) ⊘ in all bedrooms S £164-£443; D £180-£473 (incl. bkfst)✳ Facilities Spa STV FTV ⊗ ♨ 18 Gym Putt green Wi-fi in bedrooms Xmas New Year Services Lift Parking 125 Notes LB

★★★★★ 83% ◎◎ HOTEL
Fairmont St Andrews
KY16 8PN

☎ 01334 837000 📠 01334 471115

e-mail: info@standrewsbay.com

PETS: Bedrooms unattended Charges £20 per stay £50 damage deposit Public areas except dining areas on leads Exercise area adjacent

Enjoying breathtaking coastal views, this modern hotel is flanked by its two golf courses. Spacious public areas centre round a stunning two-storey atrium. The lower floor contains an open-plan lounge and restaurant, whilst the upper floor features a plush bar and the delightful Esperante fine dining restaurant and cocktail bar. Extensive conference and golfing facilities are available.

Rooms 209 en suite 8 annexe en suite (86 fmly) (57 GF) ⊘ in 195 bedrooms Facilities STV ⊗ ♨ 36 Gym Putt green Clay pigeon shooting etc can be organised Services Lift air con

★★★ ◎◎ HOTEL
St Andrews Golf
40 The Scores KY16 9AS

☎ 01334 472611 📠 01334 472188

e-mail: reception@standrews-golf.co.uk

web: www.standrews-golf.co.uk

Dir: *follow signs 'Golf Course' into Golf Place and in 200yds turn right into The Scores*

PETS: Bedrooms Charges £10 per stay charge for damage Grounds accessible on leads Facilities walks info vet info On Request fridge access Resident Pets: Killie (Weimaraner)

A genuinely warm approach to guest care is found at this delightful, family-run hotel. In a stunning location the views of the beach, golf links and coastline can be enjoyed from the inviting day rooms. There is a choice of bars and an informal atmosphere in Ma Bell's. Bedrooms come in two distinct styles with those on the higher floors offering stylish, modern design and comfort.

Rooms 22 en suite ⊘ in all bedrooms Facilities STV FTV Wi-fi in bedrooms Services Lift Parking 6 Notes Closed 26-28 Dec

★★★★ ◎◎ INN
The Inn at Lathones
Largoward KY9 1JE

☎ 01334 840494 📠 01334 840694

e-mail: lathones@theinn.co.uk

web: www.theinn.co.uk

Dir: *5m S of St Andrews on A915, 0.5m before village of Largoward on left just after hidden dip*

PETS: Bedrooms (GF) unattended Charges £10 per stay charge for damage Grounds accessible on leads Facilities walks info vet info On Request fridge access torch

This lovely country inn, parts of which are 400 years old, is full of character and individuality. The friendly staff help to create a relaxed atmosphere. Smart contemporary bedrooms are in two separate wings. The colourful, cosy restaurant is the main focus, the menu offering modern interpretations of Scottish and European dishes.

Rooms 13 annexe en suite (1 fmly) (11 GF) ⊘ S £120; D £180✳ Facilities STV TVB tea/coffee Direct dial from bedrooms Cen ht TVL Dinner Last d 9.30pm Wi-fi available Parking 35 Notes LB Closed 26 Dec & 3-16 Jan RS 24 Dec

SCOTLAND

CITY OF GLASGOW

GLASGOW   **MAP 11 NS56**

★★★★ 75% ◉◉ HOTEL

Langs Hotel

2 Port Dundas Place G2 3LD

☎ 0141 333 1500 & 352 2452 📄 0141 333 5700

e-mail: reservations@langshotels.co.uk

web: www.langshotels.co.uk

Dir: *M8 junct 16, follow signs for George Square. Hotel immediately left after Concert Square car park*

PETS: Bedrooms Charges charge for damage **Public areas**
Facilities cage storage walks info vet info **On Request** fridge
access torch towels **Restrictions** small dogs only

A sharply styled, modern city centre hotel offering a choice of restaurants for dinner. Oshi has a spacious split-level, Euro-fusion style, whilst Aurora has award-winning food in a more formal dining environment. Bedrooms, all with good facilities, have various designs and some feature interesting duplex suites. State-of-the-art spa facilities ensure guests can relax and unwind.

Rooms 100 en suite (4 fmly) ⊘ in all bedrooms S £100-£125;
D £115-£135 (incl. bkfst)✳ **Facilities Spa** STV Gym Wi-fi in bedrooms
New Year **Services** Lift **Notes** LB

★★★★ GUEST ACCOMMODATION

The Kelvingrove

944 Sauchiehall St G3 7TH

☎ 0141 339 5011 📄 0141 339 6566

e-mail: info@kelvingrovehotel.com

web: www.kelvingrove-hotel.co.uk

Dir: *M8 junct 18, 0.5m along road signed Kelvingrove Museum, on left*

PETS: Bedrooms Grounds accessible **Exercise area** 1 min walk

This friendly, well-maintained establishment is in a terrace just west of the city centre, and is easily spotted in summer with its colourful floral displays. Bedrooms, including several rooms suitable for families, are well equipped and have smart, fully tiled en suite bathrooms. There is a bright breakfast room, and the reception lounge is open 24 hours.

Rooms 22 en suite (5 fmly) (3 GF) ⊘ S £40-£70; D £70-£100✳
Facilities TVB tea/coffee Direct dial from bedrooms Cen ht **Notes** LB

★★★ GUEST HOUSE

Botanic Guest House

1 Alfred Ter, Great Western Rd G12 8RF

☎ 0141 337 7007 📄 0141 337 7007

e-mail: info@botanichotel.co.uk

Dir: *15 mins by car from Glasgow airport*

PETS: Bedrooms Charges £15 per night **Public areas**
Facilities walks info

The Botanic is located just off the Great Western Road alongside other guest accommodation and residential properties only 2 miles from the heart of the city centre. Comfortable bedrooms and well-presented bathrooms provide good value for money. A generous breakfast makes a good start to the day.

Rooms 16 rms (13 en suite) (5 fmly) (3 GF) **Facilities** TVB tea/coffee
Direct dial from bedrooms **Notes** No coaches

★★★ GUEST HOUSE

The Kelvin

15 Buckingham Ter, Great Western Rd, Hillhead G12 8EB

☎ 0141 339 7143 📄 0141 339 5215

e-mail: enquiries@kelvinhotel.com

web: www.kelvinhotel.com

Dir: *M8 junct 17, A82 Kelvinside/Dumbarton, 1m on right*

PETS: Bedrooms Exercise area nearby **Facilities** food bowl
water bowl walks info vet info **On Request** fridge access torch

Two substantial Victorian terrace houses on the west side of the city have been combined to create this friendly establishment close to the Botanical Gardens. The attractive bedrooms are comfortably proportioned and well equipped. The dining room on the first floor is the setting for hearty traditional breakfasts served at individual tables.

Rooms 21 rms (9 en suite) (5 fmly) (2 GF) ⊘ S £26-£46; D £50-£64✳
Facilities TVB tea/coffee Cen ht **Parking** 5

★★★ GUEST ACCOMMODATION

The Merchant Lodge

52 Virginia St G1 1TY

☎ 0141 552 2424 📄 0141 552 4747

e-mail: themerchant@ukonline.co.uk

web: www.merchantlodgehotel.com

Dir: *Off George Sq onto North Hanover St, towards Ingram St, onto Virginia Place & Virginia St*

PETS: Bedrooms unattended **Exercise area** 0.5m

Set within The Merchant City and close to Argyle Street, this former home of a tobacco lord features a cobbled courtyard and stone turnpike stair. The house, on five floors, has been fully modernised with pine floors, pine furniture and pleasant understated decor. Breakfast is fully self-service in a bright and cheerful lower level room.

Rooms 34 en suite 6 annexe en suite (8 fmly) (6 GF) **Facilities** TVB tea/
coffee Direct dial from bedrooms Cen ht

SCOTLAND

HIGHLAND

CARRBRIDGE   MAP 14 NH92

★★★ GUEST HOUSE
Pines Country House
Duthil PH23 3ND
☎ 01479 841220 🖨 01479 841220
e-mail: Lynn@thepines-duthil.fsnet.co.uk
Dir: *2m E of Carrbridge in Duthil on A938*
PETS: Bedrooms (GF) unattended sign **Grounds** accessible on leads disp bin **Facilities** food (pre-bookable) food bowl water bowl dog chews dog scoop/disp bags leads pet sitting dog walking washing facs cage storage walks info vet info
On Request fridge access torch towels **Resident Pets:** Corrie (English Springer Spaniel), Rhea (Golden Labrador)

A warm welcome is assured at this comfortable home in the Cairngorms National Park. The bright bedrooms are traditionally furnished and offer good amenities. Enjoyable home-cooked fare is served around a communal table. Relax in the conservatory-lounge and watch squirrels feed in the nearby woods.

Rooms 4 en suite (1 fmly) (1 GF) ⊗ S £35; D £50 **Facilities** STV TVB tea/coffee Cen ht Dinner Last d 4pm **Parking** 5 **Notes** LB No coaches

CONTIN   MAP 14 NH45

★★★ 76% ❀ COUNTRY HOUSE HOTEL
Coul House
IV14 9ES
☎ 01997 421487 🖨 01997 421945
e-mail: stay@coulhousehotel.com
Dir: *Exit A9 north onto A835. Hotel on right*
PETS: Bedrooms (GF) unattended **Charges** £5 per night **Public areas** except dining areas **Grounds** accessible **Facilities** cage storage walks info vet info **On Request** fridge access torch

This imposing mansion house is set back from the road in extensive grounds. A number of the generally spacious bedrooms have superb views of the distant mountains and all are thoughtfully equipped. The Octagonal Restaurant offers guests the chance to enjoy contemporary Scottish cuisine.

Rooms 20 en suite (3 fmly) (4 GF) ⊗ in all bedrooms S £75-£95; D £95-£210 (incl. bkfst) **Facilities** Putt green Wi-fi in bedrooms 9 hole pitch & putt New Year **Parking** 60 **Notes** LB

CORPACH   MAP 14 NN07

►►►►► **Linnhe Lochside Holidays**
(NN074771)
PH33 7NL
☎ 01397 772376 🖨 01397 772007
e-mail: relax@linnhe-lochside-holidays.co.uk
web: www.linnhe-lochside-holidays.co.uk
Dir: *On A830, 1m W of Corpach, 5m from Fort William*
PETS: Charges £5 per night £25 per week **Public areas** **Exercise area** on site dog walk area & long beach **Facilities** on site shop food food bowl water bowl dog chews cat treats dog scoop/disp bags washing facs walks info vet info **Other** prior notice required **Resident Pets:** dogs, cats, ferrets & chickens

Open Etr-Oct (rs 15 Dec-Etr shop/main wc block closed) Booking advisable school hols & peak periods Last arrival 21.00hrs Last departure 11.00hrs

An excellently maintained site in a beautiful setting on the shores of Loch Eil, with Ben Nevis to the east and the mountains and Sunart to the west. The owners have worked in harmony with nature to produce an idyllic environment, where they offer the highest standards of design and maintenance. A 5.5-acre site with 85 touring pitches, 63 hardstandings and 20 statics.

Notes no cars by tents

DAVIOT   MAP 14 NH73

►►► **Auchnahillin Caravan and Camping Centre** *(NH742386)*
IV2 5XQ
☎ 01463 772286
e-mail: info@auchnahillin.co.uk
web: www.auchnahillin.co.uk
Dir: *7m S of Inverness, just off A9 on B9154 (Daviot-East & Moy road)*
PETS: Stables onsite (loose box) **Public areas** except play area & amenity building **Exercise area** on site dog walk forests and moorland 2m **Facilities** on site shop washing facs walks info vet info **Other** prior notice required **Restrictions** no dangerous dogs (see page 7)

Open 15 Mar-Oct Booking advisable Jun-Aug Last arrival 21.00hrs Last departure 17.00hrs

Surrounded by hills and forests, this level, grassy site offers clean and spacious facilities. The owner lives in a bungalow on the site. A 10-acre site with 75 touring pitches, 4 hardstandings and 35 statics.

Notes No noise after midnight, limited facilities for disabled visitors

SCOTLAND

DINGWALL
MAP 14 NH55

►►► Dingwall Camping & Caravanning Club Site (NH555588)

Jubilee Park Rd IV15 9QZ

☎ 01349 862236

web: www.campingandcaravanningclub.co.uk

Dir: *A862 to Dingwall, right onto Hill Street, past filling station. Right onto High Street, 1st left after railway bridge. Site ahead*

PETS: Facilities walks info vet info **Other** prior notice required

Open Apr-Oct Booking advisable BH & peak periods Last arrival 21.00hrs Last departure noon

A quiet park with attractive landscaping and very good facilities maintained to a high standard. A convenient touring centre, close to the historic market town of Dingwall. A 6.5-acre site with 83 touring pitches.

FORT WILLIAM
MAP 14 NN17

★★★ 79% @ HOTEL
Moorings

Banavie PH33 7LY

☎ 01397 772797 📠 01397 772441

e-mail: reservations@moorings-fortwilliam.co.uk

web: www.moorings-fortwilliam.co.uk

Dir: *take A380 (N from Fort William), cross Caledonian Canal, 1st right*

PETS: Bedrooms Charges £5 per stay **Public areas** except at food service **Grounds** accessible **Exercise area** 100yds **Other** Pet blanket provided

Located on the Caledonian Canal next to a series of locks known as Neptune's Staircase, and close to Thomas Telford's house, this hotel with its dedicated, young staff offers friendly service. Accommodation comes in two distinct styles and the newer rooms are particularly appealing. Meals can be taken in the bars or the spacious dining room.

Rooms 27 en suite (1 fmly) (1 GF) ⊘ in 24 bedrooms S £39-£122; D £78-£138 (incl. bkfst)✱ **Facilities** STV Wi-fi available New Year **Parking** 60 **Notes LB** Closed 22-27 Dec

►►►► Glen Nevis Caravan & Camping Park (NN124722)

Glen Nevis PH33 6SX

☎ 01397 702191 📠 01397 703904

e-mail: holidays@glen-nevis.co.uk

web: www.glen-nevis.co.uk

Dir: *In northern outskirts of Fort William follow A82 to mini-rdbt. Exit for Glen Nevis. Site 2.5m on right*

PETS: Public areas Exercise area on site & 100mtrs **Facilities** on site shop food dog chews cat treats disp bags walks info vet info

Open 15 Mar-Oct (rs Mar & mid-end Oct limited shop & restaurant facilities) Booking advisable Jul-Aug Last arrival 22.00hrs Last departure noon

A tasteful site with well-screened enclosures, at the foot of Ben Nevis in the midst of some of the Highlands' most spectacular scenery; an ideal area for walking and touring. The park boasts a restaurant which offers a high standard of cooking and provides good value for money. A 30-acre site with 380 touring pitches, 150 hardstandings and 30 statics.

Notes Closed to vehicle entry 23.00hrs, quiet 23.00hrs-08.00hrs

GAIRLOCH
MAP 14 NG87

★★★ ⊜ INN
The Old Inn

Flowerdale Glen IV21 2BD

☎ 01445 712006 📠 01445 712445

e-mail: info@theoldinn.net

web: www.theoldinn.co.uk

Dir: *A832 into Gairloch, establishment on right opp Gairloch harbour*

PETS: Bedrooms Charges £5 per night **Public areas** except dining areas **Exercise area** nearby **Facilities** water bowl bedding cage storage walks info vet info **On Request** fridge access torch **Resident Pets:** Muscovy ducks

Situated close to the harbour, this well-established and lively inn has an idyllic location overlooking the burn and the old bridge. A good range of meals, many featuring seafood, are served in the bars and dining areas, and outside at picnic tables on finer days. Live music is a feature several evenings a week. Bedrooms are well equipped and attractively decorated.

Rooms 14 en suite (3 fmly) (2 GF) ⊘ S £32-£50; D £49-£95 **Facilities** STV TVB tea/coffee Direct dial from bedrooms Cen ht Dinner Last d 9.30pm Wi-fi available Pool Table **Parking** 40 **Notes LB** No coaches

GAIRLOCH CONTINUED

►►► Sands Holiday Centre (NG758784)

IV21 2DL

☎ 01445 712152 🖹 01445 712518

e-mail: litsands@aol.co.uk

web: www.highlandcaravancamping.co.uk

Dir: *3m W of Gairloch on B8021*

PETS: Public areas Exercise area dog walk adjacent
Facilities on site shop food food bowl water bowl dog chews
cat treats dog scoop/disp bags vet info space for loose box

Open 20 May-10 Sep (rs Apr-19 May & 11 Sep-mid Oct shop
& some toilets closed) Booking advisable Jul-Aug Last arrival
22.00hrs Last departure noon

Close to a sandy beach with a panoramic outlook towards Skye, a
well-maintained park with very good facilities. A large laundry and
refitted toilets make this an ideal family site. A 51-acre site with 360
touring pitches and 20 statics.

GLENCOE   MAP 14 NN15

►►► Glencoe Camping & Caravanning Club Site (NN111578)

PH49 4LA

☎ 01855 811397

web: www.campingandcaravanningclub.co.uk

Dir: *1m SE from Glencoe village on A82, follow Glencoe visitors' centre sign*

PETS: Exercise area on site dog walk Facilities on site shop
walks info vet info Other prior notice required

Open Apr-Oct Booking advisable BH & peak periods Last
arrival 21.00hrs Last departure noon

A partly sloping site with separate areas of grass and gravel hardstands.
Set in mountainous woodland one mile from the village, and adjacent
to the visitors' centre. A 40-acre site with 120 touring pitches, 55
hardstandings.

GLENFINNAN   MAP 14 NM98

★★ 75% ◉◉ SMALL HOTEL

The Prince's House

PH37 4LT

☎ 01397 722246 🖹 01397 722323

e-mail: princeshouse@glenfinnan.co.uk

web: www.glenfinnan.co.uk

Dir: *on A830, 0.5m on right past Glenfinnan Monument. 200mtrs from railway station*

PETS: Bedrooms Charges £5 per stay charge for damage
Public areas except restaurant Grounds accessible disp bin
Facilities most facilities available if pre-arranged
Resident Pets: Floren (cat)

This delightful hotel enjoys a well deserved reputation for fine food
and excellent hospitality. The hotel sits close to where 'Bonnie' Prince
Charlie raised the Jacobite standard and has inspiring views.
Comfortably appointed bedrooms offer pleasing decor and bathrooms.
Excellent local game and seafood can be enjoyed in the restaurant and
the bar.

Rooms 9 en suite (1 fmly) ⊗ in all bedrooms S £55-£75; D £85-£120
(incl. bkfst) Facilities Fishing New Year Parking 18 Notes LB Closed
Xmas & Jan-Feb (ex New Year) RS Nov-Dec & Mar

GRANTOWN-ON-SPEY   MAP 14 NJ02

►►►► Grantown-on-Spey Caravan Park (NJ028283)

Seafield Av PH26 3JQ

☎ 01479 872474 🖹 01479 873696

e-mail: warden@caravanscotland.com

web: www.caravanscotland.com

Dir: *From town turn N at Bank of Scotland, park in 0.25m*

PETS: Public areas Exercise area on site dog walk provided
various walks Facilities on site shop food bowl water bowl dog
chews cat treats washing facs walks info vet info

Open 15 Dec-Oct Booking advisable Etr, May Day, spring BH
& Jul-Aug Last arrival 22.00hrs Last departure noon

A scenic park in a mature setting near the river, surrounded by hills,
mountains, moors and woodland. The park is very well landscaped,
and is in a good location for golf, fishing, mountaineering, walking,
sailing and canoeing. Fully-serviced pitches are much sought after, and
there is a luxury toilet block. A 29-acre site with 120 touring pitches, 60
hardstandings and 45 statics.

JOHN O'GROATS MAP 15 ND37

▶▶▶ John O'Groats Caravan Site (ND382733)

KW1 4YR

☎ 01955 611329 & 07762 336359 📠 01955 611329

e-mail: info@johnogroatscampsite.co.uk

web: www.johnogroatscampsite.co.uk

Dir: *At end of A99*

PETS: Exercise area 50mtrs **Facilities** washing facs walks info vet info

Open Apr-Sep Booking advisable Last arrival 22.00hrs Last departure noon

An attractive site in an open position above the seashore and looking out towards the Orkney Islands. The passenger ferry which runs day trips to the Orkneys is nearby, and there are grey seals to watch, and sea angling organised by the site owners. A 4-acre site with 90 touring pitches, 20 hardstandings.

LOCHINVER MAP 14 NC02

★★★★ 🏵 HOTEL

Inver Lodge

IV27 4LU

☎ 01571 844496 📠 01571 844395

e-mail: stay@inverlodge.com

web: www.inverlodgehotel.com

Dir: *A835 to Lochinver, through village, left after village hall, follow private road for 0.5m*

PETS: Bedrooms (GF) unattended **Charges** charge for damage **Public areas** in front foyer lounge only **Grounds** accessible **Facilities** washing facs cage storage walks info vet info **On Request** fridge access torch towels **Resident Pets:** Sam (Cairn Terrier)

Genuine hospitality is a real feature at this delightful, purpose-built hotel. Set high on the hillside above the village all bedrooms and public rooms enjoy stunning views. There is a choice of lounges and a restaurant where chefs make use of the abundant local produce. Bedrooms are spacious, stylish and come with an impressive range of accessories. There is no night service between 11pm and 7am.

Rooms 20 en suite (11 GF) ⊘ in 18 bedrooms S £155; D £200 (incl. bkfst)✳ **Facilities** FTV Fishing Wi-fi in bedrooms **Parking** 30 **Notes LB** Closed Nov-Apr

---

MALLAIG MAP 13 NM69

★★ 70% HOTEL

West Highland

PH41 4QZ

☎ 01687 462210 📠 01687 462130

e-mail: westhighland.hotel@virgin.net

Dir: *from Fort William turn right at rdbt then 1st right up hill, from ferry left at rdbt then 1st right uphill*

PETS: Bedrooms Grounds accessible on leads disp bin **Facilities** food bowl water bowl washing facs cage storage walks info vet info **On Request** torch

Originally the town's station hotel the original building was destroyed by fire and the current hotel built on the same site in the early 20th century. Fine views over to Skye are a real feature of the public rooms which include a bright airy conservatory, whilst the attractive bedrooms are thoughtfully equipped and generally spacious.

Rooms 34 en suite (6 fmly) ⊘ in 6 bedrooms S £41-£46; D £72-£80 (incl. bkfst)✳ **Facilities** ♫ **Parking** 40 **Notes LB** Closed 16 Oct-15 Mar RS 16 Mar-1 Apr

---

MUIR OF ORD MAP 14 NH55

★★ 71% 🏵 HOTEL

Ord House

IV6 7UH

☎ 01463 870492 📠 01463 870297

e-mail: admin@ord-house.co.uk

Dir: *off A9 at Tore rdbt onto A832. 5m, through Muir of Ord. Left towards Ullapool (still A832). Hotel 0.5m on left*

PETS: Bedrooms (GF) unattended **Public areas** except restaurant **Grounds** accessible disp bin **Facilities** food (pre-bookable) food bowl water bowl dog scoop/disp bags leads washing facs walks info vet info **On Request** fridge access torch towels **Resident Pets:** Tatty (Black Labrador)

Dating back to 1637, this country-house hotel is situated peacefully in wooded grounds and offers brightly furnished and well-proportioned accommodation. Comfortable day rooms reflect the character and

CONTINUED

MUIR OF ORD CONTINUED

charm of the house, with inviting lounges, a cosy snug bar and an elegant dining room where wide-ranging, creative menus are offered.

Rooms 12 en suite (3 GF) S £40; D £104 (incl. bkfst)❄ **Facilities** no TV in bdrms ⚓ Putt green Wi-fi in bedrooms Clay pigeon shooting **Parking** 30 **Notes** LB Closed Nov-Apr

NAIRN   MAP 14 NH85

▶▶▶ **Nairn Camping & Caravanning Club Site** (NH847551)

Delnies Wood IV12 5NX

☎ 01667 455281

web: www.campingandcaravanningclub.co.uk

Dir: *Off A96 (Inverness to Aberdeen road). 2m W of Nairn*

PETS: Public areas except buildings **Exercise area** on site dog walks woods **Facilities** vet info

Open Apr-Oct Booking advisable BHs & peak periods Last arrival 21.00hrs Last departure noon

An attractive site set amongst pine trees, with facilities maintained to a good standard. The park is close to Nairn with its beaches, shopping, golf and leisure activities. A 14-acre site with 75 touring pitches.

NEWTONMORE   MAP 14 NN79

★★★★ GUEST HOUSE

Crubenbeg House

Falls of Truim PH20 1BE

☎ 01540 673300

e-mail: enquiries@crubenbeghouse.com

web: www.crubenbeghouse.com

Dir: *4m S of Newtonmore. Off A9 for Crubenmore, over railway bridge & right, signed*

PETS: Bedrooms (GF) **Public areas Grounds** accessible disp bin **Facilities** food (pre-bookable) food bowl water bowl dog chews feeding mat dog scoop/disp bags leads pet sitting dog walking washing facs cage storage walks info vet info **On Request** fridge access torch towels **Resident Pets:** Rajah (Saluki-Alsatian cross)

Set in peaceful rural location, Crubenbeg House has stunning country views and is well located for touring the Highlands. The attractive bedrooms are individually styled and well equipped, while the ground-floor bedroom provides easier access. You can enjoy a dram in front of the fire in the inviting lounge, while breakfast features the best of local produce in the adjacent dining room.

Rooms 4 rms (3 en suite) (1 pri facs) (1 GF) ⊗ S £30-£36; D £50-£80 **Facilities** STV TVB tea/coffee Licensed Cen ht Dinner Last d 4pm **Parking** 10 **Notes** LB No children No coaches

ONICH   MAP 14 NN06

★★★ 81% ⚜ HOTEL

Onich

PH33 6RY

☎ 01855 821214 📄 01855 821484

e-mail: enquiries@onich-fortwilliam.co.uk

web: www.onich-fortwilliam.co.uk

Dir: *beside A82, 2m N of Ballachulish Bridge*

PETS: Bedrooms unattended **Charges** £5 per stay per night **Public areas** except at food service on leads **Grounds** accessible disp bin **Facilities** washing facs cage storage walks info vet info pet blanket **On Request** fridge access torch towels

Genuine hospitality is part of the appeal of this hotel, which lies right beside Loch Linnhe with gardens extending to shores. Nicely presented public areas include a choice of inviting lounges and contrasting bars, and views of the loch can be enjoyed from the attractive restaurant. Bedrooms, with pleasing colour schemes, are comfortably modern.

Rooms 26 en suite (6 fmly) ⊗ in 21 bedrooms **Facilities** STV Games room **Parking** 50 **Notes** LB Closed 22-27 Dec

PLOCKTON   MAP 14 NG83

★★ 75% HOTEL

Haven

3 Innes St IV52 8TW

☎ 01599 544223 & 544334 📄 01599 544467

e-mail: reception@havenhotelplockton.co.uk

web: www.havenhotelplockton.co.uk

Dir: *off A87 just before Kyle of Lochalsh, after Balmacara signed to Plockton, hotel on main road just before lochside*

PETS: Bedrooms Charges £10 per night **Grounds** on leads disp bin **Exercise area** countryside **Facilities** vet info

A delightful hotel situated in this picturesque west Highland village and only a short walk from the seashore. A choice of eating options includes an attractive restaurant offering an imaginative dinner menu, or Motley's the popular bistro. Bedrooms are all smartly presented and include two spacious family rooms.

Rooms 15 en suite (1 fmly) ⊗ in all bedrooms **Parking** 5 **Notes** LB

POOLEWE MAP 14 NG88

►►► Inverewe Camping & Caravanning Club Site (NG862812)

Inverewe Gardens IV22 2LF

☎ 01445 781249

web: www.campingandcaravanningclub.co.uk

Dir: On A832, N of Poolewe village

PETS: Public areas except buildings Facilities walks info vet info
Other prior notice required

Open Apr-Oct Booking advisable BH & peak period Last arrival
21.00hrs Last departure noon

A well-run site located in Loch Ewe Bay, not far from Inverewe
Gardens. The Club has improved this site in the past few years, and
continues to upgrade the facilities. The warm waters of the Gulf Stream
attract otters and seals. A 3-acre site with 55 touring pitches, 8
hardstandings.

RESIPOLE (LOCH SUNART) MAP 13 NM76

►►►► Resipole Farm (NM725639)

PH36 4HX

☎ 01967 431235 📠 01967 431777

e-mail: info@resipole.co.uk

web: www.resipole.co.uk

Dir: From Corran Ferry take A861. Park 8m W of Strontian

PETS: Public areas on leads Exercise area on site walks through
woods shore line nearby Facilities on site shop food dog chews
cat treats disp bags walks info vet info

Open Apr-Oct Booking advisable bookings only for elecetric
hook ups Last arrival 22.00hrs Last departure 11.00hrs

A quiet, relaxing park in beautiful surroundings, with deer frequently
sighted, and of great interest to naturalists. Situated on the saltwater
Loch Sunart in the Ardnamurchan Peninsula, and offering a great deal
of space and privacy. An 8-acre site with 85 touring pitches, 30
hardstandings and 9 statics.

ROSEMARKIE MAP 14 NH75

►►► Rosemarkie Camping & Caravanning Club Site (NH739569)

Ness Rd East IV10 8SE

☎ 01381 621117

web: www.campingandcaravanningclub.co.uk

Dir: Take A832. A9 at Tore rdbt. Through Avoch, Fortrose then
right at police house. Down Ness Rd. 1st left, small turn signed
Golf & Caravan site

PETS: Public areas except buildings Exercise area on site
Facilities walks info vet info Other prior notice required

Open Apr-Oct Booking advisable BH & peak period Last arrival
21.00hrs Last departure noon

A superb club site set along the water's edge, with beautiful views over
the bay where resident dolphins swim. Two excellent toilet blocks,
including a disabled room, and a family room with combined facilities,
have greatly enhanced the facilities here. A smart reception area sets
the standard for this very clean and well-maintained site. A 4-acre site
with 60 touring pitches.

SCOURIE MAP 14 NC14

★★ 78% HOTEL
Scourie

IV27 4SX

☎ 01971 502396 📠 01971 502423

e-mail: patrick@scourie-hotel.co.uk

Dir: N'bound on A894. Hotel in village on left

PETS: Bedrooms (GF) unattended Charges charge for damage
Public areas except dining area Grounds accessible disp bin
Exercise area 200yds Facilities cage storage walks info vet info
On Request fridge access Restrictions Telephone for details
Resident Pets: Molly (Springer Spaniel), Jessie & Clemmie (cats),
Minstrel & Angus (horses)

This well-established hotel is an angler's paradise with extensive fishing
rights available on a 25,000-acre estate. Public areas include a choice
of comfortable lounges, a cosy bar and a smart dining room offering
wholesome fare. The bedrooms are comfortable and generally
spacious and the resident proprietors and their staff create a relaxed
and friendly atmosphere.

Rooms 18 rms (17 en suite) 2 annexe en suite (2 fmly) (5 GF) ⊗ in all
bedrooms S £31-£41; D £66-£86 (incl. bkfst)✳ Facilities no TV in bdrms
Fishing Wi-fi available Sea, trout & salmon fishing Parking 30
Notes Closed mid Oct-end Mar

SCOTLAND

SCOTLAND

SOUTH BALLACHULISH MAP 14 NN05

★★★★ GUEST HOUSE
Lyn-Leven
West Laroch PH49 4JP
☎ 01855 811392 📠 01855 811600
e-mail: macleodcilla@aol.com
web: www.lynleven.co.uk
Dir: *Off A82 signed on left West Laroch*
PETS: Bedrooms Exercise area nearby
Genuine Highland hospitality and high standards are part of the appeal of this comfortable guest house. The attractive bedrooms vary in size, are well equipped, offering many thoughtful extra touches. There is a spacious lounge and a smart dining room where delicious home-cooked evening meals and breakfasts are served at individual tables.

Rooms 8 en suite 4 annexe en suite (3 fmly) (12 GF) ⊗ S £30-£50; D £50-£64✱ **Facilities** TVB tea/coffee Licensed Cen ht TVL Dinner Last d 7pm **Parking** 12 **Notes LB** Closed Xmas

SPEAN BRIDGE MAP 14 NN28

★★★★★  GUEST HOUSE
The Smiddy House
Roy Bridge Rd PH34 4EU
☎ 01397 712335 📠 01397 712043
e-mail: enquiry@smiddyhouse.co.uk
web: www.smiddyhouse.co.uk
Dir: *In village centre, A82 onto A86*
PETS: Bedrooms Charges £3 per night **Exercise area** 0.5m
Resident Pets: Cara (King Charles Cavalier)
Set within the 'Great Glen', which stretches from Fort William to Inverness, this was once the village smithy, and is now a friendly guest house. The attractive bedrooms, which are named after Scottish places and whiskies, are comfortably furnished and well equipped. Delicious evening meals are served in the Russell's Bistro, which has achieved two AA Rosettes.

Rooms 4 en suite (1 fmly) ⊗ S £55-£70; D £65-£80 **Facilities** TVB tea/coffee Licensed Dinner Last d 9.30pm **Parking** 15 **Notes** Closed Nov

★★★★ GUEST HOUSE
Distant Hills Guest House
Roy Bridge Rd PH34 4EU
☎ 01397 712452 📠 01397 712452
e-mail: enquiry@distanthills.com
web: www.distanthills.com
Dir: *A82 onto A86 at Spean Bridge, 0.5m on right*
PETS: Bedrooms (GF) **Charges** £5 per night £35 per week charge for damage **Public areas** except dining room on leads **Grounds** accessible on leads disp bin **Exercise area** 0.5m **Facilities** walks info vet info **Resident Pets:** Sox (cat)
A friendly welcome is assured at this family-run guest house set in a large, well-tended garden. Bedrooms are maintained to a high standard with modern appointments. There is a spacious split-level lounge, with access to the garden. Enjoyable home-cooked evening meals (by arrangement) and hearty Scottish breakfasts are served at individual tables in the peaceful dining room.

Rooms 7 en suite (1 fmly) (7 GF) ⊗ D £60-£80✱ **Facilities** TVB tea/coffee Cen ht TVL Dinner Last d 24hrs notice **Parking** 11 **Notes** No coaches

★★★ FARM HOUSE
Achnabobane *(NN195811)*
PH34 4EX
☎ 01397 712919 Mr and Mrs N Ockenden
e-mail: enquiries@achnabobane.co.uk
web: www.achnabobane.co.uk
Dir: *2m S of Spean Bridge on A82*
PETS: Bedrooms (GF) **Charges** charge for damage **Public areas** except lounge & restaurant on leads **Grounds** accessible **Facilities** dog scoop/disp bags cage storage walks info vet info **On Request** fridge access torch towels **Resident Pets:** Morse (Cavalier King Charles Spaniel), Bea, Korky & Dyllon (cats), 10 chickens, 1 cockerel

With breathtaking views of Ben Nevis, Aonach Mhor and the Grey Corries, the farmhouse offers comfortable, good-value accommodation in a friendly family environment. Bedrooms are traditional in style and well equipped. Breakfast and evening meals are served in the conservatory-dining room. Pets welcome.

Rooms 4 rms (1 en suite) (1 fmly) (1 GF) ⊗ S £28; D £56✱ **Facilities** STV TV3B tea/coffee Cen ht TVL Dinner Last d 1pm **Parking** 5 **Notes** Closed Xmas

STRONTIAN
MAP 14 NM86

★★★ ◎◎ COUNTRY HOUSE HOTEL

Kilcamb Lodge

PH36 4HY

☎ 01967 402257 📄 01967 402041

e-mail: enquiries@kilcamblodge.co.uk

web: www.kilcamblodge.co.uk

Dir: *off A861, via Corran Ferry*

PETS: Bedrooms sign **Charges** dogs £5 per night £30 per week charge for damage **Grounds** accessible 22 acre grounds disp bin **Facilities** food (pre-bookable) dog chews dog scoop/disp bags washing facs cage storage walks info vet info **On Request** fridge access torch towels

This historic house on the shores of Loch Sunart was one of the first stone buildings in the area and was used as military barracks around the time of the Jacobite uprising. Accommodation is provided in tastefully decorated rooms with high quality fabrics. Accomplished cooking, utilising much local produce, can be enjoyed in the stylish dining room. Warm hospitality is assured.

Rooms 10 en suite ⊘ in all bedrooms S £85-£120; D £150-£250 (incl. bkfst) **Facilities** Fishing Wi-fi available Boating Hiking Bird, whale and otter watching Xmas New Year **Parking** 18 **Notes** LB No children 12yrs Closed 2 Jan-1 Feb

TAIN
MAP 14 NH78

▶▶▶ **Dornoch Firth Caravan Park** *(NH749843)*

Meikle Ferry South IV19 1JX

☎ 01862 892292

e-mail: will@dornochfirth.co.uk

web: www.dornochfirth.co.uk

Dir: *Follow A9 N past Tain to Meikle ferry rdbt, straight across onto A836 then immediate 1st right*

PETS: Charges £1 per night **Public areas** except play ground **Exercise area** on site large grassland area **Facilities** walks info vet info **Other** prior notice required **Restrictions** no dangerous breeds (see page 7) **Resident Pets:** Mac (Springer Spaniel)

Open all year (rs Nov-Mar static caravans closed) Booking advisable Jul-Aug Last arrival 22.00hrs Last departure noon

A pleasant family site with open views of Dornoch Firth and the lovely coastal and country scenery. The immaculately maintained facilities

and pretty flower beds make this a delightful base for touring the immediate vicinity with its many places of interest. A 3.5-acre site with 30 touring pitches, 10 hardstandings and 30 statics.

TONGUE
MAP 14 NC55

★★ 74% ◎ HOTEL

Ben Loyal

Main St IV27 4XE

☎ 01847 611216 📄 01847 611212

e-mail: benloyalhotel@btinternet.com

web: www.benloyal.co.uk

Dir: *at junct of A838/A836. Hotel by Royal Bank of Scotland*

PETS: Bedrooms unattended **Charges** charge for damage **Public areas** bar only & not at meal times **Grounds** accessible disp bin **Facilities** walks info vet info **Resident Pets:** Jasper (Cocker Spaniel), Beanie (cat)

Enjoying a super location close to Ben Loyal and with views of the Kyle of Tongue, this hotel more often that not marks the welcome completion of a stunning highland and coastal drive. Bedrooms are thoughtfully equipped and brightly decorated whilst day rooms extend to a traditionally styled dining room and a cosy bar. Extensive menus ensure there's something for everyone. Staff are especially friendly and provide useful local information.

Rooms 11 en suite ⊘ in all bedrooms S £35-£40; D £70-£80 (incl. bkfst) ✳ **Facilities** Fishing Fly fishing tuition and equipment **Parking** 20 **Notes** Closed 30 Nov-1 Mar

ULLAPOOL
MAP 14 NH19

▶▶▶ **Broomfield Holiday Park** *(NH123939)*

West Shore St IV26 2UT

☎ 01854 612020 & 612664 📄 01854 613151

e-mail: sross@broomfieldhp.com

web: www.broomfieldhp.com

Dir: *Take 2nd right past harbour*

PETS: Public areas except play area & toilet on leads **Exercise area** on site beach **Facilities** washing facs walks info vet info

Open Etr/Apr-Sep Booking advisable for group bookings only Last departure noon

Set right on the water's edge of Loch Broom and the open sea, with lovely views of the Summer Isles. The park is close to the harbour and town centre with their restaurants, bars and shops. A 12-acre site with 140 touring pitches.

Notes no noise at night

SCOTLAND

WHITEBRIDGE MAP 14 NH41

★★ 68% HOTEL
Whitebridge

IV2 6UN

☎ 01456 486226 ≣ 01456 486413

e-mail: info@whitebridgehotel.co.uk

Dir: *off A9 onto B851, follow signs to Fort Augustus. Off A82 onto B862 at Fort Augustus*

PETS: Bedrooms Public areas except restaurant on leads **Grounds** accessible **Facilities** water bowl walks info vet info

Close to Loch Ness and set amid rugged mountain and moorland scenery this hotel is popular with tourists, fishermen and deerstalkers. Guests have a choice of more formal dining in the restaurant or lighter meals in the popular cosy bar. Bedrooms are thoughtfully equipped and brightly furnished.

Rooms 12 en suite (3 fmly) ⊛ in all bedrooms S £38-£44; D £58-£66 (incl. bkfst) **Facilities** Fishing Wi-fi in bedrooms **Parking** 32 **Notes** Closed 11 Dec - 9 Jan

MIDLOTHIAN

ROSLIN MAP 11 NT26

★★★ INN
The Original Roslin Inn

4 Main St EH25 9LE

☎ 0131 440 2384 ≣ 0131 440 2514

e-mail: enquiries@theoriginalhotel.co.uk

Dir: *Off city bypass at Straiton for A703, Inn is close to Roslin Chapel*

PETS: Bedrooms Grounds accessible **Exercise area** on site 10yds

Whether you find yourself on the Da Vinci Code trail or in the area on business, this property is within easy distance of the famous Roslin Chapel which is well worth the visit. A delightful village inn offers well-equipped bedrooms with upgraded en suites. Four of the rooms have four-poster beds. The Grail Restaurant, the lounge and conservatory offer a comprehensive selection of dining options.

Rooms 6 en suite (2 fmly) ⊛ **Facilities** STV TVB tea/coffee Cen ht Dinner Last d 9.30pm **Parking** 8

MORAY

ARCHIESTOWN MAP 15 NJ24

★★ 83% ⚘ SMALL HOTEL
Archiestown

AB38 7QL

☎ 01340 810218 ≣ 01340 810239

e-mail: jah@archiestownhotel.co.uk

web: www.archiestownhotel.co.uk

Dir: *A95 Craigellachie, follow B9102 to Archiestown, 4m*

PETS: Bedrooms Charges £5 per night charge for damage **Grounds** accessible disp bin **Exercise area** adjacent **Facilities** food bowl water bowl washing facs cage storage walks info vet info **On Request** fridge access torch towels **Resident Pets:** Dax & Sam (cats)

Set in the heart of this Speyside village this small hotel is popular with anglers and locals alike. It is rightly noted for its great hospitality, attentive service and good food. Cosy and comfortable public rooms include a choice of lounges (there is no bar as such) and a bistro offering an inviting choice of dishes at both lunch and dinner.

Rooms 11 en suite (1 fmly) ⊛ in all bedrooms S £60-£75; D £80-£120 (incl. bkfst)✳ **Facilities** ⤴ Wi-fi in bedrooms New Year **Parking** 20 **Notes** LB Closed 24-27 Dec & 3 Jan-9 Feb

CRAIGELLACHIE MAP 15 NJ24

►►► **Speyside Camping & Caravanning Club Site** *(NJ257449)*

AB38 9SD

☎ 01340 810414

web: www.campingandcaravanningclub.co.uk

Dir: *From S exit A9 at Carrbridge, A95 to Grantown-on-Spey, leave Aberlour on A941. Take next left onto B9102 signed Archiestown. Site 3m on left*

PETS: Public areas except buildings **Exercise area** on site **Facilities** walks info vet info **Other** prior notice required

Open Apr-Oct Booking advisable BH & peak periods Last arrival 21.00hrs Last departure noon

A very nice rural site with views across meadowland towards Speyside, and the usual high Club standards. Hardstandings are well screened on an upper level, and grass pitches with more open views are sited lower down. A 7-acre site with 75 touring pitches, 17 hardstandings.

NORTH AYRSHIRE

KILWINNING

MAP 10 NS34

★★★ 75% HOTEL

Montgreenan Mansion House

Montgreenan Estate KA13 7QZ

☎ 01294 850005 📄 01294 850397

e-mail: reservations@montgreenanhotel.com

web: www.montgreenanhotel.com

Dir: *hotel signs 4m N of Irvine on A736 & on A737*

PETS: Bedrooms unattended Public areas Grounds accessible Exercise area on site adjacent Resident Pets: Blackie (cat), 2 Highland cows

In a peaceful setting of 48 acres of parkland and woods, this 19th-century mansion retains many of its original features. Public areas include a splendid drawing room, a library, a club-style bar and a restaurant. Accommodation ranges from compact modern rooms to the well-proportioned classical rooms of the original house.

Rooms 21 en suite (1 fmly) ⌀ in 16 bedrooms Facilities STV ⌀ 5 ⌀ ⌀ Putt green ch fac Parking 50 Notes LB

NORTH LANARKSHIRE

CUMBERNAULD

MAP 11 NS77

★★★★ 76% HOTEL

Westerwood

1 St Andrews Dr, Westerwood G68 0EW

☎ 01236 457171 📄 01236 738478

e-mail: westerwood@qhotels.co.uk

web: www.qhotels.co.uk

PETS: Bedrooms unattended Charges £10 per night Grounds accessible Exercise area on site on site Other Pet food on request

This stylish, contemporary hotel enjoys an elevated position within 400 acres at the foot of the Campsie Hills. Accommodation is provided in spacious, bright bedrooms, many with super bathrooms, and day rooms include sumptuous lounges, an airy restaurant and extensive golf, fitness and conference facilities.

Rooms 148 en suite (14 fmly) (49 GF) ⌀ in all bedrooms S £80-£130; D £85-£145 (incl. bkfst)✲ Facilities Spa STV ⌀ ⌀ 18 ⌀ Gym Putt green Wi-fi in bedrooms Beauty salon Hairdresser Ice fountain Relaxation room Sauna Steam room Xmas New Year Services Lift air con Parking 200 Notes LB

★★ 84% HOTEL

Castlecary House

Castlecary Rd, Castlecary G68 0HD

☎ 01324 840233 📄 01324 841608

e-mail: enquiries@castlecaryhotel.com

web: www.castlecaryhotel.com

Dir: *off A80 onto B816 between Glasgow and Stirling, the hotel is by the Castlecary Arches*

PETS: Bedrooms unattended Grounds accessible Exercise area 100yds

Close to the Forth Clyde Canal and convenient for the M80, this popular hotel provides a versatile range of accommodation, within purpose-built units in the grounds and also in an extension to the original house. The attractive and spacious restaurant offers a short fixed-price menu, and enjoyable meals are also served in the busy bars.

Rooms 60 rms (55 en suite) (3 fmly) S £70-£90; D £70-£90 (incl. bkfst)✲ Facilities Wi-fi available Services Lift Parking 100 Notes RS 1 Jan

PERTH & KINROSS

ALYTH

MAP 15 NO24

★★★★★ 🛏 🍴 GUEST ACCOMMODATION

Tigh Na Leigh Guesthouse

22-24 Airlie St PH11 8AJ

☎ 01828 632372 📄 01828 632279

e-mail: bandcblack@yahoo.co.uk

web: www.tighnaleigh.co.uk

Dir: *In town centre on B952*

PETS: Bedrooms Charges £5 per night Public areas (GF) except dining room Grounds accessible Exercise area 200yds Facilities food bowl water bowl dog chews dog scoop/disp bags washing facs cage storage walks info vet info On Request fridge access torch towels Resident Pets: Tom & Eddie (cats)

Situated in the heart of this country town, Tigh Na Leigh is Gaelic for "The house of the Doctor or Physician". Its location and somewhat sombre façade are in stunning contrast to what lies inside. The house has been completely restored to blend its Victorian architecture with contemporary interior design. Bedrooms include a superb suite and state-of-the-art bathrooms. Public rooms offer three entirely different lounges, whilst delicious meals are served in the conservatory/dining room overlooking a spectacular landscaped garden.

Rooms 6 en suite (1 GF) ⌀ S £37.50; D £80-£110 Facilities FTV TV5B tea/coffee Cen ht TVL Dinner Last d 8pm Wi-fi available Parking 5 Notes No children 12yrs Closed Nov-Feb

SCOTLAND

SCOTLAND

BLAIR ATHOLL

MAP 14 NN86

►►►►► Blair Castle Caravan Park

(NN874656)

PH18 5SR

☎ 01796 481263 📄 01796 481587

e-mail: mail@blaircastlecaravanpark.co.uk
web: www.blaircastlecaravanpark.co.uk

Dir: *From A9 junct with B8079 at Aldclune, then NE to Blair Atholl. Park on right after crossing bridge in village*

PETS: Charges £1 per night **Public areas** except reception & toilet blocks **Exercise area** on site dog walk adjacent 20mtrs **Facilities** on site shop food dog scoop/disp bags walks info vet info **Other** prior notice required **Restrictions** no dangerous dogs (see page 7)

Open Mar-Nov Booking advisable BH & Jul-Aug Last arrival 21.30hrs Last departure noon

Attractive site set in impressive seclusion within the Atholl estate, surrounded by mature woodland and the River Tilt. Although a large park, the various groups of pitches are located throughout the extensive parkland, and each has its own sanitary block with all-cubicled facilities of a very high standard. This park is particularly suitable for the larger type of motorhome. A 32-acre site with 280 touring pitches and 101 statics.

KINCLAVEN

MAP 11 NO13

★★★★ ◉◉ COUNTRY HOUSE HOTEL
Ballathie House

PH1 4QN

☎ 01250 883268 📄 01250 883396

e-mail: email@ballathiehousehotel.com
web: www.ballathiehousehotel.com

Dir: *from A9 2m N of Perth, B9099 through Stanley & signed, or off A93 at Beech Hedge follow signs for Ballathie 2.5m*

PETS: Bedrooms (GF) **Charges** £10 per pet per stay charge for damage **Grounds** accessible disp bin **Facilities** water bowl dog chews dog biscuit on arrival vet info **On Request** fridge access towels **Resident Pets:** Sam (Cocker Spaniel)

Set in delightful grounds, this splendid Scottish mansion house combines classical grandeur with modern comfort. Bedrooms range

from well-proportioned master rooms to modern standard rooms, and many boast antique furniture and art deco bathrooms. For the ultimate, request one of the Riverside Rooms, a purpose-built development right on the banks of the river, complete with balconies and terraces. The elegant restaurant has views over the River Tay.

Rooms 25 en suite 16 annexe en suite (2 fmly) (10 GF) ⊘ in all bedrooms S £85-£98; D £170-£240 (incl. bkfst)✳ **Facilities** FTV Fishing ⌣ Putt green Xmas New Year **Services** Lift **Parking** 50 **Notes** LB

KINROSS

MAP 11 NO10

★★★★ 75% ◉ HOTEL
The Green Hotel

2 The Muirs KY13 8AS

☎ 01577 863467 📄 01577 863180

e-mail: reservations@green-hotel.com
web: www.green-hotel.com

Dir: *M90 junct 6 follow Kinross signs, onto A922, hotel on this road*

PETS: Bedrooms (GF) **Stables** nearby (4m) **Public areas** except bar, restaurant & lounge **Grounds** accessible on leads **Exercise area** across road **Facilities** cage storage walks info vet info **On Request** fridge access towels **Resident Pets:** Samantha & Shuna (Cocker Spaniels)

A long-established hotel offering a wide range of indoor and outdoor activities. Public areas include a classical restaurant, a choice of bars and a well-stocked gift shop. The comfortable, well-equipped bedrooms, most of which are generously proportioned, boast attractive colour schemes and smart modern furnishings.

Rooms 46 en suite (4 fmly) (14 GF) ⊘ in all bedrooms S £65-£95; D £90-£150 (incl. bkfst) **Facilities** STV ⊙ supervised ♨ 36 ⌣ Fishing Squash Gym ⌣ Putt green Wi-fi in bedrooms Petanque Curling in season New Year **Parking** 60 **Notes** LB Closed 23-24 & 26-28 Dec RS 25 Dec

PERTH

MAP 11 NO12

★★★★ BED & BREAKFAST
Westview

49 Dunkeld Rd PH1 5RP

☎ 01738 627787 📄 01738 447790

e-mail: angiewestview@aol.com

Dir: *On A912, 0.5m NW from town centre opp Royal Bank of Scotland*

PETS: Bedrooms Exercise area 5 mins walk **Other** many guests bring tropical fish for showing in local competition **Resident Pets:** William Wallace & Flora MacDonald (Yorkshire Terriers)

Expect a warm welcome from enthusiastic owner Angie Livingstone. She is a fan of Victoriana, and her house captures that period, one feature being the teddies on the stairs. Best use is made of available space in the bedrooms, which are full of character. Public areas include an inviting lounge and a dining room.

CONTINUED

Westview

Rooms 5 rms (3 en suite) (1 fmly) (1 GF) ✿ **Facilities** STV TVB tea/coffee Cen ht TVL Dinner Last d 12.30pm **Parking** 4 **Notes** ✿

PITLOCHRY

MAP 14 NN95

★★★ 85% ✿ COUNTRY HOUSE HOTEL

Green Park

Clunie Bridge Rd PH16 5JY

☎ 01796 473248 ▤ 01796 473520

e-mail: bookings@thegreenpark.co.uk

web: www.thegreenpark.co.uk

Dir: *turn off A9 at Pitlochry, follow signs 0.25m through town*

PETS: Bedrooms (GF) unattended **Grounds** accessible disp bin **Exercise area** adjacent **Facilities** disp bags washing facs cage storage walks info vet info **On Request** fridge access torch towels

Guests return year after year to this lovely hotel that is situated in a stunning setting on the shores of Loch Faskally. Most of the thoughtfully designed bedrooms, including a splendid new wing, the restaurant and the comfortable lounges enjoy these views. Dinner utilises fresh produce, much of it grown in the kitchen garden.

Rooms 51 en suite (16 GF) ✿ in all bedrooms S £64-£87; D £128-£174 (incl. bkfst & dinner)✳ **Facilities** Putt green New Year **Parking** 51 **Notes** LB

★★★ 85% ✿ COUNTRY HOUSE HOTEL

Pine Trees

Strathview Ter PH16 5QR

☎ 01796 472121 ▤ 01796 472460

e-mail: info@pinetreeshotel.co.uk

web: www.pinetreeshotel.co.uk

Dir: *along main street (Atholl Rd), into Larchwood Rd, follow hotel signs*

PETS: Bedrooms unattended **Charges** £5 per night charge for damage **Public areas** lounge only on leads **Grounds** accessible on leads disp bin **Exercise area** 0.75m **Facilities** water bowl bedding dog chews cage storage walks info vet info **On Request** fridge access torch towels

Set in ten acres of tree-studded grounds high above the town, this fine Victorian mansion retains many fine features including wood panelling, ornate ceilings and a wonderful marble staircase. The atmosphere is refined and relaxing, with public rooms looking onto the lawns. Bedrooms come in a variety of sizes and many are well proportioned. Staff are friendly and keen to please.

Rooms 20 en suite (3 fmly) ✿ in all bedrooms S £57-£80; D £114-£170 (incl. bkfst & dinner)✳ **Facilities** STV FTV Xmas New Year **Parking** 40 **Notes** LB No children 12yrs

▶▶▶▶ **Milton of Fonab Caravan Site**

(NN945573)

Bridge Rd PH16 5NA

☎ 01796 472882 ▤ 01796 474363

e-mail: info@fonab.co.uk

web: www.fonab.co.uk

Dir: *0.5m S of town off A924*

PETS: Public areas Exercise area on site area provided park 0.5m **Facilities** on site shop dog chews cat treats disp bags vet info

Open Apr-Oct Booking advisable BH & Jul-Aug Last arrival 21.00hrs Last departure 13.00hrs

Set on the banks of the River Tummel, with extensive views down the river valley to the mountains, this park is close to the centre of Pitlochry, adjacent to the Pitlochry Festival Theatre. The sanitary facilities are exceptionally good, with most contained in combined shower/wash basin and toilet cubicles. A 15-acre site with 154 touring pitches and 36 statics.

Notes ✿ Couples & families only, no motor cycles

ST FILLANS MAP 11 NN62

★★★ 83% ◎◎ HOTEL

The Four Seasons Hotel

Loch Earn PH6 2NF

☎ 01764 685333 📄 01764 685444

e-mail: info@thefourseasonshotel.co.uk

web: www.thefourseasonshotel.co.uk

Dir: on A85, towards W of village facing Loch

PETS: Bedrooms (GF) unattended **Charges** Charge for damage **Public areas** except restaurants **Grounds** accessible disp bin **Facilities** food (pre-bookable) food bowl water bowl dog chews walks info vet info **On Request** fridge access torch towels **Restrictions** Telephone for details **Resident Pets:** Sham & Pagne (Münsterlanders)

Set on the edge of Loch Earn, this welcoming hotel and many of its bedrooms benefit from fine views. There is a choice of lounges, including a library, warmed by log fires during winter. Local produce is used to good effect in both the Meall Reamhar restaurant and the more informal Tarken Room.

Rooms 12 en suite 6 annexe en suite (7 fmly) ⊛ in 5 bedrooms S £44-£94; D £88-£138 (incl. bkfst)✳ **Facilities** Wi-fi available Xmas New Year **Parking** 40 **Notes LB** Closed 2 Jan-Feb RS Nov, Dec, Mar

★★★ 74% ◎ SMALL HOTEL

Achray House

PH6 2NF

☎ 01764 685231 📄 01764 685320

e-mail: info@achray-house.co.uk

Dir: follow A85 towards Crainlarich, from Stirling follow A9 then B822 at Braco, B827 to Comrie. Turn left onto A85 to St Fillans

PETS: Bedrooms (GF) unattended **Charges** £5 per night charge for damage **Public areas** except eating area **Grounds** accessible disp bin **Exercise area** opposite **Facilities** food (pre-bookable) food bowl water bowl leads pet sitting dog walking cage storage walks info vet info **On Request** fridge access torch towels **Resident Pets:** Corrie & Millie (Retrievers)

A friendly holiday hotel set in gardens overlooking picturesque Loch Earn, Achray House offers smart, attractive and well-equipped bedrooms. An interesting range of freshly prepared dishes is served both in the conservatory and in the adjoining dining rooms.

Rooms 8 en suite 2 annexe en suite (2 fmly) (3 GF) ⊛ in all bedrooms S £40-£60; D £70-£90 (incl. bkfst)✳ **Facilities** ch fac Xmas New Year **Parking** 30 **Notes LB**

SCONE MAP 11 NO12

►►► Camping & Caravanning Club Site

(NO108274)

Scone Palace PH2 6BB

☎ 01738 552323

web: www.campingandcaravanningclub.co.uk

Dir: Follow signs for Scone Palace, once through Perth continue for 2m. Turn left, follow site signs. 1m left onto Racecourse Road. Site entrance from car park

PETS: Facilities walks info vet info **Other** prior notice required

Open Mar-Oct Booking advisable BH & peak periods Last arrival 21.00hrs Last departure noon

A delightful woodland site, sheltered and well screened from the adjacent Scone racecourse. The two amenity blocks are built of timber and blend in well with the surroundings of mature trees. Super pitches add to the park's appeal. A 16-acre site with 150 touring pitches, 40 hardstandings.

SCOTTISH BORDERS

CRAILING   MAP 12 NT62

★★★★ GUEST HOUSE

Crailing Old School B&B

TD8 6TL

☎ 01835 850382

e-mail: jean.player@virgin.net

web: www.crailingoldschool.co.uk

Dir: *A698 onto B6400 signed Nisbet, Crailing Old School also signed*

PETS: Sep Accom kennel with run **Stables** 0.5m **Charges** £2 per night **Exercise area** 0.2m

This delightful rural retreat, built in 1887 as the village school, has been imaginatively renovated to combine Victorian features with modern comforts. The spacious bedrooms are beautifully maintained and decorated, and filled with homely extras. The lodge annexe suite located 10 yards from the house offers easier ground-floor access. The best of local produce produces tasty breakfasts, served in the stylish lounge-dining room (evening meals by arrangement).

Rooms 3 rms (1 en suite) 1 annexe en suite (1 GF) ⊗ S £30-£35; D £60-£70✳ **Facilities** TVB tea/coffee Cen ht TVL Dinner Last d 7.30pm **Parking** 7 **Notes** LB No children 9yrs Closed 24-27 Dec & 2 wks Feb and Nov

GALASHIELS   MAP 12 NT43

★★★ 73% HOTEL

Kingsknowes

Selkirk Rd TD1 3HY

☎ 01896 758375 📠 01896 750377

e-mail: enq@kingsknowes.co.uk

web: www.kingsknowes.co.uk

Dir: *off A7 at Galashiels/Selkirk rdbt*

PETS: Bedrooms unattended **Public areas** except at meal times **Exercise area** nearby **Resident Pets:** Isla & Hector (Labradors)

An imposing turreted mansion, this hotel lies in attractive gardens on the outskirts of town close to the River Tweed. It boasts elegant public areas and many spacious bedrooms, some with excellent views. There is a choice of bars, one with a popular menu to supplement the restaurant.

Rooms 12 en suite (2 fmly) ⊗ in all bedrooms S fr £65; D fr £95 (incl. bkfst)✳ **Facilities** STV Wi-fi available **Parking** 65 **Notes** LB

★★ FARM HOUSE

Over Langshaw (NT524400)

Langshaw TD1 2PE

☎ 01896 860244 📠 01896 860668 Mrs S Bergius

e-mail: bergius@overlangshaw.fsnet.co.uk

Dir: *3m N of Galashiels. A7 N from Galashiels, 1m right signed Langshaw, right at T-junct into Langshaw, left signed Earlston, Over Langshaw 1m, signed*

PETS: Bedrooms Grounds accessible **Exercise area** on site

There are fine panoramic views from this organic hillside farm. It offers two comfortable and spacious bedrooms. Hearty breakfasts are provided at individual tables in the lounge and a friendly welcome is guaranteed.

Rooms 2 en suite (1 fmly) (1 GF) ⊗ **Facilities** tea/coffee Cen ht TVL Dinner Last d at breakfast **Parking** 4 **Notes** 500 acres dairy/sheep/organic ⊛

JEDBURGH   MAP 12 NT62

★★ GUEST HOUSE

Ferniehirst Mill Lodge

TD8 6PQ

☎ 01835 863279

e-mail: ferniehirstmill@aol.com

web: www.ferniehirstmill.co.uk

Dir: *2.5m S on A68, onto private track to end*

PETS: Bedrooms (GF) unattended **Stables** on site **Charges** £6-£12 per night for horses **Grounds** accessible disp bin **Facilities** washing facs cage storage walks info vet info **On Request** fridge access torch towels **Resident Pets:** Arctic-maremma (Sheepdog), Flight (Whippet)

Reached by a narrow farm track and a rustic wooden bridge, this chalet-style house has a secluded setting by the River Jed where wildlife abounds. Bedrooms are small and functional but there is a comfortable lounge in which to relax. Excellent home-cooked dinners and hearty breakfasts are served in the cosy dining room.

Rooms 7 en suite (1 GF) ⊗ S £27; D £54 **Facilities** tea/coffee Direct dial from bedrooms Licensed Cen ht TVL Dinner Last d 5pm Fishing Riding **Parking** 10 **Notes** No coaches

SCOTLAND

SCOTLAND

JEDBURGH CONTINUED

►►► Jedburgh Camping & Caravanning Club Site *(NT658219)*

Elliot Park, Edinburgh Rd TD8 6EF

☎ 01835 863393

web: www.campingandcaravanningclub.co.uk

Dir: *Site opposite Edinburgh & Jedburgh Woollen Mills. N of Jedburgh on A68 (Newcastle-Edinburgh road)*

PETS: Exercise area country park **Facilities** walks info vet info **Other** prior notice required

Open Apr-Oct Booking advisable BH & peak periods Last arrival 21.00hrs Last departure noon

A touring site on the northern edge of town, nestling at the foot of cliffs close to Jed Water. Hardstandings are a welcome feature for caravans A 3-acre site with 60 touring pitches, 20 hardstandings.

KELSO   MAP 12 NT73

★★★ 83% ◉◉ HOTEL
The Roxburghe Hotel & Golf Course

Heiton TD5 8JZ

☎ 01573 450331 📄 01573 450611

e-mail: hotel@roxburghe.net

web: www.roxburghe.net

Dir: *from A68 Jedburgh take A698 to Heiton, 3m SW of Kelso*

PETS: Bedrooms courtyard rooms only **Sep Accom** Kennel **Public areas**

Outdoor sporting pursuits are popular at this impressive Jacobean mansion owned by the Duke of Roxburghe and set in 500 acres of woods and parkland. Gracious public areas are the perfect settings for afternoon teas and carefully prepared meals. Bedrooms are individually designed, with some of the superior rooms having their own fires.

Rooms 16 en suite 6 annexe en suite (3 fmly) (3 GF) ⊘ in all bedrooms S £120-£140; D £160-£296 (incl. bkfst)✳ **Facilities** STV ♨ 18 Fishing ᴥ Putt green Clay shooting Health & beauty saloon Mountain bike hire Falconry Archery Xmas New Year **Parking** 150 **Notes** LB

LAUDER   MAP 12 NT54

★★★★ ⚏ ⇔ INN
Black Bull

Market Place TD2 6SR

☎ 01578 722208 📄 01578 722419

e-mail: enquiries@blackbull-lauder.com

web: www.blackbull-lauder.com

Dir: *On A68 in village centre*

PETS: Bedrooms Charges £5 per stay charge for damage **Public areas** bar & reception only **Facilities** water bowl cage storage walks info vet info **On Request** fridge access torch towels **Resident Pets:** Ben & Zak (German Shorthaired Pointers)

This 18th-century coaching inn has been completely transformed. The lovely bedrooms are furnished in the period character and thoughtfully equipped with modern amenities. All with wooden floors, the cosy bar and four dining areas are charming, the main dining room being a former chapel. A tremendous range of food makes this a destination gastro pub.

Rooms 8 en suite (2 fmly) ⊘ S £55-£60; D £80-£95 **Facilities** TVB tea/coffee Direct dial from bedrooms Cen ht Dinner Last d 9pm **Parking** 8 **Notes** LB Closed 1st 3 wks of Feb

►►► Lauder Camping & Caravanning Club Site *(NT509535)*

Carfraemill, Oxton TD2 6RA

☎ 01578 750697

web: www.campingandcaravanningclub.co.uk

Dir: *From Lauder, right at rdbt onto A697, then left at Lodge Hotel (signed). Site on right behind Carfraemill Hotel*

PETS: Public areas except buildings **Exercise area** on site by river **Facilities** walks info vet info **Other** prior notice required

Open Mar-Oct Booking advisable BHs & peak periods Last arrival 21.00hrs Last departure noon

A meadowland site with good facilities housed in pine lodge buildings, and pleasant surroundings. Ideal either as a touring base or transit site, it is extremely well maintained. There are four wooden chalets for hire A 5-acre site with 60 touring pitches, 9 hardstandings.

►►► Thirlestane Castle Caravan & Camping Site *(NT536473)*

Thirlestane Castle TD2 6RU

☎ 01578 718884 & 07976 231032

e-mail: thirlestanepark@btconnect.com

web: www.thirlestanecastlepark.co.uk

Dir: *Signed off A68 & A697, just S of Lauder*

PETS: Public areas on leads **Facilities** walks info vet info **Restrictions** no Pitt Bull Terriers

Open Apr-1 Oct Booking advisable Jul-Aug Last arrival 22.00hrs Last departure noon

Set in the grounds of the impressive Thirlestane Castle, with mainly level grassy pitches. The park and facilities are kept in sparkling condition. A 5-acre site with 60 touring pitches and 15 statics.

Notes ⊛

PEEBLES   MAP 11 NT24

★★★★ ®® COUNTRY HOUSE HOTEL

Cringletie House

Edinburgh Rd EH45 8PL

☎ 01721 725750 📄 01721 725751

e-mail: enquiries@cringletie.com

web: www.cringletie.com

Dir: *2m N on A703*

PETS: Bedrooms unattended **Charges** £10 per night **Grounds** accessible **Exercise area** on site **Other** All dogs welcomed with a dog biscuit **Resident Pets:** Daisy (cat)

This long-established hotel is a romantic baronial mansion set in 28 acres of gardens and woodland with stunning views from all rooms. Delightful public rooms include a cocktail lounge with adjoining conservatory, whilst the first-floor restaurant is graced by a magnificent hand-painted ceiling. Bedrooms, many of them particularly spacious, are very attractively furnished.

Rooms 13 en suite (2 GF) ⊘ in all bedrooms S £140-£245; D £200-£290 (incl. bkfst)✳ **Facilities** STV 🏌 Putt green Wi-fi in bedrooms Petanque, Giant chess & draughts Xmas New Year **Services** Lift **Parking** 30 **Notes** LB

★★★ 83% ®® COUNTRY HOUSE HOTEL

Castle Venlaw

Edinburgh Rd EH45 8QG

☎ 01721 720384 📄 01721 724066

e-mail: stay@venlaw.co.uk

web: www.venlaw.co.uk

Dir: *off A703 Peebles/Edinburgh road, 0.75m N of Peebles*

PETS: Bedrooms unattended **Charges** £4.50 per night charge for damage **Grounds** accessible disp bin **Exercise area** 20mtrs **Facilities** washing facs cage storage walks info vet info **On Request** fridge access torch

This 18th-century castle is set in four acres of landscaped gardens, set high above the town. Most bedrooms are spacious and all have smart modern bathrooms, but those in the Romantic and Four-poster rooms are stunning and worth asking for. There is a cosy library bar and classically elegant restaurant. Service is friendly and obliging.

Rooms 12 en suite (3 fmly) ⊘ in all bedrooms S £73-£115; D £126-£230 (incl. bkfst) **Facilities** STV Wi-fi in bedrooms Xmas New Year **Parking** 25 **Notes** LB

★★★ 77% HOTEL

Tontine

High St EH45 8AJ

☎ 01721 720892 📄 01721 729732

e-mail: info@tontinehotel.com

web: www.tontinehotel.com

Dir: *in town centre, on High St*

PETS: Bedrooms unattended **Exercise area** Tweed Green behind Hotel **Other** certain rooms only

Conveniently situated in the main street, this long-established hotel offers comfortable public rooms including an elegant Adam restaurant, inviting lounge and 'clubby' bar. Bedrooms - contained in the original house and the river-facing wing - offer a smart, classical style of accommodation. However the lasting impression is the excellent level of hospitality and guest care.

Rooms 36 en suite (3 fmly) ⊘ in 20 bedrooms S £45-£60; D £80-£120 (incl. bkfst) **Facilities** FTV Wi-fi in bedrooms Xmas New Year **Parking** 24 **Notes** LB

SCOTLAND

SCOTLAND

PEEBLES CONTINUED

★★★ 74% HOTEL

Park

Innerleithen Rd EH45 8BA

☎ 01721 720451 📄 01721 723510

e-mail: reserve@parkpeebles.co.uk

Dir: *in town centre opposite filling station*

PETS: Bedrooms unattended sign **Stables** nearby (2m)
Public areas except at food service **Grounds** accessible disp bin
Exercise area 30yds **Facilities** dog scoop/disp bags walks info
vet info **On Request** fridge access torch

This hotel offers pleasant, well-equipped bedrooms of various sizes -
those in the original house are particularly spacious. Public areas enjoy
views of the gardens and include a tartan-clad bar, a relaxing lounge
and a spacious wood-panelled restaurant. Guests can use the extensive
leisure facilities on offer at the sister hotel, The Hydro.

Rooms 24 en suite ⊘ in all bedrooms S £85-£110; D £156-£210 (incl.
bkfst & dinner)✳ **Facilities** STV Putt green Wi-fi available Use of facilities
of Peebles Hotel Hydro Xmas New Year **Services** Lift **Parking** 50

▶▶▶▶ **Crossburn Caravan Park** (NT248417)

Edinburgh Rd EH45 8ED

☎ 01721 720501 📄 01721 720501

e-mail: enquiries@crossburncaravans.co.uk

web: www.crossburncaravans.com

Dir: *0.5m N of Peebles on A703*

PETS: Public areas except shop on leads **Exercise area** on site
dog walk 2m **Facilities** on site shop walks info vet info
Other max 2 dogs **Resident Pets:** Zara (Rhodesian Ridgeback),
Ginty (Jack Russell)

Open Apr-Oct Booking advisable Jul-Aug Last arrival 21.00hrs
Last departure 14.00hrs

A peaceful site in a relatively quiet location, despite the proximity of the
main road which partly borders the site, as does the Eddleston Water.
There are lovely views, and the park is well stocked with trees, flowers and
shrubs. Facilities are maintained to a high standard, and fully-serviced
pitches are available. A large caravan dealership is on the same site. A
6-acre site with 45 touring pitches, 15 hardstandings and 85 statics.

ST BOSWELLS

MAP 12 NT53

★★★ 72% SMALL HOTEL

Buccleuch Arms

The Green TD6 0EW

☎ 01835 822243 📄 01835 823965

e-mail: info@buccleucharms.com

web: www.buccleucharms.com

Dir: *on A68, 8m N of Jedburgh*

PETS: Bedrooms Stables on site **Charges** £5 per night
Grounds accessible **Exercise area** on site **Resident Pets:** Jasper
& Monty (Black Labradors), Kelly (Springer), Becca, Jasper (Golden
Labradors)

Formerly a coaching inn, this long-established hotel stands is the ideal
spot for relaxation. The three-year refurbishment program is still
underway and has already seen the transformation of all the bedrooms
and en suite bathrooms; each room is individually designed with
striking fabrics and colour combinations. The lounge bar is a popular
eating venue and complements the attractive restaurant. Morning
coffees and afternoon teas are served in the comfortable lounge with
its open fire.

Rooms 19 en suite (1 fmly) ⊘ in all bedrooms S £60-£76; D £95 (incl.
bkfst)✳ **Facilities** 🏊 Xmas New Year **Parking** 50 **Notes LB** Closed
25 Dec

SOUTH AYRSHIRE

AYR

MAP 10 NS32

★★★ 79% HOTEL

Savoy Park

THE INDEPENDENTS
HOTEL ASSOCIATION

16 Racecourse Rd KA7 2UT

☎ 01292 266112 📄 01292 611488

e-mail: mail@savoypark.com

Dir: *from A77 follow A70 (Holmston Road) for 2m, through
Parkhouse Street, left into Beresford Terrace, 1st right into
Bellevue Road*

PETS: Bedrooms Grounds accessible

This well-established hotel retains many of its traditional values
including friendly, attentive service. Public rooms feature impressive
panelled walls, ornate ceilings and open fires. The restaurant is
reminiscent of a Highland shooting lodge and offers a wide ranging,
good value menu to suit all tastes. The large superior bedrooms retain
a classical elegance while others are smart and modern; all have well
equipped modern bathrooms.

Rooms 15 en suite (3 fmly) ⊘ in all bedrooms S £60-£80; D £70-£115
(incl. bkfst) **Facilities** STV ch fac Xmas New Year **Parking** 60 **Notes LB**

BALLANTRAE   MAP 10 NX08

★★★★ HOTEL

Glenapp Castle

KA26 0NZ

RELAIS & CHATEAUX

☎ 01465 831212 📄 01465 831000

e-mail: enquiries@glenappcastle.com

web: www.glenappcastle.com

Dir: *1m from A77 near Ballantrae*

PETS: Bedrooms Grounds accessible **Exercise area** on site
Resident Pets: Midge (Springer Spaniel)

Friendly hospitality and attentive service prevail at this stunning Victorian castle, set in extensive private grounds to the south of the village. Impeccably furnished bedrooms are graced with antiques and period pieces. Breathtaking views of Arran and Ailsa Craig can be enjoyed from the delightful, sumptuous day rooms and from many of the bedrooms. Accomplished cooking using quality local ingredients is a feature of all meals, with dinner a well crafted and imaginative no-choice five course menu. Make a point of walking round the wonderful grounds, to include the azalea lake and walled vegetable gardens with their fine restored greenhouses.

Rooms 17 en suite (2 fmly) (7 GF) ⊘ in all bedrooms S £255-£455; D £375-£575 (incl. bkfst & dinner)✱ **Facilities** STV 🐾 🌳 Wi-fi available New Year **Services** Lift **Parking** 20 **Notes** Closed Jan & Feb

---

BARRHILL   MAP 10 NX28

▶▶▶▶ **Barrhill Holiday Park** *(NX216835)*

KA26 0PZ

☎ 01465 821355 📄 01465 821355

e-mail: windsorholidaypark@barrhillgirvan.freeserve.co.uk

web: www.windsorholidaypark.com

Dir: *On A714 (Newton Stewart to Girvan road). 1m N of Barrhill*

PETS: Public areas Exercise area on site end of park & in 1m
Facilities on site shop dog scoop/disp bags washing facs walks info vet info

Open Mar-Nov (rs Nov-Feb closed Tue to Thu) Booking advisable

A small, friendly park in a tranquil rural location, screened from the A714 by trees. The park is terraced and well landscaped, and a high quality amenity block includes disabled facilities. A 6-acre site with 30 touring pitches, 9 hardstandings and 29 statics.

Notes 🐾

MAYBOLE   MAP 10 NS20

▶▶▶ **Culzean Castle C&C Club Site** *(NS247103)*

Culzean Castle KA19 8JX

☎ 01655 760627

web: www.campingandcaravanningclub.co.uk

Dir: *From N on A77 in Maybole turn right onto B7023 (signed Culzean & Maidens), left in 100yds. Site 4m on right*

PETS: Exercise area on site dog walks **Facilities** walks info vet info **Other** prior notice required

Open Mar-Oct Booking advisable BH & peak period Last arrival 21.00hrs Last departure noon

A mainly level grass park with some gently sloping pitches and hard stands along the bed of an old railway, situated at the entrance to the castle and country park. The park is surrounded by trees on three sides and has lovely views over Culzean Bay. A 10-acre site with 90 touring pitches, 27 hardstandings.

TURNBERRY   MAP 10 NS20

★★★★★ HOTEL

Westin Turnberry Resort

KA26 9LT

WESTIN HOTELS & RESORTS

☎ 01655 331000 📄 01655 331706

e-mail: turnberry@westin.com

web: www.westin.com/turnberry

Dir: *from Glasgow take A77/M77 S towards Stranraer, 2m past Kirkoswald, follow signs for A719/Turnberry. Hotel 500mtrs on right*

PETS: Bedrooms Public areas foyer only **Grounds** accessible **Exercise area** on site

This famous hotel enjoys magnificent views over to Arran, Ailsa Craig and the Mull of Kintyre. Facilities include a world-renowned golf course, the excellent Colin Montgomerie Golf Academy, a luxurious spa and a host of outdoor and country pursuits. Elegant bedrooms and suites are located in the main hotel, while adjacent lodges provide spacious, well-equipped accommodation. The Ailsa lounge is very welcoming, and in addition to the elegant main restaurant for dining, there is a Mediterranean Terrace Brasserie and the relaxed Clubhouse.

Rooms 130 en suite 89 annexe en suite (9 fmly) (16 GF) ⊘ in all bedrooms S £230-£375; D £250-£395 (incl. bkfst)✱ **Facilities** **Spa** STV ③ supervised ⌁ 36 🌳 Fishing Riding Gym Putt green Wi-fi available Leisure club, Outdoor activity centre, Colin Montgomerie Golf Academy Xmas **Services** Lift **Parking** 200 **Notes** LB Closed various days in Dec

SCOTLAND

SOUTH LANARKSHIRE

ABINGTON
MAP 11 NS92

▶▶▶ Mount View Caravan Park *(NS935235)*
ML12 6RW

☎ 01864 502808 📄 01864 502808
e-mail: info@mountviewcaravanpark.co.uk
web: www.mountviewcaravanpark.co.uk
Dir: *M74 junct 13 onto A702 S into Abington. Left into Station Road, over river & railway. Park on right*

PETS: Public areas on leads **Exercise area** public walks adjacent **Facilities** vet info **Other** prior notice required
Resident Pets: Holly (Retriever)

Open Mar-Oct Booking advisable

A developing park, surrounded by the Southern Uplands and handily located between Carlisle and Glasgow. It is an excellent stopover site for those travelling between Scotland and the South. The West Coast railway passes beside the park. A 5.5-acre site with 51 touring pitches, 51 hardstandings and 20 statics.

ABINGTON MOTORWAY SERVICE AREA (M74)
MAP 11 NS92

BUDGET HOTEL
Days Inn Abington
ML12 6RG

DAYS INN

☎ 01864 502782 📄 01864 502759
e-mail: abington.hotel@welcomebreak.co.uk
web: www.daysinn.com
Dir: *M74 junct 13, accessible from N'bound and S'bound carriageways*

PETS: Bedrooms unattended **Grounds** accessible

This modern building offers accommodation in smart, spacious and well-equipped bedrooms, suitable for families and business travellers, and all with en suite bathrooms. Continental breakfast is available and other refreshments may be taken at the nearby family restaurant. For further details see the Hotel Groups page.

Rooms 52 en suite

BIGGAR
MAP 11 NT03

★★★ 83% ®® COUNTRY HOUSE HOTEL
Shieldhill Castle
Quothquan ML12 6NA

☎ 01899 220035 📄 01899 221092
e-mail: enquiries@shieldhill.co.uk
web: www.shieldhill.co.uk
Dir: *A702 onto B7016 (Biggar to Carnwath road), after 2m left into Shieldhill Road. Hotel 1.5m on right*

PETS: Bedrooms unattended **Stables** nearby (5m)
Charges charge for damage **Grounds** accessible on leads **disp bin Facilities** washing facs cage storage walks info vet info
On Request fridge access torch towels **Resident Pets:** Mutley (Springer/Cocker Spaniel)

Food and wine are an important focus at this imposing fortified country mansion dating back almost 800 years. Public room are atmospheric and include the classical Chancellor's restaurant, oak-panelled lounge and the Gun Room bar that offers its own menu. Bedrooms, many with feature baths, are spacious and comfortable. A friendly welcome is assured, even from the estate's dogs!

Rooms 16 en suite ⊘ in all bedrooms S fr £90; D £100-£250 (incl. bkfst)
☀ **Facilities** 🛶 Cycling Clay shoot Hot air balooning Falconry Laser & game bird shooting Xmas New Year **Parking** 50 **Notes LB**

KIRKMUIRHILL   MAP 11 NS74

★★★ FARM HOUSE
Dykecroft *(NS776419)*

ML11 0JQ

☎ 01555 892226 📠 01555 892226 Mrs I H McInally

e-mail: dykecroft.bandb@ tiscali.co.uk

Dir: *M74 junct 9/10, B7086 W for 1.5m, 1st bungalow on left past Boghead*

PETS: Bedrooms Public areas Grounds accessible
Exercise area nearby **Resident Pets:** Jan (Border Collie), Vicky (Jack Russell)

A friendly welcome is assured at this modern bungalow, situated in an open rural location on the road to Strathaven. The comfortable bedrooms are traditionally furnished, and there is a bright airy lounge-dining room with lovely country views.

Rooms 3 rms (3 GF) ⊘ S £25-£26; D £45-£46✳ **Facilities** tea/coffee Cen ht TVL **Parking** 4 **Notes** 60 acres sheep 🐾

NEW LANARK   MAP 11 NS84

★★★ 82% HOTEL
New Lanark Mill Hotel

Mill One, New Lanark Mills ML11 9DB

☎ 01555 667200 📠 01555 667222

e-mail: hotel@newlanark.org

web: www.newlanark.org

Dir: *signed from all major roads, M74 junct 7 & M8*

PETS: Bedrooms unattended **Charges** £10 per night charge for damage **Grounds** accessible **Facilities** cage storage vet info

Originally built as a cotton mill in the 18th-century, this hotel forms part of a fully restored village, now a World Heritage Site. There's a bright modern style throughout which contrasts nicely with features from the original mill. There is a comfortable foyer-lounge with a galleried restaurant above. The hotel enjoys stunning views over the River Clyde.

Rooms 38 en suite (2 fmly) ⊘ in 28 bedrooms **Facilities** Fishing about 1m away **Services** Lift **Parking** 75 **Notes** LB

STIRLING

BALMAHA   MAP 10 NS49

►►►► Milarrochy Bay C&C Club Site
(NN407927)

Milarrochy Bay G63 0AL

☎ 01360 870236

web: www.campingandcaravanningclub.co.uk

Dir: *A811 (Balloch to Stirling road) take Drymen turn. In Drymen take B837 for Balmaha. In 5m road turns sharp right up steep hill. Site in 1.5m*

PETS: Public areas except buildings **Exercise area** on site
Facilities walks info vet info **Other** prior notice required

Open Mar-Oct Booking advisable BHs & peak periods Last arrival 21.00hrs Last departure noon

On the quieter side of Loch Lomond next to the 75,000-acre Queen Elizabeth Forest, this attractive site offers very good facilities. Disabled toilets and family rooms are appointed to a high standard. A 12-acre site with 150 touring pitches, 23 hardstandings.

BLAIRLOGIE   MAP 11 NS89

►►►► Witches Craig Caravan & Camping
Park *(NS821968)*

FK9 5PX

☎ 01786 474947 📠 01786 447286

e-mail: info@witchescraig.co.uk

web: www.witchescraig.co.uk

Dir: *3m NE of Stirling on A91 (Hillfoots-St Andrews road)*

PETS: Public areas except amenity block & play ground
Exercise area on site wood **Facilities** vet info

Open Apr-Oct Booking advisable Jul-Aug Last arrival 21.00hrs Last departure 13.00hrs

In an attractive setting with direct access to the lower slopes of the dramatic Ochil Hills, this is a well-maintained family-run park. It is in the centre of 'Braveheart' country, with easy access to historical sites and many popular attractions. A 5-acre site with 60 touring pitches, 26 hardstandings.

SCOTLAND

LOCHEARNHEAD

MAP 11 NN52

★★★ GUEST HOUSE
Mansewood Country House

FK19 8NS

☎ 01567 830213

e-mail: stay@mansewoodcountryhouse.co.uk

Dir: *A84 N to Lochearnhead, 1st building on left*

PETS: Bedrooms dogs accepted in log cabins only

Mansewood Country House is a spacious former manse that dates back to the 18th century and lies in a well-tended garden to the south of the village. Bedrooms are well appointed and equipped and offer high standards of comfort. Refreshments can be enjoyed in the cosy bar or the elegant lounge, and meals prepared with flair are served in the attractive restaurant. There is also a log cabin where pets are allowed.

Rooms 6 en suite (1 GF) ⊗ S £40; D £60✳ **Facilities** TVB tea/coffee Licensed Cen ht TVL Dinner Last d 7.15pm Wi-fi available **Parking** 6 **Notes LB** No coaches

---

STIRLING

MAP 11 NS79

★★★★ 76% HOTEL
Paramount Stirling Highland

PARAMOUNT
GROUP OF HOTELS

Spittal St FK8 1DU

☎ 01786 272727 ▤ 01786 272829

e-mail: stirling@paramount-hotels.co.uk

web: www.paramount-hotels.co.uk

Dir: *take A84 into Stirling. Follow Stirling Castle signs as far as Albert Hall. Left and left again, following Castle signs*

PETS: Bedrooms Charges £15 per dog **Exercise area** 1m **Facilities** water bowl food bowl

Enjoying a location close to the castle and historic old town, this atmospheric hotel was previously the High School. Public rooms have been converted from the original classrooms and retain many interesting features. Bedrooms are more modern in style and comfortably equipped.

Rooms 96 en suite (4 fmly) ⊗ in 67 bedrooms S £60-£145✳ **Facilities Spa** STV ⊛ Squash Gym Wi-fi available Steam room Dance Studio Beauty therapist Xmas New Year **Services** Lift **Parking** 96

STRATHYRE

MAP 11 NN51

★★★★★ ◉◉ RESTAURANT WITH ROOMS
Creagan House

FK18 8ND

☎ 01877 384638 ▤ 01877 384319

e-mail: eatandstay@creaganhouse.co.uk

web: www.creaganhouse.co.uk

Dir: *0.25m N of Strathyre on A84*

PETS: Bedrooms (GF) unattended **Grounds** accessible disp bin **Exercise area** park nearby **Facilities** food bowl water bowl leads washing facs cage storage walks info vet info **On Request** fridge access torch towels **Resident Pets:** Budd (Gordon Setter), Raffles (visiting African Grey Parrot)

Originally a farmhouse dating from the 17th century, Creagan House has operated as a restaurant with rooms for many years. The baronial-style dining room provides a wonderful setting for sympathetic cooking. Warm hospitality and attentive service are the highlights of any stay.

Rooms 5 en suite (1 fmly) (1 GF) **Facilities** tea/coffee Dinner Last d 8.30pm **Parking** 26 **Notes** Closed 21 Jan-9 Mar & 4-23 Nov RS 24 Nov-20 Dec

WEST DUNBARTONSHIRE

BALLOCH
MAP 10 NS38

★★★ GUEST ACCOMMODATION
Sunnyside
35 Main St G83 9JX
☎ 01389 750282 & 07717 397548
e-mail: enquiries@sunnysidebb.co.uk
Dir: *From A82 take A811 then A813 for 1 mile, over mini-rdbt 150mtrs on left*

PETS: Bedrooms (GF) unattended **Charges** £5 per stay charge for damage **Public areas** except main family room on leads **Grounds** accessible disp bin **Exercise area** 350yds **Facilities** food (pre-bookable) food bowl water bowl bedding dog chews disp bags leads washing facs cage storage walks info vet info **On Request** fridge access torch towels

Set in its own grounds well back from the road by Loch Lomond, Sunnyside is an attractive, traditional detached house, parts of which date back to the 1830s. Bedrooms are attractively decorated and provide comfortable modern accommodation. The dining room is located on the ground floor, and is an appropriate setting for hearty Scottish breakfasts.

Rooms 6 en suite (2 fmly) (1 GF) ⊘ S £25-£40; D £40-£54✳
Facilities TVB tea/coffee Cen ht **Parking** 8

▶▶▶▶ Lomond Woods Holiday Park
(NS383816)
Old Luss Rd G83 8QP
☎ 01389 755000 📠 01389 755563
e-mail: lomondwoods@holiday-parks.co.uk
web: www.holiday-parks.co.uk
Dir: *From A82, 17m N of Glasgow, take A811(Stirling to Balloch road). Left at 1st rdbt, follow holiday park signs, 150yds on left*

PETS: Charges 50p per night **Public areas** except play area **Exercise area** on site perimeter walk provided 450yds **Facilities** walks info vet info **Other** prior notice required **Resident Pets:** Jack & Cody (Labradors)

Open all year Booking advisable all dates Last arrival 21.00hrs Last departure noon

A mature park with well-laid out pitches screened by trees and shrubs, surrounded by woodland and hills. The park is within walking distance of 'Loch Lomond Shores', a complex of leisure and retailing experiences which is the main gateway to Scotland's first National Park. Amenities include an inspiring audio-visual show, open-top bus tours, and loch cruises. A 13-acre site with 110 touring pitches and 35 statics.

WEST LOTHIAN

EAST CALDER
MAP 11 NT06

▶▶▶ Linwater Caravan Park *(NT104696)*
West Clifton EH53 0HT
☎ 0131 333 3326 📠 0131 333 1952
e-mail: linwater@supanet.com
web: www.linwater.co.uk
Dir: *M9 junct 1, signed from B7030 or from Wilkieston on A71*

PETS: Public areas except toilet block **Exercise area** on site walks to parks & canal 1m **Facilities** walks info vet info **Other** prior notice required **Restrictions** Telephone for details **Resident Pets:** Mimi (Black Labrador), Minnow (Cocker Spaniel), Treagh (Deerhound), Cobbles (cat), sheep, pigs, ducks & hens

Open late Mar-late Oct Booking advisable BHs & Aug Last arrival 21.00hrs Last departure noon

A farmland park in a peaceful rural area within easy reach of Edinburgh. The very good facilities are housed in a Scandinavian-style building, and are well maintained by resident owners. Nearby are plenty of pleasant woodland walks. A 5-acre site with 60 touring pitches, 11 hardstandings.

LINLITHGOW
MAP 11 NS97

★★★★ GUEST HOUSE
Bomains Farm
Bo'Ness EH49 7RQ
☎ 01506 822188 & 822861 📠 01506 824433
e-mail: bunty.kirk@onetel.net
web: www.bomains.co.uk
Dir: *A706 1.5m N towards Bo Ness, left at golf course x-rds, 1st farm on right*

PETS: Bedrooms unattended by arrangement **Stables** on site **Charges** £5 per night **Grounds** accessible **Exercise area** adjacent **Resident Pets:** Laddie (Jack Russell), Zana (German Shepherd)

From its elevated location this friendly farmhouse has stunning views of the Firth of Forth. The bedrooms which vary in size are beautifully decorated, well equipped and enhanced by quality fabrics, with many thoughtful extra touches. Delicious home-cooked fare featuring the best of local produce is served a stylish lounge-dining room.

Rooms 5 rms (4 en suite) (1 pri facs) ⊘ S £30-£40; D fr £50✳
Facilities STV TVB tea/coffee Cen ht TVL Dinner Last d 5.30pm **Parking** 8 **Notes** No coaches

SCOTTISH ISLANDS
Isle of Arran

LOCHRANZA   MAP 10 NR95

▶▶▶ Lochranza Caravan & Camping Site

(NR942500)
KA27 8HL
☎ 01770 830273
e-mail: office@lochgolf.demon.co.uk
web: www.arran.net/lochranza

Dir: *On A84 at N of island, beside Kintyre ferry & 14m M of Brodick for ferry to Ardrossan*

PETS: Public areas on leads **Exercise area** on site **Facilities** on site shop food vet info

Open mid Mar-Oct Booking advisable Whit & Aug Last arrival 22.00hrs Last departure 13.00hrs

Attractive park in a beautiful location, run by friendly family owners. The park is adjacent to an 18-hole golf course, opposite the famous Arran Distillery, between tree-lined hills on the edge of the village. Golf and ferry packages can be arranged. A 2.5-acre site with 60 touring pitches, 10 hardstandings.

Notes ⊛ No fires

Isle of Mull

TOBERMORY   MAP 13 NM55

★★★ ◉◉ SMALL HOTEL
Highland Cottage

Breadalbane St PA75 6PD
☎ 01688 302030
e-mail: davidandjo@highlandcottage.co.uk
web: www.highlandcottage.co.uk

Dir: *A848 Craignure/Fishnish ferry terminal, pass Tobermory signs, straight on at mini rdbt across narrow bridge, turn right. Hotel on right opposite fire station*

PETS: Bedrooms Facilities washing facs cage storage walks info vet info **On Request** fridge access torch towels **Restrictions** no large hairy dogs (German Shepherds, St. Bernards etc)

Providing the highest level of natural and unassuming hospitality, this delightful little gem lies high above the island's capital. Don't be fooled by its side street location, a stunning view over the bay is just a few metres away. "A country house hotel in town" it is an Aladdin's Cave of collectables and treasures, as well as masses of books and magazines. There are two inviting lounges, one with an honesty bar. The cosy dining room offers memorable dinners and splendid breakfasts. Bedrooms are individual; some have four-posters and all are comprehensively equipped to include video TVs and music centres.

Rooms 6 en suite (1 GF) ⊛ in all bedrooms S fr £110; D £140-£185 (incl. bkfst)✳ **Facilities** STV Wi-fi available **Parking** 6 **Notes** No children 10yrs Closed Nov-Feb

★★ 76% ◉ HOTEL
Tobermory

53 Main St PA75 6NT

☎ 01688 302091 🖹 01688 302254

e-mail: tobhotel@tinyworld.co.uk

web: www.thetobermoryhotel.com

Dir: *on waterfront, overlooking Tobermory Bay*

PETS: Bedrooms (GF) **Charges** charge for damage
Exercise areas nearby **Facilities** cage storage walks info vet info
On Request towels

This friendly hotel, with its pretty pink frontage, sits on the seafront amid other brightly coloured, picture-postcard buildings. There is a comfortable and relaxing lounge where drinks are served (there is no bar) prior to dining in the stylish restaurant. Bedrooms come in a variety of sizes; all are bright and vibrant with the superior rooms having video TVs.

Rooms 16 rms (15 en suite) (3 fmly) (2 GF) ⊘ in all bedrooms
S £32-£59; D £64-£114 (incl. bkfst)✳ **Facilities** New Year **Notes** LB
Closed Xmas

SHETLAND

LERWICK   MAP 16 HU44

★★★★ GUEST HOUSE
Glen Orchy House

20 Knab Rd ZE1 0AX

☎ 01595 692031 🖹 01595 692031

e-mail: glenorchy.house@virgin.net

Dir: *Next to coastguard station*

PETS: Bedrooms unattended **Exercise area** 20yds
Facilities water bowl on request

This welcoming and well-presented house lies above the town with views over the Knab, and is within easy walking distance of the town centre. Bedrooms are modern in design and there is a choice of lounges with books and board games, one with an honesty bar. Substantial breakfasts are served, and the restaurant offers a delicious Thai menu.

Rooms 24 en suite (4 fmly) (4 GF) ⊘ S £50; D £80 **Facilities** STV FTV
TVB tea/coffee Licensed Cen ht Dinner Last d 9pm Wi-fi available
Parking 10 **Notes** No coaches

Isle of Skye

PORTREE   MAP 13 NG44

★★ 75% ◉ HOTEL
Rosedale

Beaumont Crescent IV51 9DB

☎ 01478 613131 🖹 01478 612531

e-mail: rosedalehotelsky@aol.com

web: www.rosedalehotelskye.co.uk

Dir: *follow directions to village centre & harbour*

PETS: Bedrooms (GF) **Facilities** cage storage walks info vet info
On Request fridge access torch

The atmosphere is wonderfully warm at this delightful family-run waterfront hotel. A labyrinth of stairs and corridors connects the comfortable lounges, bar and charming restaurant, which are set on different levels. The restaurant offers fine views of the bay. Modern bedrooms offer a good range of amenities.

Rooms 18 en suite (1 fmly) (3 GF) ⊘ in all bedrooms S £30-£55;
D £60-£140 (incl. bkfst)✳ **Parking** 2 **Notes** LB Closed Nov-mid Mar

---

STAFFIN   MAP 13 NG46

►► **Staffin Camping & Caravanning**

(NG492670)

IV51 9JX

☎ 01470 562213 🖹 01470 562705

e-mail: staffin@namacleod.freeserve.co.uk

web: www.staffincampsite.co.uk

Dir: *On A855, 16m N of Portree*

PETS: Public areas except toilet block **Exercise area** adjacent
Facilities walks info vet info **Resident Pets:** Henry (Briard),
Peasan (cat)

Open Apr-Oct Booking advisable Jul-Aug Last arrival 22.00hrs
Last departure 11.00hrs

A large sloping grassy site with level hardstandings for motor homes and caravans, close to the village of Staffin. The toilet block is appointed to a very good standard. A 2.5-acre site with 50 touring pitches, 18 hardstandings.

Notes ⊕ No music after 23.00hrs

SCOTLAND

Wales

ANGLESEY, ISLE OF

AMLWCH
MAP 06 SH49

★★ 76% HOTEL
Lastra Farm
Penrhyd LL68 9TF
☎ 01407 830906 📄 01407 832522
e-mail: booking@lastra-hotel.com
web: www.lastra-hotel.com
Dir: *after 'Welcome to Amlwch' sign turn left. Straight across main road, left at T-junct on to Rhosgoch Rd*
PETS: Bedrooms (GF) unattended Charges £2.50 per night charge for damage Public areas except restaurant Grounds accessible disp bin Facilities food bowl water bowl cage storage walks info vet info On Request fridge access towels
This 17th-century farmhouse offers pine-furnished, colourfully decorated bedrooms. There is also a comfortable lounge and a cosy bar. A wide range of good-value food is available either in the restaurant or Granary's Bistro. The hotel can cater for functions in a separate purpose built suite.
Rooms 5 en suite 3 annexe en suite (1 fmly) (3 GF) ⊘ in all bedrooms Parking 40

BEAUMARIS
MAP 06 SH67

★★★ 74% HOTEL
Best Western Bulkeley Hotel
Castle St LL58 8AW
☎ 01248 810415 📄 01248 810146
e-mail: reception@thebulkeleyhotel.com
Dir: *from M56 & M6 take A5 or A55 coast road*
PETS: Bedrooms unattended Charges £10 per night charge for damage Public areas lounge & bar on leads Grounds accessible on leads disp bin Exercise area 2 mins walk Facilities water bowl walks info vet info On Request torch towels

A Grade I listed hotel built in 1831, the Bulkeley has fine views from many rooms. Well-equipped bedrooms are generally spacious, with pretty fabrics and wallpapers. There is a choice of bars, an all-day coffee lounge and a health club. Regular jazz evenings, a resident pianist and friendly staff create a relaxed atmosphere.

Rooms 43 en suite (11 fmly) S £80-£110; D £115-£185 (incl. bkfst)✳
Facilities Wi-fi in bedrooms Hair & Beauty Salon New Year Services Lift
Parking 25 Notes LB

★★ 84% ⦿ HOTEL
Bishopsgate House
54 Castle St LL58 8BB
☎ 01248 810302 📄 01248 810166
e-mail: hazel@bishopsgatehotel.co.uk
Dir: *from Menai Bridge onto A545 to Beaumaris. Hotel on left in main street*
PETS: Bedrooms Charges £5 per night charge for damage
Resident Pets: Pollyann Jane (cat)
This immaculately maintained, privately owned and personally run small hotel dates back to 1760. It features fine examples of wood panelling and a Chinese Chippendale staircase. Thoughtfully furnished bedrooms are attractively decorated and two have four-poster beds. Quality cooking is served in the elegant restaurant and guests have a comfortable lounge and cosy bar to relax in.
Rooms 9 en suite S £55; D £85 (incl. bkfst)✳ Parking 8

DULAS
MAP 06 SH48

▶▶▶▶ Tyddyn Isaf Caravan Park (SH486873)
Lligwy Bay LL70 9PQ
☎ 01248 410203 📄 01248 410667
e-mail: enquiries@tyddynisaf.demon.co.uk
web: www.tyddynisaf.demon.co.uk
Dir: *Take A5025 through Benllech to Moelfre rdbt, left towards Amlwch to Brynrefail village. Turn right opposite craft shop. Park 0.5m down lane on right*
PETS: Public areas on leads except shop, bar & play area
Exercise area on site surrounding walks adjacent Facilities on site shop food bowl water bowl dog scoop/disp bags walks info vet info space for loose box Other prior notice required
Resident Pets: Labrador, cat, sheep & cattle
Open Mar-Oct (rs Mar-Jul & Sep-Oct Bar & shop opening limited) Booking advisable May bank hol & Jun-Aug Last arrival 22.00hrs Last departure 11.00hrs
A beautifully situated, very spacious family park on quite steeply rising ground adjacent to a sandy beach, with magnificent views overlooking Lligwy Bay. Access to the beach is by private footpath (lengthy from some pitches), or by car for the less energetic. The park has very good toilet facilities, a well-stocked shop, and a clubhouse serving meals and takeaway food. Reception is a long, steep walk from the entrance and many pitches. A 16-acre site with 80 touring pitches, 20 hardstandings and 56 statics.
Notes ⊛ no groups

WALES

HOLYHEAD MAP 06 SH28

★★ GUEST HOUSE
Wavecrest
93 Newry St LL65 1HU
☎ 01407 763637 📄 01407 764862
e-mail: cwavecrest@aol.com
web: www.holyheadhotels.com
Dir: *Left at end A55, 600yds turn by railings, premises 100yds up hill on right*
PETS: Bedrooms Grounds accessible **Exercise area** 20yds
Resident Pets: Purdi (Staffordshire Bull Terrier)

Well located for the Irish ferry terminals and within easy walking distance of the town centre, the Wavecrest is proving to be a popular overnight stop-off. Pretty bedrooms are equipped with satellite television and other modern facilities. There is a comfortable lounge and evening meals may be booked in advance.

Rooms 4 rms (2 en suite) (3 fmly) ⊘ **Facilities** STV TVB tea/coffee Cen ht TVL Dinner Last d 3pm **Parking** 1 **Notes** No coaches Closed 24-31 Dec ⊛

LLANBEDRGOCH MAP 06 SH58

▶▶▶ **Ty Newydd Leisure Park** *(SH508813)*
LL76 8TZ
☎ 01248 450677 📄 01248 450711
e-mail: mike@tynewydd.com
web: www.tynewydd.com
Dir: *A5025 from Brittania Bridge. Through Pentraeth, bear left at layby. Site 0.75m on right*
PETS: Public areas except pool, bar, restaurant **Exercise area** on site adjacent **Facilities** on site shop food food bowl water bowl dog chews cat treats dog scoop/disp bags washing facs dog grooming walks info vet info

Open Whit-mid Sep (rs Mar-Whit & mid Sep-Oct club/shop wknds only,outdoor pool closed) Booking advisable Etr, Whit & Jul-Aug Last arrival 23.30hrs Last departure 10.00hrs

A low-density park with many facilities including a heated outdoor pool, a club with restaurant, and a good playground. A 4-acre site with 48 touring pitches, 15 hardstandings and 62 statics.

PENTRAETH MAP 06 SH57

▶▶▶ **Rhos Caravan Park** *(SH517794)*
Rhos Farm LL75 8DZ
☎ 01248 450214 📄 01248 450214
web: www.rhoscaravanpark.co.uk
Dir: *Site on left of A5025, 1m N of Pentraeth*
PETS: Charges 50p per night **Public areas** except toilets & play area **Exercise area** on site 4 acre field & in 0.5m **Facilities** walks info vet info **Other** prior notice required **Resident Pets:** Tess (Springer Spaniel), Jack (Chocolate Labrador)

Open Etr-Oct (rs Mar shop restricted) Booking advisable Spring bank hol & Jul-Aug Last arrival 22.00hrs Last departure 16.00hrs

A warm welcome awaits families at this spacious park on level, grassy ground with easy access to the main road to Amlwch. This 200-acre working farm has a games room, two play areas and farm animals to keep children amused, with good beaches, pubs, restaurants and shops nearby. The two toilet blocks are kept to a good standard by enthusiastic owners, who are constantly improving the facilities. A 15-acre site with 98 touring pitches and 66 statics.

RHOSNEIGR MAP 06 SH37

▶▶▶ **Ty Hen** *(SH323737)*
Station Rd LL64 5QZ
☎ 01407 810331 📄 01407 810331
e-mail: bernardtyhen@hotmail.com
web: www.tyhen.com
Dir: *A55 across Anglesey. At exit 5 follow signs to Rhosneigr, at clock turn right. Entrance adjacent to Rhosneigr railway station*
PETS: Public areas except pool, play area & toilets on leads **Exercise area** on site **Facilities** walks info vet info
Resident Pets: Twix, Thomas & Suzie (cats), Phebe & Maisey (Shetland Ponies), Percy & Petal (Donkeys)

Open mid Mar-Oct Booking advisable all year Last arrival 21.00hrs Last departure noon

Attractive seaside position near a large fishing lake and riding stables, in lovely countryside. A smart toilet block offers a welcome amenity at this popular family park, where friendly owners are always on hand. A 7.5-acre site with 38 touring pitches, 5 hardstandings and 42 statics.

Notes 1 motor vehicle per pitch, children in tents/tourers/statics by 22.00hrs

WALES

BRIDGEND

CARDIFF

BRIDGEND   MAP 03 SS97

★★★ 73% HOTEL

Best Western Heronston

Ewenny Rd CF35 5AW

☎ 01656 668811 & 666084 📠 01656 767391

e-mail: reservations@heronston-hotel.demon.co.uk

web: www.bw-heronstonhotel.co.uk

Dir: *M4 junct 35, follow signs for Porthcawl, at 5th rdbt turn left towards Ogmore-by-Sea (B4265) hotel 200yds on left*

PETS: Bedrooms Charges £10 per night charge for damage **Grounds** accessible on leads **Facilities** walks info vet info

Situated within easy reach of the town centre and the M4, this large modern hotel offers spacious well-equipped accommodation, including no-smoking bedrooms and ground floor rooms. Public areas include an open-plan lounge/bar, attractive restaurant and a smart leisure & fitness club. The hotel also has a choice of function/conference rooms and ample parking is available.

Rooms 75 en suite (4 fmly) (37 GF) ⊘ in 21 bedrooms S £65-£105; D £79-£115 (incl. bkfst)✳ **Facilities** STV ⊗ ⌁ supervised Gym Wi-fi in bedrooms Steamroom Xmas New Year **Services** Lift **Parking** 160 **Notes** LB

SARN PARK MOTORWAY   MAP 03 SS98
SERVICE AREA (M4)

BUDGET HOTEL

Days Inn Cardiff West

Sarn Park Services CF32 9RW

☎ 01656 659218 📠 01656 768665

e-mail: daysinncardiff@tiscali.co.uk

web: www.daysinn.com

Dir: *M4 junct 36*

PETS: Bedrooms Grounds accessible

This modern building offers accommodation in smart, spacious and well-equipped bedrooms, suitable for families and business travellers, and all with en suite bathrooms. Continental breakfast is available and other refreshments may be taken at the nearby family restaurant. For further details see the Hotel Groups page.

Rooms 40 en suite

CARDIFF   MAP 03 ST17

★★★★ 70% ⊛ HOTEL

Copthorne Hotel Cardiff-Caerdydd

Copthorne Way, Culverhouse Cross CF5 6DA

☎ 029 2059 9100 📠 029 2059 9080

e-mail: reservations.cardiff@mill-cop.com

web: www.copthorne.com

Dir: *M4 junct 33, A4232 for 2.5m towards Cardiff West. Then A48 W to Cowbridge*

PETS: Bedrooms (GF) **Public areas** except restaurant on leads **Grounds** accessible on leads **Facilities** cage storage walks info vet info **On Request** fridge access torch towels

A comfortable, popular and modern hotel, conveniently located for the airport and city. Bedrooms are a good size and some have a private lounge. Public areas are smartly presented with features including a gym, pool, meeting rooms and a comfortable restaurant with views of the adjacent lake.

Rooms 135 en suite (14 fmly) (27 GF) ⊘ in all bedrooms S £59-£200; D £69-£230 **Facilities** STV ⊗ Gym Wi-fi available Sauna Steam room ♫ New Year **Services** Lift **Parking** 225 **Notes** LB

★★★★ GUEST ACCOMMODATION

The Big Sleep Cardiff

Bute Ter CF10 2FE

☎ 029 2063 6363 📠 029 2063 6364

e-mail: bookings.cardiff@thebigsleephotel.com

Dir: *Opp Cardiff International Arena*

PETS: Bedrooms

Part of the Cardiff skyline, this city-centre establishment offers well-equipped bedrooms ranging from standard to penthouse, with spectacular views over the city towards the bay. There is a bar on the ground floor and secure parking. Choose between a continental breakfast or Breakfast to Go, an alternative for travellers making an early start.

Rooms 81 en suite (6 fmly) ⊘ in 60 bedrooms **Facilities** STV TVB tea/coffee Direct dial from bedrooms Lift Cen ht **Parking** 20

WALES

CARMARTHENSHIRE

CROSS HANDS MAP 02 SN51

►►► Black Lion Caravan & Camping Park

(SN572129)

78 Black Lion Rd, Gorslas SA14 6RU

☎ 01269 845365

e-mail: blacklionsite@aol.com

web: www.caravansite.com

Dir: *M4 junct 49 onto A48 to Cross Hands rdbt, right onto A476 (Llandeilo). 0.5m at Gorslas sharp right into Black Lion Rd. Site 0.5m on right, (follow brown tourist signs from Cross Hands rdbt)*

PETS: Charges 1st dog free, £2 per extra dog per night
Public areas except play areas on leads **Exercise area** on site
Facilities washing facs walks info vet info space for loose box
Other prior notice required

Open Apr-Oct (rs Oct-Mar main toilet block closed) Booking advisable Last arrival 22.00hrs Last departure 11.00hrs

Cheerful and friendly owners keep this improving park clean and well maintained. The very good toilet and shower facilities include a separate room for disabled guests, and this is a popular overnight stop for people travelling on the Irish ferries. The National Botanic Garden of Wales is about 10 minutes' drive away. A 12-acre site with 45 touring pitches, 10 hardstandings.

CWMDUAD MAP 02 SN33

★★★ GUEST HOUSE
Neuadd-Wen

SA33 6XJ

☎ 01267 281438 📠 01267 281438

e-mail: goodbourn@neuaddwen.plus.com

Dir: *On A484, 9m N of Carmarthen, towards Cardigan*

PETS: Bedrooms (GF) **Charges** charge for damage
Public areas except dining room **Grounds** accessible disp bin
Exercise area field adjacent **Facilities** water bowl bedding
feeding mat washing facs walks info vet info **On Request** fridge
access torch towels

Excellent customer care is assured at this combined Post Office and house situated in pretty gardens in an unspoiled village. Bedrooms are filled with thoughtful extras and there is a choice of lounges. One bedroom is in a carefully renovated Victorian toll cottage across the road. There is an attractive dining room that serves imaginative dinners using fresh local produce.

Rooms 9 rms (6 en suite) 1 annexe en suite (2 fmly) (2 GF) ⊗
S £22-£26; D £44-£52 **Facilities** TV9B tea/coffee Direct dial from
bedrooms Licensed Cen ht TVL Dinner Last d 5pm **Parking** 12
Notes LB No coaches

HARFORD MAP 02 SN64

►►► Springwater Lakes *(SN637430)*

SA19 8DT

☎ 01558 650788 📠 01558 650788

Dir: *4m E of Lampeter on A482, entrance well signed on right*

PETS: Charges 1st dog free, £1.50 per extra dog per night
Public areas on leads **Exercise area** on site **Facilities** vet info
Other prior notice required

Open Mar-Oct Booking advisable Jun-Aug Last arrival 20.00hrs Last departure 11.00hrs

In a rural setting overlooked by the Cambrian Mountains, this park is adjoined on each side by four spring-fed and well-stocked fishing lakes. All pitches have hardstandings, electricity and TV hook-ups, and there is a small and very clean toilet block and a shop. A 20-acre site with 20 touring pitches, 12 hardstandings.

Notes 🐾 children must be supervised around lakes

LLANDOVERY MAP 03 SN73

►►► Erwlon Caravan & Camping Park

(SN776343)

Brecon Rd SA20 0RD

☎ 01550 721021

e-mail: peter@erwlon.fsnet.co.uk

Dir: *0.5m E of Llandovery on A40*

PETS: Stables nearby (1m) (loose box) **Charges**
Public areas on leads **Exercise area** on site fenced area provided
250 acre farm & public footpaths adjacent **Facilities** washing facs
walks info vet info

Open all year Booking advisable BHs Last arrival anytime Last departure noon

Long-established family-run site set beside a brook in the Brecon Beacons foothills. The town of Llandovery and the hills overlooking the Towy Valley are a short walk away. A superb facilities block with cubicled washrooms, family and disabled rooms is part of ongoing improvements. An 8-acre site with 75 touring pitches, 15 hardstandings.

Notes 🐾 Quiet after 22.30hrs

WALES

LLANELLI

MAP 02 SN50

★★★ 75% HOTEL

Best Western Diplomat Hotel

Felinfoel SA15 3PJ

☎ 01554 756156 📠 01554 751649

e-mail: reservations@diplomat-hotel-wales.com

web: www.diplomat-hotel-wales.com

Dir: *M4 junct 48 onto A4138 then B4303, hotel 0.75m on right*

PETS: Bedrooms unattended Charges £5 per night
Public areas except restaurant on leads Grounds accessible on leads disp bin Facilities cage storage walks info vet info
On Request fridge access torch towels Resident Pets: Heidi & Duke (Labrador Alsatian cross)

This Victorian mansion, set in mature grounds, has been extended over the years to provide a comfortable and relaxing hotel. The well-appointed bedrooms are located in the main house and there is also a wing of comfortable modern bedrooms. Public areas include Trubshaw's restaurant, a large function suite and a modern leisure centre.

Rooms 42 en suite 8 annexe en suite (2 fmly) (4 GF) ⊘ in 42 bedrooms S £60-£70; D £80-£90 (incl. bkfst)✳ Facilities ⓣ supervised Gym ♫ Xmas New Year Services Lift Parking 250 Notes LB

See advert on opposite page

NEWCASTLE EMLYN

MAP 02 SN34

▶▶▶ Argoed Meadow Caravan and Camping Site *(SN268415)*

Argoed Farm SA38 9JL

☎ 01239 710690

web: www.cenarthcamping.co.uk

PETS: Stables nearby (3m) (loose box) Public areas on leads
Exercise area on site 7 acre field & 2 mins walk
Facilities washing facs walks info vet info Other prior notice required

Open all year Booking advisable

Pleasant open meadowland on the banks of the River Teifi, very close to Cenarth Falls gorge. A 3-acre site with 30 touring pitches, 5 hardstandings.

Notes ⊛

▶▶▶ Dolbryn Camping & Caravanning

(SN298382)

Capel Iwan Rd SA38 9LP

☎ 01239 710683

e-mail: dolbryn@btinternet.com

web: www.dolbryn.co.uk

Dir: *A484 (Carmarthan to Cardigan road). At Newcastle Emlyn (signed) turn to Capel Iwan. Follow signs*

PETS: Stables nearby (3m) Public areas on leads under strict control Exercise area on site large field Facilities walks info vet info Other prior notice required

Open Mar-Nov Booking advisable Last arrival 23.30hrs Last departure 19.00hrs

A secluded park set in a peaceful valley with a stream, ponds, mature trees and an abundance of wildlife in 13 acres, that include a vineyard and plenty of nature walks. The toilets and showers are located in rustic farm outbuildings. The cosy bar offers a chance to get together with fellow campers, or take part in family activities. A 6-acre site with 60 touring pitches.

Notes ⊛ quiet after 23.30hrs

▶▶▶ Moelfryn Caravan & Camping Site

(SN321370)

Ty-Cefn, Pant-y-Bwlch SA38 9JE

☎ 01559 371231 📠 01559 371231

e-mail: moelfryn@tinyonline.co.uk

Dir: *A484 from Carmarthen towards Cynwyl Elfed. Pass Blue Bell Inn on right, 200yds take left fork onto B4333 towards Hermon. In 7m brown sign on left. Turn left, site on right*

PETS: Public areas except shower block & play area Facilities on site shop vet info Restrictions Telephone for details
Resident Pets: Kai (German Shepherd), 3 cats & 2 horses

Open Mar-10 Jan Booking advisable Jul-Aug Last arrival 22.00hrs Last departure noon

A small family-run park in an elevated location overlooking the valley of the River Teifi. Pitches are level and spacious, and well screened by hedging and mature trees. Facilities are well maintained, clean and tidy, and the playing field is well away from the touring area. A 3-acre site with 25 touring pitches, 13 hardstandings.

Notes ⊛

RHANDIRMWYN   MAP 03 SN74

►►► Rhandirmwyn Camping & Caravanning Club Site *(SN779435)*

SA20 0NT

☎ 01550 760257

web: www.campingandcaravanningclub.co.uk

Dir: *From Llandovery take A483, turn left signed Rhandirmwyn for 7m, left at post office, site on left before river*

PETS: **Exercise area** on site dog walks **Facilities** walks info vet info **Other** prior notice required

Open Mar-Oct Booking advisable BH & peak periods Last arrival 21.00hrs Last departure noon

On the banks of the Afon Tywi near Towy Forest and the Llyn Brianne reservoir, this secluded park has superb views from all pitches. The park is divided into paddocks by mature hedging, and facilities and grounds are very well tended. An 11-acre site with 90 touring pitches, 17 hardstandings.

CEREDIGION

ABERYSTWYTH   MAP 06 SN58

★★ 80% HOTEL

Marine Hotel & Leisure Suite

The Promenade SY23 2BX

☎ 01970 612444 ▤ 01970 617435

e-mail: marinehotel1@btconnect.com

web: www.marinehotelaberystwyth.co.uk

Dir: *from W on A44. From N or S Wales on A487. On seafront, west of pier*

PETS: **Bedrooms Charges** £5 per night **Exercise area** park

The Marine is a privately owned hotel situated on the promenade overlooking Cardigan Bay. Bedrooms have been tastefully decorated, some have four-poster beds and many have sea views. The reception rooms are comfortable and relaxing, and meals are served in the elegant dining room or the bar.

Rooms 48 rms (47 en suite) (9 fmly) ⊘ in all bedrooms S £35-£65; D £55-£105 (incl. bkfst) **Facilities** Gym Wi-fi in bedrooms Steam room Xmas New Year **Services** Lift **Parking** 27 (charged) **Notes** LB

★★★★ GUEST HOUSE

Llety Ceiro Country House

Peggy Ln, Bow St, Llandre SY24 5AB

☎ 01970 821900 ▤ 01970 820966

e-mail: marinehotel1@btconnect.com

Dir: *4m NE of Aberystwyth. Off A487 onto B4353 for 300yds*

PETS: **Bedrooms** unattended **Public areas** except restaurant **Grounds** accessible

Located north of Aberystwyth, this house is immaculately maintained throughout. Bedrooms are equipped with a range of thoughtful extras in addition to smart modern bathrooms. A spacious conservatory lounge is available in addition to an attractive dining room, and bicycle hire is also available.

Rooms 11 en suite (2 fmly) (3 GF) ⊘ S £35-£65; D £50-£85 **Facilities** TVB tea/coffee Direct dial from bedrooms Licensed Cen ht TVL Dinner Last d 8pm Free use of facilities at sister hotel **Parking** 21 **Notes** LB

WALES

ABERYSTWYTH CONTINUED

★★★ GUEST HOUSE
Queensbridge Hotel
Promenade, Victoria Ter SY23 2DH
☎ 01970 612343 📠 01970 617452
Dir: *500yds N of town centre near Constitution Hill*
PETS: Bedrooms Charges £5 per night
The friendly Queensbridge is on the promenade at the north end of the town. The bedrooms, some suitable for families, have modern facilities and many have fine sea views. There is a comfortable lounge, and a bar where snacks are available. A lift serves all floors.

Rooms 15 en suite (2 fmly) ⊗ S £35-£55; D £65-£85✳ **Facilities** TVB tea/coffee Direct dial from bedrooms Licensed Lift Cen ht TVL Golf **Parking** 6 **Notes** LB

BETTWS EVAN   MAP 02 SN34

►►► Pilbach Holiday Park *(SN306476)*
SA44 5RT
☎ 01239 851434 📠 01239 851969
e-mail: info@pilbach.com
web: www.pilbach.com
Dir: *S on A487, turn left onto B4333*
PETS: Charges £2-£4 per night **Public areas Exercise area** on site dog walk area **Facilities** on site shop food bowl water bowl washing facs walks info vet info **Other** prior notice required **Restrictions** no large dogs

Open Mar-Oct (rs Mar-Spring BH & Oct swimming pool closed) Booking advisable Spring BH & Jul-Aug Last arrival 22.00hrs Last departure noon

Set in secluded countryside, with two separate paddocks and pitches clearly marked in the grass, close to nearby seaside resorts. It has a heated outdoor swimming pool, and entertainment in the club two or three times a week in high season. A 15-acre site with 65 touring pitches, 10 hardstandings and 70 statics.

CROSS INN   MAP 02 SN35

►►► Cardigan Bay Camping & Caravanning Club Site *(SN383566)*
Llwynhelyg SA44 6LW
☎ 01545 560029
web: www.campingandcaravanningclub.co.uk
Dir: *Left from A487 (Cardigan-Aberystwyth) at Synod Inn. Take A486 signed New Quay. In village of Cross Inn, left after Penrhiwgaled Arms Pub. Site 0.75m on right*
PETS: Public areas except buildings **Exercise area** on site **Facilities** walks info vet info **Other** prior notice required

Open Mar-Oct Booking advisable BH & peak periods Last arrival 21.00hrs Last departure noon

An excellent, attractive touring site in an elevated rural position with extensive country views. A footpath from the site joins the coastal walk, and the pretty village of New Quay is only a short drive away. A 14-acre site with 90 touring pitches, 6 hardstandings.

EGLWYSFACH   MAP 06 SN69

★★★ COUNTRY HOUSE HOTEL
Ynyshir Hall
SY20 8TA
☎ 01654 781209 & 781268 📠 01654 781366
e-mail: ynyshir@relaischateaux.com
web: www.vonessenhotels.co.uk
Dir: *off A487, 5.5m S of Machynlleth, signed from main road*
PETS: Bedrooms (GF) unattended sign **Sep Accom** outside kennel **Charges** £3 per night £21 per week charge for damage **Grounds** accessible **Facilities** food (pre-bookable) food bowl water bowl walks info vet info **On Request** torch towels **Other** dogs in ground floor only **Resident Pets:** Oscar (Bermese Mountain Dog)

Set in beautifully landscaped grounds and surrounded by a RSBP reserve, Ynyshir Hall is a haven of calm. Lavishly styled bedrooms, each individually themed around a great painter, provide high standards of luxury and comfort. Lounge and bar have different moods, and both feature abundant fresh flowers. The dining room offers outstanding cooking using best ingredients with modern flair.

Rooms 7 en suite 2 annexe en suite ⊘ in all bedrooms S £180-£250; D £180-£375 (incl. bkfst)✶ **Facilities** ⬞ Xmas New Year **Parking** 20 **Notes** LB No children 9yrs Closed 5-29 Jan

---

GWBERT-ON-SEA   MAP 02 SN15

★★★ 77% HOTEL
The Cliff Hotel

SA43 1PP

☎ 01239 613241 📠 01239 615391

e-mail: reservations@cliffhotel.com

Dir: off A487 into Cardigan, follow signs to Gwbert, 3m to hotel

PETS: Bedrooms Stables on site **Charges** £5 per night **Grounds** accessible **Exercise area** 20yds

Set in 30 acres of grounds with a 9-hole golf course, and enjoying a cliff-top location overlooking Cardigan Bay, this hotel commands superb sea views. Bedrooms in the main building offer excellent bay views and there is also a wing of 22 modern rooms. Public areas are spacious and comprise a choice of bars, lounges and the fine dining restaurant. The spa offers a wide range of up-to-the-minute leisure facilities.

Rooms 70 en suite (6 fmly) (5 GF) ⊘ in all bedrooms **Facilities** Spa STV ⊗ ↺ ↓9 Fishing Gym **Services** Lift **Parking** 150 **Notes**

LAMPETER   MAP 02 SN54

★★★ 86% ◉◉ COUNTRY HOUSE HOTEL
Best Western Falcondale Mansion

SA48 7RX

☎ 01570 422910 📠 01570 423559

e-mail: info@falcondalehotel.com

web: www.falcondalehotel.com

Dir: 800yds W of High St A475 or 1.5m NW of Lampeter A482

PETS: Bedrooms unattended sign **Charges** £6 per night **Public areas** except dining areas **Exercise area** nearby **Facilities** food (pre-bookable) food bowl water bowl bedding dog scoop/disp bags leads dog walking on request cage storage walks info vet info **On Request** fridge access torch towels **Restrictions** Telephone for details **Resident Pets:** Chloe & Truffles (cats), Pudgeley & Major (Cocker Spaniels)

Built in the Italianate style, this charming Victorian property is set in extensive grounds and beautiful parkland. The individually-styled

---

bedrooms are generally spacious, well equipped and tastefully decorated. Bars and lounges are similarly well appointed with additional facilities including a conservatory and function room. Guests have a choice of either the Valley Restaurant for fine dining or the less formal Peterwells Brasserie.

Rooms 20 en suite (2 fmly) ⊘ in 16 bedrooms S £95-£120; D £130-£168 (incl. bkfst)✶ **Facilities** ⬞ Wi-fi in bedrooms Xmas **Services** Lift **Parking** 60

CONWY

ABERGELE   MAP 06 SH97

►►► Roberts Caravan Park (SH937740)

Waterloo Service Station, Penrefail Crossroads LL22 8PN

☎ 01745 833265

e-mail: gailyroberts@btinternet.com

Dir: From Abergele take A548 for 2m, turn left onto B5381 signed St Asaph, park entrance at filling station

PETS: Charges £1 per night **Public areas** except toilets **Exercise area** on site small dog run **Facilities** on site shop dog chews cat treats litter disp bags walks info vet info

Open Mar-Oct Booking advisable BH & Jul-Aug

A pretty hillside park with countryside views towards the coast. The spacious serviced pitches and excellent toilet facilities enhance this beautifully landscaped park, and will appeal to those seeking peace and relaxation. The friendly owners are always on hand. A filling station and shop are handily placed at the entrance. A 3-acre site with 60 touring pitches.

BETWS-Y-COED   MAP 06 SH75

★★★ 77% ◉ COUNTRY HOUSE HOTEL
Craig-y-Dderwen Riverside Hotel

LL24 0AS

☎ 01690 710293 📠 01690 710362

e-mail: info@snowdoniahotel.com

web: www.snowdoniahotel.com

Dir: A5 to town, cross Waterloo Bridge, take 1st left

PETS: Bedrooms unattended **Charges** £7.50 per night **Public areas** except restaurant & bistro **Grounds** accessible **Exercise area** on site 16 acres of fields **Facilities** food **Resident Pets:** Reggy, Snowy & Delilah (cats)

This Victorian country-house hotel is set in well-maintained grounds alongside the River Conwy, at the end of a tree-lined drive. Very pleasant views can be enjoyed from many rooms, and two of the bedrooms have four-poster beds. There are comfortable lounges and the atmosphere is tranquil and relaxing.

Rooms 16 en suite (2 fmly) (1 GF) ⊘ in 13 bedrooms S £70-£90; D £80-£160 (incl. bkfst)✶ **Facilities** STV ⬞ Wi-fi in bedrooms Badminton Volleyball New Year **Parking** 50 **Notes** Closed 23-26 Dec & 2 Jan-1 Feb

COLWYN BAY MAP 06 SH87

★★★★ GUEST HOUSE
Whitehall Hotel

51 Cayley Promenade, Rhos-on-Sea LL28 4EP
☎ 01492 547296
e-mail: mossd.cymru@virgin.net
web: www.whitehall-hotel.co.uk

Dir: *A55 onto B5115 Brompton Av, right at rdbt onto Whitehall Rd to seafront*

PETS: Bedrooms Grounds accessible **Exercise area** adjacent **Facilities** pets in one bedroom only

Overlooking Rhos-on-Sea promenade, this popular, family-run establishment is convenient for shopping and local amenities. Attractively appointed bedrooms include family rooms and a room on ground floor level. All benefit from an excellent range of facilities such as video and CD players, as well as air-conditioning. Facilities include a bar and a foyer lounge. Home cooked dinners are available.

Rooms 12 rms (10 en suite) (2 pri facs) (4 fmly) ⊗ **Facilities** STV TVB tea/coffee Direct dial from bedrooms Licensed Cen ht TVL Dinner Last d 4.30pm **Parking** 5

★★★ GUEST HOUSE
The Northwood

47 Rhos Rd, Rhos-on-Sea LL28 4RS
☎ 01492 549931
e-mail: welcome@thenorthwood.co.uk
web: www.thenorthwood.co.uk

Dir: *A55 onto B5115 Brompton Av, over rdbt, 2nd right*

PETS: Bedrooms (GF) unattended sign **Charges** £2.50-£5.50 per night charge for damage **Public areas** except dining room & lounge **Grounds** accessible disp bin **Exercise area** 10mtrs **Facilities** food (pre-bookable) food bowl water bowl dog chews cat treats feeding mat litter dog scoop/disp bags leads pet sitting dog walking washing facs cage storage walks info vet info **On Request** fridge access torch towels **Resident Pets:** Sticky and Fluffy (lovebirds), Sam (cat)

A short walk from the seafront and shops, the Northwood has a warm and friendly atmosphere and welcomes back many regular guests. Bedrooms are furnished in modern style and freshly prepared meals

can be enjoyed in the spacious dining room/bar while light refreshments are offered in the lounge.

Rooms 11 rms (10 en suite) (1 pri facs) (3 fmly) (2 GF) ⊗ S £30-£35; D £60-£66 **Facilities** TVB tea/coffee Licensed TVL Dinner Last d 7pm Wi-fi available **Parking** 12 **Notes LB** No coaches

CONWY MAP 06 SH77

★★★ 78% ◉◉ HOTEL
Castle Hotel Conwy

High St LL32 8DB

WELSH RAREBITS

☎ 01492 582800 📠 01492 582300
e-mail: mail@castlewales.co.uk
web: www.castlewales.co.uk

Dir: *A55 junct 18, follow town centre signs, cross estuary (castle on left). Right then left at mini-rdbts onto one-way system. Right at Town Wall Gate, right onto Berry St then along High St on left*

PETS: Bedrooms Charges £5 per night **Exercise area** 50mtrs **Facilities** food (pre-bookable) pet sitting dog walking dog grooming cage storage walks info vet info **On Request** fridge access torch towels **Restrictions** no breeds larger than Labrador **Resident Pets:** Tizzy (Cocker Spaniel)

This family-run, 16th-century hotel is one of Conwy's most distinguished buildings and offers a relaxed and friendly atmosphere. Bedrooms are appointed to an impressive standard and include a stunning suite. Public areas include a popular modern bar and the award-winning Shakespeare's restaurant.

Rooms 28 en suite (2 fmly) ⊗ in 20 bedrooms S £77-£95; D £110-£350 (incl. bkfst) **Facilities** STV Wi-fi in bedrooms New Year **Parking** 34 **Notes LB**

★★★ 78% ⍟ HOTEL

Groes Inn

WELSH RAREBITS

Tyn-y-Groes LL32 8TN

☎ 01492 650545 📄 01492 650855

e-mail: enquries@thegroes.com

web: www.groesinn.com

Dir: *A55, over Old Conwy Bridge, 1st left through Castle Walls on B5106 (Trefriw road), hotel 2m on right.*

PETS: Bedrooms unattended **Stables** by arrangement **Charges** £10 per night **Exercise area** adjacent **Other** pets in two bedrooms only

This inn dates back in part to the 16th century and has charming features. It offers a choice of bars and has a beautifully appointed restaurant, with a conservatory extension opening on to the lovely rear garden. The comfortable, well-equipped bedrooms are contained in a separate building; some have balconies or private terraces. The inn has a deservedly good reputation for its food.

Rooms 14 en suite (1 fmly) (6 GF) S £79-£145; D £95-£175 (incl. bkfst)✱ **Facilities** STV Wi-fi in bedrooms New Year **Parking** 100 **Notes** LB

★★★★★ 🏠 GUEST ACCOMMODATION

The Old Rectory Country House

Llanrwst Rd, Llansanffraid Glan Conwy LL28 5LF

☎ 01492 580611

e-mail: info@oldrectorycountryhouse.co.uk

web: www.oldrectorycountryhouse.co.uk

Dir: *0.5m S from A470/A55 junct on left, by 30mph sign*

PETS: Bedrooms (GF) unattended **Exercise area** 15mtrs **Facilities** washing facs cage storage walks info vet info **On Request** fridge access torch towels **Restrictions** no breeds larger than a Labrador; pets in coach house only

This very welcoming accommodation has fine views over the Conwy estuary and towards Snowdonia. The elegant day rooms are luxurious and afternoon tea is available in the lounge. Bedrooms share the delightful views and are thoughtfully furnished, and the genuine hospitality creates a real home from home.

Rooms 4 en suite 2 annexe en suite ⊘ S £79-£109; D £99-£159 **Facilities** TVB tea/coffee Direct dial from bedrooms Cen ht **Parking** 10 **Notes** LB No children 5yrs Closed 14 Dec-15 Jan

★★★★★ ⍟ 🛏 GUEST ACCOMMODATION

Sychnant Pass House

Sychnant Pass Rd LL32 8BJ

☎ 01492 596868 📄 01492 585486

e-mail: bre@sychnant-pass-house.co.uk

web: www.sychnant-pass-house.co.uk

Dir: *1.75m W of Conwy. Off A547 Bangor Rd in town onto Mount Pleasant & Sychnant Pass Rd, 1.75m on right near top of hill*

PETS: Bedrooms (GF) unattended **Charges** charge for damage **Public areas** except restaurant & leisure area **Grounds** accessible disp bin **Facilities** food (pre-bookable) water bowl bedding dog chews dog scoop/disp bags washing facs walks info vet info **On Request** fridge access torch towels **Resident Pets:** Morris, Peter & Wellington (cats), Nellie, Molly, Maisie & Millie (dogs)

Fine views are to be had from this Edwardian house set in landscaped grounds. Bedrooms, including suites and four poster rooms, are individually furnished and equipped with a range of thoughtful extras. Lounges, warmed by open fires in the chillier months, are comfortable and inviting, and imaginative dinners and suppers are served in the attractive dining room.

Rooms 12 en suite (3 fmly) (2 GF) ⊘ S £75-£160; D £95-£180✱ **Facilities** TVB tea/coffee Cen ht Dinner Last d 8.30pm Wi-fi available 🐾 Sauna Solarium Gymnasium **Parking** 30 **Notes** LB Closed 24-26 Dec & Jan

LLANDDULAS   MAP 06 SH97

►►►► Bron-Y-Wendon Caravan Park

(SH785903)

Wern Rd LL22 8HG

☎ 01492 512903 📄 01492 512903

e-mail: stay@northwales-holidays.co.uk

web: www.northwales-holidays.co.uk

Dir: *Take A55 W. Turn right at sign for Llanddulas A547 junct 23, then sharp right. 200yds, under A55 bridge. Park on left*

PETS: Charges £1 per night **Exercise area** at rear of the site **Facilities** walks info vet info

Open all year Booking advisable BH Last arrival anytime Last departure 11.00hrs

A good quality site with sea views from every pitch, and excellent purpose-built toilet facilities. Staff are helpful and friendly, and everything from landscaping to maintenance has a stamp of excellence. An ideal seaside base for touring Snowdonia, with lots of activities available nearby. An 8-acre site with 130 touring pitches, 85 hardstandings.

LLANDUDNO   MAP 06 SH78

★★ 80% SMALL HOTEL

Epperstone

15 Abbey Rd LL30 2EE

☎ 01492 878746 📄 01492 871223

e-mail: epperstonehotel@btconnect.com

Dir: *A55-A470 to Mostyn Street. Left at rdbt, 4th right into York Rd. Hotel on junct of York Rd & Abbey Rd*

PETS: Bedrooms (GF) **Public areas** except restaurant **Grounds** accessible disp bin **Exercise area** all around **Facilities** water bowl cage storage walks info vet info **On Request** fridge access torch

This delightful hotel is located in wonderful gardens in a residential part of town, within easy walking distance of the seafront and shopping area. Bedrooms are attractively decorated and thoughtfully equipped. A Victorian-style conservatory are available. A daily changing menu is offered in the bright dining room.

Rooms 8 en suite (5 fmly) (1 GF) ⊗ in all bedrooms S £27-£35; D £54-£70 (incl. bkfst)✳ **Facilities** STV Wi-fi available Xmas **Parking** 8 **Notes** LB No children 5yrs

★★ 76% HOTEL

Sunnymede

West Pde LL30 2BD

☎ 01492 877130 📄 01492 871824

e-mail: sunnymedehotel@yahoo.co.uk

Dir: *from A55 follow Llandudno & Deganwy signs. At 1st rdbt after Deganwy take 1st exit towards sea. Left at corner, then 400yds*

PETS: Bedrooms unattended **Public areas** except restaurant & library **Exercise area** 10yds **Resident Pets:** Sassy, Candy & Radar (rescue dogs)

Sunnymede is a friendly family-run hotel located on town's West Shore. Many rooms have views over the Conwy Estuary and Snowdonia. The modern bedrooms are attractively decorated and well equipped. Bar and lounge areas are particularly comfortable and attractive.

Rooms 15 en suite (3 fmly) (4 GF) ⊗ in all bedrooms S £54-£122; D £108-£122 (incl. bkfst & dinner)✳ **Facilities** Xmas **Parking** 18 **Notes** LB No children 3yrs Closed Jan-Feb & Nov RS Xmas

★★★ GUEST HOUSE

Vine House

23 Church Walks LL30 2HG

☎ 01492 876493 & 07977 059220

e-mail: gavin.jacob@tesco.net

Dir: *By Great Orme tram station*

PETS: Bedrooms Charges £3 per night **Public areas** except dining room **Exercise area** nearby **Facilities** washing facs cage storage walks info vet info **On Request** fridge access torch towels **Other** mobile phone number required if pets are left unattended in rooms **Resident Pets:** tropical fish

Vine House is a friendly family-run house located a short walk from the seafront and pier, opposite the historic tram station. Bedrooms vary in size and style and include some spacious, stylish refurbished rooms with separate sitting areas and modern bathrooms. All rooms have views of the sea or the Orme.

Rooms 4 rms (2 en suite) (2 pri facs) (1 fmly) ⊗ S £25-£31; D £44-£56 **Facilities** TVB tea/coffee Wi-fi available **Notes** LB No coaches ⊜

LLANRWST

MAP 06 SH86

★★★ 74% HOTEL

Maenan Abbey

Maenan LL26 0UL

☎ 01492 660247 📠 01492 660734

e-mail: reservations@manab.co.uk

Dir: *3m N on A470*

PETS: Please telephone for details

Set in its own spacious grounds, this privately owned hotel was built as an abbey in 1850 on the site of a 13th-century monastery. It is now a popular venue for weddings as the grounds and magnificent galleried staircase make an ideal backdrop for photographs. Bedrooms include a large suite and are equipped with modern facilities. Meals are served in the bar and newly refurbished restaurant.

Rooms 14 en suite (2 fmly) **Facilities** Fishing guided mountain walks **Parking** 60

▶▶▶ Bodnant Caravan Park *(SH805609)*

Nebo Rd LL26 0SD

☎ 01492 640248

e-mail: ermin@bodnant-caravan-park.co.uk

web: www.bodnant-caravan-park.co.uk

Dir: *S in Llanrwst, turn off A470 opposite Birmingham garage onto B5427 signed Nebo. Site 300yds on right, opposite leisure centre*

PETS: **Charges** 30p per dog per night **Public areas** except play area **Exercise area** on site fenced area, illuminated short dog walk Gwydyr Forest 1m **Facilities** walks info vet info **Other** prior notice required Pets' store 0.25m, kennels nearby Resident Pets: Dani, Besi, Bobi & Loli (working dogs), cats, sheep & fowl

Open Mar-end Oct (rs Mar- only 1 toilet block open if weather bad) Booking advisable Etr, May Day, spring bank hol & Jul-Aug Last arrival 21.00hrs Last departure 11.00hrs

This stunningly attractive park is filled with flower beds, and the landscape includes shrubberies and trees. The statics are unobtrusively sited, and the toilet blocks are very well kept. There is a separate playing field and rally field. A 5-acre site with 54 touring pitches and 2 statics.

Notes Main gates locked 23.00hrs-08.00hrs, no noise after 22.50hrs

---

TAL-Y-BONT (NEAR CONWY)
MAP 06 SH76

▶ Tynterfyn Touring Caravan Park *(SH768692)*

LL32 8YX

☎ 01492 660525

Dir: *5m S of Conwy on B5106, road sign Tal-y-Bont, 1st on left*

PETS: **Charges** 50p per night **Public areas** except play area **Exercise area** on site large field National Park adjacent **Facilities** food bowl water bowl walks info vet info **Other** prior notice required Resident Pets: Nel & Suzie (Border Collies)

Open Mar-Oct (tent pitches only for 28 days in year) Booking advisable BH & Jul-Aug Last arrival 22.00hrs Last departure noon

A quiet, secluded little park set in the beautiful Conwy Valley, and run by family owners. The grounds are tended with care, and the older-style toilet facilities sparkle. There is lots of room for children and dogs to run around. A 2-acre site with 15 touring pitches, 4 hardstandings.

Notes 🈯

WALES

TREFRIW   MAP 06 SH76

DENBIGHSHIRE

★★★★ GUEST ACCOMMODATION
Hafod Country House

LL27 0RQ

☎ 01492 640029 📠 01492 641351

e-mail: stay@hafod-house.co.uk

Dir: *On B5106 entering Trefriw from S, house on right*

PETS: Bedrooms unattended **Charges** £6 per night £37.50 per week **Public areas** bar only **Grounds** accessible disp bin **Facilities** food (pre-bookable) food bowl water bowl dog chews dog scoop/disp bags leads washing facs cage storage walks info vet info **On Request** fridge access torch towels
Resident Pets: Ilsa (Deerhound)

This former farmhouse is personally run and friendly with a wealth of charm and character. The tasteful bedrooms feature period furnishings and thoughtful extras such as fresh fruit. There is a comfortable sitting room and a cosy bar. The fixed-price menu is imaginative and makes good use of fresh, local produce while the breakfast menu offers a wide choice.

Rooms 6 en suite ⊗ S £40-£52.50; D £70-£95✱ **Facilities** TVB tea/coffee Direct dial from bedrooms Cen ht Dinner Last d 9pm **Parking** 14
Notes LB No children 11yrs Closed Jan RS Feb-Mar

CORWEN   MAP 06 SJ04

★★★★★ 🍴 GUEST HOUSE
Bron-y-Graig

LL21 0DR

☎ 01490 413007 📠 01490 413007

e-mail: business@north-wales-hotel.co.uk

web: www.north-wales-hotel.co.uk

Dir: *On A5 on E edge of Corwen*

PETS: Bedrooms Public areas except restaurant
Exercise area nearby **Resident Pets:** Jodie (Labrador), Tiptoes (cat)

A short walk from the town centre, this impressive Victorian house retains many original features including fireplaces, stained glass and a tiled floor in the entrance hall. Bedrooms, complemented by luxurious bathrooms, are thoughtfully furnished, and two are in a renovated coach house. Ground-floor areas include a traditionally furnished dining room and a comfortable lounge. A warm welcome, attentive service and imaginative food is assured.

Rooms 8 en suite 2 annexe en suite (3 fmly) ⊗ S £39-£49; D £59✱
Facilities STV TVB tea/coffee Direct dial from bedrooms Licensed Cen ht Dinner Last d 9.30pm Fishing **Parking** 15 **Notes LB** ch fac

[U]

Powys Country House

Holyhead Rd, Bonwm LL21 9EG

☎ 01490 412367 📠 01490 412367

e-mail: info@powyscountryhouse.co.uk

Dir: *On A5 1m E from Corwen, on left*

PETS: Bedrooms Grounds accessible **Exercise area** 100mtrs, paddock **Other** assist dogs in B&B, other dogs in cottage
Resident Pets: Louis (Leowberger), Tara (cross)

At the time of going to press the rating for this establishment had not been confirmed. Please check the AA website www.theAA.com for up-to-date information.

Rooms 4 en suite (2 fmly) ⊗ S £40-£45; D £55-£65✱ **Facilities** STV FTV TVB tea/coffee Cen ht TVL 🛁 **Parking** 12 **Notes LB** No children 3yrs Closed end Nov-end Mar

WALES

►► Llawr-Betws Farm Caravan Park

(SJ016424)

LL21 0HD

☎ 01490 460224 & 460296

web: www.ukparks.co.uk/llawrbetws

Dir: *3m W of Corwen off A494 (Bala road)*

PETS: **Public areas** **Facilities** walks info vet info

Open Mar-Oct Booking advisable BH & Jul-Aug Last arrival 23.00hrs Last departure noon

A quiet grassy park with mature trees and gently sloping pitches. The friendly owners keep the facilities in good condition. A 12.5-acre site with 35 touring pitches and 68 statics.

Notes ✉

LLANGOLLEN   MAP 07 SJ24

►► Penddol Caravan Park (SJ209427)

Abbey Rd LL20 8SS

☎ 01978 861851

Dir: *From Llangollen on A542, Abbey Rd, turn into Eisteddfodd Pavilion, then over humpback bridge. Site on left*

PETS: **Public areas** **Exercise area** adjacent field **Facilities** vet info

Open Mar-Oct Booking advisable BHs Last departure 16.00hrs

An elevated adults-only park enjoying panoramic views across the beautiful Vale of Llangollen. The Llangollen canal runs alongside this tidy park, offering scenic walks and horse drawn barge trips. Nearby is the Eisteddfod Pavilion, and the Llangollen steam railway. A 2.25-acre site with 30 touring pitches.

Notes ✉ Adults only

RHUALLT   MAP 06 SJ07

►►► Penisar Mynydd Caravan Park

(SJ093770)

Caerwys Rd LL17 0TY

☎ 01745 582227 📄 01745 582227

e-mail: penisarmynydd@btinternet.com

Dir: *From Llandudno take 1st left at top of Rhuallt Hill (junct 29). From Chester take junct 29, follow signs for Dyserth, park 500yds on right*

PETS: **Charges** £1 per night **Public areas** on leads **Exercise area** on site rally field available when not in use walks nearby **Facilities** vet info

Open Mar-Jan Booking advisable BH Last arrival 22.00hrs

A very tranquil, attractively laid-out park set in three grassy paddocks with superb facilities block including a disabled room and dishwashing area. The majority of pitches are super pitches. Everything is immaculately maintained, and the amenities of the seaside resort of Rhyll are close by. A 6.75-acre site with 75 touring pitches, 75 hardstandings.

Notes ✉

RUABON   MAP 07 SJ34

►►► James' Caravan Park (SJ300434)

LL14 6DW

☎ 01978 820148 📄 01978 820148

e-mail: ray@carastay.demon.co.uk

Dir: *0.5m W of the A483/A539 junct to Llangollen*

PETS: **Charges** £2 per night **Public areas** on leads **Exercise area** on site **Facilities** walks info vet info **Other** prior notice required

Open all year Booking advisable BHs Last arrival 21.00hrs Last departure 11.00hrs

A well-landscaped park on a former farm, with modern heated toilet facilities. Old farm buildings house a collection of restored original farm machinery, and the village shop, four pubs, take away and launderette are a ten-minute walk away. A 6-acre site with 40 touring pitches, 4 hardstandings.

Notes ✉

RUTHIN   MAP 06 SJ15

★★★★ GUEST ACCOMMODATION

Eyarth Station

Llanfair Dyffryn Clwyd LL15 2EE

☎ 01824 703643 📄 01824 707464

e-mail: stay@eyarthstation.com

Dir: *1m S of Ruthin. Off A525 onto lane, 600yds to Eyarth Station*

PETS: **Bedrooms** (GF) **Sep Accom** **Charges** £6 per night charge for damage **Public areas** except dining room & lounge on leads **Grounds** accessible on leads disp bin **Exercise area** 20yds **Facilities** food bowl water bowl feeding mat dog scoop/disp bags leads washing facs cage storage walks info vet info **On Request** fridge access torch towels **Restrictions** no Rottweilers or Pitt Bull Terriers

Until 1964 and the Beeching cuts, this was a sleepy country station. A comfortable lounge and outdoor swimming pool occupy the space once taken up by the railway and platforms. Bedrooms are carefully decorated and full of thoughtful extras. Family rooms are available, and two rooms are in the former stationmaster's house adjoining the main building.

Rooms 4 en suite 2 annexe en suite (2 fmly) (4 GF) ⊘ S £50; D £70-£75✳ **Facilities** TV1B tea/coffee Cen ht TVL Dinner Last d 7pm ⚡ **Parking** 6 **Notes** LB

WALES

WALES

FLINTSHIRE

MOLD

MAP 07 SJ26

★★★ 73% HOTEL

Beaufort Park Hotel

Alltami Rd, New Brighton CH7 6RQ

☎ 01352 758646 📄 01352 757132

e-mail: info@beaufortparkhotel.co.uk

web: www.beaufortparkhotel.co.uk

Dir: *A55/A494. Through Alltami lights, over mini rdbt by petrol station towards Mold, A5119. Hotel 100yds on right*

PETS: Bedrooms

This large, modern hotel is conveniently located a short drive from the North Wales Expressway and offers various styles of spacious accommodation. There are extensive public areas, and several meeting and function rooms are available. There is a wide choice of meals in the formal restaurant and in the popular Arches bar.

Rooms 105 en suite (8 fmly) (32 GF) ⊘ in 92 bedrooms S £70-£95; D £95-£110 (incl. bkfst)✳ **Facilities** STV Squash Wi-fi available ♫ Xmas New Year **Parking** 200 **Notes LB**

GWYNEDD

ABERDYFI

MAP 06 SN69

★★ 82% ⚉ SMALL HOTEL

Penhelig Arms Hotel & Restaurant

WELSH RAREBITS

LL35 0LT

☎ 01654 767215 📄 01654 767690

e-mail: info@penheligarms.com

web: www.penheligarms.com

Dir: *take A493 coastal road, hotel faces Penhelig harbour*

PETS: Bedrooms unattended **Charges** £4 per night **Public areas** except restaurant **Grounds** accessible **Exercise area** 25yds

Situated opposite the old harbour, this delightful 18th-century hotel overlooks the Dyfi Estuary. The well-maintained bedrooms have good quality furnishings and modern facilities. Some are situated in a purpose built cliff top annexe, whilst a self-contained family suite is located in an adjacent cottage. The public bar retains its original character and is much loved by locals who enjoy the real ale selections and the excellent food, with its emphasis on seafood.

Rooms 10 en suite 5 annexe en suite (5 fmly) ⊘ in all bedrooms S £55; D £90-£140 (incl. bkfst) **Facilities** Wi-fi in bedrooms New Year **Parking** 14 **Notes LB** Closed 25 & 26 Dec

ABERSOCH

MAP 06 SH32

►►► **Deucoch Touring & Camping Park**

(SH303269)

Sarn Bach LL53 7LD

☎ 01758 713293

Dir: *From Abersoch take Sarn Bach road, at x-rds turn right, site on right in 800yds*

PETS: Stables nearby **Public areas** except shower block **Exercise area** 1m **Facilities** walks info vet info **Other** prior notice required **Resident Pets:** Chara (Samoyed)

Open Mar-Oct Booking advisable school hols Last arrival 22.00hrs Last departure 11.00hrs

A sheltered site with sweeping views of Cardigan Bay and the mountains, just a mile from Abersoch and a long sandy beach. The facilities block is well maintained, and this site is of special interest to watersports enthusiasts and those touring the Llyn Peninsula. A 5-acre site with 68 touring pitches, 10 hardstandings.

Notes ⊗ Families only

►►► **Rhydolion** (SH284275)

Rhydolion, LLangian LL53 7LR

☎ 01758 712342

e-mail: enquiries@rhydolion.co.uk

web: www.rhydolion.co.uk/caravan_camping.htm

Dir: *From A499 take unclassified road to Llangian for 1m, turn left into & through Llangian. Site 1.5m after road fork towards Hell's Mouth/Porth Neigwl*

PETS: Public areas Exercise area lane adjacent **Facilities** vet info **Other** prior notice required

Open Mar-Oct Booking advisable Last arrival 22.00hrs Last departure noon

A peaceful park with good views, on a working farm close to the long sandy surfers beach at Hell's Mouth. The toilet block is kept to a high standard by the friendly owners, and nearby Abersoch is a mecca for boat owners and water sports enthusiasts. A new campers' kitchen and laundry are useful additions. A 1.5-acre site with 28 touring pitches.

Notes ⊗ Families and couples only

BALA MAP 06 SH93

►►►► **Pen-y-Bont** *(SH932350)*

Llangynog Rd LL23 7PH

☎ 01678 520549 📠 01678 520006

e-mail: penybont-bala@btconnect.com

web: www.penybont-bala.co.uk

Dir: *From A494 take B4391. Site 0.75m on right*

PETS: Charges £1 per night **Public areas Exercise area** nearby **Facilities** on site shop food food bowl water bowl dog chews cat treats dog scoop/disp bags leads washing facs walks info vet info

Open Mar-Oct Booking advisable BH & school hols Last arrival 21.00hrs Last departure noon

A very attractively landscaped park in a woodland country setting, very close to the River Dee and Bala Lake. The park offers excellent facilities, and most pitches have water and electricity. Lake Bala is famous for its water sports, with the River Tryweryn catering for enthusiasts of canoe slalom and white-water rafting. A 7-acre site with 95 touring pitches, 59 hardstandings.

Notes No camp fires, quiet after 22.30hrs

►►► **Bala Camping & Caravanning Club Site** *(SH962391)*

Crynierth Caravan Park, Cefn-Ddwysarn LL23 7LN

☎ 01678 530324

web: www.campingandcaravanningclub.co.uk

Dir: *A5 onto A494 to Bala. Through Bethal & Sarnau. Right at sign onto unclassified road, site 400yds on left*

PETS: Public areas except buildings **Exercise area** on site **Facilities** walks info vet info **Other** prior notice required

Open Mar-Oct Booking advisable BH & peak periods Last arrival 21.00hrs Last departure noon

A quiet pleasant park with interesting views and high class facilities, set back from the main road in a very secluded position. Lake Bala offers great appeal for the water sports enthusiast, as does the nearby River Tryweryn, a leading slalom course in white-water rafting. A 4-acre site with 50 touring pitches, 8 hardstandings.

►►► **Tyn Cornel Camping & Caravan Park** *(SH895400)*

Frongoch LL23 7NU

☎ 01678 520759 📠 01678 520759

e-mail: peter.tooth@talk21.com

web: www.tyncornel.co.uk

Dir: *From Bala take A4212 (Porthmadog road) for 4m. Site on left before National Whitewater Centre*

PETS: Stables nearby (4m) (loose box) **Charges** £1 per night **Public areas** except shop & toilet block **Exercise area** on site 4 acre field area adjacent **Facilities** on site shop walks info vet info **Other** prior notice required **Resident Pets:** China (Labrador), Mrs Cat (cat)

Open Mar-Oct Booking advisable at all times Last arrival 21.00hrs Last departure noon

A delightful riverside park with mountain views, popular with those seeking a base for river kayaks and canoes, with access to the nearby White Water Centre and riverside walk with tearoom. The helpful, resident owners keep the modern facilities, including a new laundry and dishwashing room, spotlessly clean. A 10-acre site with 37 touring pitches.

Notes Quiet after 23.00hrs & silence after mdnt

BARMOUTH MAP 06 SH61

★★★★ 🛏 GUEST ACCOMMODATION
Llwyndu Farmhouse

Llanaber LL42 1RR

☎ 01341 280144

e-mail: intouch@llwyndu-farmhouse.co.uk

web: www.llwyndu-farmhouse.co.uk

Dir: *A496 towards Harlech where street lights end, on outskirts of Barmouth, take next right*

PETS: Bedrooms unattended **Exercise area** only at meal times **Exercise area** nearby **Facilities** washing facs cage storage walks info vet info **On Request** fridge access torch towels **Resident Pets:** Juke (Jack Russell), Lampshade & Suzy (cats), Holly & Melody (horses)

This converted 16th-century farmhouse retains many original features including inglenook fireplaces, exposed beams and timbers. There is a

CONTINUED

WALES

BARMOUTH *CONTINUED*

cosy lounge and meals are enjoyed at individual tables in the character dining room. Bedrooms are modern and well equipped, and some have four-poster beds. Four rooms are in nearby buildings.

Rooms 3 en suite 4 annexe en suite (2 fmly) ⊘ S £88; D £88-£94✴
Facilities TVB tea/coffee Cen ht TVL Dinner Last d 6.30pm **Parking** 10
Notes LB Closed 25-26 Dec RS Sun

►►► Trawsdir Touring Caravan & Camping Park *(SH596198)*

Caerddaniel Caravan Park, Llanaber LL42 1RR
☎ 01341 280999 & 280611 📠 01341 280740
e-mail: enquiries@barmouthholidays.co.uk
web: www.barmouthholidays.co.uk

Dir: *3m N of Barmouth on A496, just past Wayside pub on right*

PETS: Public areas Exercise area on site dog field provided
Facilities on site shop food food bowl water bowl dog chews cat treats litter dog scoop/disp bags washing facs vet info space for loose box

Open Mar-Oct Booking advisable Etr, Whitsun & Jul-Aug Last arrival 21.00hrs Last departure noon

A good quality park on a working sheep farm with views to the sea and hills, and very accessible to motor traffic. The modern facilities are very clean and well maintained, and tents and caravans have their own designated areas divided by dry-stone walls. A 15-acre site with 70 touring pitches, 40 hardstandings.

Notes Families & couples only

BEDDGELERT   MAP 06 SH54

★★★ 75% HOTEL
The Royal Goat

LL55 4YE
☎ 01766 890224 📠 01766 890422
e-mail: info@royalgoathotel.co.uk
web: www.royalgoathotel.co.uk

THE CIRCLE
Selected Individual Hotels

Dir: *On A498 at Beddgelert*

PETS: Bedrooms Charges £6 per night **Grounds** accessible
Exercise area 100yds

An impressive building steeped in history, the Royal Goat provides well-equipped accommodation. Attractively appointed, comfortable public areas include a choice of bars and restaurants, a residents' lounge and function rooms.

Rooms 32 en suite (4 fmly) ⊘ in 20 bedrooms **Facilities** Fishing
Services Lift **Parking** 100 **Notes** LB Closed Jan-1 Mar RS Nov-1 Jan

---

★★★★ 🛏 GUEST ACCOMMODATION
Sygun Fawr Country House

LL55 4NE
☎ 01766 890258 📠 01766 890258
e-mail: sygunfawr@aol.com
web: www.sygunfawr.co.uk

Dir: *A498 N, turn right over river at brown sign onto lane*

PETS: Bedrooms unattended **Charges** £4 per night
Public areas except restaurant **Grounds** accessible
Exercise area adjacent field

Sygun Fawr is set in a spectacular location within the Snowdonia National Park. The surrounding countryside and immaculate gardens are a mass of colour in the spring. Bedrooms are neat and pretty and many have superb views. Stone walls and exposed timbers abound, and a cosy bar and several comfortable sitting rooms are provided.

Rooms 11 en suite (1 GF) ⊘ S £57; D £75-£99✴ **Facilities** tea/coffee
Cen ht TVL Dinner Last d 8pm **Parking** 20 **Notes** LB Closed Jan

---

CAERNARFON   MAP 06 SH46

►►► Plas Gwyn Caravan Park *(SH523632)*

Llanrug LL55 2AQ
☎ 01286 672619
e-mail: info@plasgwyn.co.uk
web: www.plasgwyn.co.uk

Dir: *A4086, 3m E of Caernarfon*

PETS: Charges 50p per night **Public areas Exercise area** on site field available **Facilities** on site shop walks info vet info
Other prior notice required **Resident Pets:** Megan (Labrador), Kiri (Bison Frisé), Millie (Springer Spaniel), Beth (Cocker Spaniel)

Open Mar-Oct Booking advisable BH Last arrival 22.00hrs Last departure 11.30hrs

A secluded park handy for the beaches, historic Caernarfon, and for walking. The site is set within the grounds of Plas Gwyn House, a Georgian property with colonial additions, and the friendly owners are constantly improving the facilities. A 1.5-acre site with 27 touring pitches, 4 hardstandings and 18 statics.

▶▶▶ Riverside Camping *(SH505630)*

Seiont Nurseries, Pont Rug LL55 2BB

☎ 01286 678781 📄 01286 677223

e-mail: brenda@riversidecamping.co.uk

web: www.riversidecamping.co.uk

Dir: *2m from Caernarfon on right of A4086 towards Llanberis, also signed Seiont Nurseries*

PETS: Charges £2 per night £14 per week **Public areas** except restaurant & garden centre on leads **Exercise area** on site walk along disused railway **Other** prior notice required

Open Etr-end Oct Booking advisable BH & May-Aug Last arrival anytime Last departure noon

Set in the grounds of a large garden centre beside the small River Seiont, this park is approached by an impressive tree-lined drive. Facilities are very good, and include a café/restaurant and laundry. A 4.5-acre site with 60 touring pitches, 4 hardstandings.

Notes 🐾 No fires, no loud music

▶▶ Cwm Cadnant Valley *(SH487628)*

Cwm Cadnant Valley, Llanberis Rd LL55 2DF

☎ 01286 673196 📄 01286 675941

e-mail: aa@cwmcadnant.co.uk

web: www.cwmcadnant.co.uk

Dir: *On outskirts of Caernarfon on A4086 towards Llanberis, next to fire station*

PETS: Public areas except toilets, shower block & laundry **Exercise area** on site area at rear of site woodland 200yds **Facilities** vet info **Other** prior notice required

Open 14 Mar-3 Nov Booking advisable BH & Jul-Aug Last arrival 22.00hrs Last departure 11.00hrs

Set in an attractive wooded valley with a stream is this terraced site with secluded pitches. It is located on the outskirts of Caernarfon, close to the main Caernarfon-Llanberis road. A 4.5-acre site with 60 touring pitches.

CRICCIETH   MAP 06 SH43

▶▶▶▶ Eisteddfa *(SH518394)*

Eisteddfa Lodge, Pentrefelin LL52 0PT

☎ 01766 522696

e-mail: eisteddfa@criccieth.co.uk

web: www.eisteddfapark.co.uk

Dir: *From Porthmadog take A497 towards Criccieth. After approx 3.5m, through Pentrefelin, park signed 1st right after Plas Gwyn Nursing Home*

PETS: Charges 50p per night **Public areas Exercise area** on site **Facilities** walks info vet info **Other** prior notice required

Open Mar-Oct Booking advisable bank & school hols Last arrival 22.30hrs Last departure 11.00hrs

A quiet, secluded park on elevated ground, sheltered by the Snowdonia Mountains and with lovely views of Cardigan Bay. The owners are carefully improving the park whilst preserving its unspoilt beauty, and are keen to welcome families, who will appreciate the cubicled facilities. There's a field and play area, and woodland walks, with Criccieth nearby. An 11-acre site with 100 touring pitches, 17 hardstandings.

Notes 🐾

▶ Tyddyn Morthwyl Camping & Caravan Site *(SH488402)*

LL52 0NF

☎ 01766 522115

e-mail: trumper@henstabl147freeserve.co.uk

Dir: *1.5m N of Criccieth on B4411*

PETS: Public areas certain areas only, must be on leads **Exercise area** adjacent paths **Facilities** vet info **Resident Pets:** Charlie (cat), cattle, sheep.

Open Etr-Oct (rs Mar & Oct) Booking advisable Spring bank hol & Jul-Aug Last departure 14.00hrs

A quiet sheltered site with level grass pitches in three fields. The simple facilities include some electric hook-ups, and the sea is close by. A 10-acre site with 60 touring pitches and 22 statics.

Notes 🐾

DOLGELLAU   MAP 06 SH71

★★★ 80% ◉◉ HOTEL

Penmaenuchaf Hall

WELSH RAREBITS

Penmaenpool LL40 1YB

☎ 01341 422129 📄 01341 422787

e-mail: relax@penhall.co.uk

web: www.penhall.co.uk

Dir: *off A470 onto A493 to Tywyn. Hotel approx 1m on left*

PETS: Bedrooms Charges £5 per night **Public areas** in hall/lounge only **Grounds** accessible on leads disp bin 21 acres of grounds **Facilities** food (pre-bookable) food bowl water bowl dog chews cat treats washing facs cage storage walks info vet info **On Request** fridge access torch towels **Other** treats left on pets own beds at night

Built in 1860, this impressive hall stands in 20 acres of formal gardens, grounds and woodland and enjoys magnificent views across the River Mawddach. Careful restoration has created a comfortable and welcoming hotel. Fresh produce cooked in modern British style is served in the panelled restaurant.

Rooms 14 en suite (2 fmly) ∅ in all bedrooms S £90-£135; D £135-£205 (incl. bkfst) ✳ **Facilities** STV Fishing ↩ Complimentary salmon & trout fishing ch fac Xmas New Year **Parking** 30 **Notes LB** No children 6yrs

WALES

DOLGELLAU CONTINUED

★★★ 77% ⊕ HOTEL

Dolserau Hall

LL40 2AG

☎ 01341 422522 📠 01341 422400

e-mail: welcome@dolserau.co.uk

web: www.dolserau.co.uk

Dir: *1.5m outside Dolgellau between A494 to Bala and A470 to Dinas Mawddy*

PETS: Bedrooms (GF) unattended **Grounds** accessible disp bin **Exercise area** adjacent **Facilities** walks info vet info **Resident Pets:** Charlie (Golden Retriever)

This privately owned, friendly hotel lies in attractive grounds extending to the river and is surrounded by green fields. Several comfortable lounges are provided and welcoming log fires are lit during cold weather. The smart bedrooms are spacious, well equipped and comfortable. A varied menu offers very competently prepared dishes.

Rooms 15 en suite 5 annexe en suite (1 fmly) (3 GF) ⊘ in all bedrooms S £83; D £154-£178 (incl. bkfst & dinner)✳ **Facilities** STV Fishing Xmas New Year **Services** Lift **Parking** 40 **Notes LB** No children 8yrs Closed Dec-Jan (ex Xmas & New Year)

FFESTINIOG · MAP 06 SH74

★★★★ BED & BREAKFAST

Ty Clwb

The Square LL41 4LS

☎ 01766 762658 📠 01766 762658

e-mail: tyclwb@talk21.com

web: www.tyclwb.co.uk

Dir: *On B4391 in of Ffestiniog, opp church*

PETS: Bedrooms unattended **Public areas** except dining room **Grounds** accessible disp bin **Exercise area** 100yds **Facilities** water bowl dog chews dog scoop/disp bags washing facs cage storage walks info vet info **On Request** fridge access torch towels **Resident Pets:** Ben (Lurcher/Old English Sheepdog cross), Caspar (Border Collie)

Located opposite the historic church, this elegant house has been carefully modernised and is immaculately maintained throughout. Bedrooms are thoughtfully furnished and in addition to an attractive dining room, a spacious lounge with sun patio provides stunning views of the surrounding mountain range.

Rooms 3 en suite ⊘ D £48-£60 **Facilities** tea/coffee Cen ht TVL

★★★ GUEST ACCOMMODATION

Morannedd

Blaenau Rd LL41 4LG

☎ 01766 762734

e-mail: morannedd@talk21.com

Dir: *At edge of village on A470 towards Blaenau Ffestiniog*

PETS: Bedrooms Public areas except dining room **Grounds** accessible **Exercise area** surrounding countryside **Resident Pets:** Tessa (cat)

This guest house is set in the Snowdonia National Park and is well located for touring north Wales. A friendly welcome is offered and the atmosphere is relaxed and informal. Bedrooms are smart and modern and a cosy lounge is available. Hearty home cooking is a definite draw.

Rooms 4 en suite ⊘ **Facilities** TVB tea/coffee Cen ht **Notes** Closed Xmas ⊛

HARLECH · MAP 06 SH33

★★★ 80% ⊕⊕ HOTEL

Maes y Neuadd Country House

> WELSH
> RAREBITS

LL47 6YA

☎ 01766 780200 📠 01766 780211

e-mail: maes@neuadd.com

web: www.neuadd.com

Dir: *3m NE of Harlech, signed on unclassified road, off B4573*

PETS: Bedrooms (GF) **Charges** £7.50 per night charge for damage **Grounds** accessible on leads disp bin **Facilities** bedding dog scoop/disp bags pet sitting washing facs walks info vet info **On Request** fridge access torch towels **Resident Pets:** Lili (Cocker Spaniel), Eric (Old English Sheepdog), Felix & Arthur (cats), Salt & Pepper (Zebra finches)

This 14th-century hotel enjoys fine views over the mountains and across the bay to the Lleyn Peninsula. The team here is committed to restoring some of the hidden features of the house. Bedrooms, some in an adjacent coach house, are individually furnished and many boast fine antique pieces. Public areas display a similar welcoming charm, including the restaurant, which serves many locally-sourced and home-grown ingredients.

Rooms 15 en suite (5 fmly) (3 GF) ⊘ in all bedrooms D £98-£190 (incl. bkfst) **Facilities** ⤴ Wi-fi available Clay pigeon Cooking tuition Garden breaks Xmas New Year **Parking** 50 **Notes LB**

★★★★ GUEST HOUSE
Pensarn Hall Country Guest House

Pensarn LL45 2HS

☎ 01341 241236

e-mail: welcome@pensarn-hall.co.uk

Dir: *S on A496 past Harlech. After 1.75m, Pensarn Hall on left*

PETS: Bedrooms Charges £5 per night **Exercise area** 1m

This lovely Victorian country house stands in spacious gardens overlooking the Artro Estuary and Shell Island. The house has an interesting history, including connections with David Lloyd-George. It provides friendly hospitality as well as thoughtfully equipped accommodation, including a room with a four-poster bed.

Rooms 7 en suite (1 fmly) ⊘ **Facilities** TVB tea/coffee Cen ht TVL **Parking** 8 **Notes** No children 2yrs No coaches

---

LLANBEDR
MAP 06 SH52

★★ 69% SMALL HOTEL
Ty Mawr

LL45 2NH

☎ 01341 241440 ▤ 01341 241440

e-mail: tymawrhotel@onetel.com

web: www.tymawrhotel.org.uk

Dir: *from Barmouth A496 (Harlech road). In Llanbedr turn right after bridge, hotel 50yds on left, brown tourist signs on junct*

PETS: Bedrooms unattended **Public areas** except dining room **Grounds** accessible disp bin **Exercise area** 200yds **Facilities** water bowl cage storage walks info vet info **On Request** fridge access towels **Resident Pets:** Carlo (Welsh Sheepdog), Chelly (Border Collie), Tara (Sheepdog), Lola (rabbit), Dolce & Prada (budgies)

Located in a picturesque village, this family-run hotel has a relaxed, friendly atmosphere. The pleasant grounds opposite the River Artro makes a popular beer garden during fine weather. The attractive, cane-furnished bar offers a blackboard selection of food and a good choice of real ales. A more formal menu is available in the restaurant. Bedrooms are smart and brightly decorated.

Rooms 10 en suite (2 fmly) ⊘ in all bedrooms S £35-£45; D £65-£70 (incl. bkfst)✳ **Facilities** STV **Parking** 30 **Notes** LB Closed 24-26 Dec

---

LLANDWROG
MAP 06 SH45

►►►► White Tower Caravan Park *(SH453582)*

LL54 5UH

☎ 01286 830649 & 07802 562785 ▤ 01286 830649

e-mail: whitetower@supanet.com

web: www.whitetower.supanet.com

Dir: *1.5m from village along Tai'r Eglwys road. From Caernarfon take A487 Porthmadog road. Cross rdbt, take 1st right. Park 3m on right*

PETS: Public areas Exercise area 100mtrs **Facilities** walks info vet info

Open 1 Mar-10 Jan (rs Mar-mid May & Sep-Oct bar open wknds only) Booking advisable BH & Jul-Aug Last arrival 23.00hrs Last departure noon

There are lovely views of Snowdonia from this park located just 2 miles from the nearest beach at Dinas Dinlle. A well-maintained toilet block has key access, and the hard pitches have water and electricity. Popular amenities include an outdoor heated swimming pool, a lounge bar with family room, and a games and TV room. A 6-acre site with 104 touring pitches, 80 hardstandings and 54 statics.

LLANRUG
MAP 06 SH56

►►► Llys Derwen Caravan & Camping Site

(SH539629)

Ffordd Bryngwyn LL55 4RD

☎ 01286 673322

e-mail: llysderwen@aol.com

web: www.llysderwen.co.uk

Dir: *From A55 junct 13 (Caernarfon) take A4086 to Llanberis, through Llanrug, turn right at pub, site 60yds on right*

PETS: Public areas on leads **Exercise area** on site **Facilities** walks info vet info **Resident Pets:** Else, Rosy, Lacey, Buffy, Brenna, Ria, Odin (Bernese Mountain Dogs), Sian (Jack Russell)

Open Mar-Oct Booking advisable Last arrival 10.30hrs Last departure noon

A pleasant site set in woodland within easy reach of Caernarfon, Snowdon, Anglesey and the Lleyn Peninsula. A 5-acre site with 30 touring pitches and 2 statics.

Notes ⊜

LLANYSTUMDWY

MAP 06 SH43

►►► Llanystumdwy Camping & Caravanning Club Site (SH469384)

Tyddyn Sianel LL52 0LS

☎ 01766 522855

web: www.campingandcaravanningclub.co.uk

Dir: *From Criccieth take A497 W, 2nd right to Llanystumdwy, site on right*

PETS: Public areas Facilities walks info vet info **Other** prior notice required

Open Mar-Oct Booking advisable BH & peak period Last arrival 21.00hrs Last departure noon

An attractive site close to one of many beaches in the area, and with lovely mountain and sea views. There is a good range of well-maintained facilities, and the mainly sloping site is handy for walking in the Snowdonia National Park or on the local network of quiet country lanes. A 4-acre site with 70 touring pitches, 4 hardstandings.

PORTHMADOG

MAP 06 SH53

★★★ 70% HOTEL

Royal Sportsman

131 High St LL49 9HB

☎ 01766 512015 📠 01766 512490

e-mail: enquiries@royalsportsman.co.uk

Dir: *by rdbt, at A497 & A487 junct*

PETS: Bedrooms (GF) unattended **Stables** nearby

Charges £3.50 per night charge for damage **Public areas** except dining room **Grounds** accessible disp bin **Facilities** food (pre-bookable) food bowl water bowl pet sitting dog walking dog grooming (can be arranged) walks info vet info

On Request fridge access torch **Resident Pets:** Gelert (Sheepdog)

Ideally located in the centre of Porthmadog, this former coaching inn dates from the Victorian era and has been restored into a friendly, privately owned and personally run hotel. Rooms are tastefully decorated and well equipped, and some are in an annexe close to the hotel. There is a large comfortable lounge and a wide range of meals is served in the bar or restaurant.

Rooms 19 en suite 9 annexe en suite (7 fmly) (9 GF) ✆ in all bedrooms S £49-£64; D £78-£89 (incl. bkfst)✳ **Facilities** STV Wi-fi in bedrooms Xmas New Year **Parking** 18 **Notes** LB

★★★★★ FARM HOUSE

Tyddyn Du Farm Holiday Suites (SH691398)

Gellilydan, Ffestiniog LL41 4RB

☎ 01766 590281 📠 01766 590281 Mrs P Williams

e-mail: theaa@snowdoniafarm.com

web: www.snowdonia-farm-holidays-wales.co.uk

Dir: *1st farmhouse on left after junct A487 & A470, near Gellilydan*

PETS: Bedrooms (GF) sign **Sep Accom** meshed compound by arrangement **Charges** £3 per night £20 per week charge for damage **Public areas** except dining room **Grounds** accessible disp bin **Facilities** food (pre-bookable) dog scoop/disp bags leads washing facs cage storage walks info vet info

On Request fridge access torch towels **Resident Pets:** Spot, Sam & Gel (Border Collies), 5 Shetland ponies, sheep

Superbly located on an elevated position with stunning views of the surrounding countryside, this 400-year-old stone property provides a range of spacious, beautifully furnished and equipped bedrooms, converted from former stables and barns. Superb breakfasts are served in a cosy pine-furnished dining room in the main house, and a lounge with log fire is available. Families and pets are especially welcome.

Rooms 4 en suite (4 fmly) (4 GF) ✆ **Facilities** TVB tea/coffee Cen ht TVL Dinner Last d 5pm 🐴 Ponies & chickens **Parking** 10 **Notes** 150 acres organic/sheep RS Xmas

---

TYWYN

MAP 06 SH50

★★★★ FARM HOUSE

Eisteddfa (SH651055)

Eisteddfa, Abergynolwyn LL36 9UP

☎ 01654 782385 📠 01654 782228 Mrs G Pugh

Dir: *5m NE of Tywyn on B4405 nr Dolgoch Falls*

PETS: Bedrooms Charges £10 per stay **Public areas Grounds** accessible

Eisteddfa is a modern stone bungalow situated less than a mile from Abergynolwyn, in a spot ideal for walking or for visiting the local railway. Rooms are well equipped, and the lounge and dining room look over the valley.

Rooms 3 rms (2 en suite) (3 GF) **Facilities** STV TVB tea/coffee Cen ht TVL **Notes** 1200 acres mixed Closed Dec-Feb

MONMOUTHSHIRE

ABERGAVENNY

MAP 03 SO21

★★★ 79% ⓦⓦ COUNTRY HOUSE HOTEL

Llansantffraed Court

> WELSH
> RAREBITS

Llanvihangel Gobion NP7 9BA

☎ 01873 840678 🗎 01873 840674

e-mail: reception@llch.co.uk

web: www.llch.co.uk

Dir: *at A465/A40 Abergavenny junct take B4598 signed Usk (do not join A40). Continue towards Raglan, hotel on left in 4.5m*

PETS: Bedrooms unattended **Charges** £20 per night **Public areas** except dining area **Exercise area** on site **Facilities** dog walking

In a commanding position and in its own extensive grounds, this very impressive property, now a privately owned country house hotel, has enviable views of the Brecon Beacons. Extensive public areas include a relaxing lounge and a spacious restaurant offering imaginative and enjoyable dishes. Bedrooms are comfortably furnished and have modern facilities.

Rooms 21 en suite (1 fmly) ⊘ in all bedrooms S £86-£115; D £115-£175 (incl. bkfst) **Facilities** STV ⤺ Fishing ⤸ Putt green Wi-fi in bedrooms Clay pigeon shooting school ch fac **Services** Lift **Parking** 250 **Notes** LB

★★★ 75% ⓦ HOTEL

Angel

15 Cross St NP7 5EN

☎ 01873 857121 🗎 01873 858059

e-mail: mail@angelhotelabergavenny.com

web: www.angelhotelabergavenny.com

Dir: *follow town centre signs from rdbt, S of Abergavenny, past rail and bus stations. Turn left by hotel*

PETS: Bedrooms unattended sign **Charges** £10 per night **Public areas** except restaurant on leads **Grounds** accessible on leads **Exercise area** 50mtrs **Facilities** water bowl bedding pet sitting dog walking cage storage walks info vet info **On Request** towels

This has long been a popular venue for both local people and visitors; the two traditional function rooms and a ballroom are in regular use. In addition there is a comfortable lounge, a relaxed bar and an award-winning restaurant.

Rooms 29 en suite (2 fmly) ⊘ in all bedrooms S £60-£100; D £85-£150 (incl. bkfst)✳ **Facilities** STV Wi-fi in bedrooms ♫ Xmas New Year **Parking** 30 **Notes** LB Closed 25 Dec RS 24, 26 & 27 Dec

★★★ FARM HOUSE

Hardwick Farm *(SO306115)*

NP7 9BT

☎ 01873 853513 & 854238 🗎 01873 854238 Mrs A Price

e-mail: carol.hardwickfarm@virgin.net

Dir: *1m from Abergavenny, off A4042, farm sign on right*

PETS: Bedrooms Charges £5 per night **Public areas Grounds** accessible **Facilities** washing facs walks info vet info **On Request** torch

Quietly located in the Usk valley with wonderful views, this large family-run farmhouse provides warm hospitality. The spacious bedrooms are comfortably furnished, well equipped, and include one suitable for a family. Farmhouse breakfasts are served at separate tables, in the traditionally furnished dining room.

Rooms 2 en suite (1 fmly) ⊘ S £40; D £58✳ **Facilities** TVB tea/coffee Cen ht **Parking** 2 **Notes** LB 230 acres dairy mixed Closed Xmas ✆

►►► Pyscodlyn Farm Caravan & Camping Site *(SO266155)*

Llanwenarth Citra NP7 7ER

☎ 01873 853271 🗎 01873 853271

e-mail: pyscodlyn.farm@virgin.net

web: www.pyscodlyncaravanpark.com

Dir: *From Abergavenny take A40 (Brecon road), site 1.5m from entrance of Nevill Hall Hospital, on left 50yds past phone box*

PETS: Stables on site (loose box) **Public areas Exercise area** on site adjacent field **Facilities** washing facs vet info

Open Apr-Oct Booking advisable BH

With its outstanding views of the mountains, this quiet park in the Brecon Beacons National Park makes a pleasant venue for country lovers. The Sugarloaf Mountain and the River Usk are within easy walking distance, and despite being a working farm, dogs are welcome. A 4.5-acre site with 60 touring pitches and 6 statics.

WALES

WALES

★★★ GUEST HOUSE
Church Farm
Mitchel Troy NP25 4HZ
☎ 01600 712176
e-mail: info@churchfarmguesthouse.eclipse.co.uk
Dir: *From Ross-on-Wye/Monmmouth on A40 turn left onto B4293 signed Trelleck, just before tunnel. 150yds turn left follow Mitchel Troy signs, on main road, on left, 200yds before campsite*
PETS: Bedrooms Public areas except dining room
Grounds accessible **Facilities** cage storage walks info vet info
On Request fridge access **Resident Pets:** Ollie (Labrador)

Located in the village of Mitchel Troy, this 16th-century former farmhouse retains many original features including exposed beams and open fireplaces. There is a range of bedrooms and a spacious lounge, and breakfast is served in the traditionally furnished dining room. Dinner is available by prior arrangement.

Rooms 9 rms (7 en suite) (2 pri facs) (3 fmly) ⊗ S £28-£30; D £56-£60
Facilities TV2B tea/coffee Cen ht TVL Dinner Last d noon **Parking** 12
Notes LB No coaches Closed Xmas ⊛

★★★★★ ⊕⊕ 🍴
RESTAURANT WITH ROOMS
The Bell at Skenfrith
NP7 8UH
☎ 01600 750235 📠 01600 750525
e-mail: enquiries@skenfrith.co.uk
web: www.skenfrith.co.uk
Dir: *On B4521 in Skenfrith, opposite castle*
PETS: Bedrooms Charges £5 per dog per night
Public areas except restaurant **Grounds** accessible
Facilities water bowl walks info vet info **On Request** torch
Resident Pets: Millie (Yellow Labrador)

The Bell is a beautifully restored, 17th-century former coaching inn which still retains much of its original charm and character. It is peacefully situated on the banks of the Monnow, a tributary of the River Wye, and is ideally placed for exploring the numerous delights of the counties of Herefordshire and Monmouthshire. Natural materials have been used to create a relaxing atmosphere, while the bedrooms, which include full suites and rooms with four-poster beds, are stylish, luxurious and equipped with DVD players.

Rooms 8 en suite ⊗ D £105-£185✳ **Facilities** TVB tea/coffee Direct dial from bedrooms Cen ht Dinner Last d 9.30pm Wi-fi available **Parking** 36
Notes No children 8yrs Closed last wk Jan-1st wk Feb RS Oct-Mar

★★★ 70% HOTEL
The Abbey Hotel
Tintern, Nr Chepstow NP16 6SF
☎ 01291 689777 📠 01291 689727
e-mail: info@theabbey-hotel.co.uk
web: www.theabbey-hotel.co.uk
Dir: *M48 junct 2/A466, hotel opposite the abbey ruins*
PETS: Bedrooms Charges £5 per night **Public areas** except restaurant on leads **Grounds** accessible on leads **Facilities** water bowl vet info **Restrictions** small-medium dogs only
Resident Pets: Shelly, Jake & Misty (Jack Russells)

Appointed to a high standard and commanding stunning views of nearby Tintern Abbey, this friendly hotel provides modern bedrooms, including a family suite. Diners are spoilt for choice between the brasserie with its carvery, the more formal carte service for dinner, and the pleasant hotel bar where lighter meal options are on offer.

Rooms 23 en suite ⊗ in 7 bedrooms S £50-£55; D £80-£125 (incl. bkfst) ✳ **Facilities** STV Fishing Wi-fi in bedrooms Xmas New Year **Parking** 60
Notes LB

★★ 67% HOTEL
Parva Farmhouse
Monmouth Rd NP16 6SQ
☎ 01291 689411 📠 01291 689941
e-mail: parvahoteltintern@fsmail.net
Dir: *1m from Tintern Abbey on A466 Monmouth Road. Last hotel in village on right*
PETS: Bedrooms Charges £3 per night **Public areas** except restaurant **Grounds** accessible **Exercise area** on site adjacent
Resident Pets: Frodo (Border Terrier cross)

This relaxed and friendly hotel is situated on a sweep of the River Wye with far reaching views of the valley. Originally a farmhouse dating from the 17th century, many of the original features have been retained. The lounge is full of character and has a fire in colder months, and the Inglenook Restaurant has a cosy atmosphere. The individually designed bedrooms are tastefully decorated and enjoy pleasant views; one has a four-poster.

Rooms 8 en suite (2 fmly) ⊗ in all bedrooms S £45-£60; D £63-£85 (incl. bkfst) ✳ **Parking** 8 **Notes** No children 12yrs

NEATH PORT TALBOT

PORT TALBOT   MAP 03 SS79

★★★ 72% HOTEL

Best Western Aberavon Beach

SA12 6QP

☎ 01639 884949 🖷 01639 897885

e-mail: sales@aberavonbeach.com

web: www.aberavonbeach.com

Dir: *M4 junct 41/A48 & follow signs for Aberavon Beach & Hollywood Park*

PETS: Bedrooms unattended **Charges** charge for damage **Public areas** except restaurant on leads **Grounds** accessible on leads **Exercise area** 100yds Aberavon Beach (restricted access May-Sep) **Facilities** water bowl walks info vet info **On Request** fridge access **Restrictions** no dangerous breeds (see page 7)

This friendly, purpose-built hotel enjoys a prominent position on the seafront overlooking Swansea Bay. Bedrooms, many of which have sea views, are comfortably appointed and thoughtfully equipped. Public areas include a leisure suite with swimming pool, open-plan bar and restaurant and a selection of function rooms.

Rooms 52 en suite (6 fmly) ⊘ in 40 bedrooms S £69-£115; D £79-£125 (incl. bkfst)✱ **Facilities** FTV 🏊 Wi-fi in bedrooms All weather leisure centre 🎵 Xmas New Year **Services** Lift **Parking** 150

NEWPORT

ST BRIDES WENTLOOGE   MAP 03 ST28

★★★★★ 🏵 ➡ INN

The Inn at the Elm Tree

NP10 8SQ

☎ 01633 680225 🖷 01633 681035

e-mail: inn@the-elm-tree.co.uk

Dir: *4m SW of Newport. On B4239 in St Brides village*

PETS: Bedrooms unattended **Charges** £10 per night **Grounds** accessible **Exercise area** 10mtrs **Other** pet food on request

A stylish barn conversion on the tranquil Wentlooge Levels. Individually decorated bedrooms combine the traditional and the contemporary:- hand-made brass beds, beamed ceilings and sumptuous fabrics blend with minimalist bathrooms (some with a jacuzzi), ISDN lines and business services. The restaurant offers an extensive choice including seafood and game in season, with the emphasis on quality ingredients.

Rooms 10 en suite (1 fmly) (2 GF) ⊘ S £80-£90; D £90-£130✱ **Facilities** TVB tea/coffee Direct dial from bedrooms Cen ht Dinner Last d 9.30pm **Notes LB**

PEMBROKESHIRE

BROAD HAVEN   MAP 02 SM81

►►► **Creampots Touring Caravan & Camping Park** *(SM882131)*

Broadway SA62 3TU

☎ 01437 781776

web: www.creampots.co.uk

Dir: *From Haverfordwest take B4341 to Broadway. Turn left signed Milford Haven. Park 2nd entrance, 500yds on right*

PETS: Public areas except play areas **Exercise area** beach 1.5m **Facilities** walks info vet info **Other** prior notice required

Open Apr-Oct Booking advisable BH & Jul-Aug Last arrival 21.00hrs Last departure noon

Set just outside the Pembrokeshire National Park, this quiet site is just 1.5m from a safe sandy beach at Broad Haven, and the coastal footpath. The park is well laid out and carefully maintained, and the toilet block offers a good standard of facilities. The new owners welcome families. An 8-acre site with 71 touring pitches, 14 hardstandings and 1 static.

FISHGUARD   MAP 02 SM93

►►► **Gwaun Vale Touring Park** *(SM977356)*

Llanychaer SA65 9TA

☎ 01348 874698

e-mail: margaret.harries@talk21.com

Dir: *From Fishguard take B4313. Site 1.5m on right*

PETS: Public areas except play area, toilet block, laundry on leads **Exercise area** on site fenced area provided adjacent **Facilities** on site shop walks info vet info

Open Apr-Oct Booking advisable Jul-Aug Last arrival anytime Last departure noon

Located at the opening of the beautiful Gwaun Valley, this well-kept park is set on the hillside with pitches tiered on two levels. There are lovely views of the surrounding countryside, and good facilities. A 1.75-acre site with 29 touring pitches, 5 hardstandings.

Notes 🐾

WALES

HASGUARD CROSS

MAP 02 SM80

►►► Hasguard Cross Caravan Park

(SM850108)

SA62 3SL

☎ 01437 781443 📄 01437 781443

e-mail: hasguard@aol.com

web: www.hasguardcross.co.uk

Dir: *From Haverfordwest take B4327 towards Dale. After 7m turn right at x-rds & site is 1st entrance on right*

PETS: Public areas except pub **Exercise area** on site long fenced run provided beach 2m **Facilities** vet info **Other** prior notice required

Open all year (rs Aug Tent field for 28 days) Booking advisable Spring bank hol & Jun-Aug Last arrival 21.00hrs Last departure 10.00hrs

A very clean, efficient and well-run site in Pembrokeshire National Park with views of surrounding hills just 1.5m from sea and beach at Little Haven. The toilet and shower facilities are immaculately clean, and there is a licensed bar (evenings only) serving a good choice of food. A 4.5-acre site with 12 touring pitches and 42 statics.

Notes ⊜

►►► Redlands Touring Caravan & Camping Park *(SM853109)*

SA62 3SJ

☎ 01437 781300

e-mail: info@redlandscamping.co.uk

web: www.redlandstouring.co.uk

Dir: *From Haverfordwest take B4327 towards Dale. Site 7m on right*

PETS: Charges 1st dog free, 2nd dog 60p per night **Public areas** on leads **Exercise area** on site dog walk area provided **Facilities** on site shop dog tethers walks info vet info

Open Mar-Dec (rs off peak-shop closed) Booking advisable BH & Jul-Aug Last arrival 21.00hrs Last departure 11.30hrs

A family owned and run park set in five acres of level grassland with tree-lined borders, close to many sandy beaches and the famous coastal footpath. Ideal for exploring the Pembrokeshire National Park. A 6-acre site with 64 touring pitches, 11 hardstandings.

Notes ⊜ No commercial vans

HAVERFORDWEST

MAP 02 SM91

★★ 67% HOTEL

Hotel Mariners

Mariners Square SA61 2DU

☎ 01437 763353 📄 01437 764258

Dir: *follow town centre signs, over bridge, up High St, 1st turning on right, hotel at the end*

PETS: Bedrooms Exercise area 1m

Located a few minutes walk from the town centre, this privately owned and friendly hotel is reputed to date back to 1625. The bedrooms are equipped with modern facilities and are soundly maintained. A good range of food is offered in the popular bar, which is a focus for the town. The restaurant offers a more formal dining option. Facilities include a choice of meeting rooms.

Rooms 28 en suite (5 fmly) ⊗ in 16 bedrooms **Facilities** STV **Parking** 50 **Notes** LB Closed 25-Dec-2 Jan

★★★★ GUEST ACCOMMODATION

College Guest House

93 Hill St, St Thomas Green SA61 1QL

☎ 01437 763710 📄 01437 763710

e-mail: colinlarby@aol.com

Dir: *In town centre, signs for St Thomas Green car park*

PETS: Bedrooms unattended **Charges** charge for damage **Public areas** except restaurant **Grounds** accessible disp bin **Exercise area** 90mtrs **Facilities** food bowl water bowl feeding mat dog scoop/disp bags leads pet sitting washing facs cage storage walks info vet info **On Request** fridge access torch towels **Resident Pets:** Bartie (Jack Russell Collie cross), Zag & Alfie (cats)

Located in a mainly residential area within easy walking distance of the attractions, this impressive Georgian house has been upgraded to offer good levels of comfort and facilities. There is range of practically equipped bedrooms, along with public areas that include a spacious lounge (with internet access) and an attractive pine-furnished dining room, the setting for comprehensive breakfasts.

Rooms 8 en suite (4 fmly) ⊗ **Facilities** TVB tea/coffee Cen ht TVL **Parking** 2

MANORBIER
MAP 02 SS09

★★ 71% HOTEL
Castle Mead
SA70 7TA

THE CIRCLE
Selected Individual Hotels
GREAT BRITAIN

☎ 01834 871358 📄 01834 871358

e-mail: castlemeadhotel@aol.com

web: www.castlemeadhotel.com

Dir: *A4139 towards Pembroke, turn onto B4585 into village & follow signs to beach & castle. Hotel on left above beach*

PETS: Bedrooms (GF) **Charges** charge for damage
Grounds accessible disp bin **Exercise area** 500yds beach
Facilities walks info vet info **On Request** fridge access torch
Resident Pets: Rosie (Border Collie), Max & Polly (cats)

Benefiting from a superb location with spectacular views of the bay, the Norman church and Manorbier Castle, this family-run hotel is friendly and welcoming. Bedrooms which include some in a converted former coach house, are generally quite spacious and have modern facilities. Public areas include a sea view restaurant, bar and residents' lounge, as well as an extensive garden.

Rooms 5 en suite 3 annexe en suite (2 fmly) (3 GF) ⊘ in all bedrooms
S fr £45; D fr £80 (incl. bkfst) **Parking** 20 **Notes** LB Closed Dec-Feb
RS Nov

ROSEBUSH
MAP 02 SN02

►► Rosebush Caravan Park *(SN073293)*
Rhoslwyn SA66 7QT

☎ 01437 532206 & 07831 223166 📄 01437 532206

Dir: *From A40 near Marbeth take B4313, between Haverfordwest and Cardigan B4329, 1m*

PETS: Public areas Exercise area on site **Facilities** on site shop
food walks info vet info **Other** prior notice required

Open 14 Mar-Oct Booking advisable peak season Last arrival 23.00hrs Last departure noon

A most attractive park with a large ornamental lake at its centre and good landscaping. Set off the main tourist track, it offers lovely views of the Presely Hills which can be reached by a scenic walk. Rosebush is a quiet village with a handy pub, and the park owner also runs the village shop. Due to the deep lake on site, children are not accepted. A 12-acre site with 65 touring pitches and 15 statics.

Notes ⊛ Adults only

ST DAVID'S
MAP 02 SM72

★★★ 79% ◉◉ COUNTRY HOUSE HOTEL
Warpool Court
SA62 6BN

WELSH
RAREBITS

☎ 01437 720300 📄 01437 720676

e-mail: info@warpoolcourthotel.com

web: www.warpoolcourthotel.com

Dir: *At Cross Square left by Cartref Restaurant (Goat St). Pass Farmers Arms pub, after 400mtrs left, follow hotel signs, entrance on right*

PETS: Bedrooms unattended **Charges** £10 per night
Grounds accessible disp bin **Facilities** water bowl washing facs
cage storage walks info vet info **On Request** fridge access torch
towels

Originally the cathedral choir school, Warpool Court Hotel is set in landscaped gardens looking out to sea and is within easy walking distance of the Pembrokeshire coastal path. The lounges are spacious and comfortable and bedrooms are well furnished and equipped with modern facilities. The restaurant offers delightful cuisine.

Rooms 25 en suite (3 fmly) ⊘ in all bedrooms S £100-£115; D £150-£220
(incl. bkfst)✶ **Facilities** ৲ ☙ ৬ Xmas New Year **Parking** 100
Notes LB Closed Jan

►►►► Caerfai Bay Caravan & Tent Park
(SM759244)

Caerfai Bay SA62 6QT

☎ 01437 720274 📄 01437 720577

e-mail: info@caerfaibay.co.uk

web: www.caerfaibay.co.uk

Dir: *At St David's turn off A487 at Visitor Centre/Grove Hotel. Follow signs for Caerfai Bay. Right at end of road*

PETS: Public areas except buildings **Exercise area** coastal path
Facilities walks info vet info **Other** prior notice required, no dogs
in July & August

Open Mar-mid Nov Booking advisable school hols Last arrival 21.00hrs Last departure 11.00hrs

Magnificent coastal scenery and an outlook over St Bride's Bay can be enjoyed from this delightful site, located just 300yds from a bathing beach. The facilities include four en suite family rooms which are an asset to the park. There is a farm shop very close by. A 10-acre site with 117 touring pitches, 9 hardstandings and 32 statics.

WALES

WALES

►► St David's Camping & Caravanning Club Site (SM805305)

Dwr Cwmdig, Berea SA62 6DW

☎ 01348 831376

web: www.campingandcaravanningclub.co.uk

Dir: *S on A487, right at Glyncheryn Farmers Stores in Croesgoch. After 1m turn right follow signs to Abereiddy. At x-roads left. Site 75yds on left*

PETS: Public areas except buildings **Facilities** walks info vet info **Other** prior notice required

Open Apr-Oct Booking advisable BH & peak periods Last arrival 21.00hrs Last departure noon

An immaculately kept small site in open country near the Pembrokeshire Coastal Path. The slightly sloping grass has a few hardstandings for motor homes, and plenty of electric hook-ups. A 4-acre site with 40 touring pitches, 4 hardstandings.

SAUNDERSFOOT   MAP 02 SN10

★★★★ GUEST HOUSE
Vine Cottage

The Ridgeway SA69 9LA

☎ 01834 814422

e-mail: enquiries@vinecottageguesthouse.co.uk

web: www.vinecottageguesthouse.co.uk

Dir: *A477 S onto A478, left onto B4316, after railway bridge right signed Saundersfoot, cottage 100yds beyond 30mph sign*

PETS: Bedrooms (GF) **Charges** £5 per stay charge for damage **Public areas** except dining room **Grounds** accessible disp bin **Facilities** dog chews feeding mat dog scoop/disp bags leads washing facs cage storage walks info vet info **On Request** fridge access torch towels **Restrictions** no Pitt Bull Terriers **Resident Pets:** Ruby & Hegan (English Springer Spaniels)

There is a warm welcome that awaits all guests at this pleasant former farmhouse, which is conveniently located on the outskirts of Saundersfoot yet within easy walking distance of the village. A feature is the extensive mature gardens which display some rare and exotic plants, also a summer house at the rear of the garden where guests can sit and relax in the warmer evenings. Bedrooms, which include a

ground-floor room, are modern and well equipped, and some are suitable for families. There is a comfortable, airy lounge, and meals are served in the cosy dining room.

Rooms 5 en suite (2 fmly) (1 GF) ⊘ S £35-£63; D £56-£70✳ **Facilities** TVB tea/coffee Cen ht Dinner Last d 10am **Parking** 10 **Notes LB** No children 6yrs No coaches ⊕

SOLVA   MAP 02 SM82

★★★★★ FARM HOUSE
Lochmeyler Farm Guest House (SM855275)

Llandeloy SA62 6LL

☎ 01348 837724 📠 01348 837622 Mrs M Jones

e-mail: stay@lochmeyler.co.uk

web: www.lochmeyler.co.uk

Dir: *From Haverfordwest A487 St David's Rd to Penycwm, right to Llandeloy*

PETS: Bedrooms Exercise area nearby **Resident Pets:** George (Labrador), Patch (Collie), Sooty (Cocker Spaniel)

Located on a 220-acre dairy farm in an Area of Outstanding Natural Beauty, this farmhouse provides high levels of comfort and excellent facilities. The spacious bedrooms, some in converted outbuildings, are equipped with a wealth of thoughtful extras and four have private sitting rooms. Comprehensive breakfasts are served in the dining room and two sumptuous lounges are also available.

Rooms 11 en suite (11 fmly) (5 GF) ⊘ S £27.50-£55; D £55-£80 **Facilities** TVB tea/coffee Direct dial from bedrooms Licensed Cen ht TVL Dinner Last d 2pm **Parking** 11 **Notes LB** No children 14yrs 220 acres dairy Closed Xmas & New Year

TAVERNSPITE MAP 02 SN11

►►► Pantglas Farm Caravan Park *(SN175122)*

SA34 0NS

☎ 01834 831618 📄 01834 831193

e-mail: pantglasfarm@btinternet.com

web: www.pantglasfarm.co.uk

Dir: *Leave A477 to Tenby at Red Roses x-roads onto B4314 to Tavernspite. Take middle road at village pumps. Site 0.5m on left*

PETS: Charges £1.50 per night £10.50 per week

Public areas except play area **Exercise area** on site large grass field available except play area **Facilities** disp bags washing facs walks info vet info **Other** prior notice required

Open Mar to end Oct Booking advisable Spring bank hol & Jul-Aug Last arrival 20.00hrs Last departure 10.30hrs

A quiet site in a rural location with pitches located in three enclosures, and views across the rolling countryside towards Carmarthen Bay. There is a large activity play area for children, an indoor games room, and a licensed bar, and the toilet facilities are well maintained. The park is well situated for exploring the beautiful surrounding area and the coastline. A 10-acre site with 86 touring pitches, 3 hardstandings.

Notes ✐

WOLF'S CASTLE MAP 02 SM92

★★ 76% ◉ COUNTRY HOUSE HOTEL

Wolfscastle Country Hotel

> WELSH RAREBITS

SA62 5LZ

☎ 01437 741688 & 741225 📄 01437 741383

e-mail: enquiries@wolfscastle.com

web: www.wolfscastle.com

Dir: *on A40 in village at top of hill. 6m N of Haverfordwest*

PETS: Bedrooms unattended **Charges** £5 per night

Grounds accessible **Restrictions** executive rooms not available for dogs

This large stone house dates back to the mid-19th century and commands a regal position in the village. Now a friendly, privately owned and personally run hotel, it provides modern, well-maintained and equipped bedrooms. There is a pleasant bar and an attractive restaurant, which has a well-deserved reputation for its food.

Rooms 20 en suite 1 annexe en suite (2 fmly) ⊘ in all bedrooms S £65-£85; D £95-£125 (incl. bkfst)✳ **Facilities** STV Wi-fi in bedrooms **Parking** 60 **Notes** LB Closed 24-26 Dec

---

BRECON MAP 03 SO02

★★ 65% HOTEL

Lansdowne Hotel & Restaurant

The Watton LD3 7EG

☎ 01874 623321 📄 01874 610438

e-mail: reception@lansdownehotel.co.uk

Dir: *A40/A470 onto B4601*

PETS: Bedrooms Charges £2.50 per night **Exercise area** 2 min walk

Now a privately owned and personally run hotel, this Georgian house is conveniently located close to the town centre. The accommodation is well equipped and includes family rooms and a bedroom on ground floor level. There is a comfortable lounge and an attractive split level dining room containing a bar.

Rooms 9 en suite (2 fmly) (1 GF) ⊘ in all bedrooms S £40; D £60 (incl. bkfst)✳ **Notes** No children 5yrs

★★★★ ◉◉ 🍴 INN

The Felin Fach Griffin

Felin Fach LD3 0UB

☎ 01874 620111 📄 01874 620120

e-mail: enquiries@eatdrinksleep.ltd.uk

web: www.eatdrinksleep.ltd.uk

Dir: *4m NE of Brecon on A470*

PETS: Bedrooms unattended **Public areas** except dining room **Grounds** accessible **Facilities** water bowl bedding

This delightful inn stands in an extensive garden at the northern end of Felin Fach village. The public areas have a wealth of rustic charm and provide the setting for the excellent food. Service and hospitality are commendable. The bedrooms are carefully appointed and have modern equipment and facilities.

Rooms 7 en suite (1 fmly) **Facilities** tea/coffee Direct dial from bedrooms Cen ht Dinner Last d 9.30pm 🍴 **Parking** 61 **Notes** No coaches Closed 25-26 Dec RS Mon (ex BH's)

WALES

BRECON CONTINUED

⌖ 🐾 🐕 🏠

★★★ GUEST ACCOMMODATION
Borderers
47 The Watton LD3 7EG
☎ 01874 623559
e-mail: info@borderers.com
web: www.borderers.com
Dir: *200yds SE of town centre on B4601, opp church*
PETS: Bedrooms unattended **Exercise area** nearby
Resident Pets: Ella (Black Labrador), Breagh (Chocolate Labrador)
This guest house was originally a 17th-century drovers' inn. The courtyard, now a car park, is surrounded by many of the bedrooms, and pretty hanging baskets are seen everywhere. The non-smoking bedrooms are attractively decorated with rich floral fabrics. A room suitable for easier access is available.

Rooms 4 rms (3 en suite) (1 pri facs) 5 annexe en suite (2 fmly) (4 GF) ⊘ S £35-£55; D £50-£55✳ **Facilities** TVB tea/coffee Cen ht **Parking** 6

►►►► Brynich Caravan Park *(SO069278)*
Brynich LD3 7SH
☎ 01874 623325 📄 01874 623325
e-mail: holidays@brynich.co.uk
web: www.brynich.co.uk
Dir: *2km E of Brecon on A470, 200mtrs from junct with A40*
PETS: Charges £1 per dog per night **Public areas** except play areas **Exercise area** on site 4 acre wooded walk along brook **Facilities** on site shop food food bowl water bowl disp bags vet info **Other** prior notice required

Open 24 Mar-28 Oct Booking advisable bank & school hols, wknds Jun-Sep Last arrival 20.00hrs Last departure noon
AA Campsite of the Year for Wales 2007. An attractive and well-managed park with views across open countryside towards the Brecon Beacons. Families in particular will enjoy the facilities on offer here, including the centrally placed toddlers play area, large well equipped indoor play-barn, extensive recreation field and adventure playground for older children, and there's an excellent restaurant in a 17th-century converted barn. Brecon is 1.5 miles away. A 20-acre site with 130 touring pitches, 35 hardstandings.

Notes No rollerskates, skateboards or motorized scooters, only environmentally friendly ground sheets

BUILTH WELLS
MAP 03 SO05

⌖ 🐾 🐕 🏠

★★★ 75% HOTEL
Caer Beris Manor
THE INDEPENDENTS
LD2 3NP
☎ 01982 552601 📄 01982 552586
e-mail: caerberis@btconnect.com
web: www.caerberis.co.uk
Dir: *from town centre follow A483/Llandovery signs. Hotel on left*
PETS: Bedrooms unattended (well behaved only) **Charges** £5 per night **Public areas** except restaurant **Exercise area** on site

With extensive landscaped grounds, guests can expect a relaxing stay at this friendly and privately owned hotel. Bedrooms are individually decorated and furnished to retain an atmosphere of a bygone era. A spacious, comfortable lounge and a lounge bar also retain this atmosphere together with the elegant restaurant, complete with 16th-century panelling.

Rooms 23 en suite (1 fmly) (3 GF) S £69-£79; D £109-£129 (incl. bkfst) **Facilities** STV Fishing Riding Gym 🛥 Wi-fi available Clay pigeon shooting Xmas New Year **Parking** 32 **Notes** LB

WALES

▶▶▶ Fforest Fields Caravan & Camping Park (SO100535)

Hundred House LD1 5RT

☎ 01982 570406

e-mail: office@fforestfields.co.uk

web: www.fforestfields.co.uk

Dir: *From town follow New Radnor signs on A481. 4m to signed entrance on right, 0.5m before Hundred House village*

PETS: **Public areas** except toilets **Exercise area** on site woods adjacent **Facilities** washing facs walks info vet info **Other** prior notice required **Restrictions** max 2 dogs unless by prior arrangement, no noisy or aggressive dogs

Open Etr & Apr-Oct (rs Nov-Mar toilets & showers closed) Booking advisable BHs & Jul-Aug Last arrival 21.00hrs Last departure 18.00hrs

A sheltered park in a hidden valley with wonderful views and plenty of wildlife. Set in unspoilt countryside, this is a peaceful park with delightful hill walks beginning on site. The historic town of Builth Wells and the Royal Welsh Showground are only 4 miles away, and there are plenty of outdoor activities in the vicinity. A 7-acre site with 60 touring pitches, 15 hardstandings.

Notes 🐾

CRICKHOWELL   MAP 03 SO21

★★★ 79% ◉◉ HOTEL

Bear

NP8 1BW

[WELSH RAREBITS]

☎ 01873 810408 📄 01873 811696

e-mail: bearhotel@aol.com

Dir: *on A40 between Abergavenny & Brecon*

PETS: **Bedrooms** (GF) unattended **Public areas** except restaurant **Grounds** accessible on leads **Facilities** food bowl water bowl dog chews freshly cooked chicked offered to all visiting dogs washing facs walks info vet info **On Request** fridge access towels **Resident Pets:** Magic (Cat)

A favourite with locals as well as visitors, the character and friendliness of this 15th-century coaching inn are renowned. The bedrooms come in a variety of sizes and standards including some with four-posters. The bar and restaurant are furnished in keeping with the style of the building and provide comfortable areas in which to enjoy some of the very popular dishes that use the finest locally-sourced ingredients.

Rooms 21 en suite 13 annexe en suite (6 fmly) ⊘ in 29 bedrooms S £68-£125; D £86-£158 (incl. bkfst)✷ **Facilities** Wi-fi in bedrooms Xmas New Year **Parking** 45 **Notes** RS 25 Dec

---

CRIGGION   MAP 07 SJ21

★★★★ FARM HOUSE

Brimford House (SJ310150)

SY5 9AU

☎ 01938 570235 Mrs Dawson

e-mail: info@brimford.co.uk

Dir: *Off B4393 after Crew Green turn left for Criggion Brimford 1st on left after the pub*

PETS: **Bedrooms** **Public areas** except dining room **Grounds** accessible **Facilities** cage storage vet info **On Request** fridge access torch towels **Resident Pets:** Emma (Black Labrador), Cally (Golden Labrador)

This elegant Georgian house stands in lovely open countryside and is a good base for touring central Wales and the Marches. Bedrooms are spacious, and thoughtful extras enhance guest comfort. A cheery log fire burns in the lounge during colder weather and the hospitality is equally warm, providing a relaxing atmosphere throughout.

Rooms 3 en suite ⊘ S £40-£60; D £55-£65 **Facilities** TVB tea/coffee Cen ht TVL Fishing **Parking** 4 **Notes** LB 250 acres Arable, beef

---

ERWOOD   MAP 03 SO04

★★★★ BED & BREAKFAST

Hafod-Y-Garreg

LD2 3TQ

☎ 01982 560400

e-mail: john-annie@hafod-y.wanadoo.co.uk

web: www.hafodygarreg.co.uk

Dir: *1m S of Erwood. Off A470 at Trericket Mill, sharp right, up track past cream farmhouse towards pine forest, through gate*

PETS: **Bedrooms** **Public areas** **Exercise area** nearby **Facilities** walks info vet info **On Request** torch **Restrictions** no puppies **Resident Pets:** Ginger (cat), Rosie (goat), chickens

This remote Grade II listed farmhouse dates in part from 1401 and is the oldest surviving traditional house in Wales. It has tremendous character and has been furnished and decorated to befit its age, while the bedrooms have modern facilities. There is an impressive dining room and a lounge with an open fireplace. Warm hospitality from John and Annie McKay is another major strength here.

Rooms 2 en suite (1 fmly) D £60 **Facilities** TVB tea/coffee Cen ht Dinner Last d Day before **Parking** 6 **Notes** LB Closed Xmas 🐾

HAY-ON-WYE

MAP 03 SO24

★★★ 71% ◉ HOTEL

The Swan-at-Hay

WELSH RAREBITS

Church St HR3 5DQ

☎ 01497 821188 🗎 01497 821424

e-mail: info@theswanathay.co.uk

Dir: *In centre of Hay on B4350*

PETS: **Bedrooms** Charges £6 per night **Public areas** public bar only **Exercise area** 20yds **Facilities** pet food by arrangement

This former coaching inn dates back to the 1800s and is only a short walk from the town centre. Bedrooms are well equipped - some are located in either the main hotel and others in converted cottages across the courtyard. Spacious, relaxing public areas include a comfortable lounge, a choice of bars and a more formal restaurant. There is also a large function room and a smaller meeting room.

Rooms 15 en suite 4 annexe en suite (1 fmly) (2 GF) ⊗ in all bedrooms S £70-£80; D £100-£150 (incl. bkfst) **Facilities** Fishing Wi-fi available New Year **Parking** 18 **Notes** LB

★★ 69% HOTEL

Baskerville Arms

Clyro HR3 5RZ

☎ 01497 820670 🗎 01497 821609

e-mail: info@baskervillearms.co.uk

Dir: *from Hereford follow Brecon A438 into Clyro. Hotel signed*

PETS: **Bedrooms** Charges £4 per night **Public areas** except restaurant **Exercise area** on site

Situated near Hay-on-Wye in the peaceful village of Clyro, this former Georgian coaching inn is personally run by its friendly and enthusiastic owners. Bedrooms offer a range of styles while public areas include a bar with a village inn atmosphere, a separate restaurant and a comfortable residents' lounge. There is also a large function room, plus a meeting room.

Rooms 13 en suite (1 fmly) ⊗ in 12 bedrooms S £45-£49; D £62.50-£79 (incl. bkfst)✱ **Facilities** Wi-fi available Xmas New Year **Parking** 12 **Notes** LB

LLANDRINDOD WELLS

MAP 03 SO06

►►► **Disserth Caravan & Camping Park**

(SO035583)

Disserth, Howey LD1 6NL

☎ 01597 860277 🗎 01597 860147

e-mail: m.hobbs@virgin.net

web: www.disserth.com

Dir: *1m off A483, between Howey & Newbridge-on-Wye, by 13th-century church*

PETS: **Public areas** except reception & bar **Exercise area** adjacent fields with footpaths **Facilities** vet info **Other** prior notice required, horses by arrangement **Resident Pets:** Jake (Lakeland/ Terrier cross), Jack & Oscar (cats), Mildred (Berkshire sow)

Open Mar-Oct Booking advisable BH & Royal Welsh Show Last arrival 22.00hrs Last departure noon

A delightfully secluded and predominantly adult park nestling in a beautiful valley on the banks of the River Ithon, a tributary of the River Wye. This little park is next to a 13th-century church, and has a small bar open at weekends and busy periods. The chalet toilet block offers spacious combined cubicles. A 4-acre site with 30 touring pitches and 23 statics.

Notes ⊛

LLANGAMMARCH WELLS

MAP 03 SN94

★★★ ◎◎ ◉ COUNTRY HOUSE HOTEL

The Lake Country House & Spa

PRIDE OF BRITAIN HOTELS

LD4 4BS

☎ 01591 620202 & 620474 🗎 01591 620457

e-mail: info@lakecountryhouse.co.uk

web: www.lakecountryhouse.co.uk

Dir: *W from Builth Wells on A483 to Garth (approx 6m). Left for Llangammarch Wells, follow hotel signs*

PETS: **Bedrooms** Charges £6 per night **Grounds** accessible **Exercise area** on site **Resident Pets:** Belle (Labrador), Cassie (Collie/Labrador)

Expect good old-fashioned values and hospitality at this Victorian country house hotel. In fact, the service is so traditionally English, guests may believe they have a butler! The establishment offers a 9-hole, par 3 golf course, 50 acres of wooded grounds and a spa where the hot tub overlooks the lake. Bedrooms, some located in an annexe, and some at ground-floor level, are individually styled and have many extra comforts. Traditional afternoon teas are served in the lounge and award-winning cuisine is provided in the spacious and elegant restaurant.

Rooms 30 en suite (7 GF) ⊗ in all bedrooms S £115-£180; D £170-£250 (incl. bkfst)✱ **Facilities** Spa STV ⑨ ♨ ♪ Fishing ♥ Putt green Wi-fi available Archery Horse riding Mountain biking Quad biking Xmas **Parking** 72 **Notes** LB

LLANGURIG — MAP 06 SN97

★★★★ GUEST HOUSE
Old Vicarage

SY18 6RN

☎ 01686 440280 📄 01686 440280

e-mail: theoldvicarage@llangurig.fslife.co.uk

web: www.theoldvicaragellangurig.co.uk

Dir: A44 into Llangurig, 1st right, 100yds on left

PETS: Bedrooms Charges £1 per night **Public areas** except dining areas on leads **Grounds** accessible on leads disp bin **Exercise area** 100yds **Facilities** water bowl feeding mat washing facs cage storage walks info vet info **On Request** torch towels **Resident Pets:** Polly (Red Chow)

Set in the heart of this quiet village, the Old Vicarage offers attractively furnished, well-equipped bedrooms. A small bar serves the dining room and two lounges, where there are collections of porcelain and antiques. Evening meals and afternoon teas make good use of local produce.

Rooms 4 en suite (1 fmly) ⊗ S £30-£40; D £50-£54 **Facilities** TVB tea/coffee Licensed Cen ht TVL Dinner Last d 5pm **Parking** 5 **Notes** LB No coaches Closed Xmas & New Year ⊗

LLANWDDYN — MAP 06 SJ01

★★★ 75% ⊛ COUNTRY HOUSE HOTEL
Lake Vyrnwy

Lake Vyrnwy SY10 0LY

CLASSIC BRITISH HOTELS

☎ 01691 870692 📄 01691 870259

e-mail: res@lakevyrnwy.com

web: www.lakevyrnwy.com

Dir: on A4393, 200yds past dam turn sharp right into drive

PETS: Bedrooms (GF) unattended **Sep Accom** heated kennels **Charges** £10 per night charge for damage **Grounds** accessible on leads **Exercise area** 5 mins walk **Facilities** cage storage walks info vet info **On Request** fridge access torch towels **Other** designated bedrooms only (only well behaved dogs may be left unattended) **Resident Pets:** 3 Black Labradors

This fine country-house hotel lies in 26,000 acres of woodland above Lake Vyrnwy. It provides a wide range of bedrooms, most with superb views and many with four-poster beds and balconies. The extensive public rooms are elegantly furnished and include a terrace, a choice of bars serving meals and the more formal dining in the restaurant.

Rooms 38 en suite (4 fmly) S £170-£215; D £195-£240 (incl. bkfst & dinner)✳ **Facilities** Spa STV ⊰ Fishing Wi-fi available Archery Bird watching Buggy racing Canoeing/kayaking Clay shooting Sailing Xmas New Year **Parking** 70

LLYSWEN — MAP 03 SO13

★★★★ 85% ⊛⊛ COUNTRY HOUSE HOTEL
Llangoed Hall

WELSH RAREBITS

LD3 0YP

☎ 01874 754525 📄 01874 754545

e-mail: enquiries@llangoedhall.com

web: www.llangoedhall.com

Dir: A470 through village for 2m. Hotel drive on right

PETS: Sep Accom Kennels **Charges** £10 per night (kennels) £15 per night (bedrooms) **Exercise area** 17 acres of parkland **Facilities** pet food water bowls food bowls bedding **Other** paddock for horses

Set against the stunning backdrop of the Black Mountains and the Wye Valley, this imposing country house is a haven of peace and quiet. The interior is no less impressive, with a noteworthy art collection complementing the many antiques featured in day rooms and bedrooms. Comfortable, spacious bedrooms and suites are matched by equally inviting lounges.

Rooms 23 en suite **Facilities** STV ⊰ Fishing ⊱ Maze Clay pigeon shooting ♫ **Parking** 80 **Notes** LB ⊗ No children 8yrs

MACHYNLLETH — MAP 06 SH70

★★★ 70% ⊛ HOTEL
Wynnstay

Maengwyn St SY20 8AE

☎ 01654 702941 📄 01654 703884

e-mail: info@wynnstay-hotel.com

web: www.wynnstay-hotel.com

Dir: at junct of A487/A489, in town centre

PETS: Bedrooms unattended **Sep Accom** kennels **Charges** £5 per night **Public areas** except restaurant **Grounds** accessible

Long established, this former posting house lies in the centre of this historic town. Bedrooms, some with four-poster beds, have modern facilities and include family rooms. There is a comfortable lounge bar area and a good range of food and wines is available. Guests can also dine in the Wynnstay Pizzeria or the restaurant, which offers more formal dining.

Rooms 23 en suite (3 fmly) ⊗ in all bedrooms S £55-£95; D £85-£115 (incl. bkfst) **Facilities** STV Wi-fi available Clay shooting Game shooting Mountain biking Xmas New Year **Parking** 40 **Notes** LB

WALES

MONTGOMERY   MAP 07 SO29

★★ 79% ⊛ HOTEL

Dragon

SY15 6PA

☎ 01686 668359 📄 0870 011 8227

e-mail: reception@dragonhotel.com

web: www.dragonhotel.com

Dir: *behind town hall*

PETS: Bedrooms unattended **Stables** nearby (0.5m)
Public areas except dining room on leads **Grounds** accessible
on leads **Facilities** pet sitting & dog walking must be pre-booked
vet info **On Request** torch towels

This fine 17th-century coaching inn stands in the centre of
Montgomery. Beams and timbers from the nearby castle, which was
destroyed by Cromwell, are visible in the lounge and bar. A wide
choice of soundly prepared, wholesome food is available in both the
restaurant and bar. Bedrooms are well equipped and family rooms are
available.

Rooms 20 en suite (6 fmly) ⊘ in 18 bedrooms S £51-£61;
D £87.50-£97.50 (incl. bkfst)✷ **Facilities** ⊙ Wi-fi available ♫ Xmas New
Year **Parking** 21 **Notes** LB

RHONDDA CYNON TAFF

PONTYPRIDD   MAP 03 ST08

★★★ 73% HOTEL

Llechwen Hall

Llanfabon CF37 4HP

☎ 01443 742050 & 743020 📄 01443 742189

e-mail: llechwen@aol.com

web: www.llechwen.com

Dir: *A470 N towards Merthyr Tydfil, then A472, then A4054 for
Cilfynydd. After 0.25m, left at hotel sign*

PETS: Bedrooms (GF) unattended **Stables** nearby (2m)
Grounds accessible on leads disp bin **Facilities** cage storage
walks info vet info **On Request** fridge access torch towels
Resident Pets: Charles & William (Cavalier King Charles Spaniels)

Set on top of a hill with a stunning approach, this establishment has
served many purposes in its 200-year-old history, which includes a
private school and a magistrates' court. Bedrooms are individually
decorated and well equipped, and some are situated in the
comfortable coach house nearby. The Victorian-style public areas are
attractively appointed and the hotel is a popular venue for weddings.

Rooms 12 en suite 8 annexe en suite (11 fmly) (4 GF) ⊘ in 8 bedrooms
S £68.95-£73.95; D £92.90-£122.90 (incl. bkfst)✷ **Facilities** Xmas New
Year **Parking** 100 **Notes** Closed 25-28 Dec

SWANSEA

PORT EINON   MAP 02 SS48

►►► Carreglwyd Camping & Caravan Park

(SS465863)

SA3 1NN

☎ 01792 390795 📄 01792 390796

Dir: *A4118 to Port Einon, site adjacent to beach*

PETS: Public areas on leads **Exercise area** on site **Facilities** on site shop food food bowl water bowl dog chews cat treats **Resident Pets:** Brono (Black Labrador), Emma-Jane (cat)

Open Mar-Dec Booking advisable Jul-Aug, Etr, BHs Last arrival 18.00hrs Last departure 16.00hrs

Set in an unrivalled location alongside the safe sandy beach of Port Einon on the Gower Peninsula, this popular park is an ideal family holiday spot. Close to an attractive village with pubs and shops, most pitches offer sea views. The sloping ground has been partly terraced, and facilities are provided by two toilet blocks which might be stretched during busy periods. A 12-acre site with 150 touring pitches.

RHOSSILI   MAP 02 SS48

►►► Pitton Cross Caravan & Camping Park

(SS434877)

SA3 1PH

☎ 01792 390593 📄 01792 391010

e-mail: enquiries@pittoncross.co.uk

web: www.pittoncross.co.uk

Dir: *2m W of Scurlage on B4247*

PETS: Stables nearby (3m) (loose box) **Charges** £1 per night £7 per week **Public areas** on leads certain areas **Exercise area** on site adjoining field **Facilities** on site shop food food bowl water bowl disp bags leads washing facs walks info vet info **Other** prior notice required

Open Feb-Nov Booking advisable Spring BH & Jul-Aug Last arrival 20.00hrs Last departure 11.00hrs

Surrounded by farmland close to sandy Menslade Bay, which is within walking distance across the fields. This grassy park is divided by hedging into paddocks. Nearby Rhossili Beach is popular with surfers. A 6-acre site with 100 touring pitches, 21 hardstandings.

Notes quiet at all times

VALE OF GLAMORGAN

BARRY   MAP 03 ST16

★★★ 79% ◉ COUNTRY HOUSE HOTEL

Egerton Grey Country House

WELSH RAREBITS

Porthkerry CF62 3BZ

☎ 01446 711666 📄 01446 711690

e-mail: info@egertongrey.co.uk

web: www.egertongrey.co.uk

Dir: *M4 junct 33 follow signs for airport, left at rdbt for Porthkerry, after 500yds turn left down lane between thatched cottages*

PETS: Bedrooms Charges £10 per stay **Public areas** conservatory only **Grounds** accessible **Resident Pets:** Louis (Cavalier King Charles Spaniel), Puss (cat)

This former rectory enjoys a peaceful setting and views over delightful countryside with distant glimpses of the sea. The bedrooms are spacious and individually furnished. Public areas offer charm and elegance, and include an airy lounge and restaurant, which has been sympathetically converted from the billiards room.

Rooms 10 en suite (4 fmly) ⊘ in all bedrooms S £90-£120; D £140-£160 (incl. bkfst)✳ **Facilities** FTV ⛳ Putt green Wi-fi in bedrooms Xmas New Year **Parking** 40 **Notes** LB

WREXHAM

EYTON MAP 07 SJ34

►►►►► **The Plassey Leisure Park** (SJ353452)

The Plassey LL13 0SP

☎ 01978 780277 🖹 01978 780019

e-mail: enquiries@theplassey.co.uk

web: www.theplassey.co.uk

Dir: From A483 at Bangor-on-Dee exit onto B5426 for 2.5m. Park entrance signed on left

PETS: Charges £2 per dog per night £14 per dog per week **Public areas** except shops, restaurants and bars on leads **Exercise area** on site 1 acre grounds and 2 miles of walks **Facilities** on site shop food dog chews cat treats dog scoop/disp bags walks info vet info **Other** prior notice required

Open Jan-Nov Booking advisable wknds, bank & school hols Last arrival 21.00hrs Last departure 18.00hrs

A lovely park set in several hundred acres of quiet farm and meadowland in the Dee Valley. The superb toilet facilities include individual cubicles for total privacy and security, while the Edwardian farm buildings have been converted into a restaurant, coffee shop, beauty studio, and various craft outlets. There is plenty here to entertain the whole family, from scenic walks and swimming pool to free fishing, and use of the 9-hole golf course. A 10-acre site with 110 touring pitches, 45 hardstandings.

Notes No footballs, bikes or skateboards

LLANARMON DYFFRYN CEIRIOG MAP 07 SJ13

★★★ 87% ◉◉ HOTEL

West Arms

LL20 7LD

WELSH RAREBITS

☎ 01691 600665 & 600612 🖹 01691 600622

e-mail: gowestarms@aol.com

Dir: Off A483/A5 at Chirk, take B4500 to Ceiriog Valley. Llanarmon 11m at end of B4500

PETS: Bedrooms (GF) unattended **Stables** nearby (8m) **Charges** £6 per night charge for damage **Public areas** except restaurant on leads **Grounds** accessible disp bin **Exercise area** 300yds **Facilities** water bowl litter dog scoop/disp bags cage storage walks info vet info **On Request** fridge access torch towels **Resident Pets:** Marmite (Black Labrador)

Set in the beautiful Ceiriog Valley, this delightful hotel has a wealth of charm and character. There is a comfortable lounge, a room for private dining and two bars, as well as a pleasant, award-winning restaurant offering a set-price menu of freshly cooked dishes. The attractive bedrooms have a mixture of modern and period furnishings.

West Arms

Rooms 15 en suite (2 fmly) (3 GF) ⊘ in all bedrooms S £53.50-£118; D £87-£228 (incl. bkfst)✳ **Facilities** Fishing Xmas New Year **Parking** 22 **Notes** LB

★★ 76% SMALL HOTEL

The Hand at Llanarmon

LL20 7LD

☎ 01691 600666 🖹 01691 600262

e-mail: reception@thehandhotel.co.uk

web: www.thehandhotel.co.uk

Dir: Turn off A5 at Chirk onto B4500 signed Ceiriog Valley, continue for 11m

PETS: Bedrooms unattended **Stables** on site **Public areas** except restaurant **Exercise area** adjacent, country lane **Resident Pets:** Pero (Welsh Sheepdog)

This small, pleasant, privately owned and run hotel is located in the village centre and has a wealth of charm and character. Apart from warm and friendly hospitality, it provides a variety of bedroom styles, including rooms on ground floor level and two in a separate annexe building. A very good choice of well prepared food is provided.

Rooms 13 en suite (4 GF) ⊘ in all bedrooms S £45-£65; D £70-£110 (incl. bkfst)✳ **Parking** 18 **Notes** LB RS 24-26 Dec

WALES

Make travel simple
with online booking

Online booking for hotels, guest accommodation and restaurants at **www.theAA.com/travel**

Search and book online with Britain's largest travel publisher

Ireland

NORTHERN IRELAND
CO ANTRIM

BALLYMONEY MAP 01 C6

►►►► Drumaheglis Marina & Caravan Park

36 Glenstall Rd BT53 7QN

☎ 028 2766 6466 & 0227 🖹 028 2766 7659

e-mail: helen.neill@ballymoney.gov.uk

web: www.ballymoney.gov.uk

Dir: *Signed off A26, approx 1.5m outside Ballymoney towards Coleraine, off B66 S of Ballymoney*

PETS: Public areas on leads **Exercise area** on site **Facilities** vet info

Open 17 Mar-Oct Booking advisable BHs & summer months Last arrival 20.00hrs Last departure 13.00hrs

Exceptionally well-designed and laid out park beside the Lower Bann River, with very spacious pitches and two quality toilet blocks. Ideal base for touring Antrim or for watersports enthusiasts. A 16-acre site with 55 touring pitches, 55 hardstandings.

LARNE MAP 01 D5

►►► Curran Court Caravan Park

131 Curran Rd BT40 1BD

☎ 028 2827 3797 🖹 028 2826 0096

Dir: *On A2, 0.25m from ferry. From town centre follow signs for Leisure Centre, opposite Curran Court Hotel*

PETS: Public areas under supervision **Exercise area** on site **Facilities** vet info

Open Apr-Sep Booking advisable main season

A handy site for the ferry. When the reception is closed, the owners can be contacted at the Curran Court Hotel across the road. A 3-acre site with 30 touring pitches.

CO DOWN

KILLYLEAGH MAP 01 D5

►►► Delamont Country Park C&C Club Site

Delamont Country Park, Downpatrick Rd BT30 9TZ

☎ 028 4482 1833

web: www.campingandcaravanningclub.co.uk

Dir: *From Belfast take A22. Site 1m S of Killyleagh & 4m N of Downpatrick*

PETS: Facilities walks info vet info **Other** prior notice required

Open Mar-Oct Booking advisable BHs & peak periods Last arrival 21.00hrs Last departure noon

A spacious park enjoying superb views and walks, in a lovely and interesting part of the province. The facilities are of a very high order, and include fully-serviced pitches and excellent toilets. The site is close to Strangford Loch Marine Water reserve, a medieval fairy fort, and a blue flag beach. A 4.5-acre site with 63 touring pitches, 63 hardstandings.

CO LONDONDERRY

AGHADOWEY MAP 01 C6

★★ 76% HOTEL
Brown Trout Golf & Country Inn

209 Agivey Rd BT51 4AD

IRISH COUNTRY HOTELS

☎ 028 7086 8209 🖹 028 7086 8878

e-mail: bill@browntroutinn.com

Dir: *at junct of A54 & B66 junct on road to Coleraine*

PETS: Bedrooms unattended sign **Charges** charge for damage **Public areas** except restaurant on leads **Grounds** accessible **Facilities** dog scoop/disp bags leads washing facs dog grooming cage storage walks info vet info **On Request** fridge access torch towels **Resident Pets:** Muffin & Lucy (Chocolate Labrador)

Set alongside the Agivey River and featuring its own 9-hole golf course, this welcoming inn offers a choice of spacious accommodation. Comfortably furnished bedrooms are situated around a courtyard area whilst the cottage suites also have lounge areas. Home-cooked meals are served in the restaurant and lighter fare is available in the charming lounge bar which has entertainment at weekends.

Rooms 15 en suite (11 fmly) S £60-£80; D £80-£110 (incl. bkfst) **Facilities** ♨ 9 Fishing Gym Putt green Wi-fi available Game fishing ♫ Xmas New Year **Parking** 80 **Notes** LB

REPUBLIC OF IRELAND
CO CORK

BANDON · MAP 01 B2

★★★★ BED & BREAKFAST
Glebe Country House

Ballinadee
☎ 021 4778294 ◻ 021 4778456
e-mail: glebehse@indigo.ie
Dir: *Off N71 at Innishannon Bridge signed Ballinadee, 8km along river bank, left after village sign*
PETS: Please telephone for details

This lovely guest house stands in well-kept gardens, and is run with great attention to detail. Antique furnishings predominate throughout this comfortable house, which has a lounge and an elegant dining room. An interesting breakfast menu offers unusual options, and a country-house style dinner is available by arrangement.

Rooms 4 en suite (2 fmly) ⊗ S €60-€70; D €90-€110 **Facilities** tea/coffee Direct dial from bedrooms Cen ht TVL Dinner Last d noon **Parking** 10 **Notes** LB Closed 21 Dec-3 Jan

BLARNEY · MAP 01 B2

★★★★★ 🏠 ⟲ GUEST HOUSE
Ashlee Lodge

Tower
☎ 021 4385346 ◻ 021 4385726
e-mail: info@ashleelodge.com
Dir: *4km from Blarney on R617*
PETS: Bedrooms (GF) sign **Grounds** accessible on leads disp bin **Facilities** washing facs walks info vet info **On Request** fridge access towels

Ashley Lodge is a purpose-built guest house, situated in the village of Tower, close to Blarney and local pubs and restaurants. Bedrooms are decorated with comfort and elegance in mind, some with whirlpool baths, and one room has easier access. The extensive breakfast menu is memorable for Ann's home baking. You can unwind in the sauna or the outdoor hot tub. Transfers to the nearest airport and railway station can be arranged, and tee times can be booked at many of the nearby golf courses.

Rooms 10 en suite (2 fmly) (6 GF) ⊗ S €70-€150; D €100-€250 **Facilities** STV TVB tea/coffee Direct dial from bedrooms Licensed Cen ht TVL Dinner Last d 8.30pm Wi-fi available Sauna Hot tub **Parking** 12 **Notes** LB

CLONAKILTY · MAP 01 B2

★★ GUEST HOUSE
Desert House

Coast Rd
☎ 023 33331 ◻ 023 33048
e-mail: deserthouse@eircom.net
Dir: *1km E of Clonakilty. Signed on N71 at 1st rdbt, house 500 metres on left*
PETS: Bedrooms unattended **Public areas** except dining & sitting room (on lead) **Grounds** accessible on leads disp bin **Exercise area** adjacent **Facilities** washing facs cage storage walks info vet info **On Request** fridge access torch towels **Resident Pets:** Holly & Sophie (Golden Cocker Spaniels), Tess (Sheepdog), Gwen (Springer Spaniel)

This comfortable Georgian farmhouse overlooks Clonakilty Bay and is within walking distance of the town. The estuary is of great interest to bird watching enthusiasts. It is a good base for touring west Cork and Kerry.

Rooms 5 rms (4 en suite) S €45-€52; D €70-€80⁕ **Facilities** TVB tea/coffee Cen ht **Parking** 10 **Notes** No coaches

IRELAND

KINSALE | **MAP 01 B2**

★★★★★ GUEST HOUSE

Friar's Lodge

5 Friars St

☎ 086 289 5075 & 021 4777384 📄 021 4774363

e-mail: mtierney@indigo.ie

Dir: *In town centre next to parish church*

PETS: Bedrooms (GF) unattended **Charges** €10 per night
Exercisea area nearby **Facilities** walks info vet info
On Request fridge access towels

This new, purpose built property near the Friary, has been developed with every comfort in mind. Bedrooms are particularly spacious. Located on a quiet street within minutes walk of the town centre, with secure parking to the rear. A very good choice is offered from the breakfast menu.

Rooms 18 en suite (2 fmly) (4 GF) ⊘ in 4 bedrooms S €60-€80;
D €90-€140 **Facilities** STV TV available tea/coffee Direct dial from bedrooms Licensed Lift Cen ht **Parking** 20 **Notes** Closed Xmas

CO DONEGAL

DONEGAL | **MAP 01 B5**

★★★★ 86% ◉◉ HOTEL

Harvey's Point Country

Lough Eske

☎ 074 9722208 📄 074 9722352

e-mail: reservations@harveyspoint.com

web: www.harveyspoint.com

Dir: *N56 from Donegal, then 1st right (Loch Eske/Harvey's Point). Hotel approx 10 mins' drive*

PETS: Bedrooms unattended **Sep Accom** On request
Stables on site **Grounds** accessible **Resident Pets:** Paddy
(Labrador) & geese

Situated by the lakeshore, this hotel is an oasis of relaxation. Comfort and attentive guest care are the norm here. A range of particularly spacious suites are available, all making the best use of the surrounding views. The kitchen brigade maintains consistently high standards in the Dining room, with a very popular Sunday Buffet Lunch served weekly.

AA Hotel of the Year for Ireland 2007-8.

Rooms 60 en suite S €199-€235; D €290-€580 (incl. bkfst)✳
Facilities STV 2 Treatment rooms ♫ Xmas New Year **Services** Lift
Parking 300 **Notes** LB No children 10yrs Closed Mon & Tue Nov-Mar

CASHEL | **MAP 01 A4**

★★★ ◉◉ COUNTRY HOUSE HOTEL

Cashel House

☎ 095 31001 📄 095 31077

e-mail: info@cashel-house-hotel.com

web: www.cashel-house-hotel.com

RELAIS &
CHATEAUX.

Dir: *S off N59, 1.5km W of Recess, well signed*

PETS: Bedrooms unattended **Stables** on site **Charges** €20 per horse per night charge for damage **Grounds** accessible on leads disp bin **Facilities** washing facs cage storage walks info vet info
On Request fridge access torch towels

Cashel House is a mid-19th century property, standing at the head of Cashel Bay, in the heart of Connemara. Quietly secluded in award-winning gardens and woodland walks. Attentive service comes with the perfect balance of friendliness and professionalism from McEvilly family and their staff. The comfortable lounges have turf fires and antique furnishings. The restaurant offers local produce such as the famous Connemara Lamb, and fish from the nearby coast.

Rooms 32 en suite (4 fmly) (6 GF) ⊘ in 20 bedrooms
S €106.88-€151.88; D €213.75-€214.05 (incl. bkfst) ✳ **Facilities** ⌁
Xmas New Year **Parking** 40 **Notes** LB Closed 4 Jan-4 Feb

CLIFDEN | **MAP 01 A4**

★★★ 77% ◉◉ HOTEL

Ardagh

Ballyconneely Rd

☎ 095 21384 📄 095 21314

e-mail: ardaghhotel@eircom.net

IRISH COUNTRY
HOTELS

Dir: *N59 (Galway to Clifden), signed to Ballyconneely*

PETS: Bedrooms Public areas Grounds accessible

Situated at the head of Ardbear Bay, this family-run hotel makes full use of the spectacular scenery in the area. The restaurant is renowned for its cuisine, which is complemented by friendly and knowledgeable service. Many of the spacious and well-appointed bedrooms have large picture windows and plenty of comfort.

Rooms 19 en suite (2 fmly) ⊘ in all bedrooms S €112.50-€125;
D €165-€190 (incl. bkfst)✳ **Facilities** Pool room ♫ **Parking** 35
Notes LB Closed Nov-Mar

IRELAND

★★★ 70% ⓖ HOTEL
Alcock & Brown Hotel

☎ 095 21206 & 21086 📠 095 21842

e-mail: alcockandbrown@eircom.net

Dir: *take N59 from Galway via Oughterard, hotel in town centre*

PETS: Bedrooms Charges

This comfortable family owned hotel is situated on the town square. There is a cosy bar and lounge with open fire. Brown's the restaurant is attractively decorated where the dinner menu offers a wide menu with good food with many fresh, local fish specialities. Bedrooms are well appointed. The friendly and attentive staff offer good service.

Rooms 19 en suite ⊘ in all bedrooms S €75-€99; D €110-€158 (incl. bkfst)✳ **Facilities** STV ♫ New Year **Notes LB** Closed 19-26 Dec

---

GALWAY   **MAP 01 B3**

★★★★ 79% ⓖ HOTEL
Ardilaun Hotel & Leisure Club

Taylor's Hill

☎ 091 521433 📠 091 521546

e-mail: info@theardilaunhousehotel.ie

web: www.theardilaunhousehotel.ie

Dir: *N6 to Galway City West, then follow signs for N59 Clifden, then N6 towards Salthill, hotel on this road*

PETS: Bedrooms (GF) **Grounds** accessible on leads disp bin **Facilities** walks info vet info **On Request** fridge access towels

The Ardilaun is located on five acres of landscaped gardens and has undergone a major refurbishment. Bedrooms have been thoughtfully equipped and furnished and the new wing of executive rooms and suites are particularly spacious. Public areas include Camilaun restaurant overlooking the garden, comfortable lounges and Blazers bar. There are extensive banqueting and leisure facilities

Rooms 125 en suite (17 fmly) (8 GF) ⊘ in 106 bedrooms S €100-€150; D €150-€500 (incl. bkfst)✳ **Facilities Spa** STV FTV ⓧ supervised Gym Wi-fi available Treatment & analysis rooms Beauty salon Spinning room ♫ New Year **Services** Lift **Parking** 380 **Notes LB** Closed 24-26 Dec RS Closed pm 24 Dec

★★★★ GUEST ACCOMMODATION
Atlantic Heights

2 Cashelmara, Knocknacarra Cross, Salthill

☎ 091 529466 & 528830

e-mail: info@atlanticheightsgalway.com

web: www.atlanticheightsgalway.com

Dir: *4km W of city centre. 1km from Salthill promenade in upper Salthill on R336*

PETS: Bedrooms Grounds accessible **Resident Pets:** Susie (Brehony Spaniel)

Enthusiastic hosts Robbie and Madeline Mitchell take great pride in their fine balconied house with views of Galway Bay. The bedrooms have many thoughful extras, and the extensive breakfast menu, served late if required, features home baking. Laundry service available.

Rooms 6 en suite (3 fmly) ⊘ S €40-€80; D €70-€110 **Facilities** STV FTV TVB tea/coffee Direct dial from bedrooms Cen ht Wi-fi available **Parking** 6 **Notes LB** Closed Nov-Mar

---

RECESS   **MAP 01 A4**

★★★ ⓖ COUNTRY HOUSE HOTEL
Lough Inagh Lodge

Inagh Valley

☎ 095 34706 & 34694 📠 095 34708

e-mail: inagh@iol.ie

Dir: *from Recess take R344 towards Kylemore*

PETS: Bedrooms unattended **Sep Accom** kennels **Public areas Exercise area** field **Facilities** pet food on request **Resident Pets:** rex (Springer Spaniel), Sasha (cat)

MANOR HOUSE

IRELAND

This 19th-century, former fishing lodge is akin to a family home where guests are encouraged to relax and enjoy the peace. Nestled between the Connemara Mountains and fronted by a good fishing lake. Bedrooms are smartly decorated and comfortable, there is a choice of lounges with turf fires and a cosy traditional bar. The delightful restaurant specialises in dishes of the local lamb and fish from both the lake and sea.

Rooms 13 en suite (1 fmly) (4 GF) S €117-€157; D €191-€270 (incl. bkfst)✳ **Facilities** STV Fishing Hill walking Fly fishing Cycling **Services** air con **Parking** 16 **Notes LB** Closed mid Dec-mid Mar

CO KERRY

CASTLEGREGORY
MAP 01 A2

★★★ BED & BREAKFAST
Griffin's Palm Beach Country House
Goulane, Conor Pass Rd
☎ 066 7139147 ▤ 066 7139073
e-mail: griffinspalmbeach@eircom.net
Dir: *1.5km from Stradbally village*
PETS: Bedrooms (GF) **Charges** €5 per night **Grounds** accessible on leads disp bin **Exercise area** beach 0.5m **Facilities** water bowl washing facs cage storage walks info vet info **On Request** fridge access torch **Resident Pets:** Rose (Sheepdog), Pebbles (Fox Terrier)

This farmhouse is a good base for exploring the Dingle Peninsula and unspoiled beaches. The comfortable bedrooms have fine views over Brandon Bay, and the delightful garden can be enjoyed from the dining room and sitting room. Mrs Griffin offers a warm welcome and her home baking is a feature on the breakfast menu.
Rooms 8 rms (6 en suite) (2 pri facs) (3 fmly) (1 GF) ❷ S €45-€50; D €80-€90✳ **Facilities** tea/coffee Cen ht TVL **Parking** 10 **Notes** ch fac Closed Nov-Feb

CO KILDARE

ATHY
MAP 01 C3

★★★★★ BED & BREAKFAST
Coursetown Country House
Stradbally Rd
☎ 059 8631101 ▤ 059 8632740
e-mail: coursetown@hotmail.com
Dir: *3km from Athy. N78 at Athy onto R428*
PETS: Sep Accom Stables nearby (6m) **Charges** charge for damage **Grounds** accessible on leads disp bin **Facilities** washing facs cage storage vet info **On Request** fridge access towels **Resident Pets:** Casper, Millicent & Leopold (cats)
This charming Victorian country house stands on a 100-hectare tillage farm and bird sanctuary. It has been extensively refurbished, and all bedrooms are furnished to the highest standards. Convalescent or

disabled guests are especially welcome, and Iris and Jim Fox are happy to share their knowledge of the Irish countryside and its wildlife.
Rooms 5 en suite (1 GF) ❷ S €75; D €120✳ **Facilities** TVB tea/coffee Direct dial from bedrooms Cen ht TVL **Parking** 22 **Notes** No children 12yrs Closed 15 Nov-15 Mar

CO MAYO

ACHILL ISLAND
MAP 01 A4

★★★★ GUEST HOUSE
Gray's
Dugort
☎ 098 43244 & 43315
Dir: *11km NW of Achill Sound. Off R319 to Doogort*
PETS: Bedrooms (GF) **Grounds** accessible disp bin **Resident Pets:** Cuddles (Corgi), Huggy Bear & Phoebe (cats)
This welcoming guest house is in Doogort, on the northern shore of Achill Island, at the foot of the Slievemore mountains. There is a smart conservatory and various lounges, the cosy bedrooms are well appointed, and dinner is served nightly in the cheerful dining room. A self-contained villa, ideal for families, is also available.
Rooms 5 en suite 10 annexe en suite (4 fmly) (2 GF) ❷ S €55-€61; D €110✳ **Facilities** TVB tea/coffee Licensed Cen ht TVL Dinner Last d 6pm Pool Table ↳ **Parking** 30 **Notes** Closed 25 Dec-1 Jan ❸

CO ROSCOMMON

ROSCOMMON
MAP 01 B4

★★★ RESTAURANT WITH ROOMS
Gleesons Townhouse & Restaurant
Market Square
☎ 090 6626954 ▤ 090 6627425
e-mail: info@gleesonstownhouse.com
Dir: *in town centre next to Tourist office*
PETS: Bedrooms unattended **Sep Accom** kennel **Grounds** accessible (courtyard area) **Resident Pets:** Millie (Cavalier King Charles Spaniel)
This 19th-century cut-limestone town house has been very tastefully restored. The bedrooms and suites are decorated and furnished to a high standard. Dinner is served nightly in the Manse Restaurant and there is an extensive lunch and afternoon tea menu in the café or in the beautifully landscaped front courtyard. Conference facilities and secure car parking are available.
Rooms 19 rms (17 en suite) (2 pri facs) (1 fmly) ❷ in 12 bedrooms S €60-€75; D €120-€150✳ **Facilities** STV FTV TVB tea/coffee Direct dial from bedrooms Lift Cen ht TVL Dinner Last d 8:45pm Wi-fi available **Parking** 25 **Notes** LB Closed 25-26 Dec

CO TIPPERARY

NENAGH MAP 01 B3

★★★★ BED & BREAKFAST
Ashley Park House
☎ 067 38223 & 38013 ▤ 067 38013
e-mail: margaret@ashleypark.com
web: www.ashleypark.com
Dir: *6.5km N of Nenagh. Off N52 across lake, signed on left & left under arch*
PETS: Bedrooms Stables on site **Charges** horses €20 per night horses €120 per week **Public areas** except restaurants **Grounds** accessible **disp bin Exercise area** 20yds **Facilities** food bowl water bowl bedding cage storage walks info vet info **On Request** fridge access torch **Resident Pets:** Horses, ducks, peacocks, hens, lambs in spring

The attractive, colonial style farmhouse was built in 1770. Set in gardens that run down to Lake Ourna, it has spacious bedrooms with quality antique furnishings. Breakfast is served in the dining room overlooking the lake, and dinner is available by arrangement. There is a delightful walled garden, and a boat for the fishing on the lake is available.
Rooms 5 en suite (3 fmly) ⊘ S €60; D €100-€120✱ **Facilities** TVB tea/coffee Cen ht TVL Dinner Last d 9pm Wi-fi available Golf 18 Fishing **Parking** 30 **Notes** ✐

CO WATERFORD

DUNGARVAN MAP 01 C2

★★★★★ FARM HOUSE
Castle Country House *(S 192016)*
Millstreet, Cappagh
☎ 058 68049 ▤ 058 68099 Mrs J Nugent
e-mail: castlefm@iol.ie
Dir: *15km off the N25 between Dungarvan and Cappoquin. House is signed on the N72 & the R671. From the N72, take R671 for 3.5 miles; turn right at Millstreet.*
PETS: Bedrooms unattended **Grounds** accessible **Facilities** water bowl bedding washing facs cage storage walks info vet info **On Request** fridge access torch towels **Resident Pets:** Kerry (Collie)
This delightful house is in the west wing of a 15th-century castle. Guests are spoiled by host Joan Nugent who loves to cook and hunt out antiques for her visitors to enjoy. She is helped by her husband Emmett who enjoys showing off his high-tech dairy farm and is a fount of local knowledge. Bedrooms are spacious and enjoy lovely views. There is a river walk and a beautiful garden to relax in.
Rooms 5 en suite (1 fmly) ⊘ S €45-€50; D €90-€100 **Facilities** FTV TVB tea/coffee Licensed Cen ht Dinner Last d 5pm Fishing Farm tour **Parking** 11 **Notes** LB 200 acres dairy & beef Closed Dec-Feb

CO WICKLOW

DUNLAVIN MAP 01 C3

★★★★★ GUEST HOUSE
Rathsallagh House
☎ 045 403112 ▤ 045 403343
e-mail: info@rathsallagh.com
Dir: *10.5km after end of M9 left signed Dunlavin, house signed 5km*
PETS: Sep Accom 2 heated indoor pens **Charges** €20 per night **Public areas** except restaurant on leads **Grounds** accessible disp bin **Facilities** food (pre-bookable) food bowl water bowl leads 570 acres of grounds available washing facs cage storage vet info **On Request** fridge access torch towels **Resident Pets:** Becket & Tilly (Labrador), Tiki, Jodi, Truffel, Tigger & Treacle (Terriers)
Surrounded by its own 18-hole championship golf course this delightful house was converted from Queen Ann stables in 1798 and now has the new addition of spacious and luxurious bedrooms with conference and leisure facilities. Food is country-house cooking at its best, and there is a cosy bar and comfortable drawing room to relax in. Close to Curragh and Punchestown racecourses.
Rooms 17 en suite 12 annexe en suite (11 GF) ⊘ S €185; D €270-€320✱ **Facilities** FTV TVB tea/coffee Direct dial from bedrooms Licensed Cen ht TVL Dinner Last d 9pm Wi-fi available Golf 18 Snooker Sauna Golf academy with driving range **Parking** 150 **Notes** LB No children 12yrs

IRELAND

DUNLAVIN CONTINUED

⚜ 🐱 📷 📖

★★★★ FARM HOUSE
Tynte House *(N 870015)*

☎ 045 401561 📠 045 401586 Mr & Mrs J Lawler
e-mail: info@tyntehouse.com
web: www.tyntehouse.com

Dir: *N81 at Hollywood Cross, right at Dunlavin, follow finger signs for Tynte House, past market house in town centre*
PETS: Bedrooms Grounds accessible on leads disp bin
Facilities cage storage walks info vet info **On Request** fridge access torch towels **Resident Pets:** Suki (Maltese), Sasha (West Yorkshire Terrier)

The 19th-century farmhouse stands in the square of this quiet country village. The friendly hosts have carried out a lot of restoration resulting in comfortable bedrooms and a relaxing guest sitting room. Breakfast is a highlight of a visit to this house, which features Caroline's home baking.

Rooms 7 en suite (2 fmly) ⊗ in 2 bedrooms S €44-€54; D €70-€90
Facilities TVB tea/coffee Direct dial from bedrooms Cen ht TVL Golf 18 ⛳ Pool Table Playground Games room **Parking** 16 **Notes LB** 200 acres arable beef Closed 16 Dec-9 Jan

MACREDDIN   MAP 01 D3

⚜ 🐱 📷 📖 🐴

★★★★ 84% ◉◉ HOTEL
The Brooklodge Hotel & Wells Spa

☎ 0402 36444 📠 0402 36580
e-mail: brooklodge@macreddin.ie
web: www.brooklodge.com

MANOR HOUSE

Dir: *N11 to Rathnew, R752 to Rathdrum, R753 to Aughrim follow signs to Macreddin Village*
PETS: Bedrooms (GF) unattended **Sep Accom** barn
Stables on site **Public areas** small dogs only on leads
Grounds accessible on leads **Facilities** guests must supply all pet requirements **On Request** towels **Other** pets in ground floor rooms only **Resident Pets:** Rudi & Lilly (Golden Retrievers)

The Brooklodge is a luxurious country house hotel situated in Macreddin Village near Aughrim, comprising of a pub, café, organic bakery, smokehouse and equestrian centre. Comfort predominates among restful lounges, well-appointed bedrooms and mezzanine suites. The award-winning Strawberry Tree Restaurant is a truly romantic setting, specialising in organic and wild foods. The Wells spa centre offers extensive treatments and leisure facilities.

Rooms 58 en suite 32 annexe en suite (27 fmly) (4 GF) ⊗ in 28 bedrooms S €135-€275; D €180-€270 (incl. bkfst) **Facilities** Spa STV ⊛ ⊁ ⛳ 18 Riding Gym Putt green Wi-fi available Archery Clay pigeon shooting Falconry Shiatsu Massage Off road driving Xmas New Year **Services** Lift **Parking** 200 **Notes LB**

How do I find the perfect place?

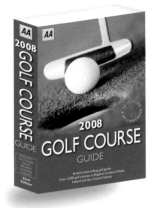

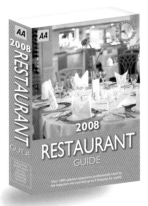

Discover new horizons with Britain's largest travel publisher

County Maps

The county map shown here will help you identify the counties within each country. You can look up each county in the guide using the county names at the top of each page. To find towns featured in the guide use the atlas and the index.

England

1 Bedfordshire
2 Berkshire
3 Bristol
4 Buckinghamshire
5 Cambridgeshire
6 Greater Manchester
7 Herefordshire
8 Hertfordshire
9 Leicestershire
10 Northamptonshire
11 Nottinghamshire
12 Rutland
13 Staffordshire
14 Warwickshire
15 West Midlands
16 Worcestershire

Scotland

17 City of Glasgow
18 Clackmannanshire
19 East Ayrshire
20 East Dunbartonshire
21 East Renfrewshire
22 Perth & Kinross
23 Renfrewshire
24 South Lanarkshire
25 West Dunbartonshire

Wales

26 Blaenau Gwent
27 Bridgend
28 Caerphilly
29 Denbighshire
30 Flintshire
31 Merthyr Tydfil
32 Monmouthshire
33 Neath Port Talbot
34 Newport
35 Rhondda Cynon Taff
36 Torfaen
37 Vale of Glamorgan
38 Wrexham

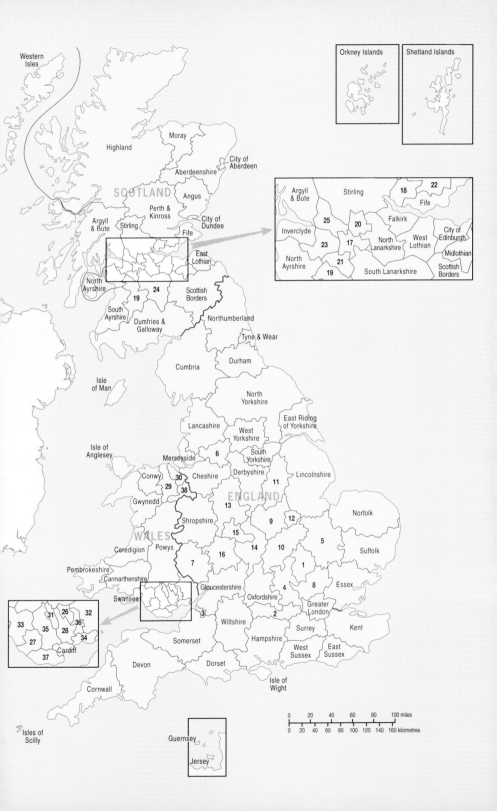

KEY TO ATLAS

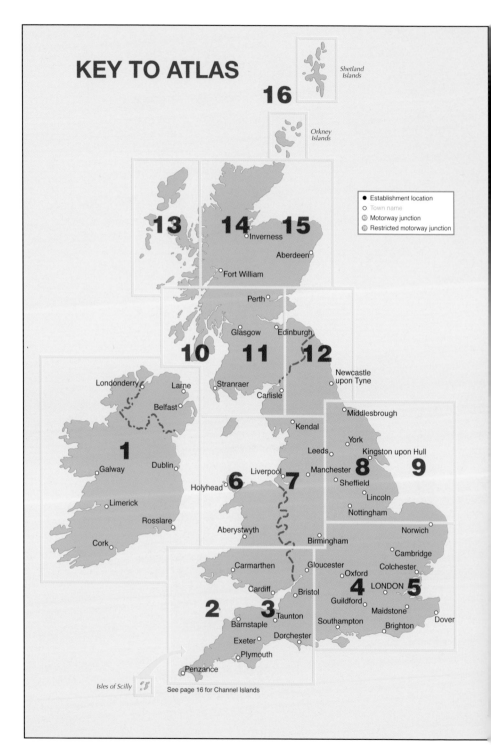

Shetland Islands

16

Orkney Islands

- ● Establishment location
- ○ Town name
- Motorway junction
- Restricted motorway junction

13

14

15
○ Inverness

Aberdeen○

○ Fort William

Perth○

Glasgow○ ○ Edinburgh

10

11

12

Newcastle
upon Tyne○

○ Londonderry ○ Larne ○ Stranraer

○ Belfast Carlisle○

Middlesbrough○

Kendal○

1

York○

Leeds○

Kingston upon Hull○

○ Galway ○ Dublin Liverpool○ **6** **7** Manchester○ **8** **9**

Holyhead○ ○ Sheffield

○ Limerick Lincoln○

Rosslare○ Nottingham○

Aberystwyth○ Norwich○

○ Cork Birmingham○

Cambridge○

Carmarthen○ Gloucester○ Colchester○

Cardiff○ ○ Oxford **4** LONDON **5**

2 **3**○ Bristol Guildford○ Maidstone○ ○ Dover

Barnstaple○ Taunton○ Southampton○ Brighton○

Exeter○ Dorchester○

○ Plymouth

○ Penzance

Isles of Scilly See page 16 for Channel Islands

© Automobile Association Developments Limited 2007

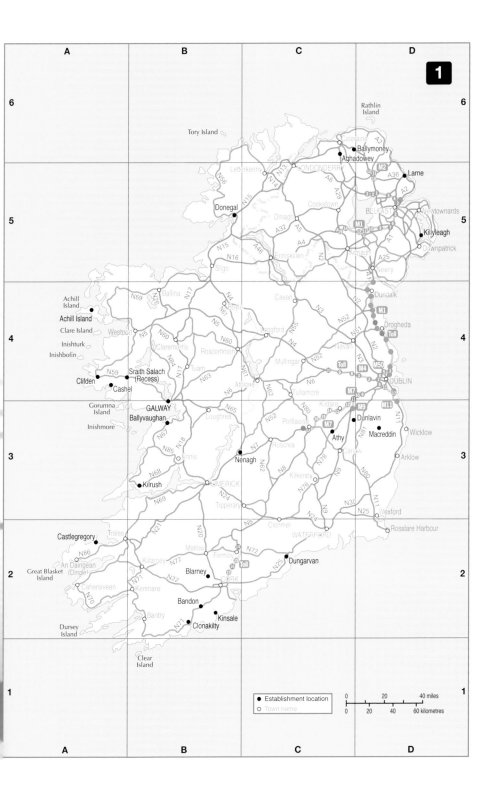

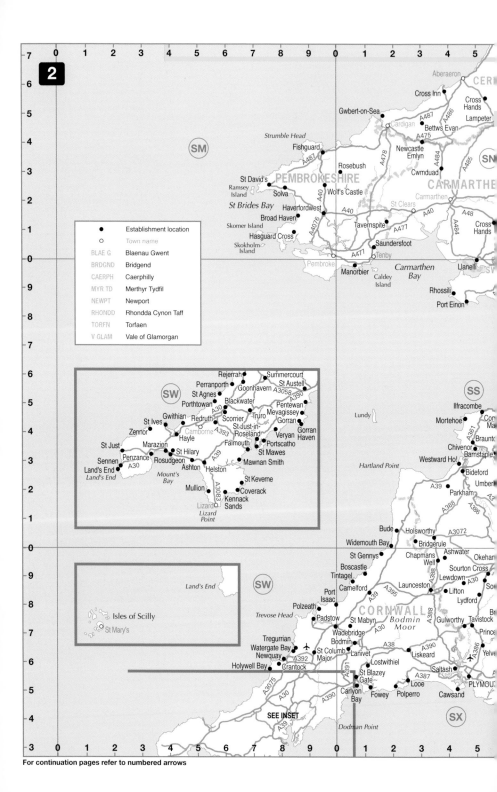

2

Legend	
●	Establishment location
○	Town name
BLAE G	Blaenau Gwent
BRDGND	Bridgend
CAERPH	Caerphilly
MYR TD	Merthyr Tydfil
NEWPT	Newport
RHONDD	Rhondda Cynon Taff
TORFN	Torfaen
V GLAM	Vale of Glamorgan

SM

SN

Aberaeron
Cross Inn
Cross Hands
Lampeter
Gwbert-on-Sea
Cardigan
Bettws Evan
Newcastle Emlyn
A487
A486
A475
A484
A485
Strumble Head
Fishguard
Rosebush
Cwmduad
CARMARTHE
A478
St David's
PEMBROKESHIRE
Ramsey Island
Solva
Wolf's Castle
A40
Carmarthen
St Clears
St Brides Bay
Haverfordwest
A40
A40
A48
Skomer Island
Broad Haven
Tavernspite
A77
A484
Cross Hands
Hasguard Cross
Saundersfoot
A4076
Skokholm Island
SY
Pembroke
A477
Tenby
Llanelli
Manorbier
Caldey Island
Carmarthen Bay
Port Einon
Rhossili

SW

Rejerrah
Summercourt
Perranporth
Goonhavern
St Austell
St Agnes
Blackwater
A3058
A390
Porthtowan
A30
Pentewan
Redruth
Scorrier
Truro
Mevagissey
St Ives
Gwithian
St Just-in-Roseland
Gorran
Zennor
Hayle
Camborne
A393
Veryan
Gorran Haven
St Just
Marazion
Falmouth
Portscatho
Penzance
St Hilary
A39
St Mawes
Sennen
Rosudgeon
Ashton
Mawnan Smith
Land's End
A30
Helston
Land's End
Mount's Bay
St Keverne
Mullion
A3083
Coverack
Lizard
Kennack Sands
Lizard Point

SS
Ilfracombe
Mortehoe
Corn Mar
Lundy
A361
Braunto
Chivenor
Barnstaple
Westward Ho!
Bideford
Hartland Point
Umber
A39
Parkham
A388
A386
Bude
Holsworthy
A3072
Widemouth Bay
Bridgerule
St Gennys
Chapmans Well
Ashwater
Okehan
Boscastle
Sourton Cross
Tintagel
Launceston
Lewdown
A30
So
Camelford
A395
A388
Port Isaac
Lifton
Lydford
Polzeath
CORNWALL
Gulworthy
Tavistock
Br
Trevose Head
Padstow
Bodmin Moor
Prince
St Mabyn
Yelve
A38
Tregurrian
Wadebridge
A30
A390
Watergate Bay
Bodmin
Liskeard
A386
Newquay
St Columb Major
Lanivet
A392
Lostwithiel
Saltash
Holywell Bay
Crantock
A391
PLYMOUTH
St Blazey Gate
A387
Carlyon Bay
Looe
A3075
A30
Fowey
Polperro
Cawsand
A39
SEE INSET
A390
Dodman Point
SX

SW
Land's End
Isles of Scilly
St Mary's

For continuation pages refer to numbered arrows

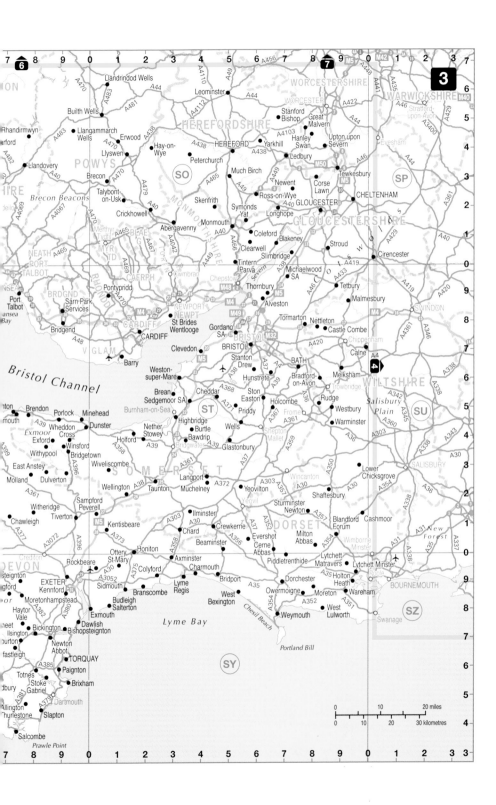

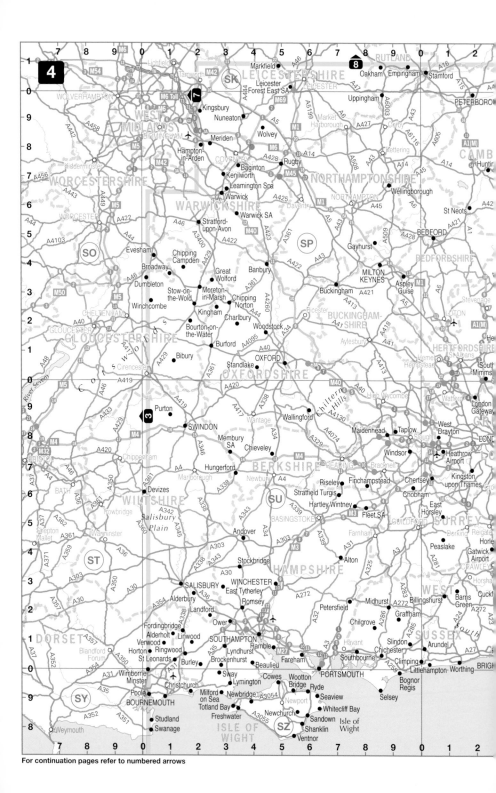

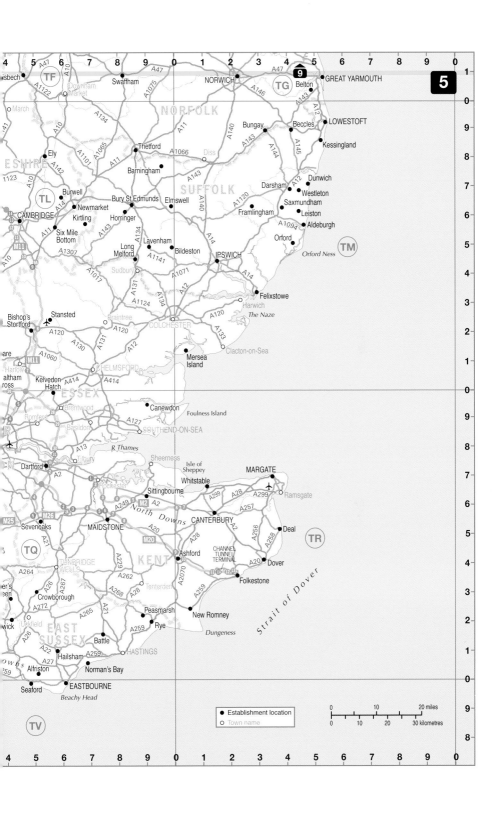

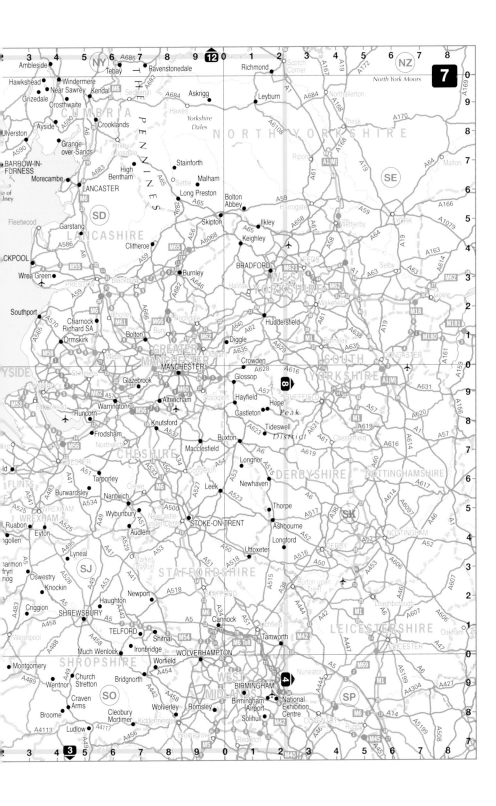

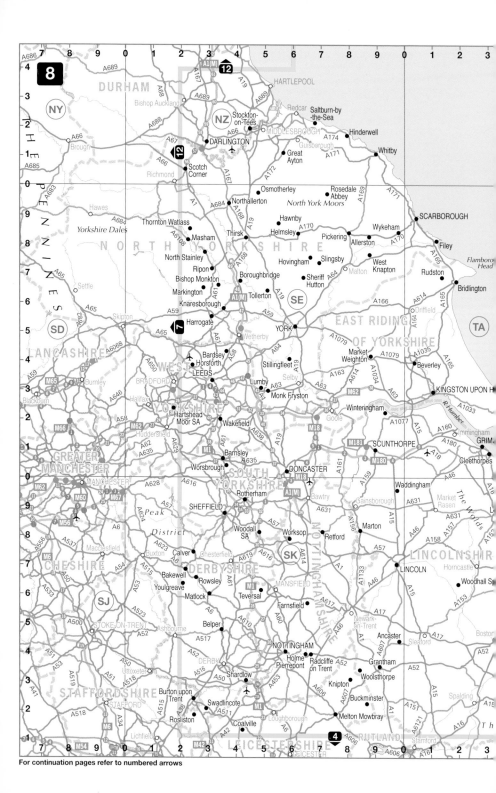

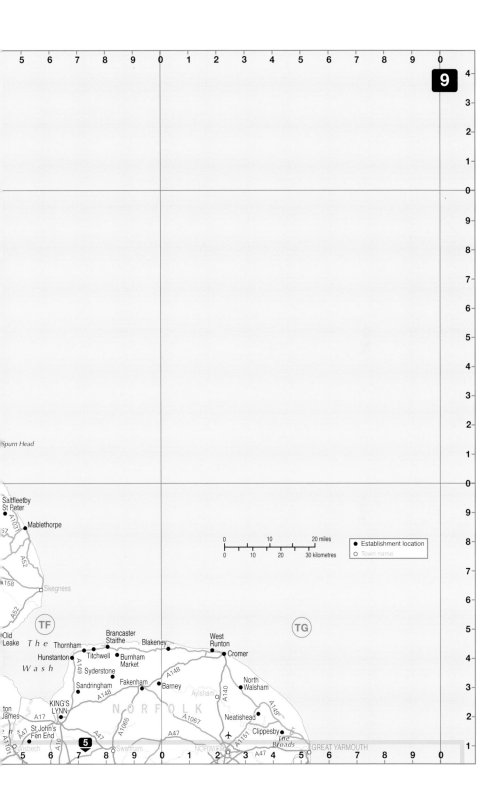

9

5 6 7 8 9 0 1 2 3 4 5 6 7 8 9 0

4
3
2
1
0

9
8
7
6
5
4
3
2

Spurn Head

1
0

Saltfleetby
St Peter

9

•Mablethorpe

8

A52

7

A158

•Skegness

6

A52

Old
Leake

TF

The   •Thornham

Brancaster
Staithe   •Blakeney

West
Runton

TG

5

4

Hunstanton•   •Titchwell •Burnham
Market   •Cromer

A149

Syderstone•

Wash

3

Sandringham•   •Fakenham   •Barney

North
Walsham•

A148

A140   Aylsham○   A140

NORFOLK

A1067

2

ton
James

KING'S
LYNN

Neatishead•

A149

St John's
Fen End

A1065

A47

Clippesby•
*The
Broads*

A1151

A47

A10

5

○Swaffham

NORWICH○

A47

GREAT YARMOUTH

1

Wisbech

5 6 7 8 9 0 1 2 3 4 5 6 7 8 9 0

0   10   20 miles
0   10   20   30 kilometres

● Establishment location
○ Town name

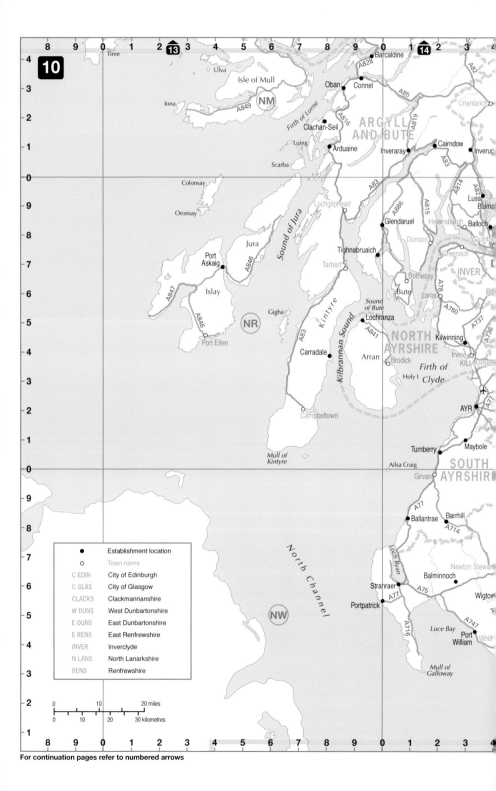

10

Tiree

Isle of Mull
Ulva

NM

Iona

A849

A816

Firth of Lorne

Oban
Connel
Barcaldine
A828

Crianlarich

A82

A85

A819

ARGYLL
AND BUTE

Clachan-Seil

Luing

Arduaine

Scarba

Inveraray

Cairndow

Inverug

A83

A83

Colonsay

A886

A815

A814

Luss
Balma

Oronsay

Lochgilphead

Glendaruel

Helensburgh

Balloch

Dumba

Dunoon

Greenock

INVER

Port
Askaig

Jura

Sound of Jura

Tighnabruaich

Tarbert

Bothesay

Bute

Largs

A78

A760

A737

A736

A847

Islay

A846

Gigha

Sound
of Bute

Lochranza

NORTH
AYRSHIRE

Kilwinning

R

A846

Port Ellen

NR

A63

Kintyre

Carradale

Kilbrannan Sound

A841

Arran

Brodick

Holy I

Irvine

KILMARNO

Firth of
Clyde

AYR

A77

Campbeltown

Turnberry

Maybole

Mull of
Kintyre

Ailsa Craig

Girvan

SOUTH
AYRSHIR

●	Establishment location
○	Town name
C EDIN	City of Edinburgh
C GLAS	City of Glasgow
CLACKS	Clackmannanshire
W DUNS	West Dunbartonshire
E DUNS	East Dunbartonshire
E RENS	East Renfrewshire
INVER	Inverclyde
N LANS	North Lanarkshire
RENS	Renfrewshire

North Channel

NW

Ballantrae

Barrhill

A714

Loch Ryan

Newton Stewar

Balminnoch

Stranraer

A77

A75

Wigtov

Portpatrick

A716

Luce Bay

A747

Port
William

Whit

Mull of
Galloway

0   10   20 miles
0   10   20   30 kilometres

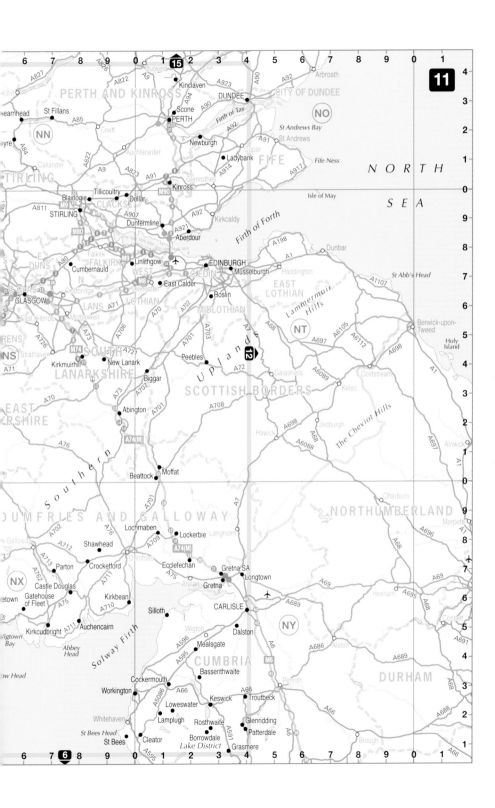

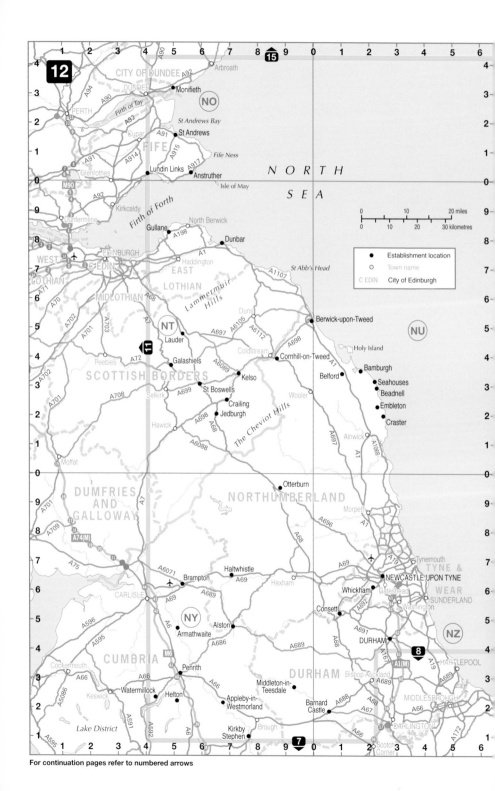

For continuation pages refer to numbered arrows

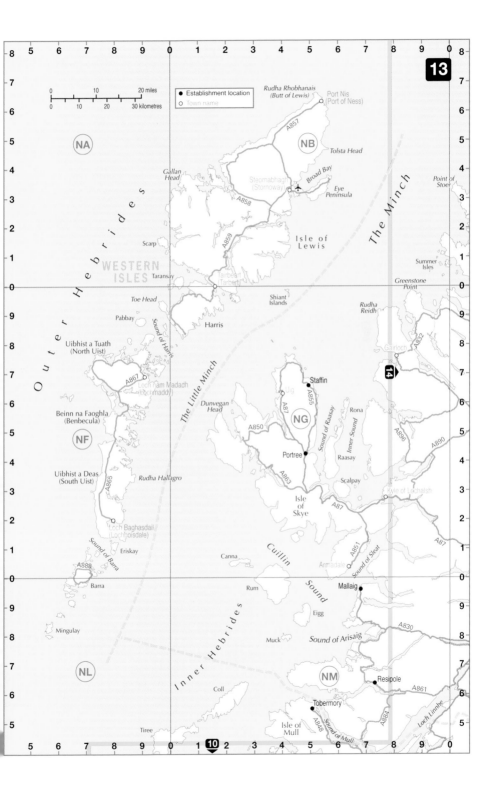

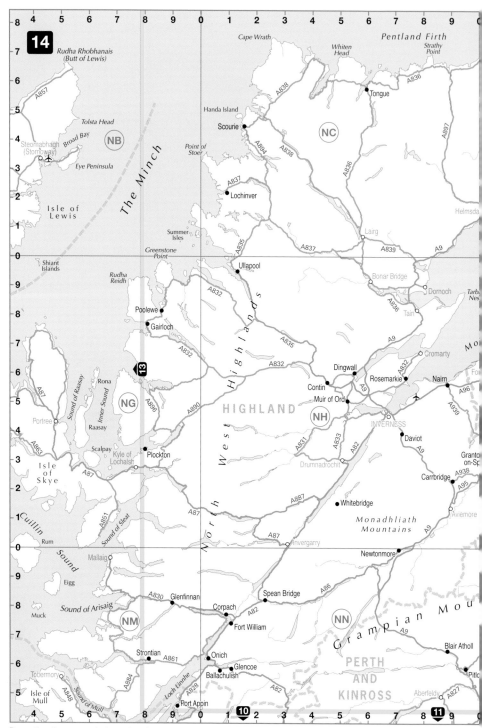

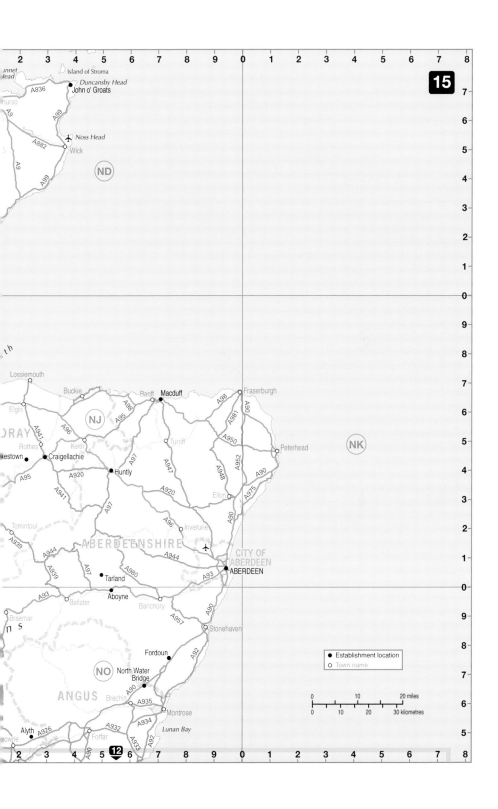

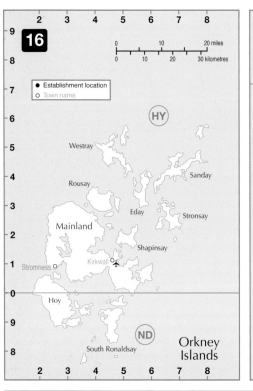

16

Establishment location
Town name

HY

Westray

Rousay

Sanday

Eday

Mainland

Stronsay

Shapinsay

Kirkwall

Stromness

Hoy

ND

South Ronaldsay

Orkney
Islands

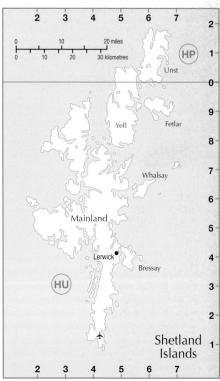

HP

Unst

Yell

Fetlar

Whalsay

Mainland

Lerwick

Bressay

HU

Shetland
Islands

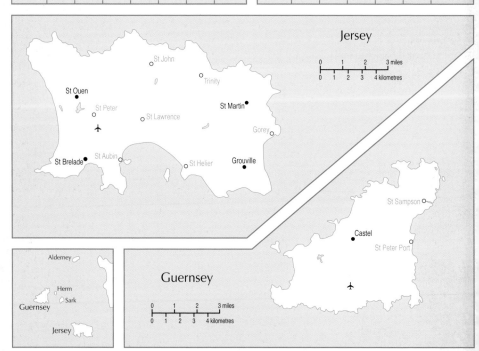

Jersey

St John

Trinity

St Ouen

St Peter

St Martin

St Lawrence

Gorey

St Brelade

St Aubin

St Helier

Grouville

St Sampson

Castel

St Peter Port

Alderney

Herm

Sark

Guernsey

Jersey

Guernsey

Index

Index

Index

Index

Index

Index

Index

Index

Index

'A perfect litter' 1958 – copyright AA/Ron Weston

The Automobile Association would like to thank the following photographers, companies and picture libraries for their assistance in the preparation of this book.

Abbreviations for the picture credits are as follows: (t) top; (b) bottom; (l) left; (r) right; (AA) AA World Travel Library.

20/21 AA/T Mackie; 304/305 S Anderson; 350/351 AA/N Jenkins; 390/391 AA/C Jones.

1b Mark Ellott; 2tl Ashley Hill-Smith; 2l Mark Stocks; 2cl Jane Croft; 2bl Kirsten Sizer; 3tr Andy Royle; 3bl Jenny Gould; 3br Susan Lambert; 5tr Andy Royle; 5b Andy Royle; 6tl Hazel Harrod; 7tr Andy Royle; 7br Lucy Hipwood; 8tl Hazel Harrod; 8b Leona Mundin; 9tr Andy Royle; 9bl Sarah Croker; 9br Jenny Gould; 10tl Hazel Harrod; 11tr Andy Royle; 11bl Jim Cook; 11br Sarah Croker; 12tl Hazel Harrod; 12tr Laura Freeman; 13tr Andy Royle; 13br Laura Freeman; 14tl Hazel Harrod; 14l Jim Cook; 14r Jane Croft; 15tr Andy Royle; 15b Andy Royle; 16b Andy Royle; 17tr Andy Royle; 17c Karen Turner; 18tl Hazel Harrod; 19tr Andy Royle; 19b Hazel Harrod; 34tr Andy Royle; 130br Graeme Main; 139br Graeme Main; 165br Graeme Main; 173br Graeme Main; 212bl Karen Tatlock; 231bl Graeme Main; 253bl Graeme Main; 256bl Graeme Main; 271bl Kirsten Sizer; 274bl Graeme Main; 291bl Andy Royle; 320bl Laura Freeman; 322bl Lisa Guy; 348bl Gemma Scott; 384bl Lisa Guy; 385br Graeme Main; 391bl Rachel Jones; 396b Claire Blackburn; 417 Graeme Main

Every effort has been made to trace the copyright holders, and we apologise in advance for any accidental errors. We would be happy to apply the corrections in the following edition of this publication.

AA Pet Friendly Places to Stay 2008

Please send this form to:
Editor, AA Pet Friendly Places to Stay,
Lifestyle Guides,
The Automobile Association,
14th Floor, Fanum House,
Basingstoke RG21 4EA

or fax: 01256 491647
or e-mail: lifestyleguides@theAA.com

Readers' Report Form

Please use this form to tell us about any establishment you have visited, whether it is in the guide or not currently listed. Feedback from readers helps us to keep our guide accurate and up to date. However, if you have a complaint to make during a visit, we do recommend that you discuss the matter with the management there and then, so that they have a chance to put things right before your visit is spoilt.

Please note that the AA does not undertake to arbitrate between you and the establishment's management, or to obtain compensation or engage in protracted correspondence.

Date:

Your name (block capitals)

Your address (block capitals)

....

....

....

....

....

e-mail address:

Comments (Please include the name & address of the establishment) ....

....

....

....

....

....

....

....

(please attach a separate sheet if necessary)

Please tick here if you DO NOT wish to receive details of AA offers or products

PTO

AA Pet Friendly Places to Stay 2008

Have you bought this guide before?   Yes   No

Do you regularly use any other accommodation, restaurant, pub or food guides?
If yes, which ones?

....

....

Why did you buy this guide? (circle all that apply)

holiday   short break   attending a show (eg Crufts)

other ....

How often do you stay in a Hotel, B&B or at a Campsite with your pets?
(circle one choice)

more than once a month   once a month   once in 2-3 months

once in six months   once a year   less than once a year

Please answer these questions to help us make improvements to the guide:

Which of these factors are most important when choosing pet-friendly
accommodation?

price   location   awards/rating   service

decor/surroundings   previous experience   recommendation   proximity to exercise area

facilities for pets   extent of freedom for pets

other (please state) ....

Do you use the location atlas?   Yes   No

What elements of the guide do you find the most useful when choosing an
establishment?

description   photo   advertisement   star/pennant rating

information on pet facilities

What do you like best about the guide?

....

....

....

Can you suggest any improvements to the guide?

....

....

....

Thank you for returning this form

Please send this form to:
Editor, AA Pet Friendly Places to Stay,
Lifestyle Guides,
The Automobile Association,
14th Floor, Fanum House,
Basingstoke RG21 4EA

Readers' Report Form

or fax: 01256 491647
or e-mail: lifestyleguides@theAA.com

Please use this form to tell us about any establishment you have visited, whether it is in the guide or not currently listed. Feedback from readers helps us to keep our guide accurate and up to date. However, if you have a complaint to make during a visit, we do recommend that you discuss the matter with the management there and then, so that they have a chance to put things right before your visit is spoilt.

Please note that the AA does not undertake to arbitrate between you and the establishment's management, or to obtain compensation or engage in protracted correspondence.

Date:

Your name (block capitals)

Your address (block capitals)

....

....

....

....

....

e-mail address:

Comments (Please include the name & address of the establishment) ....

....

....

....

....

....

....

....

(please attach a separate sheet if necessary)

Please tick here if you DO NOT wish to receive details of AA offers or products

PTO

AA Pet Friendly Places to Stay 2008

Have you bought this guide before?   Yes   No

Do you regularly use any other accommodation, restaurant, pub or food guides? If yes, which ones?

....

....

Why did you buy this guide? (circle all that apply)

holiday   short break   attending a show (eg Crufts)

other ....

How often do you stay in a Hotel, B&B or at a Campsite with your pets? (circle one choice)

more than once a month   once a month   once in 2-3 months

once in six months   once a year   less than once a year

Please answer these questions to help us make improvements to the guide:

Which of these factors are most important when choosing pet-friendly accommodation?

price   location   awards/rating   service

decor/surroundings   previous experience   recommendation   proximity to exercise area

facilities for pets   extent of freedom for pets

other (please state) ....

Do you use the location atlas?   Yes   No

What elements of the guide do you find the most useful when choosing an establishment?

description   photo   advertisement   star/pennant rating

information on pet facilities

What do you like best about the guide?

....

....

....

Can you suggest any improvements to the guide?

....

....

....

Thank you for returning this form

Please send this form to:
Editor, AA Pet Friendly Places to Stay,
Lifestyle Guides,
The Automobile Association,
14th Floor, Fanum House,
Basingstoke RG21 4EA

or fax: 01256 491647
or e-mail: lifestyleguides@theAA.com

Readers' Report Form

Please use this form to tell us about any establishment you have visited, whether it is in the guide or not currently listed. Feedback from readers helps us to keep our guide accurate and up to date. However, if you have a complaint to make during a visit, we do recommend that you discuss the matter with the management there and then, so that they have a chance to put things right before your visit is spoilt.

Please note that the AA does not undertake to arbitrate between you and the establishment's management, or to obtain compensation or engage in protracted correspondence.

Date:

Your name (block capitals)

Your address (block capitals)

....

....

....

....

....

e-mail address:

Comments (Please include the name & address of the establishment) ....

....

....

....

....

....

....

(please attach a separate sheet if necessary)

Please tick here if you DO NOT wish to receive details of AA offers or products

PTO

AA Pet Friendly Places to Stay 2008

Have you bought this guide before?   Yes   No

Do you regularly use any other accommodation, restaurant, pub or food guides? If yes, which ones?

....

....

Why did you buy this guide? (circle all that apply)

holiday   short break   attending a show (eg Crufts)

other ....

How often do you stay in a Hotel, B&B or at a Campsite with your pets? (circle one choice)

more than once a month   once a month   once in 2-3 months

once in six months   once a year   less than once a year

Please answer these questions to help us make improvements to the guide:

Which of these factors are most important when choosing pet-friendly accommodation?

price   location   awards/rating   service

decor/surroundings   previous experience   recommendation   proximity to exercise area

facilities for pets   extent of freedom for pets

other (please state) ....

Do you use the location atlas?   Yes   No

What elements of the guide do you find the most useful when choosing an establishment?

description   photo   advertisement   star/pennant rating

information on pet facilities

What do you like best about the guide?

....

....

....

Can you suggest any improvements to the guide?

....

....

....

Thank you for returning this form

How do I find the perfect place?

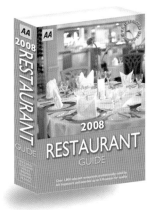

Making choices simple with Britain's largest travel publisher

PETS' PARADISE

Notes